AF477453

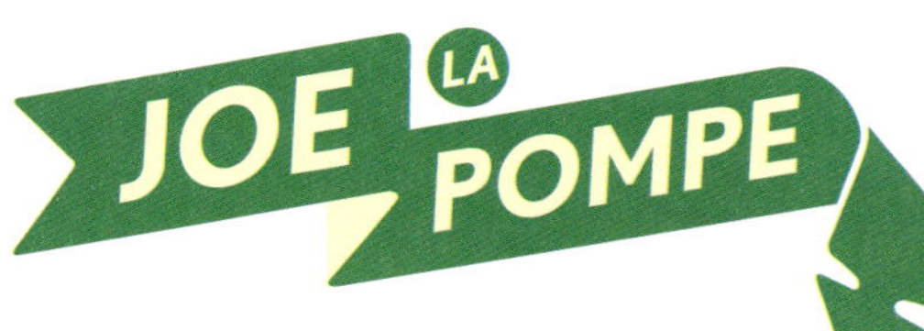

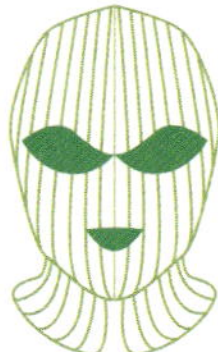

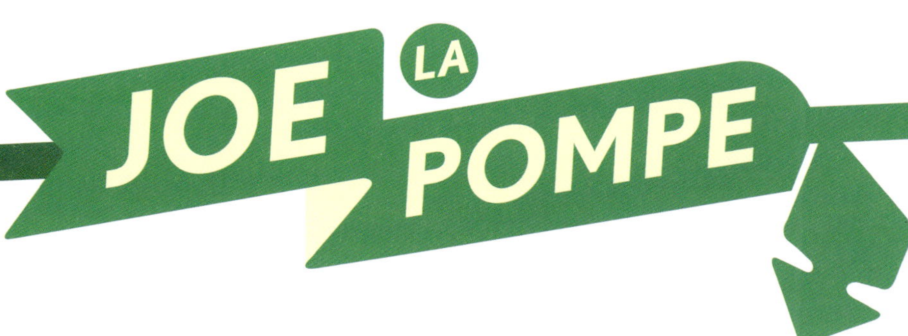

100 VISUAL IDEAS,
1000 GREAT ADS

SOMMAIRE
CONTENTS

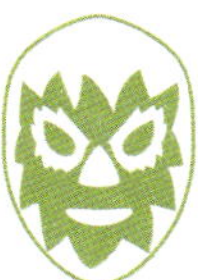

JOE CONTRE-ATTAQUE

C'est à l'enfance que remonte son obsession de la collection. Maniaque et acharné, Joe – puisqu'il se fait appeler ainsi – a d'abord accumulé les timbres, les cartes de téléphone ou les pin's avant de s'intéresser à la publicité. Biberonné par les coupures pub à la télévision, fasciné par Jean-Pierre Stevens, le mari de Ma sorcière bien-aimée qui travaille justement dans la publicité, le voilà qui en fait son métier : *« Quand j'étais enfant, je ne pensais pas que ça existait un boulot où l'on est payé pour avoir des idées »*, se souvient-il. Dans le civil, l'homme est donc créatif dans une agence de publicité. On n'en saura pas plus.

Car c'est derrière une cagoule et sous ce pseudonyme de Joe La Pompe que l'individu s'est fait connaître dans le milieu des médias et de la création. Masqué pour démasquer les copieurs. Traquant sans répit et depuis plus de 10 ans les publicités jumelles, il ne s'est pas fait que des amis – certains créatifs vexés l'auraient même menacé – et a préféré l'anonymat. D'abord sur Internet [1], puis dans un livre [2], c'est seul et à la sueur de son front que le chasseur expose son butin : toute publicité dont l'idée existe déjà,

(1) *www.joelapompe.net*
(2) *Nouveau? Le meilleur de la production et reproduction publicitaire, ed. Télémaque*

JOE STRIKES BACK

His obsession for collecting started in childhood. Fussy and fierce, Joe – as he's called – first started hoarding stamps, phonecards and lapel pins before becoming interested in advertising. Nursed on TV commercial breaks and fascinated by Darrin Stephens, the husband in Bewitched who works in advertising, he found his calling: *"When I was a kid, I never thought there was a job where you got paid for having ideas,"* he recollects. In civilian life, the man works as a creative in an advertising agency. We can't reveal any more.

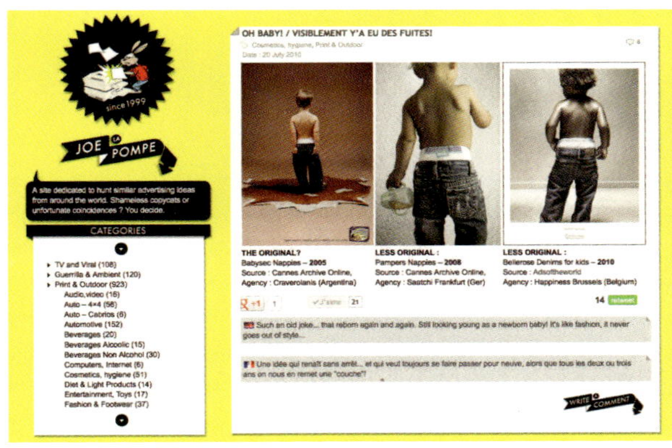

www.joelapompe.net

Because it is from behind a face mask and under the pseudonym "Joe La Pompe" – "pomper" in French means to imitate, so Joe La Pompe can be roughly translated as Joe Cribber – that the individual in question has become known in media and creative circles. He is masked to unmask copycats. Relentlessly hunting identical adverts for more than 10 years, he is not out to make new friends – some miffed creative have even threatened him – and so he prefers to

que ce soit une coïncidence, une copie, l'expression de la même bonne idée à des kilomètres ou des années d'écart, la faute à la jeunesse et au manque de culture de son auteur…

Ce sont ainsi plus de 1 000 paires – parfois même triplettes – de campagnes (surtout imprimées, mais aussi télévisées ou observées dans les rues) qui nourrissent une banque de données exceptionnelle. L'idée de départ n'était pas de dénoncer un système, mais d'ériger une collection et de « *rendre à César ce qui lui appartient et rendre hommage aux vrais créatifs* ». Si certaines images semblent réellement être des copies, beaucoup tiennent simplement au fonctionnement du monde publicitaire : « *Les produits et services qu'on vend sont les mêmes, les attentes des clients sont les mêmes, la manière de travailler, la culture des auteurs est proche…* », explique-t-il.

La collection de publicités récoltées par Joe La Pompe s'enrichit désormais d'une nouvelle typologie. Ce que rassemble le présent ouvrage, ce ne sont plus des copies, mais des images qui ont une thématique ou un symbole en commun. C'est un travail qu'il mène depuis quelques années et qui a donné lieu à des publications dans la presse professionnelle en France (CB News) et en Belgique (Média Marketing). C'est en 2009, soit 10 ans après la création de son site Internet, que Joe a rassemblé diverses publicités qui utilisaient ou détournaient l'image de la poupée Barbie qui fêtait cette année-là ses 50 ans. Depuis, il a identifié des

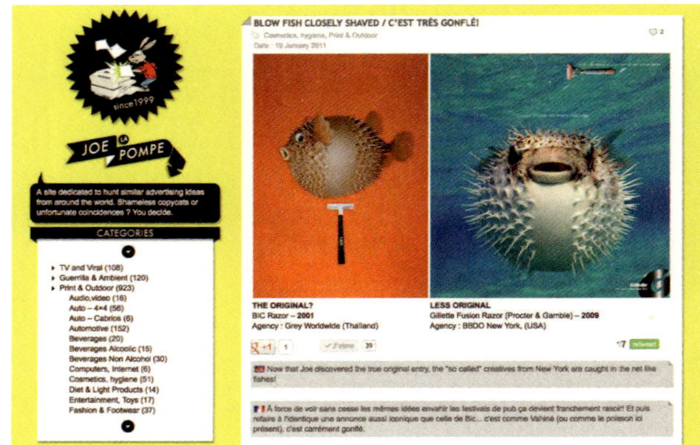

www.joelapompe.net

remain anonymous. Starting online [1], then in a book [2], it is just by the sweat of his brow that the ad buff is able to display his booty: all the advertisements for which the same concept had already existed, be it by coincidence, a copy, an expression of the same good idea miles or years apart, a mistake of youth, or because of perpetrator's lacking education.

There are millions of duplicate – sometimes even triplicate – campaigns (mainly printed but also televised and observed on the street) that have nourished this exceptional database. The original idea was not to denounce the system, but to establish a veritable collection and to *"render unto Caesar the things which are Caesar's, and to pay homage to the real creatives."* If certain images really appear to just be copies, much of the explanation simply lies in the way the advertising world works: *"The products and services that we sell are the same, client expectations are all the same, and the way we work and our educational background is quite close,"* he explains.

The advertising collection harvested by Joe La Pompe is now enriched by a new typology. What brings this presentation together is not just copies, but images that have a theme or a symbol in common. It is a vocation that has driven him for several years and has led to his work being published in the trade press in France (CB News) and in Belgium (Média Marketing). In 2009, 10 years after the creation of his website, Joe assembled various advertisements that had used or had been derived from the image of the Barbie doll that at the time was celebrating

(1) *www.joelapompe.net*
(2) *Nouveau? Le meilleur de la production et reproduction publicitaire, ed. Télémaque*

personnages, des symboles, des thèmes récurrents qui font référence dans les diverses campagnes parce que tout le monde les comprend. *« La publicité se nourrit de symboles, de repères et d'images universels que tout le monde connaît. Elle les récupère, joue avec, se les approprie, les retourne et les détourne au gré des modes, de ses besoins et de ses envies »*, détaille l'auteur.

Pour la première fois, donc, un livre fait l'inventaire des symboles les plus connus, les plus utilisés et les plus détournés. Ce sont des centaines d'heures de travail, de veille et de documentation qui ont été nécessaires à Joe pour rassembler ce matériel volumineux. Provenant en grande partie de concours internationaux, les publicités présentées ont été traduites en anglais pour en faciliter la compréhension. Puisant dans une dizaine d'années de création publicitaire du monde entier (dont certaines sources assez exotiques comme la Slovaquie, Porto Rico, la Colombie, l'Indonésie, le Vietnam, la Hongrie, la Liban, l'Ukraine, la Nouvelle-Zélande, l'Australie ou l'Afrique du Sud…), le livre met côte à côte des images qui n'avaient pas vocation à se retrouver ensemble.

De manière subjective et personnelle, Joe La Pompe a donc choisi 100 sujets et pour chacun, il a sélectionné 10 campagnes et pas une de plus ! Ce sont donc pas moins de 1 000 images qui sont ici rassemblées. Ces thèmes sont très variés : symboles, événements, personnalités (histo-riques ou fictionnelles), animaux, modes, monuments, objets, tendances…

Il ne s'agit pas d'une simple compilation, ou d'empilements superflus (du type *« les 150 meilleures*

its 50th anniversary. Since then, Joe has identified the characters, symbols and recurring themes that are frequently referenced in a wide range of campaigns mainly because everyone can identify with them. *"Advertising feeds on symbols, benchmarks and universal images that everyone knows. It scavenges, plays with, appropriates, turns upside and hijacks according to the prevailing fashions and its needs and desires,"* elaborates the author.

For the first time, therefore, here is a book that makes an inventory of the best known, most used and most often hijacked symbols. This was the result of hundreds of hours of work and careful surveillance, craftily undertaken alone by Joe, to identify the subjects and themes that needed to be put into focus, and above all to gather the copious amounts of material that was needed. Although they originate in large part from an international field, the advertisements presented here have been translated into English for the sake of readability. Drawing on a dozen years' worth of adverts from all over the world (including places as diverse as Slovakia, Puerto Rico, Columbia, Indonesia, Vietnam, Hungary, Lebanon, Ukraine, New Zealand, Australia and South Africa), this book puts images that were never meant to found together side-by-side.

In his own subjective and personal manner, Joe La Pompe has chosen 100 motifs, and for each one he has selected 10 campaigns to highlight and not one more! That is to say that not less than one thousand images have been assembled here. The themes are quite varied: symbols, events, personalities (historical or fictional), animals, patterns, monuments, objects and trends.

pubs »…), comme on en trouve beaucoup sur Internet, mais c'est avant tout une sélection, un tri, un vrai choix éditorial effectué dans les images retenues. Ce travail de documentaliste passionné – qui a fait appel à la mémoire et à la recherche acharnée de l'auteur – offre une photographie de la publicité mondiale des années 2000, sans pour autant prétendre à l'exhaustivité.

On constatera au travers des pages qu'un même thème peut déboucher sur une palette d'idées très différentes, parfois même contradictoires. Un référent identique peut être utilisé pour faire la promotion de biens très variés. Suivant les pays ou les époques, un même symbole n'aura pas la même portée ou la même signification, même si la mondialisation des références tend à une certaine unification.

Véritable catalogue, ce livre sera utile à tous les créatifs qui pourront aller voir ce qui a été fait et éviter les redites. Mine d'informations et d'inspiration, il pourra servir de guide, de boussole pour ajouter sa pierre à l'édifice publicitaire.

À l'heure d'Internet et de la prise de pouvoir du digital, ce livre se veut aussi un hommage à la publicité imprimée, laquelle garde une place spéciale dans le cœur de l'auteur et est loin d'avoir fini de nous étonner.

France Clarinval

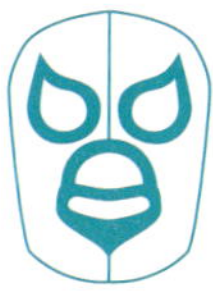

But this book is not the result of a simple compilation or yet another superfluous list (of the *"150 best ads"* variety) that lack any editorial filter – as you often find online – but rather it is first and foremost a selection – real separation of the wheat from the chaff – and a real choice of the images that Joe deemed the best. This is the work of a passionate archivist, whose well exercised memory and unrelenting research provides a snapshot of the world of advertising in the 2000s, without pretending to be totally exhaustive.

You might observe, as you progress across these pages, that the same theme can lead to a range of such different ideas, sometimes even contradictory ones. An identical originating object can be used to promote such varied goods. Depending on the country or the age, the same symbol doesn't necessarily have the same thrust or the same meaning, even if the globalisation of cultural touchstones has led to a certain degree of cultural fusion.

As a real catalogue, this book will be useful for all creatives who want to see what's already been done and to avoid repetition. As a mine of information and inspiration, it will also serve as guideposts, a roadmap, to follow those who have already made their own contribution to the field of advertising.

In the Internet age and with all things going digital, this book is also a homage to print advertising, which has kept its special place in the author's heart and is far from being finished astounding us.

France Clarinval *(translated by Aaron Grunwald)*

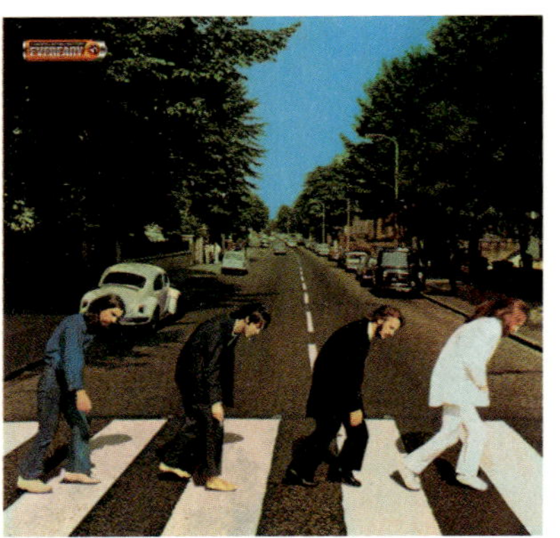

INDE INDIA (2005)
Young & Rubicam Mumbai
Eveready Batteries

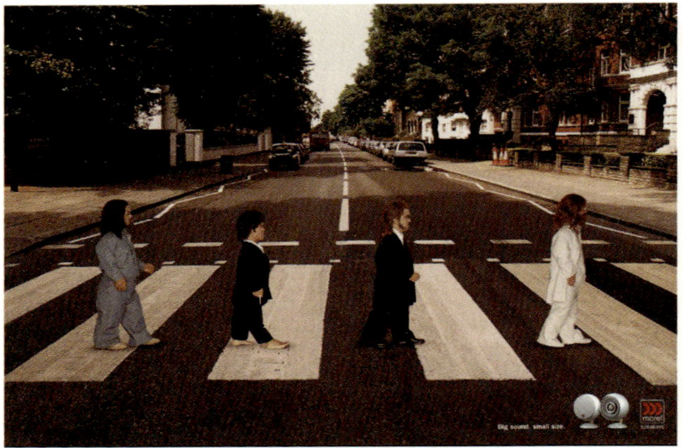

BRÉSIL BRAZIL (2003)
DM9DDB Morel Speakers
Big sound, small size

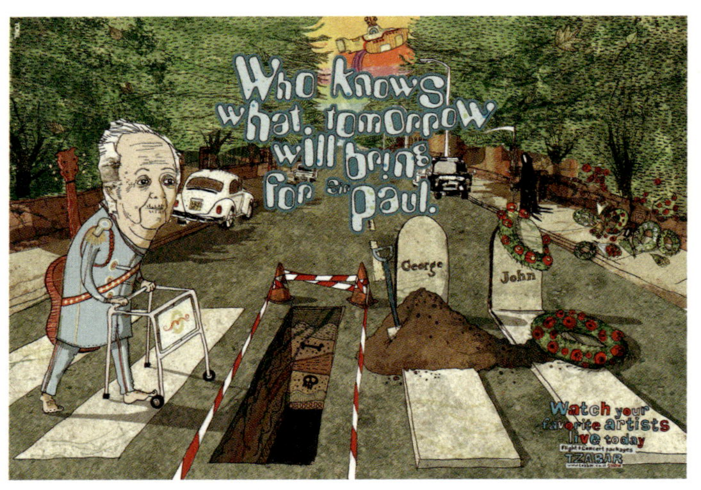

ISRAËL ISRAEL (2009)
Grey Tel Aviv Tzabar. Flights and concerts packages.
Who knows what tomorrow will bring for Sir Paul.
Watch your favorite artists live today

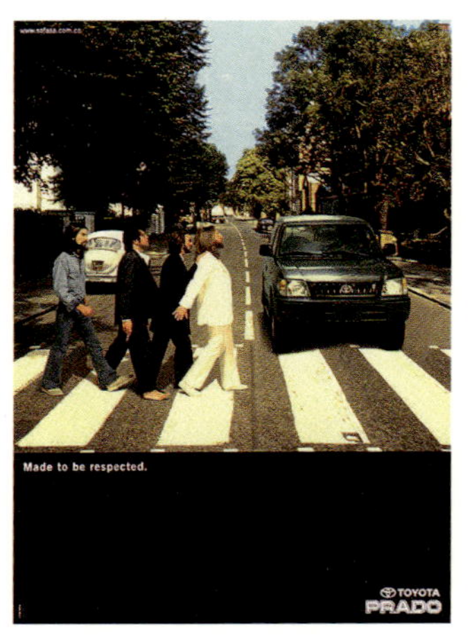

COLOMBIE COLOMBIA (2001)
Lowe Toyota Prado
Made to be respected

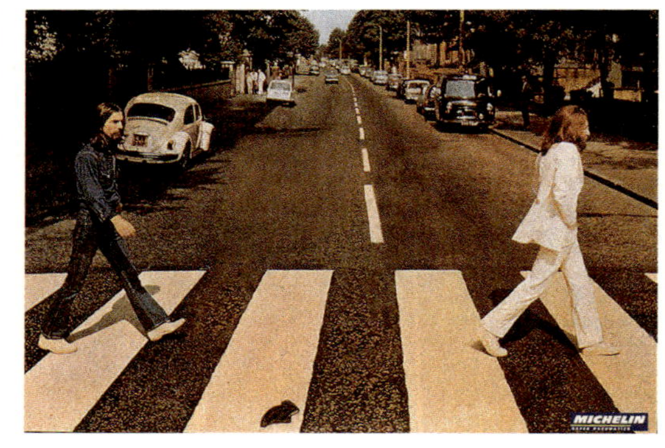

ARGENTINE ARGENTINA (2001)
EuroRSCG Michelin
Safer Pneumatics

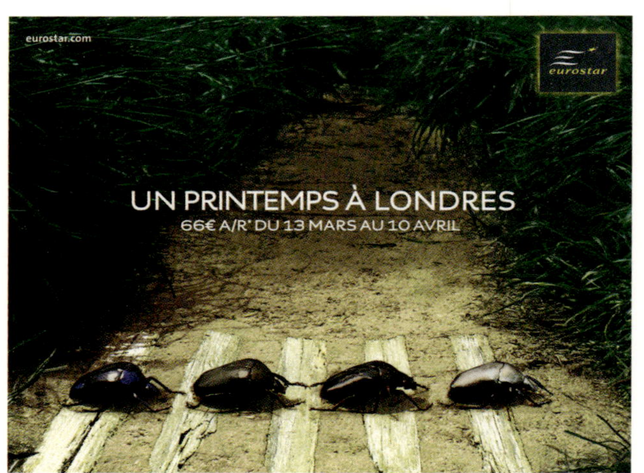

FRANCE FRANCE (2007)
Leg Eurostar
Springtime in London

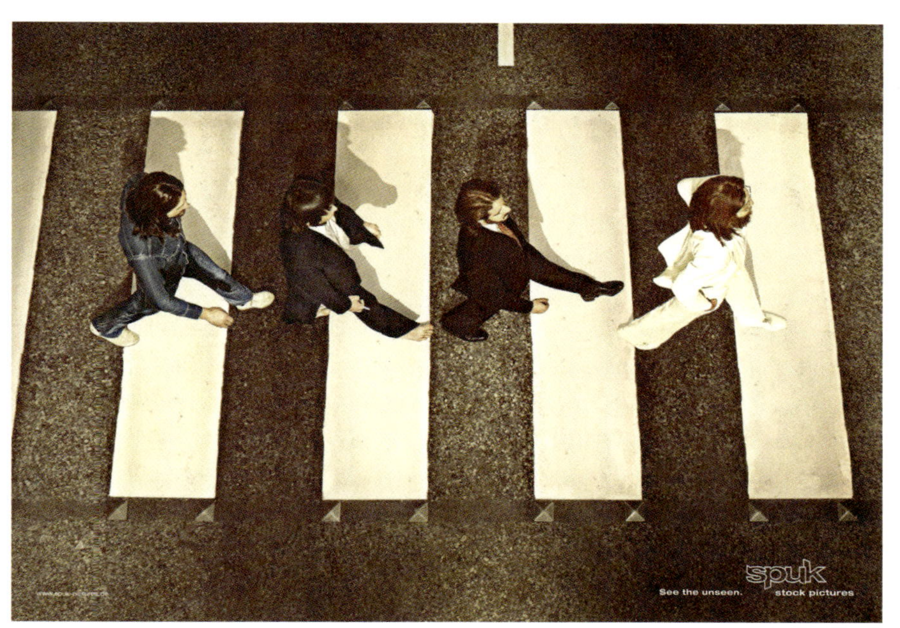

ALLEMAGNE GERMANY (2010)
BBDO Dusseldorf   Spuk stock pictures
See the unseen.

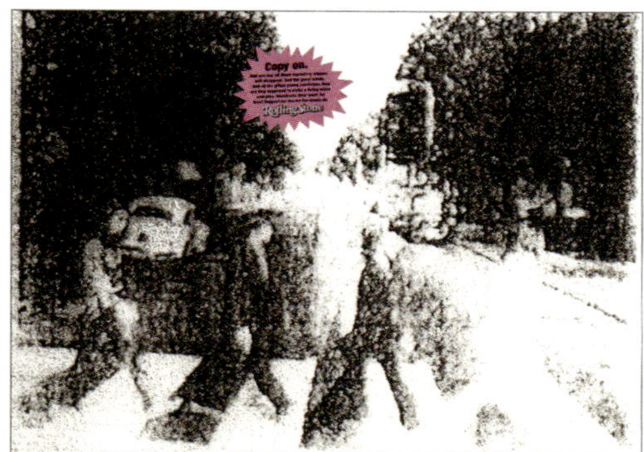

ALLEMAGNE GERMANY (2010)
Ogilvy Frankfurt   money-for-music.de
Copy on. And one day all those legendary albums will
disappear. And the great bands. And all the gifted young
musicians. How are they supposed to make a living when
everyone downloads their work for free?
Support us: money-for-music.de

ABBEY ROAD

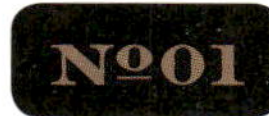

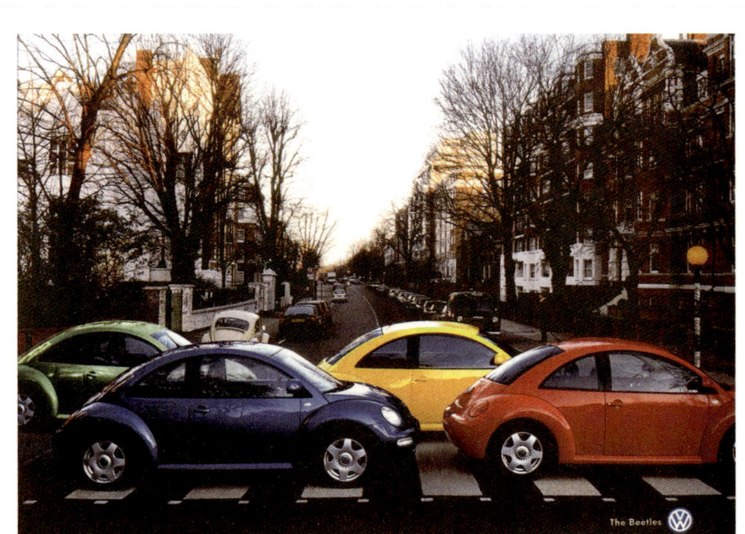

NORVÈGE NORWAY (2007)
Bates   Volkswagen
The Beetles

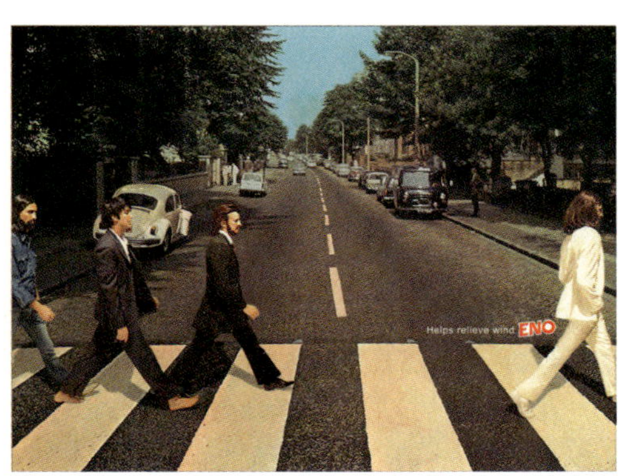

CHINE CHINA (2007)
Grey Hong Kong   ENO
Helps relieve wind

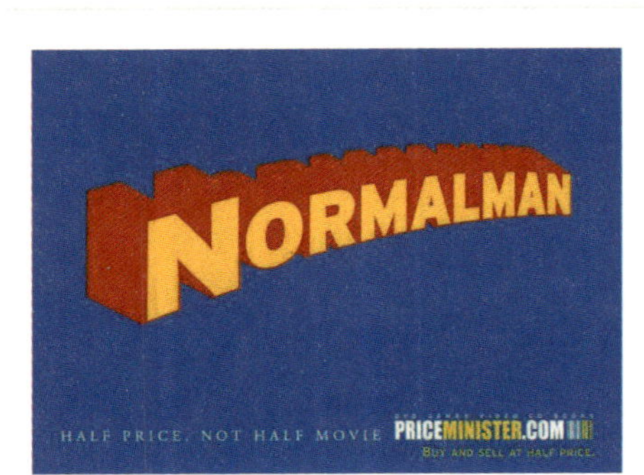

FRANCE FRANCE (2003)
Leg · Price Minister
Half price, not half movie

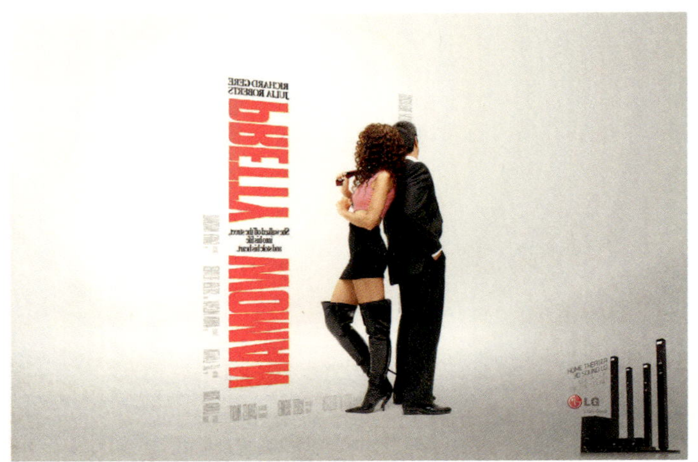

BRÉSIL BRAZIL (2012)
Young & Rubicam Sao Paulo · LG Home theater 3D sound
Every side of the sound

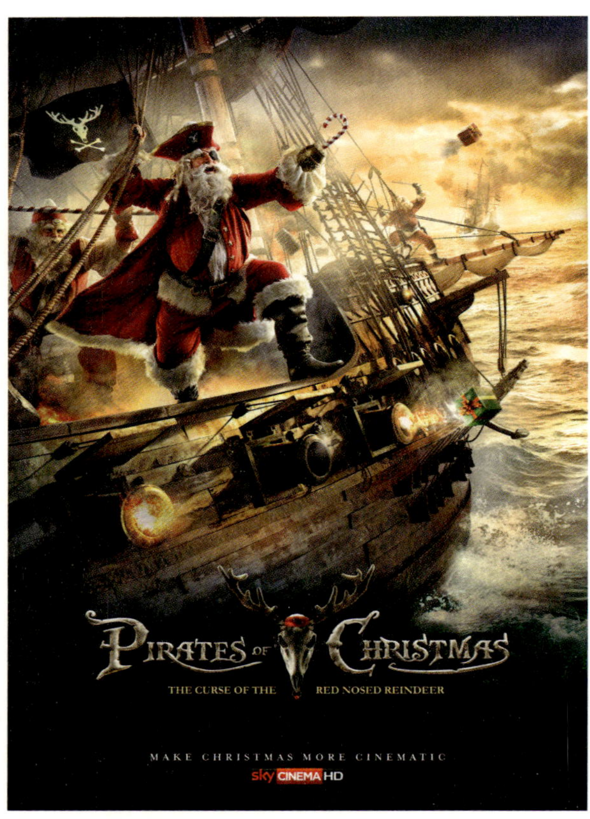

ITALIE ITALY (2012)
1861 Milan · Sky Cinema HD

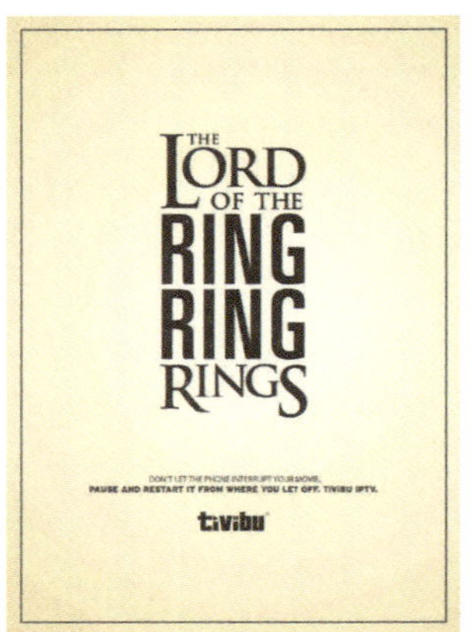

TURQUIE TURKEY (2011)
TBWA Istanbul · Tivibu
Don't let the phone interrupt
your movie

BELGIQUE BELGIUM (2000)
Euro RSCG United · Club RTL
The main film goes twice
every evening

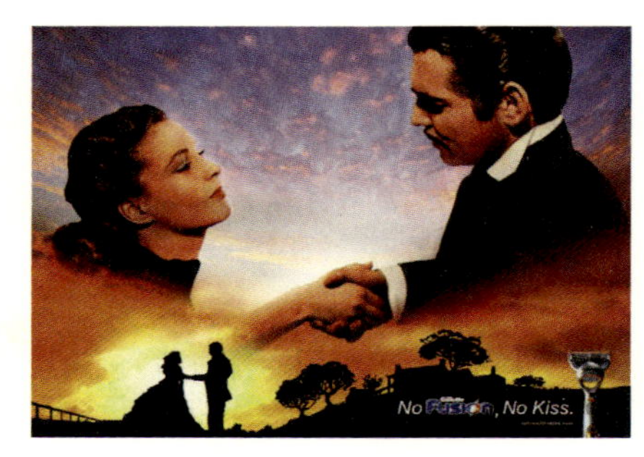

ALLEMAGNE GERMANY (2008)
BBDO · Gillette Fusion
No fusion, No kiss

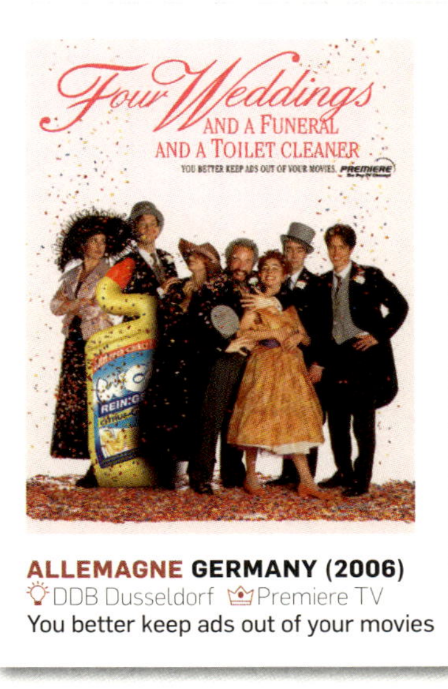

VIÊT-NAM VIETNAM (2007)
Ogilvy & Mather Megastar Cineplex
On a smaller screen you get a smaller movie

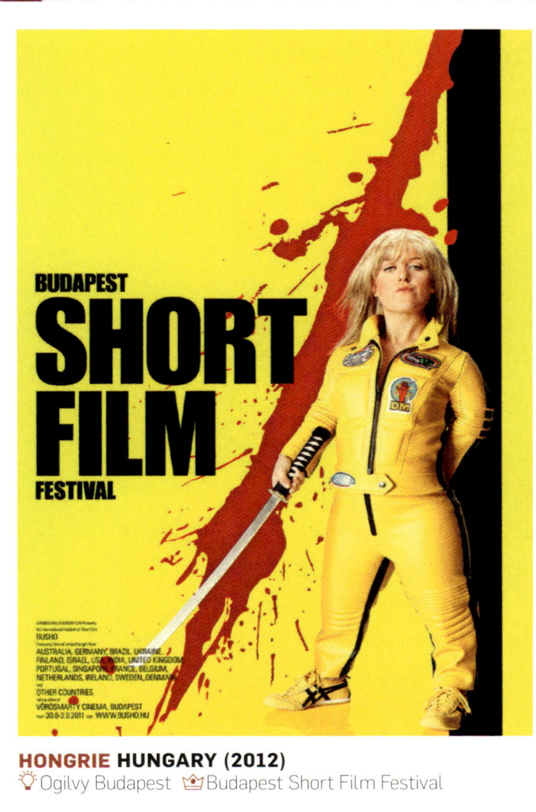

ALLEMAGNE GERMANY (2006)
DDB Dusseldorf Premiere TV
You better keep ads out of your movies

HONGRIE HUNGARY (2012)
Ogilvy Budapest Budapest Short Film Festival

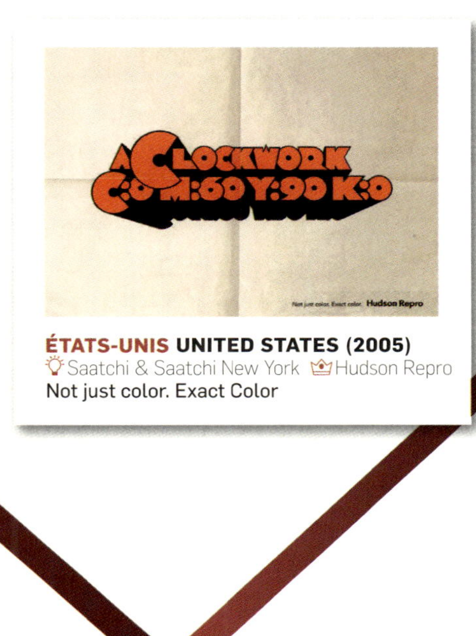

ÉTATS-UNIS UNITED STATES (2005)
Saatchi & Saatchi New York Hudson Repro
Not just color. Exact Color

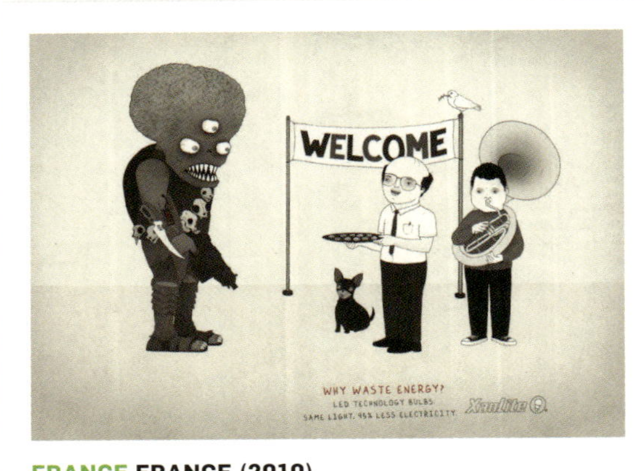

FRANCE FRANCE (2010)
Ogilvy & Mather · Xanlite LED Technology
Why waste energy?

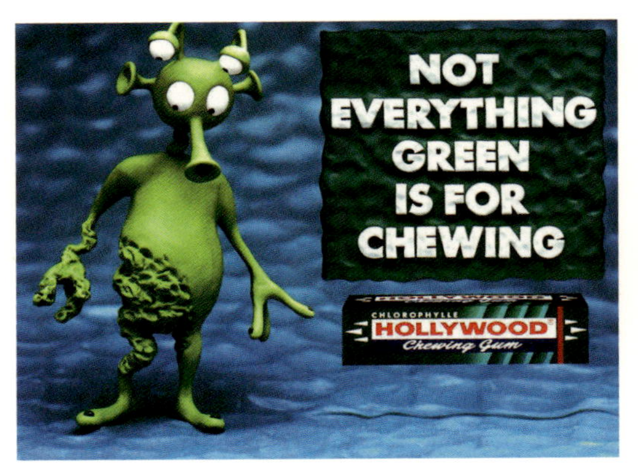

FRANCE FRANCE (1999)
BETC Euro RSCG · Hollywood Chewing-Gum

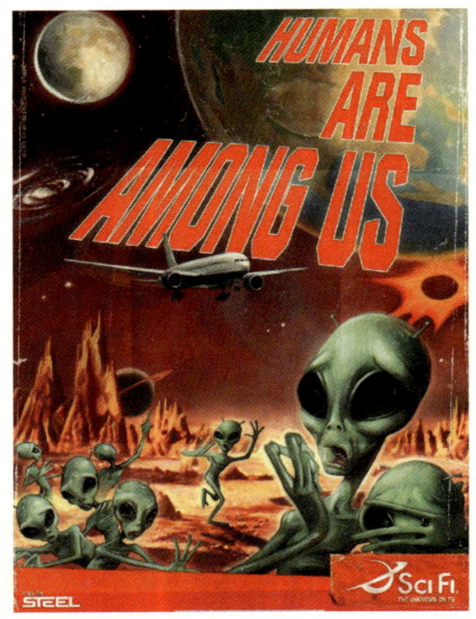

ITALIE ITALY (2009)
Saatchi & Saatchi Roma · Sci Fi

ALIENS

№ 03

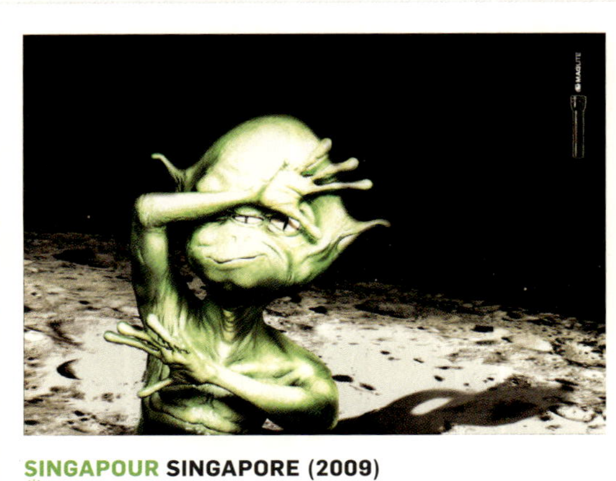

SINGAPOUR SINGAPORE (2009)
Ogilvy · Maglite

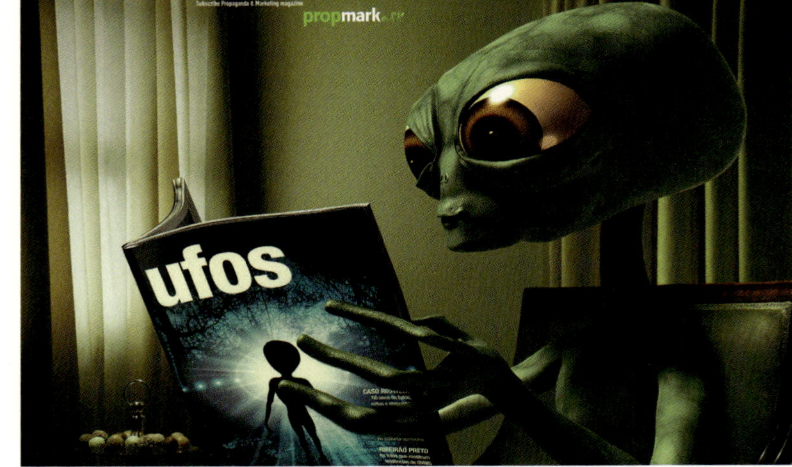

BRÉSIL BRAZIL (2008)
Neogama BBH · Propmark
If you're in advertising and marketing, what are you going to read?

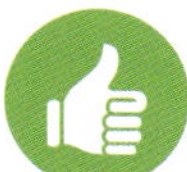

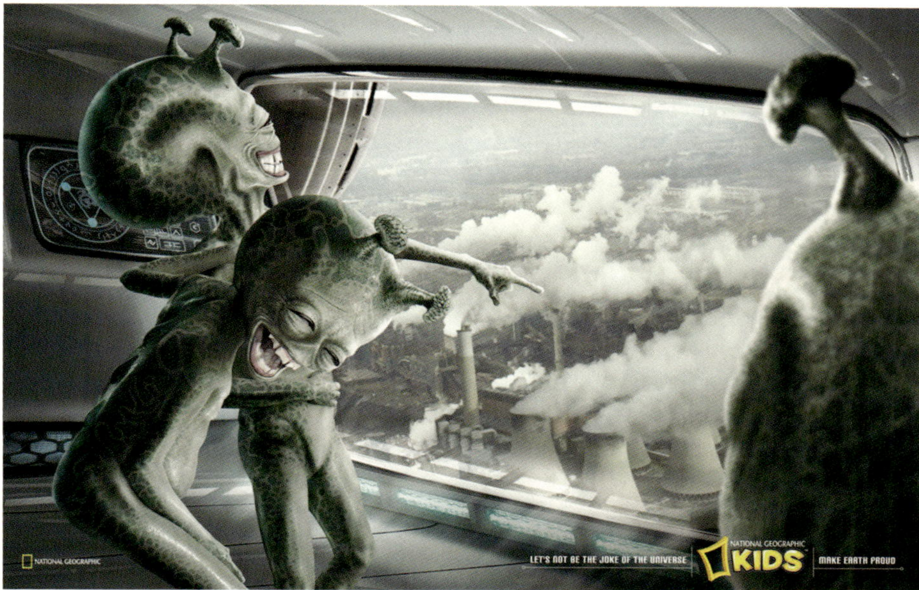

AFRIQUE DU SUD
SOUTH AFRICA (2010)
Foxp2 CapeTown
National Geographic Kids
Let's not be the joke
of the universe

« On représente toujours les
extra-terrestres comme une
menace, alors que finalement,
le pire danger, c'est nous-mêmes.
C'est donc très bien vu et, à vrai
dire, à leur place, je rigolerais
bien en voyant certains de nos
comportements. »
"Extra-terrestrials are always
represented as a threat, even
though we are our own worst
enemy. So it's very well
considered, and indeed in their
place I'd have a good laugh
at some of our behaviour."

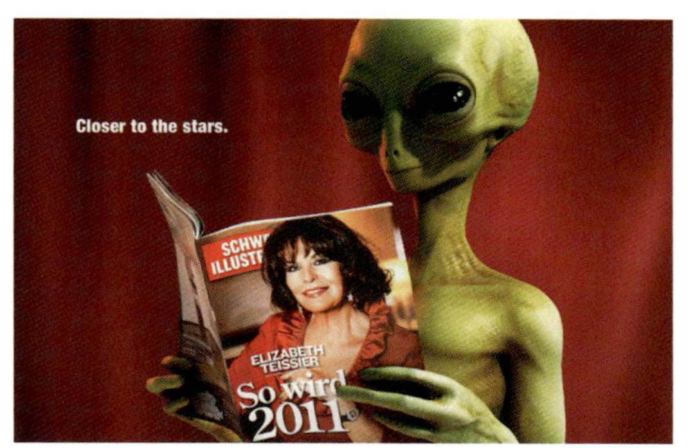

SUISSE **SWITZERLAND (2010)**
Wirz Werbung   Schweizer Illustrierte
Closer to the stars

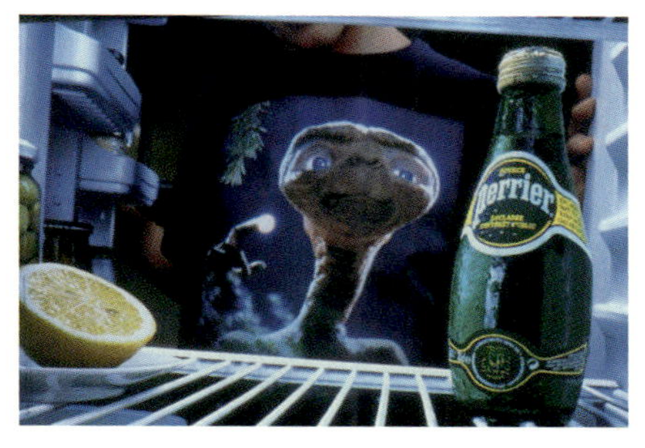

FRANCE **FRANCE (2002)**
Ogilvy & Mather   Perrier

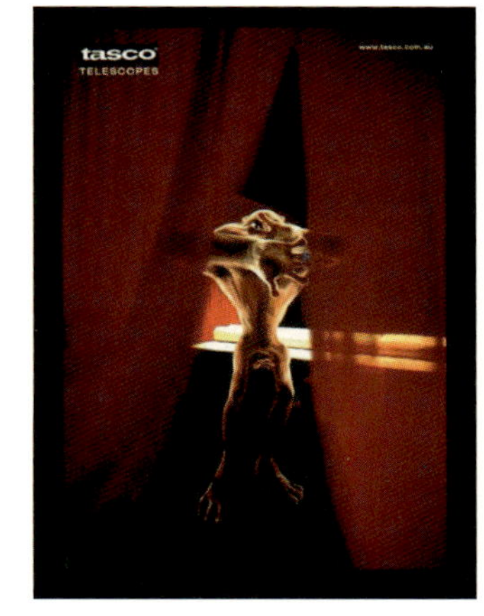

AUSTRALIE **AUSTRALIA (2002)**
Brown Melhuish Fishlock
Tasco Telescopes

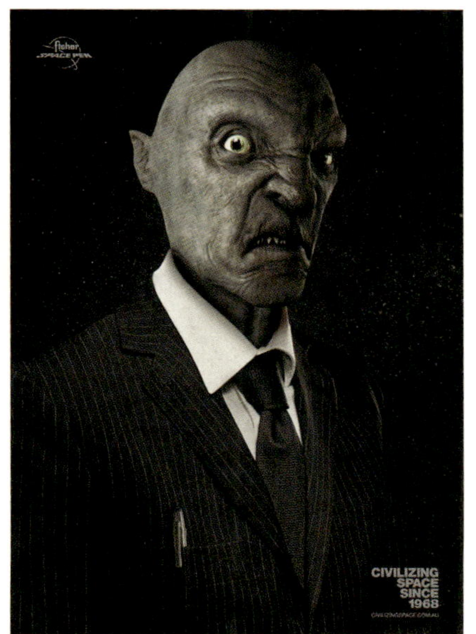

AUSTRALIE **AUSTRALIE (2009)**
Kastner & Partners, Sydney
Fischer Space Pen
Civilizing space since 1968

AUSTRALIE
AUSTRALIA (2008)
Fenton Stephens Melbourne
Gorilla Ladders
A new bread of ladders

« Sur l'échelle du rire, je mettrais
un 10/10 à celle-ci.
C'est tellement simple, poétique,
crétin et inattendu que j'ai été
séduit par l'idée. »
"On a laughter scale, I'd give this
one 10 out of 10. It is so simple,
poetic, stupid and unexpected
that I was seduced by the idea."

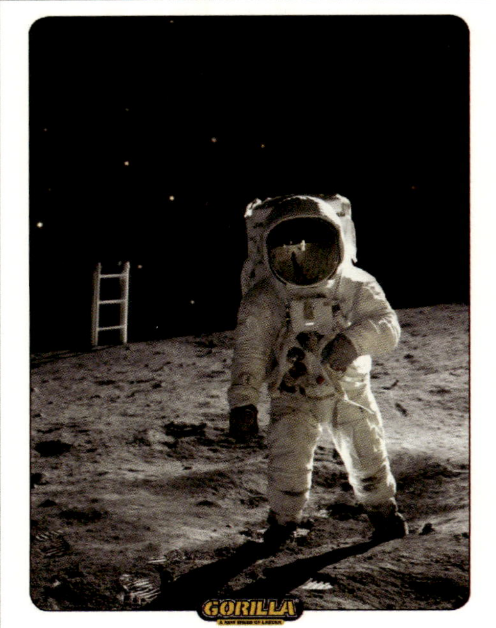

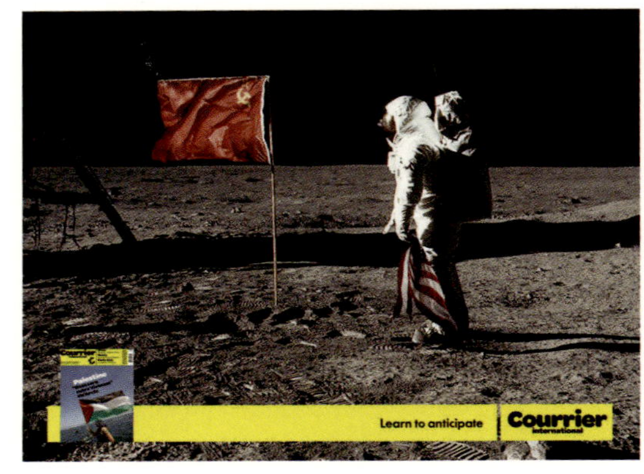

FRANCE FRANCE (2010)
Saatchi & Saatchi   Courrier International
Learn to anticipate

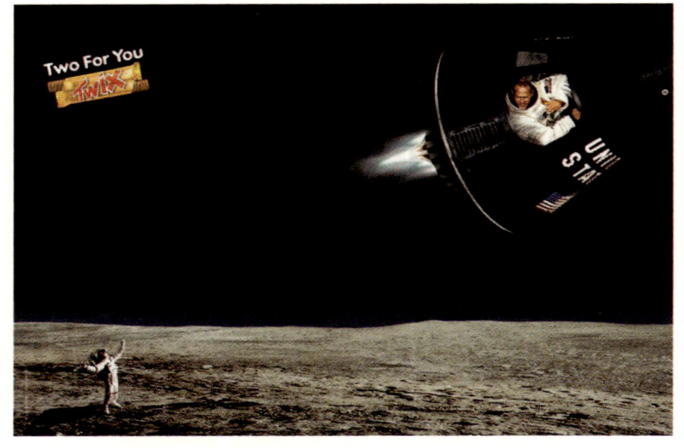

ROYAUME-UNI UNITED KINGDOM (2005)
Grey London   Twix
Two for you

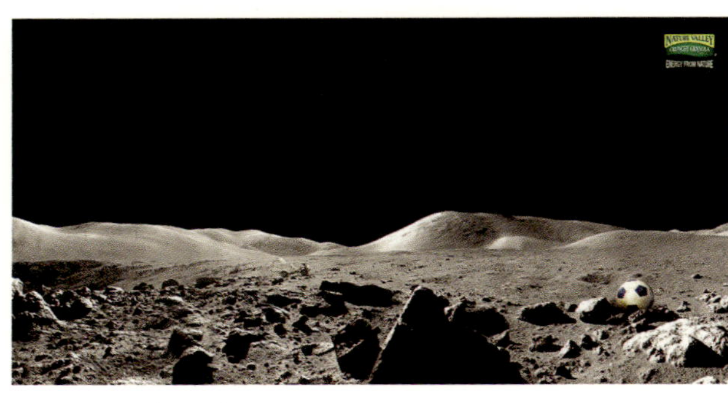

INDE INDIA (2007)
Solutions Integrated Marketing Services NewDelhi
Nature Valley Crunchy Granola
Energy from nature

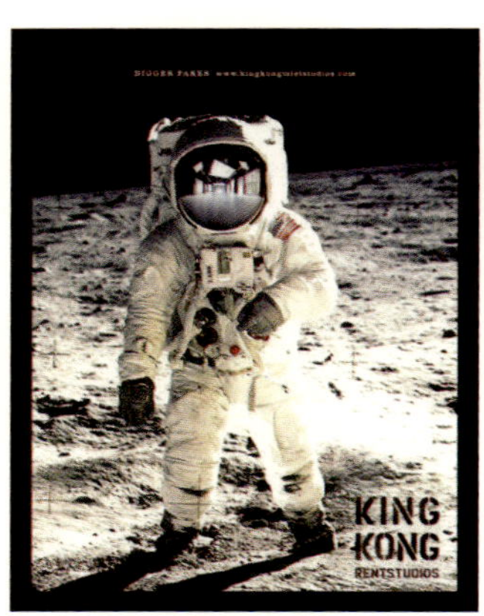

ALLEMAGNE GERMANY (2006)
BBDO   King Kong Rent Studios
Bigger Fakes

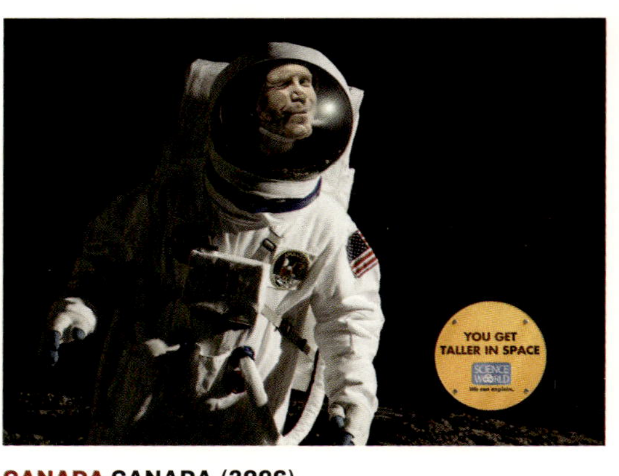

CANADA CANADA (2006)
Rethink   Science World
You get taller in space. We can explain

APOLLO MISSIONS

№ 04

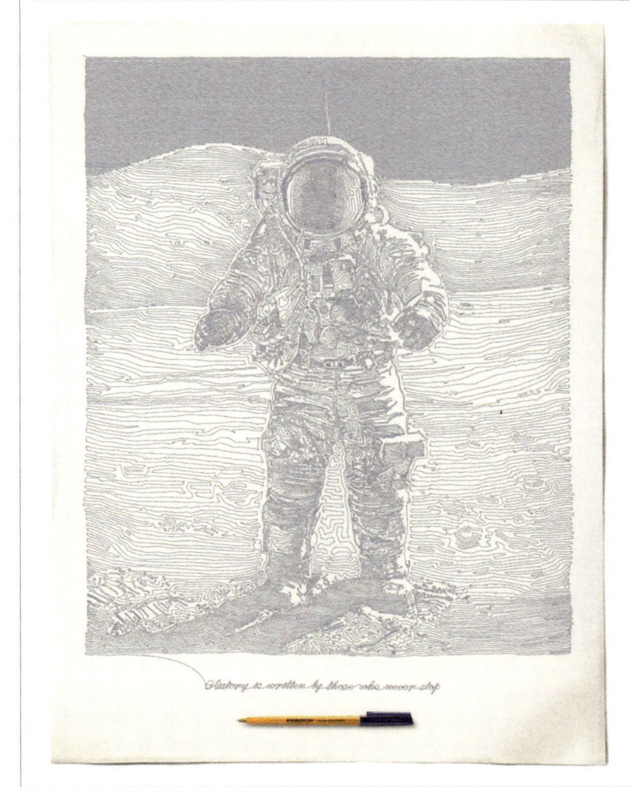

INDE INDIA (2010)
Bates Staedtler Pens
History is written by those who never stop

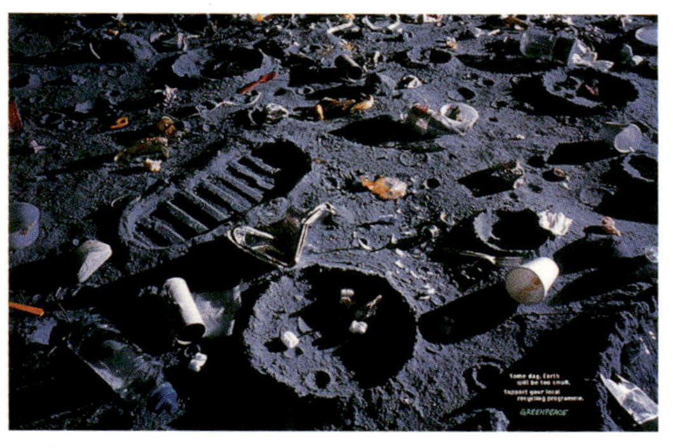

BRÉSIL BRAZIL (2001)
Giovanni FCB Greenpeace
Some day, earth will be too small.
Support your local recycling program.

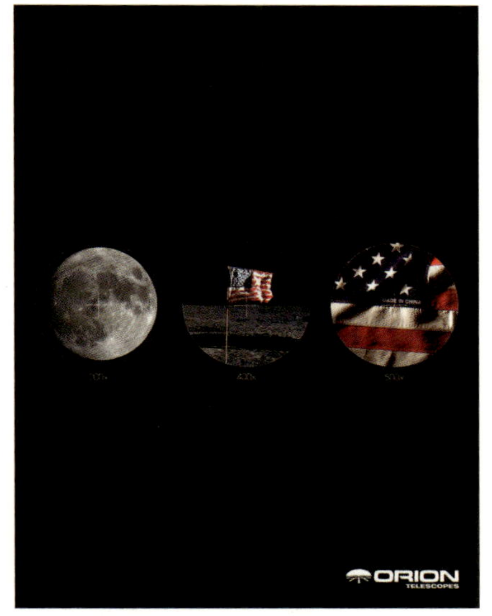

ÉTATS-UNIS UNITED STATES (2007)
Texas Creative Orion Telescopes
(on the zoom x800 we can read
"made in China" on the US Flag)

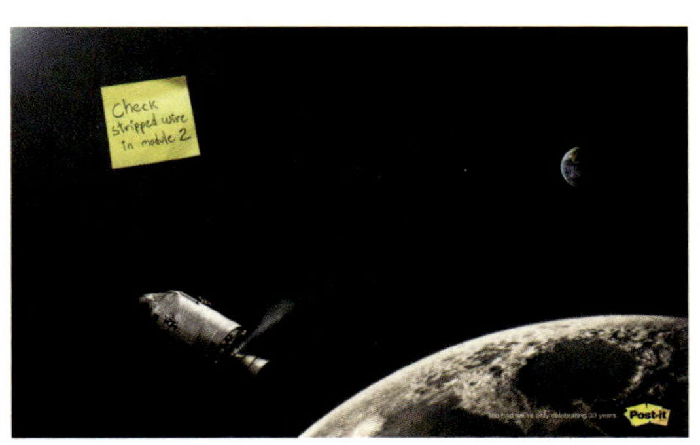

MEXIQUE MEXICO (2010)
BBDO Post-It
"Check stripped wire in module 2"
Too bad we're only celebrating 30 years

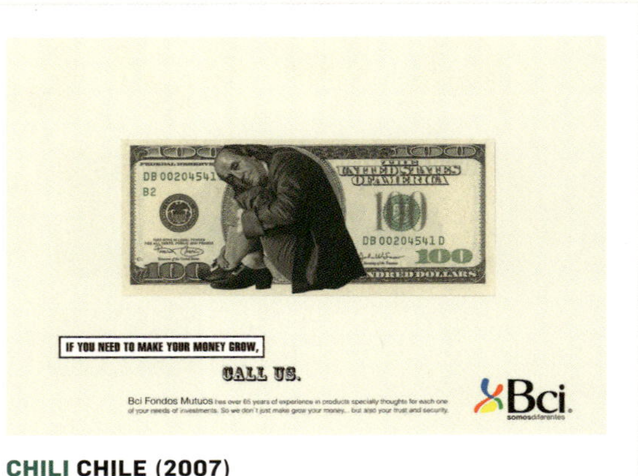

CHILI CHILE (2007)
MC Cann Erickson — BCI Mutual Funds
If you need to make your money grow call us

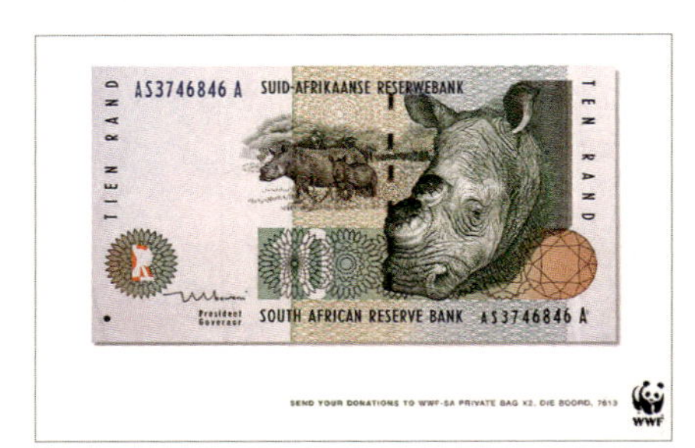

AFRIQUE DU SUD SOUTH AFRICA (2001)
Ogilvy & Mather — WWF
Send your donations to WWF

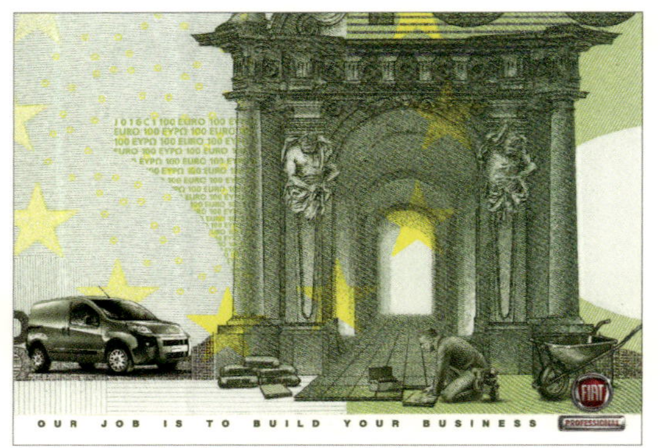

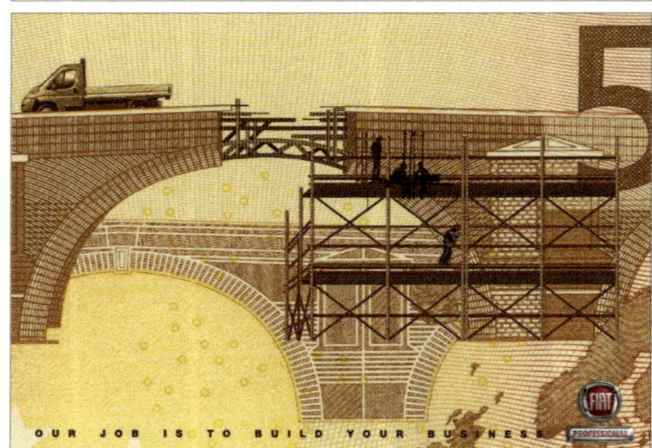

ITALIE ITALY (2009)
Leo Burnett Turin — Fiat Professionnal
Our job is to build your business

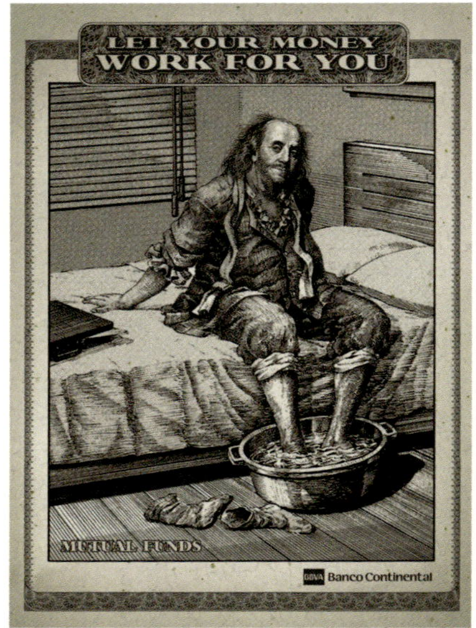

PÉROU PERU (2008)
DraftFCB — Banco Continental
Let your money work for you

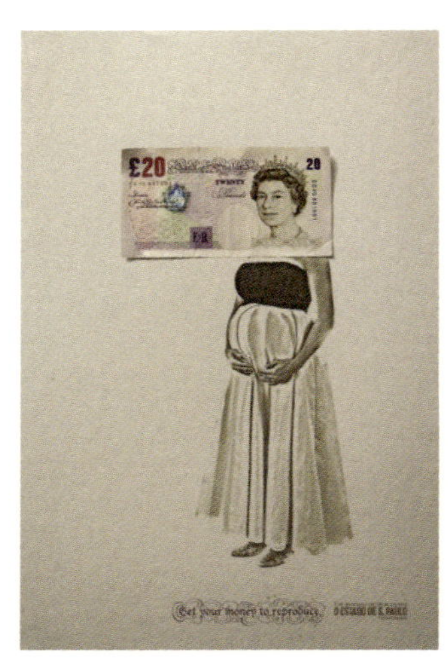

BRÉSIL BRAZIL (2007)
Talent Propaganda
O estate de Sao Paulo Newspaper
Get your money to reproduce

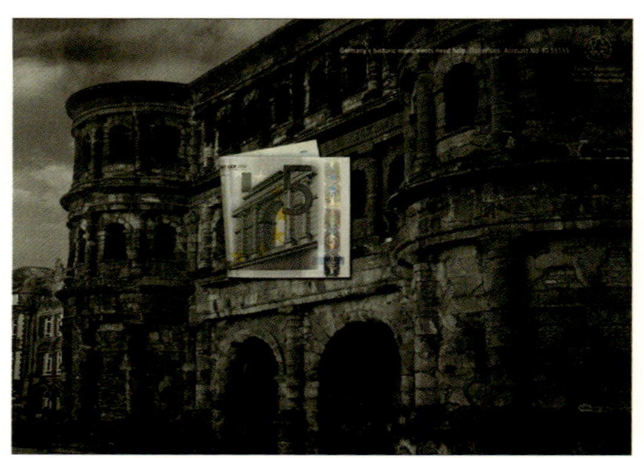

ALLEMAGNE GERMANY (2005)
Ogilvy & Mather Frankfurt
German's Historic Monuments
German's Historic Monuments need help

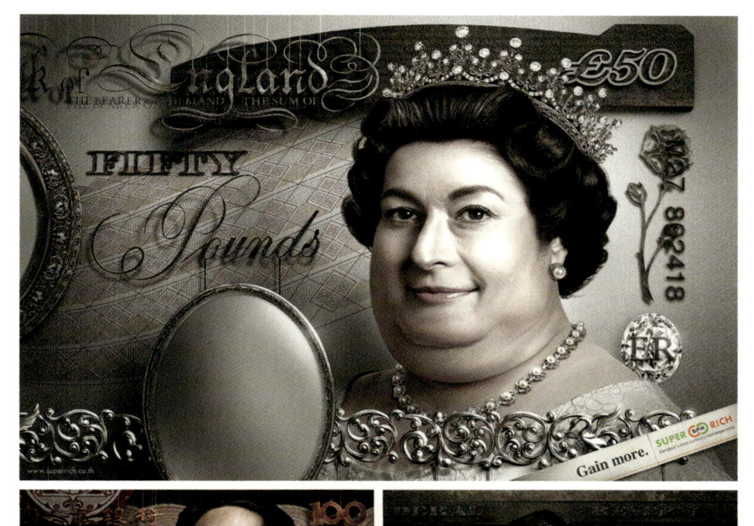
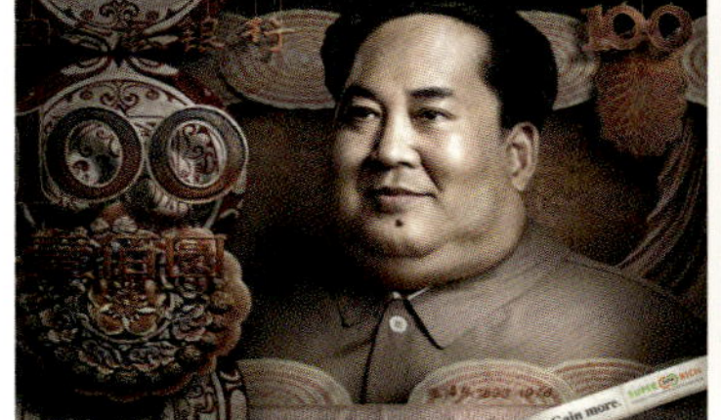
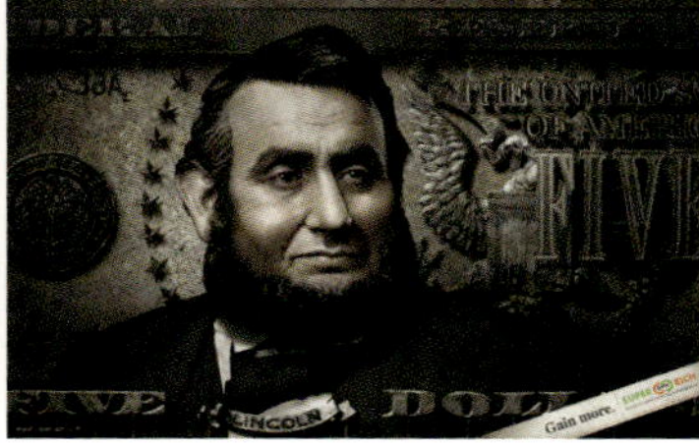

THAÏLANDE THAILAND (2011)
Ogilvy Bangkok SPR Super Rich / Currency exchange
Gain more

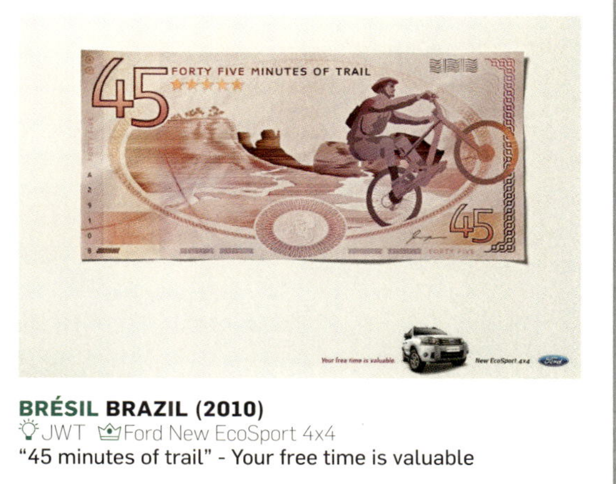

BRÉSIL BRAZIL (2010)
JWT Ford New EcoSport 4x4
"45 minutes of trail" - Your free time is valuable

ARGENT
№05
MONEY

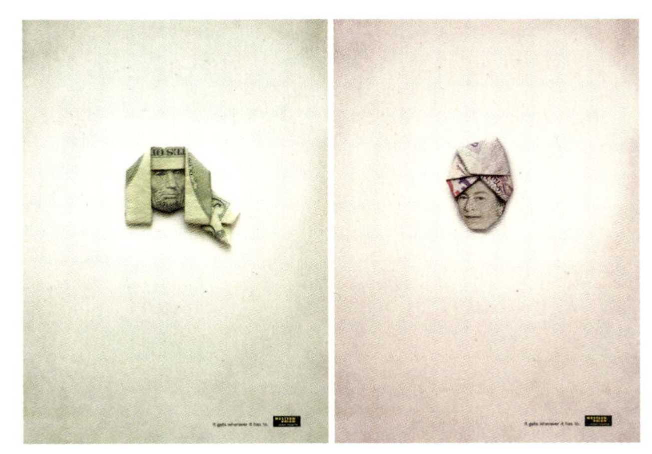

ESPAGNE SPAIN (2010)
M&C Saatchi Madrid Western Union Money Transfer
It gets wherever it has to

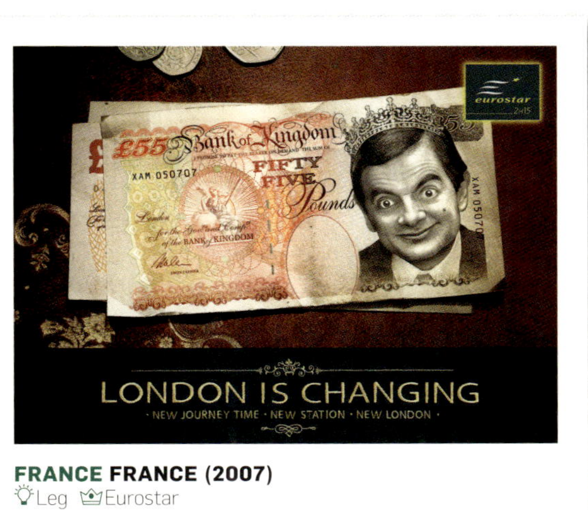

FRANCE FRANCE (2007)
Leg Eurostar

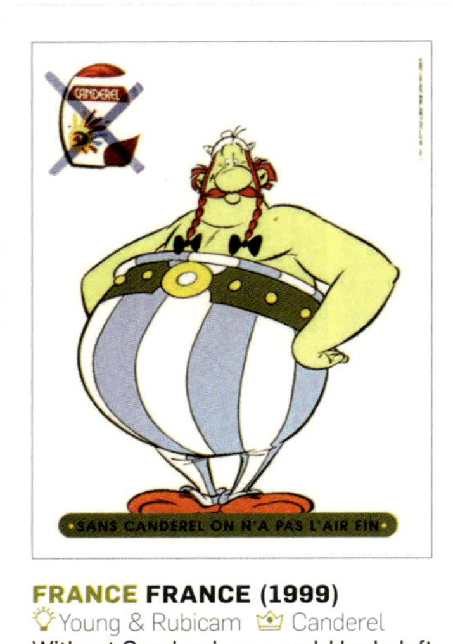

FRANCE FRANCE (1999)
Young & Rubicam   Canderel
Without Canderel, we would look daft

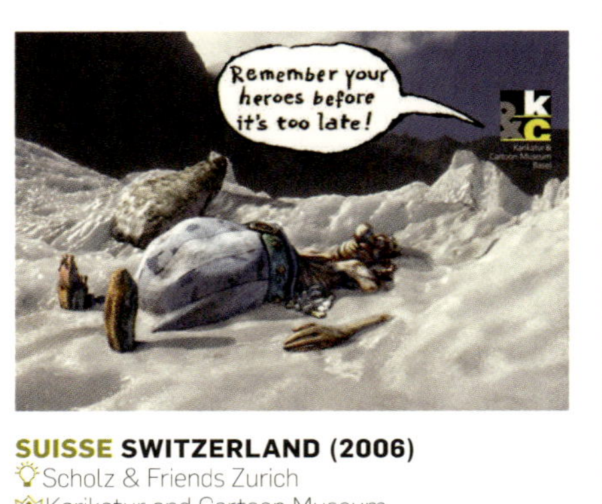

SUISSE SWITZERLAND (2006)
Scholz & Friends Zurich
Karikatur and Cartoon Museum
Remember your heroes before it's too late

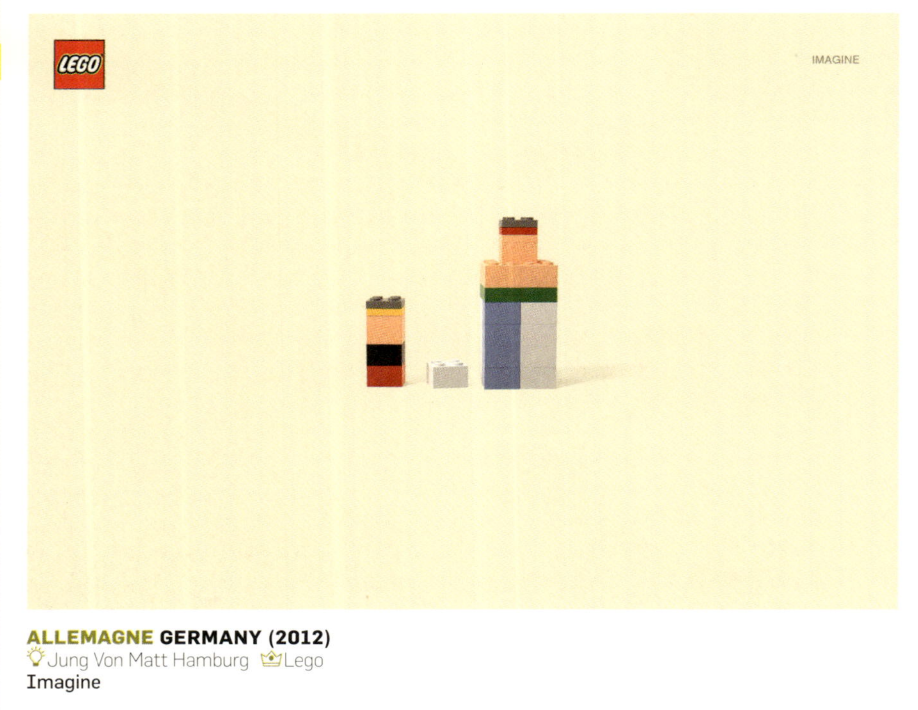

ALLEMAGNE GERMANY (2012)
Jung Von Matt Hamburg   Lego
Imagine

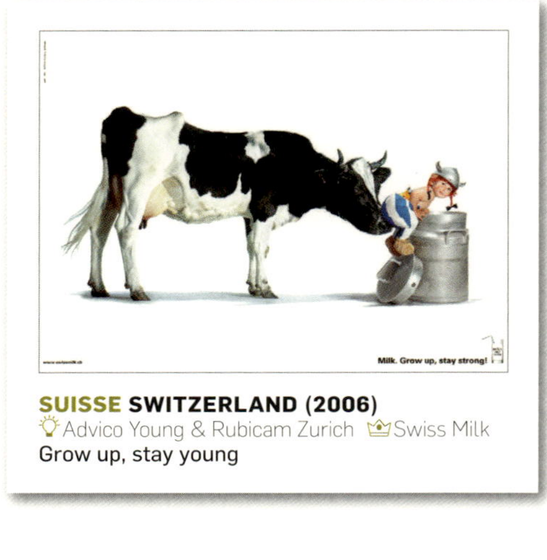

SUISSE SWITZERLAND (2006)
Advico Young & Rubicam Zurich   Swiss Milk
Grow up, stay young

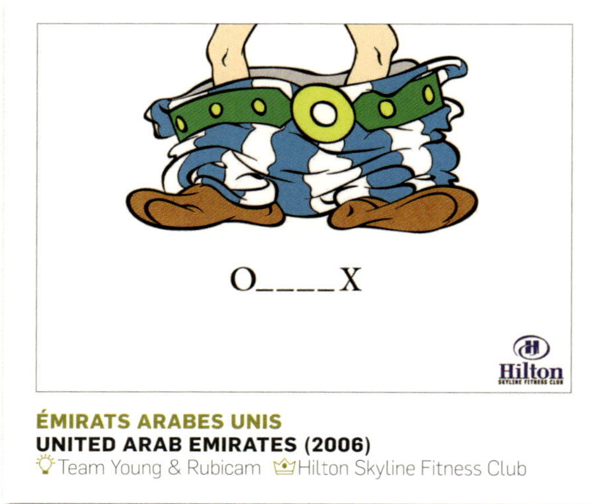

ÉMIRATS ARABES UNIS
UNITED ARAB EMIRATES (2006)
Team Young & Rubicam   Hilton Skyline Fitness Club

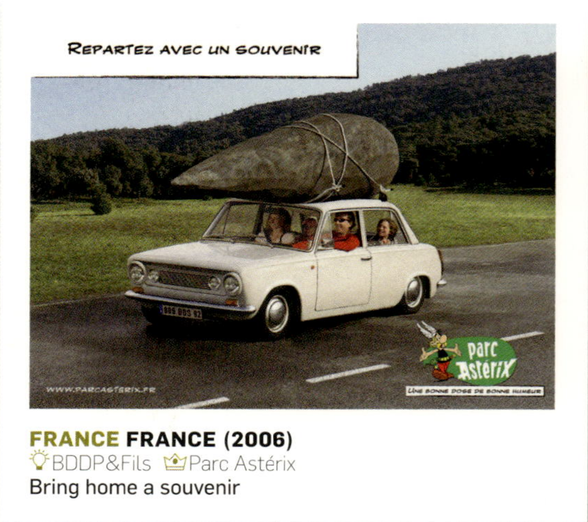

FRANCE FRANCE (2006)
BDDP&Fils   Parc Astérix
Bring home a souvenir

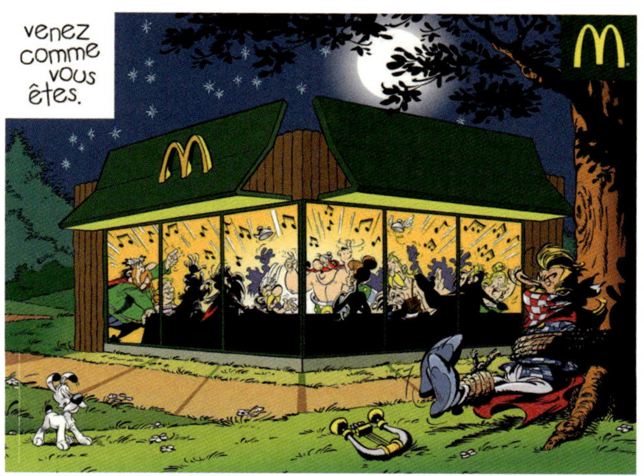

FRANCE FRANCE (2010)
BETC Euro RSCG Mc Donald's
Come as you are

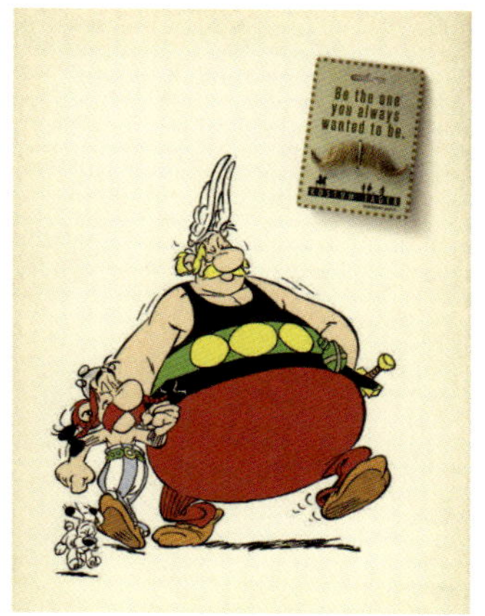

ALLEMAGNE GERMANY (2006)
Scholz & Friends
Kostum Jager (Costume Rental)
Be the one you always wanted to be

ASTERIX

№06

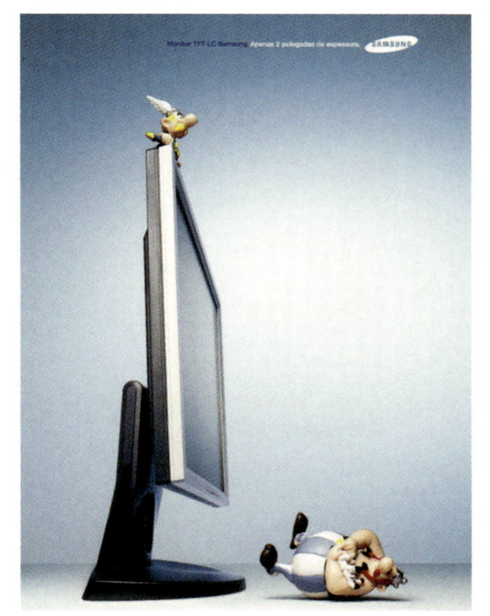

BRÉSIL BRAZIL (2003)
Giovanni FCB SaoPaulo Samsung
Flatscreen

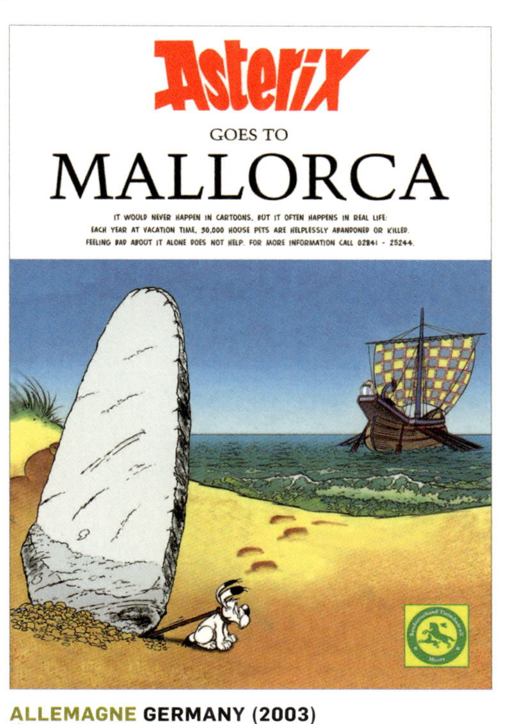

ALLEMAGNE GERMANY (2003)
H2E Society For The Prevention Of Cruelty To Animals
It would never happen in cartoons,
but it often happens in real life…

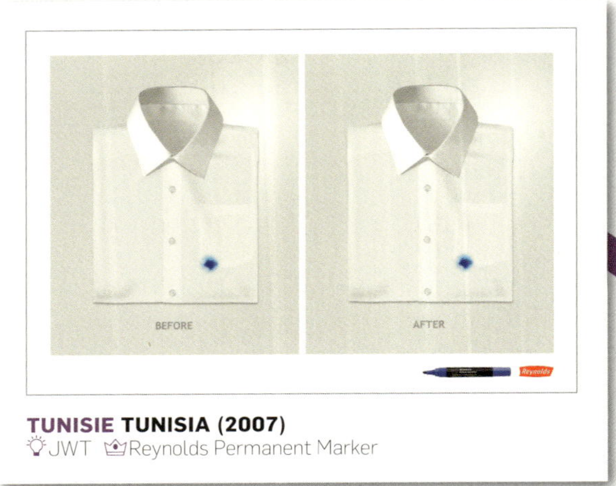

TUNISIE TUNISIA (2007)
JWT · Reynolds Permanent Marker

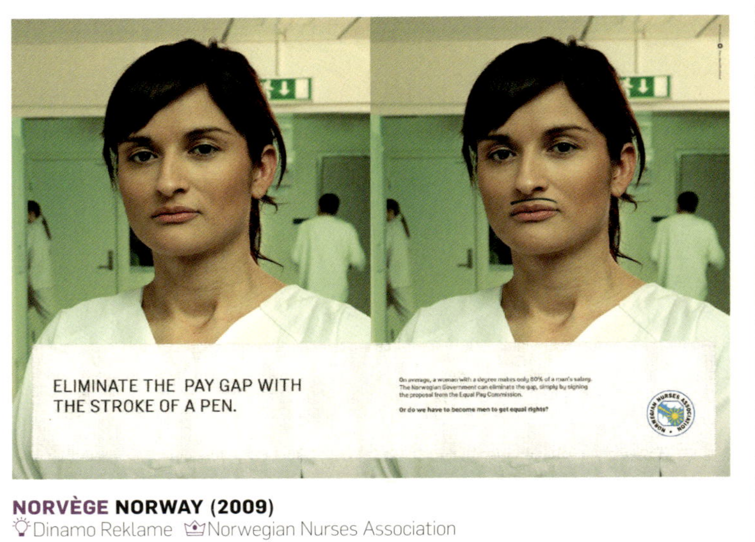

NORVÈGE NORWAY (2009)
Dinamo Reklame · Norwegian Nurses Association

AVANT/APRÈS
№ 07
BEFORE/AFTER

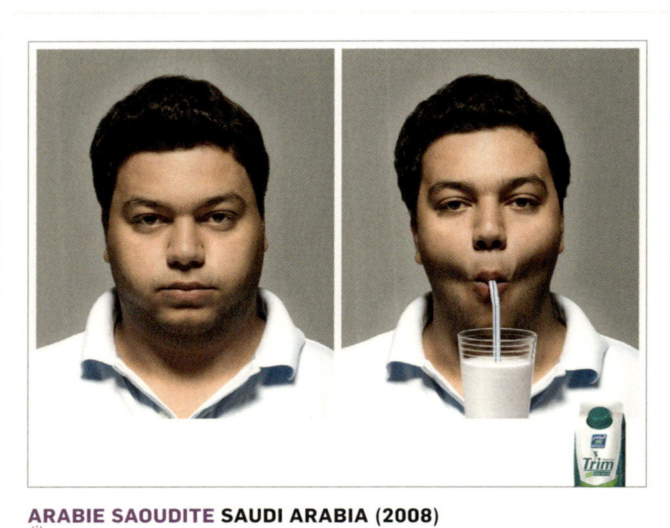

ARABIE SAOUDITE SAUDI ARABIA (2008)
Leo Burnett Jeddah · Trim Low Fat Milk

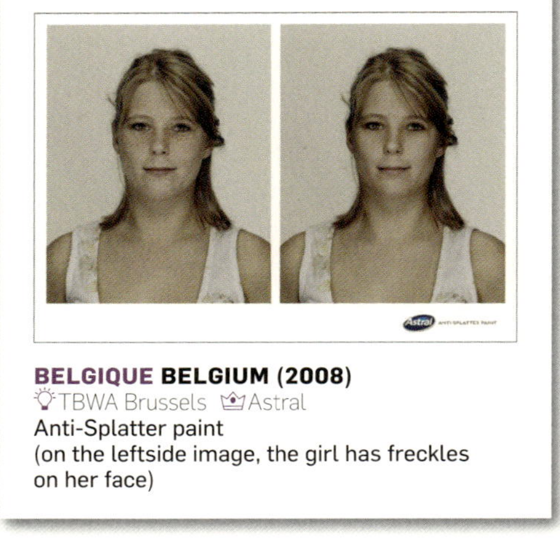

BELGIQUE BELGIUM (2008)
TBWA Brussels · Astral
Anti-Splatter paint
(on the leftside image, the girl has freckles
on her face)

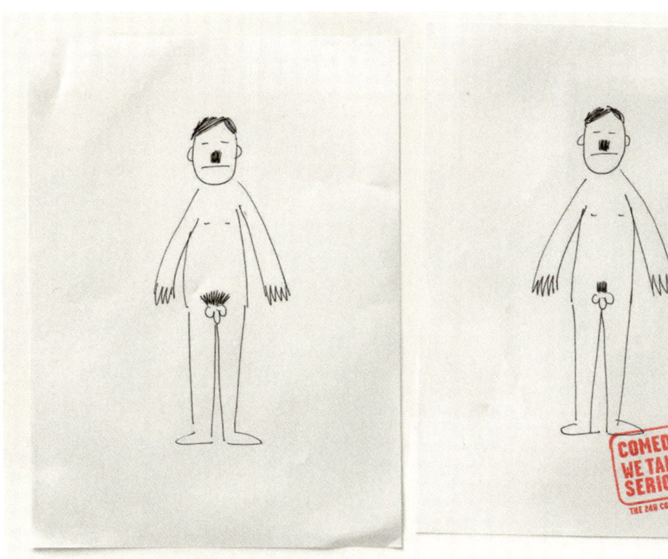

ALLEMAGNE GERMANY (2007)
Kempertrautmann Hamburg Comedy Central Channel
Comedy. We take it serious.

« J'adore cette campagne. Ça se joue sur des détails mais qui font toute la différence. C'est très difficile de faire quelque chose de drôle pour une chaîne de comédie sans tomber dans le scato, le pouet pouet ou le lourdingue. »
"I love this campaign. It plays on all the details but that is what makes all the difference. It is really hard to make something funny for a comedy channel without getting into fart jokes, clown horns and crudeness."

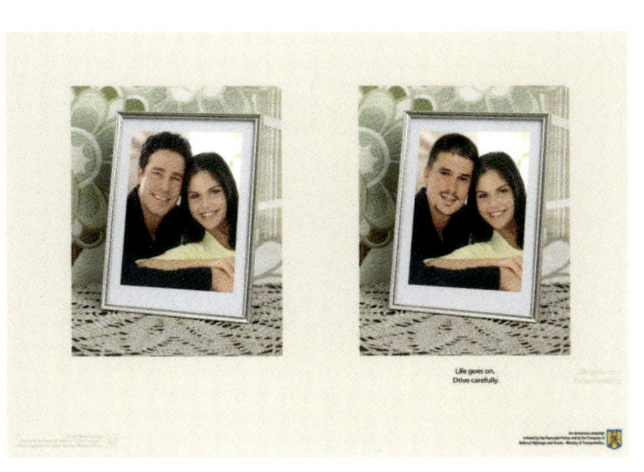

ROUMANIE ROMANIA (2007)
Mc Cann Erickson Awareness Campaign / Road Safety
Life goes on. Drive carefully
(The man on the right frame differs from the one in the left frame)

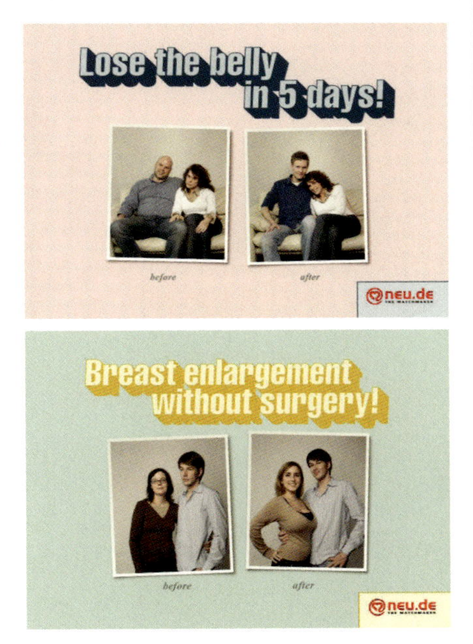

ALLEMAGNE GERMANY (2007)
Saatchi & Saatchi Frankfurt
Neu.de Matchmaking Service

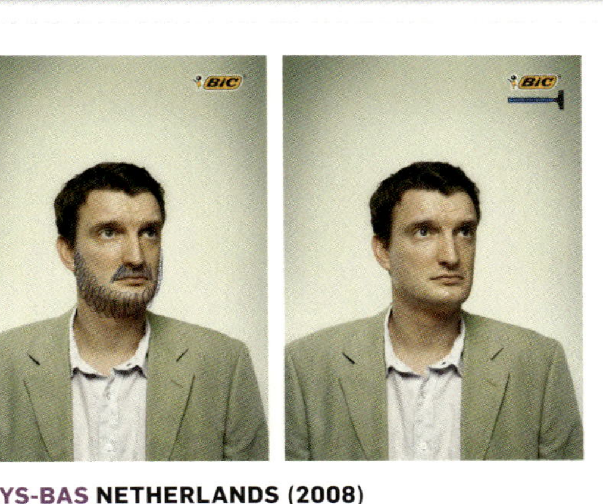

PAYS-BAS NETHERLANDS (2008)
JWT BIC
Page 1: Pens. Page 2: Shavers.

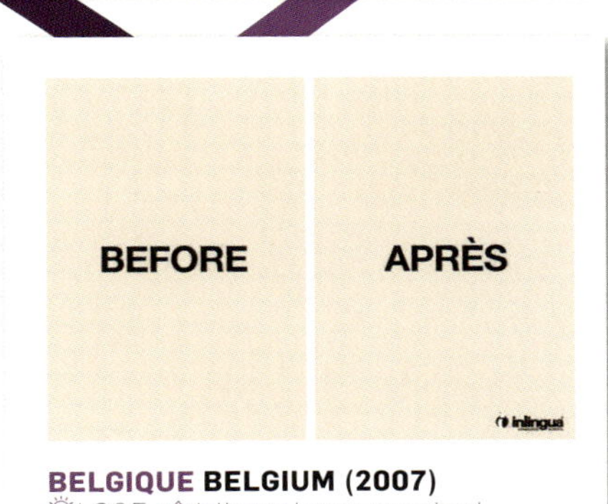

BELGIQUE BELGIUM (2007)
LG&F Inlingua language school

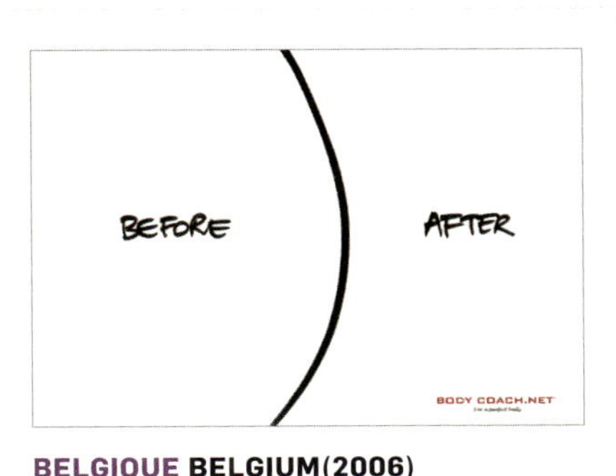

BELGIQUE BELGIUM (2006)
Duval Guillaume BodyCoach.net
For a perfect body

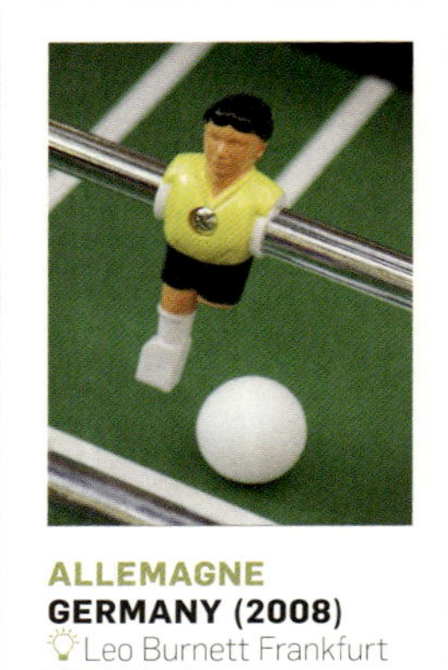

ALLEMAGNE
GERMANY (2008)
Leo Burnett Frankfurt
UNICEF
Anti Landmines campaign

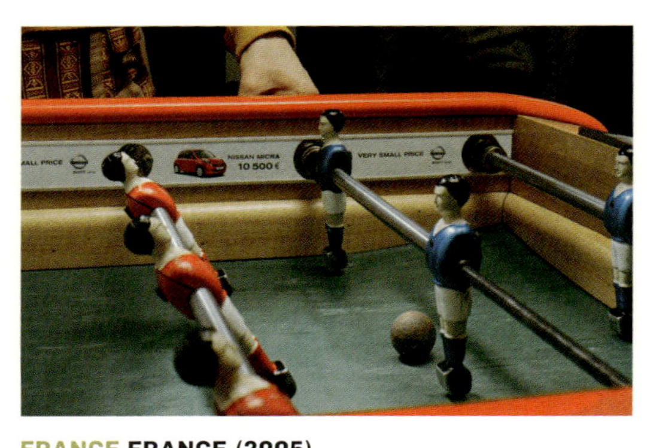

FRANCE FRANCE (2005)
TBWA G1   Nissan Micra
Very small price

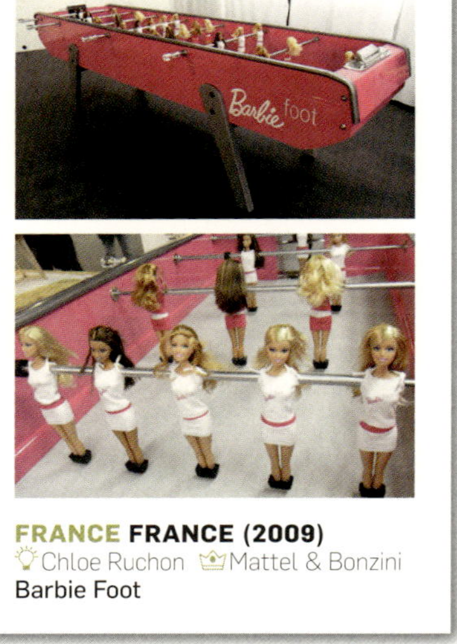

FRANCE FRANCE (2009)
Chloe Ruchon   Mattel & Bonzini
Barbie Foot

BABY-FOOT
№ 08
TABLE SOCCER

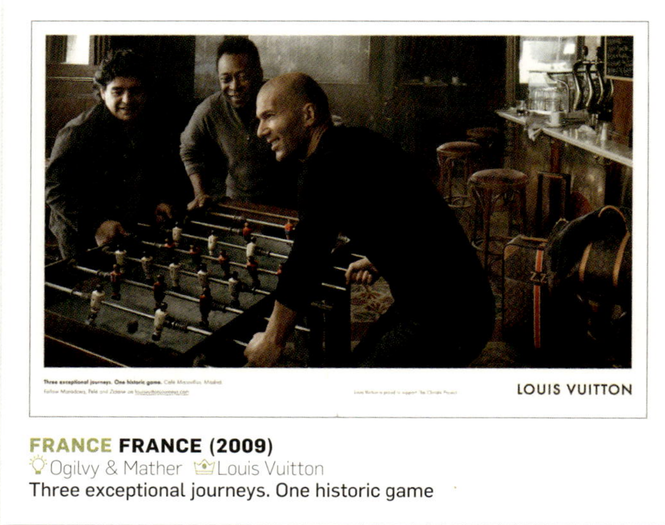

FRANCE FRANCE (2009)
Ogilvy & Mather   Louis Vuitton
Three exceptional journeys. One historic game

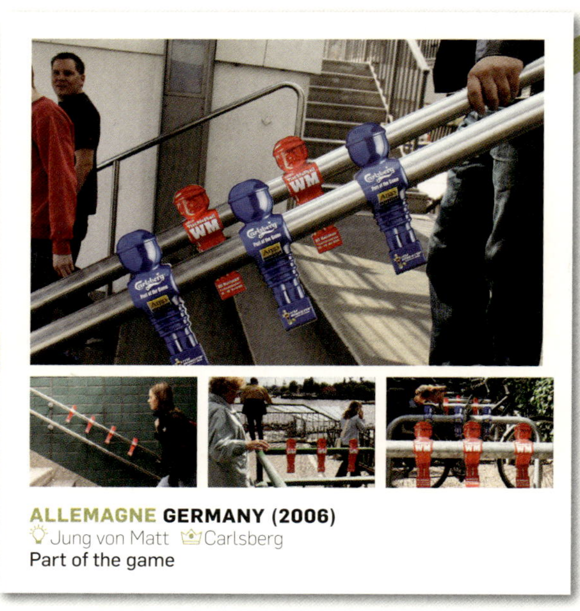

ALLEMAGNE GERMANY (2006)
Jung von Matt   Carlsberg
Part of the game

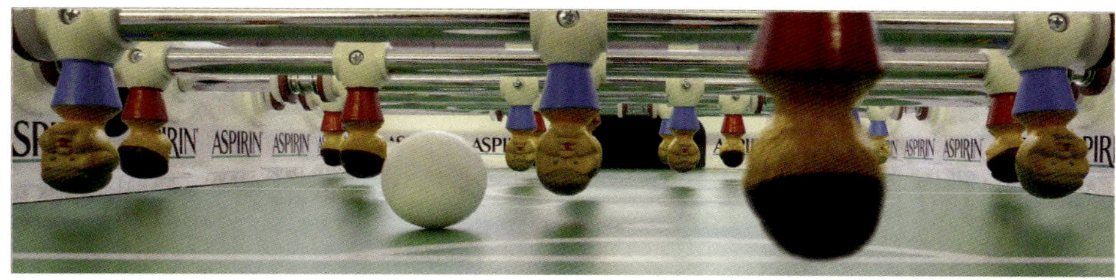

ALLEMAGNE GERMANY (2008)
BBDO Bayer Aspirin
Headache table soccer with upside down figurines

« Je trouve l'idée plutôt renversante. C'est terriblement crétin et ça marche bien. On a vraiment envie d'y jouer. Vu le Q.I. de certains footballeurs, je me demande si quand on frappe la balle ça sonne creux ? »
"I find the idea rather astonishing. It is terribly stupid and it works well. We really want to play. Given the IQ of some football players, I wonder if it sounds hollow when they the ball gets hit?"

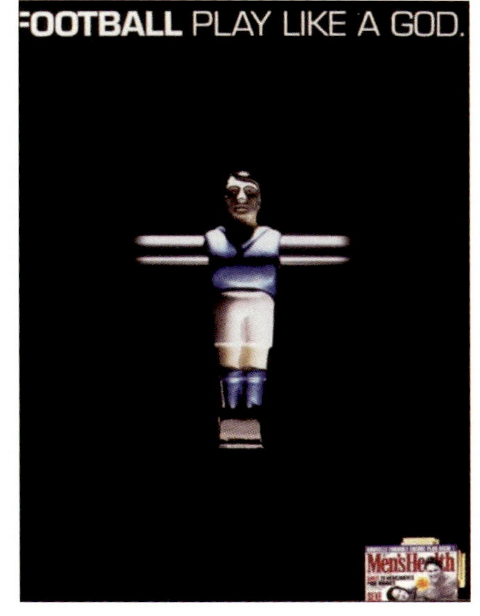

FRANCE FRANCE (2003)
Enjoy Scher Lafarge Men's Health

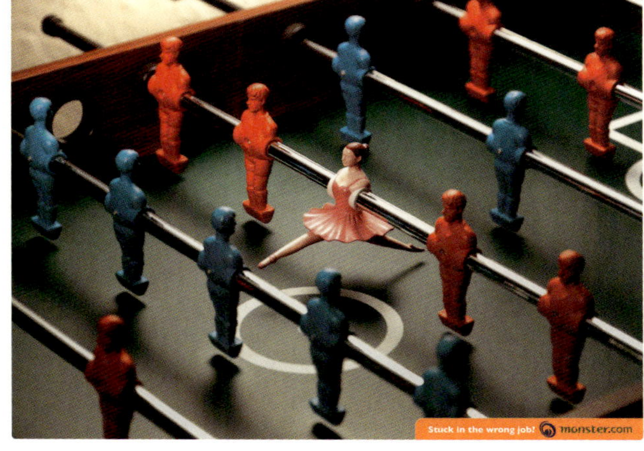

HONG KONG HONG KONG (2008)
JWT Monster.com
Stuck in the wrong job?

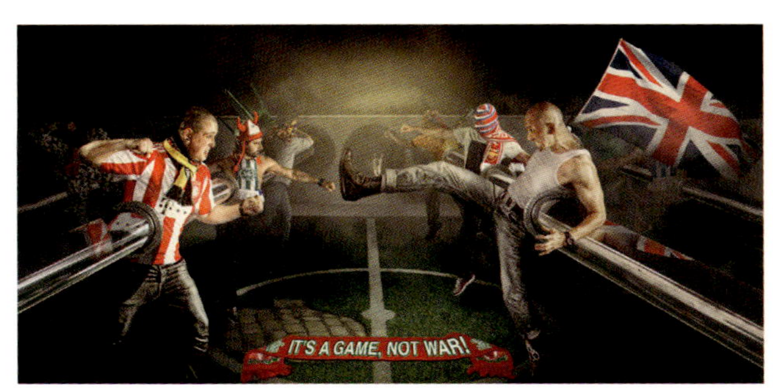

UKRAINE UKRAINE (2012)
Young & Rubicam UEFA
It's a game, not war!

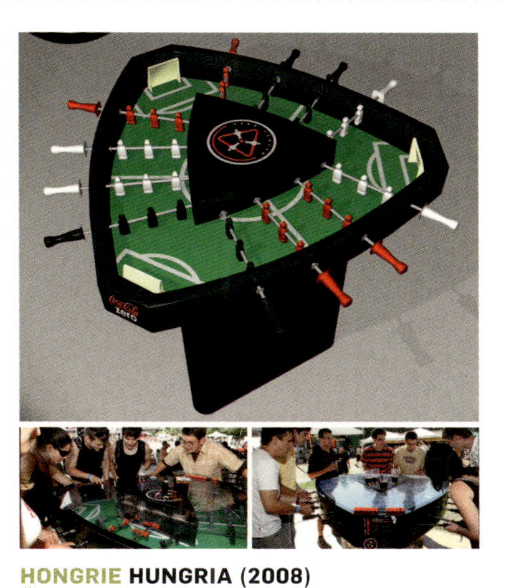

HONGRIE HUNGRIA (2008)
Leo Burnett Budapest Coke Zero
3 sided table football. Play the impossible

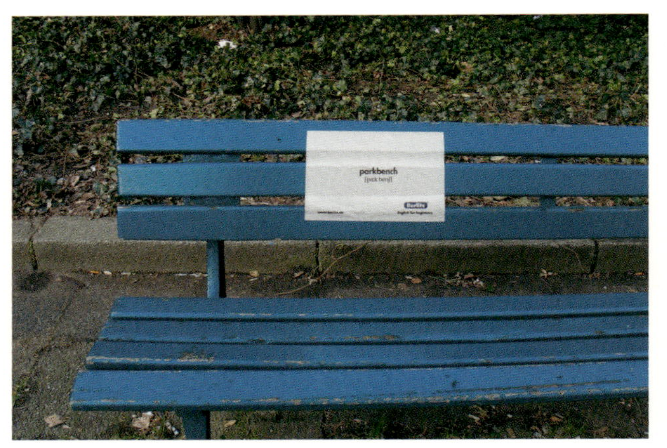

ALLEMAGNE GERMANY (2005)
DDB | Berlitz
"Parkbench" - English for beginners

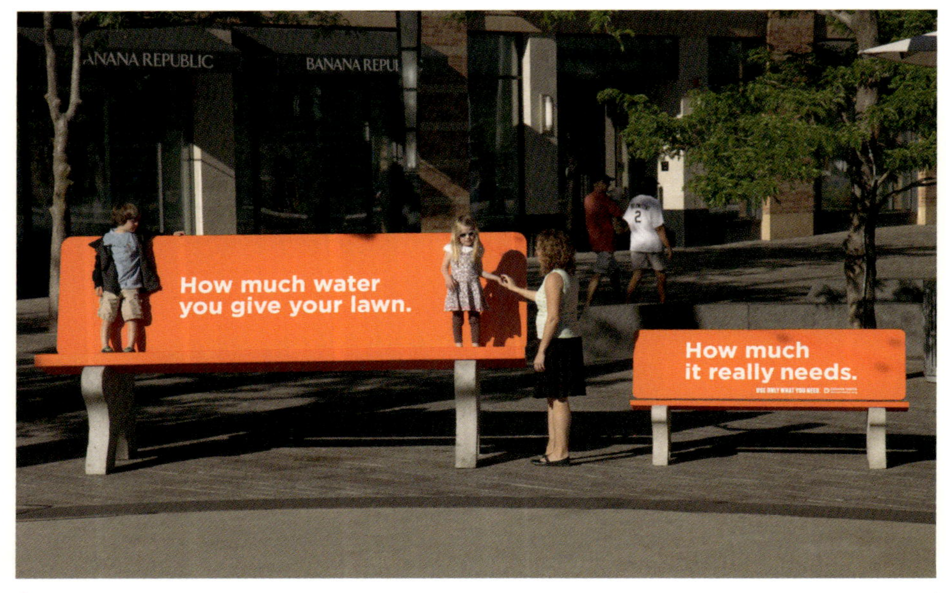

ÉTATS-UNIS UNITED STATES (2011)
Sukle Advertising | Denver Water
How much water you give your lawn. How much it really needs. Use only what you need.

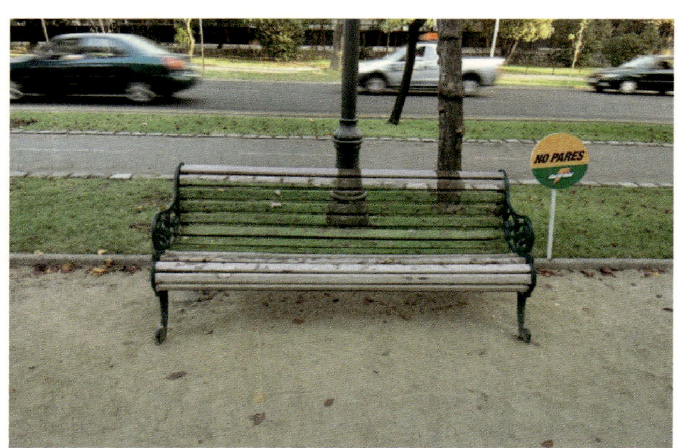

CHILI CHILE (2009)
BBDO | Gatorade
Do not stop

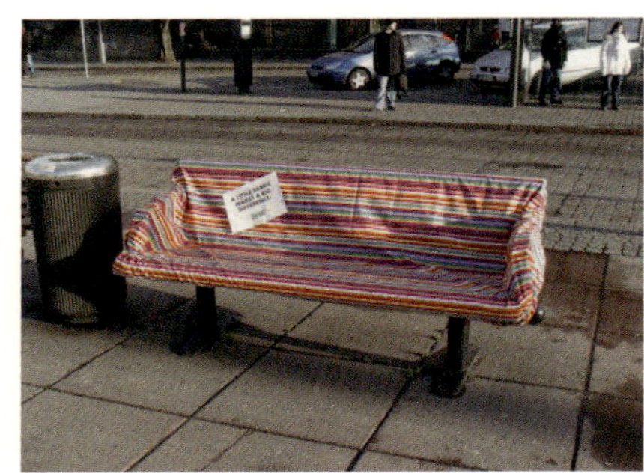

SUÈDE SWEDEN (2004)
Forsman & Bodenfors | IKEA
A little fabric makes a big difference

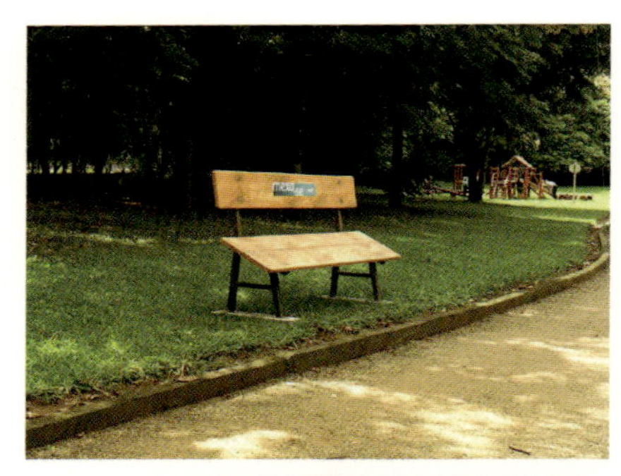

ALLEMAGNE GERMANY (2005)
DDB Sao Paulo
Companhia Athletica Sports Club

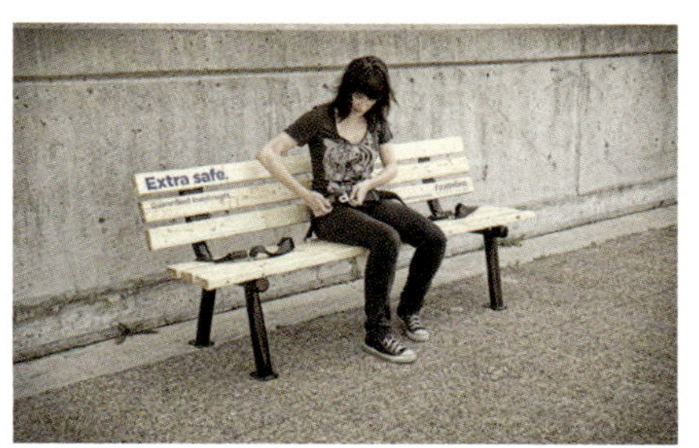

CANADA **CANADA (2009)**
TBWA Toronto First Ontario Investments
Extra Safe Guaranteed Investments

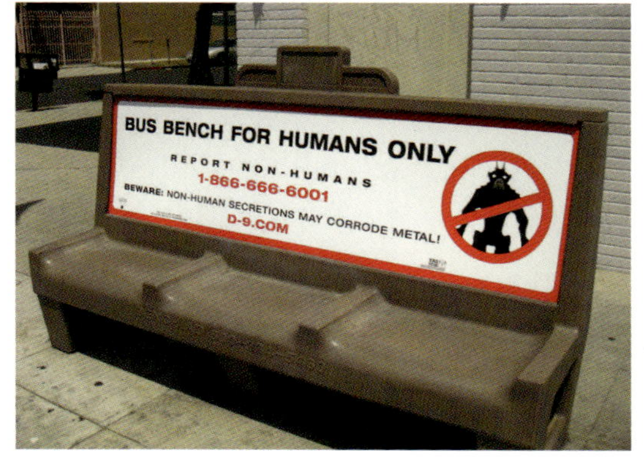

INCONNU **UNKNOWN (2009)**
Ignition Print Sony Pictures - District9 Movie

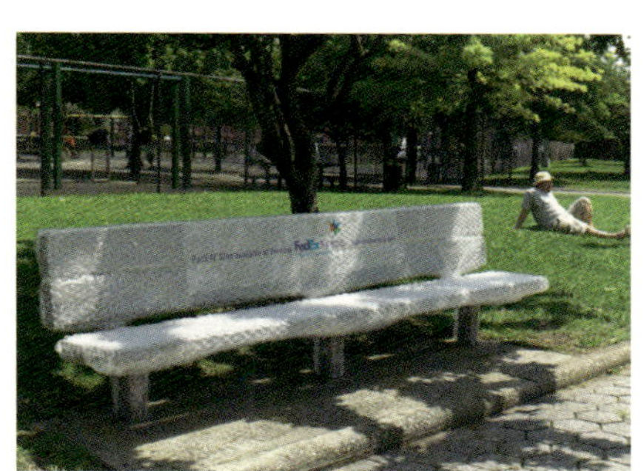

ÉTATS-UNIS **UNITED STATES (2008)**
BBDO New York FedEx Kinkos
Pack N'Ship available at the new Fedex Kinkos
(The bench is packed with bubble wrap)

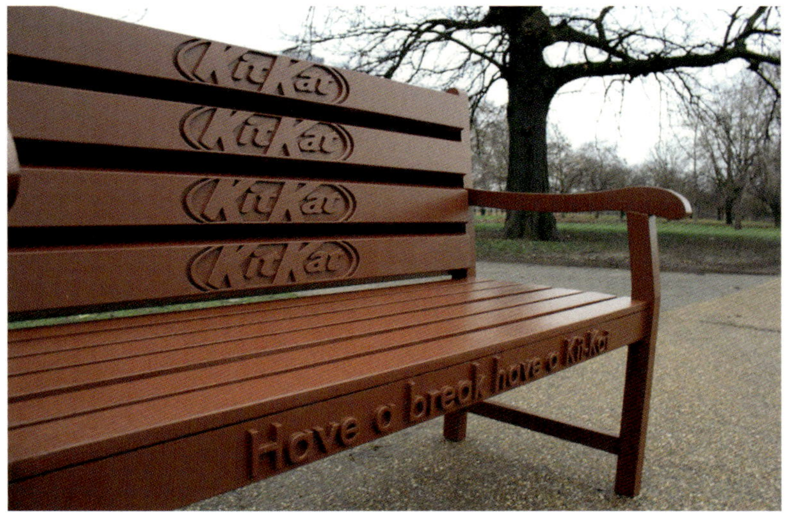

ROYAUME-UNI **UNITED KINGDOM (2008)**
JWT London Kit Kat
Have a break, have a Kit Kat

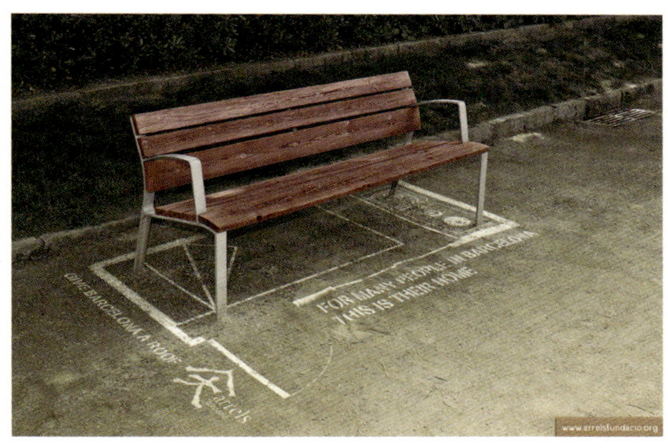

ESPAGNE **SPAIN (2010)**
Altraforma Barcelona Arrels Foundation
For many people in Barcelona this is their home
Give Barcelona a roof

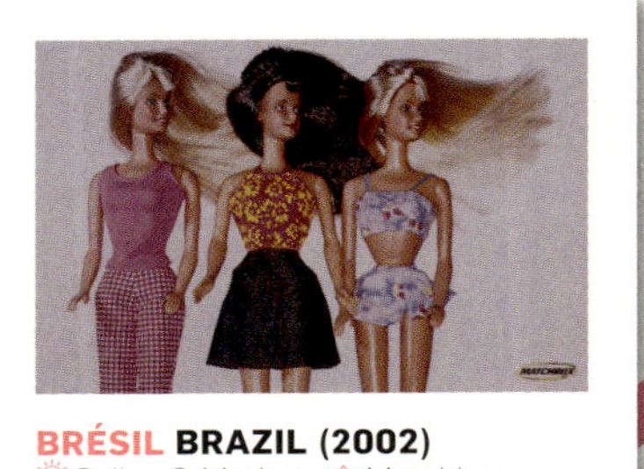

BRÉSIL BRAZIL (2002)
Ogilvy & Mather   Matchbox

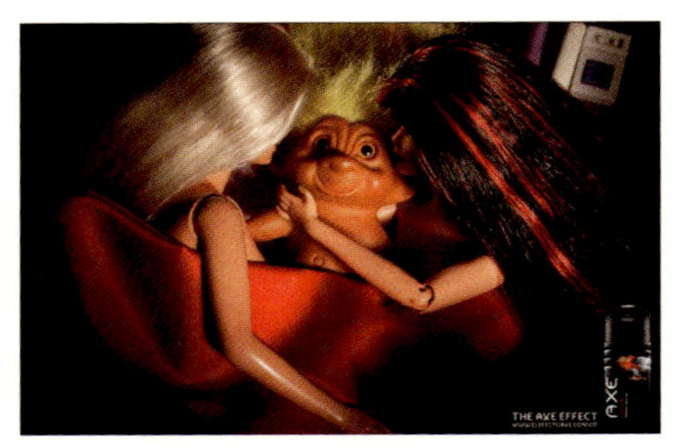

COLOMBIE COLOMBIA (2004)
Lowe   Axe Fusion
The axe effect

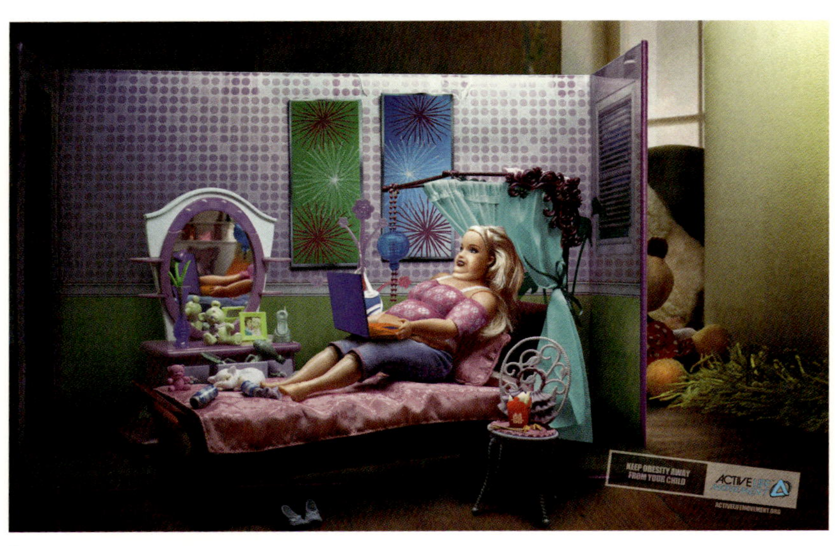

ÉTATS-UNIS UNITED STATES (2009)
Latin Works Austin   Active Life Movement
Keep obesity away from your child

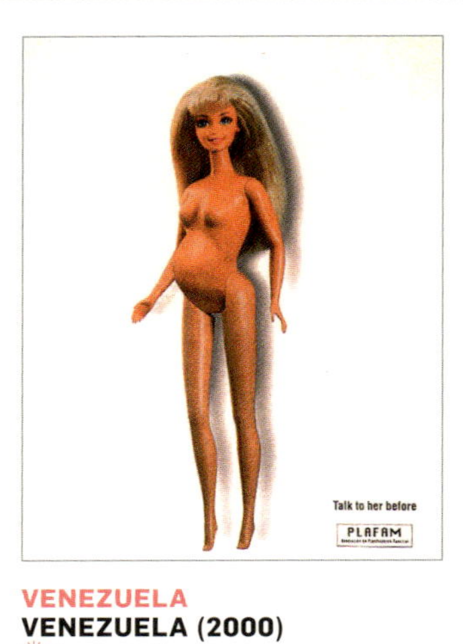

VENEZUELA
VENEZUELA (2000)
Cosar Add
Plafam Family Planning
Talk to her before

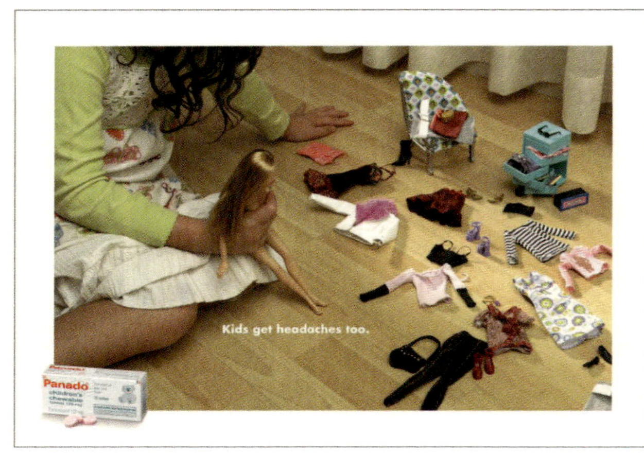

AFRIQUE DU SUD SOUTH AFRICA (2008)
DraftFCB Johannesburg   Panado Anti dolor for children
Kids get headaches too

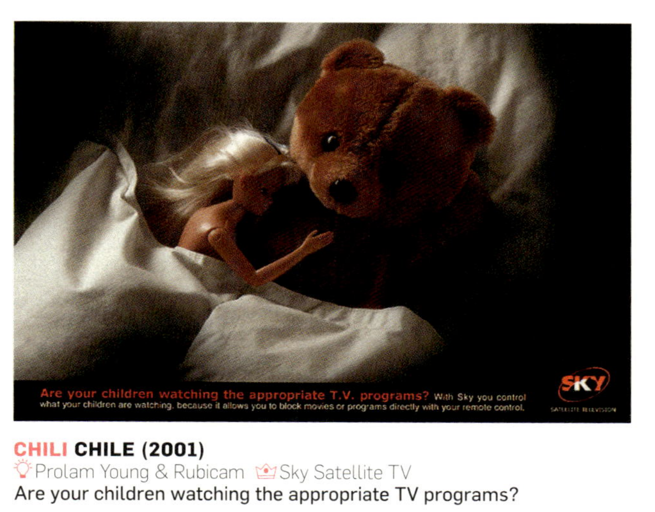

CHILI CHILE (2001)
Prolam Young & Rubicam · Sky Satellite TV
Are your children watching the appropriate TV programs?

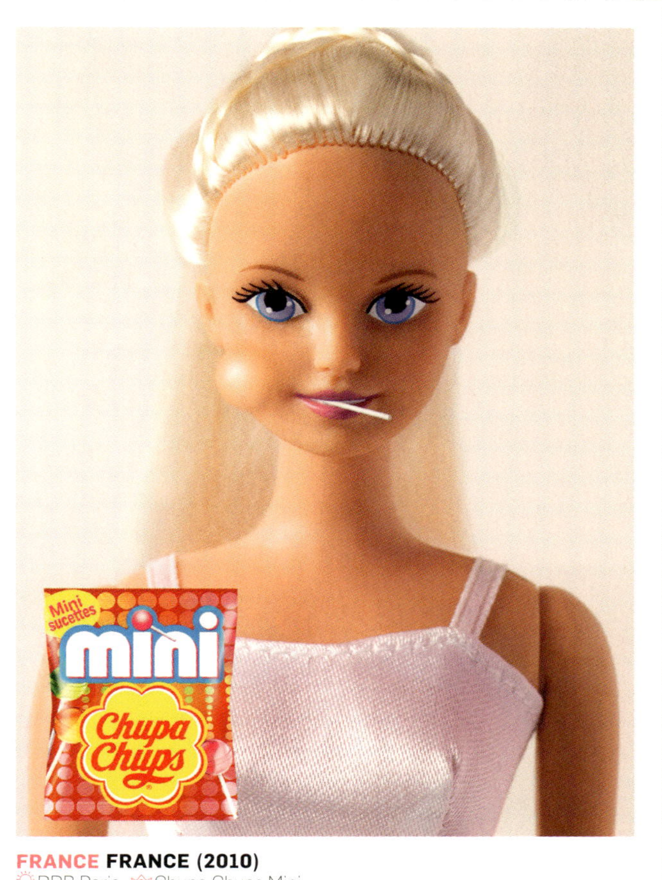

FRANCE FRANCE (2010)
DDB Paris · Chupa Chups Mini

BARBIE

№10

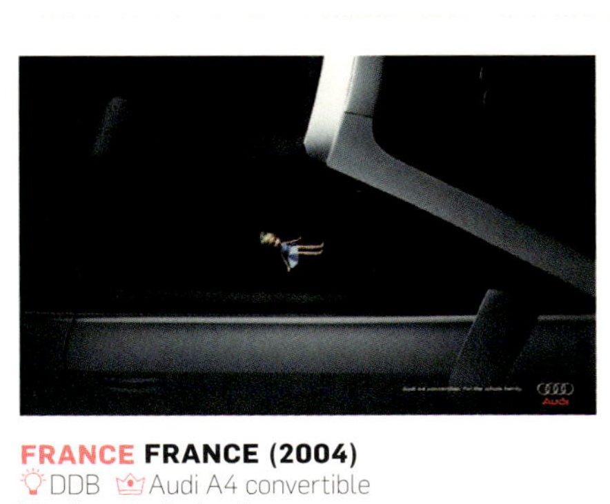

FRANCE FRANCE (2004)
DDB · Audi A4 convertible
For the whole family

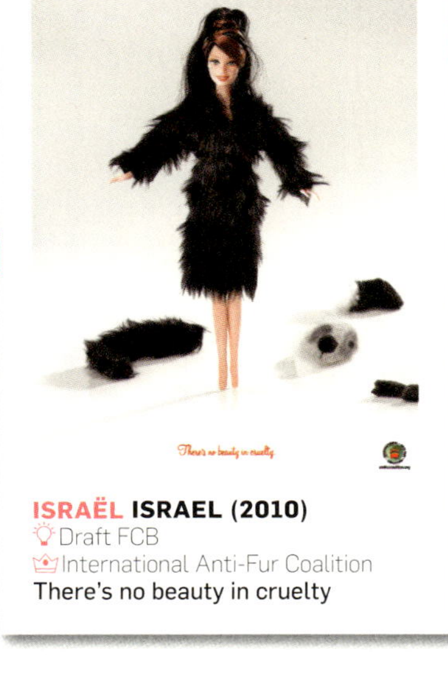

ISRAËL ISRAEL (2010)
Draft FCB · International Anti-Fur Coalition
There's no beauty in cruelty

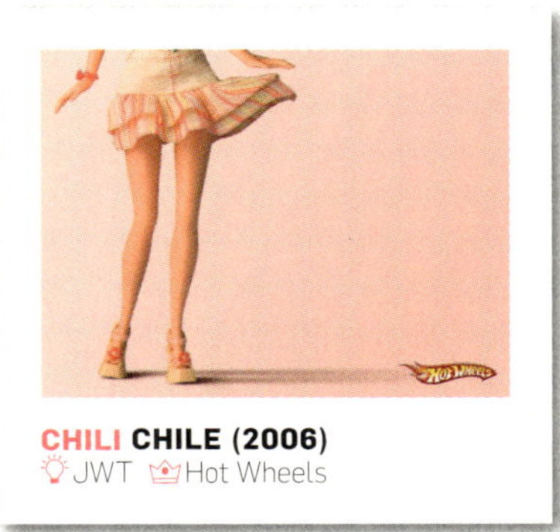

CHILI CHILE (2006)
JWT · Hot Wheels

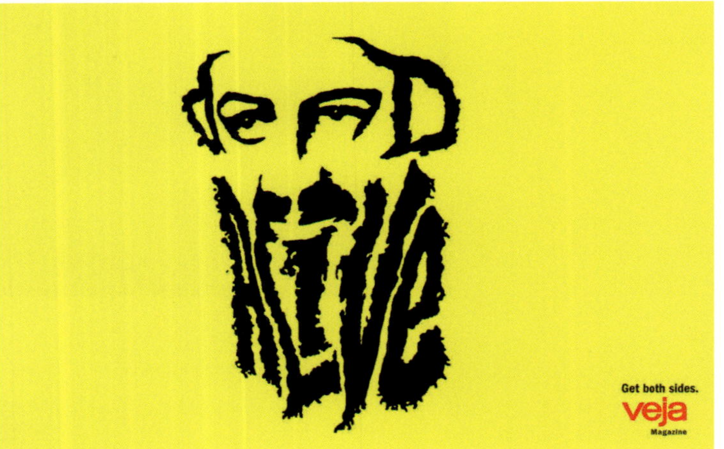

BRÉSIL BRAZIL (2004)
Almap BBDO Veja Magazine
(Dead / Alive) Get both sides

« C'est déjà étrange, suspect, inapproprié, voire de mauvais goût d'utiliser une telle icône dans la publicité. Le symbole qu'il représente est à manier avec précaution. On tombe vite dans l'anecdotique ou le caricatural. Celle-ci est un magnifique jeu typographique qui fait sens et qui se justifie pour un magazine d'actualité. »
"It's already strange, suspect, inappropriate and seen as distasteful to use such an icon in an advertisement. Here, the symbol it represents is treated with caution. It could quickly fall into the anecdotal or caricature. So, this is a magnificent turn of the typeface that makes sense and is justifiable for a news magazine."

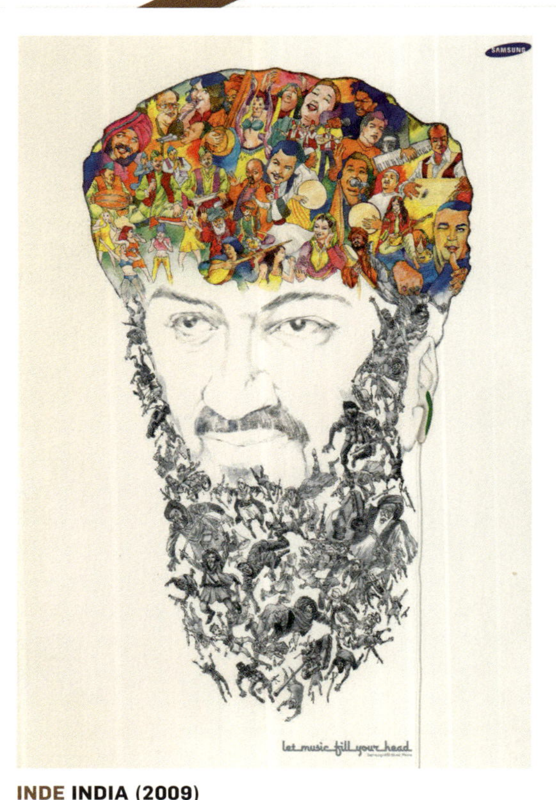

INDE INDIA (2009)
Cheil Worldwide Samsung
Let music fill your head

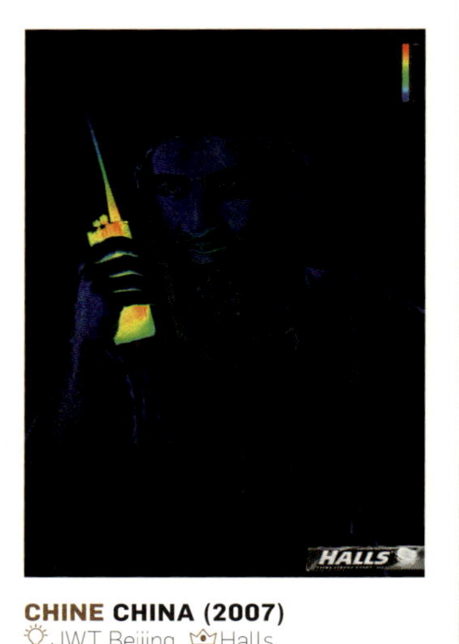

CHINE CHINA (2007)
JWT Beijing Halls

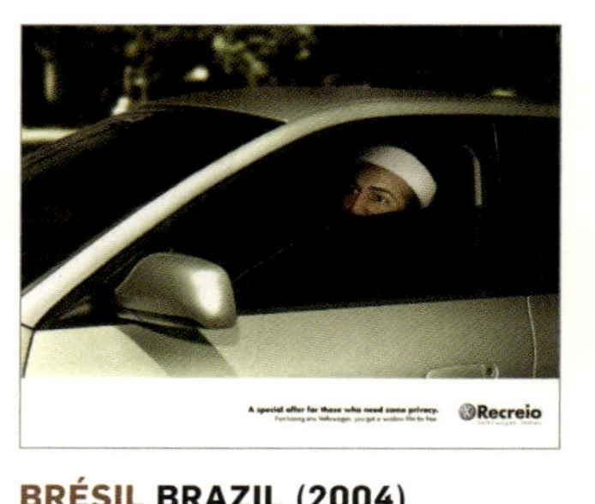

BRÉSIL BRAZIL (2004)
100% Propaganda
Recreio Volkswagen Dealer
A special offer for those who need some privacy

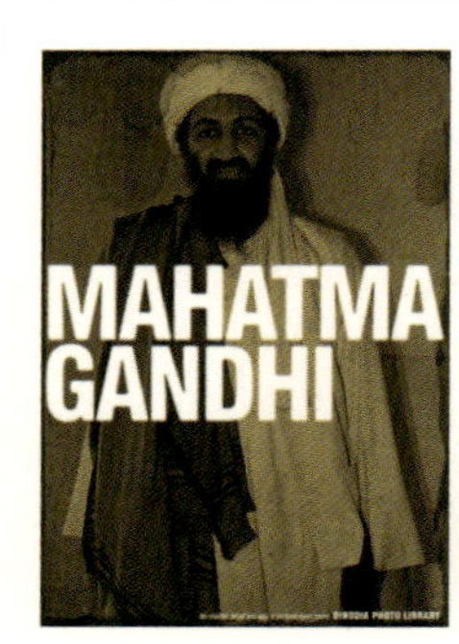

INDE INDIA (2006)
Leo Burnett
Dinodia Photo Library
No matter what you say, a picture says more

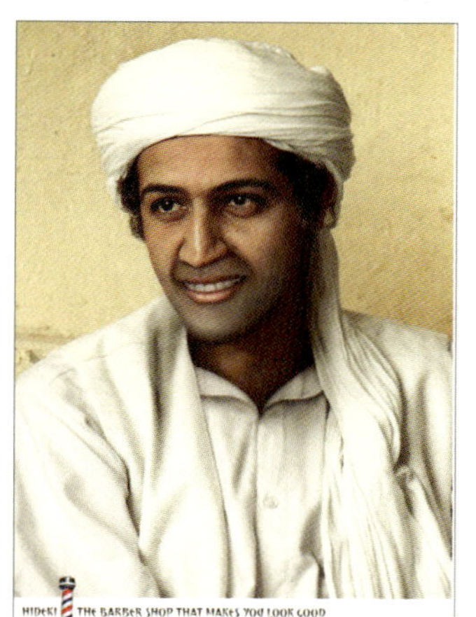

JAPON JAPAN (2006)
Ogilvy & Mather Hideki
The barber shop that makes you look good

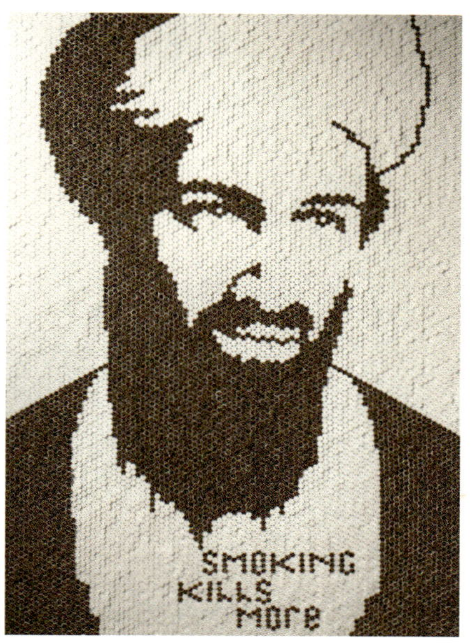

BRÉSIL BRAZIL (2008)
Saatchi & Saatchi Anti Smoking Campaign
(Portrait made out of cigarettes)
Smoking kills more

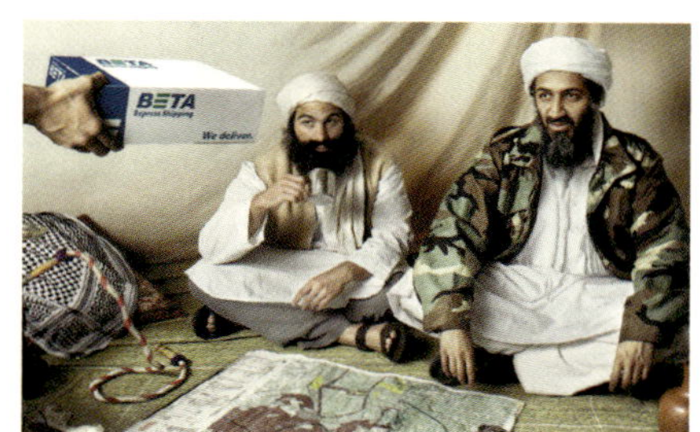

BRÉSIL BRAZIL (2008)
White Propaganda Sao Paulo
Beta Express Shipping
We deliver

BEN LADEN
Nº11
BIN LADEN

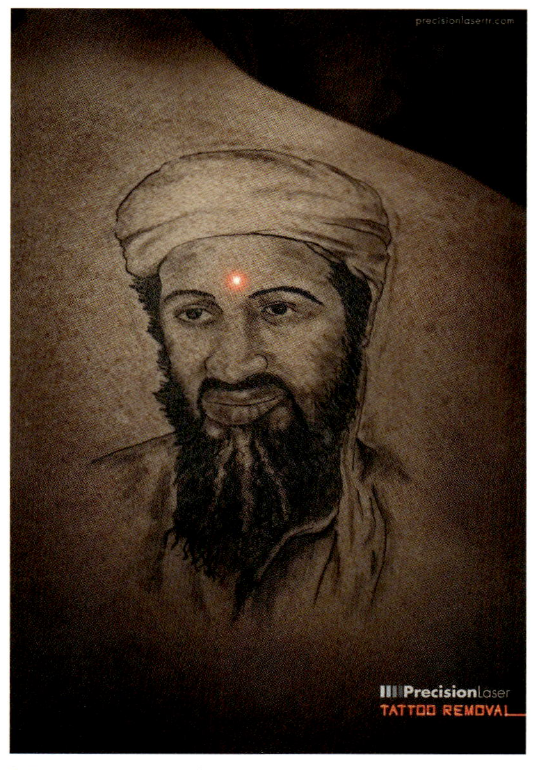

CANADA CANADA (2011)
Mc Laren Mc Cann Precision Laser Tattoo Removal

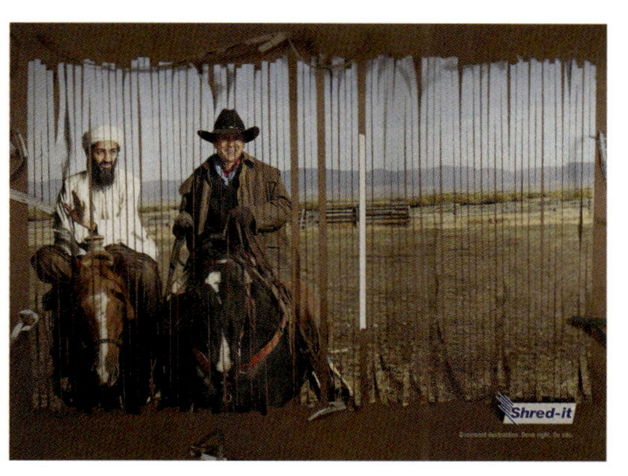

PORTO RICO PUERTO RICO (2007)
Young & Rubicam Shred-It
Document destruction. Done right. On site.

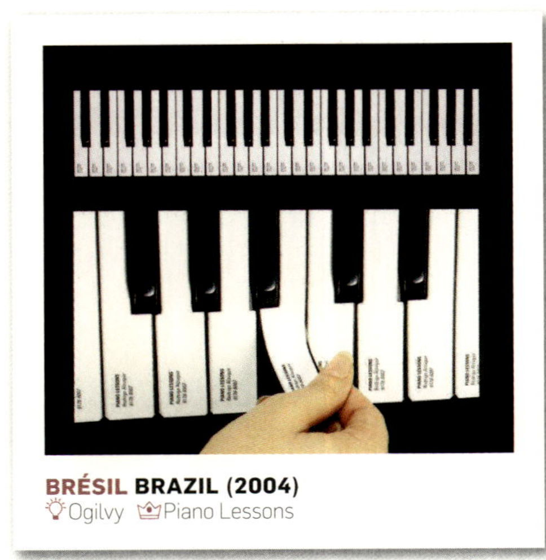

BRÉSIL BRAZIL (2004)
Ogilvy Piano Lessons

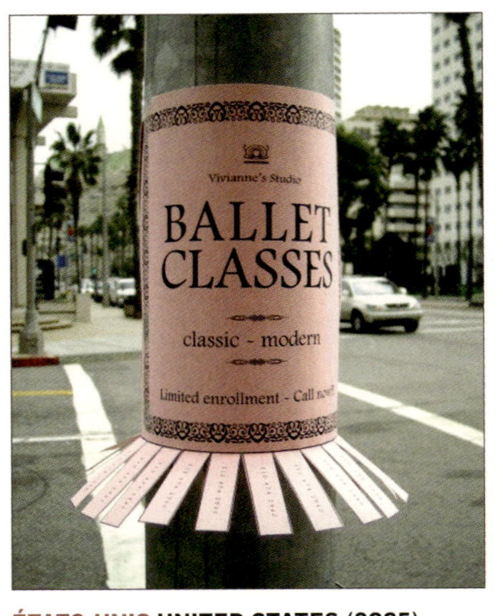

ÉTATS-UNIS UNITED STATES (2005)
Grupo Gallegos Ballet Classes

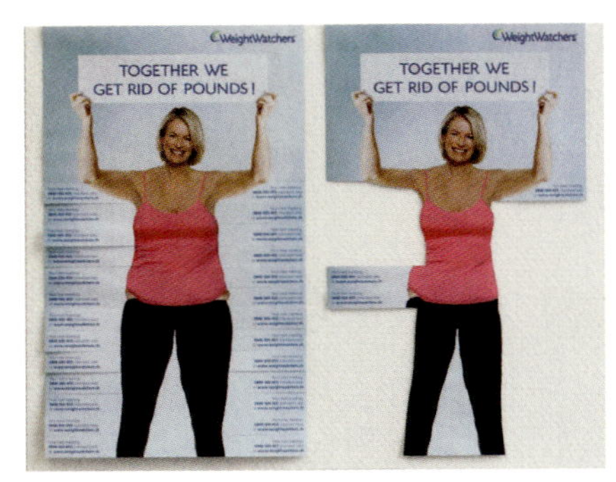

SUISSE SWITZERLAND (2009)
Euro RSCG Weight Watchers
Together we get rid of pounds

BONS À DÉCOUPER

Nº12

TEAR-OFF

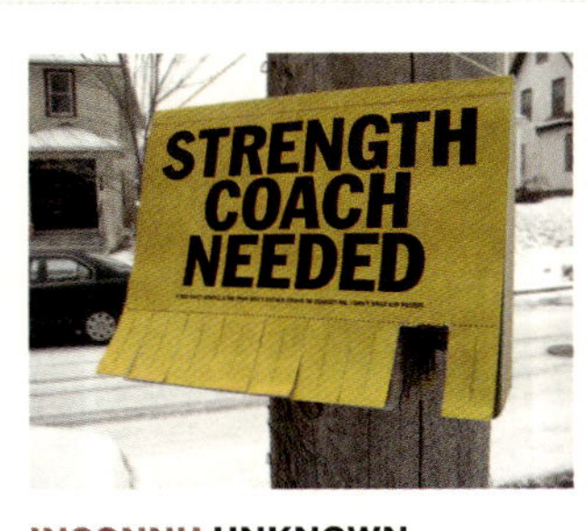

INCONNU UNKNOWN
Inconnu/unknown
Strenght Coach
Strenght coach needed.
If you can't remove a tab then don't
bother trying to contact me.
I don't want any posers

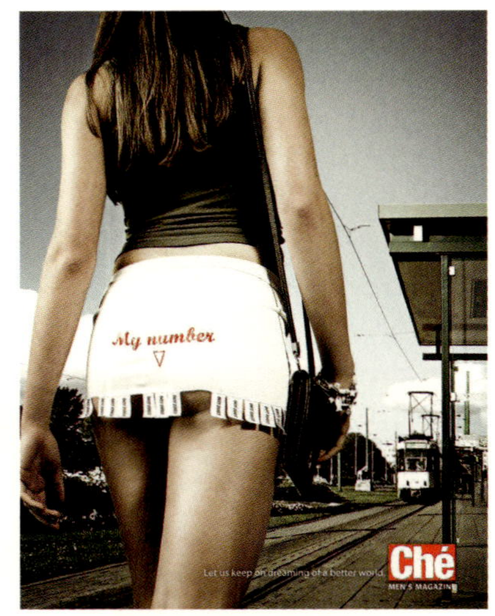

BELGIQUE BELGIUM (2007)
Duval Guillaume Antwerp
Ché Magazine Men's Magazine
(My number....)
Let us keep on dreaming of a better world

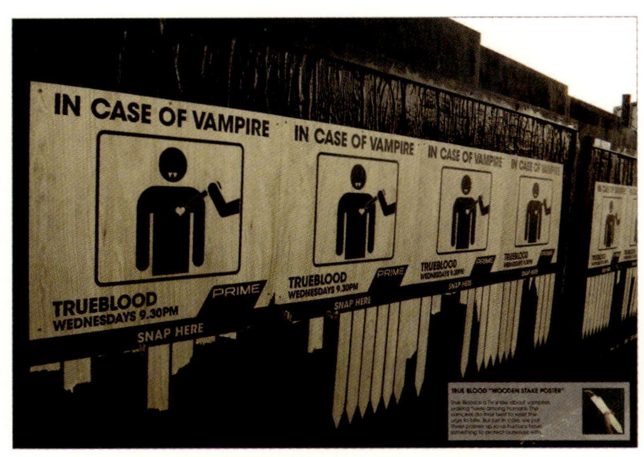

NOUVELLE-ZÉLANDE NEW ZEALAND (2009)
DraftFCB True Blood on Prime TV
In case of vampire...

SUISSE
SWITZERLAND (2008)
Ruf Lanz Zurich
McKinsey & Company
recruitment

« J'aime le côté ultra-ciblé de cette publicité. Seul le public visé est capable d'en décoder le message même si tout le monde comprend la blague. Un bon calcul pour recruter ? »
"I love the ultra-targeted aspect of this advertisement. Only the aimed-for audience is capable of decoding the message even if everyone gets the joke. A good calculation for recruiting?"

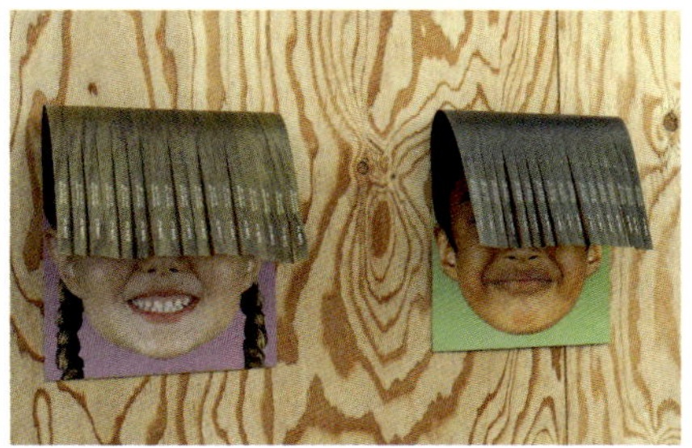
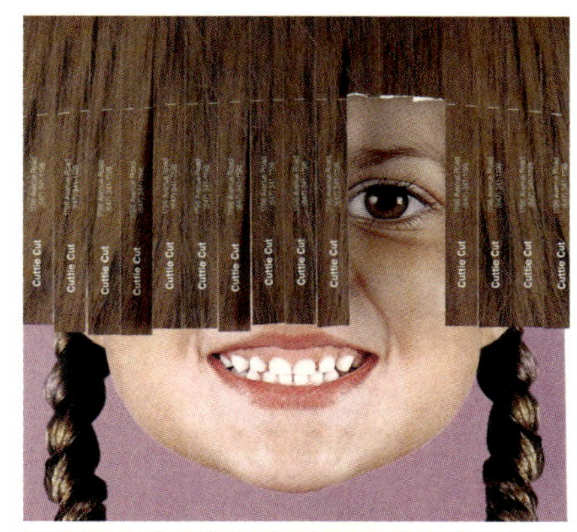

CANADA CANADA (2009)
Young & Rubicam Toronto   Cuttie Cut
Kids' Hair salon

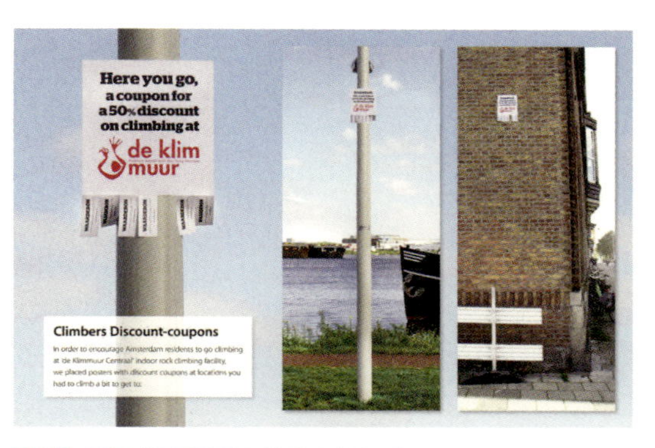

PAYS-BAS NETHERLANDS (2011)
N=5   De Klim Muur climbing wall discount coupons

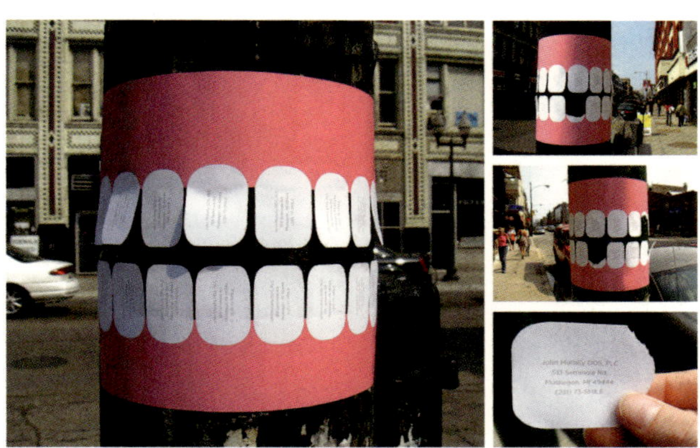

ÉTATS-UNIS UNITED STATES (2007)
Cramer-krasselt Chicago   Dr Mullally dentist

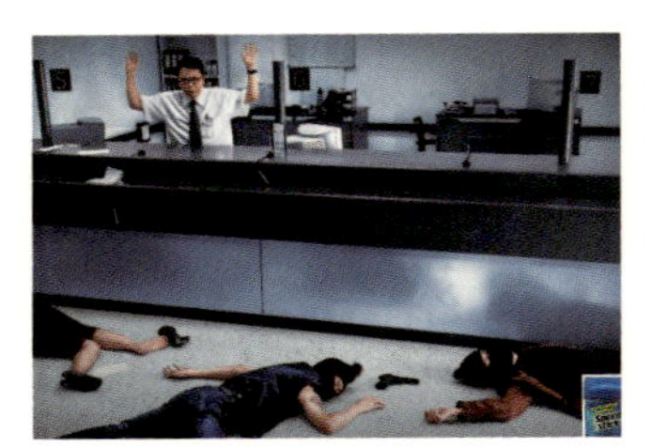

MALAISIE MALAYSIA (2005)
Young & Rubicam
Mennen Speed Stick Deodorant

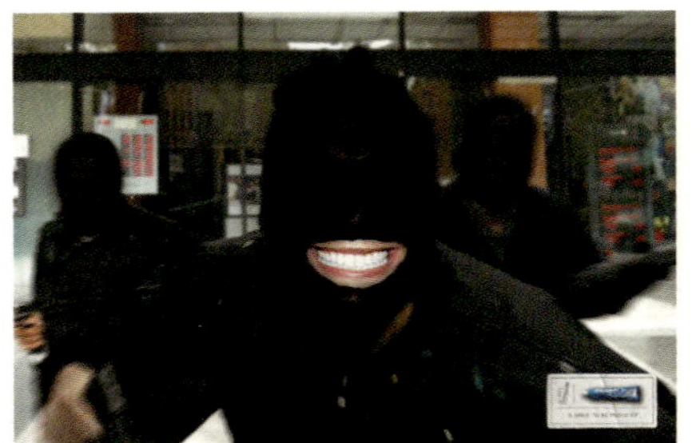

VIÊT-NAM VIETNAM (2005)
JWT Ho Chi Minh — Cres Whitening Toothpaste
A smile to be proud of

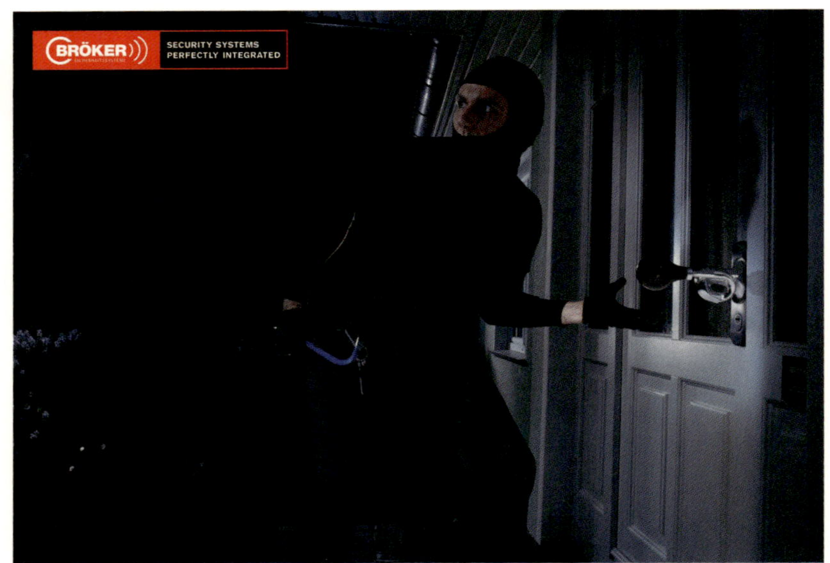

ALLEMAGNE GERMANY (2011)
Publicis Frankfurt — Bröker Alarm systems
Security systems perfectly integrated

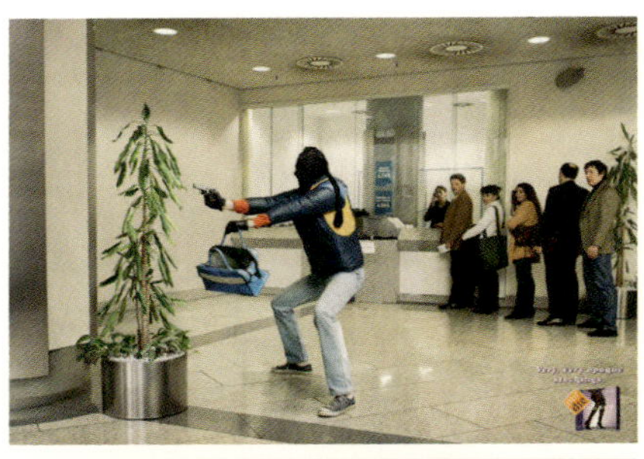
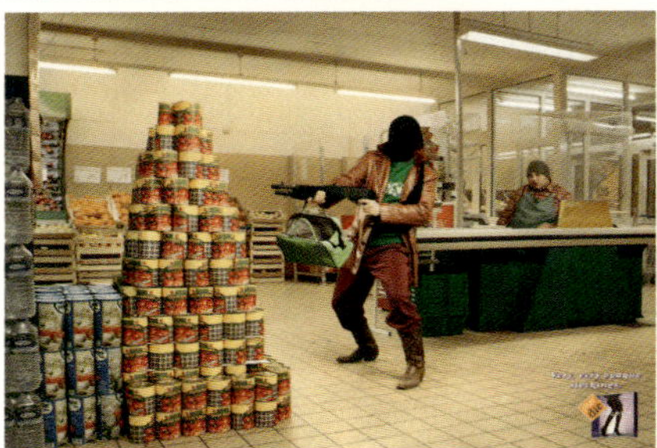
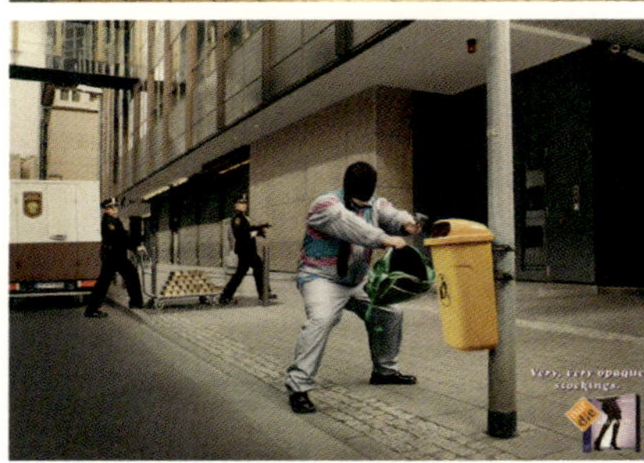

ALLEMAGNE GERMANY (2006)
Ogilvy Frankfurt — Nur Die
Very, very opaque stockings

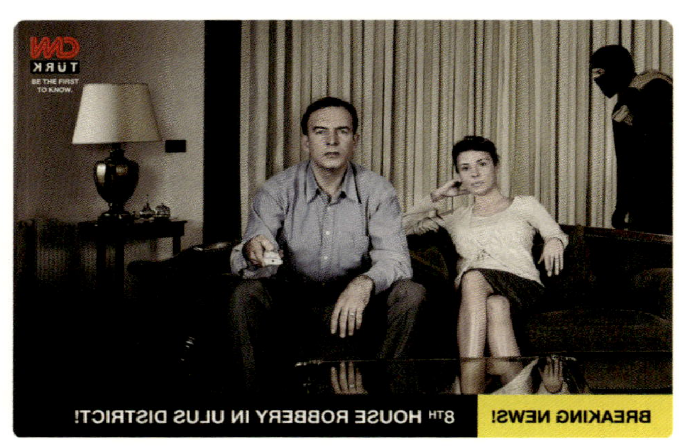

TURQUIE TURKEY (2006)
DDB & Co — CNN Turk
"Breaking news! 8th house robbery in ulus district!"
Be the first to know

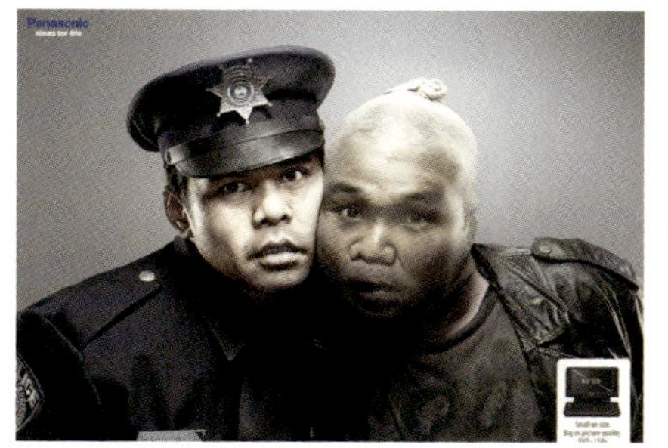

INDONÉSIE INDONESIA(2009)
Saatchi & Saatchi   Panasonic 8.5" LCD DVD
Small on size. Big on picture quality

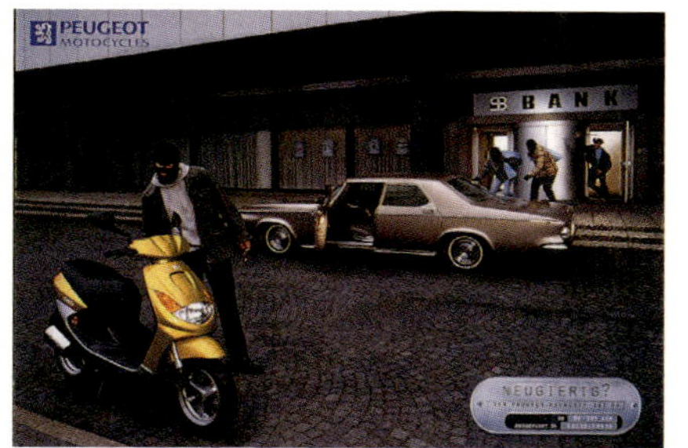

ALLEMAGNE GERMANY (1999)
Michael Conrad & Leo Burnett
Peugeot Vivacity

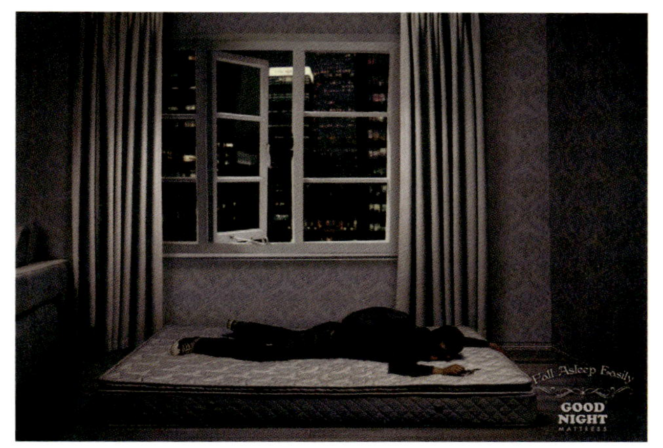

CHINE CHINA (2011)
J&J Advertising   Good Night Mattress
Fall asleep easily

BRAQUAGES ET CAMBRIOLAGES

№13

IT'S A ROBBERY

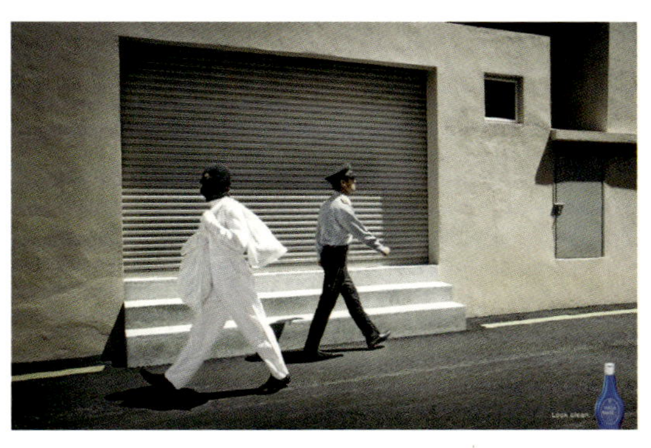

MALAISIE MALAYSIA (2008)
Grey Kuala Lumpur   Ujala Liquid Fabric Whitener
Look Clean

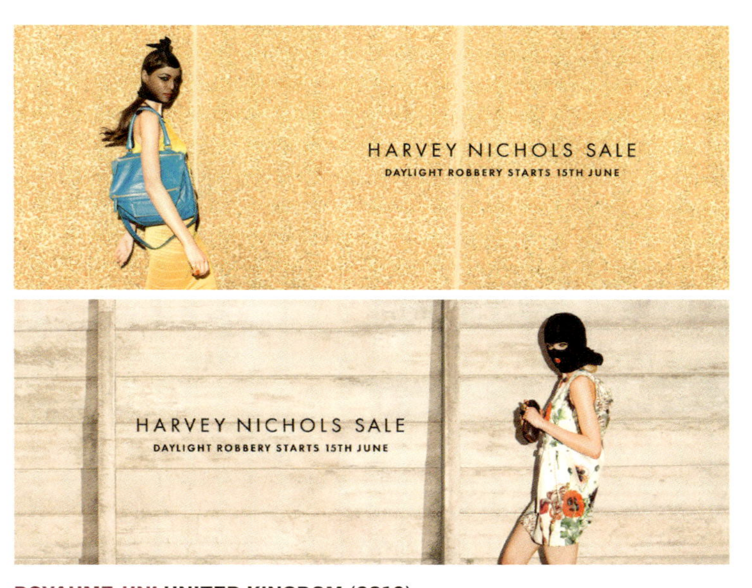

ROYAUME-UNI UNITED KINGDOM (2012)
DDB London   Harvey Nichols Sale
Daylight robbery starts 15th June

№14

SPEECH & THOUGHT BUBBLES

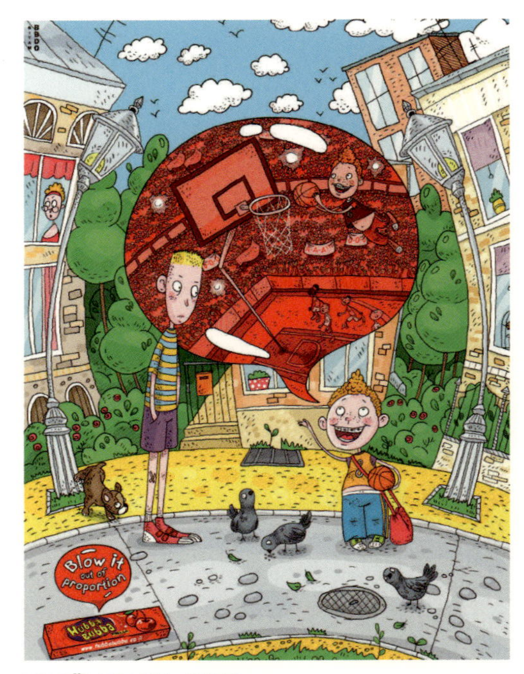
ISRAËL ISRAEL (2011)
Gitam BBDO Hubba Bubba Chewing gum
Blow it out of proportion

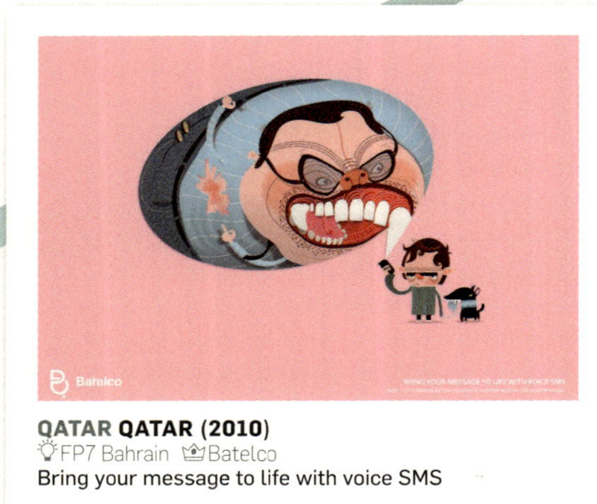
QATAR QATAR (2010)
FP7 Bahrain Batelco
Bring your message to life with voice SMS

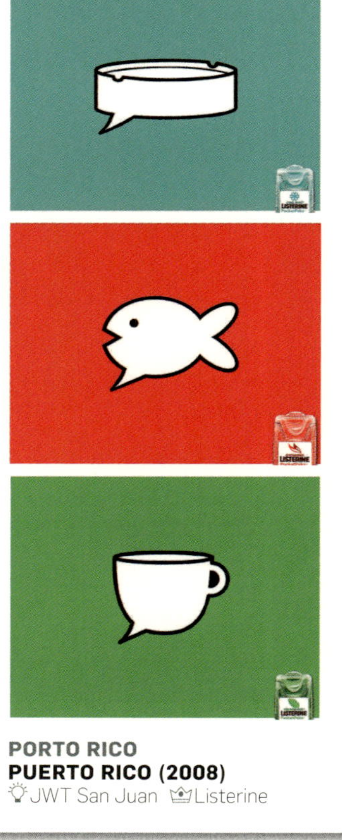
**PORTO RICO
PUERTO RICO (2008)**
JWT San Juan Listerine

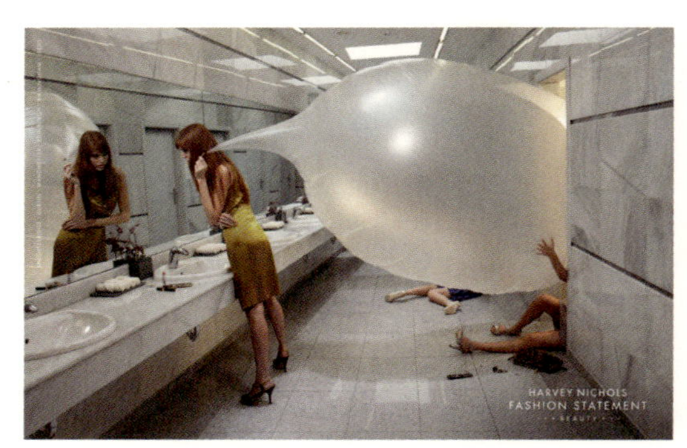
ROYAUME-UNI UNITED KINGDOM (2008)
DDB London Harvey Nichols
Fashion Statement

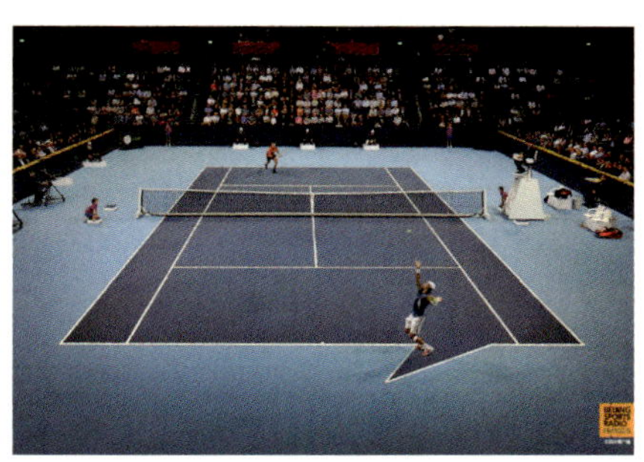

CHINE CHINA (2012)
Ogilvy & Mather Hong Kong
Beijing Sports Radio

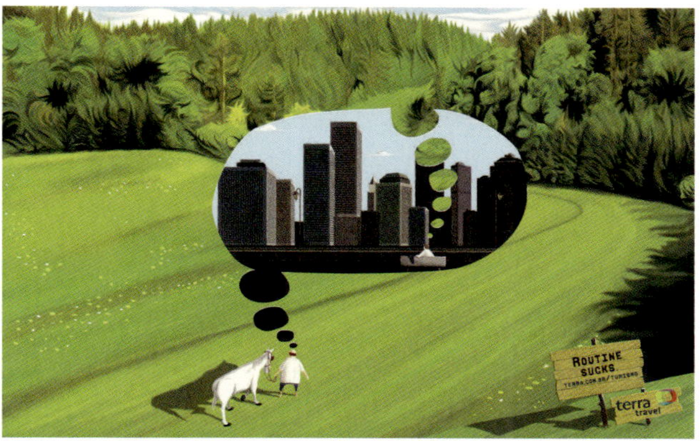

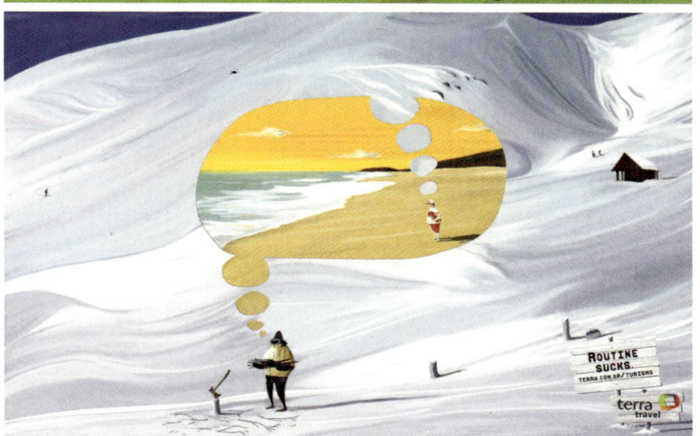

BRÉSIL BRAZIL (2009)
DDB Terra Travel
Routine Sucks

« Magnifique illustration de l'adage populaire « l'herbe est plus verte ailleurs » ou « chacun voit midi à sa porte ». Double niveau de lecture, double effet, double impact. Ça fait rêver ! »
"Magnificent illustration of the popular sayings, "the grass is always greener on the other side" and "to each his own". Double the attention grabbing, double the impression, double the impact. It makes you dream!"

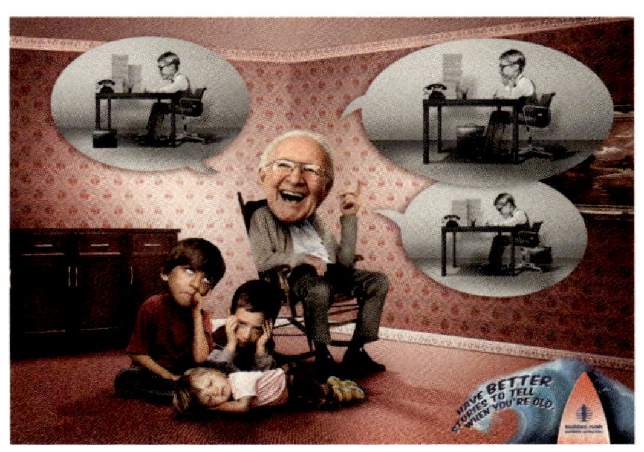

SUISSE SWITZERLAND (2010)
Advico Young & Rubicam Sudden Rush surfing trips
Have better stories to tell when you're old

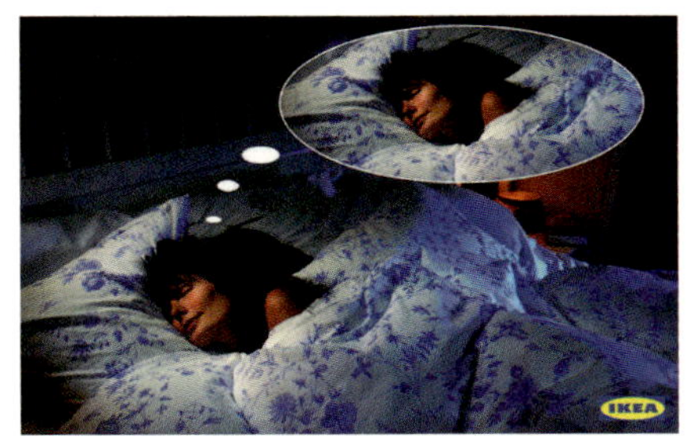

ALLEMAGNE GERMANY (2008)
DDB IKEA

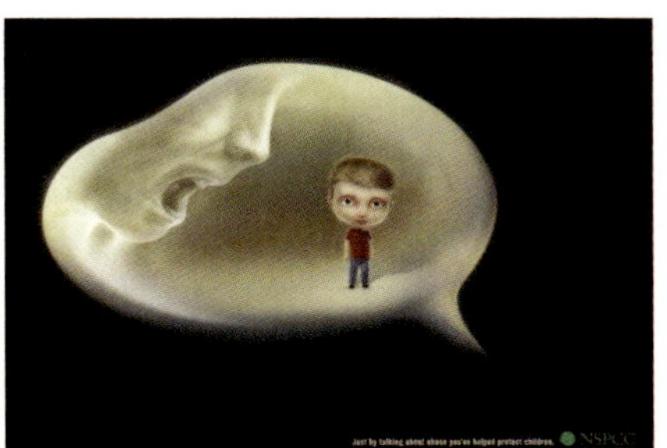

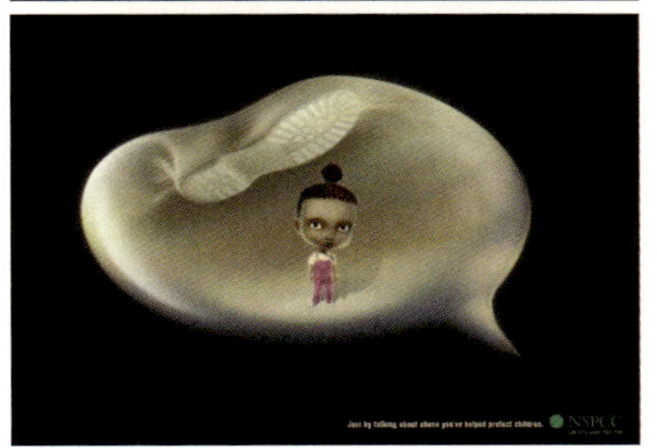

ROYAUME-UNI UNITED KINGDOM (2006)
Saatchi & Saatchi NSPCC
Just by talking about abuse you've helped protect children

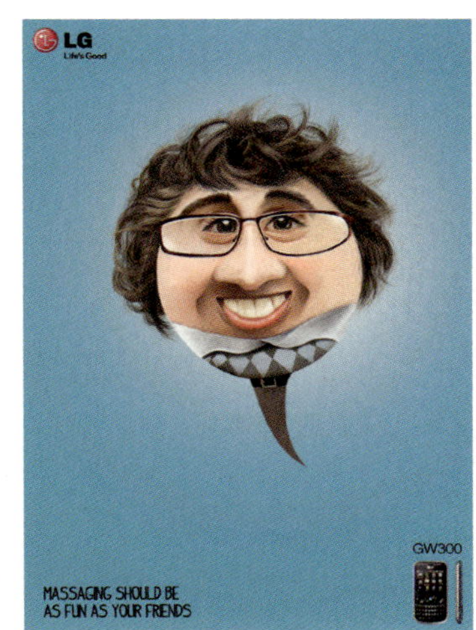

ÉGYPTE EGYPT (2011)
Media Marquee LG GW300
Messaging should be as fun as your friends

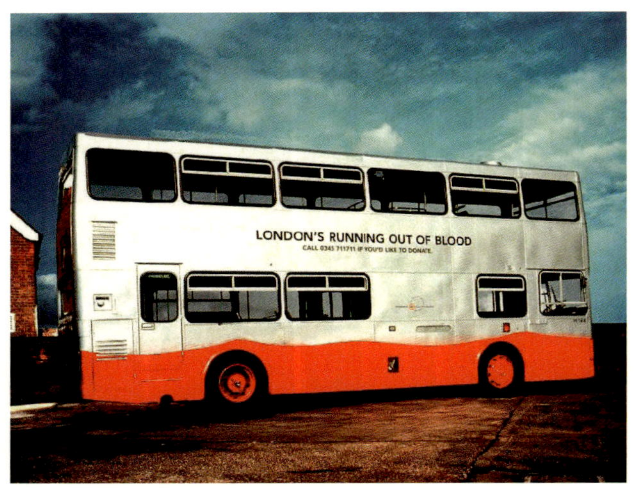

ROYAUME-UNI
UNITED KINGDOM (1999)
Lowe Howard Spink
Blood Donation
London's running out of blood

« Une idée sang pour sang pertinente qui joue avec un attribut propre au bus londonien et connu des touristes du monde entier : la couleur rouge. »
"An idea that is, ounce for ounce, one of most relevant as it plays off an integral attribute of London busses that is known by tourists the world over: the colour red."

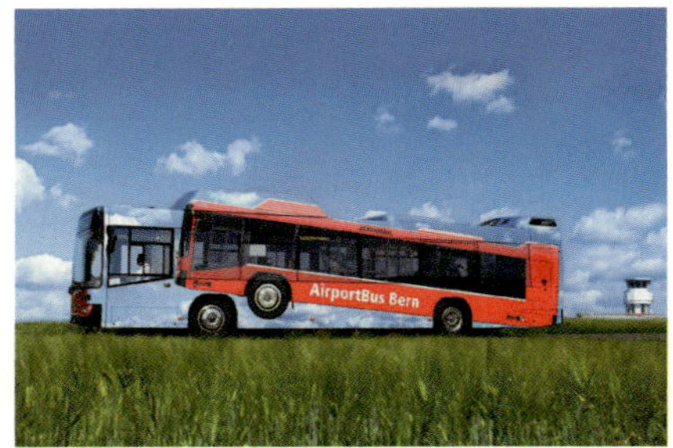

SUISSE SWITZERLAND (2009)
Neue Lgk Berne and Zurich
Airport Bus Bern

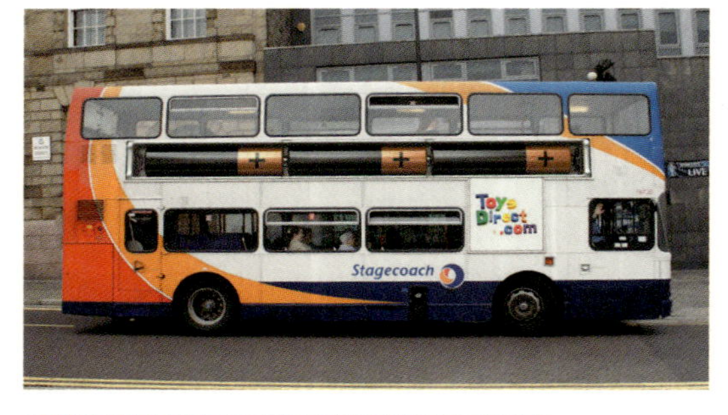

ROYAUME-UNI UNITED KINGDOM (2009)
Robson Brown Ltd ToysDirect.com

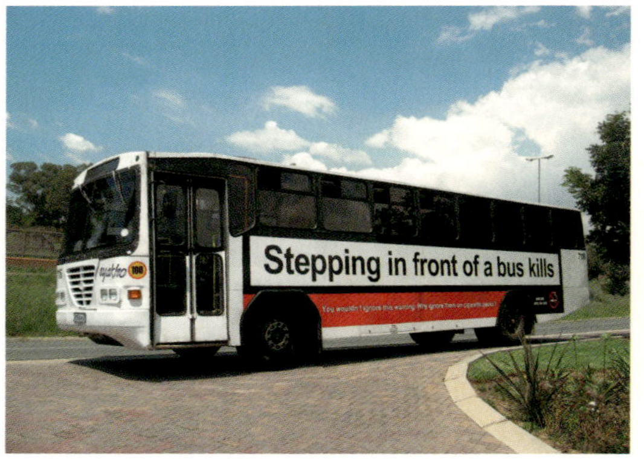

AFRIQUE DU SUD SOUTH AFRICA (2007)
Lowe Bull   Anti Tobacco campaign
Stepping in front of a bus kills You wouldn't ignore this warning. Why ignore them on cigarette packs?

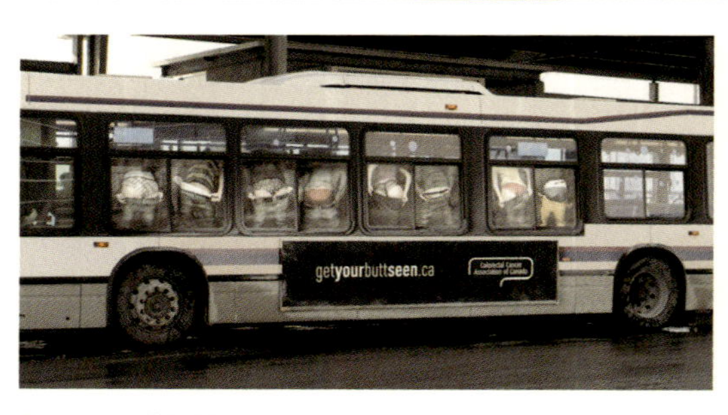

CANADA CANADA
Ogilvy Montreal   Colorectal Cancer Association of Canada
Get your butt seen

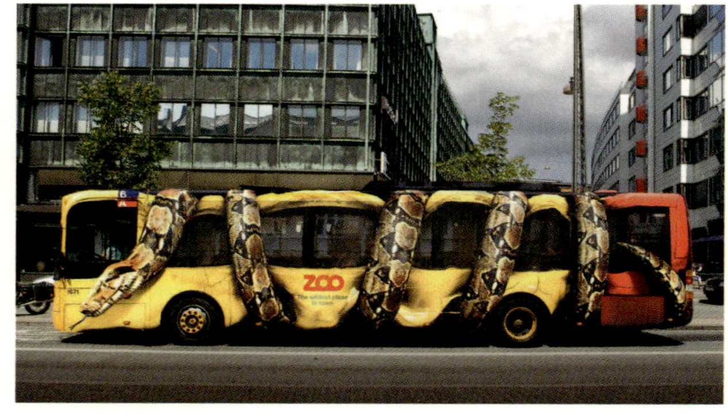

DANEMARK DENMARK (2009)
Young & Rubicam Copenhagen   Copenhagen Zoo
The wildest place in town

BUS

Nº15

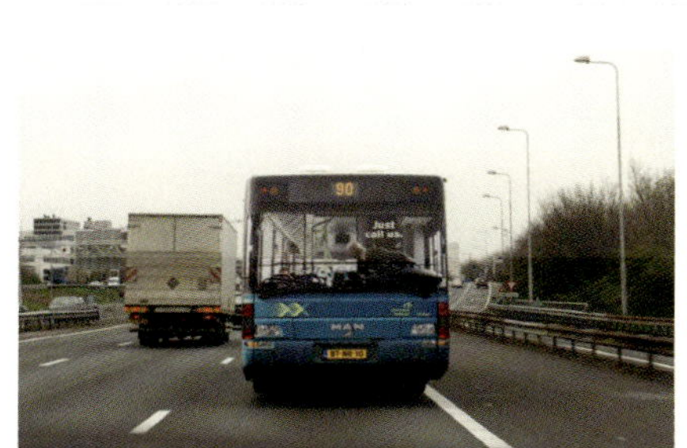

PAYS-BAS NETHERLANDS (2008)
DDB Amsterdam
Centraal Beheer Insurance Company
Just Call us

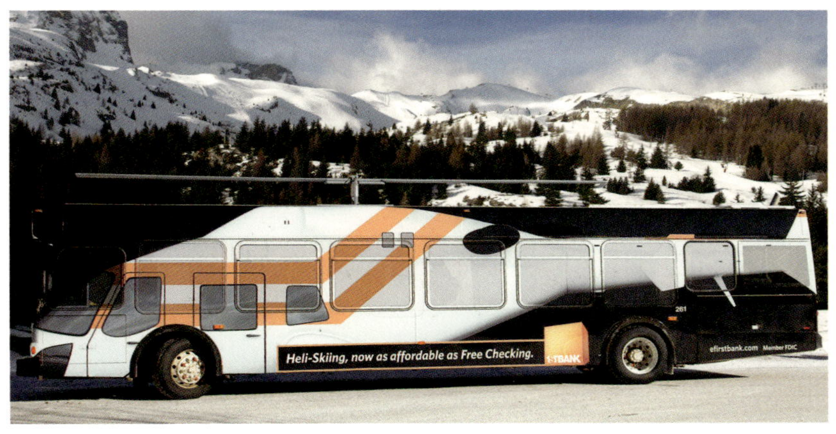

ÉTATS-UNIS UNITED STATE (2012)
TDA Boulder 1stBank
Heli-skiing, now as affordable as free checking

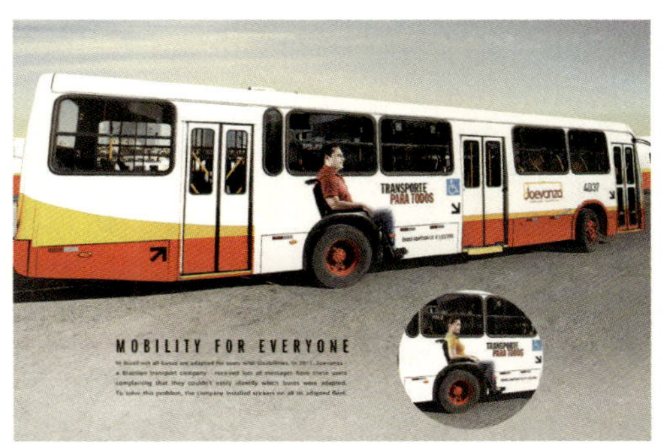

BRÉSIL BRAZIL (2012)
Propeg Joevanza Transport Company
Mobility for everyone

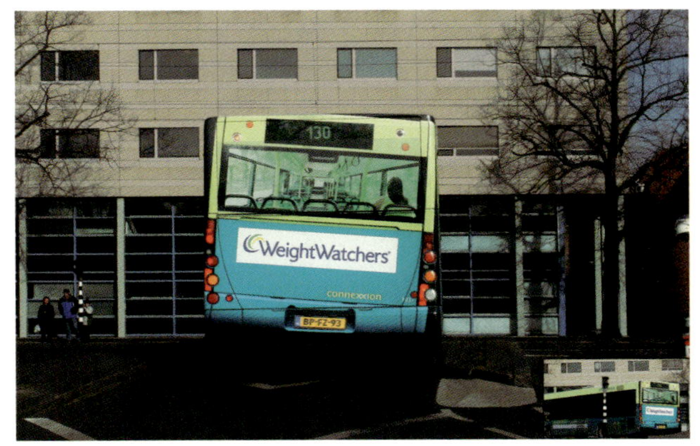

PAYS-BAS NETHERLANDS (2008)
Lowe Amsterdam Weight Watchers

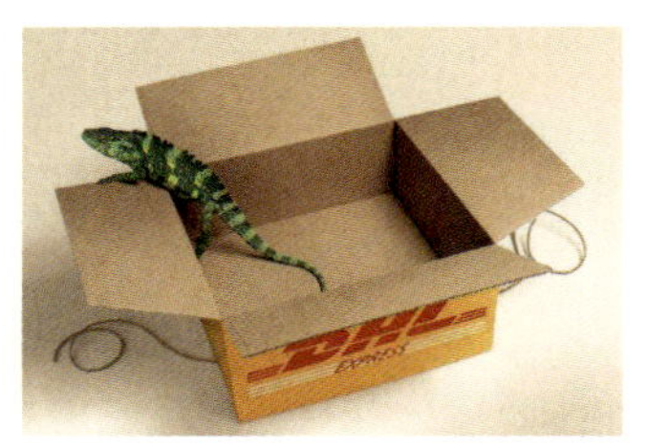

**AFRIQUE DU SUD
SOUTH AFRICA (2005)**
Ogilvy & Mather DHL Express

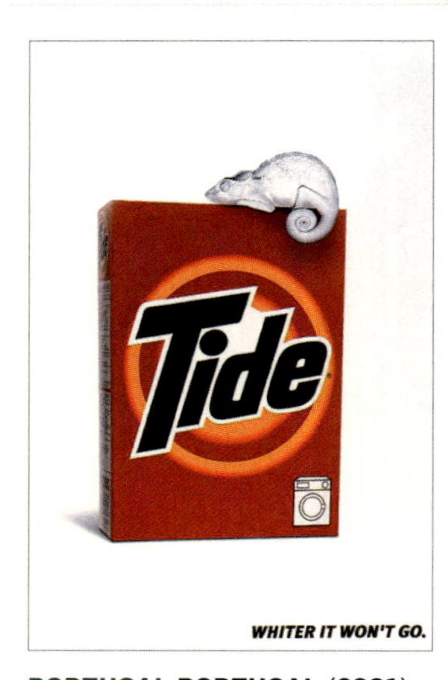

PORTUGAL PORTUGAL (2001)
Leo Burnett Tide
Whiter it won't go

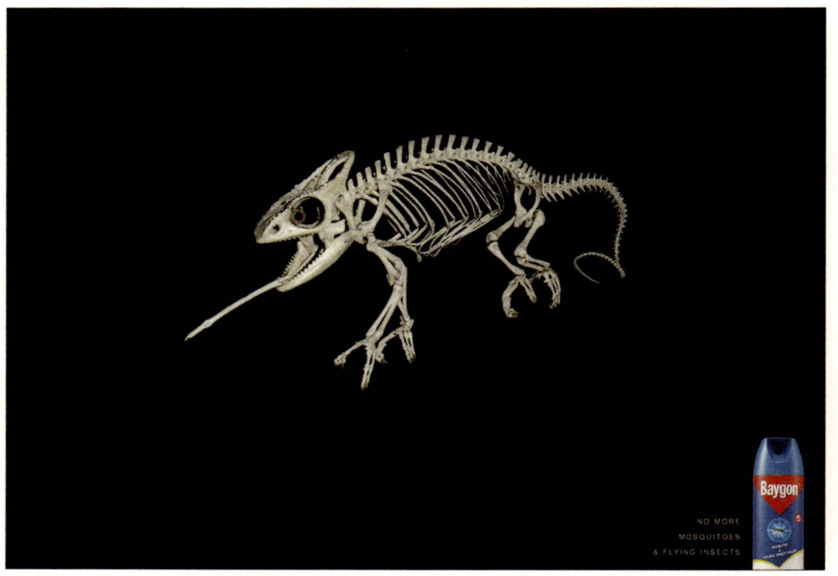

THAILANDE THAILAND
KID Bangkok Baygon
No more moquitoes and flying insects

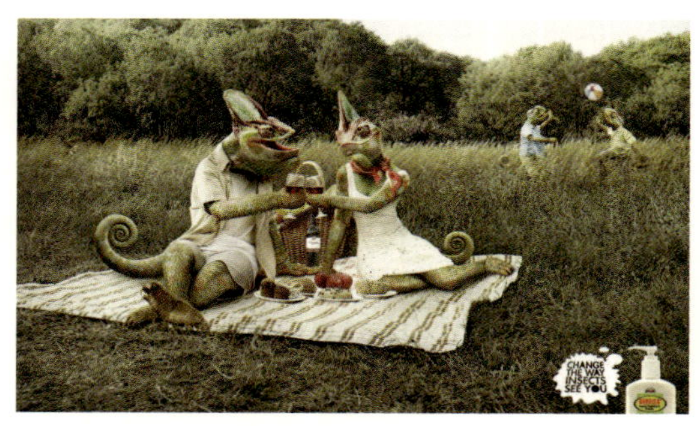

SINGAPOURE SINGAPORE (2009)
McCann Erickson Repellat
Change the way insects see you

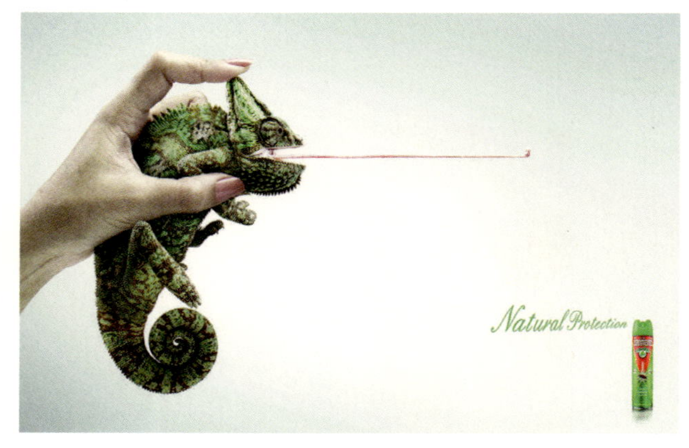

THAILANDE THAILAND (2011)
Euro RSCG Bangkok Shieldtox Naturgard
Natural protection

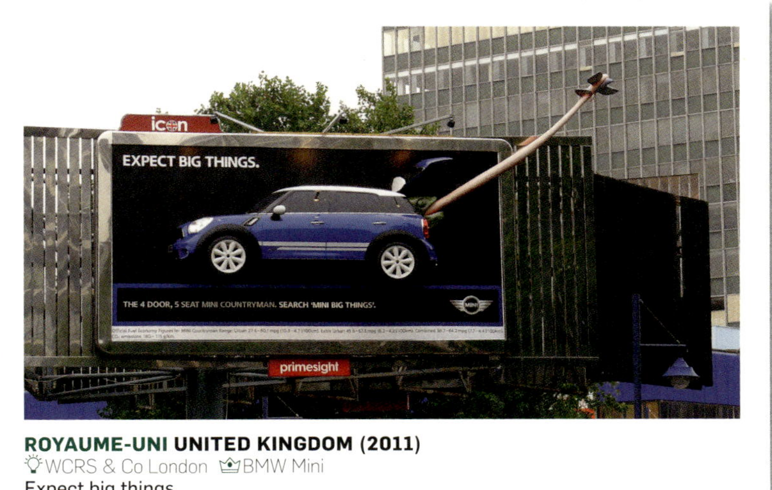

ROYAUME-UNI UNITED KINGDOM (2011)
WCRS & Co London   BMW Mini
Expect big things

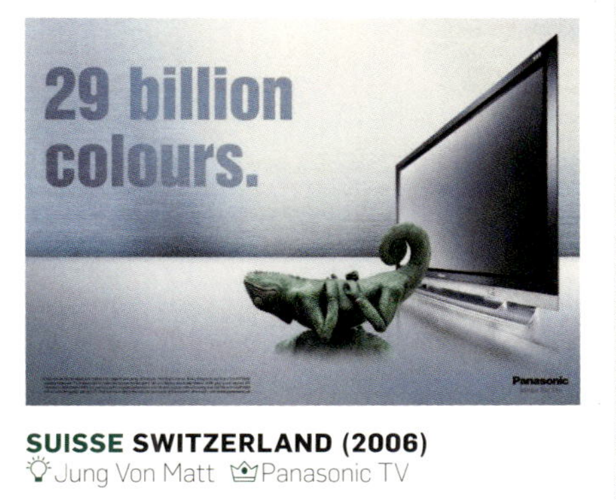

SUISSE SWITZERLAND (2006)
Jung Von Matt   Panasonic TV

CAMÉLÉONS
№ 16
CHAMELEONS

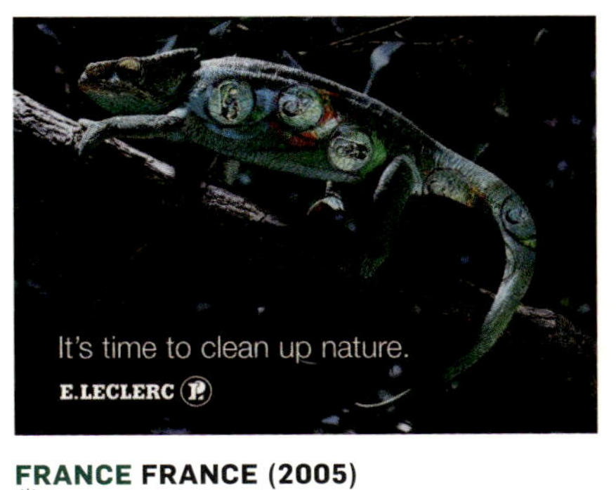

FRANCE FRANCE (2005)
Australie   E.Leclerc
It's time to clean up nature

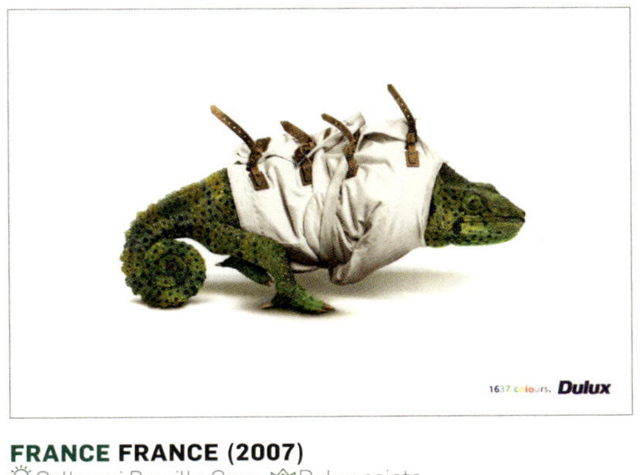

FRANCE FRANCE (2007)
Callegari Berville Grey   Dulux paints
1637 colours

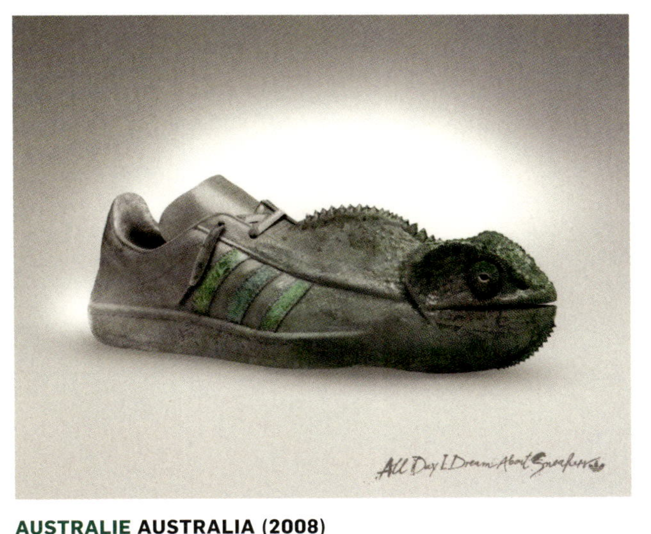

AUSTRALIE AUSTRALIA (2008)
Life Lounge Melbourne   Adidas Originals
All day I dream about sneakers

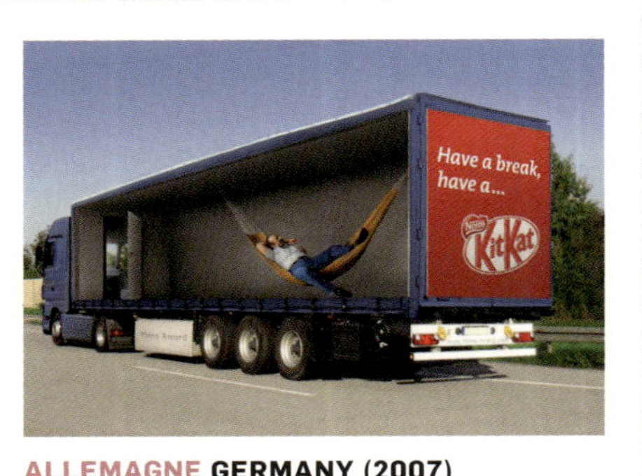

ALLEMAGNE GERMANY (2007)
DDB Dusseldorf Kit Kat
Have a break, have a Kit Kat

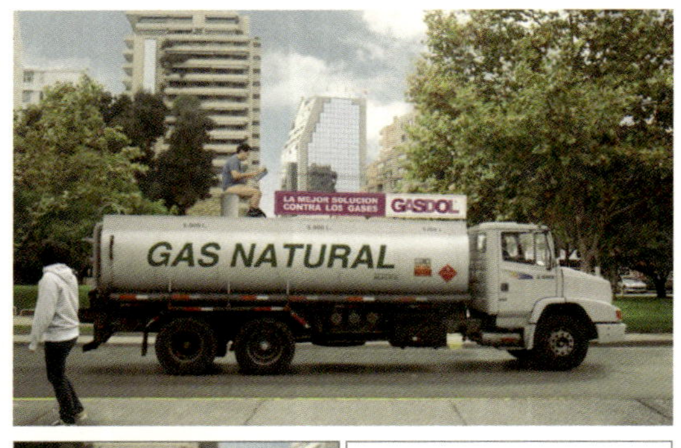

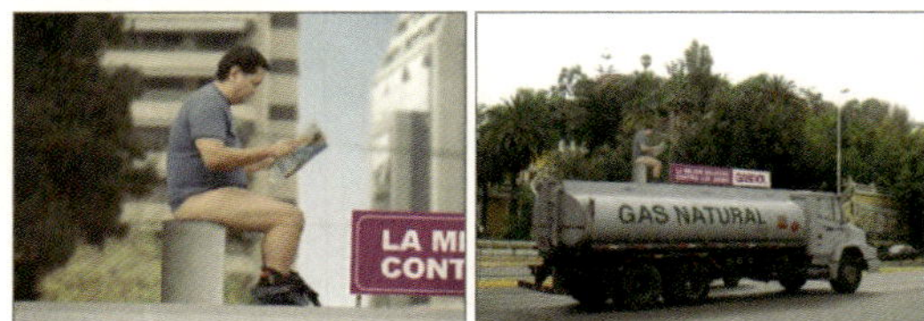

CHILI CHILE (2009)
Ogilvy Santiago Gasdol
The best solution against gas (flatulences)

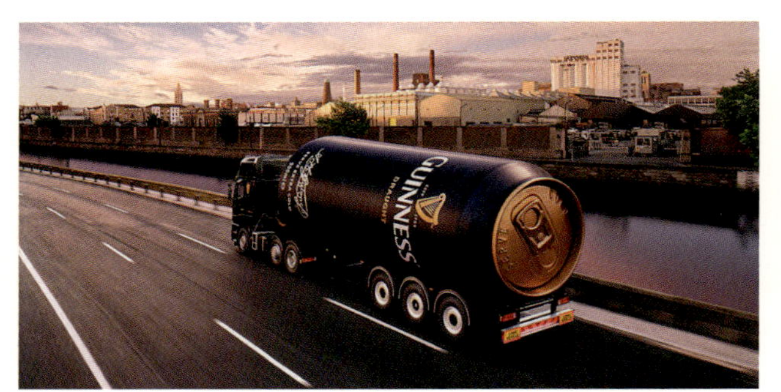

IRLANDE IRELAND (2010)
Irish International BBDO Dublin Guinness Beer

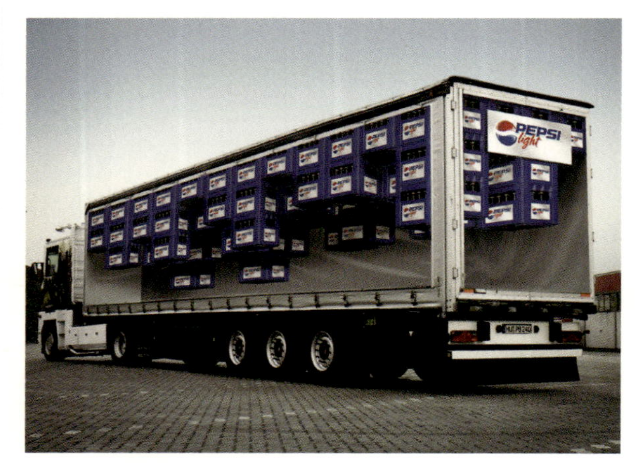

ALLEMAGNE GERMANY (2005)
BBDO Dusseldorf Pepsi Light

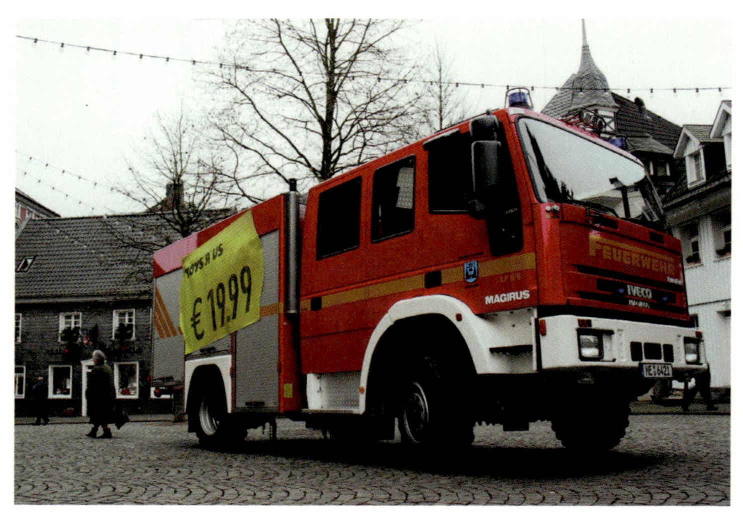

ALLEMAGNE GERMANY (2006)
Grey Dusseldorf Toy's r us

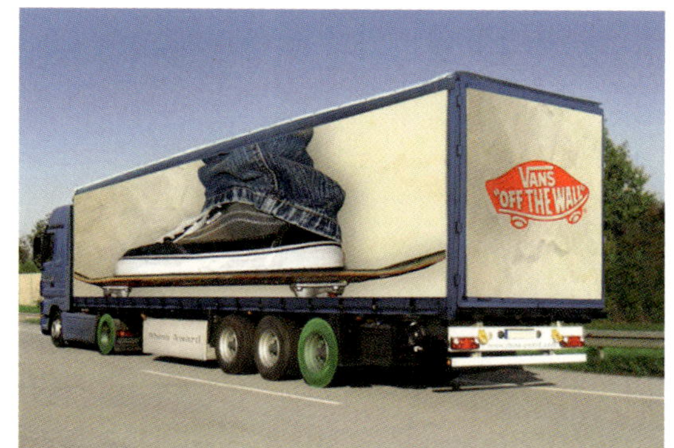

ALLEMAGNE GERMANY (2007)
DDB — Vans skateboard shoes

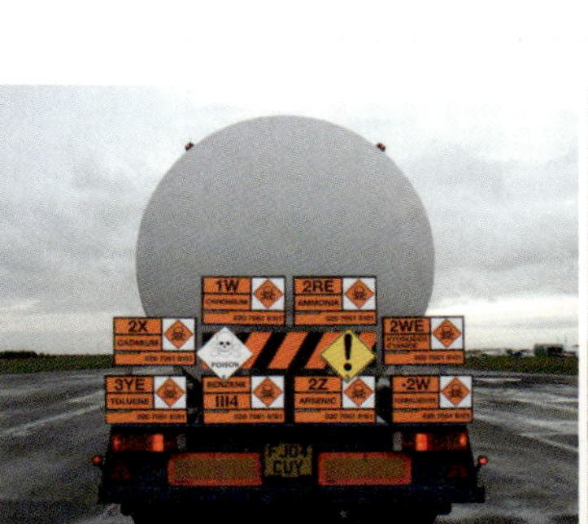
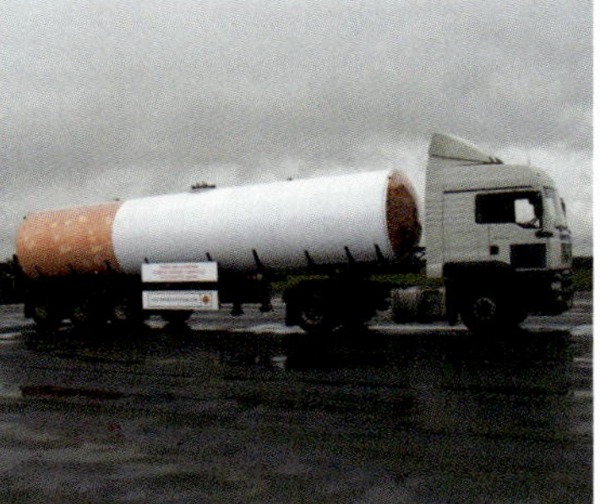

ROYAUME-UNI UNITED KINGDOM (2007)
Ogilvy London — Department Of Health / Cancer Research
Smoke is poison

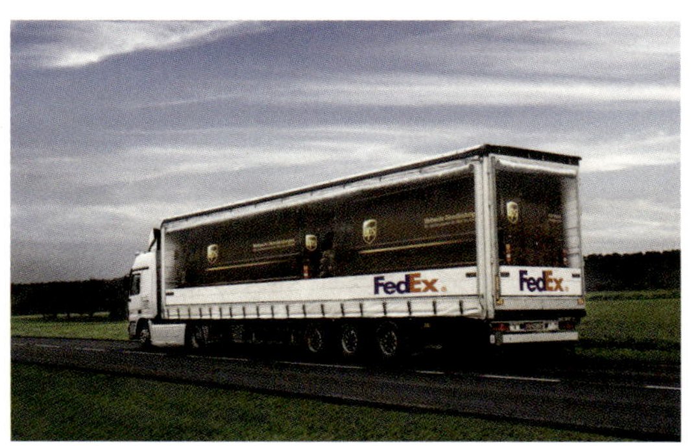

ALLEMAGNE GERMANY (2007)
BBDO — FedEx

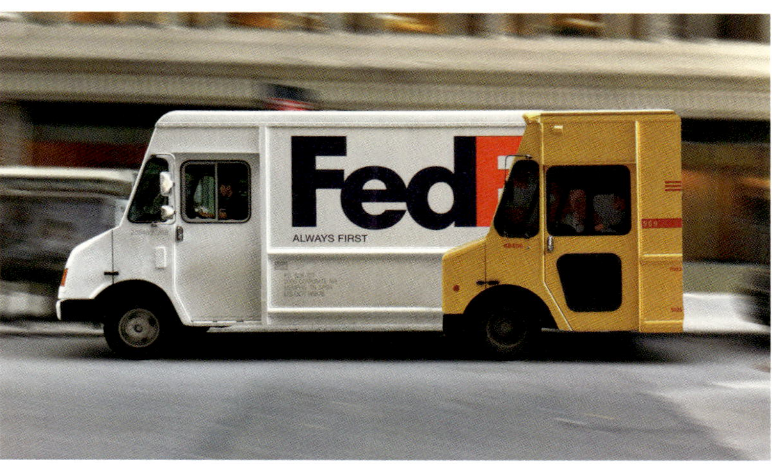

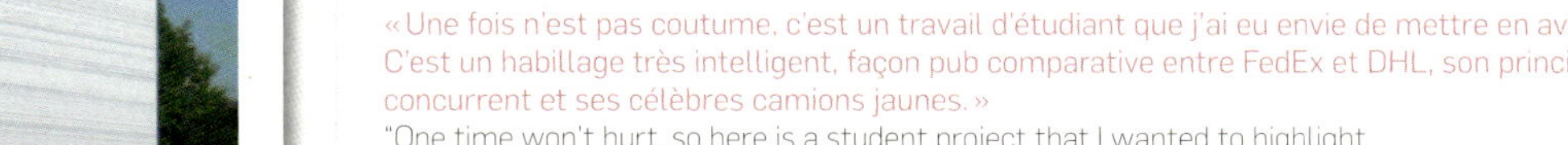

ALLEMAGNE GERMANY (2012)
Miami Ad School Hamburg Thomas Ilum and Zoe Vogelius — FedEx
Always first

« Une fois n'est pas coutume, c'est un travail d'étudiant que j'ai eu envie de mettre en avant.
C'est un habillage très intelligent, façon pub comparative entre FedEx et DHL, son principal
concurrent et ses célèbres camions jaunes. »
"One time won't hurt, so here is a student project that I wanted to highlight.
This is a very intelligent way to make an advert comparing FedEx and its principal competitor
DHL and its famous yellow trucks."

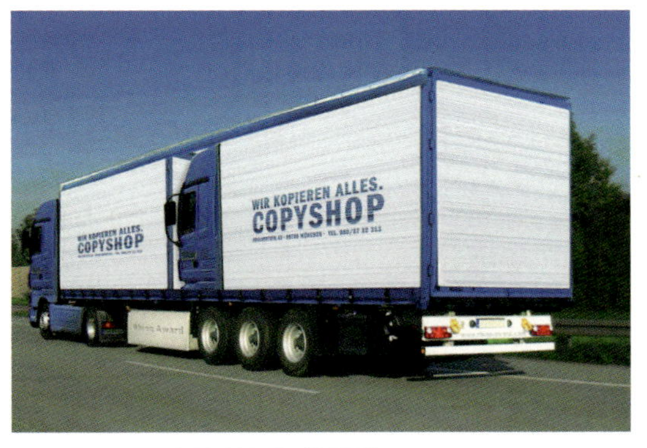

ALLEMAGNE GERMANY (2007)
.start — Copyshop

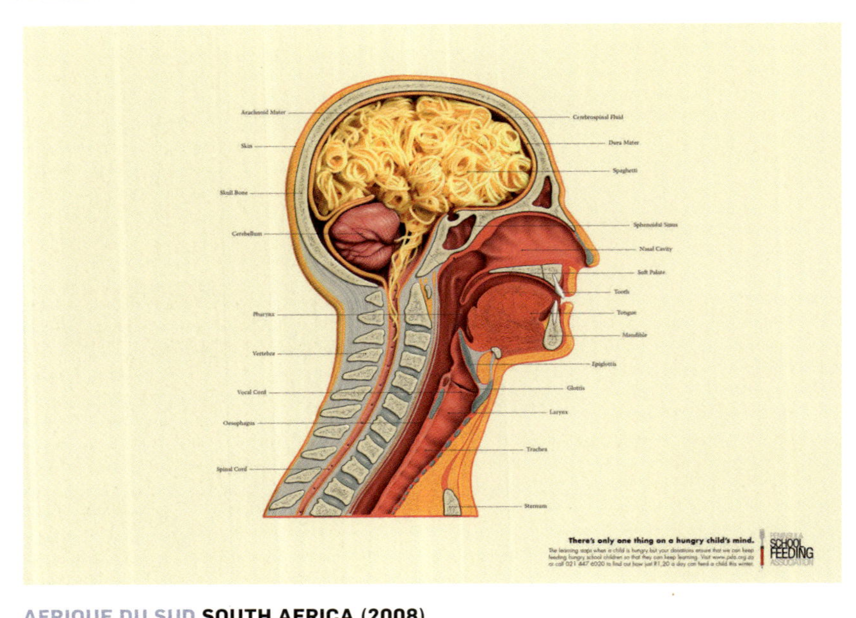

AFRIQUE DU SUD SOUTH AFRICA (2008)
Draft FCB Cape Town · School Feeding Association
There's only one thing on a hungry child's mind

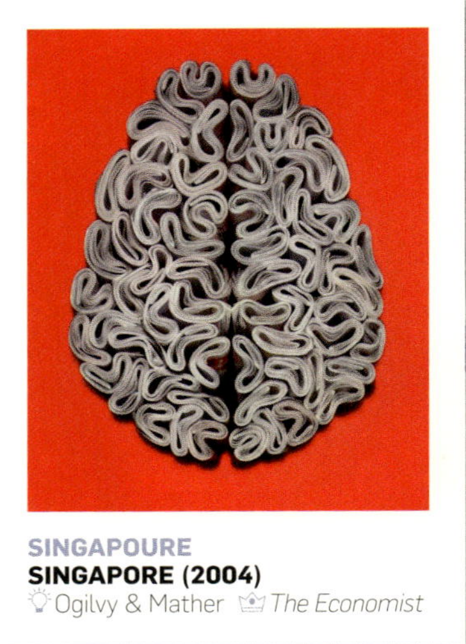

SINGAPOURE
SINGAPORE (2004)
Ogilvy & Mather · *The Economist*

CERVEAUX
№18
BRAINS

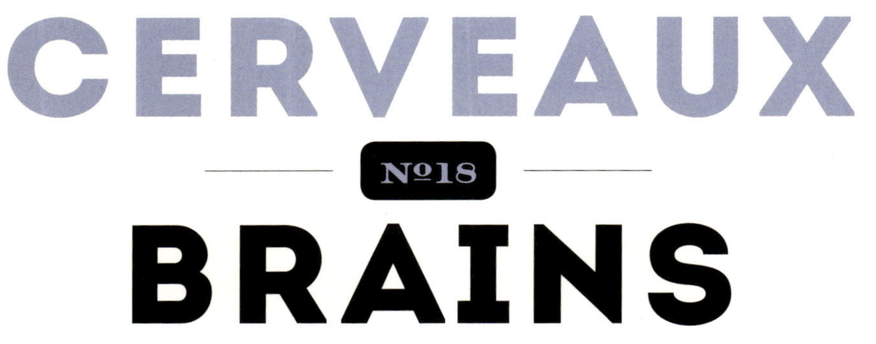

ALLEMAGNE GERMANY (2011)
Kolle Rebbe · Inlingua Language school
Get it out faster

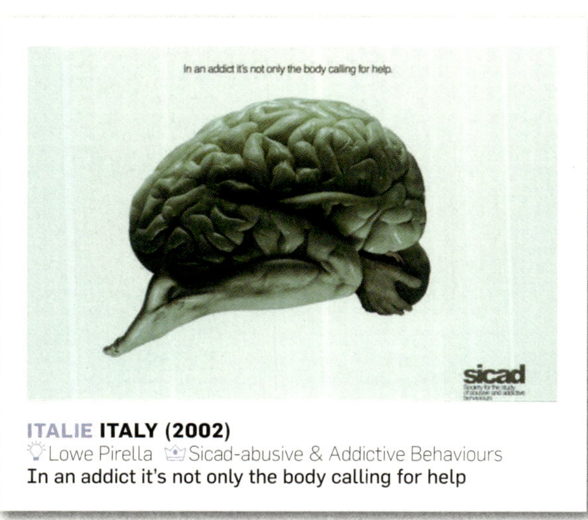

ITALIE ITALY (2002)
Lowe Pirella · Sicad-abusive & Addictive Behaviours
In an addict it's not only the body calling for help

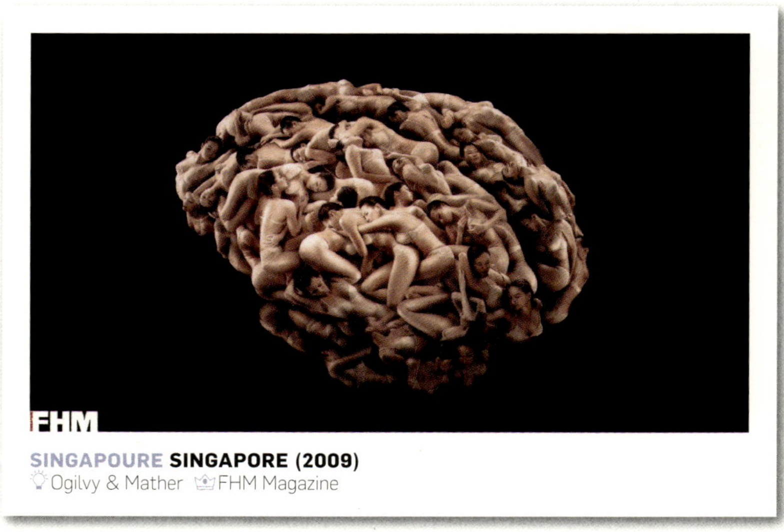

SINGAPOURE SINGAPORE (2009)
Ogilvy & Mather · FHM Magazine

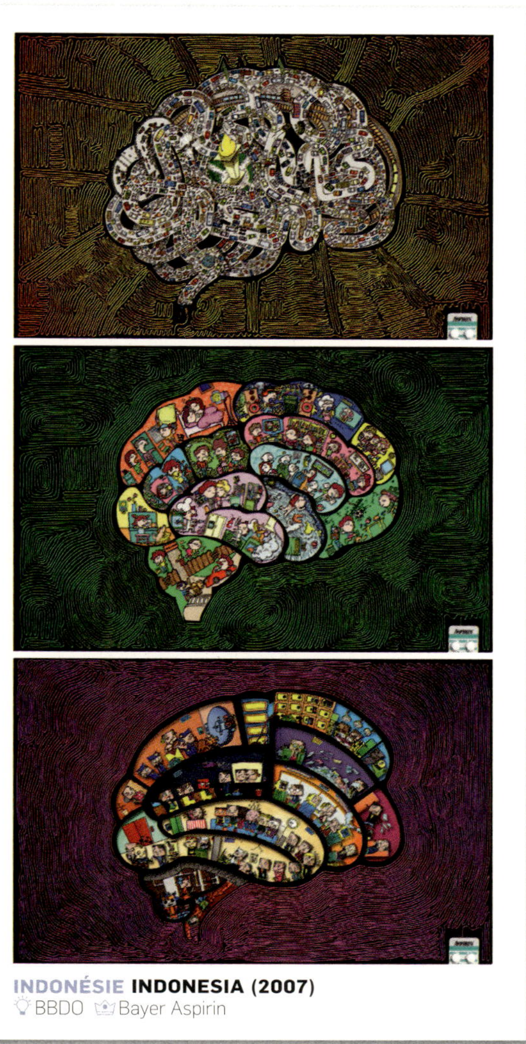

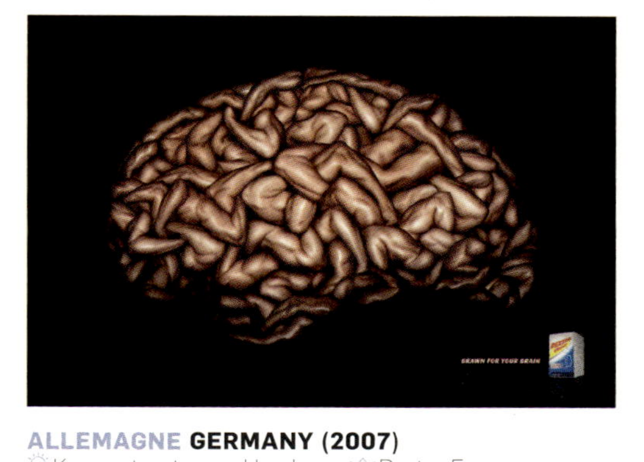

ALLEMAGNE GERMANY (2007)
Kempertrautmann Hamburg · Dextro Energy
Brawn for your brain

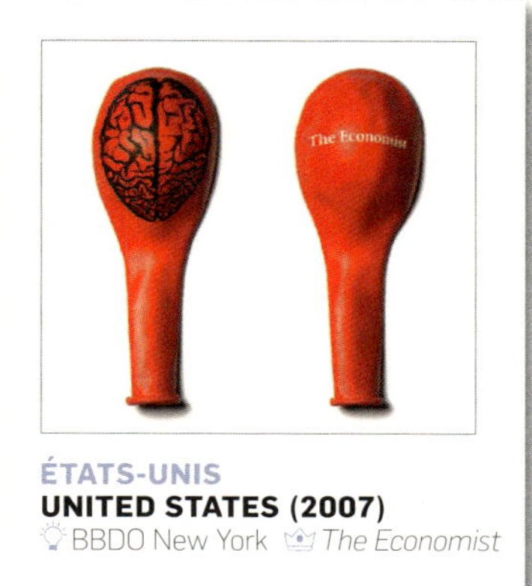

ÉTATS-UNIS
UNITED STATES (2007)
BBDO New York · *The Economist*

INDONÉSIE INDONESIA (2007)
BBDO · Bayer Aspirin

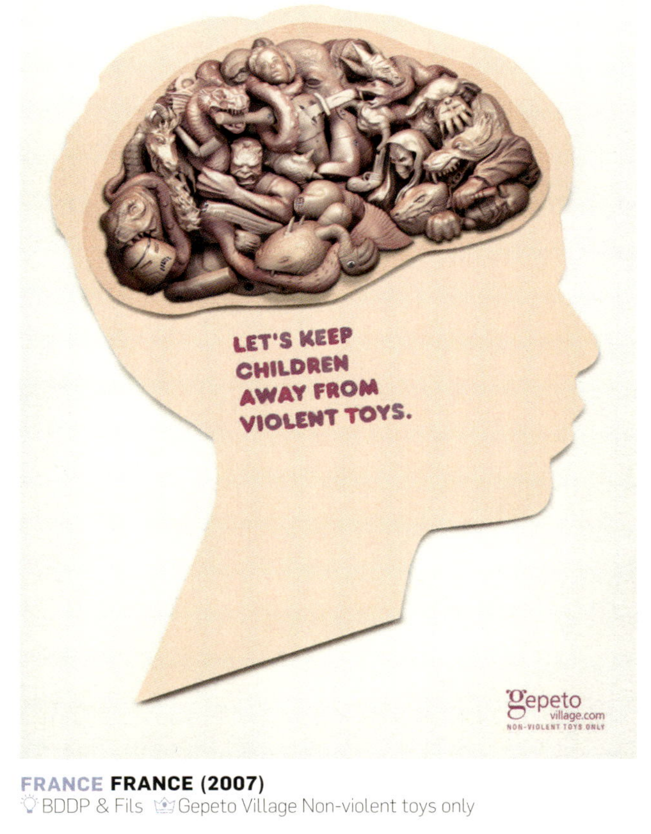

FRANCE FRANCE (2007)
BDDP & Fils · Gepeto Village Non-violent toys only

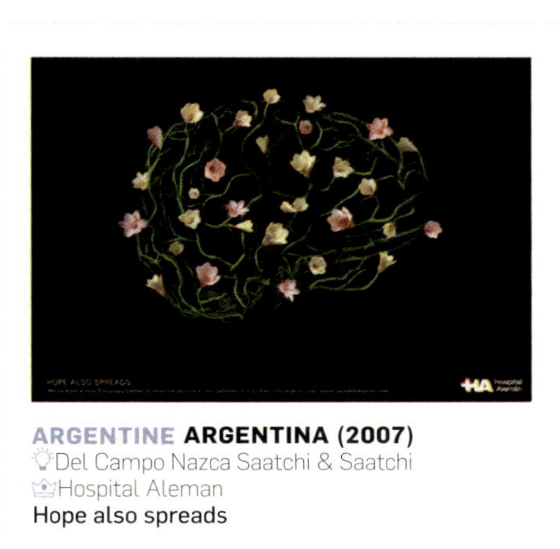

ARGENTINE ARGENTINA (2007)
Del Campo Nazca Saatchi & Saatchi
Hospital Aleman
Hope also spreads

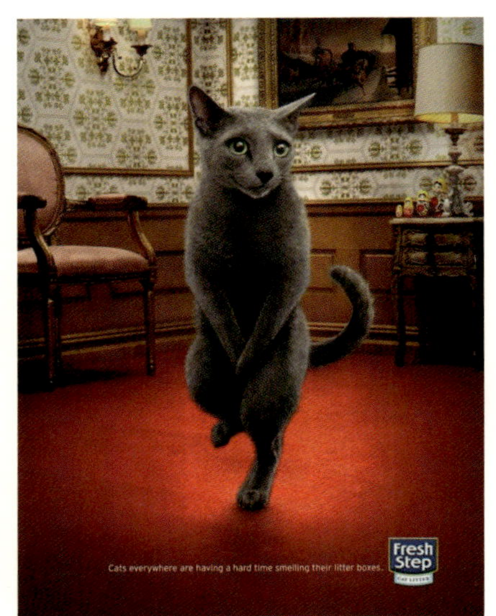

ÉTATS-UNIS UNITED STATES (2009)
DDB West · Fresh Step
Cats everywhere are having a hard time smelling their litter boxes

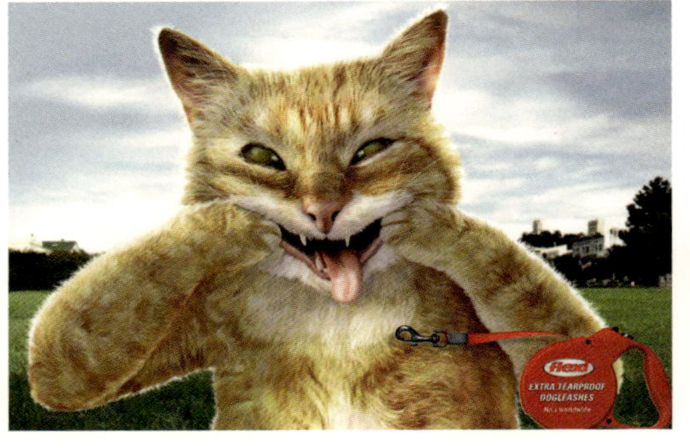

ALLEMAGNE GERMANY (2004)
Sholz & Friends · Flexi Dogleashes
Extra tearproof dogleashes

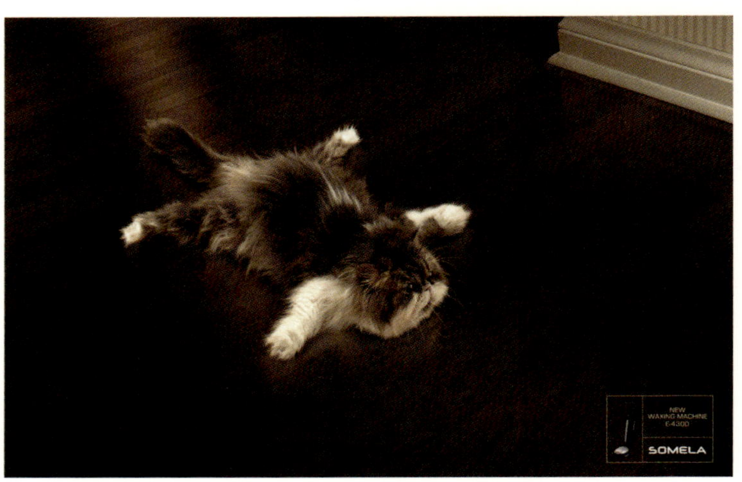

CHILI CHILE (2007)
Leo Burnett · Somela
New waxing machine E-4300

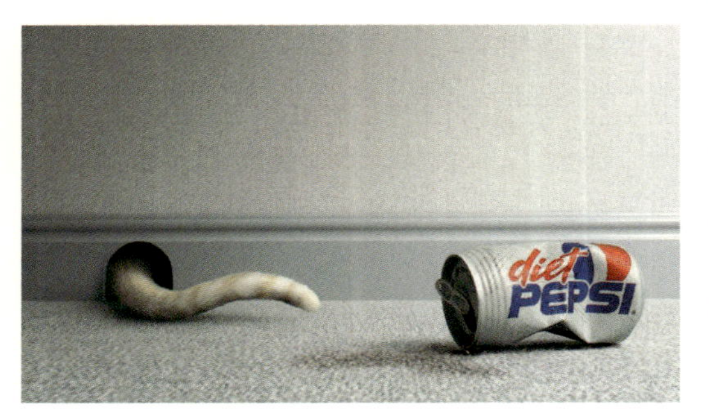

THAILANDE THAILAND (2002)
BBDO Bangkok · Pepsi Diet

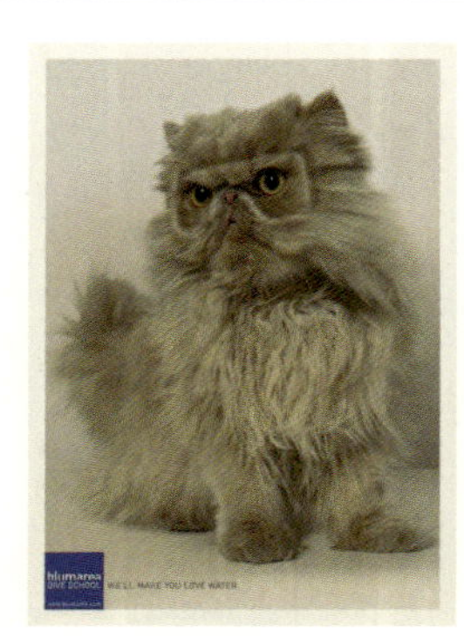

ITALIE ITALY (2005)
JWT Milan
BluMarea Dive School

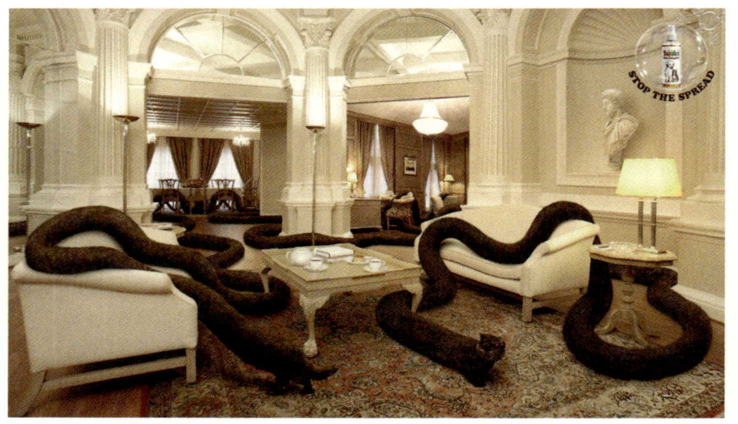

INDONESIE INDONESIA (2011)
Grey · Bubbles Pet Cologne
Stop the spread

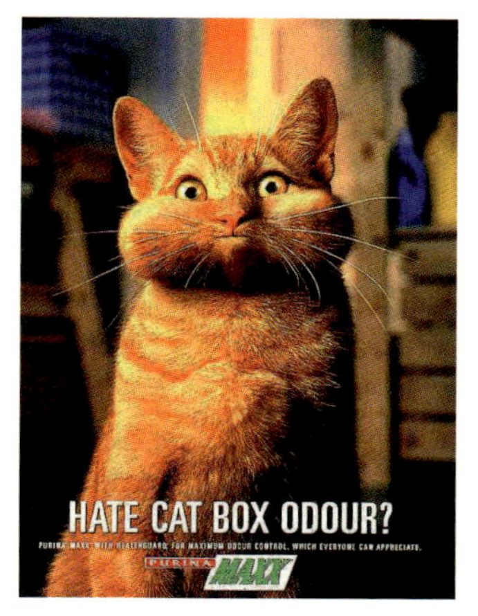

CANADA CANADA (1998)
Roche Mac Aulay & Partners
Purina Maxx
Hate cat box odour?

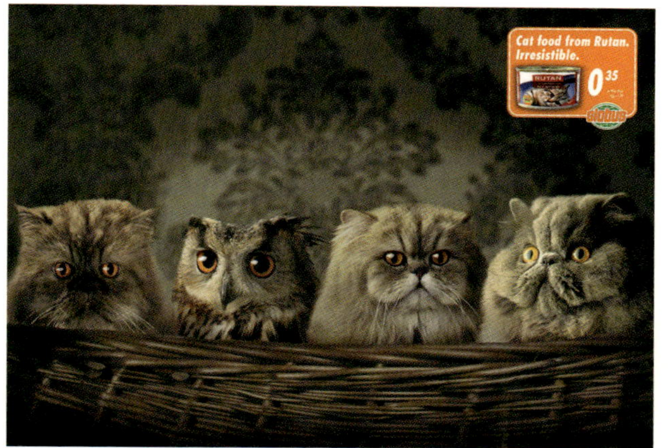

ALLEMAGNE GERMANY (2005)
Ogilvy Frankfurt Globus Supermarket
Cat food from Rutan. Irrésistible

CHATS
№19
CATS

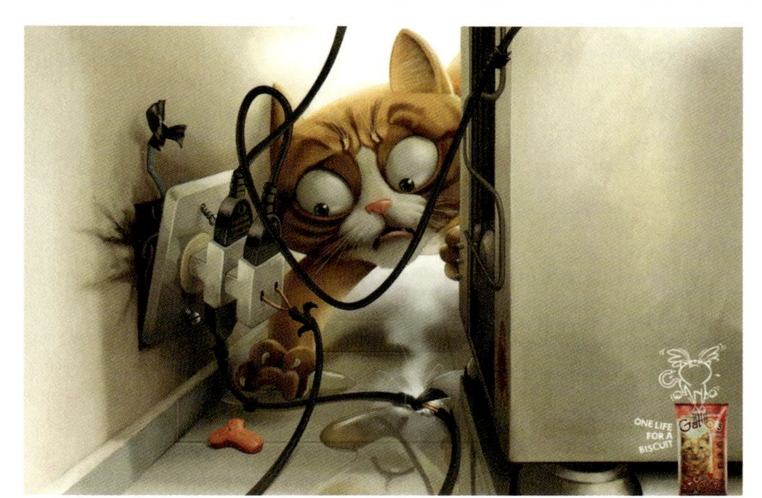

BRÉSIL BRAZIL (2011)
Z Sao Paulo Gatos
One life for a biscuit

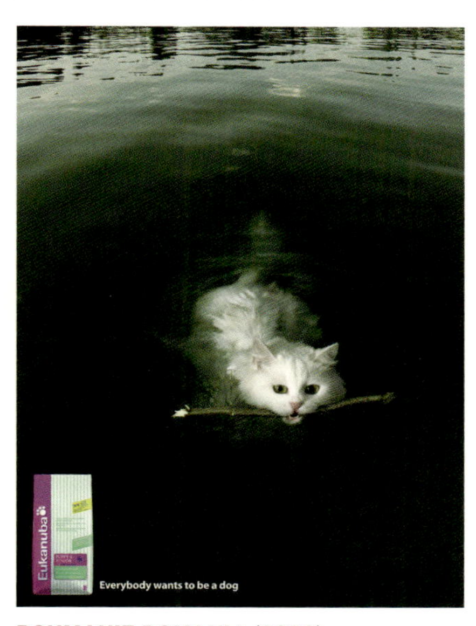

ROUMANIE ROMANIA (2006)
LeoBurnett Eukanuba Dog Food
Everybody wants to be a dog

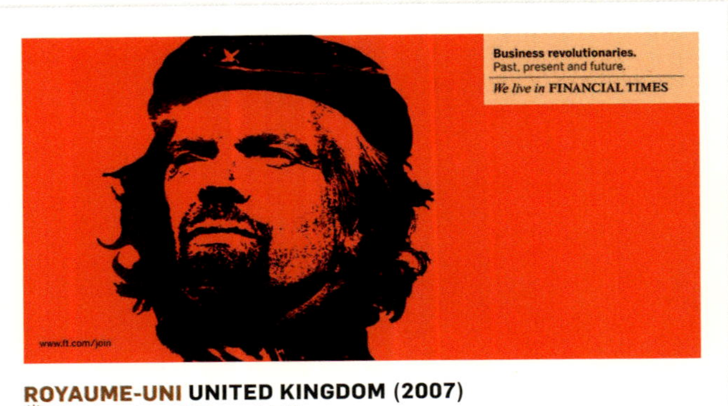

ROYAUME-UNI UNITED KINGDOM (2007)
DDB London Financial Times
Business revolutionaries. Past, present and future

CHE GUEVARA
№20

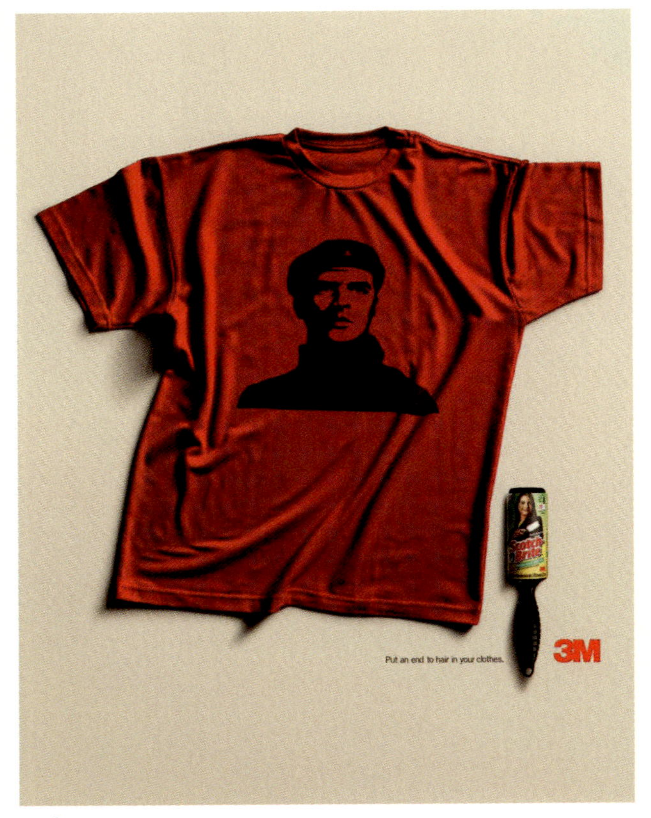

BRÉSIL BRAZIL (2008)
Matos Grey Sao Paulo 3M
Put an end to hair in your clothes

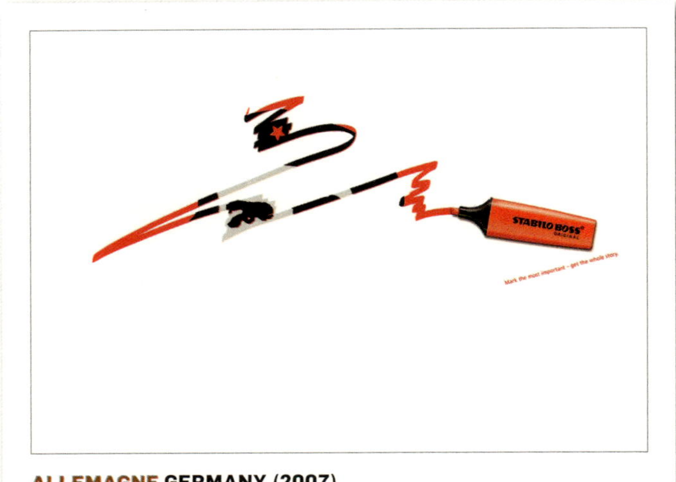

ALLEMAGNE GERMANY (2007)
Serviceplan Hamburg Stabilo
Mark the most important - get the whole story

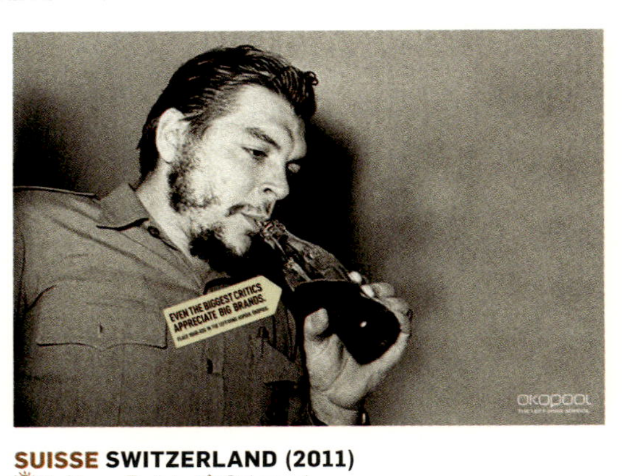

SUISSE SWITZERLAND (2011)
Ruf Lanz Zurich Oekopool
Even the biggest critics appreciate big brands.
Place your ads in the left-wing adpool Oekopool.

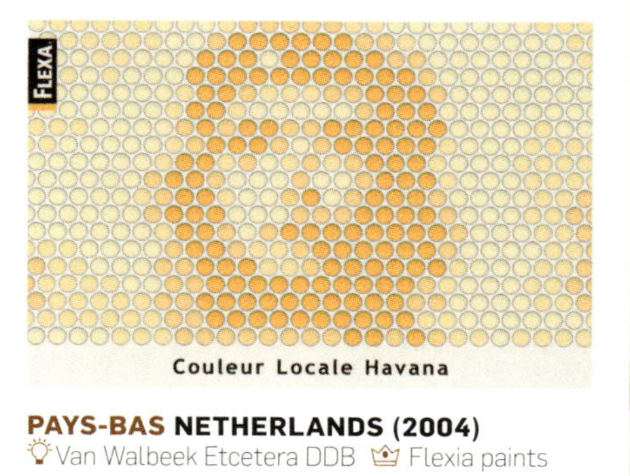

PAYS-BAS NETHERLANDS (2004)
Van Walbeek Etcetera DDB Flexia paints

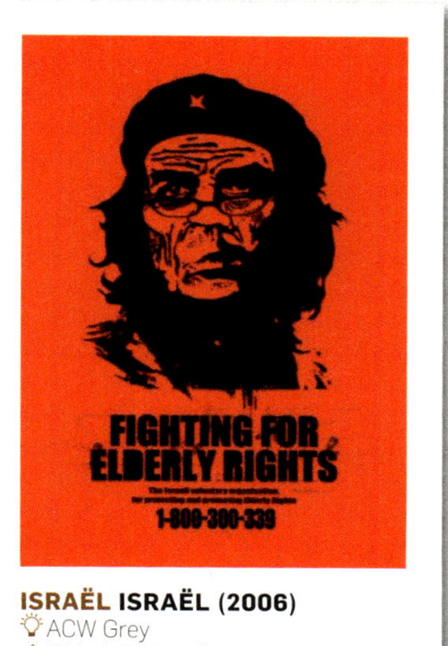

ISRAËL ISRAËL (2006)
ACW Grey
Elderly Rights Organisation

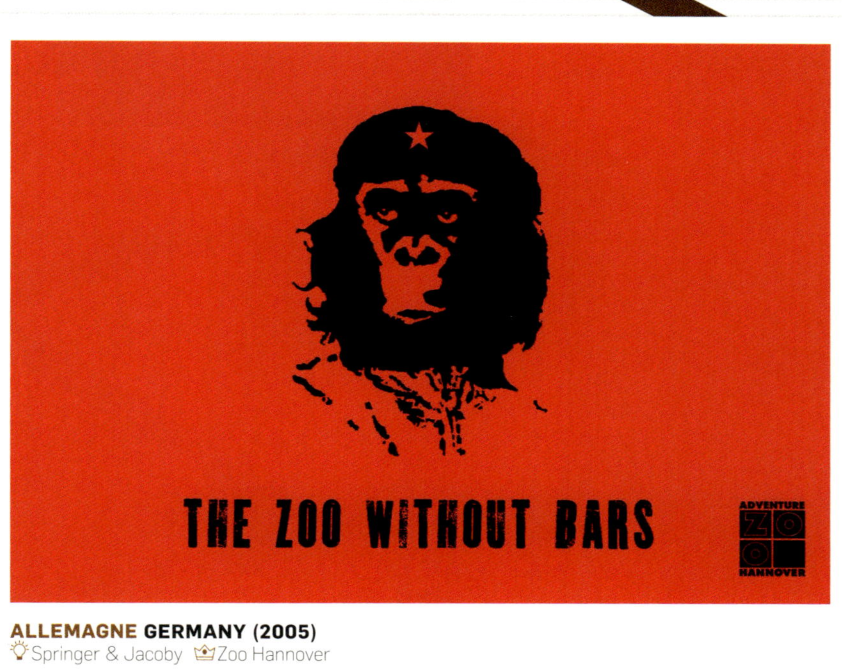

ALLEMAGNE GERMANY (2005)
Springer & Jacoby Zoo Hannover

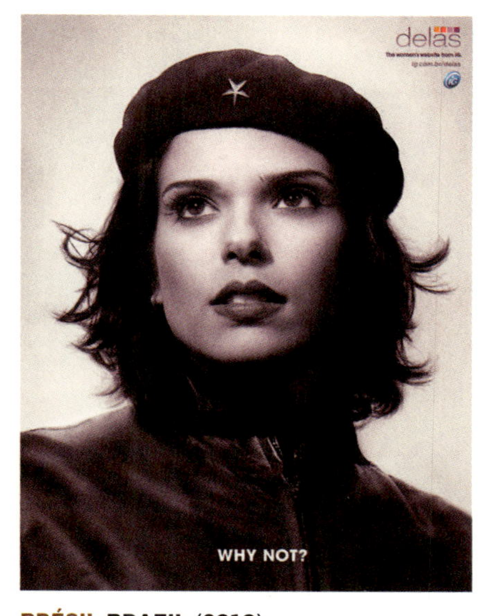

BRÉSIL BRAZIL (2010)
Lew Lara TBWA Delas Women's Channel

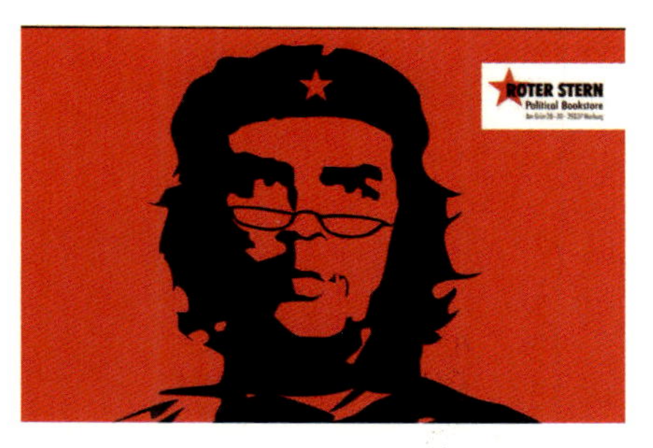

ALLEMAGNE GERMANY (2004)
Red Rabbit Roter Stern
Political bookstore

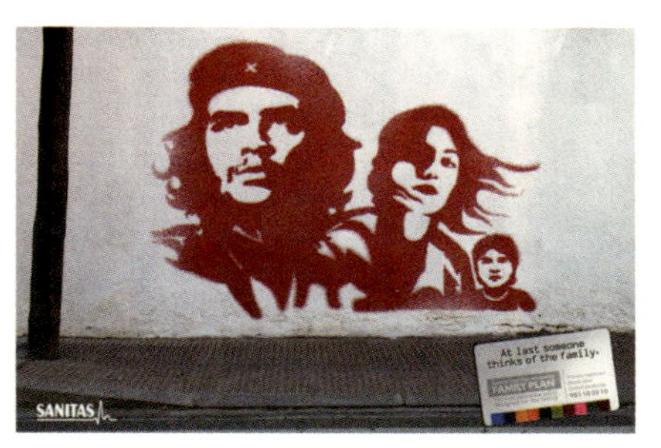

ESPAGNE SPAIN (2003)
Contrapunto Family Plan Medical Insurance
At last someone thinks of the family

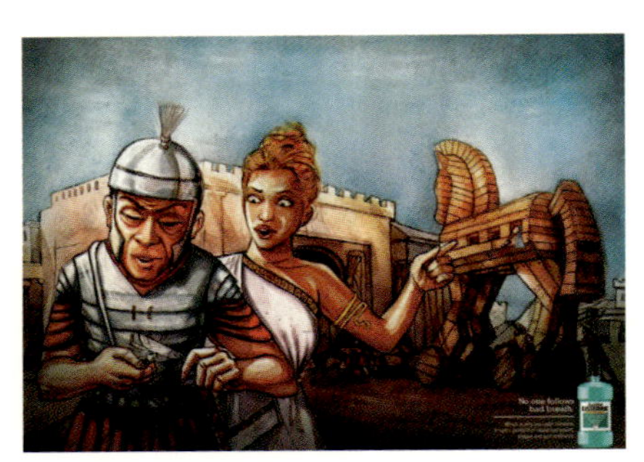

INDE INDIA (2012)
JWT Mumbai — Listerine
No one follows bad breath

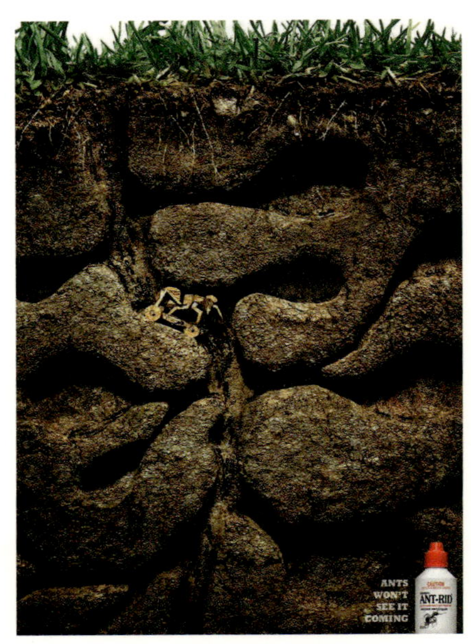

AUSTRALIE AUSTRALIA (2008)
DDB Melbourne — Ant-Rid
Ants won't see it coming

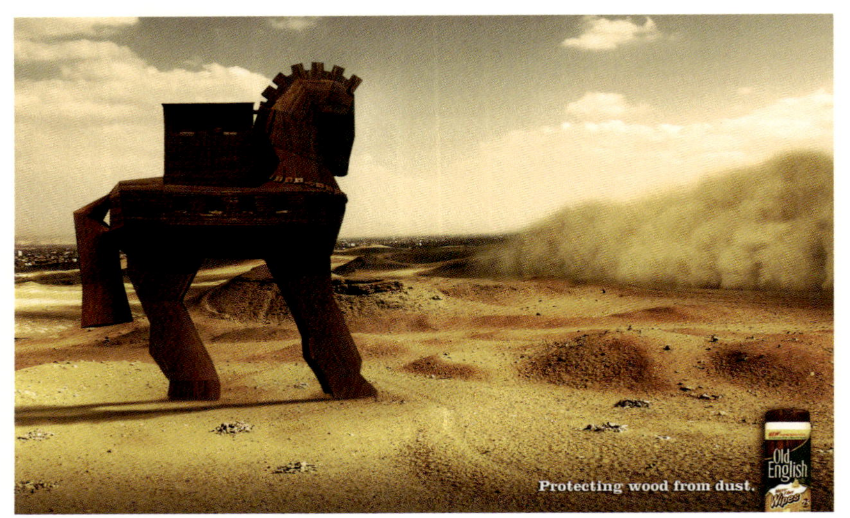

ÉTATS-UNIS UNITED STATES (2009)
Miami Ad School Student Work — Old English Wood Protection
Protecting wood from dust

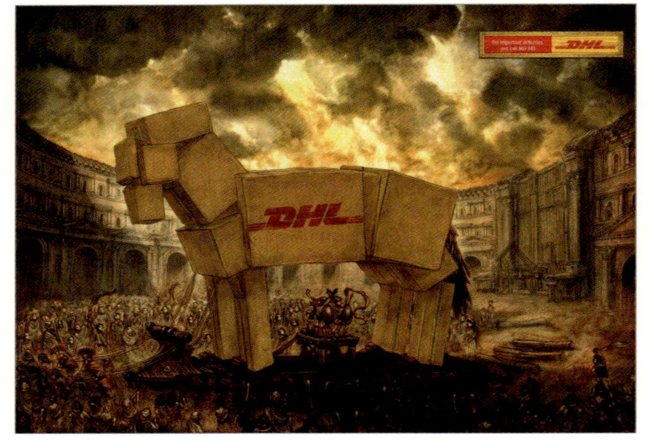

ÉMIRATS ARABES UNIS UNITED ARAB EMIRATES (2009)
Ogilvy Dubai — DHL
For important deliveries

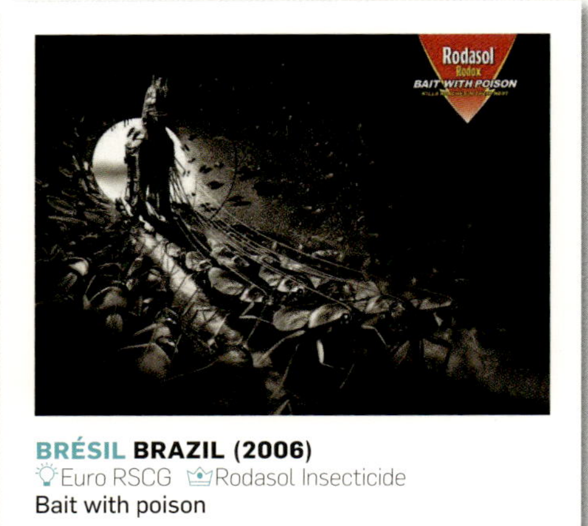

BRÉSIL BRAZIL (2006)
Euro RSCG — Rodasol Insecticide
Bait with poison

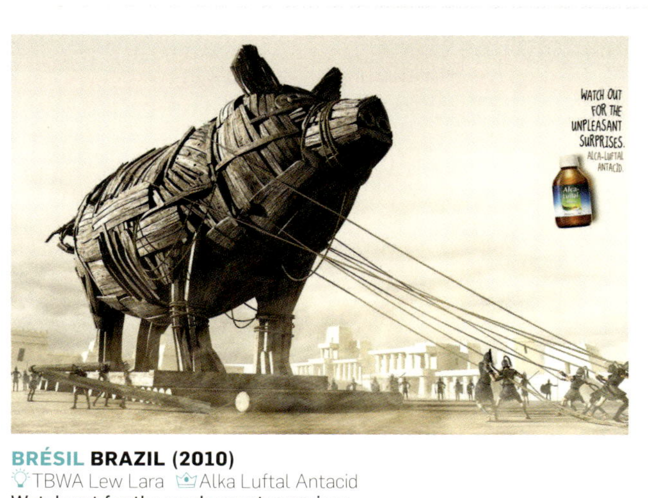

BRÉSIL BRAZIL (2010)
TBWA Lew Lara — Alka Luftal Antacid
Watch out for the unpleasant surprises

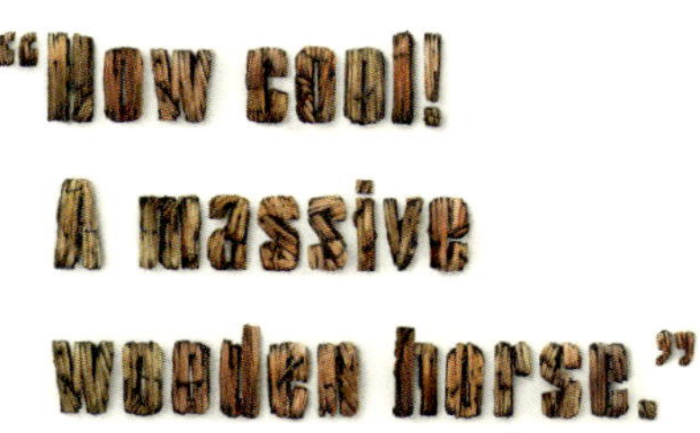

ALLEMAGNE GERMANY (2011)
DDB Berlin — Volkswagen Side Assist
See things before they get dangerous

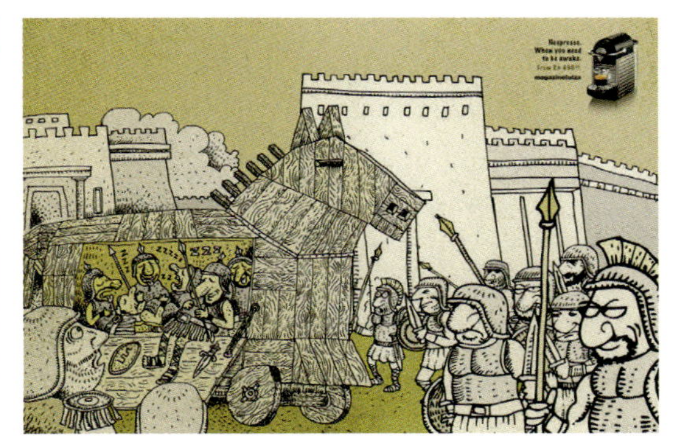

ISRAËL ISRAEL (2012)
Gitam BBDO — Hubba Bubba
Blow it out of proportion

CHEVAL DE TROIE
№21
TROJAN HORSE

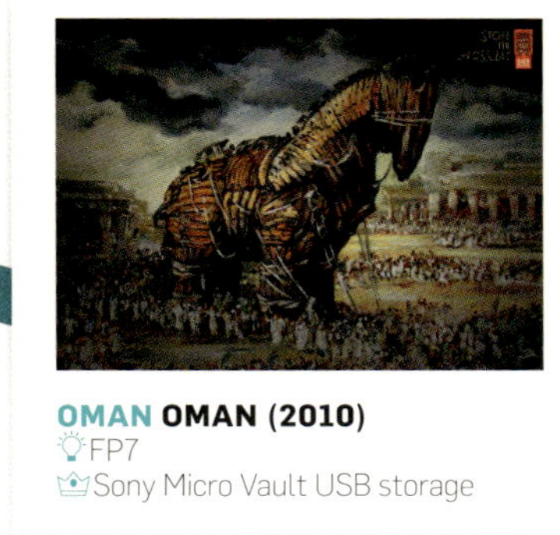

BRÉSIL BRAZIL (2010)
Ogilvy Sao Paulo — Nespresso
When you need to be awake

OMAN OMAN (2010)
FP7
Sony Micro Vault USB storage

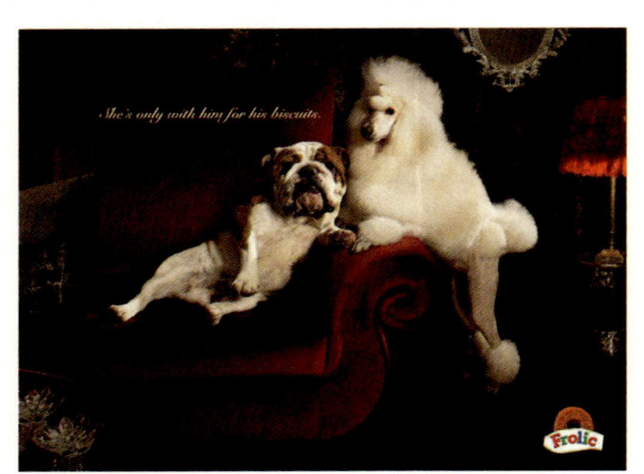

FRANCE FRANCE (2010)
CLM/BBDO Frolic
She's only with him for his biscuits

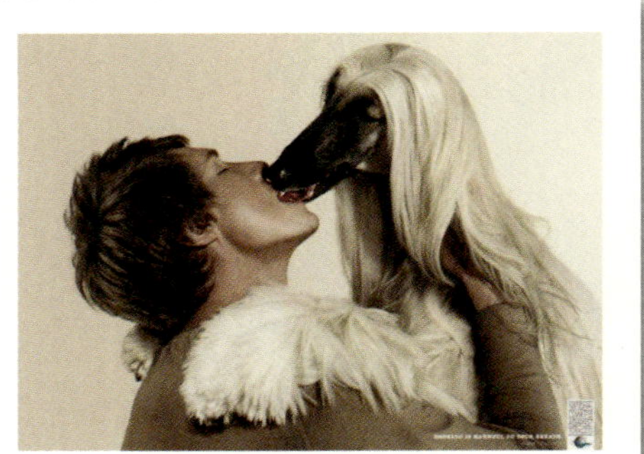

FRANCE FRANCE (2004)
TBWA Paris Anti Tobacco Campaign
Smoking is harmful to your breath

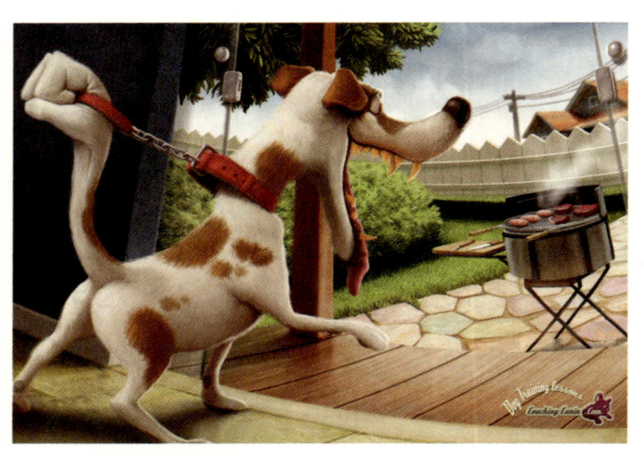

FRANCE FRANCE (2009)
Callegari Berville Grey Coaching Canin
Dog training lessons

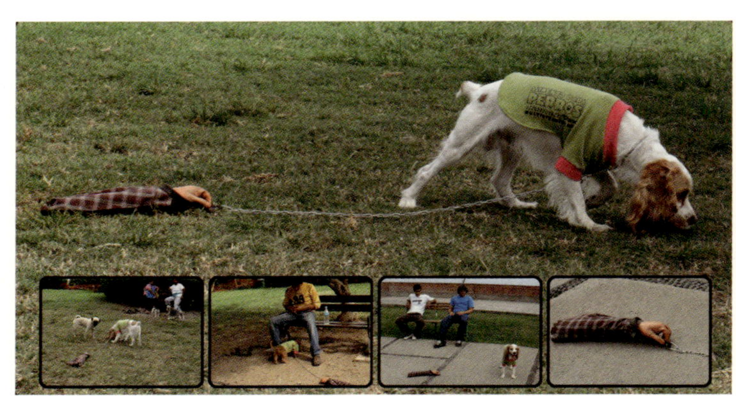

PÉROU PERU (2010)
Mayo Draft FCB Wong Dog Food
New line of dog food with full vitamins

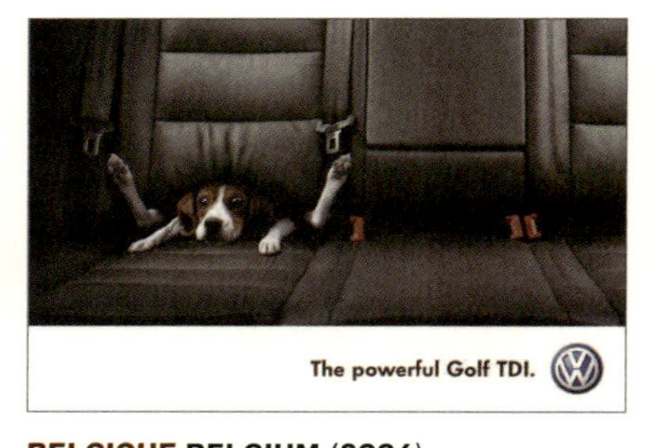

BELGIQUE BELGIUM (2004)
DDB Volkswagen Golf TDI
The powerful Golf TDI

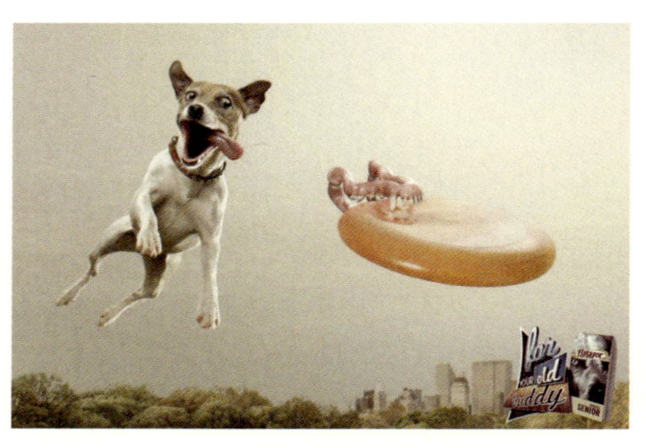

FRANCE FRANCE (2008)
TBWA Paris Flatazor Senior
For your old buddy

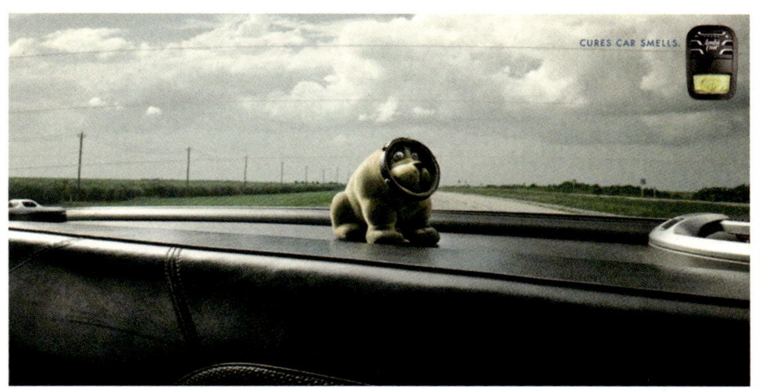

AUSTRALIE AUSTRALIA (2009)
Jay Grey Sydney   Ambi-Pur
Cures car smells

CHIENS
Nº22
DOGS

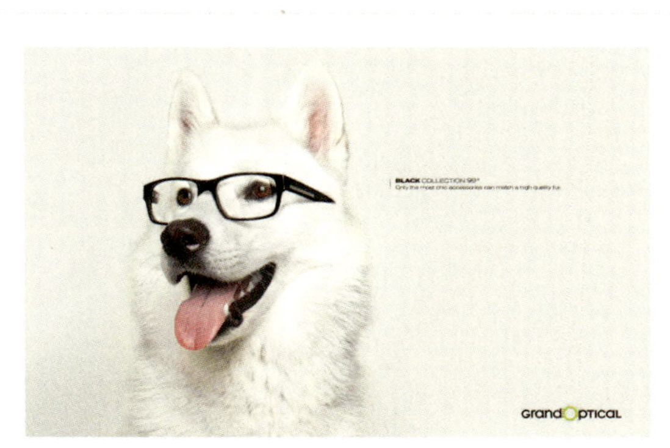

FRANCE FRANCE (2010)
Young & Rubicam   Grand Optical
Only the most chic accessories can match a high quality fur

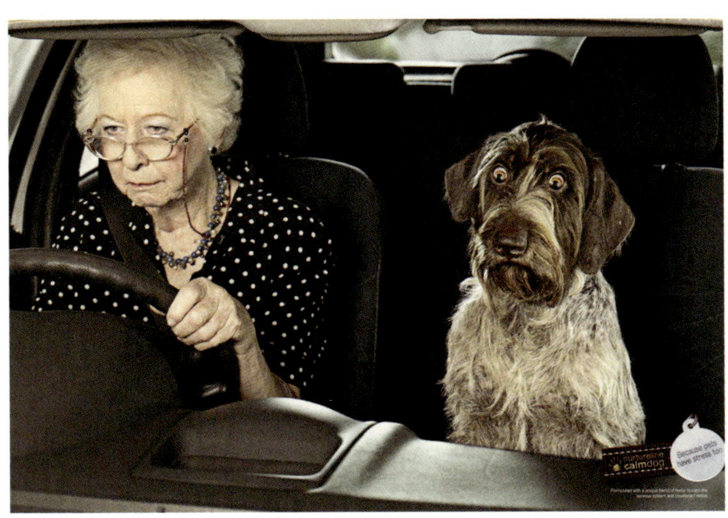

AFRIQUE DU SUD SOUTH AFRICA (2010)
Euro RSCG   Calmdog
Because pets have stress too. (Formulated with a unique blend of herbs to calm the nervous system and counteract stress)

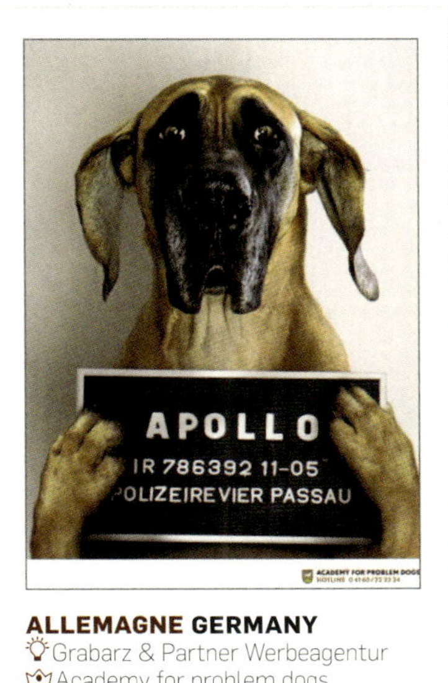

ALLEMAGNE GERMANY
Grabarz & Partner Werbeagentur
Academy for problem dogs

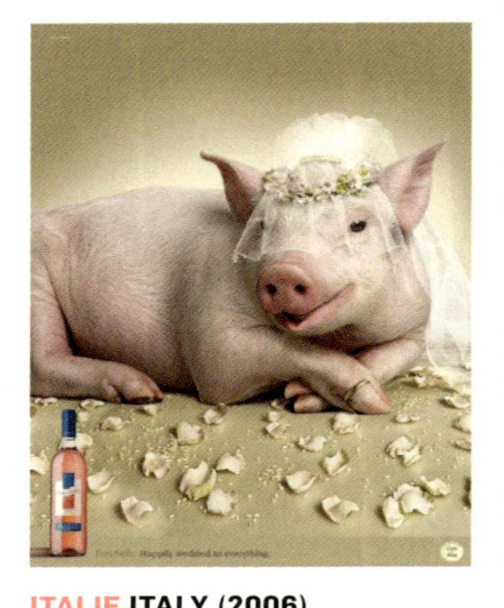

ITALIE ITALY (2006)
Cayenne Freschello Wine
Happily wedded to everything

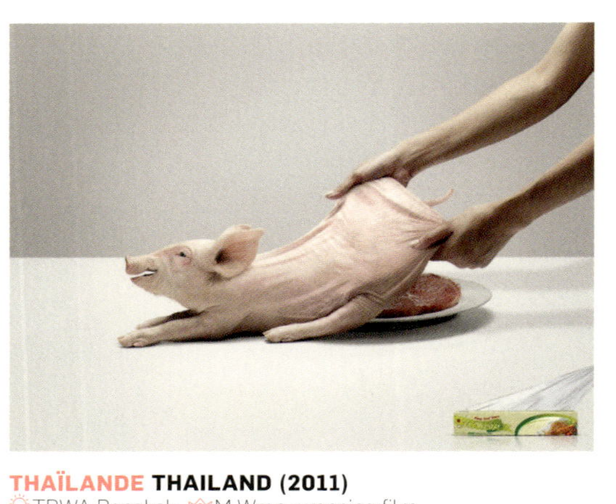

THAÏLANDE THAILAND (2011)
TBWA Bangkok M Wrap wrapping film
Keep food fresh

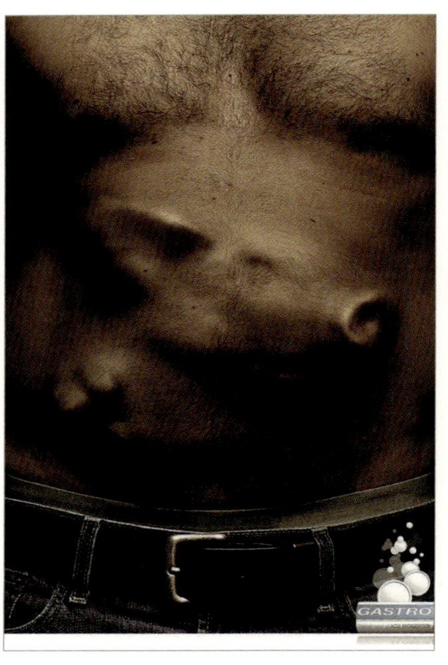

FRANCE FRANCE (2007)
Grey Paris Gastro
Instant relief of acid indigestion

COCHONS

№23

PIGS

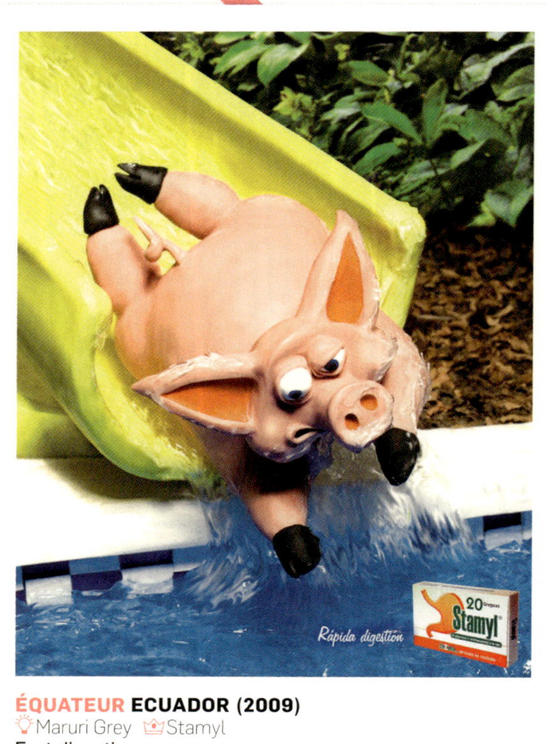

ÉQUATEUR ECUADOR (2009)
Maruri Grey Stamyl
Fast digestion

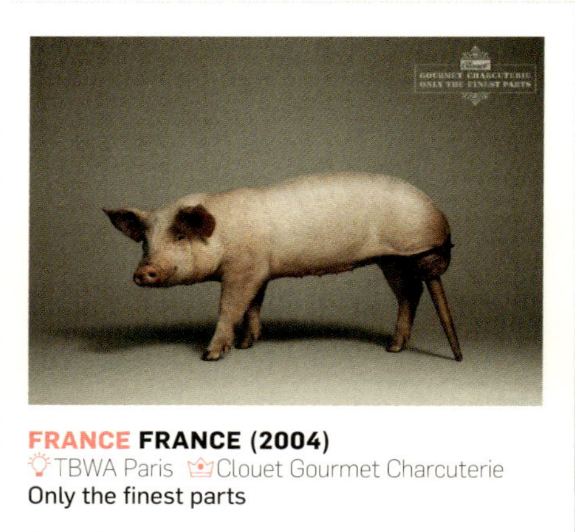

FRANCE FRANCE (2004)
TBWA Paris Clouet Gourmet Charcuterie
Only the finest parts

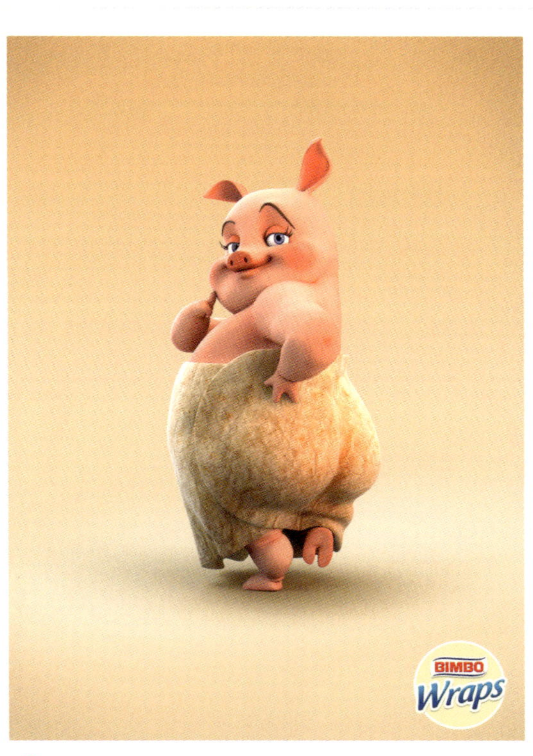

PÉROU PERU (2012)
Mc Cann — Bimbo Wraps

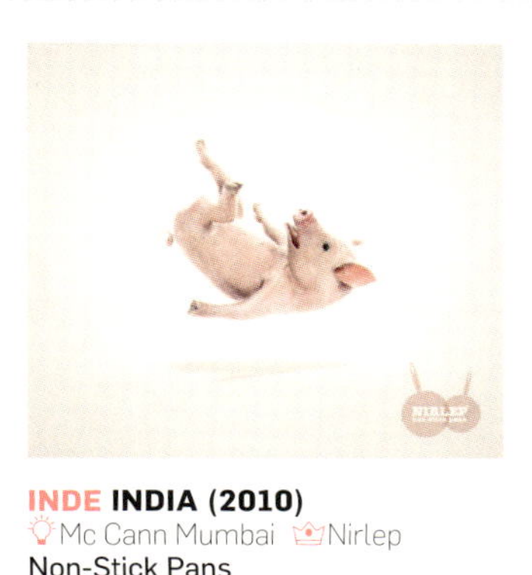

INDE INDIA (2010)
Mc Cann Mumbai — Nirlep
Non-Stick Pans

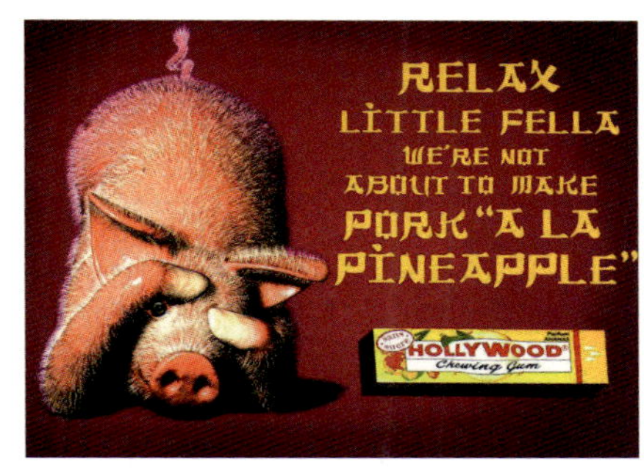

FRANCE FRANCE (1999)
BETC Euro RSCG
Hollywood Pineapple Chewing Gum
Relax little fella.
We're not about to make pork "a la pineapple"

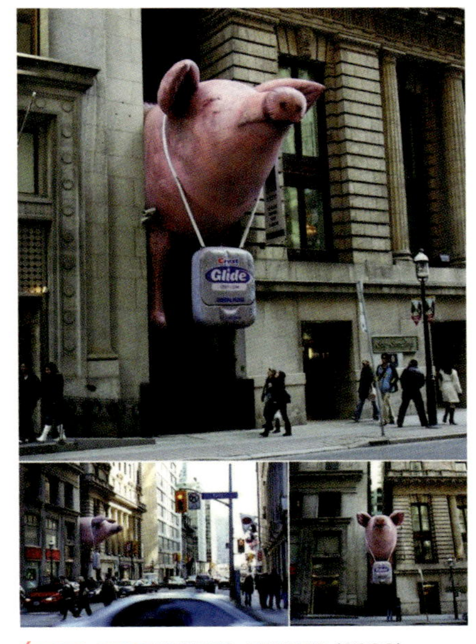

ÉTATS UNIS UNITED STATES (2008)
Saatchi & Saatchi New York
Crest Glide dental floss
When you have food stuck in your teeth

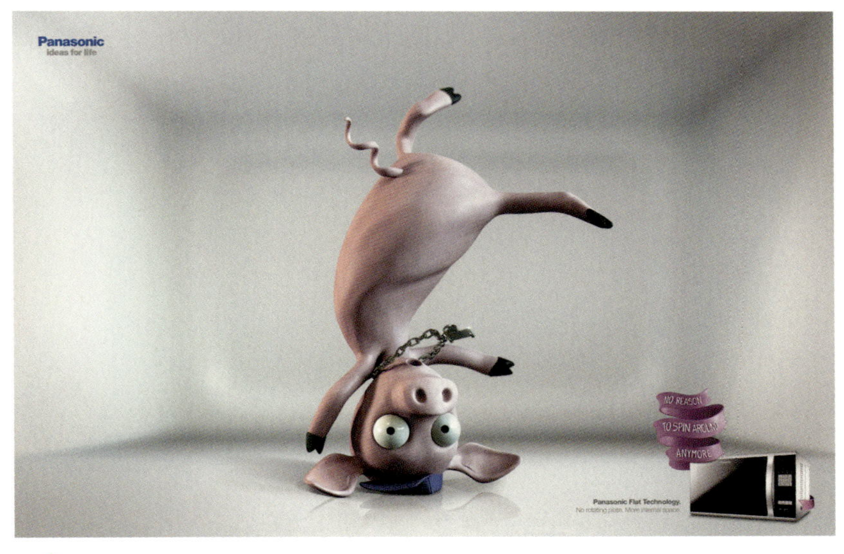

BRÉSIL BRAZIL (2012)
G2 — Panasonic Flat Technology
No rotating plate, more internal space. No reason to spin around anymore

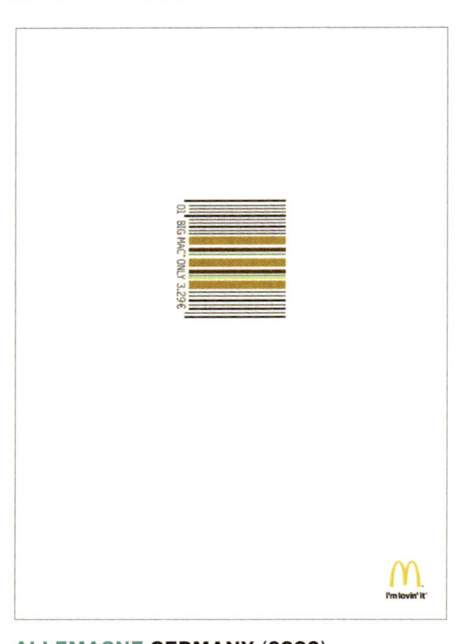

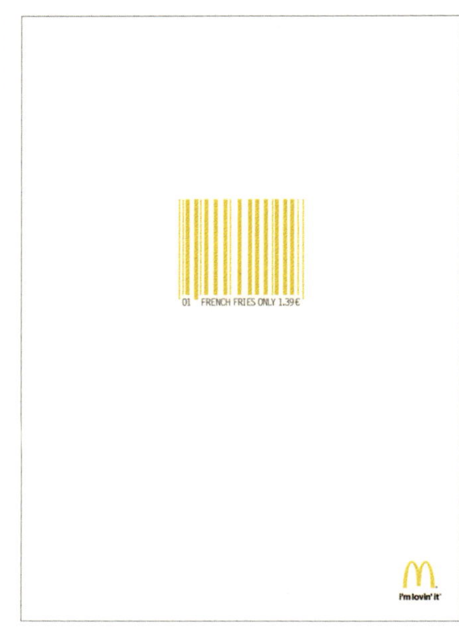

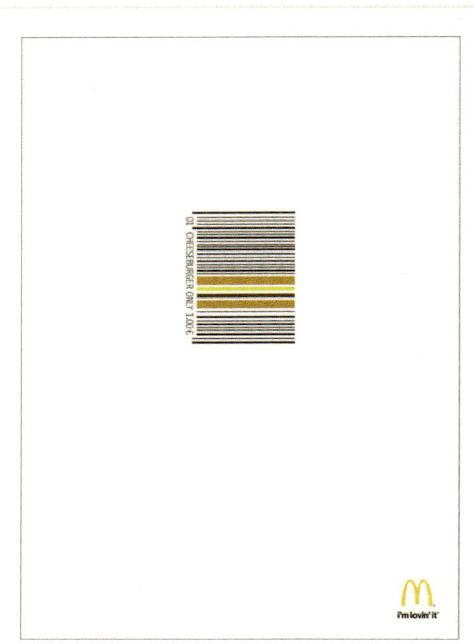

ALLEMAGNE GERMANY (2009)
Heye Group   Mc Donald's
1 - Big Mac only 3.29€ , 2 - French Fries only 1.39€ , 3 - Cheeseburger only 1.00€

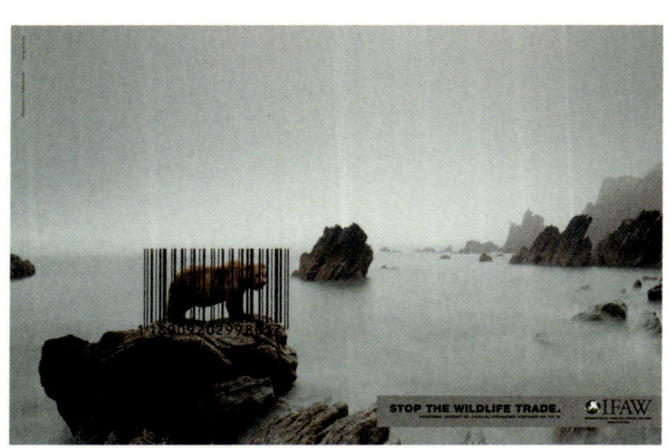

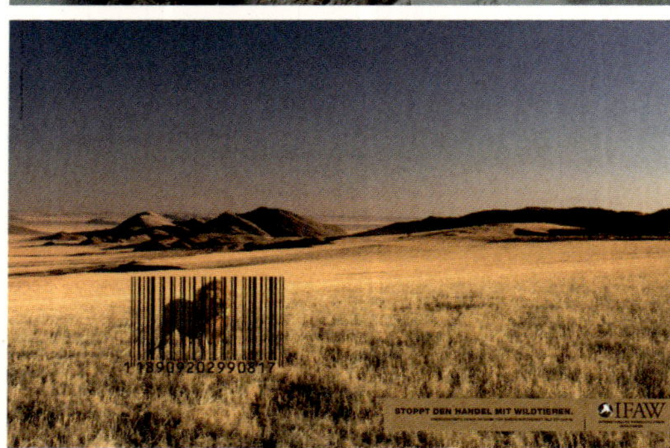

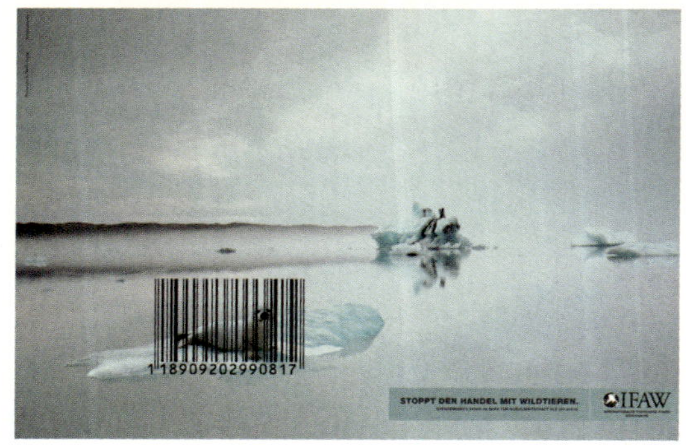

ALLEMAGNE GERMANY (2004)
Springer & Jacoby   IFAW
Stop the wildlife trade

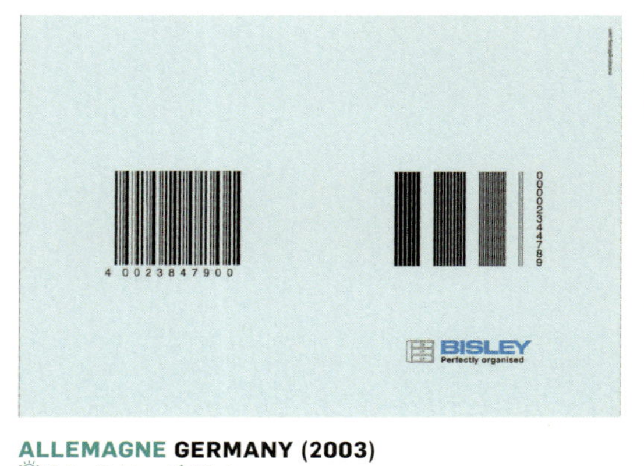

ALLEMAGNE GERMANY (2003)
Kolle Rebbe   Bisley
Perfectly Organised

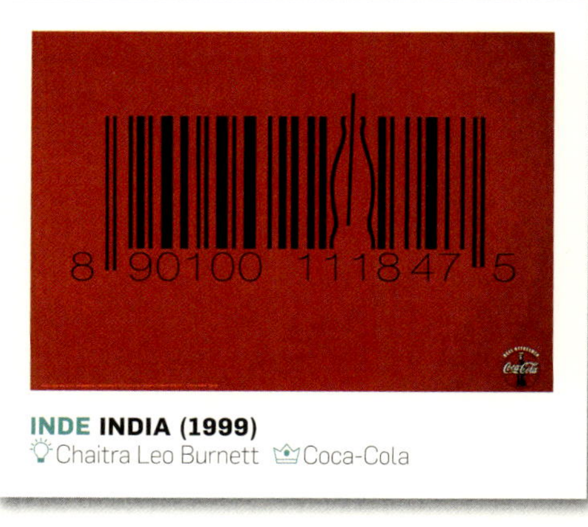

INDE INDIA (1999)
Chaitra Leo Burnett   Coca-Cola

**ÉTATS-UNIS
UNITED STATES (2008)**
Borders Perrin Norrander, Portland
Vote Appeal
Don't vote. Things are just fine
the way they are

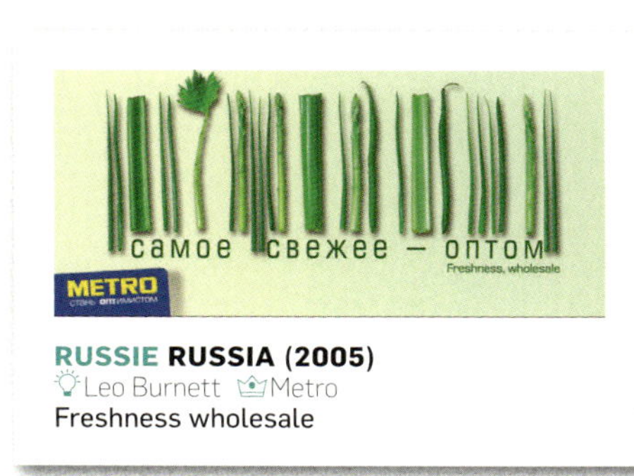

RUSSIE RUSSIA (2005)
Leo Burnett · Metro
Freshness wholesale

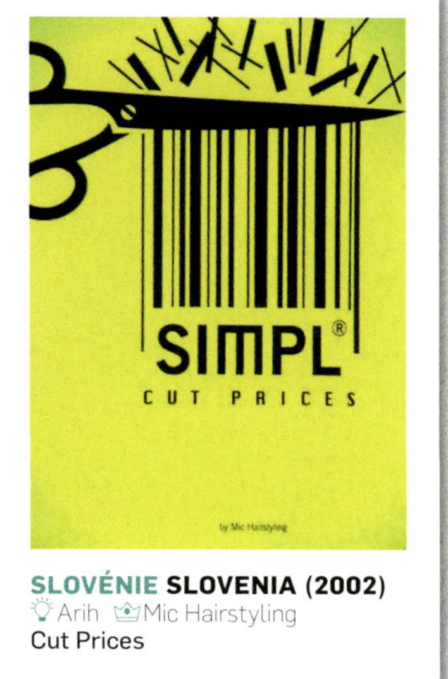

SLOVÉNIE SLOVENIA (2002)
Arih · Mic Hairstyling
Cut Prices

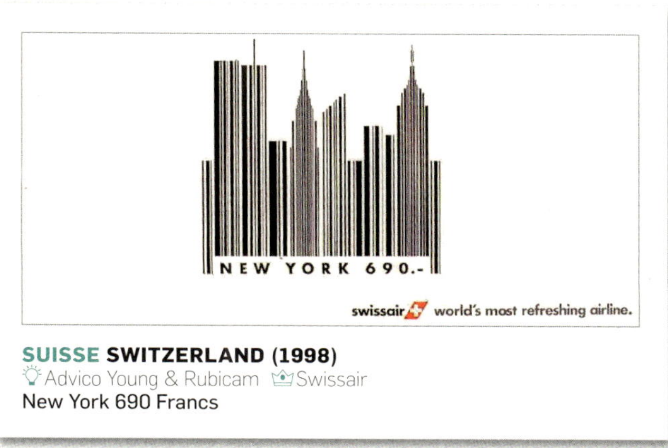

SUISSE SWITZERLAND (1998)
Advico Young & Rubicam · Swissair
New York 690 Francs

CODES BARRES
№ 24
BAR CODES

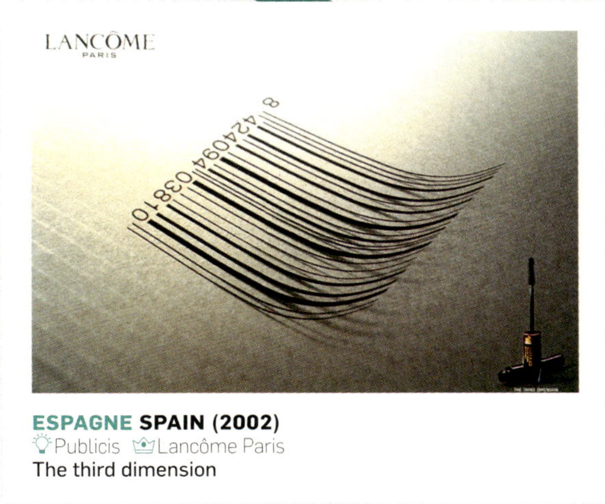

ESPAGNE SPAIN (2002)
Publicis · Lancôme Paris
The third dimension

ITALIE ITALY (2002)
Bates · Bates Agency
Creativity that sells

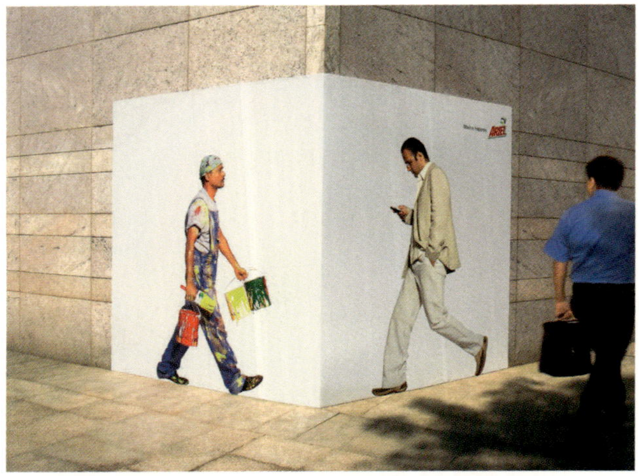

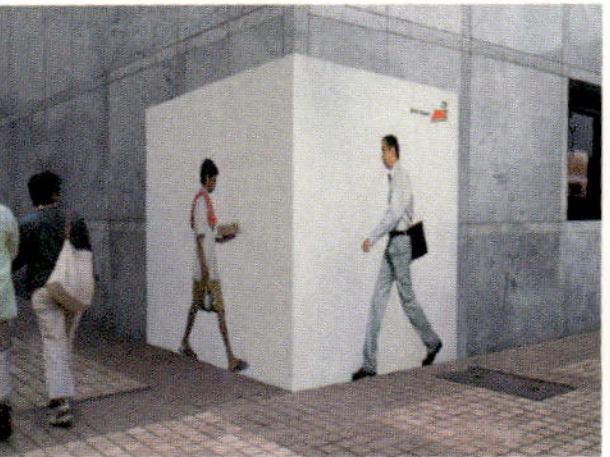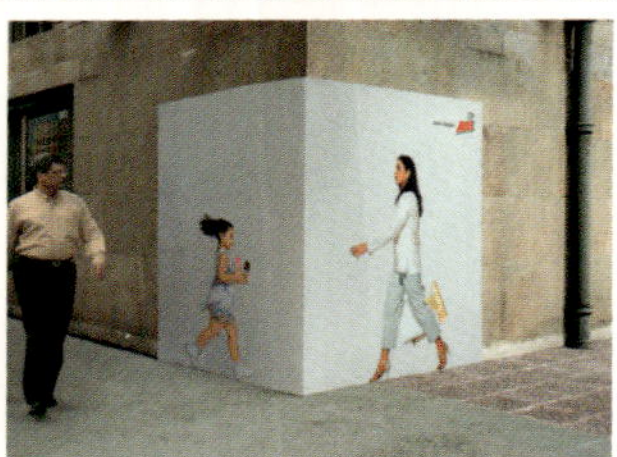

INDE **INDIA (2003)**
Saatchi & Saatchi Mumbai Ariel
Stains happen

« L'une des utilisations d'angle de rue qui, à mes yeux, se justifie le mieux. Ça rebondit sur une situation réelle qui pourrait parfaitement arriver à n'importe qui... Bref, félicitations aux créatifs et aux stratèges pour cet angle créatif. »
"One use of a street corner that, in my eyes, vindicates itself nicely. It takes a new turn on a real situation that could perfectly well happen to anyone. Quick congratulations to the creatives and to the strategists for this creative angle."

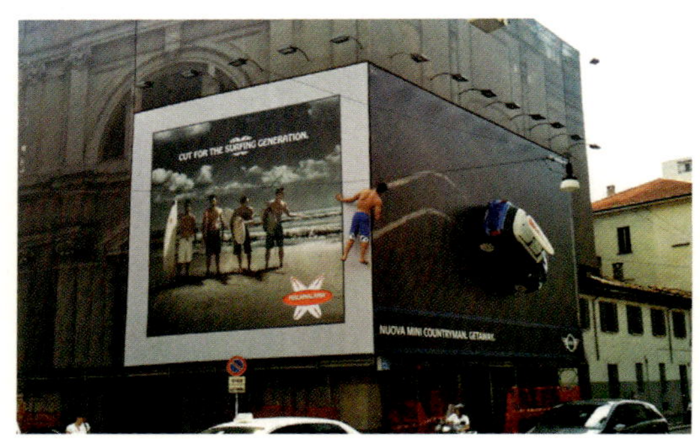

ITALIE **ITALY (2010)**
Lamar Advertising New BMW Mini Countryman
Getaway

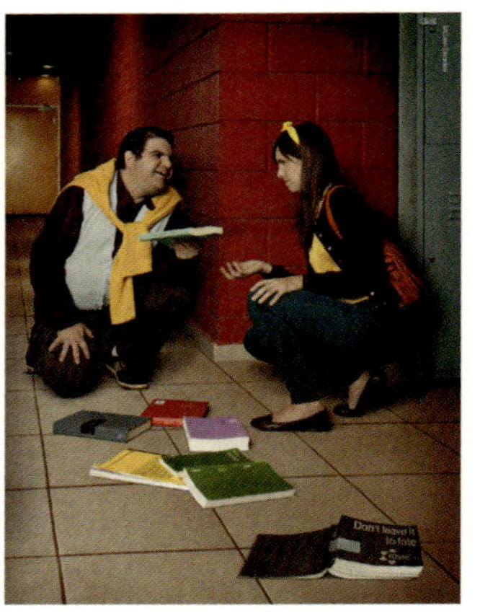

ISRAËL **ISRAEL (2011)**
Mc Cann Erickson Tel Aviv
JDate Dating Service
Don't leave it to fate

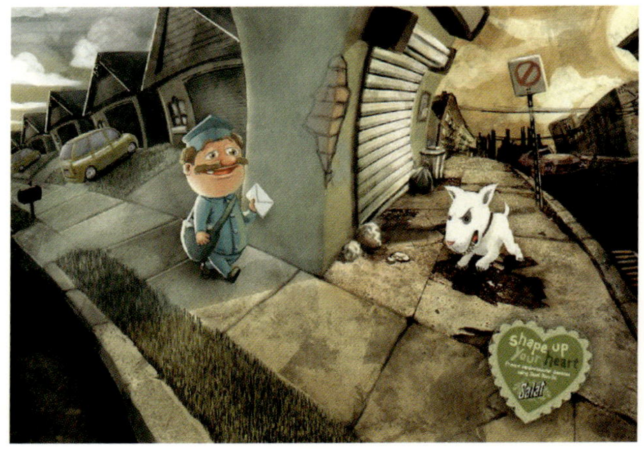

COSTA RICA **COSTA RICA (2009)**
Saatchi & Saatchi Salat
Shape up your heart

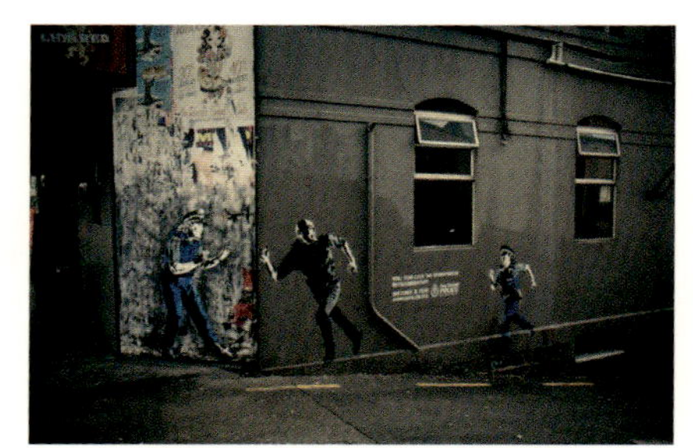

NOUVELLE-ZÉLANDE
NEW ZEALAND (2011)
M&C Saatchi New Zealand Police
You too can do something extraordinary

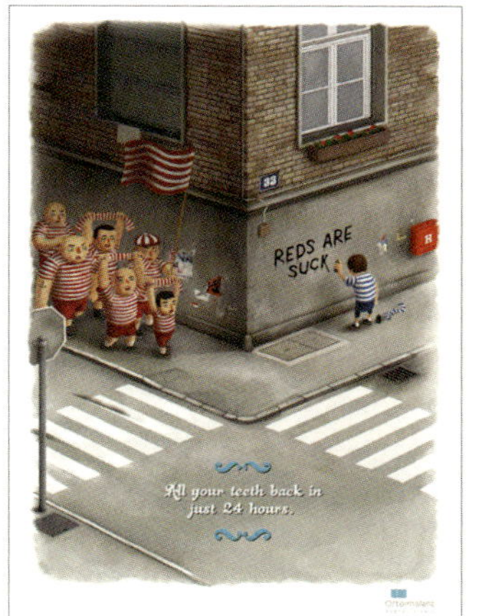

CROATIE CROATIA (2010)
Hype Zagreb
OrtoImplant dental clinic
(Reds are suck...)
All your teeth back in just 24 Hours

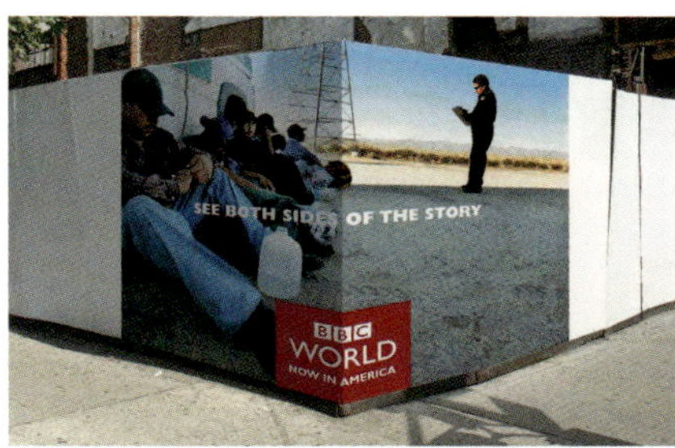

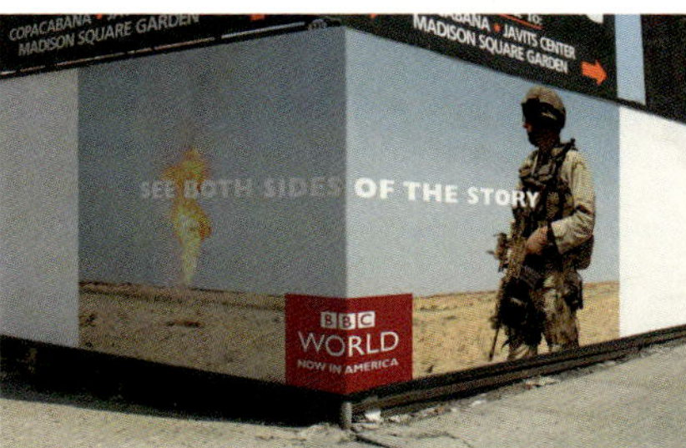

ÉTATS-UNIS UNITED STATES (2006)
BBDO New York — BBC World
See both sides of the story

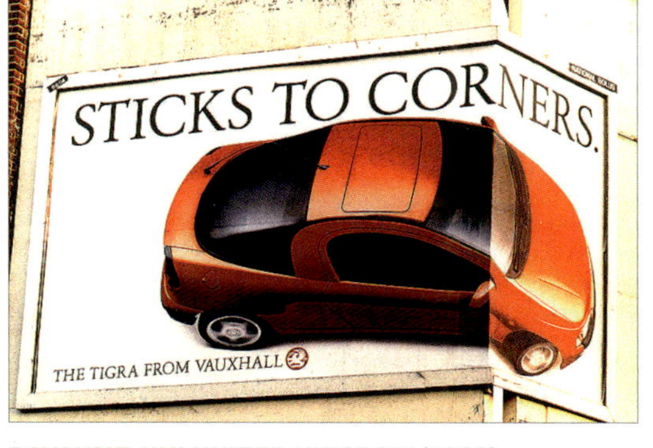

ROYAUME-UNI UNITED KINGDOM (1993)
Lowe HS — Vauxhall Tigra

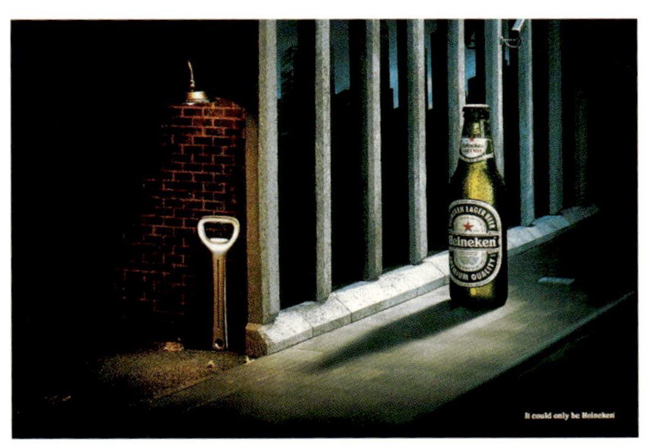

SINGAPOUR SINGAPORE (2001)
Bates — Heineken
It could only be Heineken

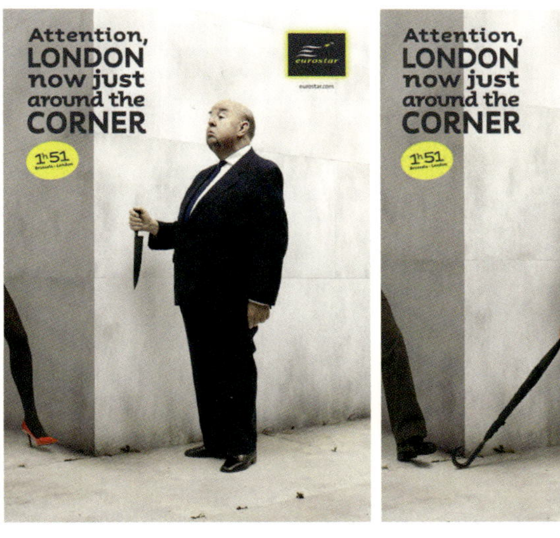

BELGIQUE BELGIUM (2007)
TBWA Brussels — Eurostar
1h51 Brussels-London. London now just around the corner

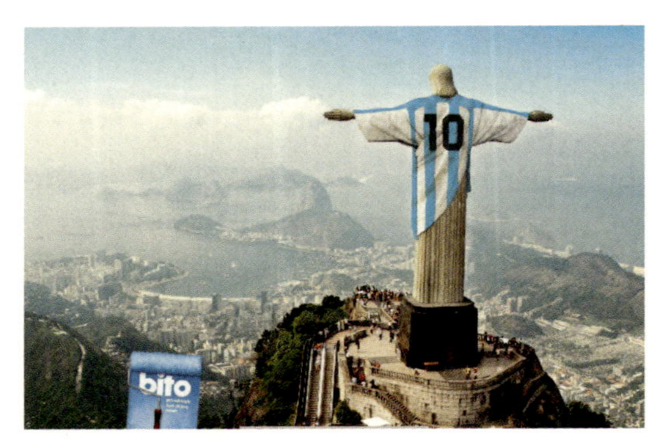

ALLEMAGNE GERMANY (2008)
Scholz & Friends Berlin Bito
Provokingly fast drying paint

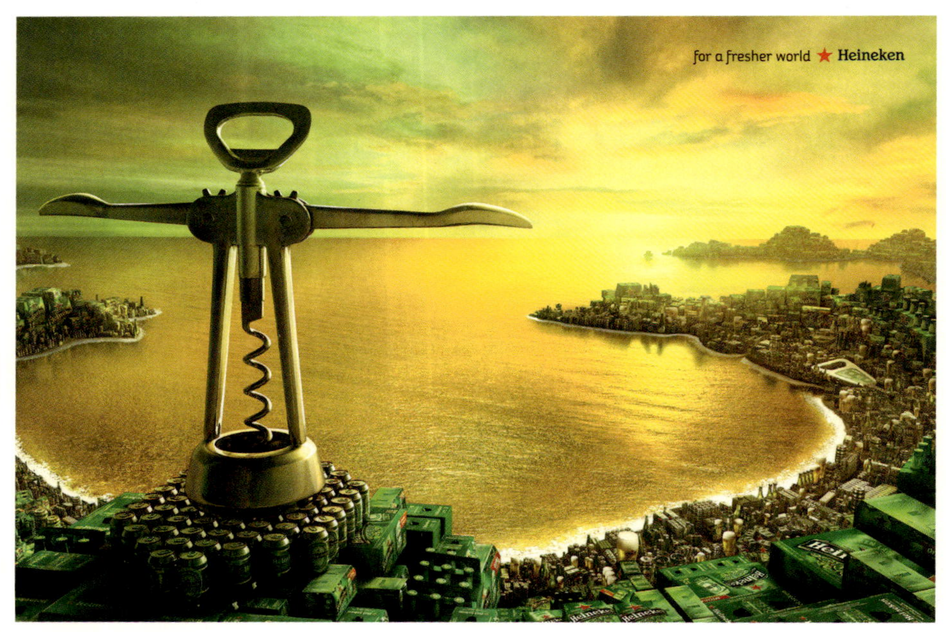

FRANCE FRANCE (2008)
Publicis Conseil Heineken
For a fresher world

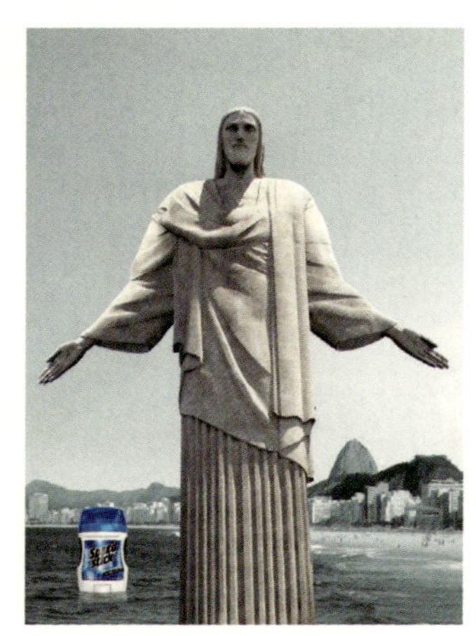

BRÉSIL BRAZIL (2010)
Universidade Presbiteriana
Mackenzie, Rubens Mendes
Speed Stick deodorant

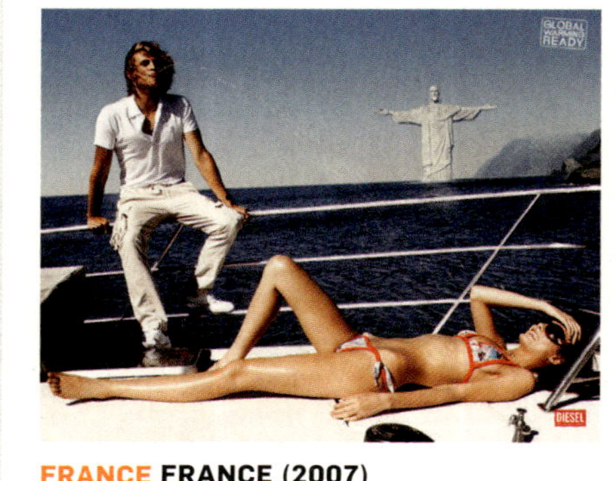

FRANCE FRANCE (2007)
Marcel Paris Diesel
Global warming ready

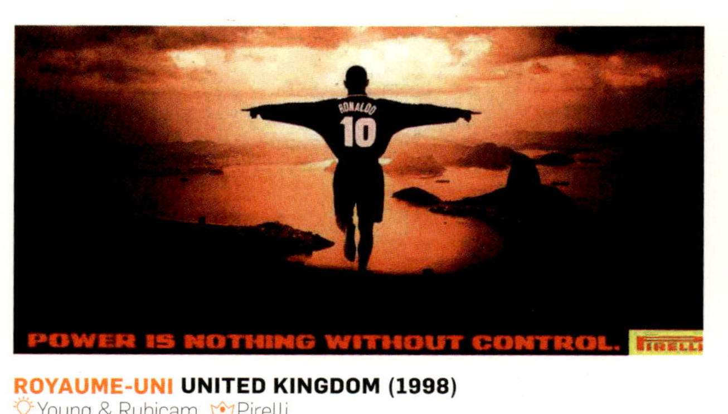

ROYAUME-UNI UNITED KINGDOM (1998)
Young & Rubicam Pirelli
Power is nothing without control

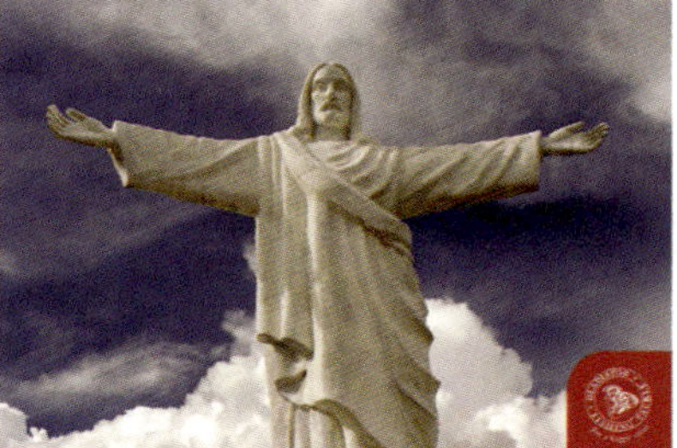

AUSTRALIE AUSTRALIA (2005)
DDB Sydney · Gladiator fishing equipment
For a bigger catch

«Ce que j'aime dans celle-ci, c'est que finalement, elle détourne très peu la statue originale. Il n'y a que la position des mains qui change, et c'est à peine perceptible. C'est un geste bien connu de tous les pêcheurs du dimanche (et je ne parle pas de ceux qui croient en Jésus).»
"What I love about this one is that it only slightly spoofs one of the world's most famous statues. It is only the hand position that is changed, but is hardly noticeable. Nonetheless, it's a hand gesture known to all avid anglers (and all those who've heard their fishy tales)."

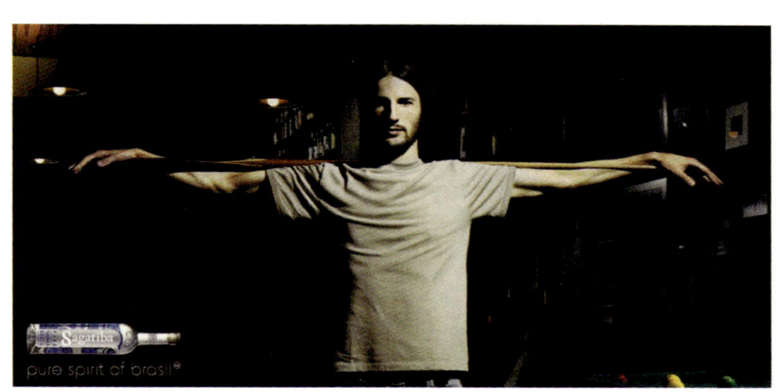

ROYAUME-UNI UNITED KINGDOM (2004)
Saatchi & Saatchi London · Sagatiba cachaça liquor
Pure spirit of brazil

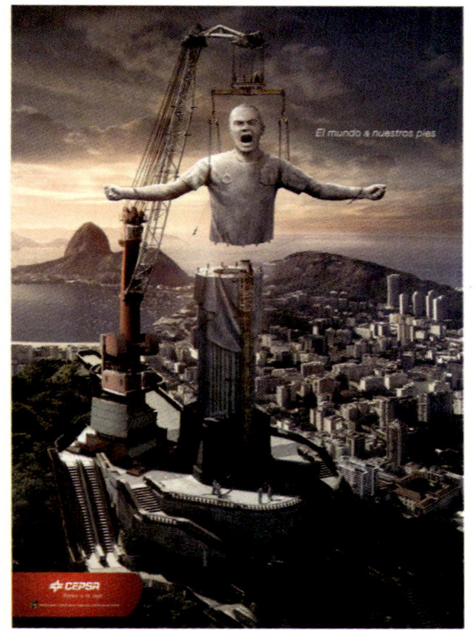

ESPAGNE SPAIN (2011)
SRA Rushmore · Cepsa
The world at our feet

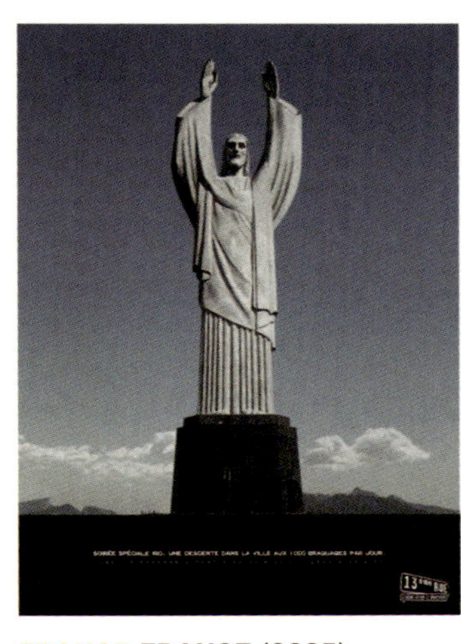

FRANCE FRANCE (2005)
BETC Euro RSCG
13th Street TV Channel
Rio night. A raid on the city with 10000 hold-ups a day

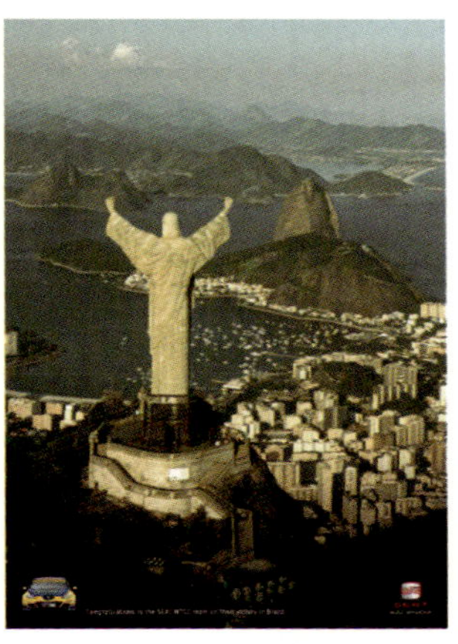

ESPAGNE SPAIN (2007)
Atletico · Seat
Congratulations to the Seat WTCC team on their victory in brazil

HONDURAS HONDURAS (2010)
Excell Ogilvy San Pedro Sula · Samsung
Optical zoom x24

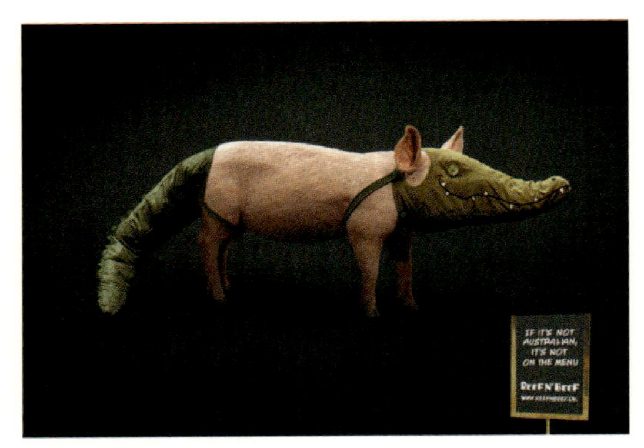

DANEMARK DENMARK (2008)
Saatchi & Saatchi Copenhagen Reef N'Beef
If it's not Australian, it's not on the menu

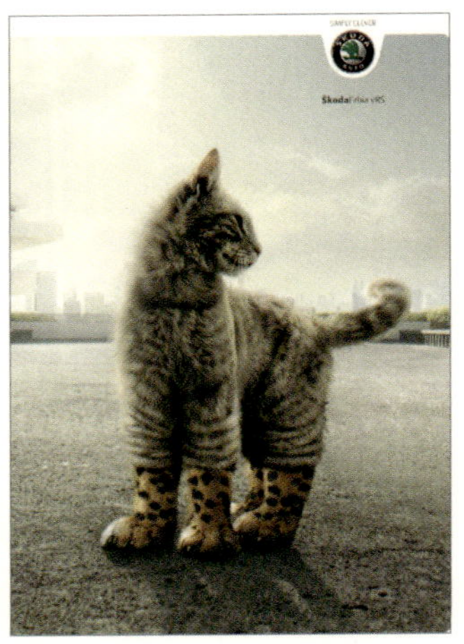

POLOGNE POLAND (2010)
Change Warsaw Skoda Fabia

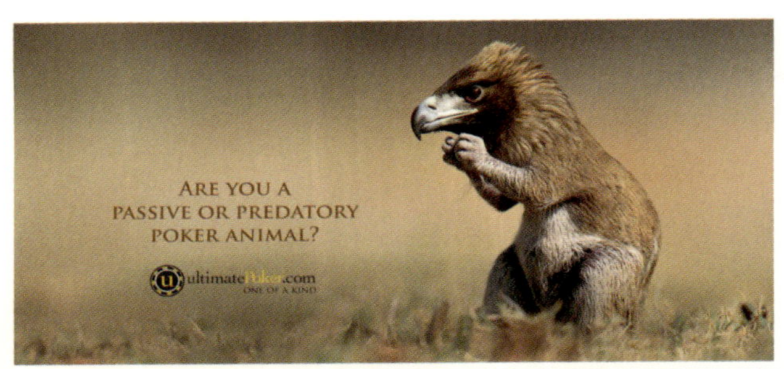

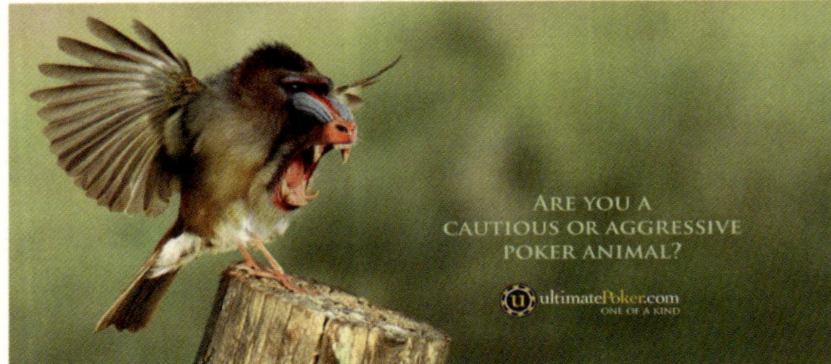

ITALIE ITALY (2007)
Pentamark Pfizer Animal Health
Are you a passive or predatory poker animal?
Are you a cautious or aggressive poker animal?

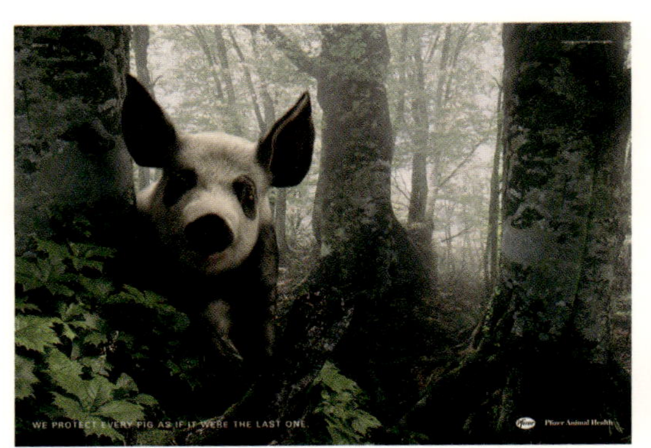

ITALIE ITALY (2007)
Pentamark Pfizer Animal Health
We protect every pig as if it where the last one

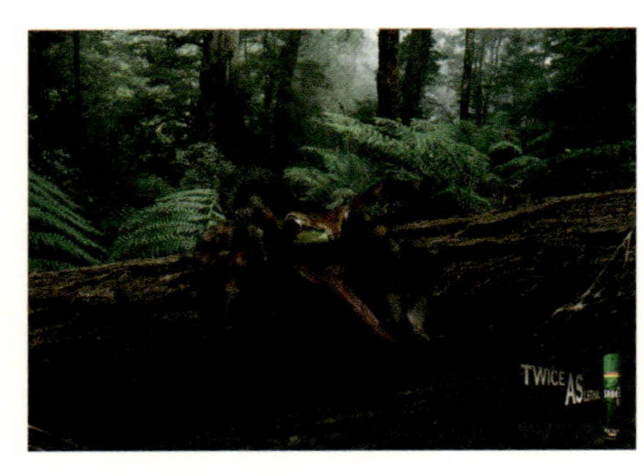

FRANCE FRANCE (2008)
Callegari Berville Grey Saniterpen
Twice as lethal

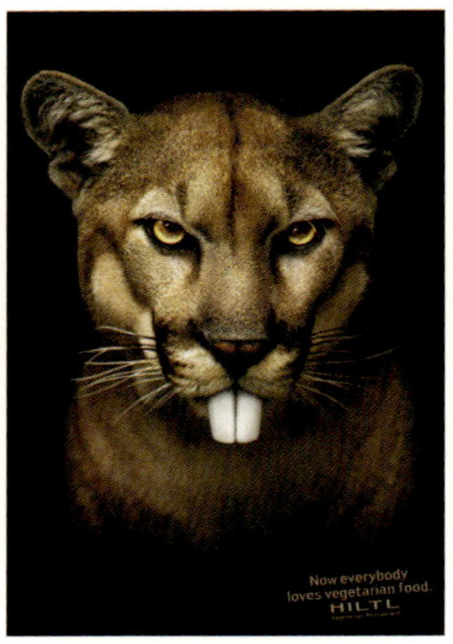

SUISSE SWITZERLAND (2010)
Ruf Lanz Zurich
Hiltl Vegetarian Restaurant
Now everybody loves vegetarian food

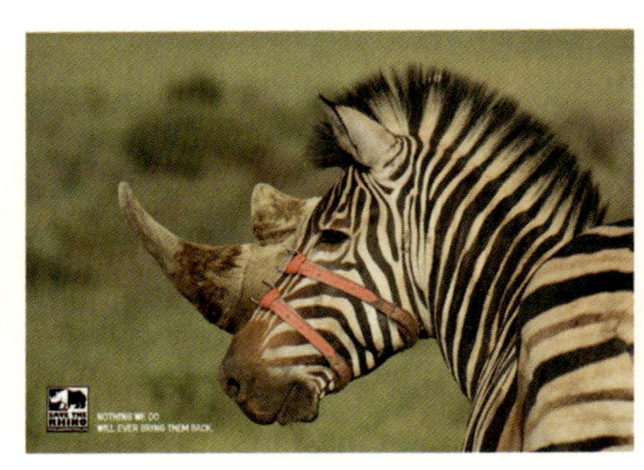

AFRIQUE DE SUD SOUTH AFRICA (2011)
Stick Johannesburg Save the Rhino
Nothing we do will ever bring them back

CROISEMENTS D'ANIMAUX

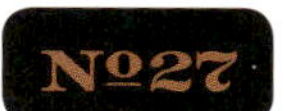

MIXED ANIMALS

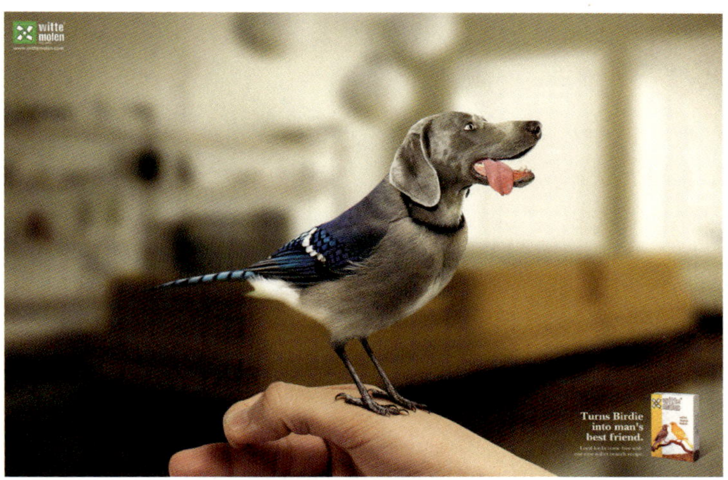

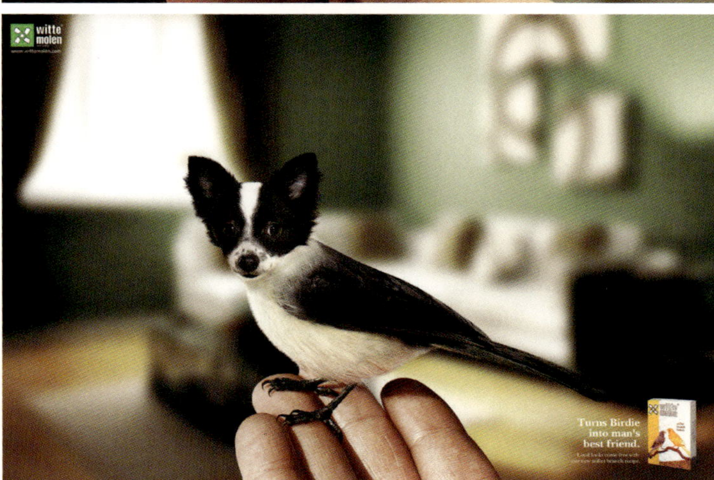

TURQUIE TURKEY (2009)
DDB Istanbul Witte Molen
Turns birdie into man's best friend

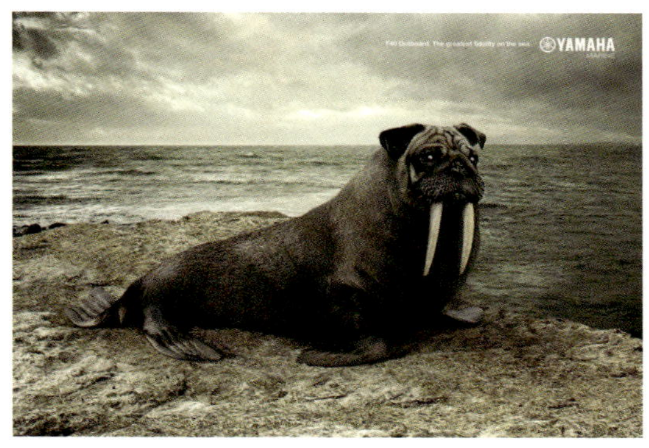

ITALIE ITALY (2010)
1861 United Yamaha Marine F40 Outboard
The greatest fidelity on the sea

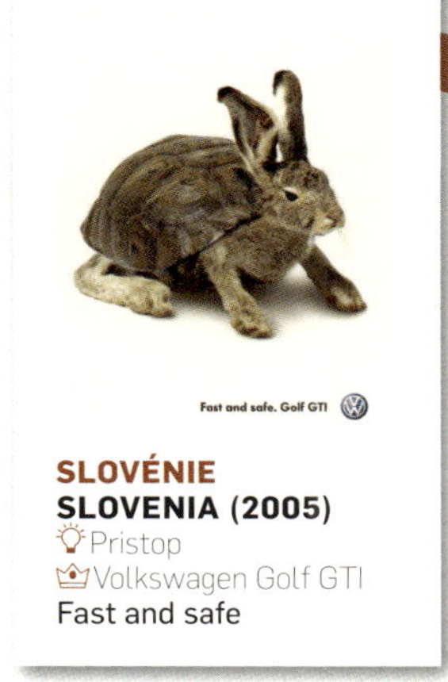

SLOVÉNIE SLOVENIA (2005)
Pristop
Volkswagen Golf GTI
Fast and safe

LE CULTE DES SEINS

Nº28

SYMBOLIZE BREASTS

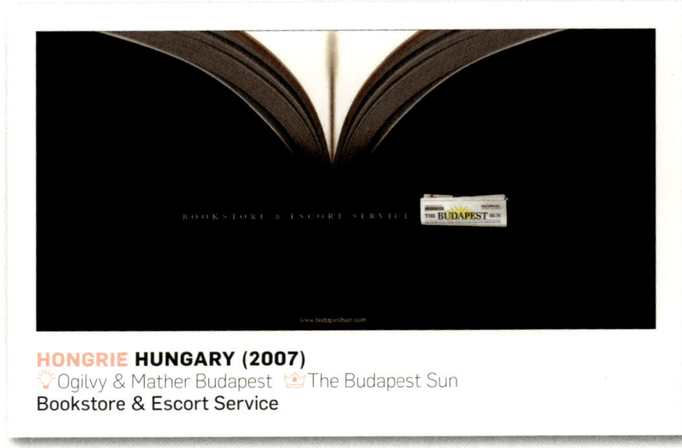

HONGRIE HUNGARY (2007)
Ogilvy & Mather Budapest — The Budapest Sun
Bookstore & Escort Service

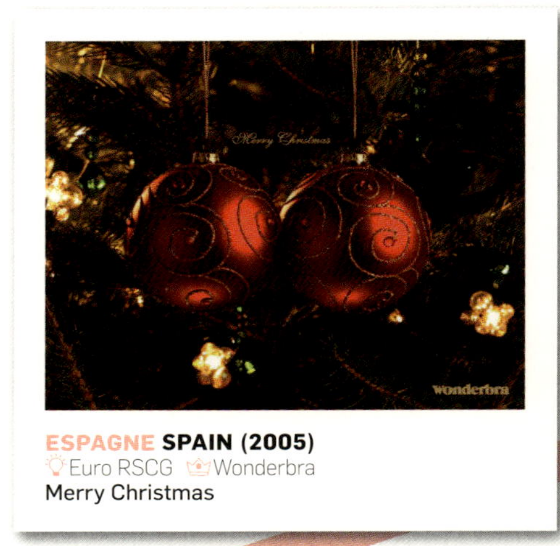

ESPAGNE SPAIN (2005)
Euro RSCG — Wonderbra
Merry Christmas

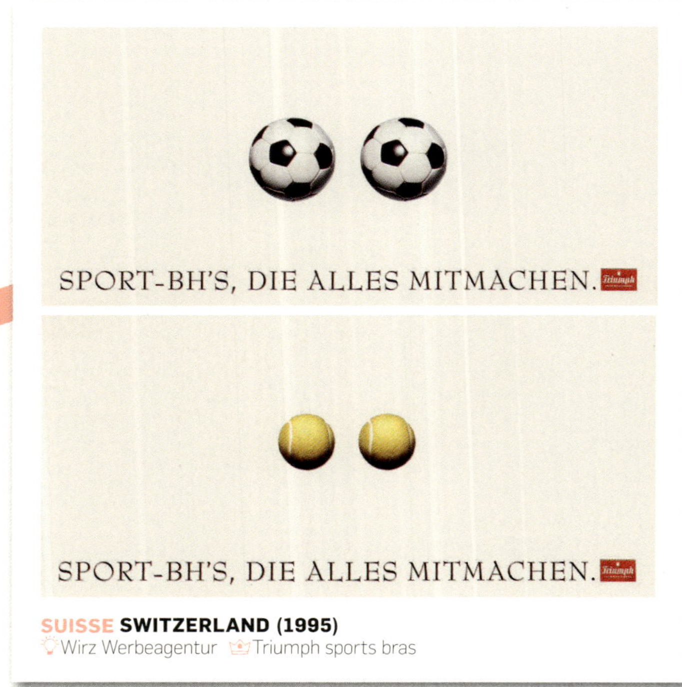

SUISSE SWITZERLAND (1995)
Wirz Werbeagentur — Triumph sports bras

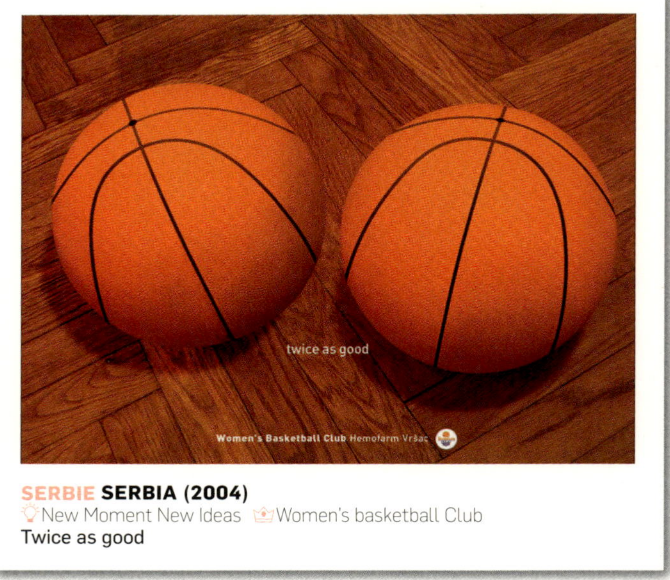

SERBIE SERBIA (2004)
New Moment New Ideas — Women's basketball Club
Twice as good

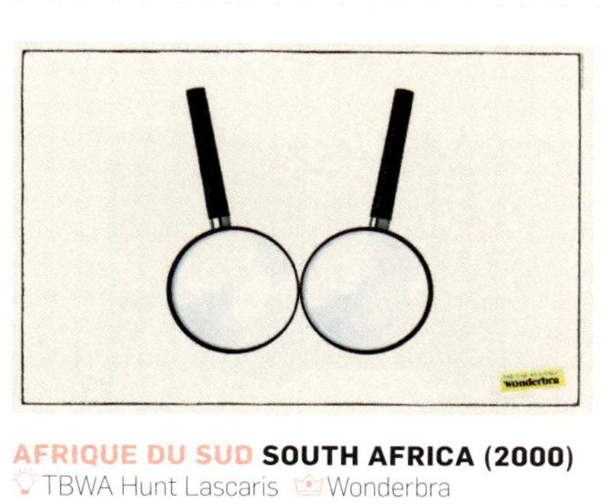

AFRIQUE DU SUD SOUTH AFRICA (2000)
TBWA Hunt Lascaris Wonderbra

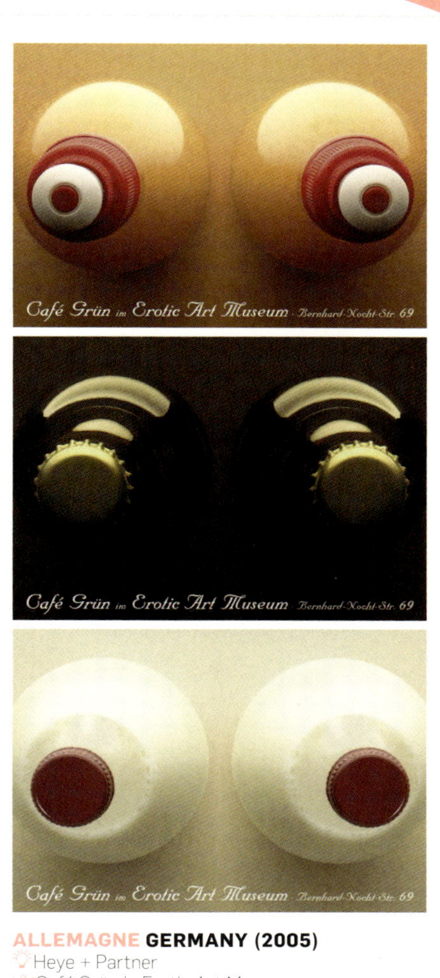

ALLEMAGNE GERMANY (2005)
Heye + Partner
Café Grün in Erotic Art Museum

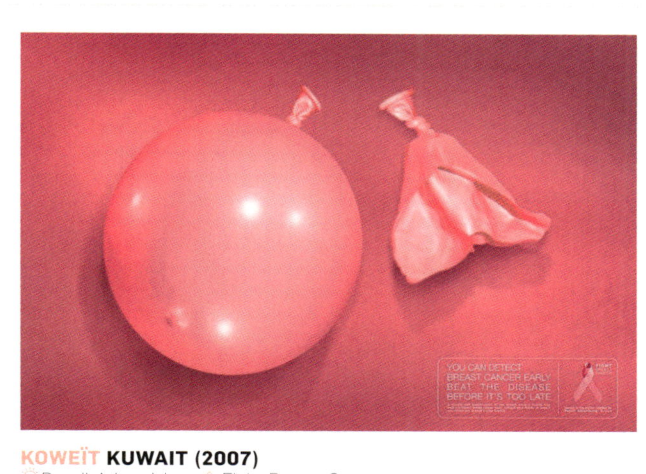

KOWEÏT KUWAIT (2007)
Pencil Advertising Fight Breast Cancer
You can detect breast cancer early

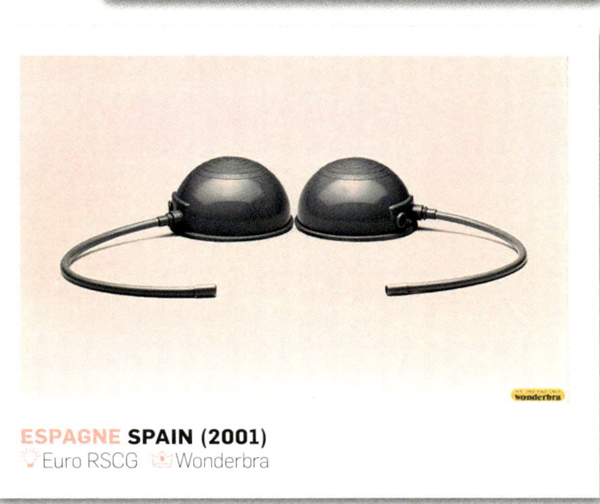

ESPAGNE SPAIN (2001)
Euro RSCG Wonderbra

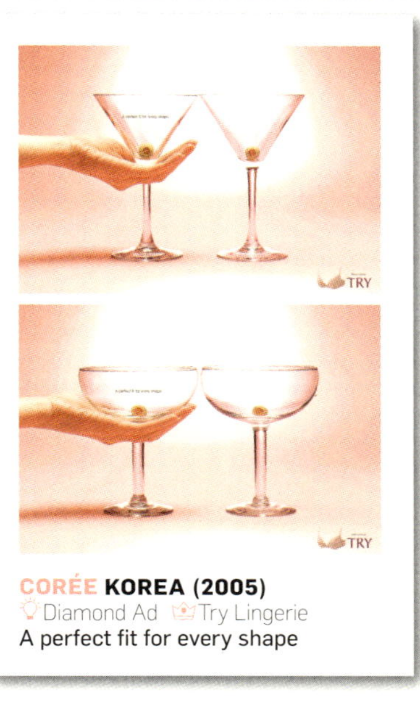

CORÉE KOREA (2005)
Diamond Ad Try Lingerie
A perfect fit for every shape

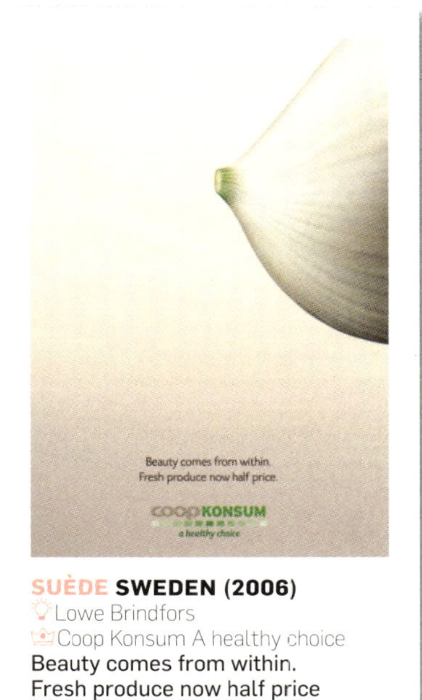

SUÈDE SWEDEN (2006)
Lowe Brindfors
Coop Konsum A healthy choice
Beauty comes from within.
Fresh produce now half price

DARK VADOR

№29

DARTH VADER

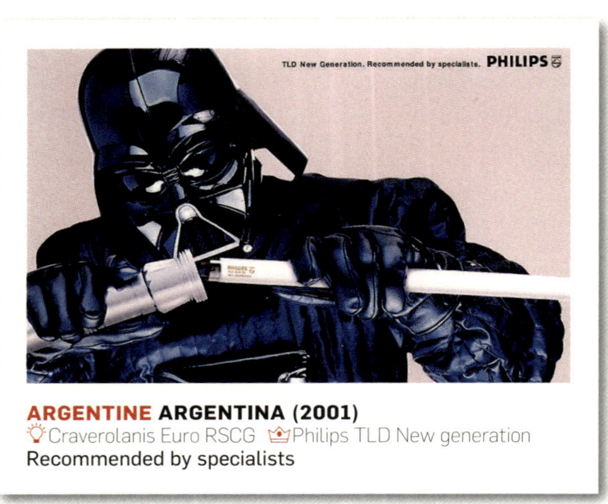

ARGENTINE ARGENTINA (2001)
Craverolanis Euro RSCG · Philips TLD New generation
Recommended by specialists

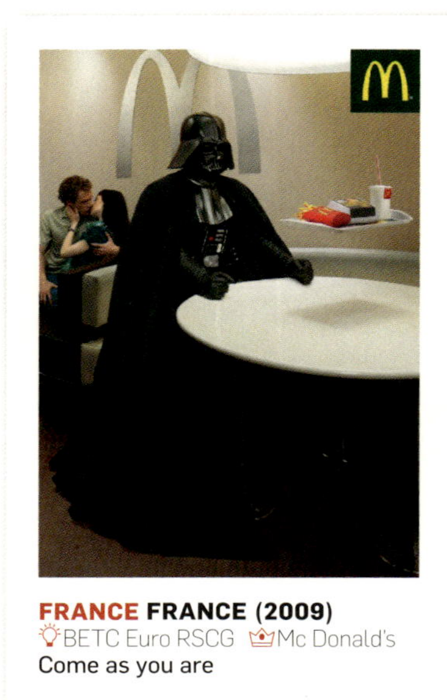

FRANCE FRANCE (2009)
BETC Euro RSCG · Mc Donald's
Come as you are

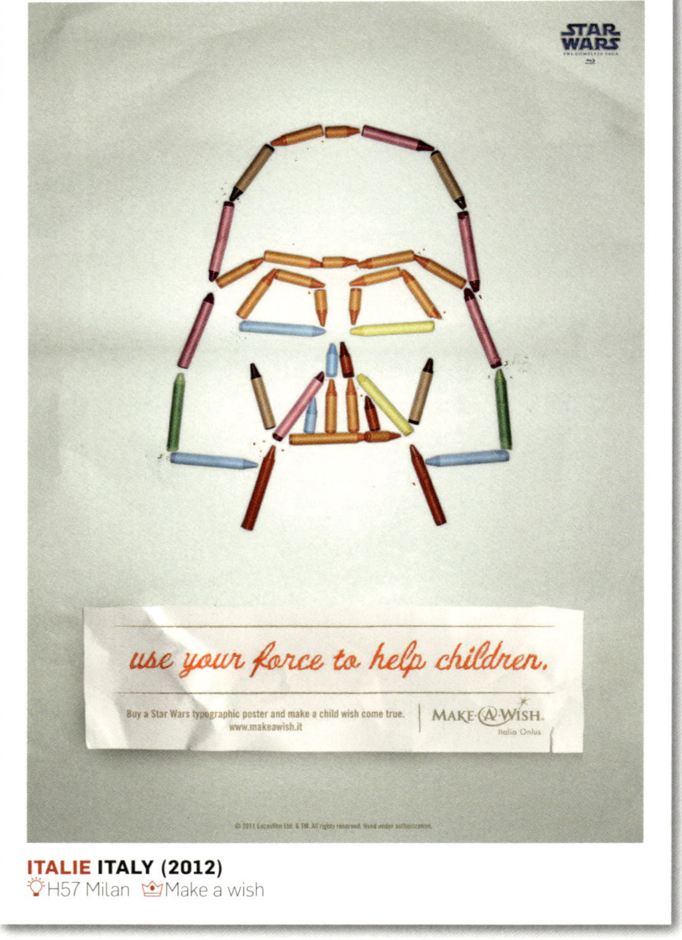

ITALIE ITALY (2012)
H57 Milan · Make a wish

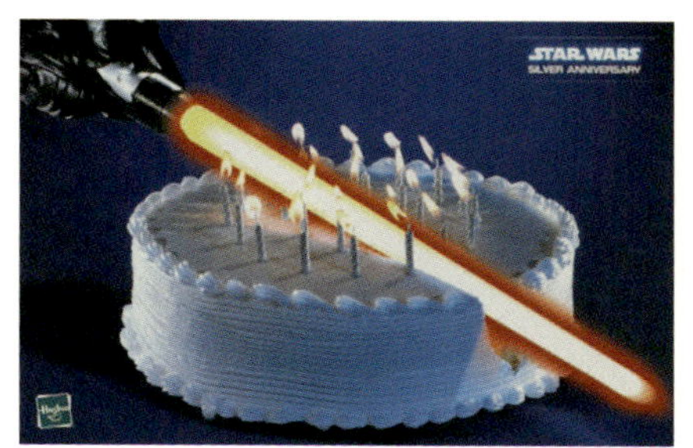

MEXIQUE MEXICO (2002)
Grey Mexico Hasbro
Star wars silver anniversary

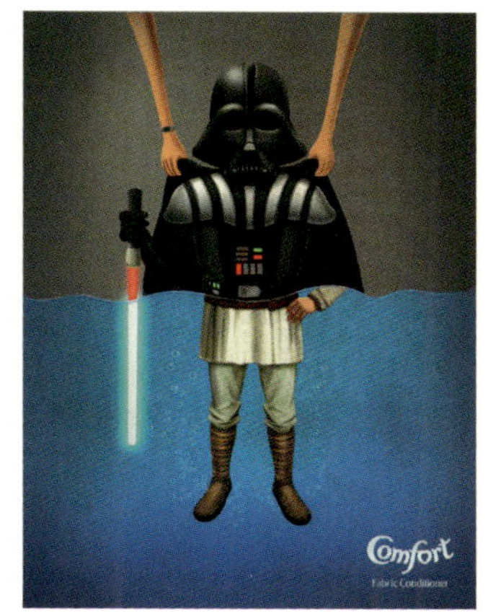

INDE INDIA (2012)
Ogilvy & Mather Mumbai
Comfort
Fabric conditioner

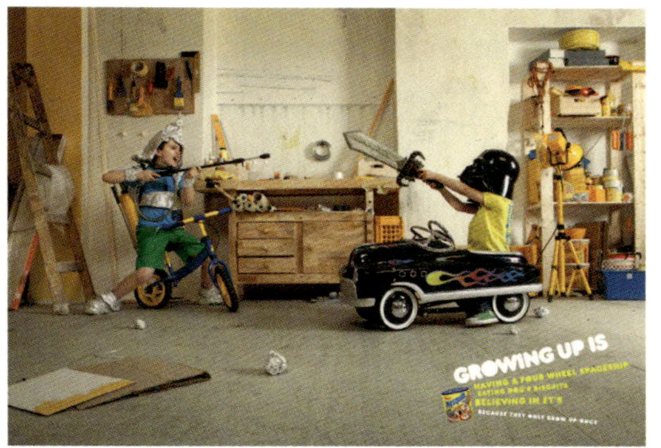

PORTUGAL PORTUGAL (2010)
McCann Erickson Nesquick
Because they only grow up once

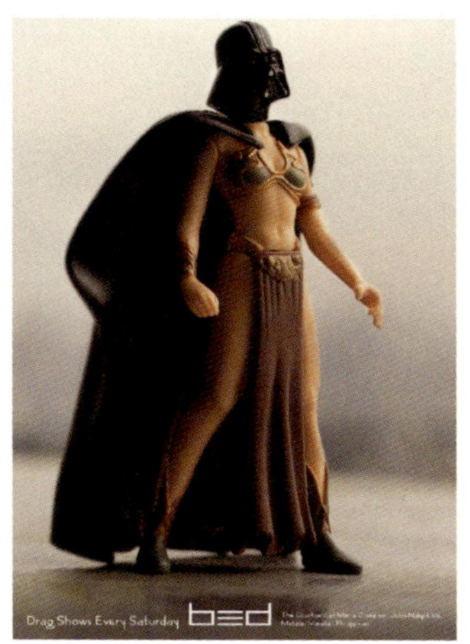

PHILIPPINES PHILIPPINES (2008)
PC&V Bed
Drag shows every saturday

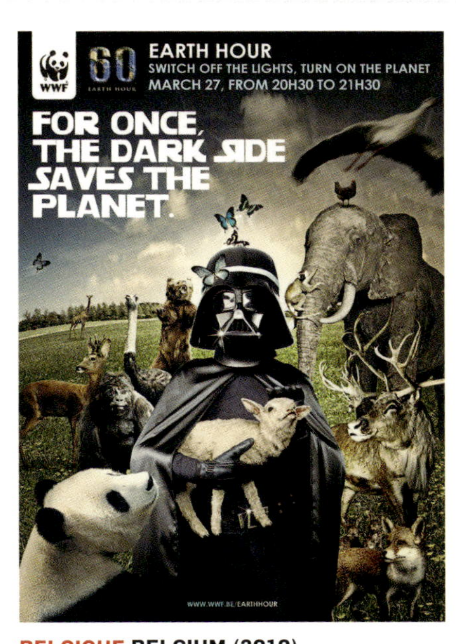

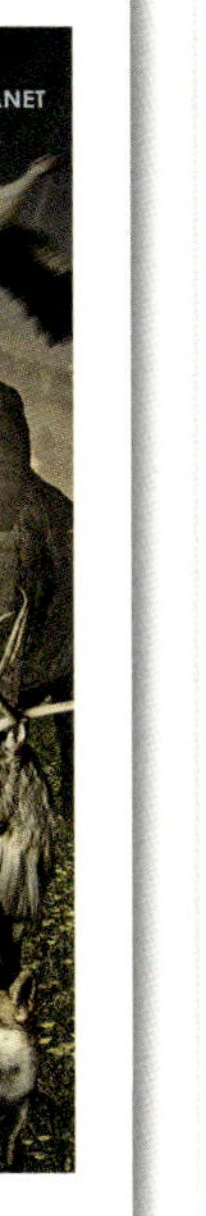

BELGIQUE BELGIUM (2010)
Germaine WWF Earth Hour.

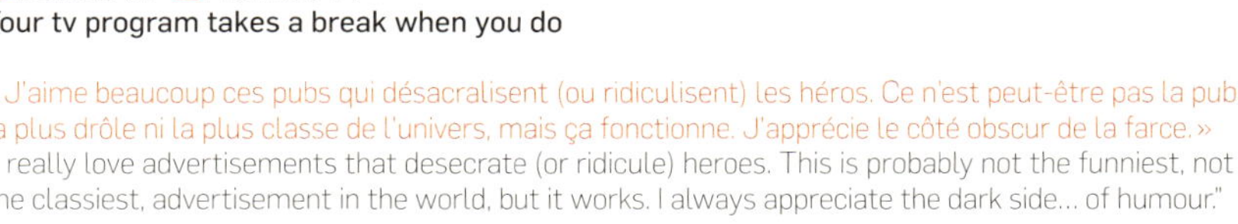

ALLEMAGNE GERMANY (2007)
DDB Berlin Premiere TV
Your tv program takes a break when you do

« J'aime beaucoup ces pubs qui désacralisent (ou ridiculisent) les héros. Ce n'est peut-être pas la pub la plus drôle ni la plus classe de l'univers, mais ça fonctionne. J'apprécie le côté obscur de la farce. »
"I really love advertisements that desecrate (or ridicule) heroes. This is probably not the funniest, not the classiest, advertisement in the world, but it works. I always appreciate the dark side… of humour."

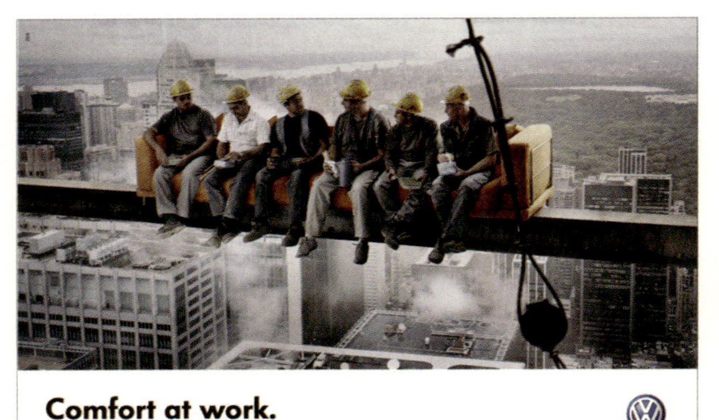

BELGIQUE BELGIUM (2007)
DDB Brussels Volkswagen commercial vehicles

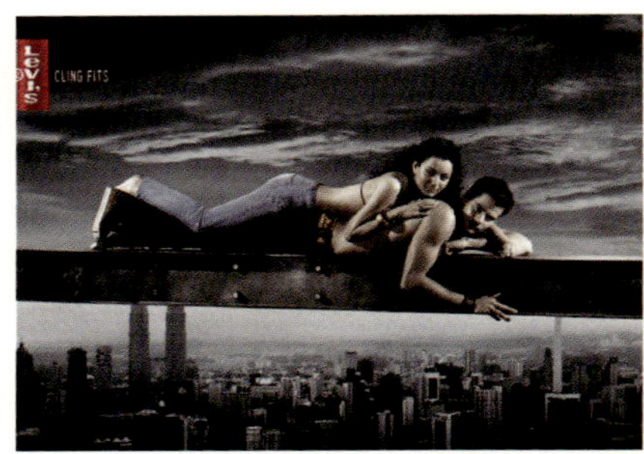

INDE INDIA (2007)
JWT Bangalore Levi's cling fits

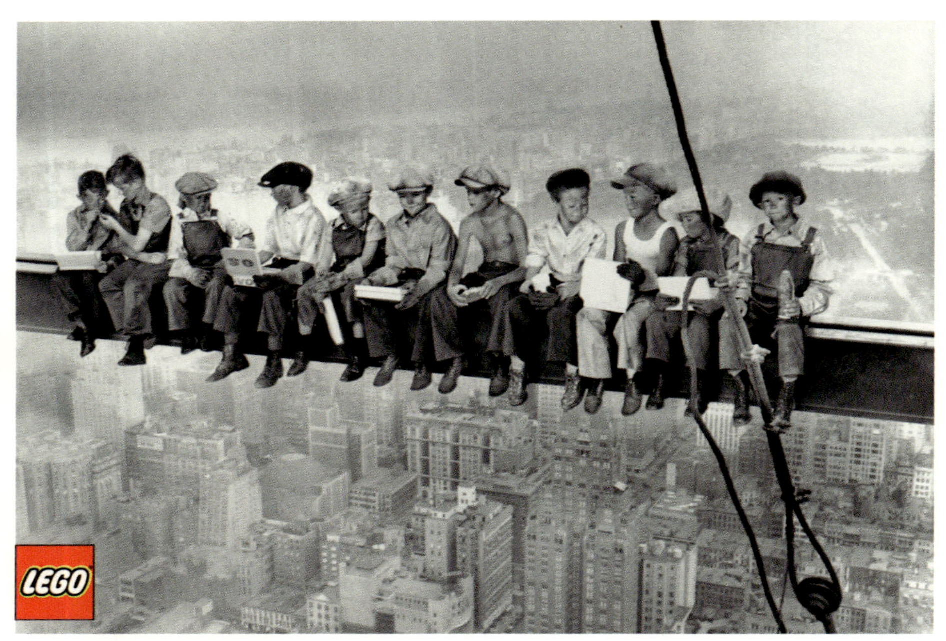

ALLEMAGNE GERMANY (2006)
Jung Von Matt Hamburg Lego
Builders of tomorrow

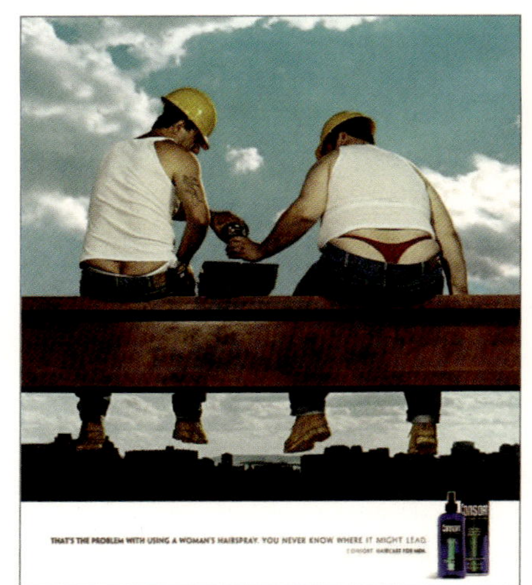

ÉTATS-UNIS UNITED STATES (2004)
Euro RSCG Consort Haircare For Men
That's the problem with using a woman's hairspray. You never know where it might lead

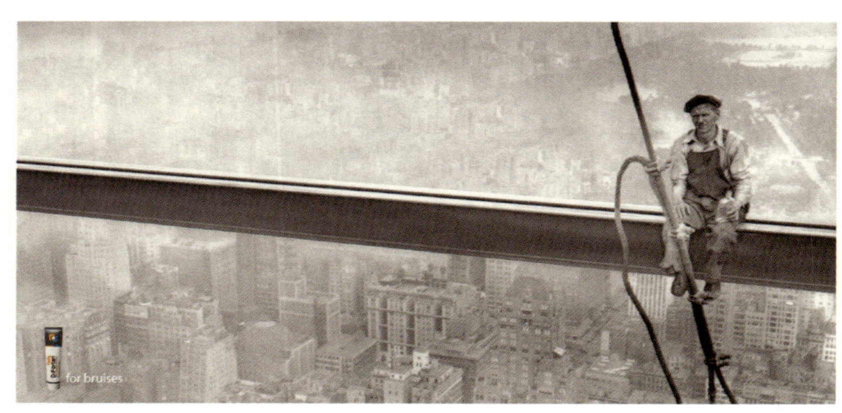

POLOGNE POLAND (2008)
TBWA Warsaw DiForlan Cream
For bruises

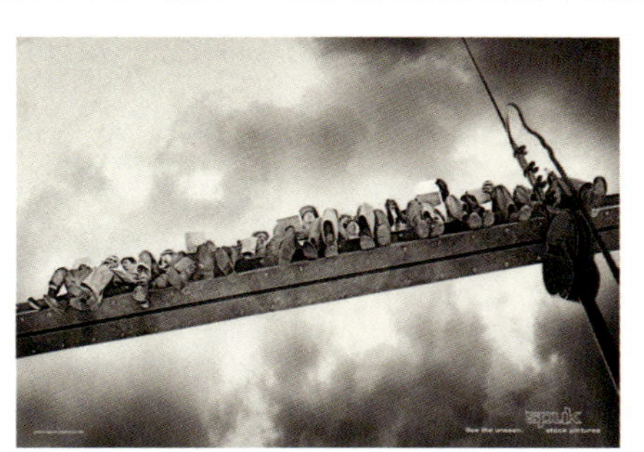

ALLEMAGNE GERMANY (2010)
BBDO Spuk stock pictures
See the unseen

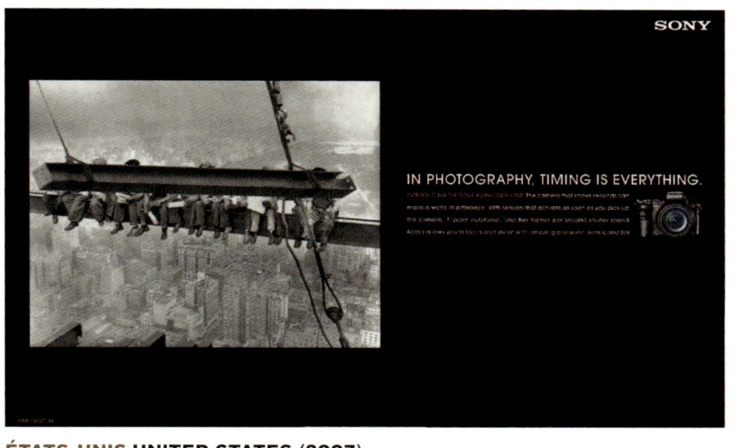

ÉTATS-UNIS UNITED STATES (2007)
BBDO New York Sony Alpha

DÉJEUNER AU SOMMET D'UN GRATTE-CIEL

№ 30

LUNCH ATOP A SKYSCRAPER

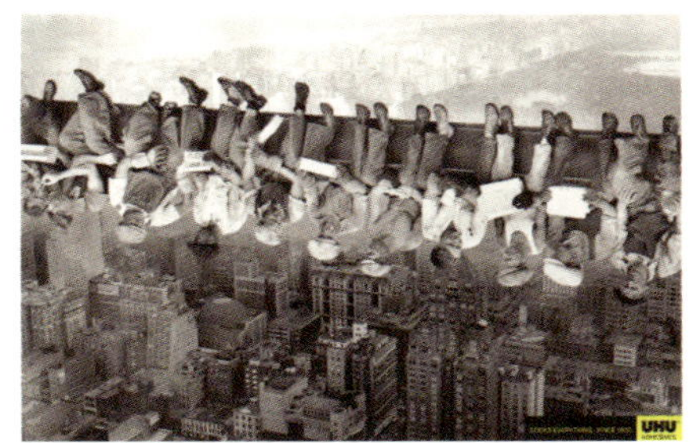

ALLEMAGNE GERMANY (2005)
BBDO Dusseldorf UHU Glue
Sticks everything since 1932

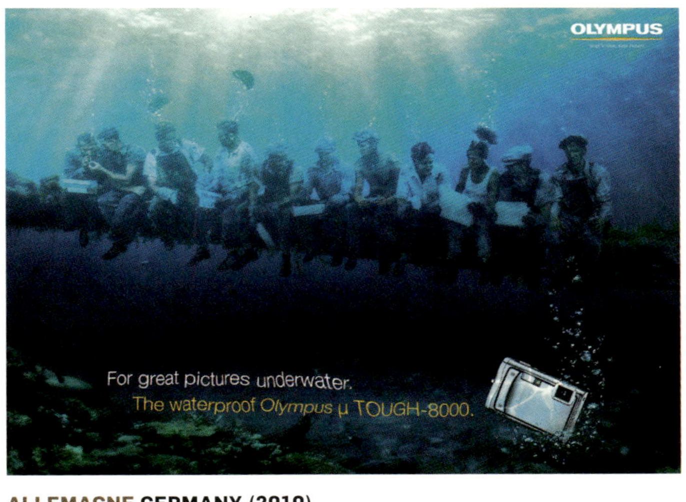

ALLEMAGNE GERMANY (2010)
Kolle Rebbe Olympus Mju Tough 8000
For great pictures underwater

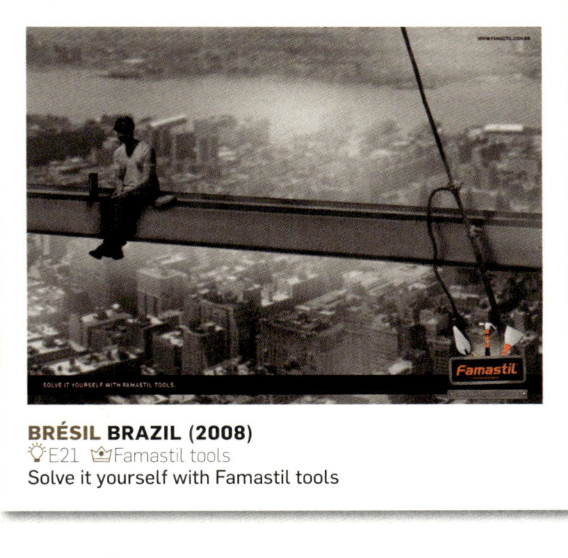

BRÉSIL BRAZIL (2008)
E21 Famastil tools
Solve it yourself with Famastil tools

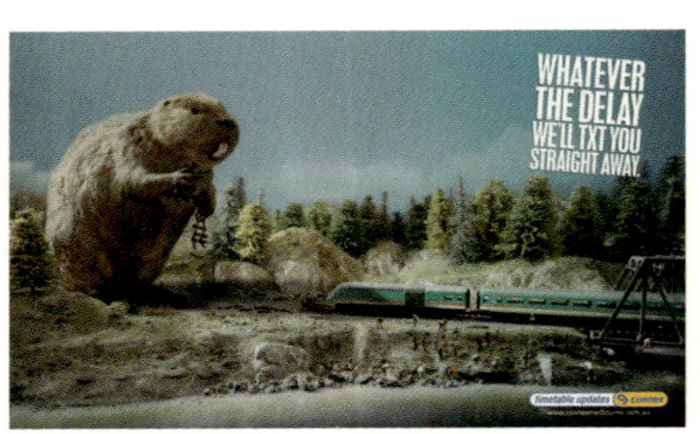

AUSTRALIE AUSTRALIA (2006)
Leo Burnett Melbourne Connex
Whatever the delay we'll text you straight away

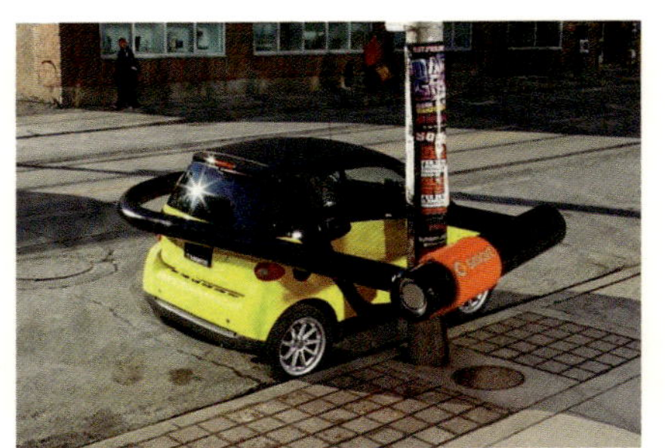

CANADA CANADA (2010)
BBDO Smart

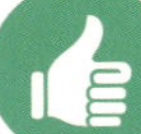

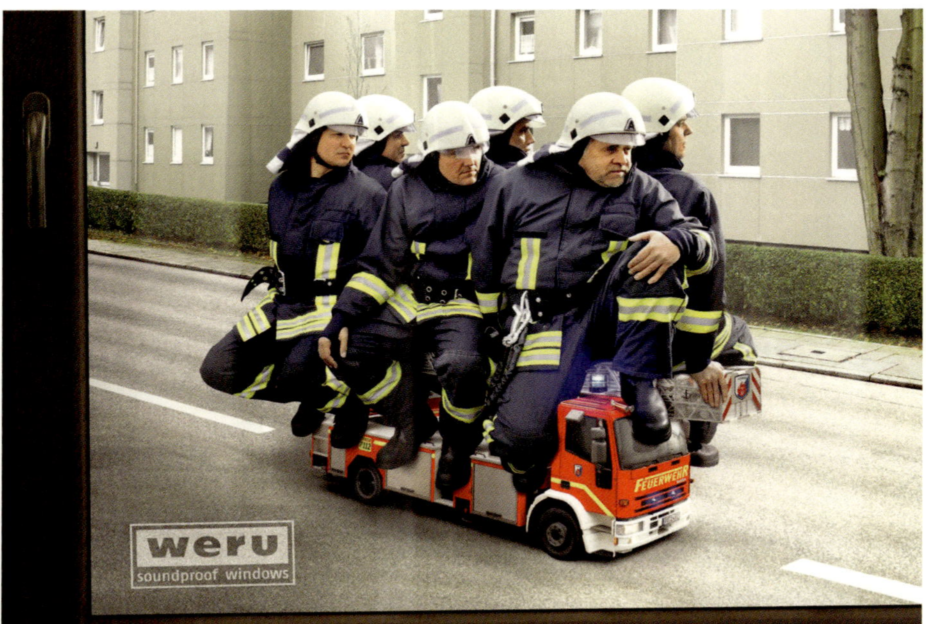

**ALLEMAGNE
GERMANY (2007)**
Scholz & Friends Weru
Soundproof windows

Sans doute l'une des campagnes les plus connues du genre et qui doit compter plus d'une dizaine de visuels révélés année après année. Les montages photo sont particulièrement réussis et crétins. C'est surprenant et drôle à la fois.
Without a doubt one of the best-known campaigns of its type and one that should count more given the dozens of such visuals released year after year. The photomontage is particularly successful and moronic. It is surprising and funny at the same time.

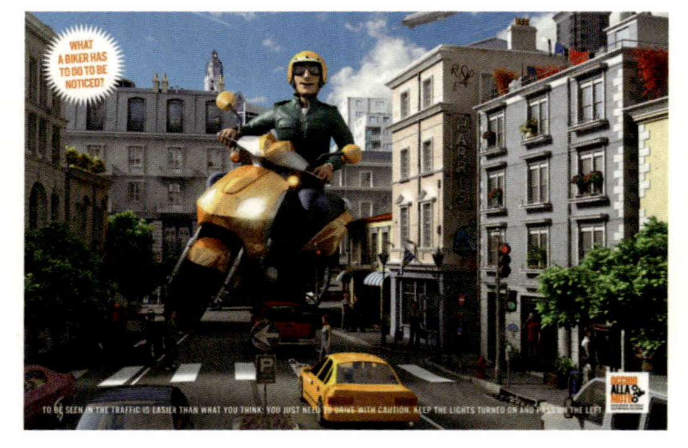

ITALIE ITALY (2010)
Ogilvy & Mather Milan Road Safety
What a biker has to do to be noticed?

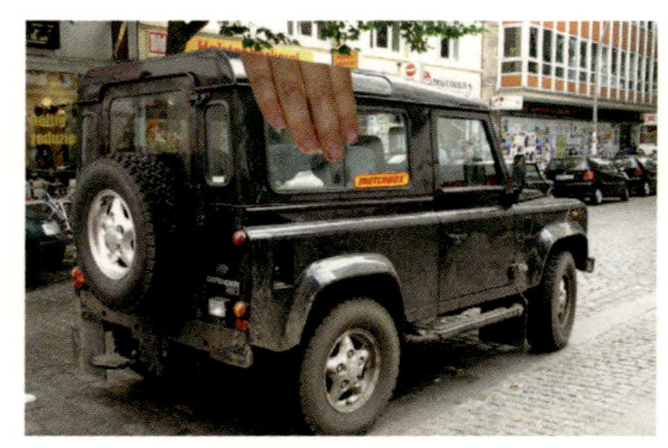

INCONNU UNKNOWN (2006)
Inconnu/unknown Matchbox

№ 31

SCALE CHANGINGS

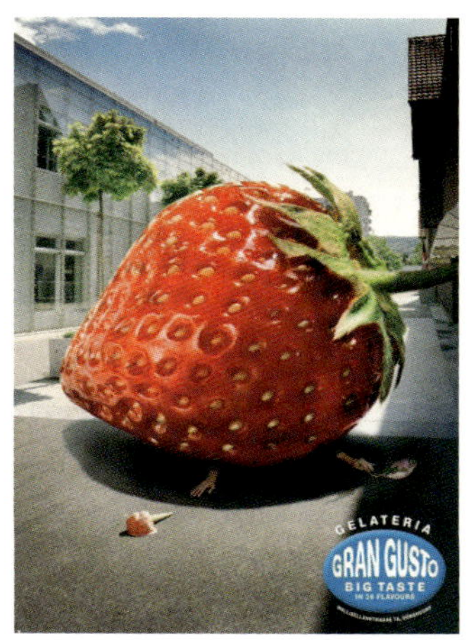

SUISSE SWITZERLAND (2005)
Young & Rubicam
Gelateria Gran Gusto
Big Taste

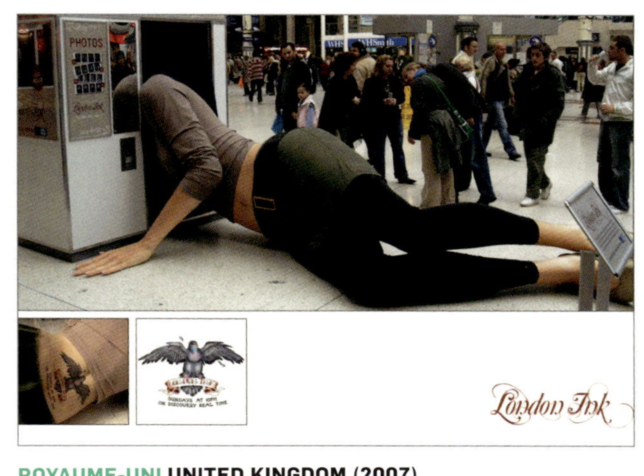

ROYAUME-UNI UNITED KINGDOM (2007)
Mother London · London Ink on Discovery RealTime

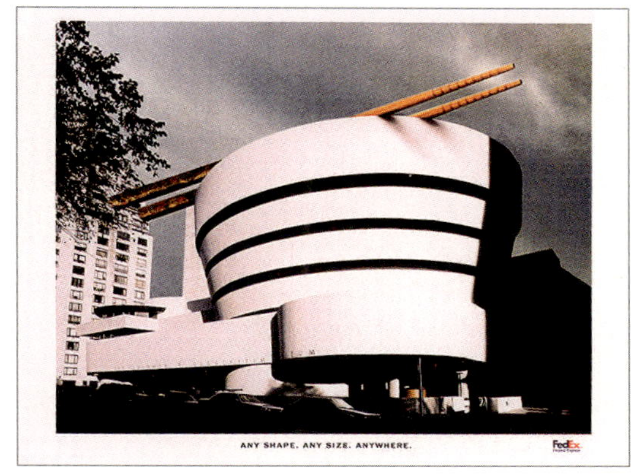

PHILIPPINES PHILIPPINES (2001)
BBDO Guerrero Ortega · FedEx
Any shape, any size, anywhere

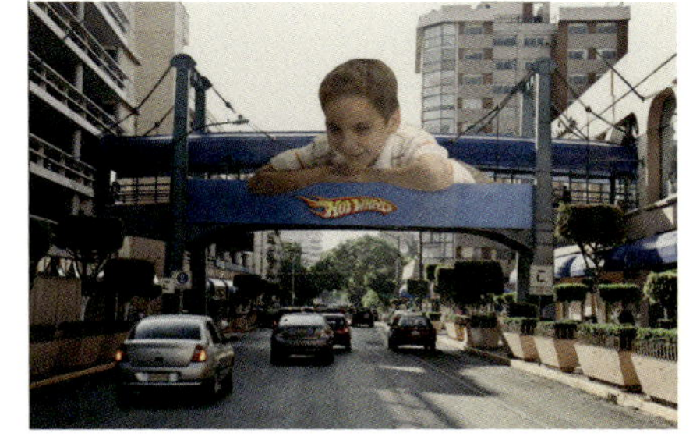

MEXIQUE MEXICO (2010)
Ogilvy & Mather · Hot Wheels

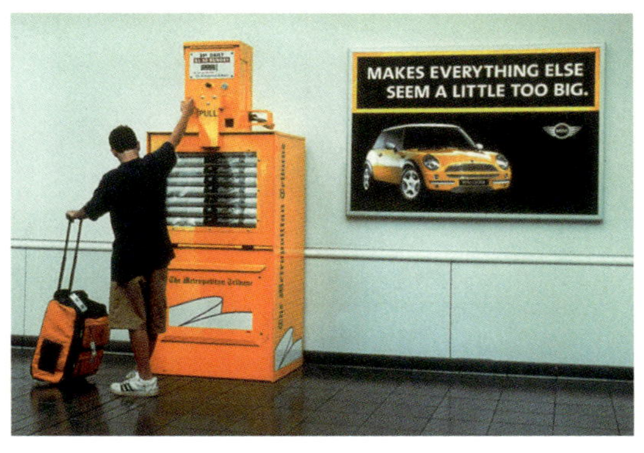

ÉTATS-UNIS UNITED STATES (2003)
Crispin Porter + Bogusky · BMW Mini

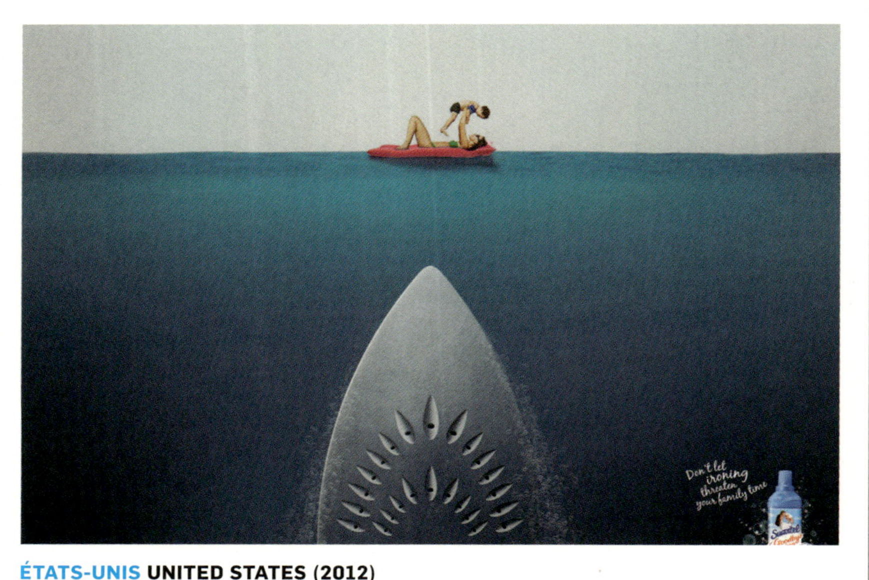

ÉTATS-UNIS UNITED STATES (2012)
Young & Rubicam New York · Suavitel. Goodbye Ironing
Don't let ironing threaten your family time

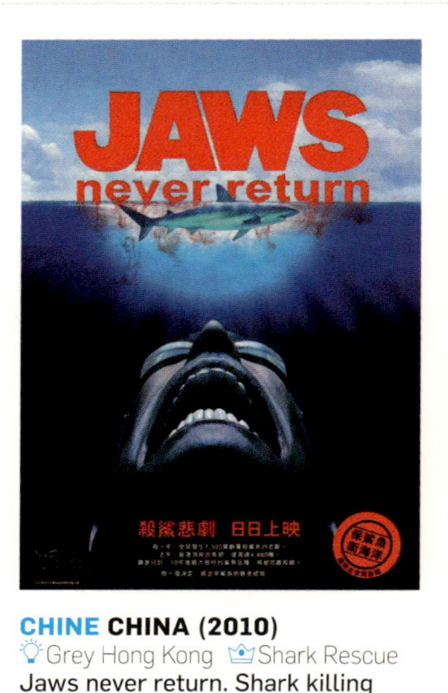

CHINE CHINA (2010)
Grey Hong Kong · Shark Rescue
Jaws never return. Shark killing
tragedies. Showing every day

LES DENTS DE LA MER

№ 32

JAWS

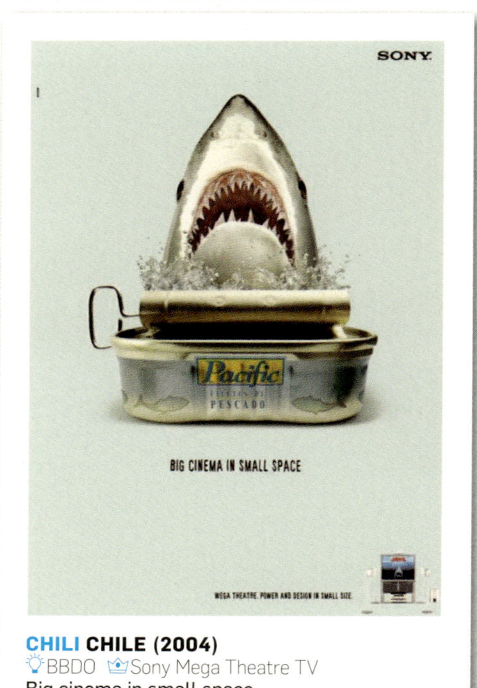

CHILI CHILE (2004)
BBDO · Sony Mega Theatre TV
Big cinema in small space

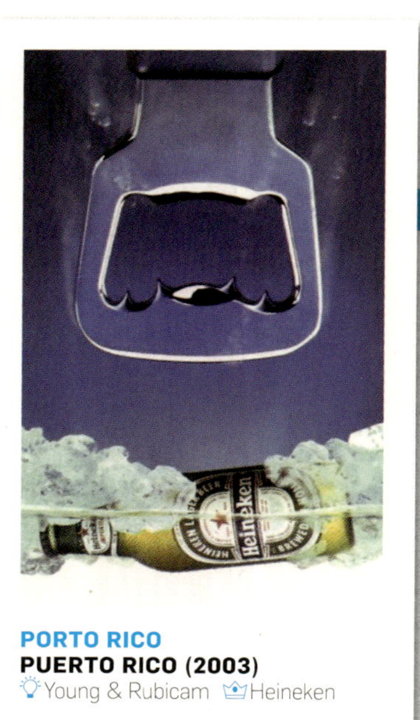

**PORTO RICO
PUERTO RICO (2003)**
Young & Rubicam · Heineken

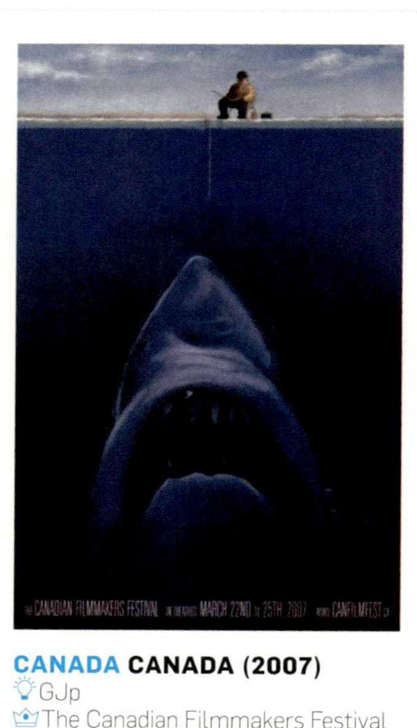

CANADA CANADA (2007)
GJp
The Canadian Filmmakers Festival

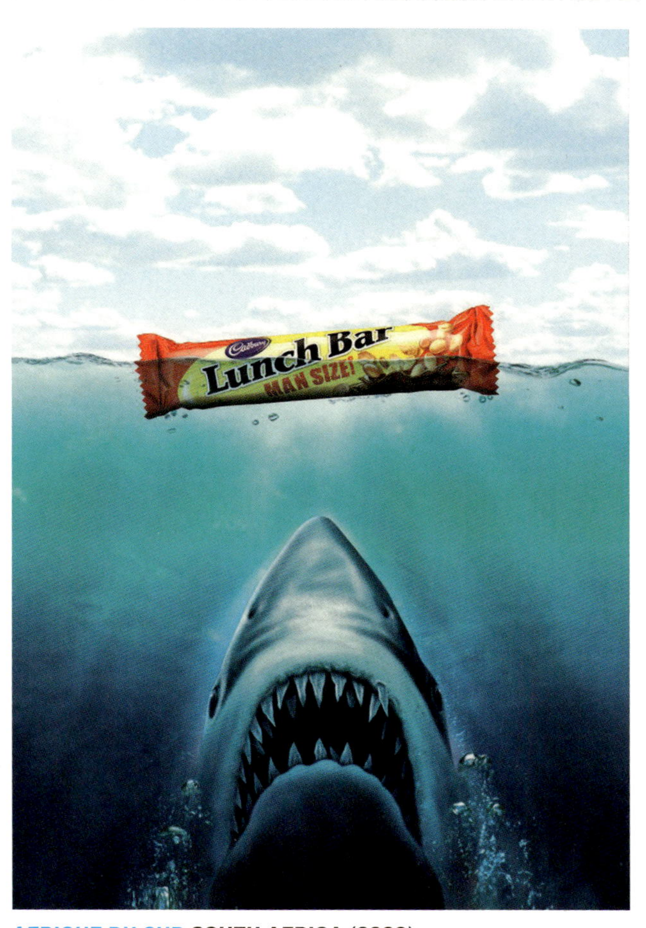

AFRIQUE DU SUD SOUTH AFRICA (2009)
Publicis — Cadbury Lunch Bar
Man size!

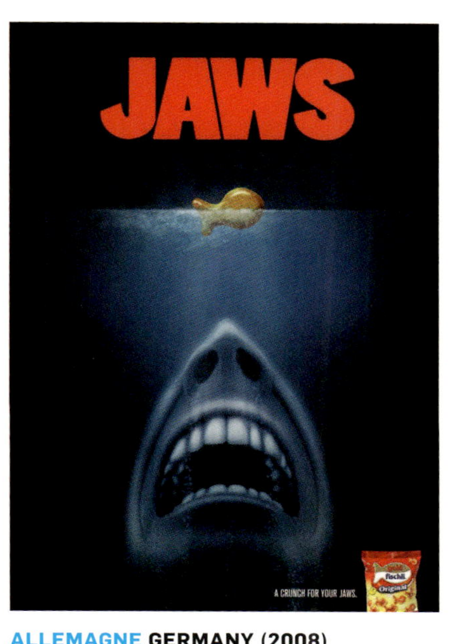

ALLEMAGNE GERMANY (2008)
Heye Group — Gold Fischli Original
A crunch for your jaws

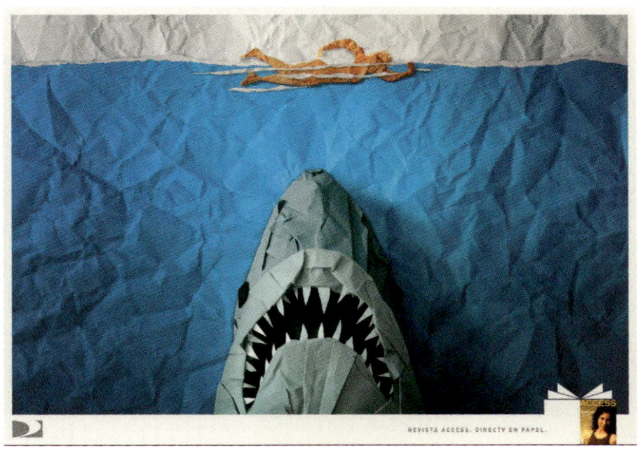

ARGENTINE ARGENTINA (2009)
Draft FCB — Access Magazine
Direct TV programs in paper format

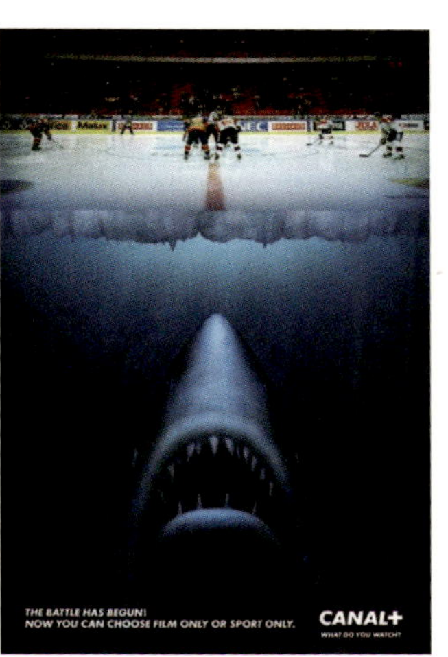

SUÈDE SWEDEN (2006)
Waters Widgren — Canal+
The battle has begun! Now you can choose film only or sport only

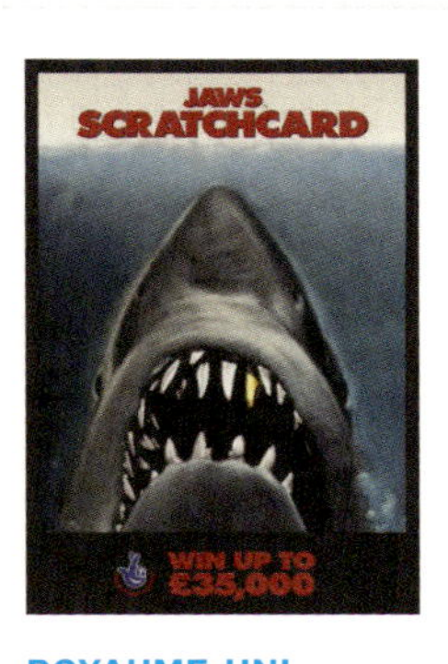

ROYAUME-UNI UNITED KINGDOM (2005)
AMV BBDO
National Lottery

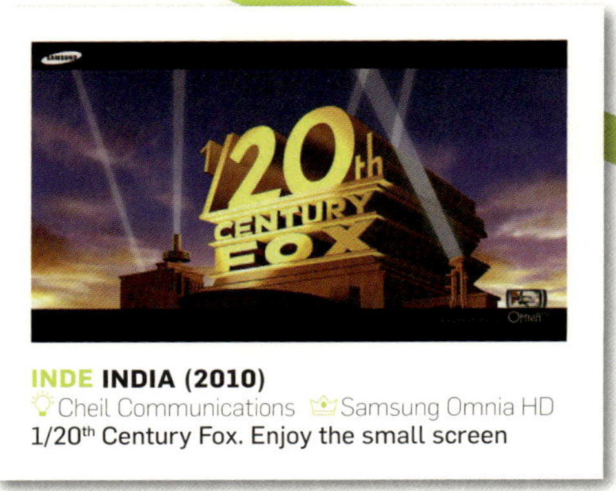

INDE INDIA (2010)
Cheil Communications Samsung Omnia HD
1/20th Century Fox. Enjoy the small screen

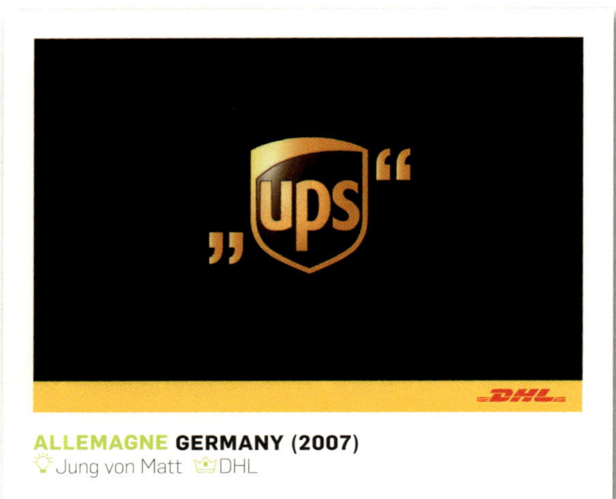

ALLEMAGNE GERMANY (2007)
Jung von Matt DHL

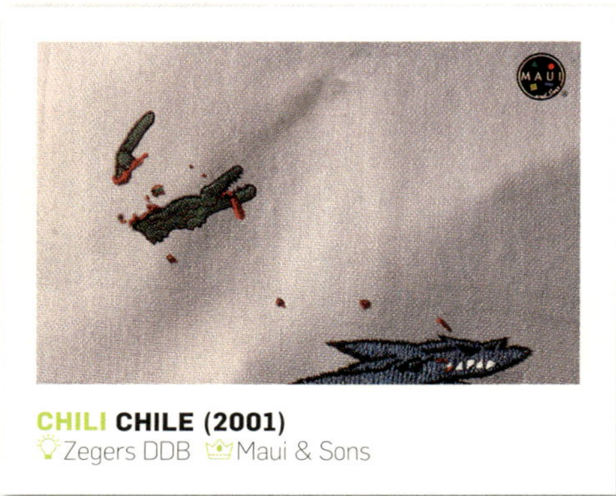

CHILI CHILE (2001)
Zegers DDB Maui & Sons

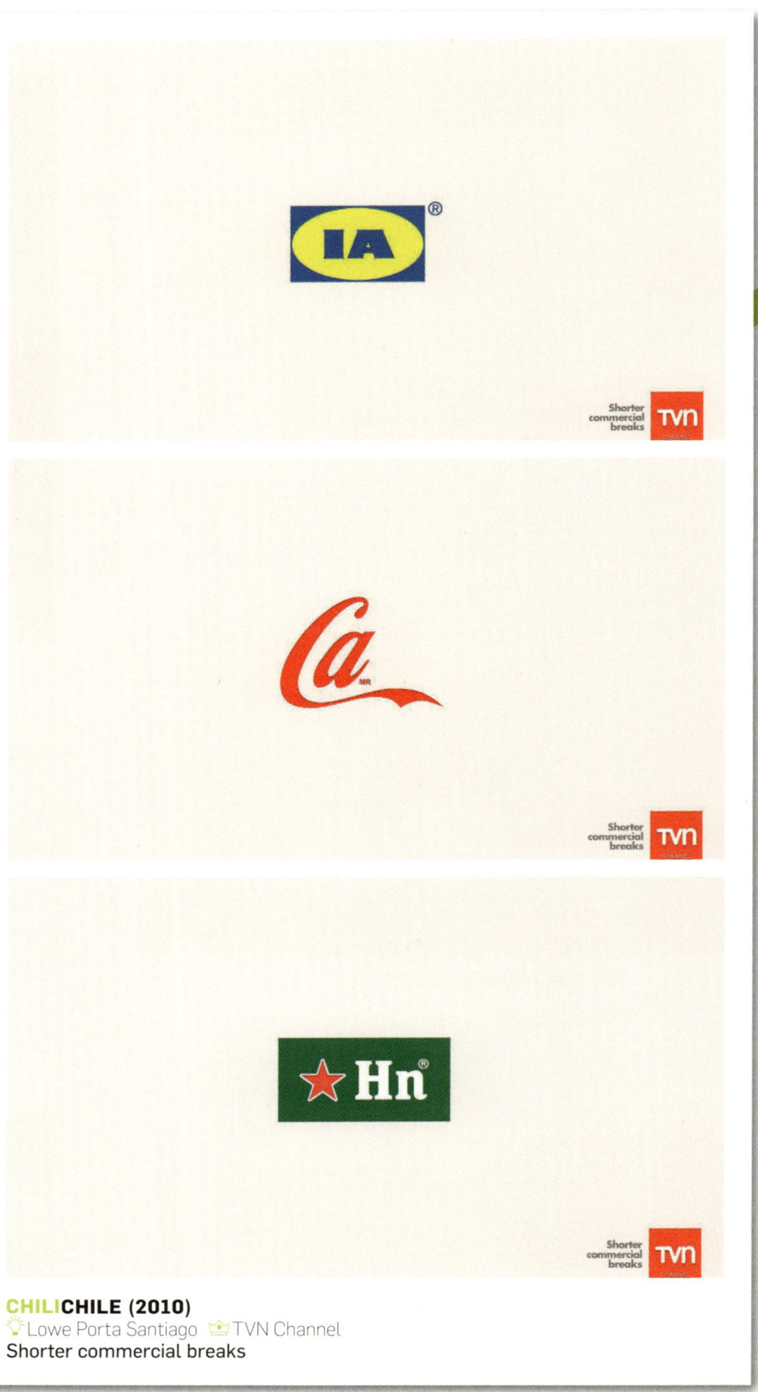

CHILI CHILE (2010)
Lowe Porta Santiago TVN Channel
Shorter commercial breaks

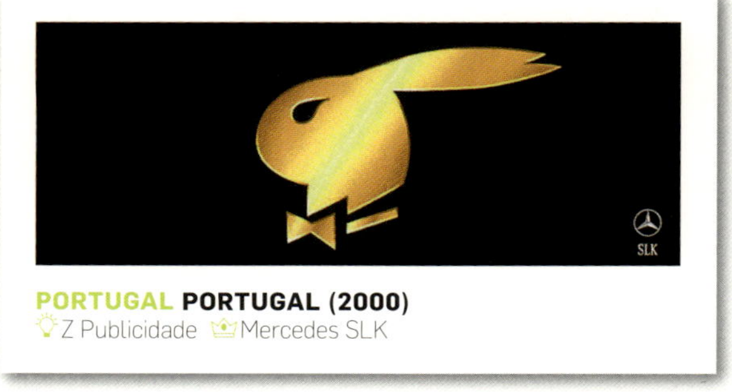

PORTUGAL PORTUGAL (2000)
Z Publicidade Mercedes SLK

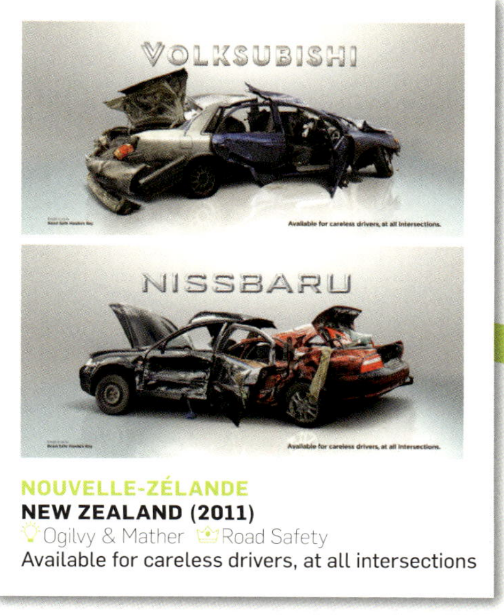

NOUVELLE-ZÉLANDE
NEW ZEALAND (2011)
Ogilvy & Mather · Road Safety
Available for careless drivers, at all intersections

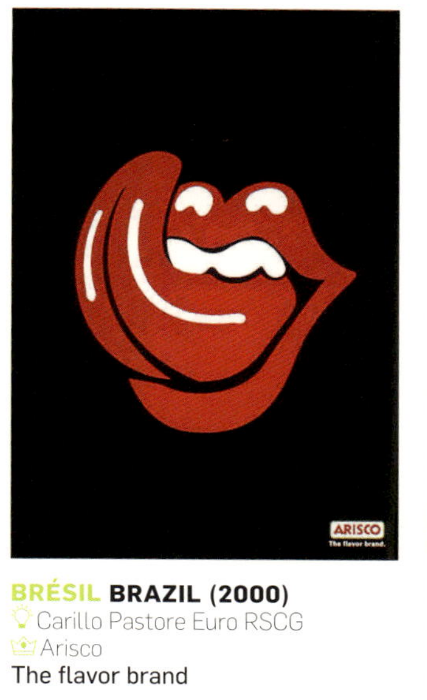

BRÉSIL BRAZIL (2000)
Carillo Pastore Euro RSCG
Arisco
The flavor brand

DÉTOURNEMENTS DE MARQUES ET LOGOS

№ 33

HIJACKED BRANDS AND LOGOS

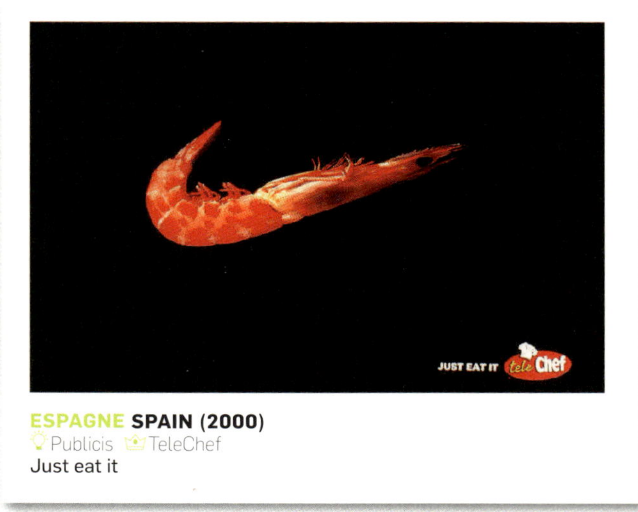

ESPAGNE SPAIN (2000)
Publicis · TeleChef
Just eat it

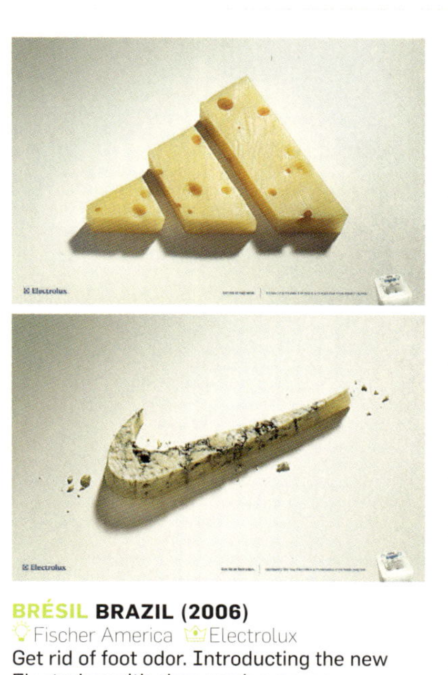

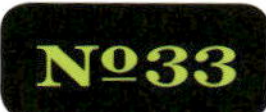

BRÉSIL BRAZIL (2006)
Fischer America · Electrolux
Get rid of foot odor. Introducing the new
Electrolux with shoe wash program

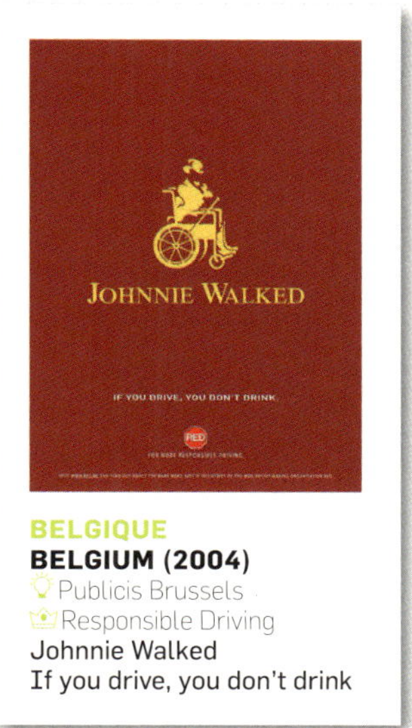

BELGIQUE
BELGIUM (2004)
Publicis Brussels
Responsible Driving
Johnnie Walked
If you drive, you don't drink

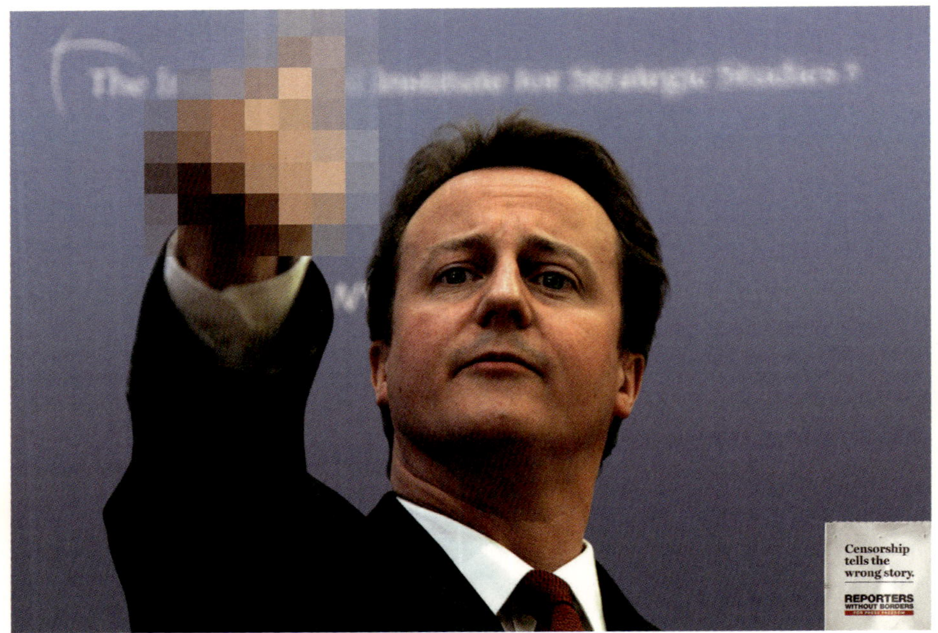

ÉMIRATS ARABES UNIS UNITED ARAB EMIRATES (2011)
Memac Ogilvy & Mather Dubai Reporters without borders
Censorship tells the wrong story

« Ma préférée, la plus gonflée et celle que je trouve la plus forte est la seule qui ne montre pas vraiment le doigt tendu. Elle ne fait que révéler notre esprit tordu. »
"My favourite, the most exaggerated and the one that I found the strongest is the only one that doesn't really show the extended finger. It only reveals our twisted mind."

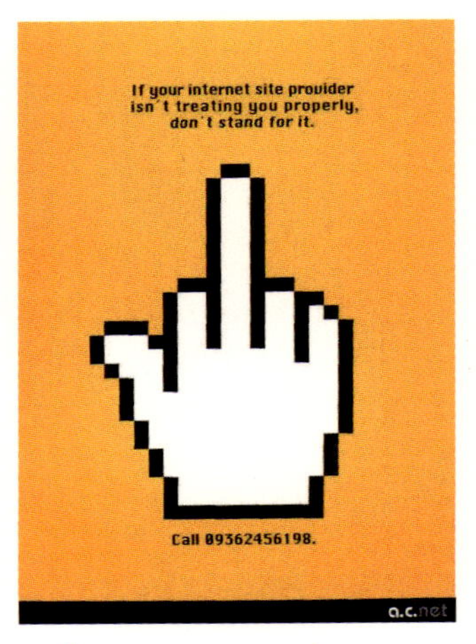

BRÉSIL BRAZIL (1999)
Z Publicidade AC Net
If your internet site provider
isn't treating you properly,
don't stand for it

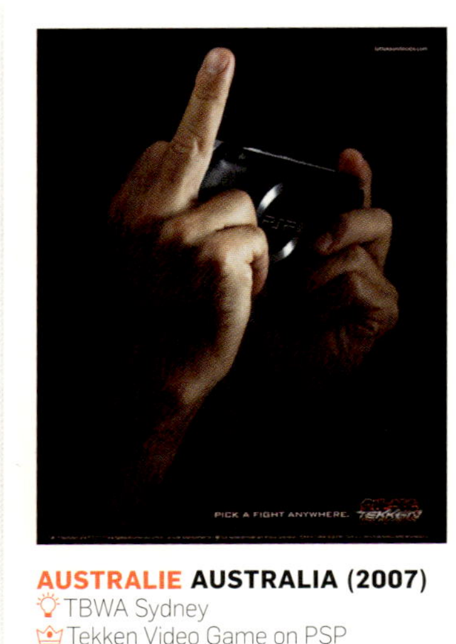

AUSTRALIE AUSTRALIA (2007)
TBWA Sydney
Tekken Video Game on PSP
Pick a fight anywhere

FRANCE FRANCE (2006)
CLM/BBDO Airwaves Chewing-gums Rock Festival

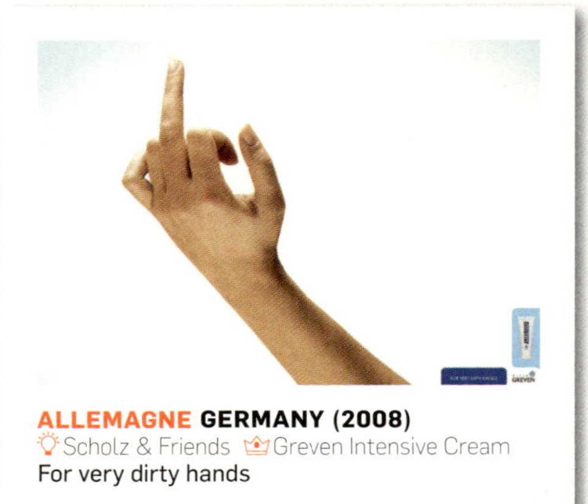

ALLEMAGNE GERMANY (2008)
Scholz & Friends Greven Intensive Cream
For very dirty hands

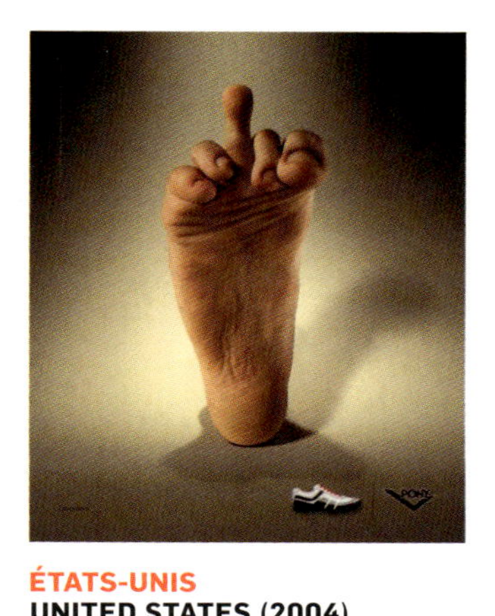

ÉTATS-UNIS
UNITED STATES (2004)
Goodby Silverstein & Partners
Pony

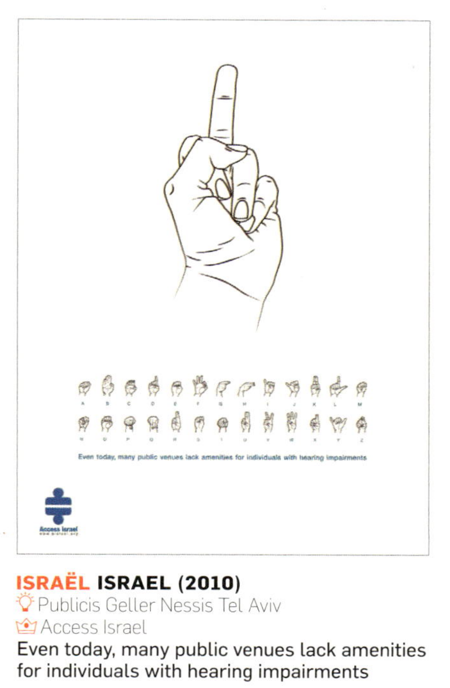

ISRAËL ISRAEL (2010)
Publicis Geller Nessis Tel Aviv
Access Israel
Even today, many public venues lack amenities for individuals with hearing impairments

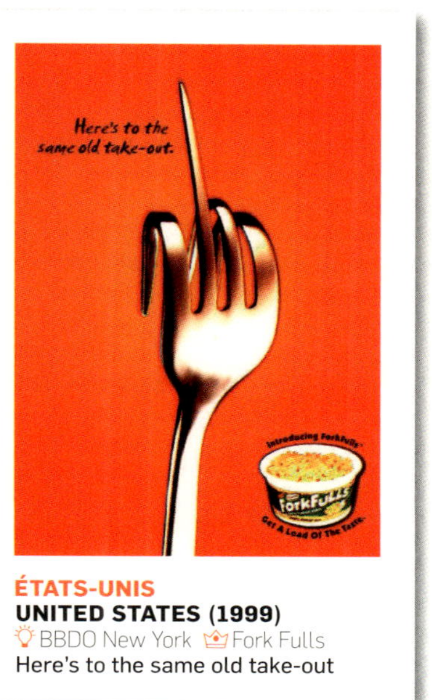

ÉTATS-UNIS
UNITED STATES (1999)
BBDO New York   Fork Fulls
Here's to the same old take-out

DOIGTS D'HONNEUR
№34
FUCK YOU SIGNS

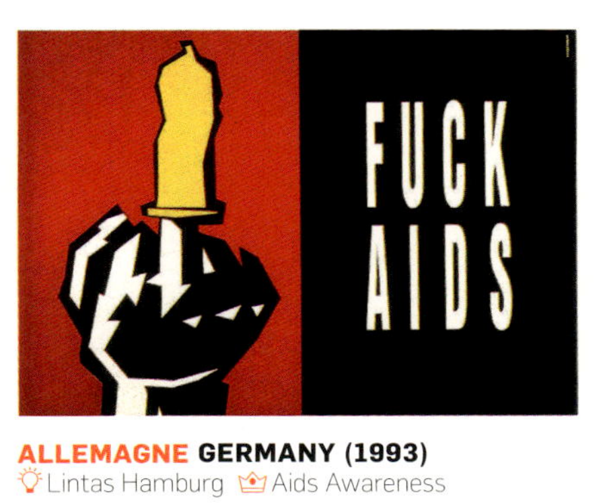

ALLEMAGNE GERMANY (1993)
Lintas Hamburg   Aids Awareness

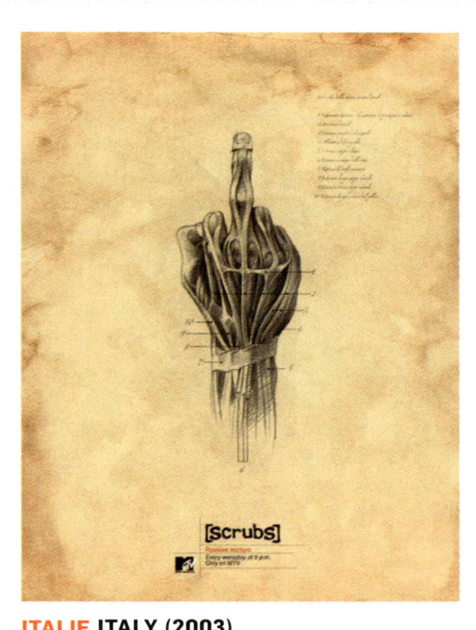

ITALIE ITALY (2003)
This is a thing Milan   MTV
Rookies doctors. Every wednesday at 9 p.m.
Only on MTV

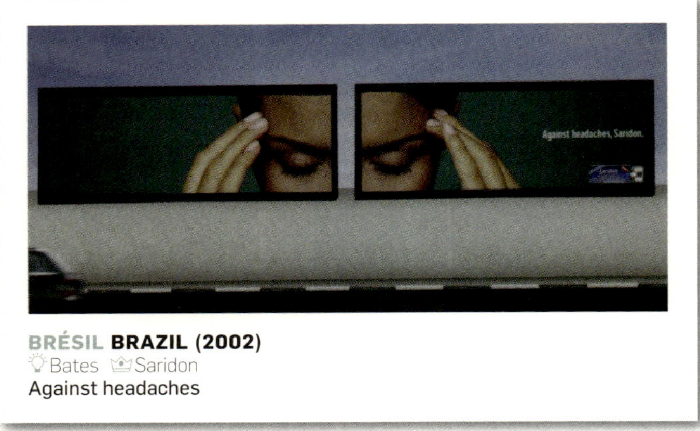

BRÉSIL BRAZIL (2002)
Bates · Saridon
Against headaches

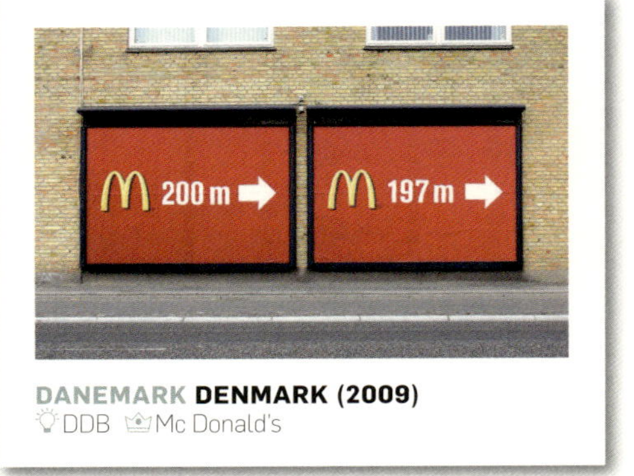

DANEMARK DENMARK (2009)
DDB · Mc Donald's

DOUBLES PANNEAUX

№ 35

DOUBLE BILLBOARDS

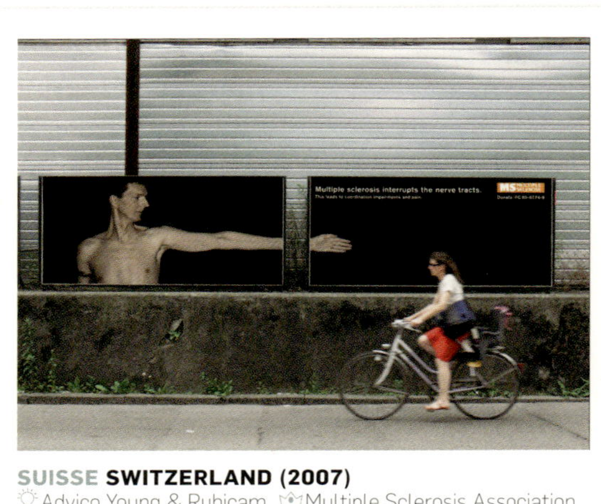

SUISSE SWITZERLAND (2007)
Advico Young & Rubicam · Multiple Sclerosis Association
Multiple sclerosis interrupts the nerve tracts

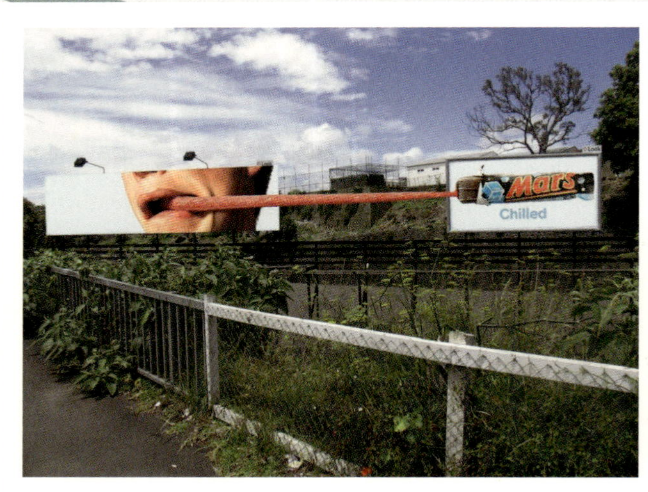

NOUVELLE ZÉLANDE NEW ZEALAND (2007)
Colenso BBDO · Mars Chilled Ice Cream

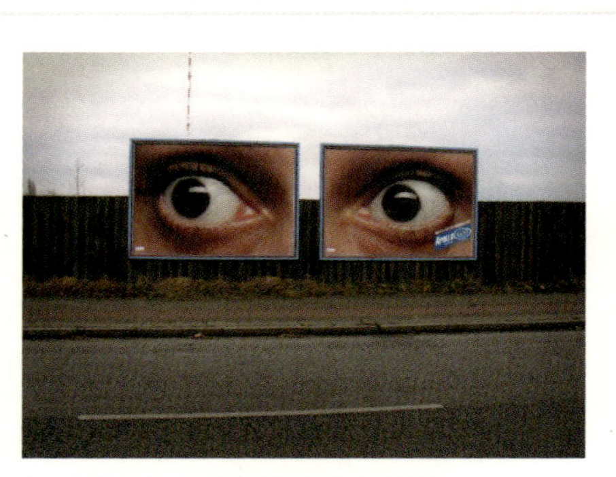

ALLEMAGNE GERMANY (2005)
Jung Von Matt · Apollo Optic
Much nicer frames at Apollo Optic

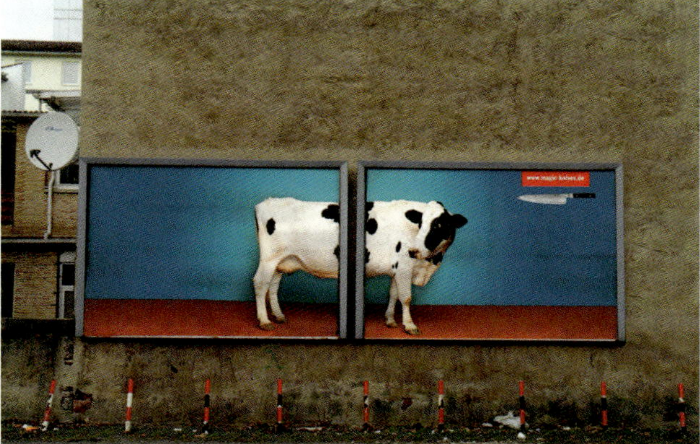

ALLEMAGNE
GERMANY (2006)
Leo Burnett Frankfurt
Magic Knives

« Ah la vache ! Ça c'est de l'effet visuel qui fonctionne tout de suite. Ce n'est pas une pub qui coupe les cheveux en quatre, mais les affiches en deux. C'est direct, simple et efficace. »
"Wow! This is a visual effect that works straight away. It's not an advert about splitting hairs, even though the display has been cut in two. It is direct, simple and effective."

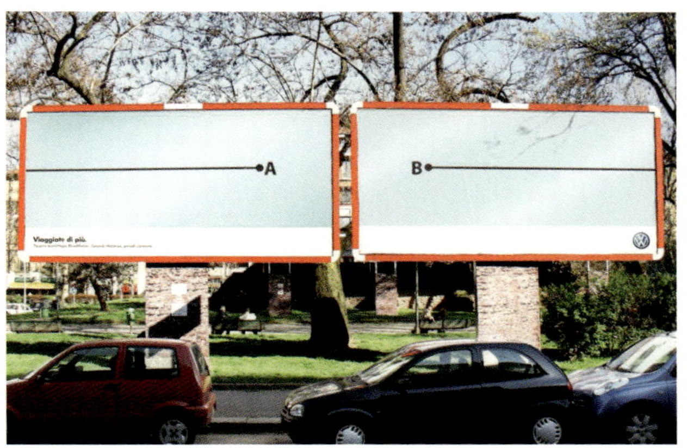

ITALIE ITALY (2007)
DDB Volkswagen Blue Motion Technology.
Travel more

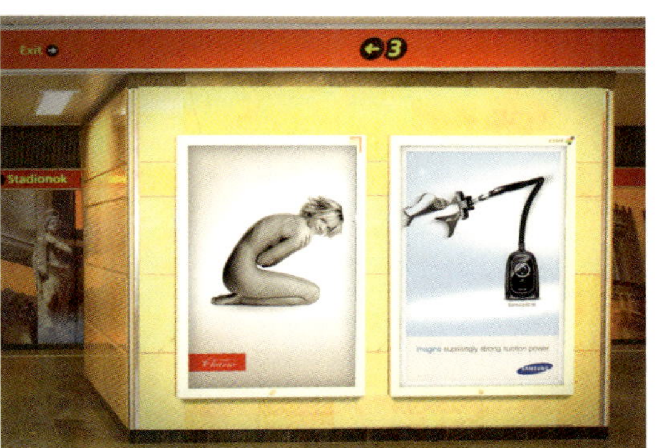

HONGRIE HUNGARY (2007)
Leo Burnett Budapest Samsung
Surprisingly strong suction power

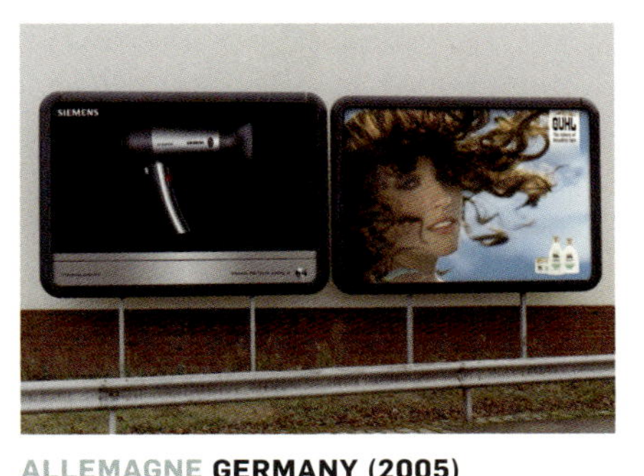

ALLEMAGNE GERMANY (2005)
Scholz & Friends Siemens Hairdryer

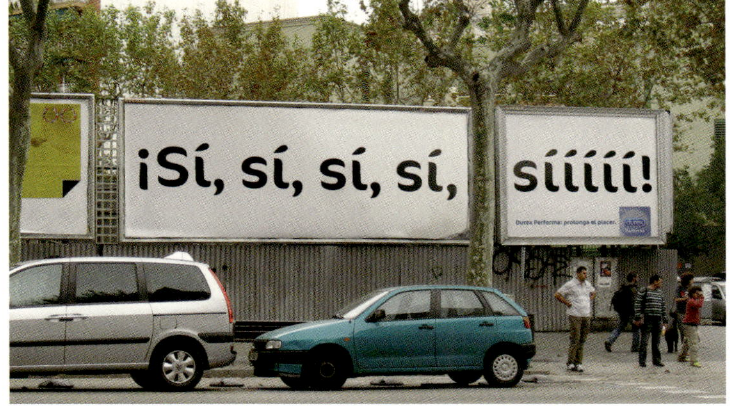

ESPAGNE SPAIN (2009)
Ciacomunicacion_ Barcelona Durex Performa Condoms
Prolonge le plaisir Prolong the pleasure

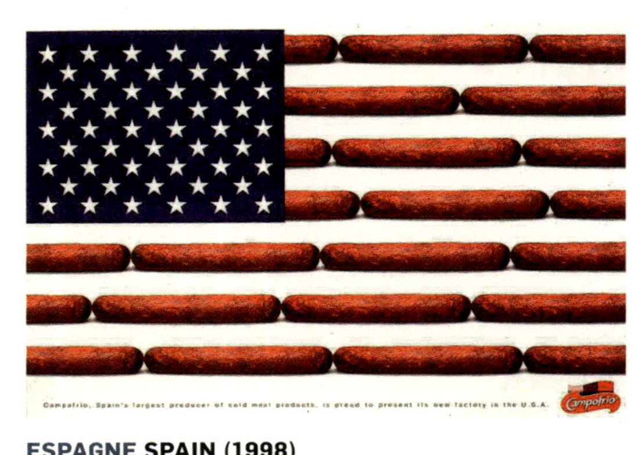

ESPAGNE SPAIN (1998)
Tiempo BBDO Campofrio
Spain's largest producer of cold meat products is proud to present its new factory in the USA

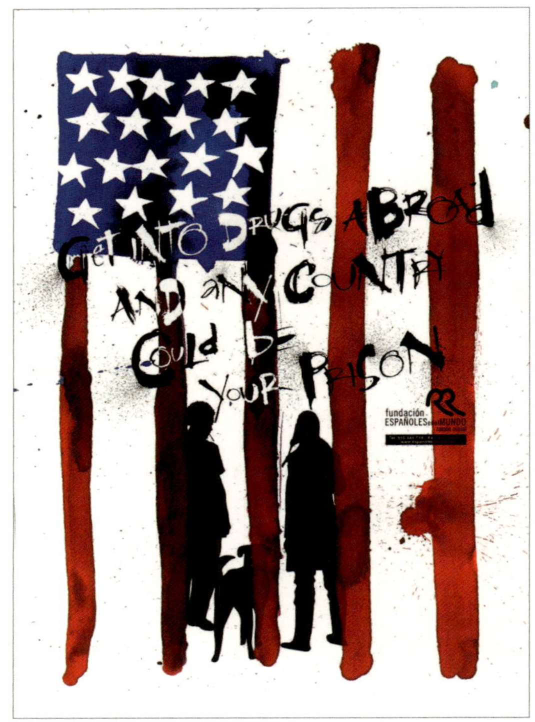

ESPAGNE SPAIN (2008)
JWT Barcelona
Fundacion Espanoles / Anti Drug Trafficking
Get into drugs abroad and any country could be your prison

DRAPEAUX AMÉRICAINS
N°36
STARS AND STRIPES

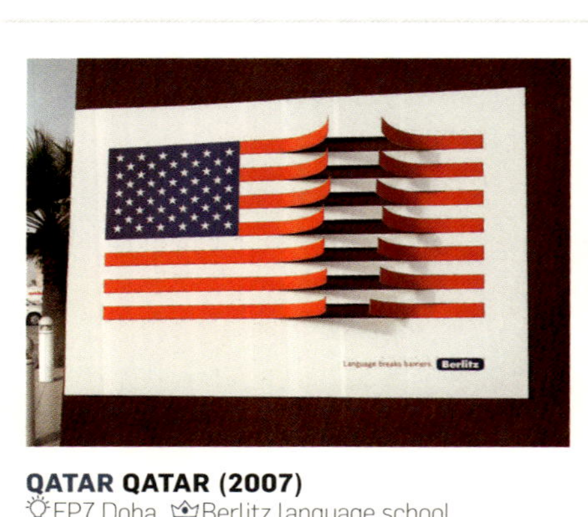
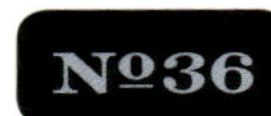

QATAR QATAR (2007)
FP7 Doha Berlitz language school
Language breaks barriers

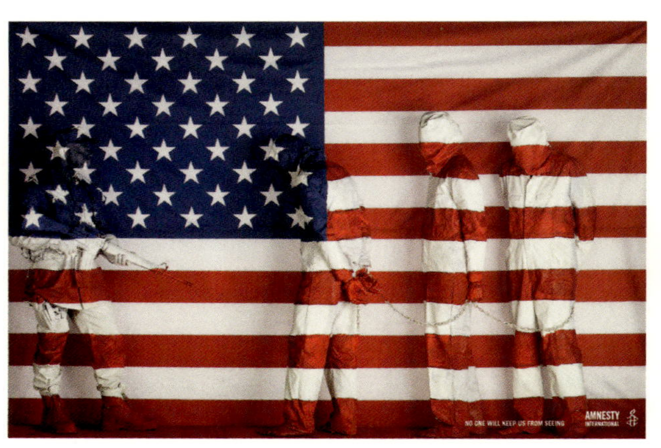

BELGIQUE BELGIUM (2008)
Air Brussels Amnesty International
No one will keep us from seeing

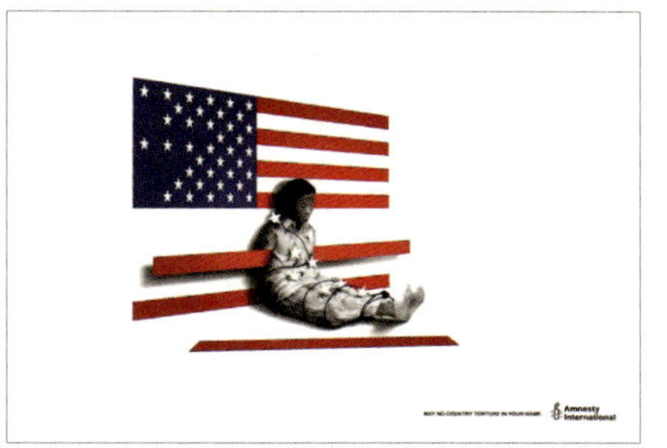

ESPAGNE SPAIN (2006)
Contrapunto · Amnesty International
May no country torture in your name

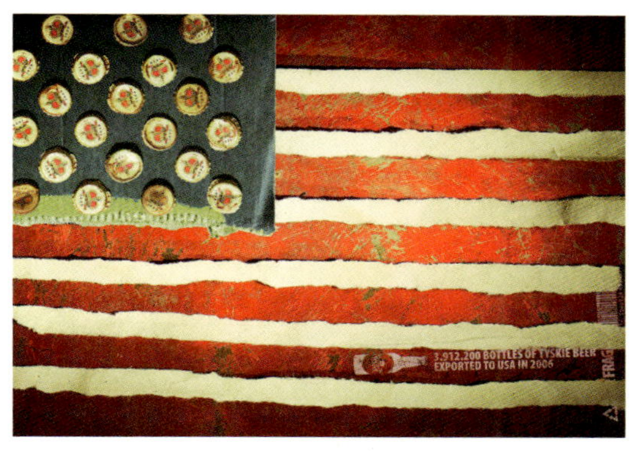

POLOGNE POLAND (2007)
DDB Warszawa · Tyskie Beer
3.912.200 Bottles of Tyskie Beer exported to USA in 2006

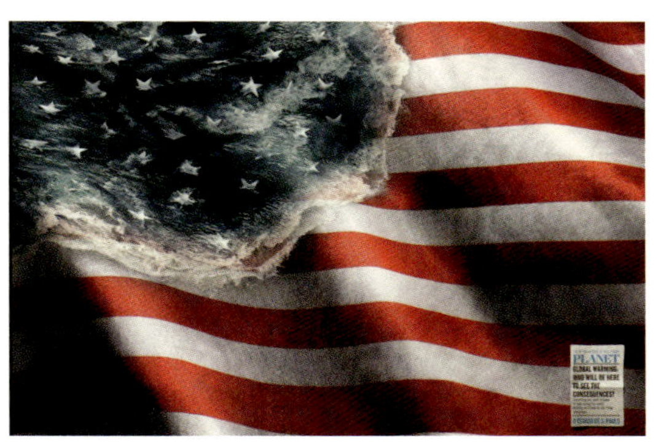

BRÉSIL BRAZIL (2011)
Young & Rubicam · O estado de Sao Paulo
Global Warming. Who will be here to see the consequences?

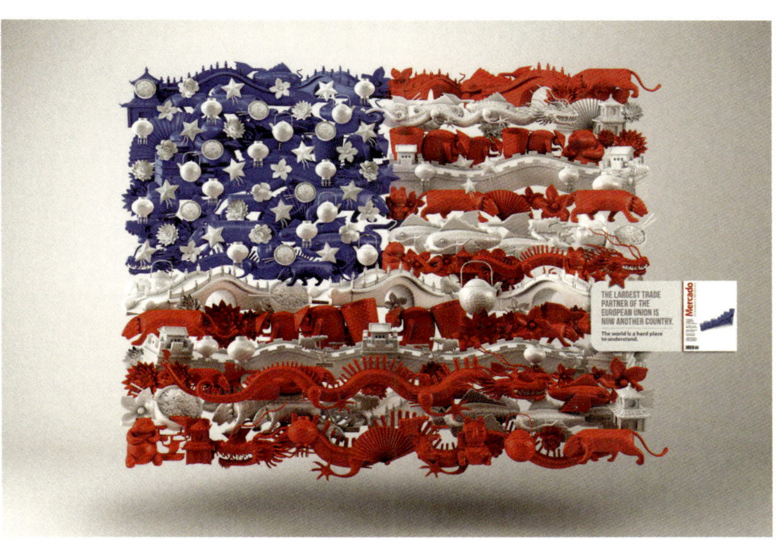

ARGENTINE ARGENTINA (2012)
JWT Buenos Aires · Mercado
The largest trade partner of the european union is now another country

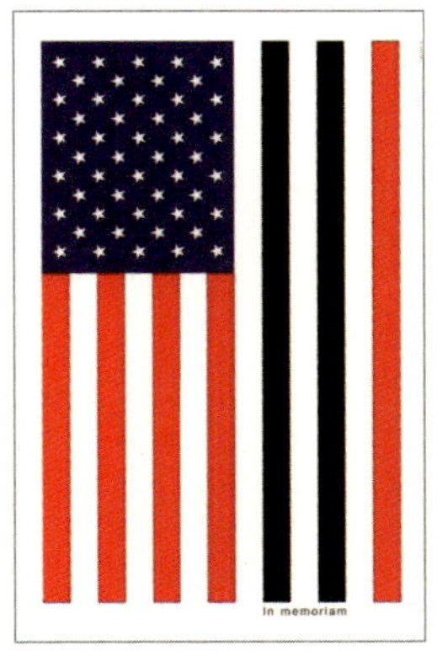

**ÉTATS UNIS
UNITED STATES (2003)**
Lowe
9/11 2nd Anniversary
In Memoriam

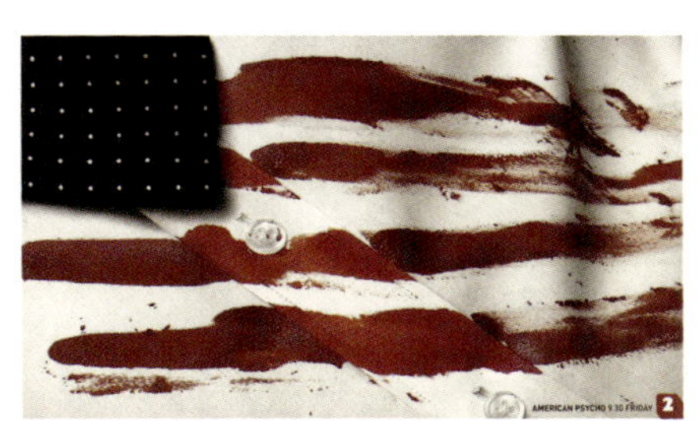

**NOUVELLE ZÉLANDE
NEW ZEALAND (2008)**
Saatchi & Saatchi
American Psycho 9.30 Friday on channel 2

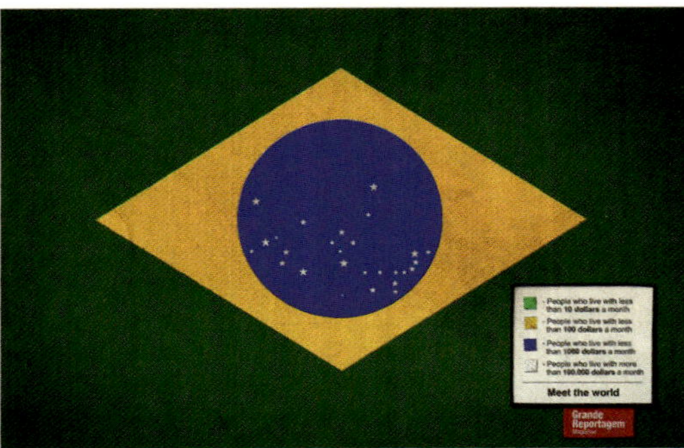

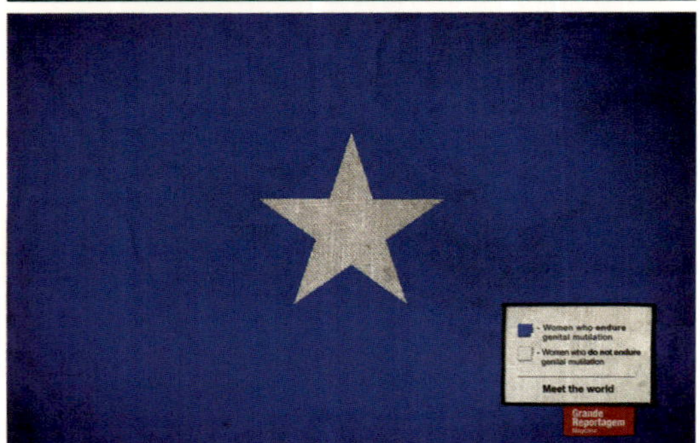

PORTUGAL PORTUGAL (2005)
FCB Lisbon · Grande Reportagem Magazine

BRAZIL
Green - Live with less than 10 dolars a month
Yellow - Live with less than 100 dolars a month
Blue - Live with less than 1000 dolars a month
White - Live with more than 100.000 dolars a month
Meet the world

SOMALIA
Blue - Women who endure genital mutilation
White - Women who do not endure genital mutilation
Meet the world

«Cette campagne est simplement au-dessus des autres par sa force, sa simplicité et son intelligence. Le symbole du drapeau est pourtant l'un des plus utilisés et des plus détournés au monde. J'en ai trouvé des centaines… C'est la croix et la bannière pour un créatif de trouver une idée originale qui n'ait jamais été faite avec un drapeau.»
"This campaign is simply above others because of its strength, its simplicity and its intelligence. The symbol of the flag is nevertheless one of the most used and most frequently misappropriated in the world. I've found hundreds. It's a tall order for a creative to find an original idea that has never been done with flag."

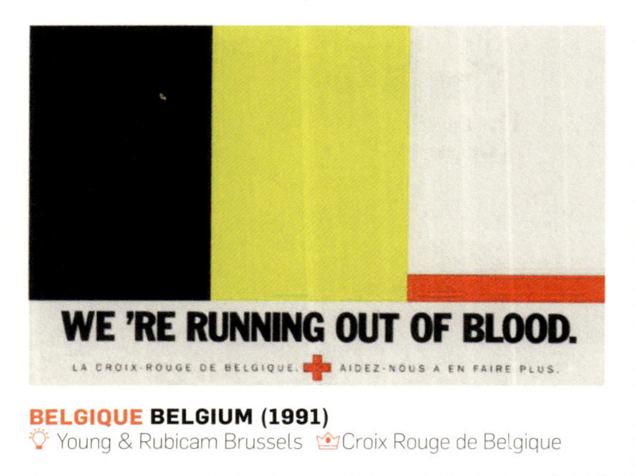

BELGIQUE BELGIUM (1991)
Young & Rubicam Brussels · Croix Rouge de Belgique

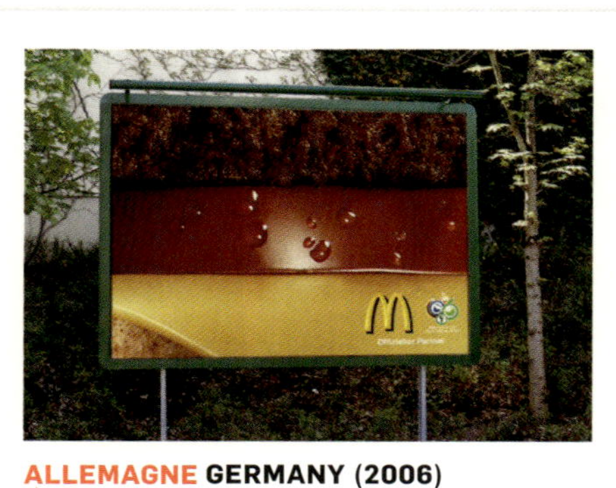

ALLEMAGNE GERMANY (2006)
Heye Group · Mc Donald's
Official partner of german soccer team

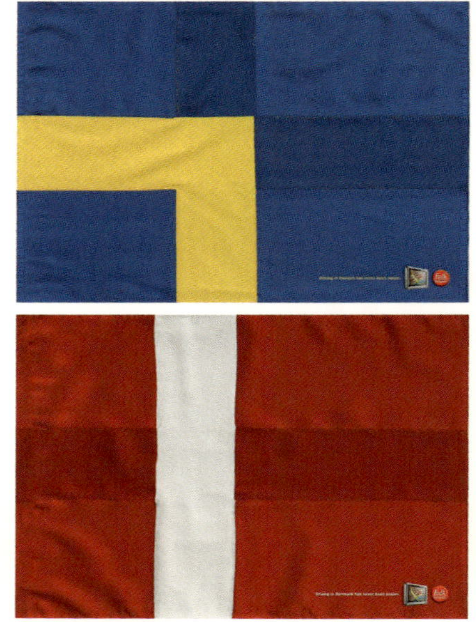

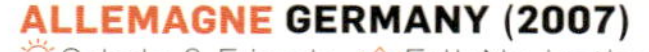

ALLEMAGNE GERMANY (2007)
Scholz & Friends · Falk Navigation System
1 - Driving in Sweden has never been easier
2 - Driving in Denmark has never been easier

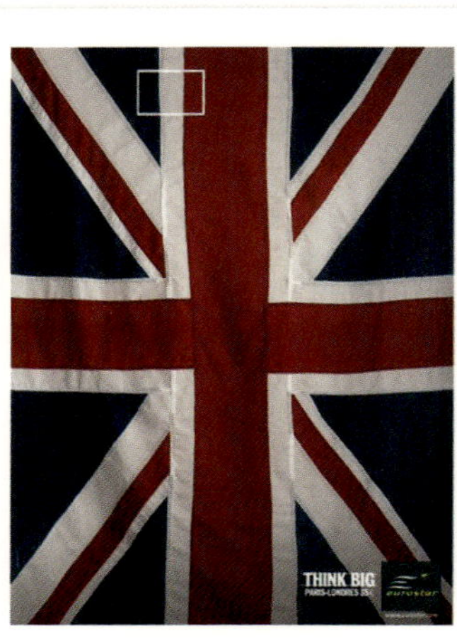

FRANCE FRANCE (2004)
Leg · Eurostar
Think Big

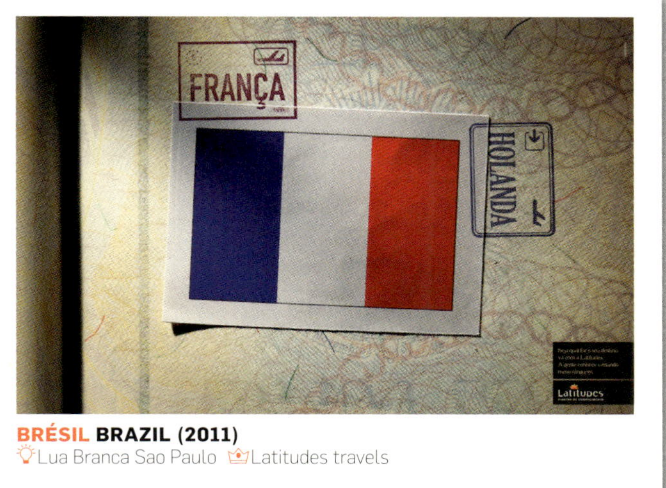
BRÉSIL BRAZIL (2011)
Lua Branca Sao Paulo · Latitudes travels

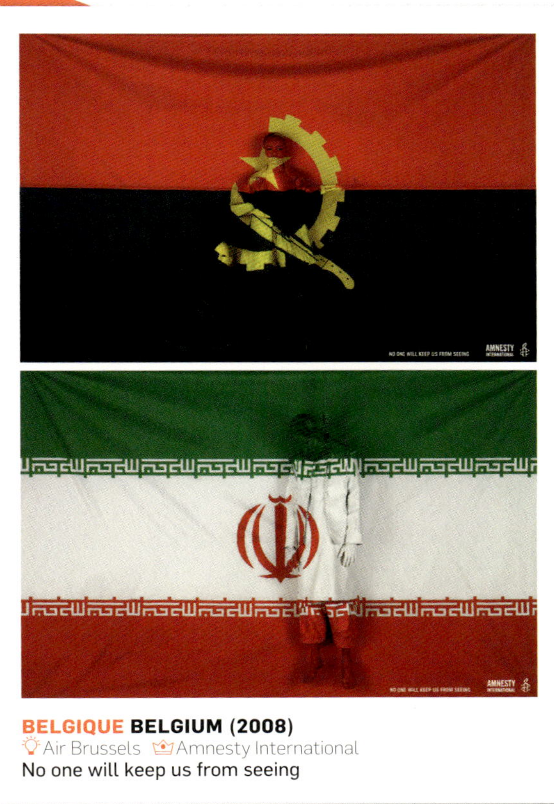
BELGIQUE BELGIUM (2008)
Air Brussels · Amnesty International
No one will keep us from seeing

DRAPEAUX DU MONDE

№ 37

WORLDWIDE FLAGS

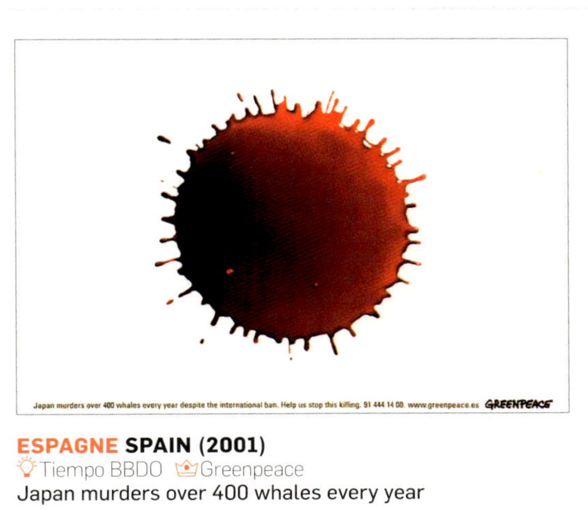
ESPAGNE SPAIN (2001)
Tiempo BBDO · Greenpeace
Japan murders over 400 whales every year

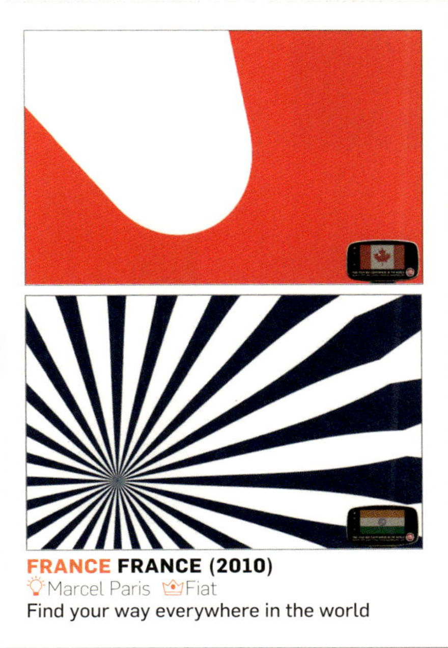
FRANCE FRANCE (2010)
Marcel Paris · Fiat
Find your way everywhere in the world

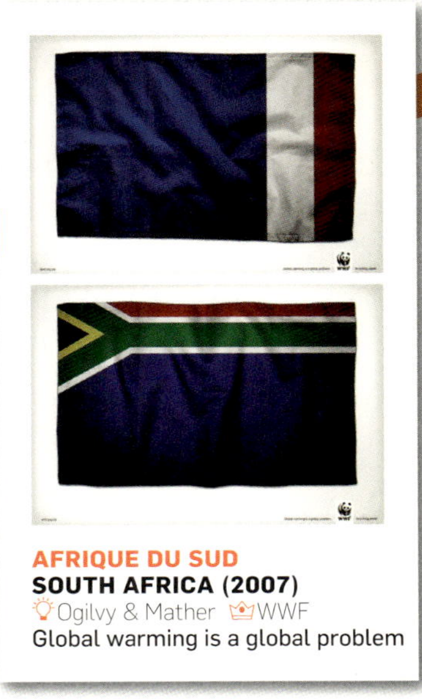
**AFRIQUE DU SUD
SOUTH AFRICA (2007)**
Ogilvy & Mather · WWF
Global warming is a global problem

EINSTEIN

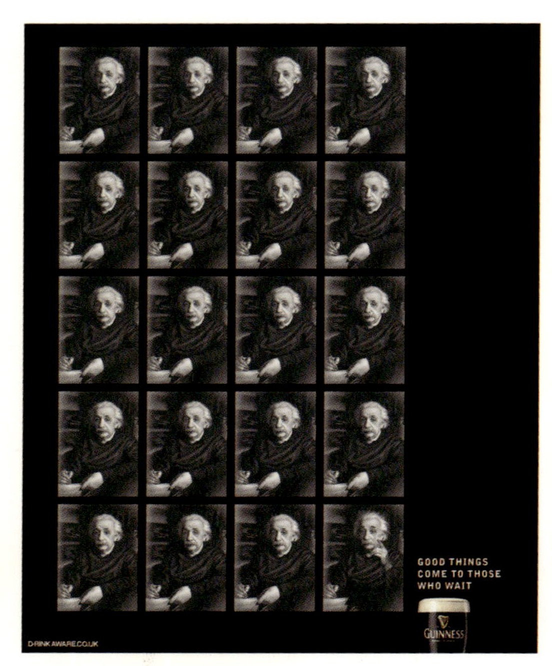

ROYAUME UNI UNITED KINGDOM (2006)
AMV BBDO London · Guinness
Good things come to those who wait

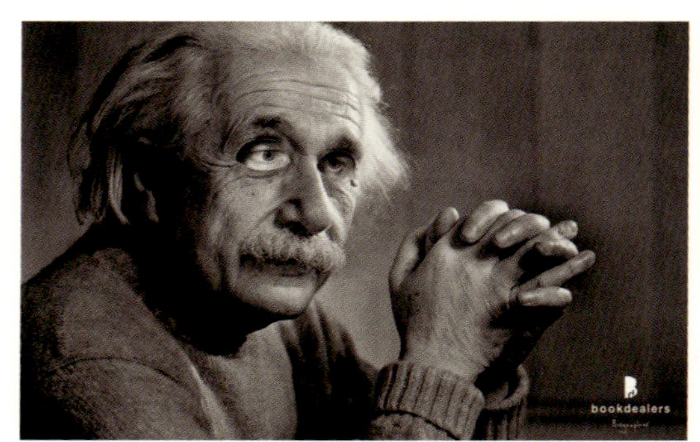

AFRIQUE DU SUD SOUTH AFRICA (2011)
Ogilvy Johannesburg · Bookdealers
Biographies

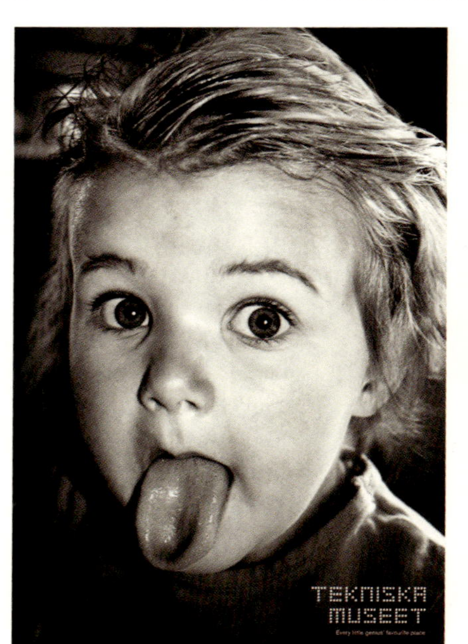

SUÈDE SWEDEN (2009)
Ruth Advertising Stockholm · Tekniska Museet
Every little genius favorite place

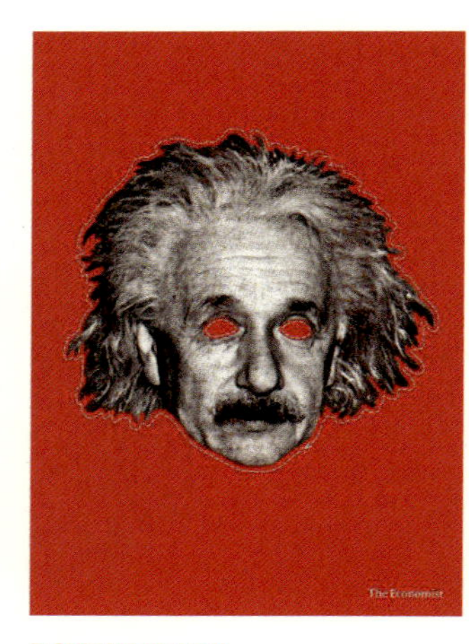

**ROYAUME UNI
UNITED KINGDOM (2005)**
AMV BBDO London
The Economist

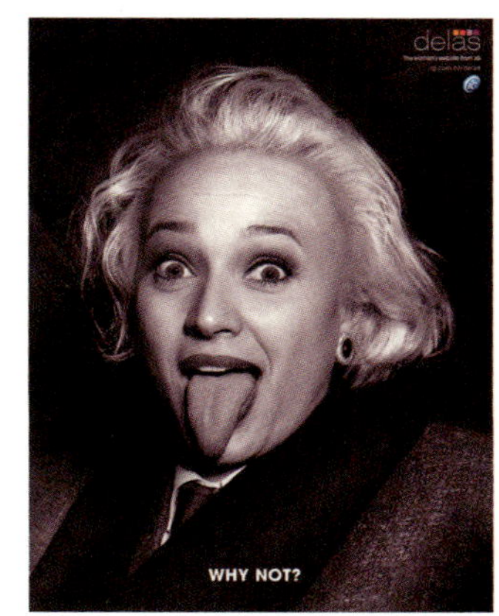

BRÉSIL BRAZIL (2010)
TBWA Lew Lara
Delas women's website from IG
Why Not?

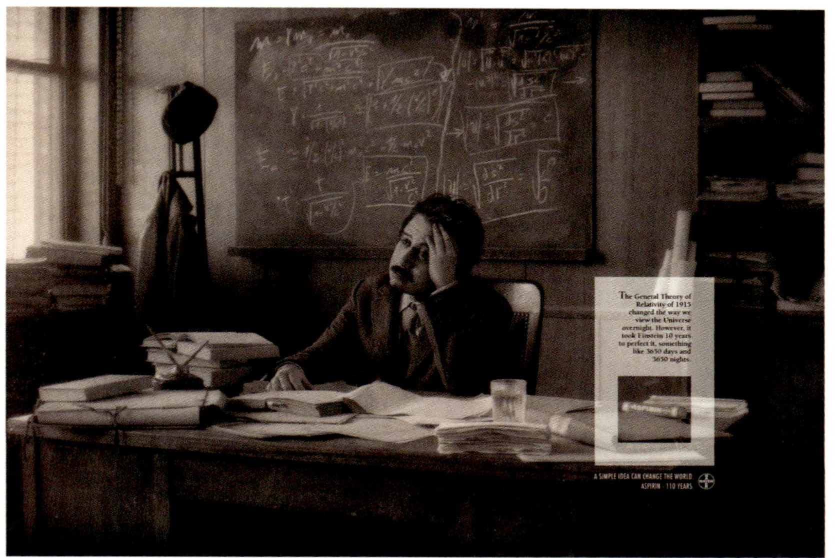

ARGENTINE ARGENTINA (2010)
Young & Rubicam Buenos Aires   Bayer Aspirin
The General Theory of Relativity of 1915 changed the way we view the universe overnight.
However, it took Einstein 10 years to perfect it, something like 3650 days and 3650 nights.
A simple idea can change the World. Aspirin - 110 years.

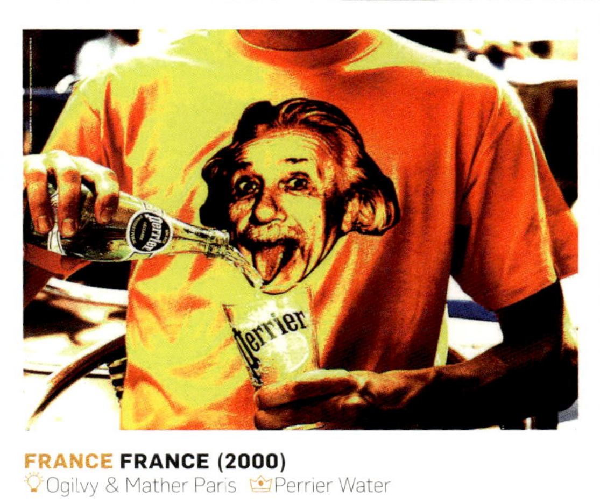

FRANCE FRANCE (2000)
Ogilvy & Mather Paris   Perrier Water

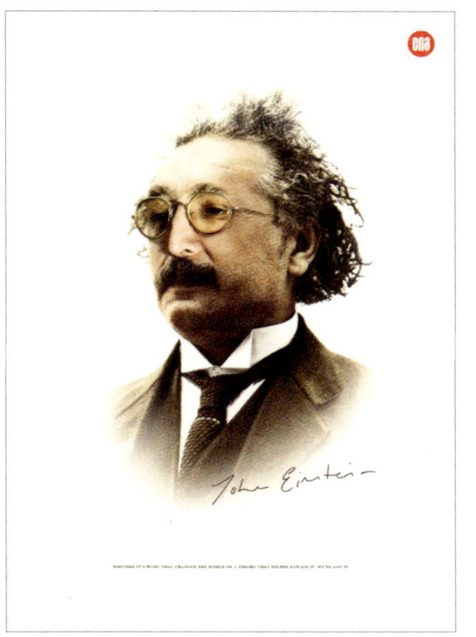

AFRIQUE DU SUD SOUTH AFRICA (2009)
The Jupiter Drawing Room   CNA
"John Einstein" Whether it's music that changed
the world or a theory that help explain it.
We've got it.

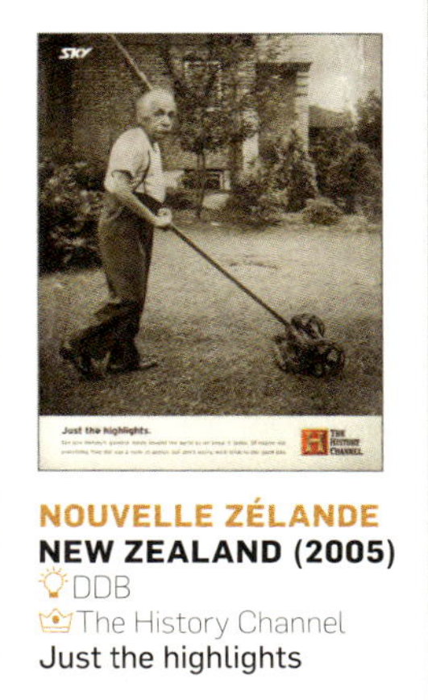

**NOUVELLE ZÉLANDE
NEW ZEALAND (2005)**
DDB
The History Channel
Just the highlights

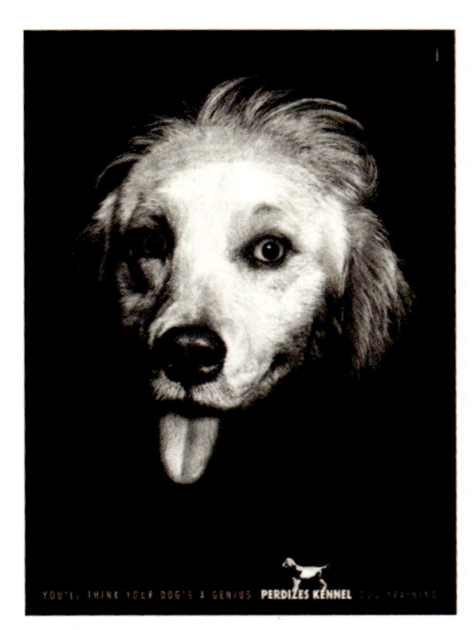

BRÉSIL BRAZIL (2003)
Bates
Perdizes Kennel Dog Training
You'll think your dog's a genius

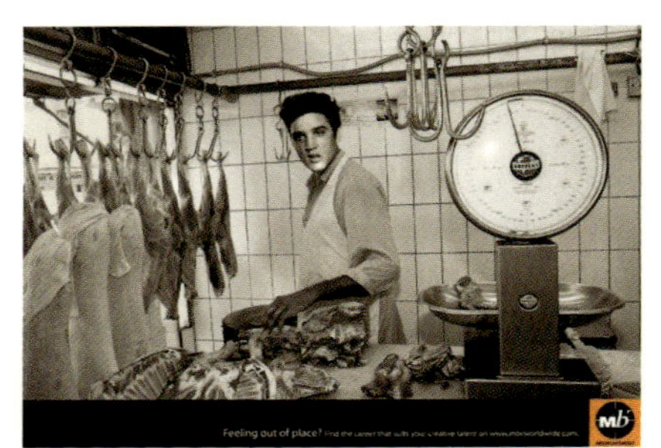

ÉMIRATS ARABES UNIS
UNITED ARAB EMIRATES (2003)
Lowe & Partners Dubai
MB Worldwide Employment agency
Feeling out of place?

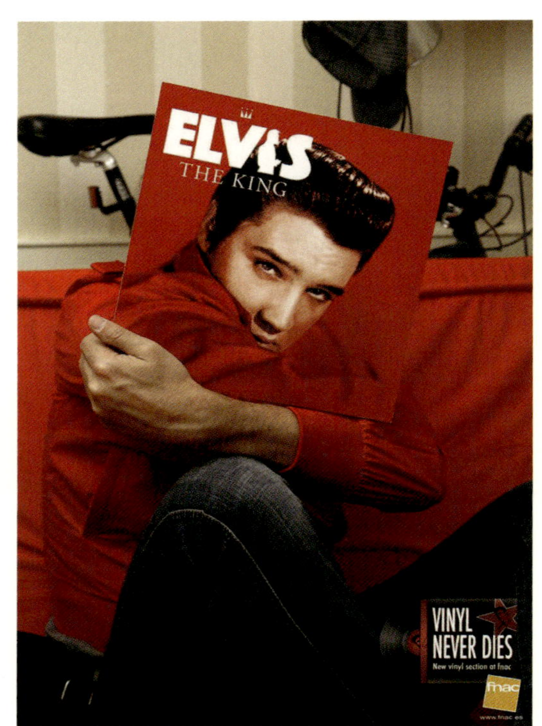

ESPAGNE SPAIN (2008)
Kitchen Madrid
Fnac
Vinyl never dies

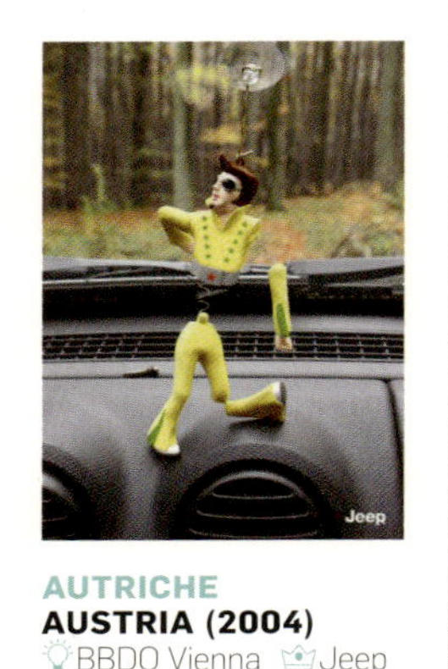

AUTRICHE
AUSTRIA (2004)
BBDO Vienna
Jeep

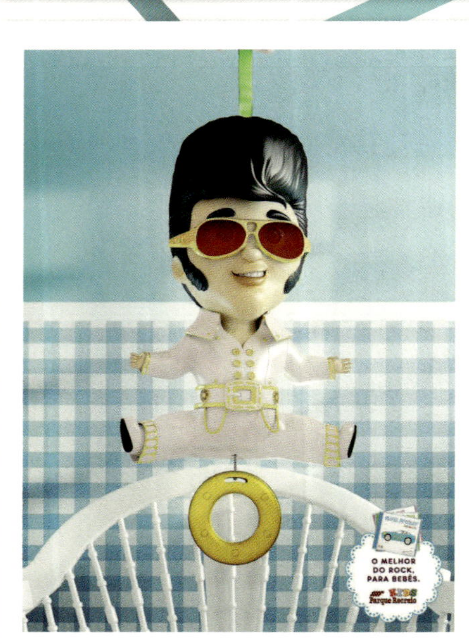

BRÉSIL BRAZIL (2012)
Mota Comunicação
Parque Recreio
"The best of pop, for babies."

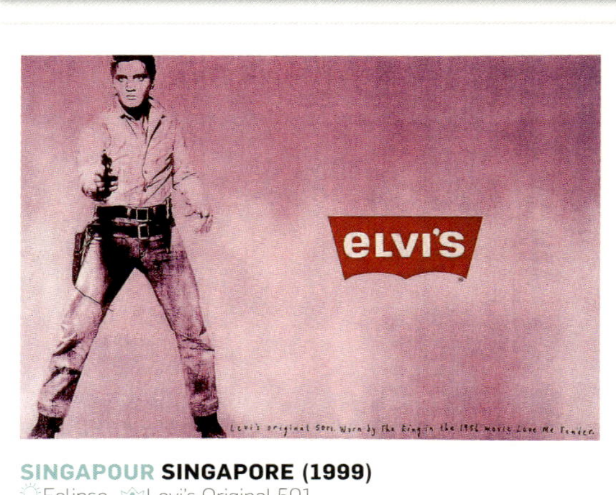

SINGAPOUR SINGAPORE (1999)
Eclipse
Levi's Original 501
Worn by the king in the 1956 movie "Love me tender"

ELVIS

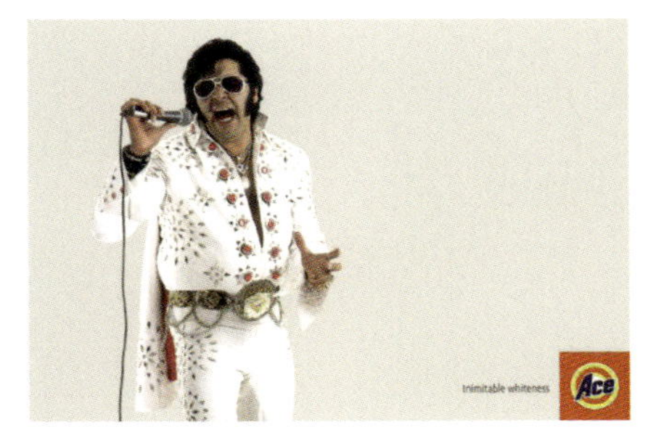

MEXIQUE MEXICO (2005)
Leo Burnett Mexico • Ace Detergent
Inimitable whiteness

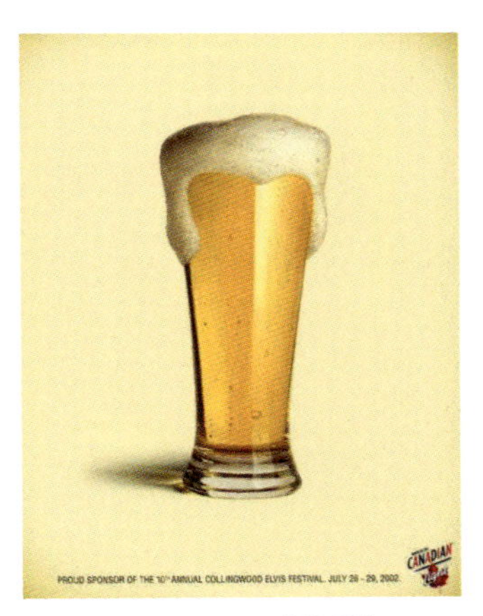

CANADA CANADA (2002)
Bensimon Byrne, Toronto
Canadian Light Beer
Proud sponsor of the 10th annual
Collingwood Elvis Festival

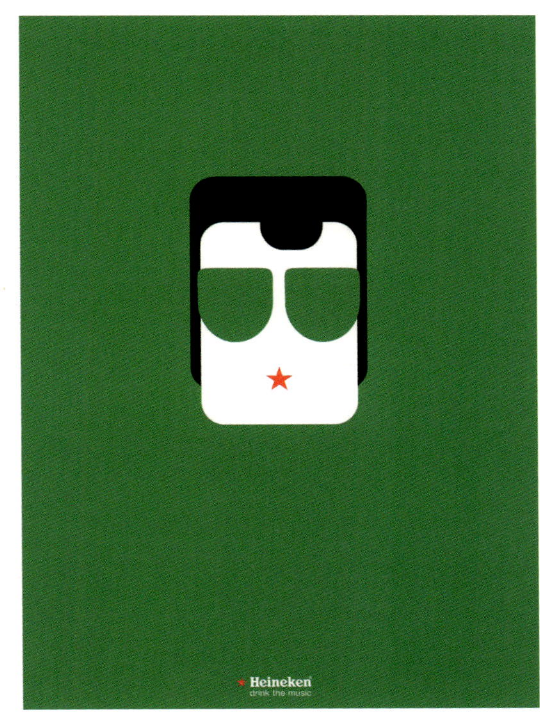

SUISSE SWITZERLAND (2006)
Publicis Zurich • Heineken
Drink the music

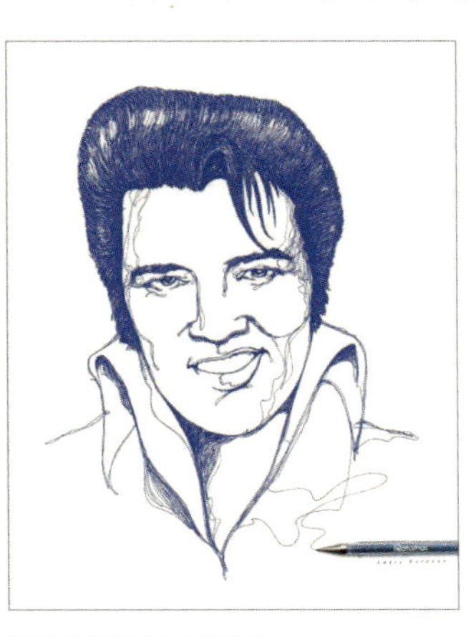

INDE INDIA (2004)
Mudra DDB New Delhi
Rotomac
Lasts forever

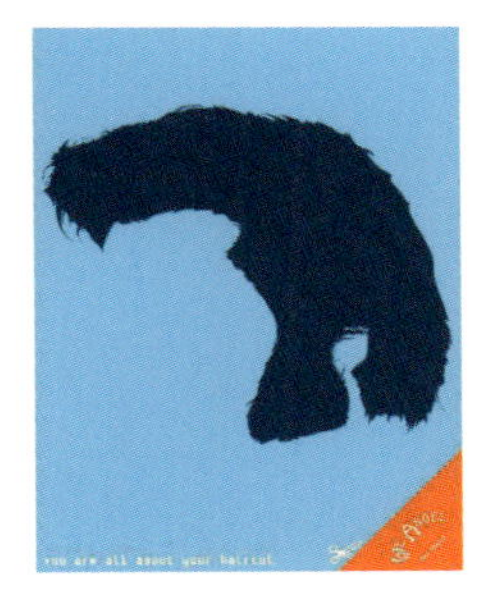

**BRÉSIL
BRAZIL (2005)**
Lowe Sao Paulo
We Angel Hair saloon
You are all about
your haircut

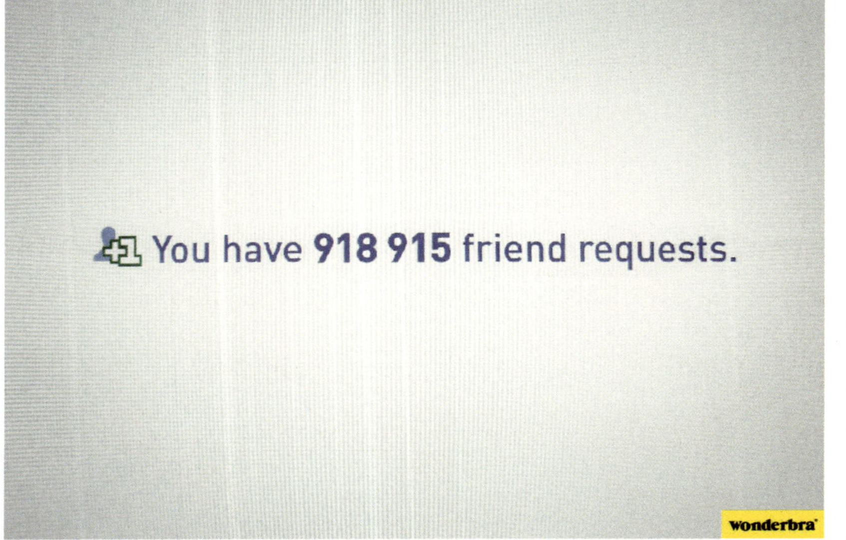

FRANCE FRANCE (2009)
Publicis Conseil Wonderbra

« Une affiche que j'ai particulièrement « liké ». Ça change de ces pubs Wonderbra qui montrent des seins en forme de ballons ou des réactions de mecs qui bavent. C'est aussi une des premières pubs qui a détourné les codes de Facebook avec humour. On n'a pas fait beaucoup mieux depuis… »
"A placement that I particularly "like". It's a change from Wonderbra adverts that show balloon shaped breasts or the reactions from drooling guys. It also was one of the first ads that put a new twist on the Facebook experience. We haven't done much better since."

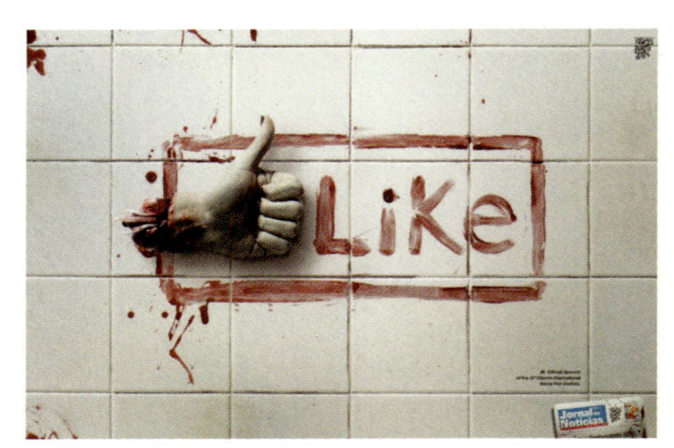

PORTUGAL PORTUGAL (2011)
Draft FCB Lisbon Jornal de Noticias
Official sponsor of the 31th Horror Film Festival

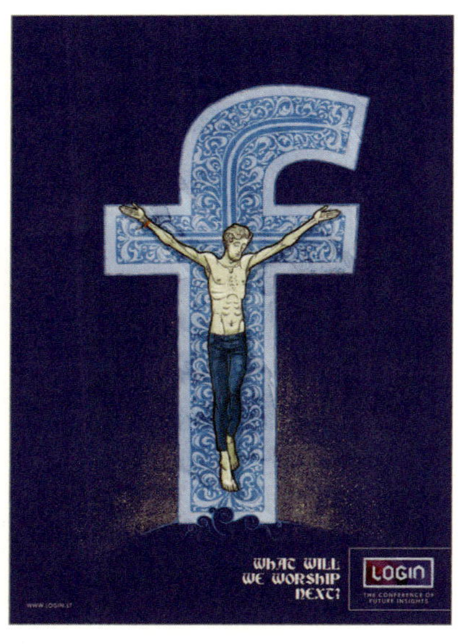

LITUANIE LITHUANIA (2012)
New Vilnius Login Conference
What will we worship next?

ISRAEL ISRAEL (2009)
Brickman Ramat Gan
Tzomet Sfarim
Face a book. Disconnect for a while.
Read a book.

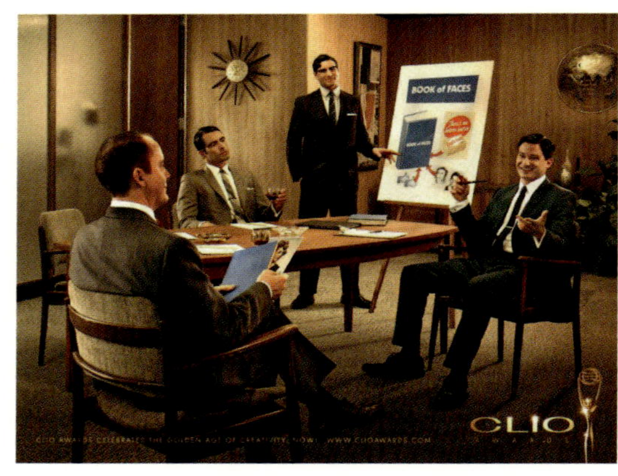

FINLANDE FINLAND (2011)
Hasan & Partners Helsinki Clio Awards
(Book of faces) Clio Awards celebrates the golden age of creativity : now!

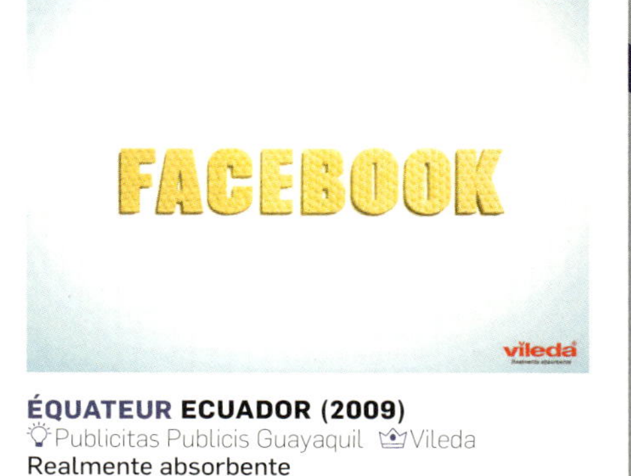

ÉQUATEUR ECUADOR (2009)
Publicitas Publicis Guayaquil — Vileda
Realmente absorbente

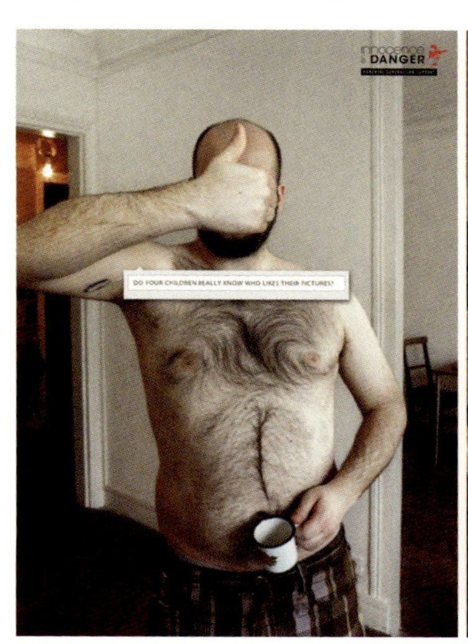
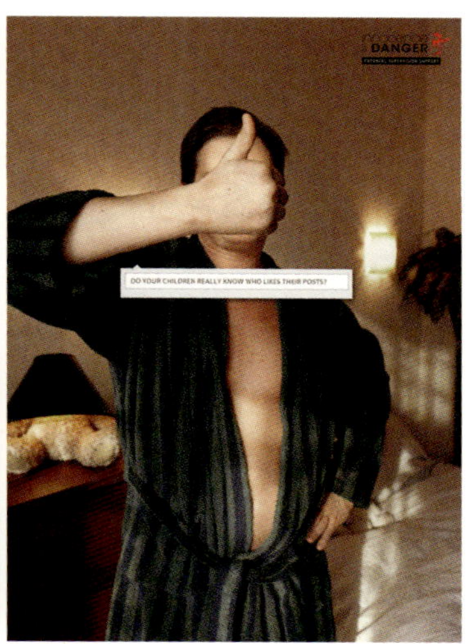

FRANCE FRANCE (2012)
Herezie Paris — Innocence in danger
Do your children really know who likes their pictures?

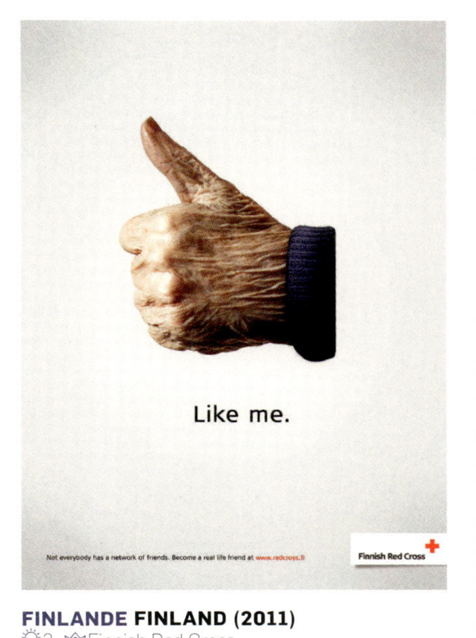

FINLANDE FINLAND (2011)
? — Finnish Red Cross
Like Me. Not everybody has a network of friends.

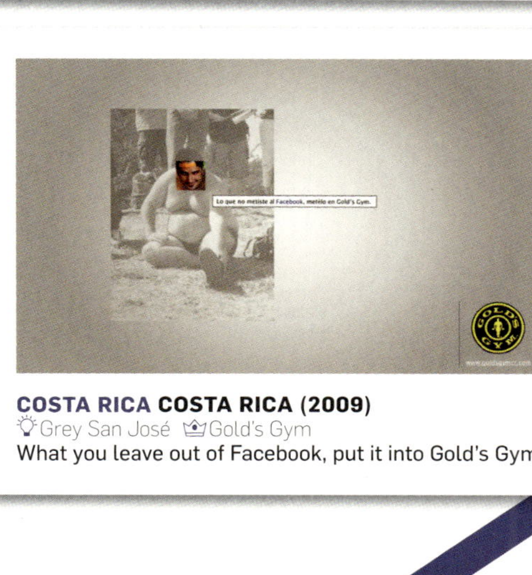

COSTA RICA COSTA RICA (2009)
Grey San José — Gold's Gym
What you leave out of Facebook, put it into Gold's Gym

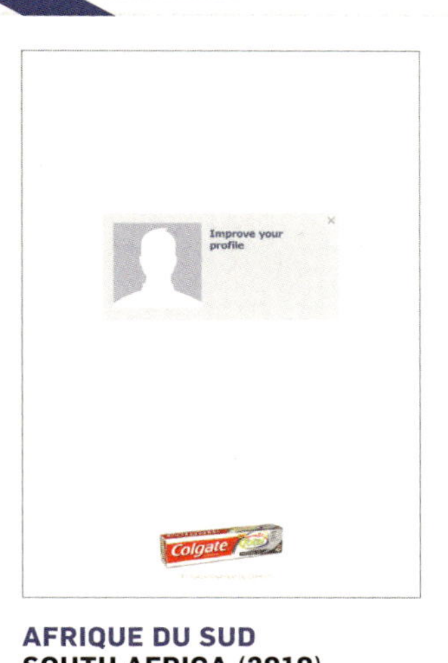

**AFRIQUE DU SUD
SOUTH AFRICA (2010)**
Young & Rubicam Johannesburg
Colgate
Improve your profile

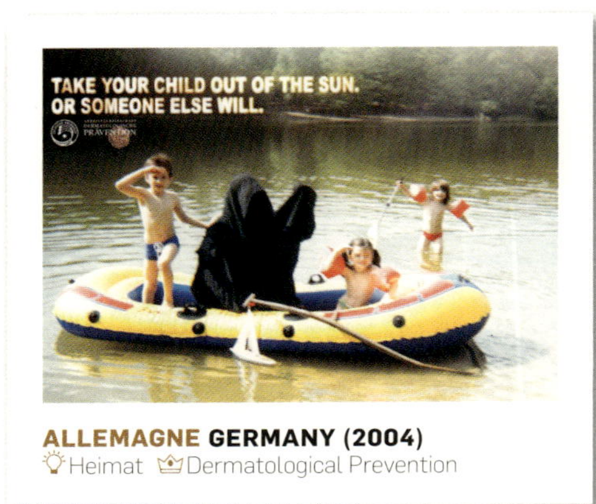

ALLEMAGNE GERMANY (2004)
Heimat — Dermatological Prevention

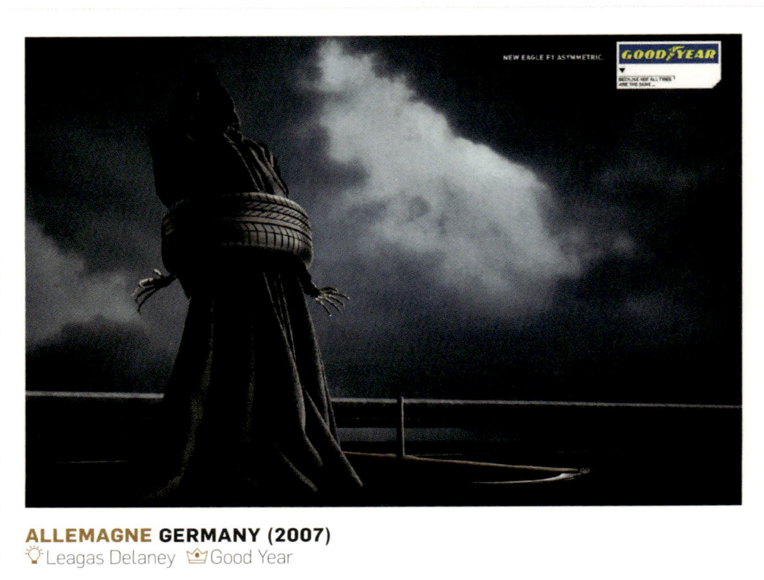

ALLEMAGNE GERMANY (2007)
Leagas Delaney — Good Year

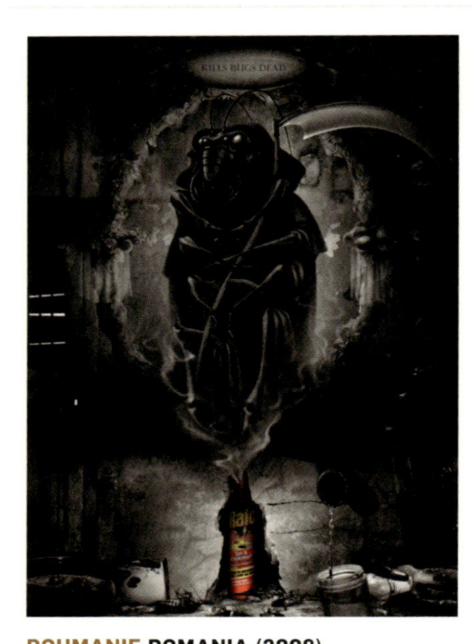

ROUMANIE ROMANIA (2008)
Draft FCB Bucharest — Raid Anti Mosquitoes

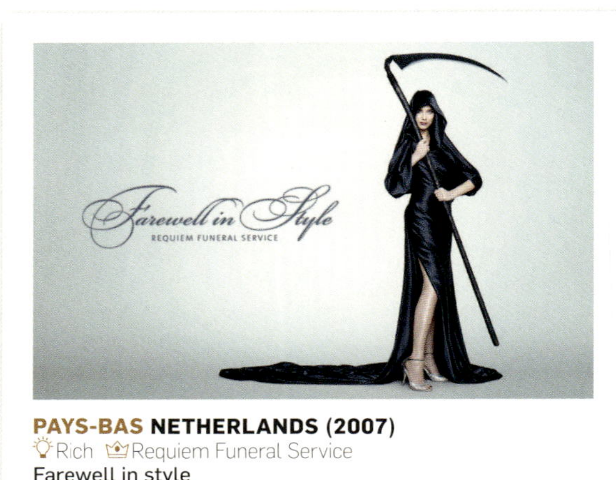

PAYS-BAS NETHERLANDS (2007)
Rich — Requiem Funeral Service
Farewell in style

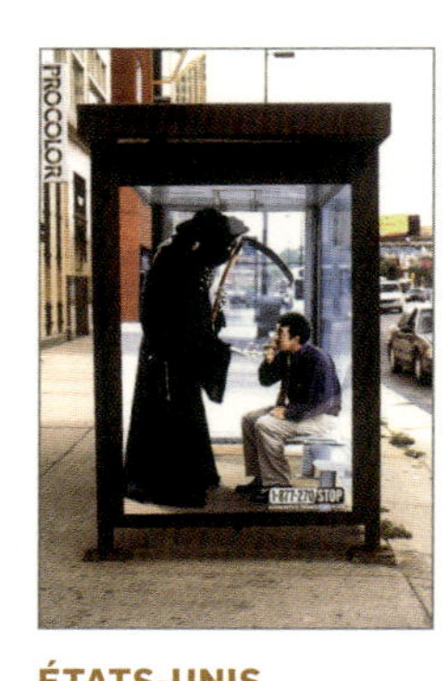

ÉTATS-UNIS UNITED STATES (2002)
Clarity Coverdale Fury — Minnesota Partnership for action against Tobacco

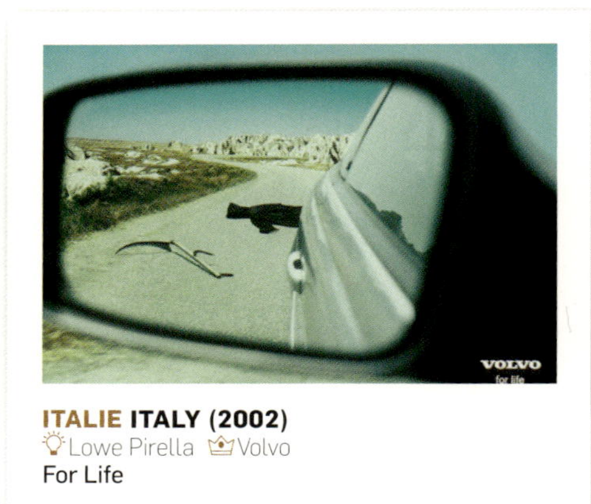

ITALIE ITALY (2002)
Lowe Pirella — Volvo
For Life

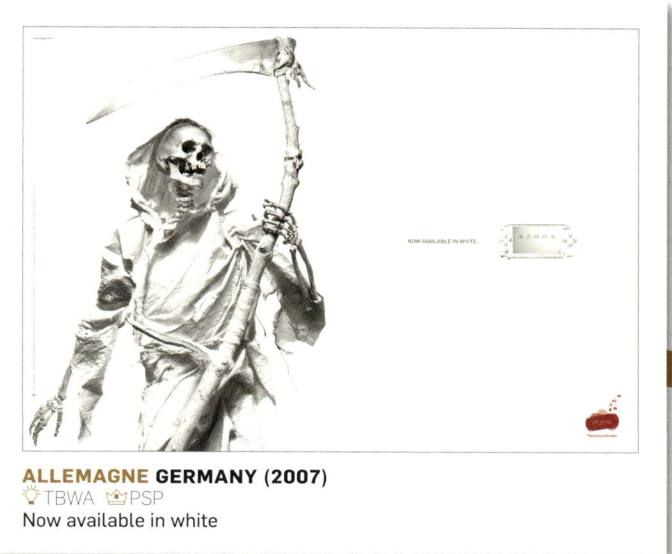

ALLEMAGNE GERMANY (2007)
TBWA PSP
Now available in white

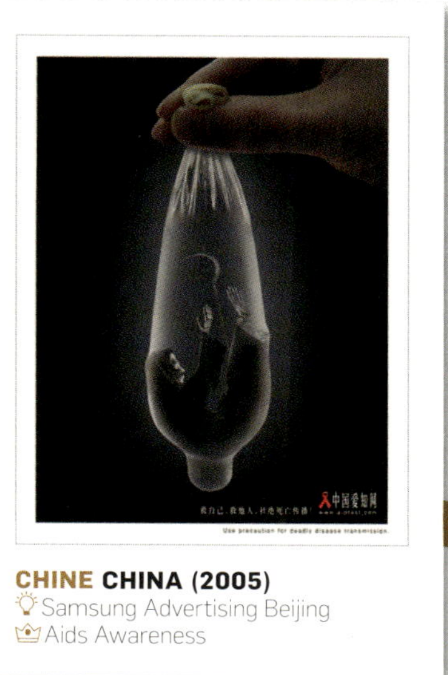

CHINE CHINA (2005)
Samsung Advertising Beijing
Aids Awareness

LA FAUCHEUSE
№ 41
THE REAPER

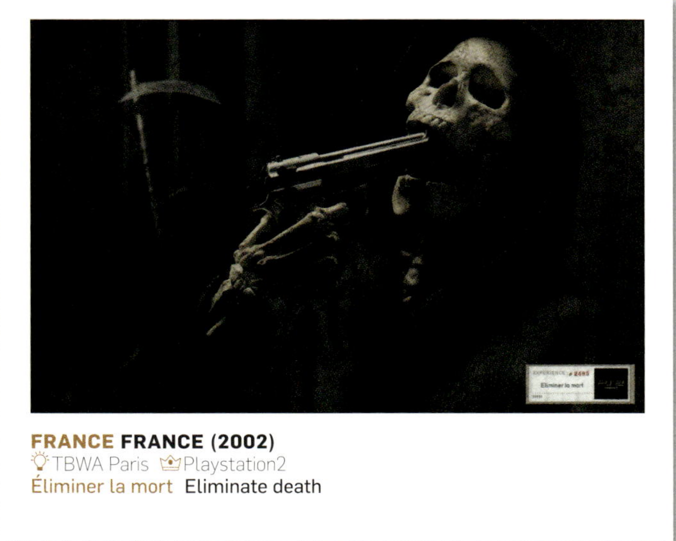

FRANCE FRANCE (2002)
TBWA Paris Playstation2
Éliminer la mort Eliminate death

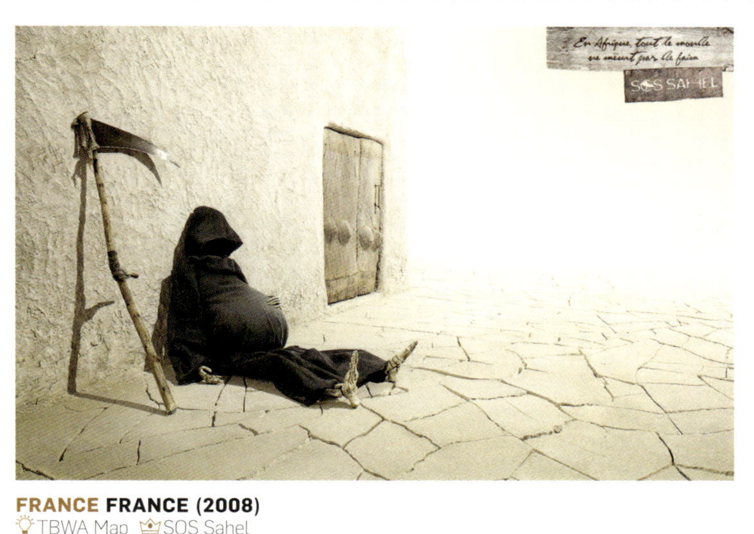

FRANCE FRANCE (2008)
TBWA Map SOS Sahel
En afrique tout le monde ne meurt pas de faim
In Africa, not everyone dies of hunger

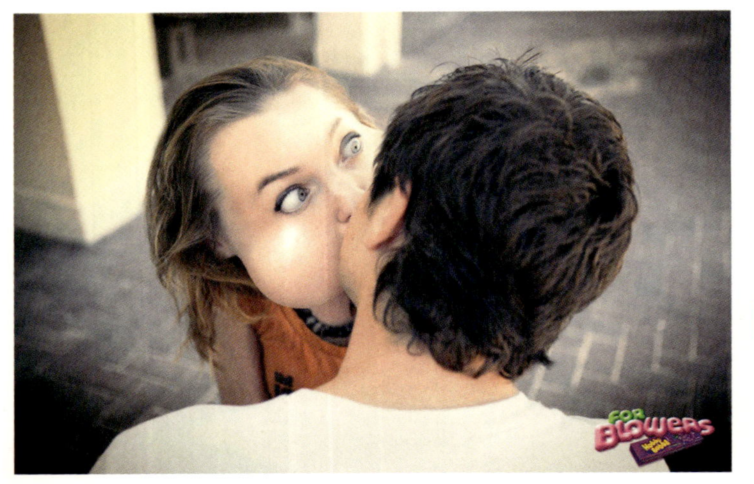

AUSTRALIE AUSTRALIA (2007)
BBDO Sydney Hubba Bubba Chewing Gum
For Blowers

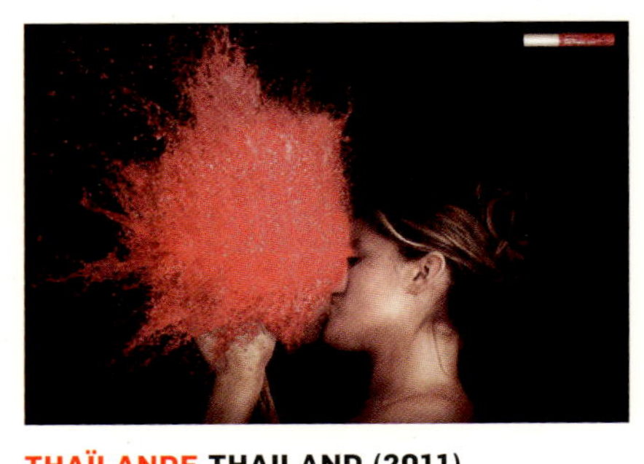

THAÏLANDE THAILAND (2011)
BBDO Bangkok Tony Moly Make Up

FRENCH KISSES

Nº42

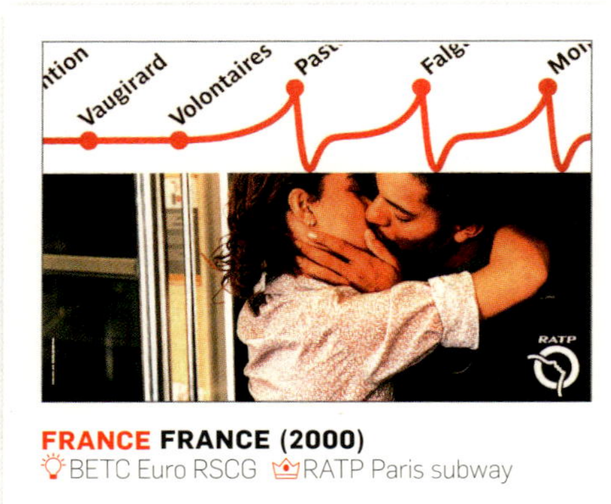

FRANCE FRANCE (2000)
BETC Euro RSCG RATP Paris subway

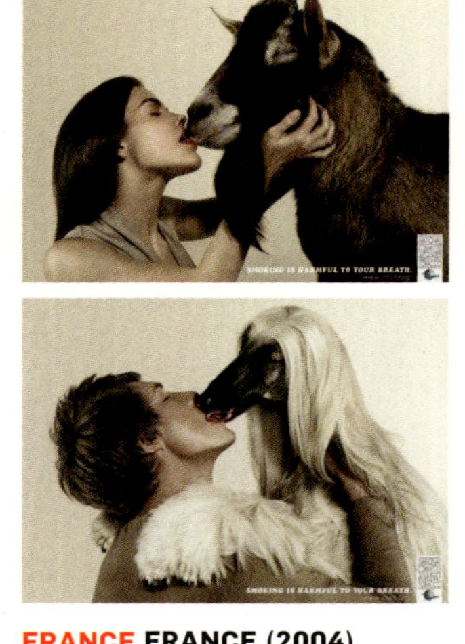

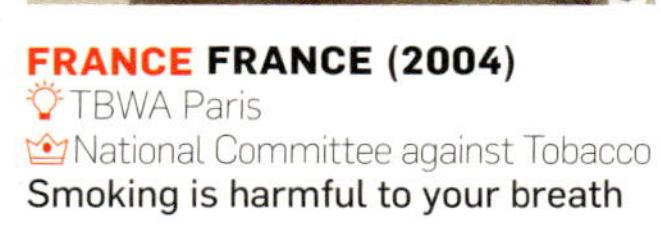

FRANCE FRANCE (2004)
TBWA Paris
National Committee against Tobacco
Smoking is harmful to your breath

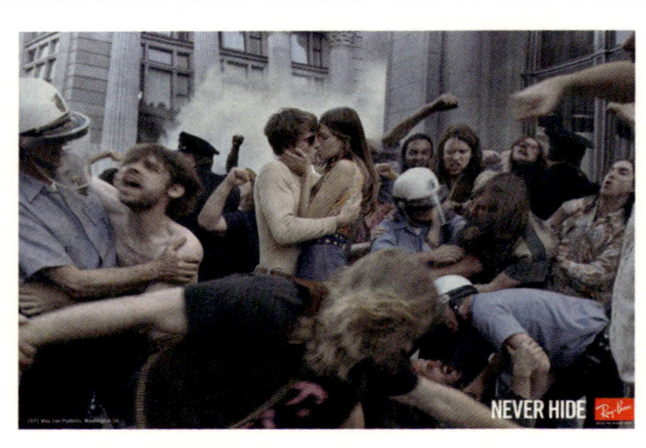

FRANCE FRANCE (2012)
Marcel Paris Ray Ban
Never Hide (1971 May Day Protests, washington DC)

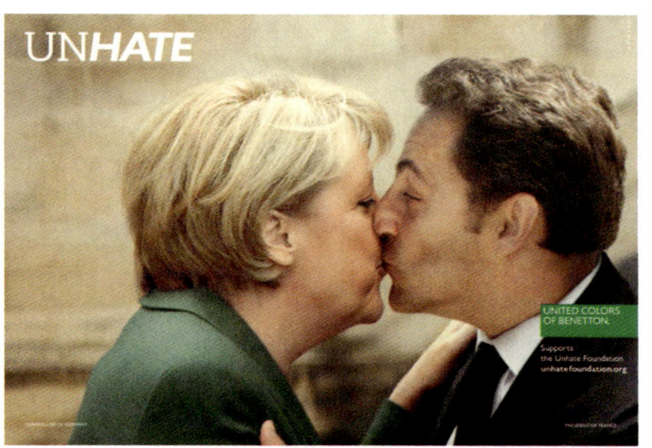

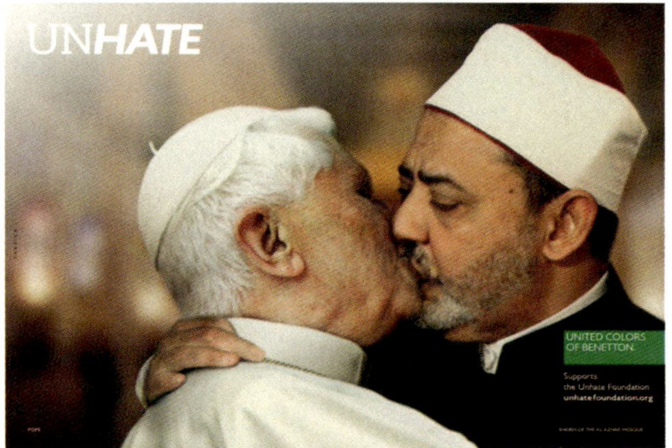

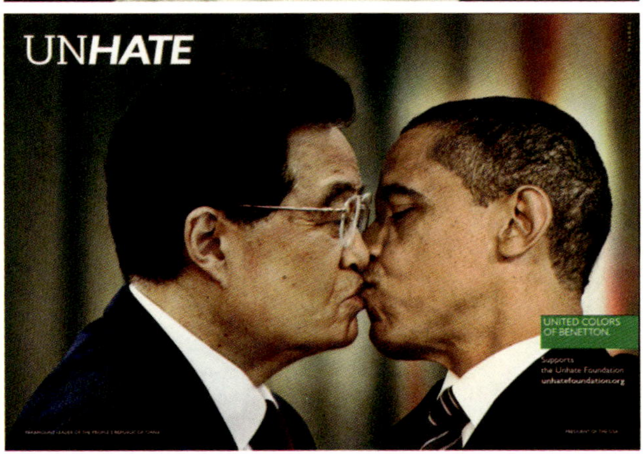

ITALIE ITALY (2011)
La Fabrica Treviso & 72andsunny Amsterdam Benetton

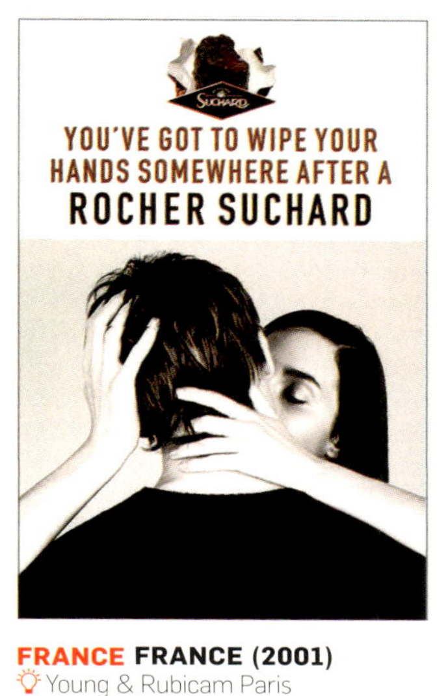

FRANCE FRANCE (2001)
Young & Rubicam Paris
Rocher Suchard

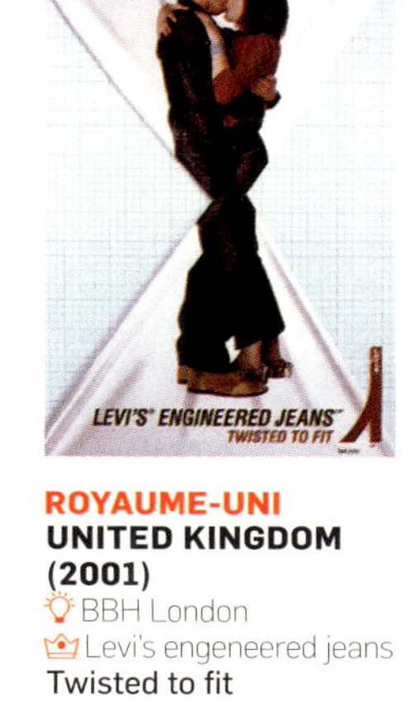

ROYAUME-UNI UNITED KINGDOM (2001)
BBH London
Levi's engeneered jeans
Twisted to fit

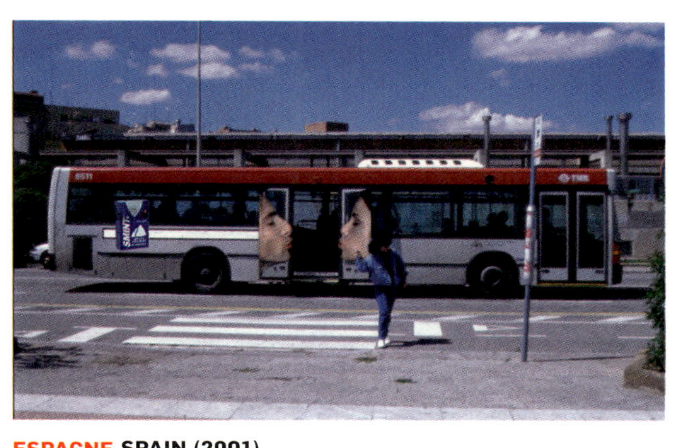

ESPAGNE SPAIN (2001)
DDB Barcelona Smint

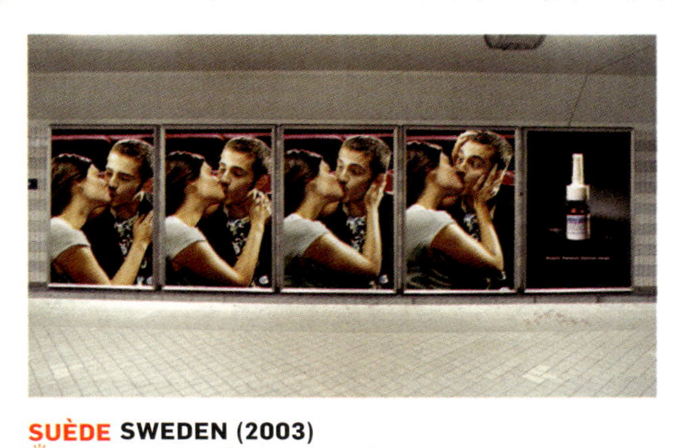

SUÈDE SWEDEN (2003)
Akestam Holst Nezeril nasal spray
Relieves blocked noses

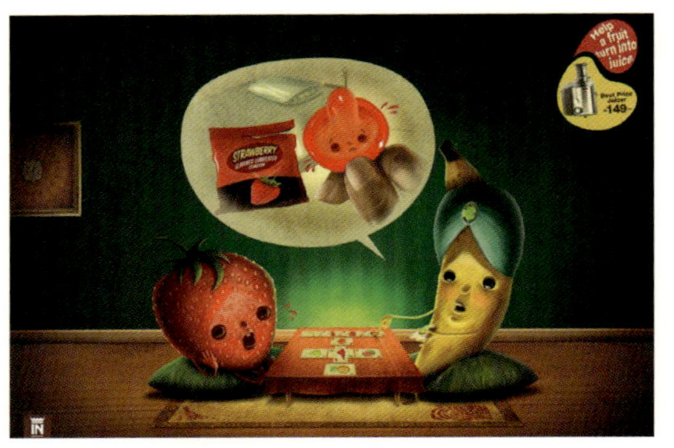

BRÉSIL BRAZIL (2011)
Propeg · Insunante - Best price juicer
Help a fruit turn into juice

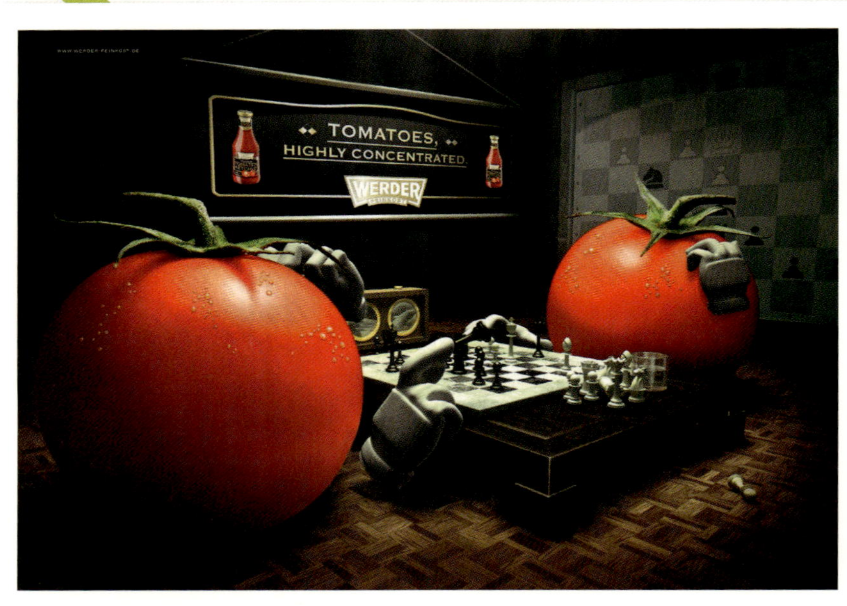

ALLEMAGNE GERMANY (2008)
Scholz & Friends Berlin · Werder Tomato Ketchup

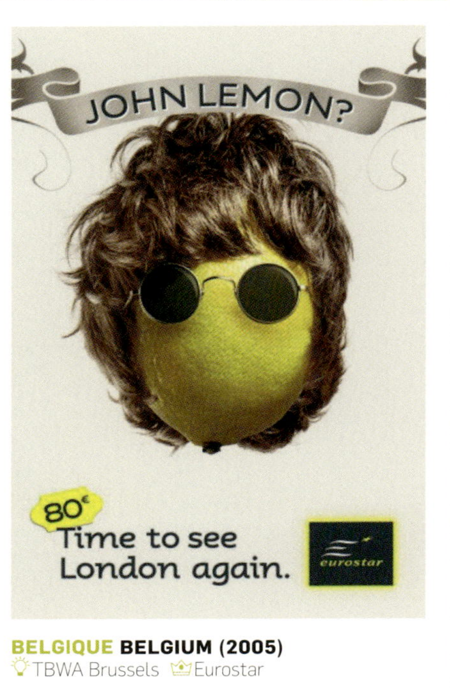

BELGIQUE BELGIUM (2005)
TBWA Brussels · Eurostar

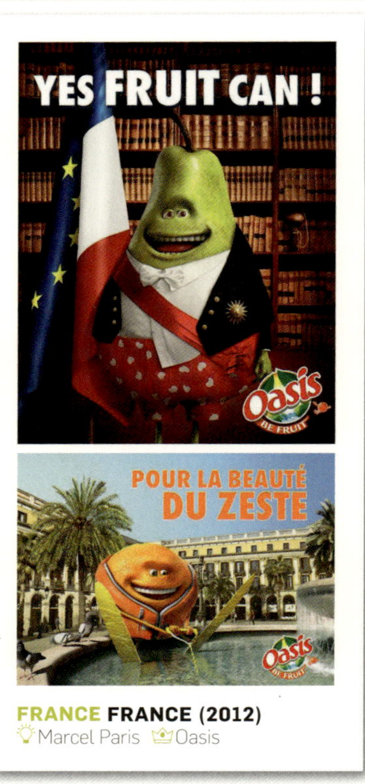

FRANCE FRANCE (2012)
Marcel Paris · Oasis

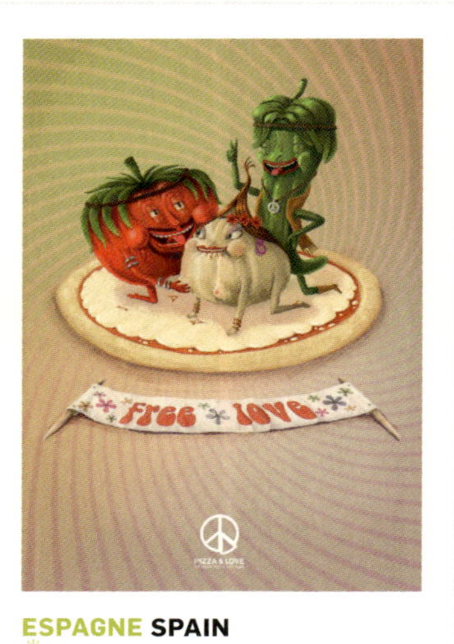

ESPAGNE SPAIN
Contrapunto
Pizza & Love Restaurant

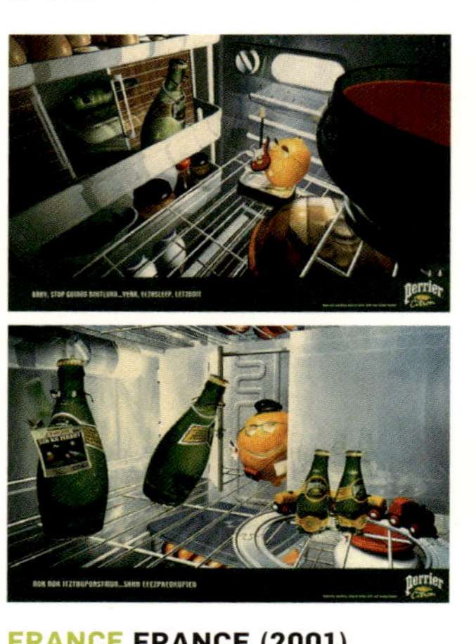

FRANCE FRANCE (2001)
Ogilvy & Mather · Perrier
Baby, stop goinon boutluru... yeah,
eezasleep, letzdoit

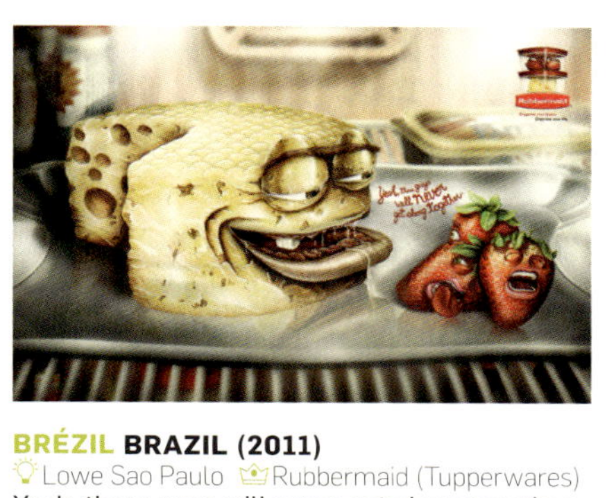
BRÉZIL BRAZIL (2011)
Lowe Sao Paulo · Rubbermaid (Tupperwares)
Yeah, these guys will never get along together

Brandt

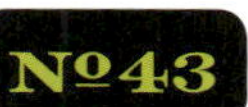

FRANCE FRANCE (2007)
DDB Paris · Brandt refrigerators
Don't let smells mix

FRUITS ET LÉGUMES HUMANISÉS

№ 43

HUMANISED FRUITS AND VEGETABLES

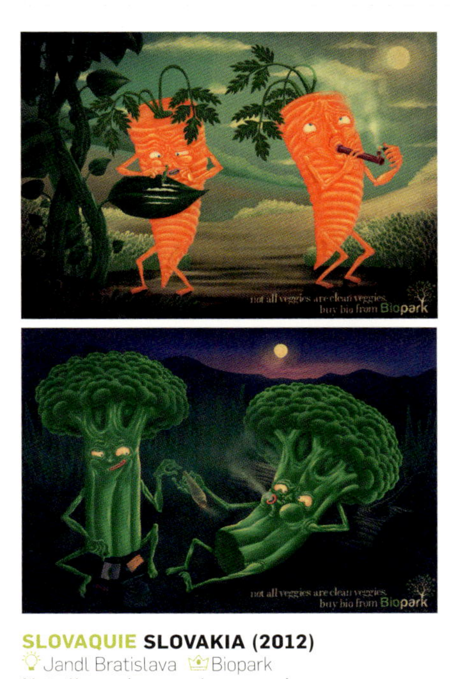

SLOVAQUIE SLOVAKIA (2012)
Jandl Bratislava · Biopark
Not all veggies are clean veggies.
Buy bio from Biopark

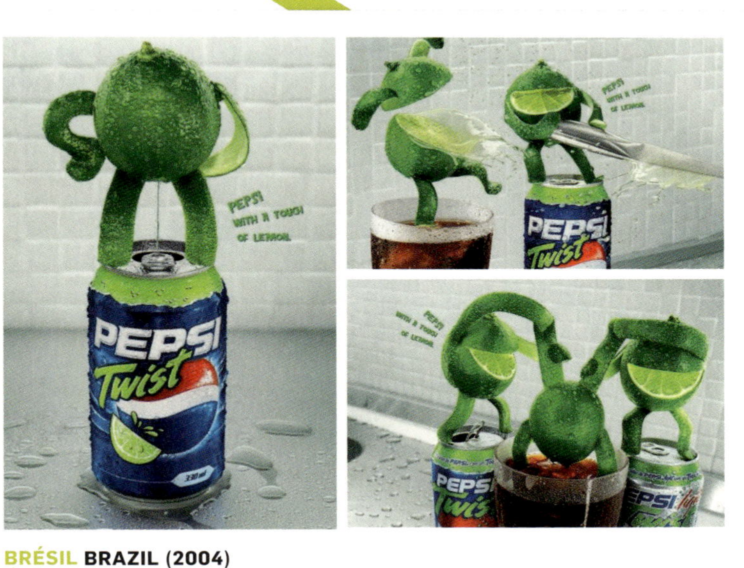

BRÉSIL BRAZIL (2004)
Almap BBDO · Pepsi Twist
With a touch of lemon

GODZILLA

№ 44

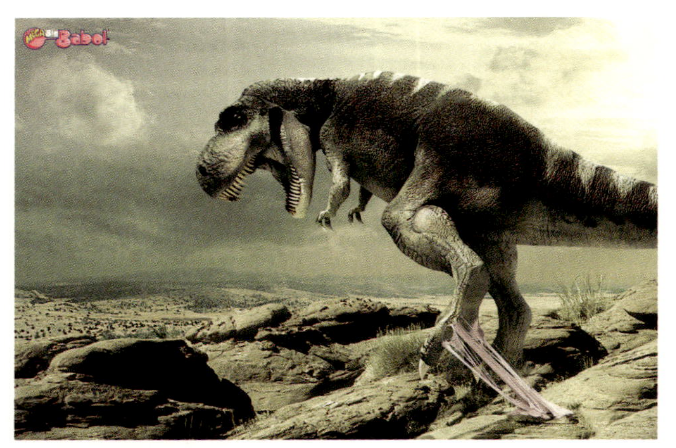

INDONÉSIE INDONESIA (2007)
Draft FCB Mega Big Babol Chewing Gum

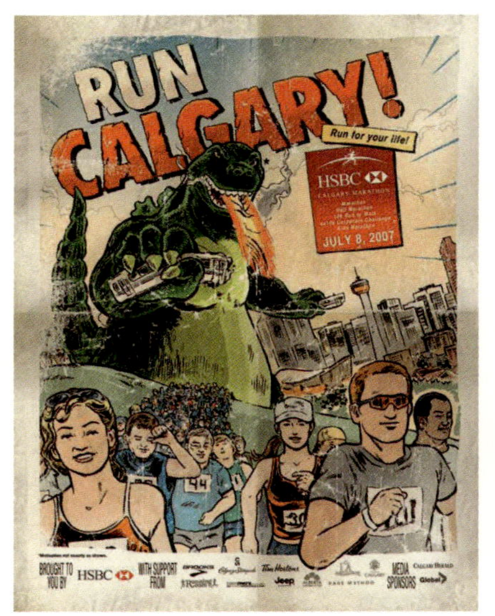

CANADA CANADA (2007)
Rare Method Calgary Marathon
Run Calgary! Run for your life

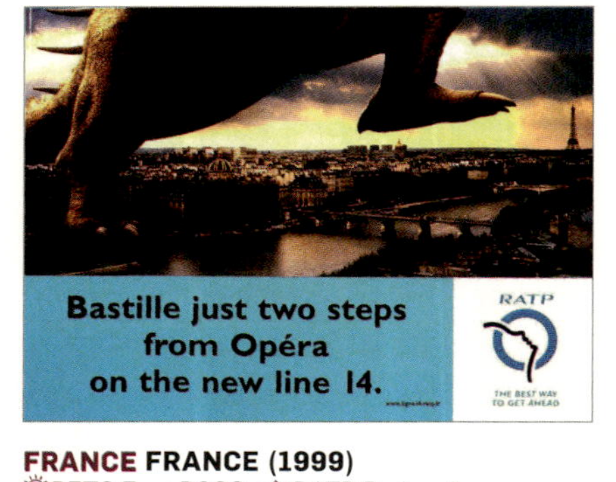

FRANCE FRANCE (1999)
BETC Euro RSCG RATP Paris subway

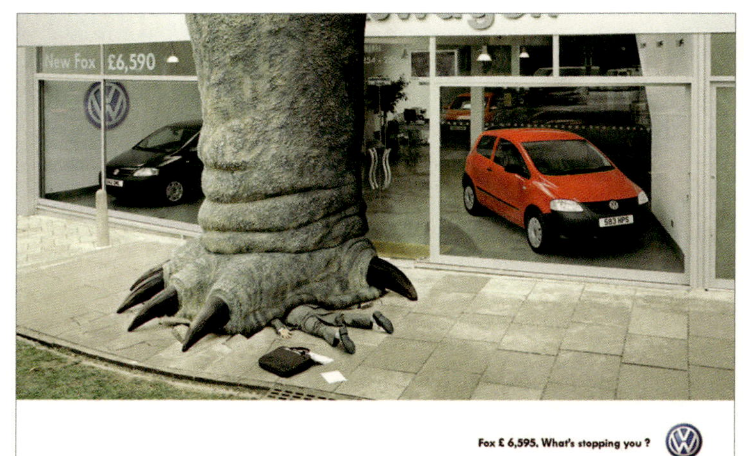

ROYAUME-UNI UNITED KINGDOM (2006)
DDB London Volkswagen Fox
6595£. What's stopping you?

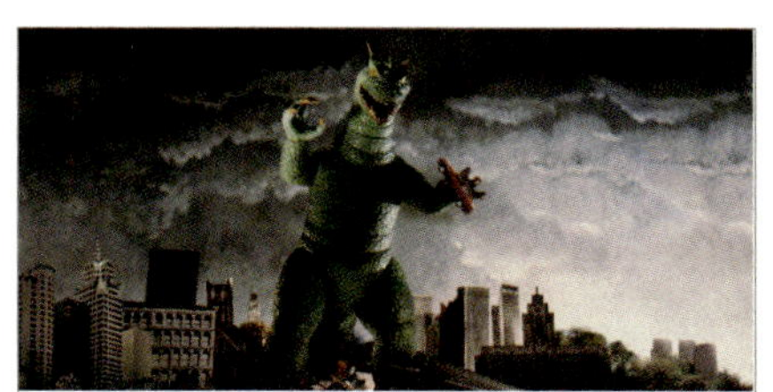

CHINE CHINA (2008)
BBDO · Shanghai Metro
Stay Below

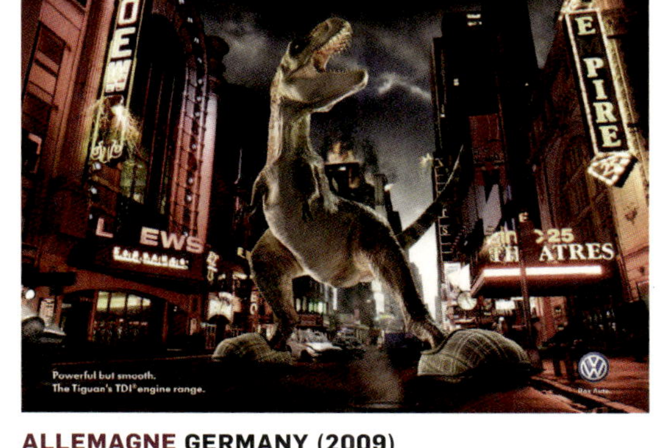

ALLEMAGNE GERMANY (2009)
Grabarz + Partner Hamburg · Volkswagen Tiguan TDI
Powerful but smooth

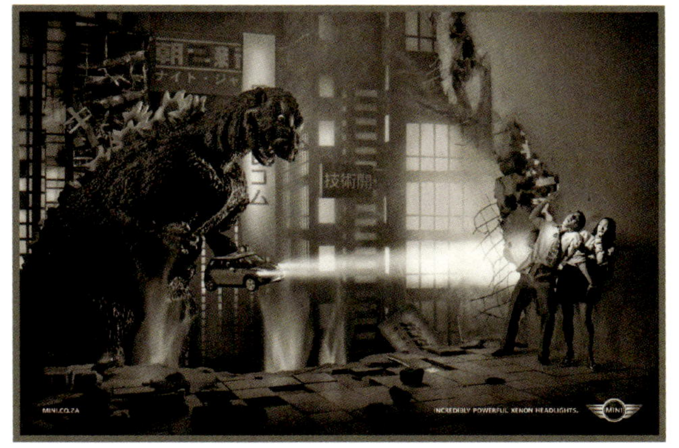

AFRIQUE DU SUD SOUTH AFRICA (2008)
King James · BMW Mini
Incredibly powerful xenon headlights

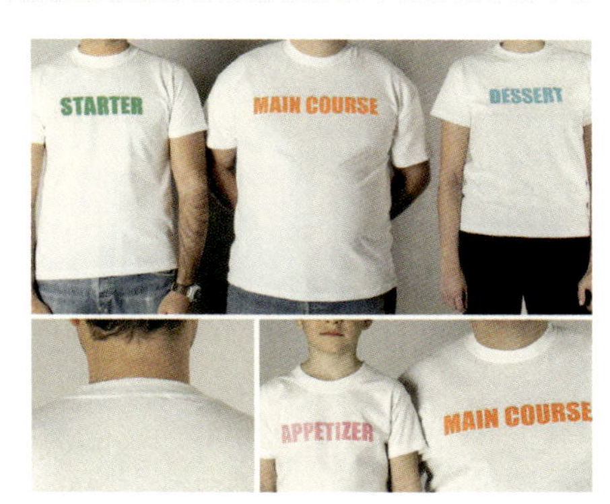

ESPAGNE SPAIN (2004)
Leo Burnett · Sitges Fantasy Film Festival
Godzilla's 50th anniversary

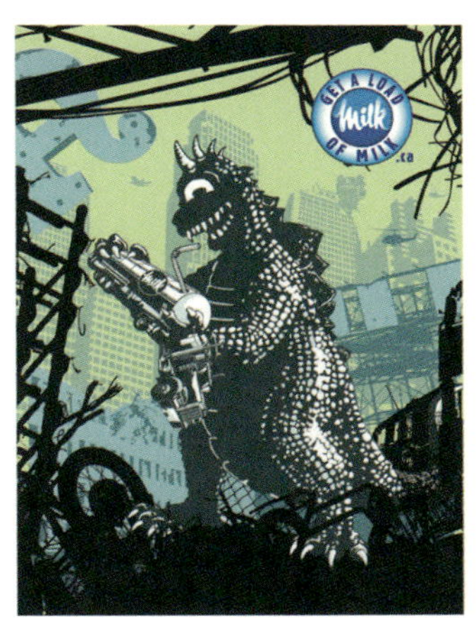

CANADA CANADA (2007)
Due North · Milk
Get a load of milk

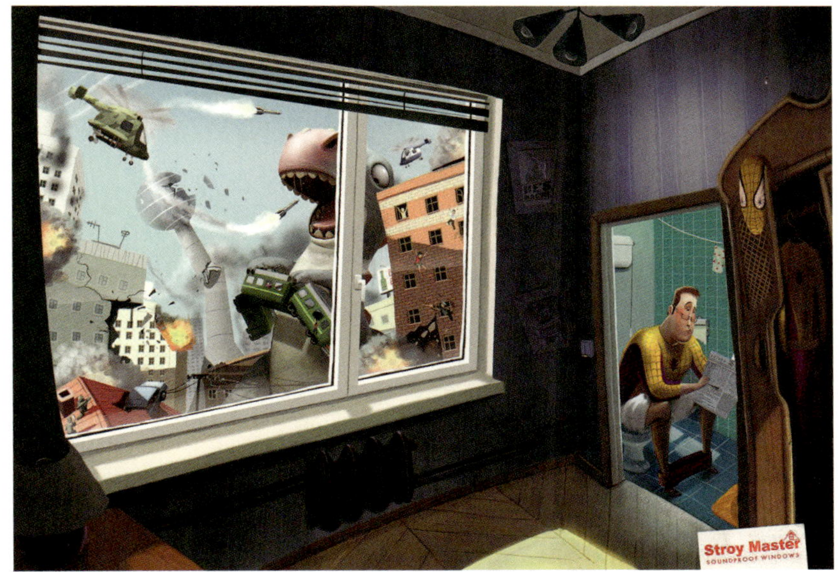

RUSSIE RUSSIA (2011)
BBDO Moscow · Story Master
Soundproof windows

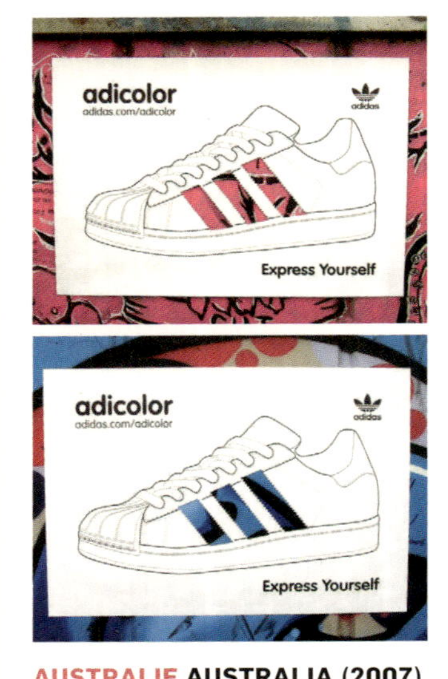

AUSTRALIE AUSTRALIA (2007)
Smart Melbourne
Adidas Adicolor
Express Yourself

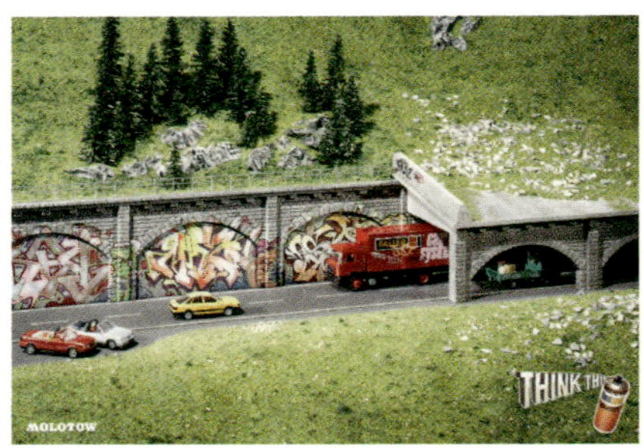

FRANCE FRANCE (2008)
TBWA Map Molotow Spray Paints
Think Thin

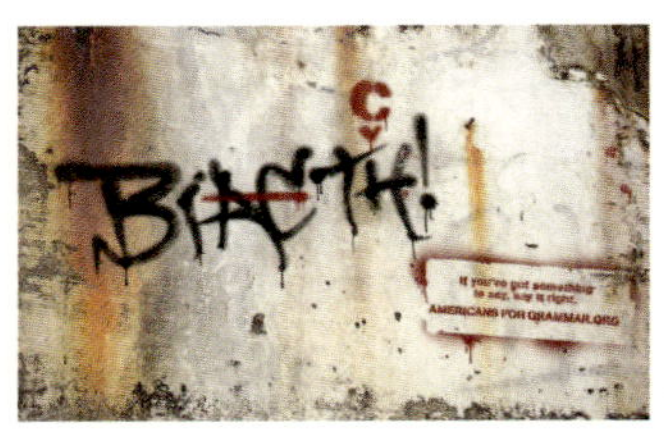

**ÉTATS-UNIS
UNITED STATES (2012)**
Young & Rubicam Chicago
Americans for Grammar
If you've got something to say,
say it right

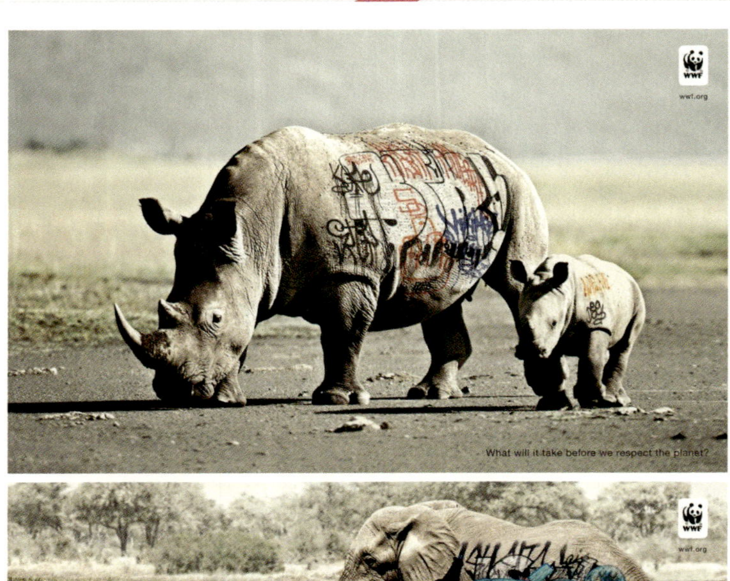

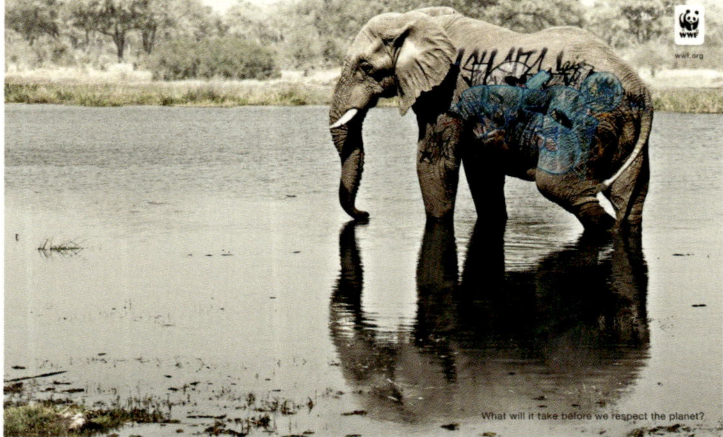

FRANCE FRANCE (2010)
Ogilvy & Mather Paris WWF
What will it take before we respect the planet?

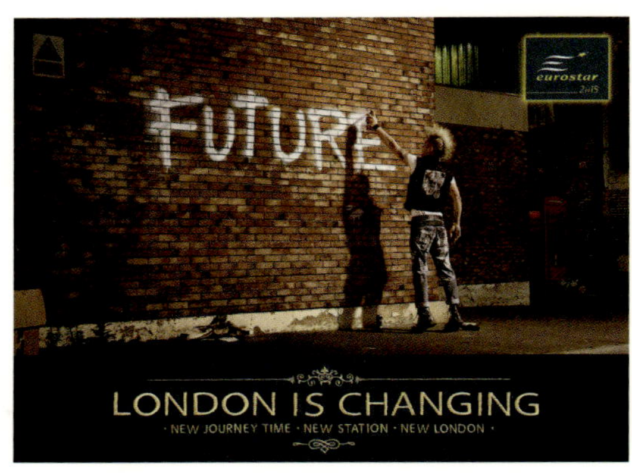

FRANCE FRANCE (2007)
Leg Eurostar
New journey time, new station, new london

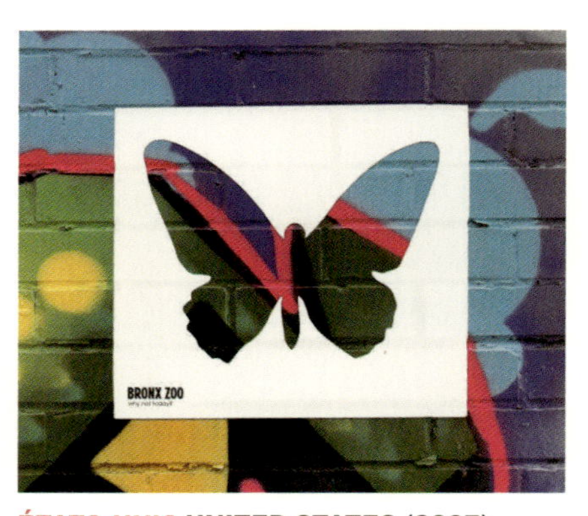

ÉTATS-UNIS UNITED STATES (2007)
Young & Rubicam New York Bronx Zoo
Why not today?

GRAFFITIS

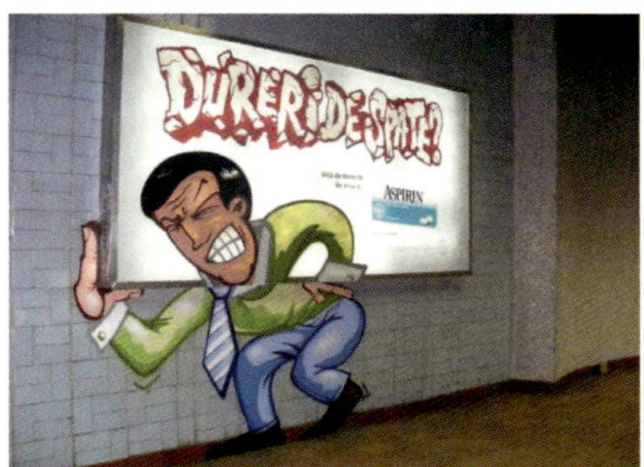

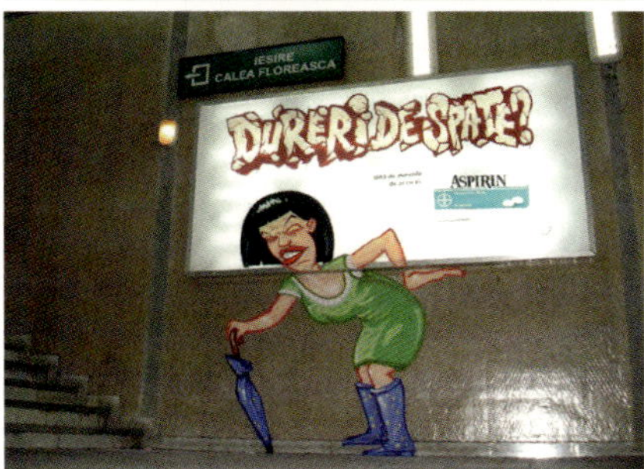

ROUMANIE ROMANIA (2009)
BBDO Bucharest · Bayer Aspirin
Back Pain?

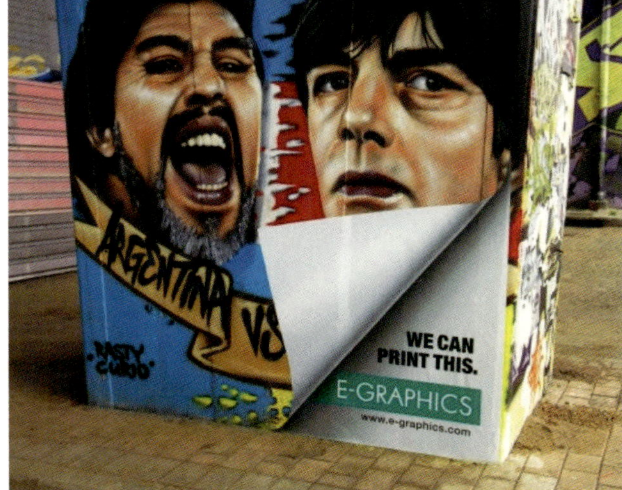

AFRIQUE DU SUD SOUTH AFRICA (2011)
TBWA Hunt Lascaris · E-Graphics

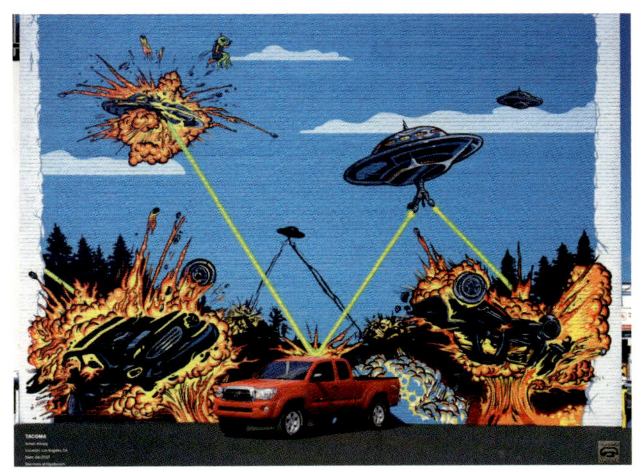

ÉTATS-UNIS UNITED STATES (2007)
Saatchi & Saatchi Los Angeles · Toyota Tacoma

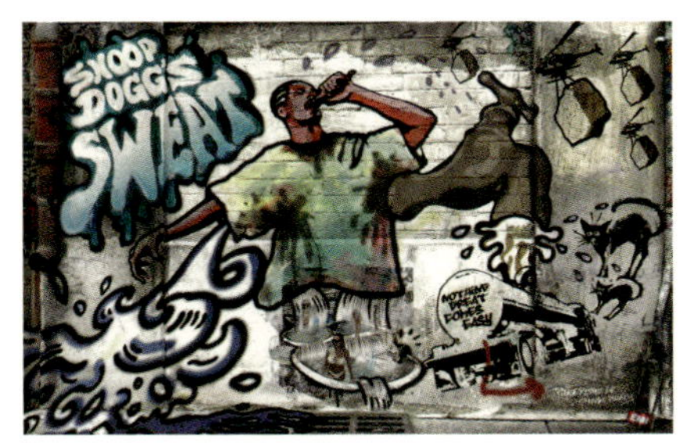

FRANCE FRANCE (2005)
TBWA Paris · EMI
Snoop dog's sweat - Nothing great comes easy
Please respect artists, stop music piracy

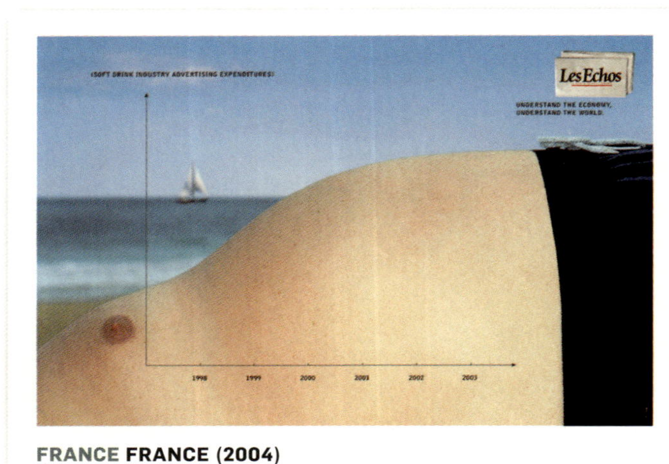

FRANCE FRANCE (2004)
BDDP&Fils   *Les Echos* newspaper
(Soft drink industry advertising expenditures... 1998, 1999, 2000...)
Understand the economy, understand the world

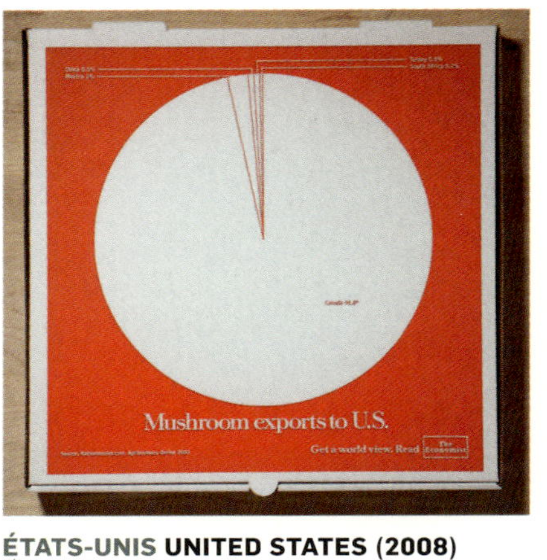

ÉTATS-UNIS UNITED STATES (2008)
BBDO New York   *The Economist*
(Branded pizza boxes targeted to students)
Mushroom exports to US
(China 0,5%, Mexico 2% ...)
Get a world view. Read The Economist

GRAPHIQUES

№46

DATA VISUALISATION

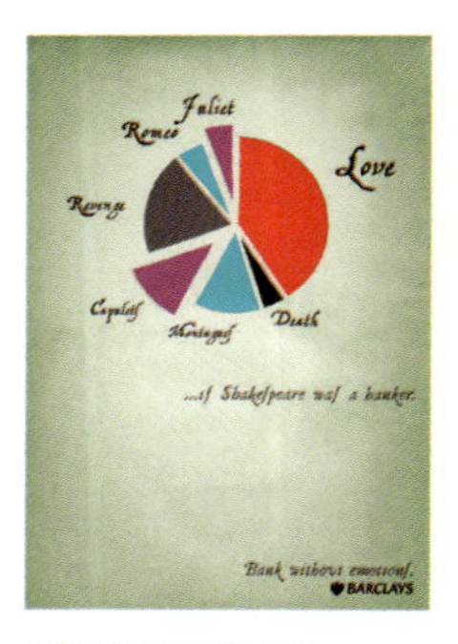

RUSSIE RUSSIA
SAA Moscow
Barclays Bank
If shakespeare was
a banker...
Bank without emotions

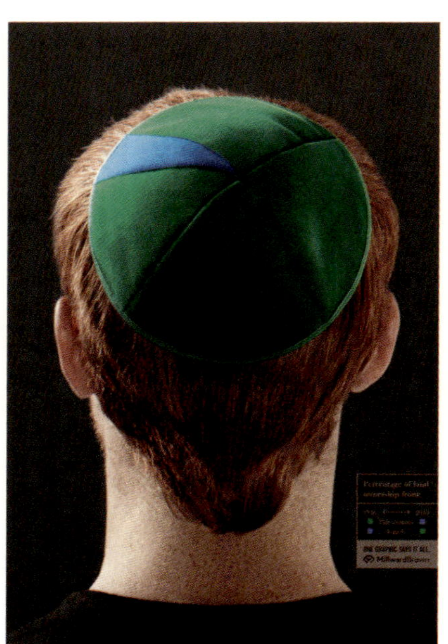

BRÉSIL BRAZIL (2011)
Young & Rubicam   Millward Brown
Percentage of land ownership from
1946 (Palestinians: Green / Israeli: Blue)
2010 (Palestinians: Blue / Israeli: Green)
One graphic says it all

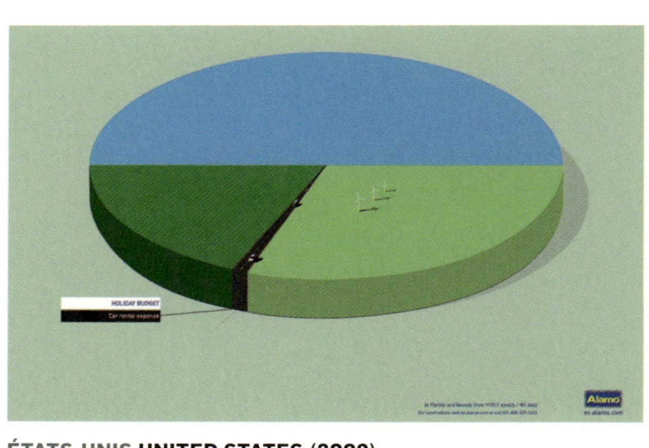

ÉTATS-UNIS UNITED STATES (2009)
DPH Miami   Alamo Car Rental
Holiday Budget / Car Rental expense

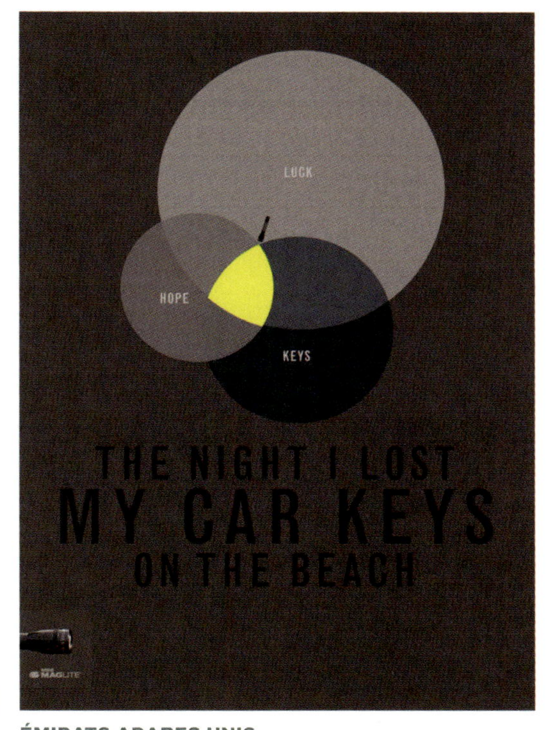

ÉMIRATS ARABES UNIS
UNITED ARAB EMIRATES (2008)
FP7 Dubai　Maglite

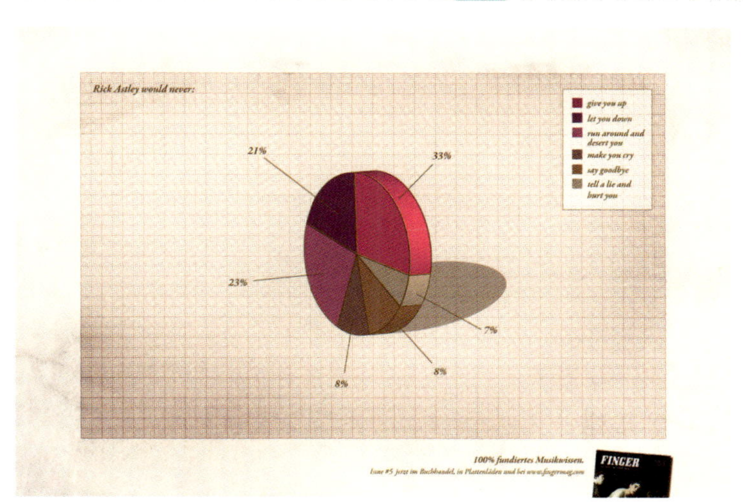

SUISSE SWITZERLAND (2008)
KSB Springer & Jacoby Zurich　Finger Music Magazine
Rick astley would never :
- Give you up
- Let you down
- Run around and desert you
- Make you cry
- Say goodbye
- Tell a lie and hurt you

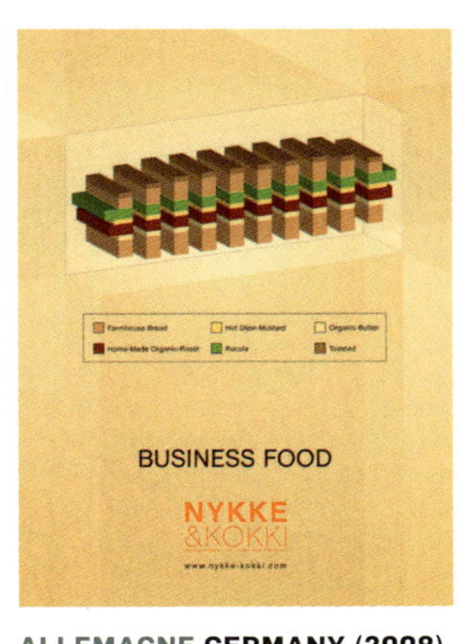

ALLEMAGNE GERMANY (2008)
Scholz & Friends Hamburg
Nykke & Kokki Business Food

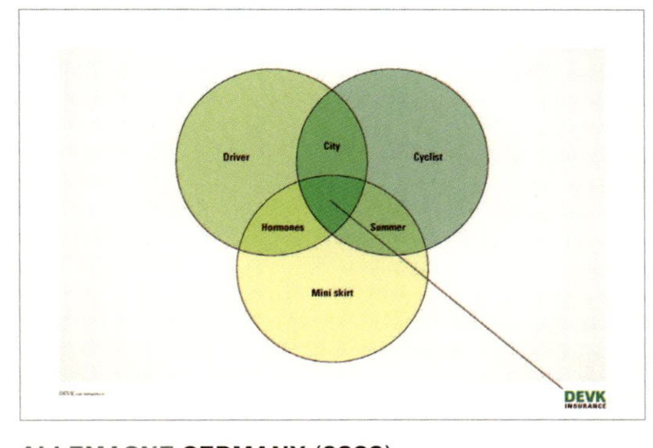

ALLEMAGNE GERMANY (2009)
Grabarz and partner Hamburg　Devk Car Insurance
Driver / City / Cyclist / Summer / Mini Skirt / Hormones

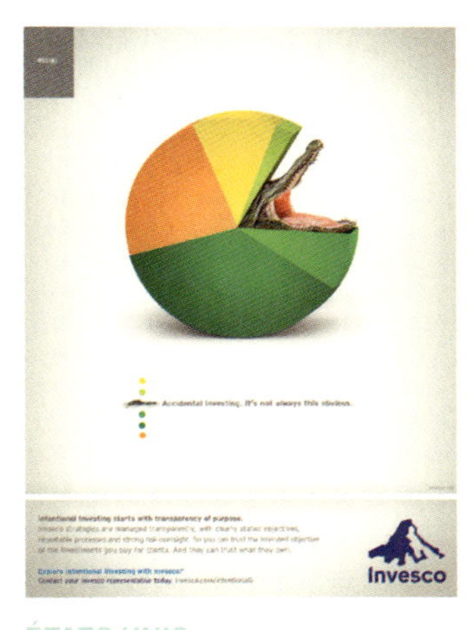

ÉTATS UNIS
UNITED STATES (2012)
Leo Burnett Chicago　Invesco
Accidental investing.
It's not always this obvious

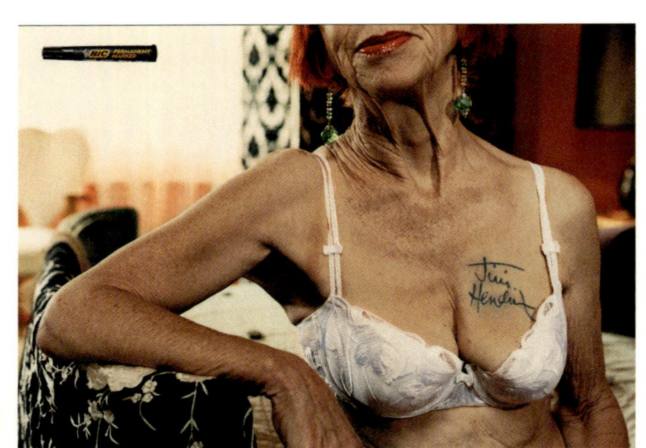

FRANCE FRANCE (2004)
TBWA Paris Bic Permanent Marker
"Jimi Hendrix"

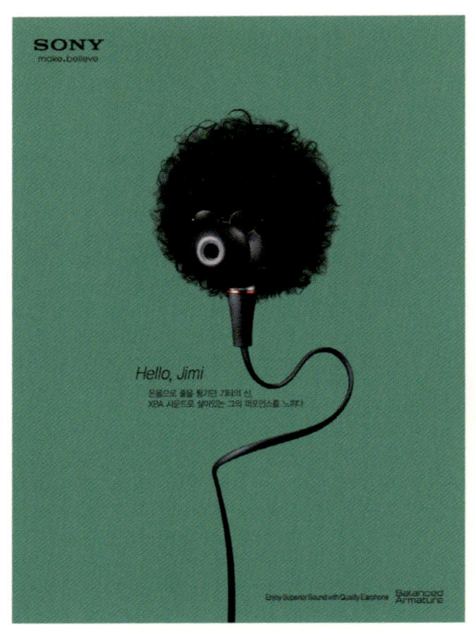

CORÉE DU SUD SOUTH KOREA (2012)
Welcomm Publicis
Sony Superior sound quality Earphone
Hello, Jimi

HENDRIX

№ 47

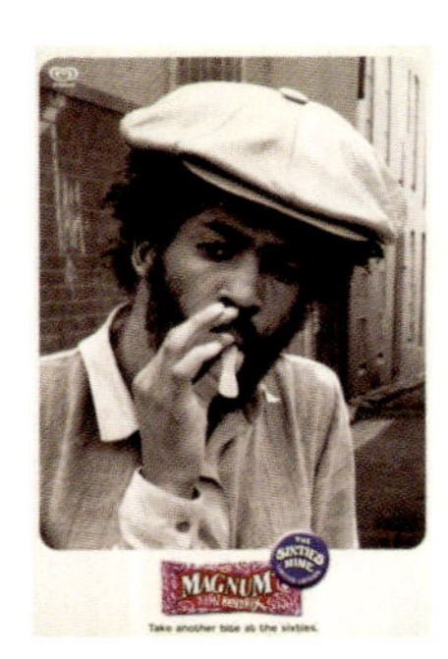

AUSTRALIE AUSTRALIA (2003)
McCann Erickson Sydney
Magnum
"The Sixties Nine"
Take another bite
at the sixties

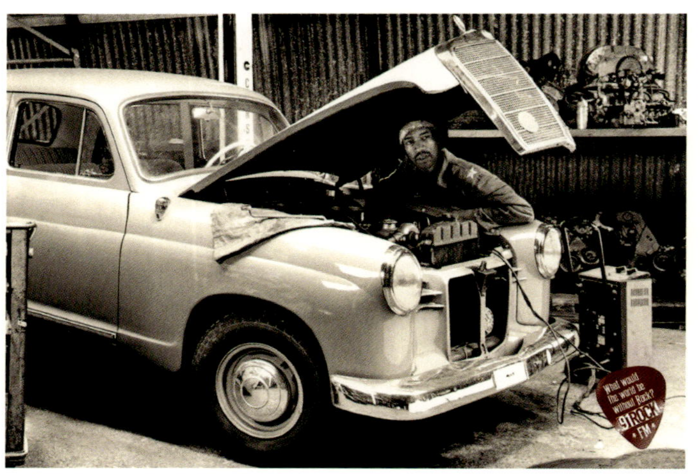

BRÉSIL BRAZIL (2010)
JWT Sao Paulo 91 Rock FM
What would the world be without Rock?

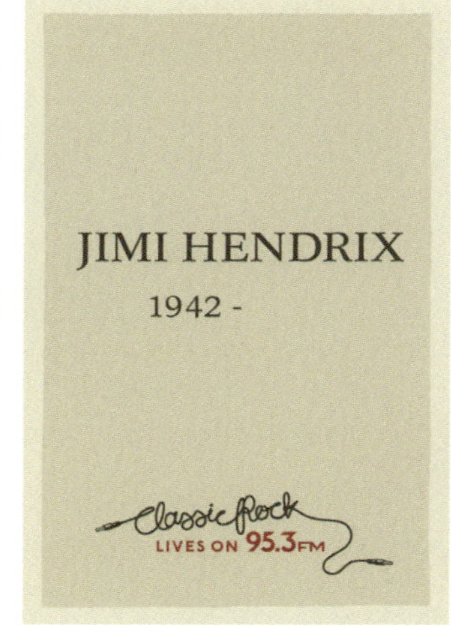

AUSTRALIE AUSTRALIA (2010)
Three Drunk Monkeys 95.3FM
Classic Rock lives on 93.3FM

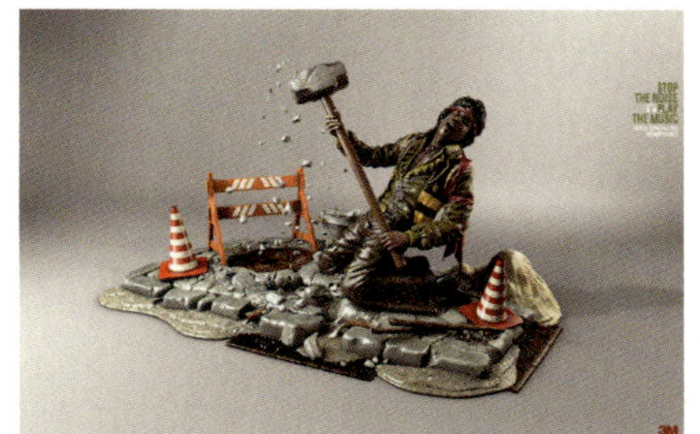

BRÉSIL BRAZIL (2012)
Grey 141 3M Noise canceling headphones
Stop The Noise. Play the music

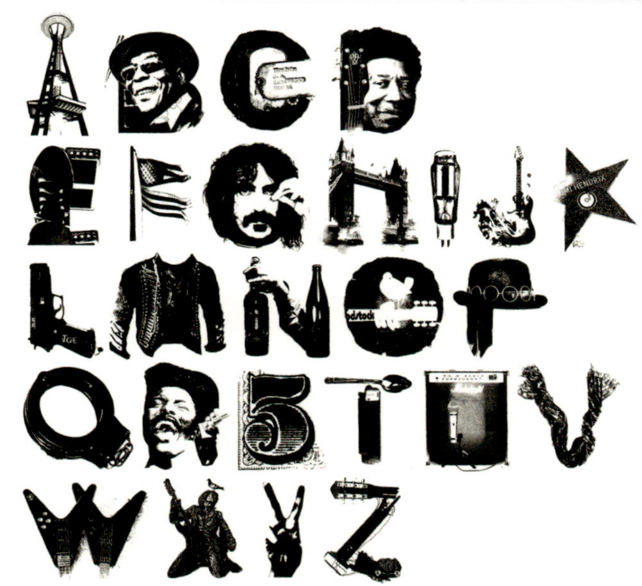

BRÉSIL BRAZIL (2011)
Almap BBDO Billboard Magazine
"Jimi Hendrix Typography" Music. Read what it's made of

« La pub est souvent considérée comme le parent pauvre de la typographie. Par rapport à l'édition, on est souvent affligé par la pauvreté dans l'originalité des polices choisies. Ici, au contraire, la typo est magnifiée et intégrée au centre de l'idée. Bref, la typo retrouve vraiment ses lettres de noblesse. »
"Advertising is often considered the red-headed stepchild of typography. Compared with publishing we are often troubled by the dearth of originality of fonts that are selected. Here on the contrary, the typeface is magnified and integrated at the centre of the idea. In short, type has really found its grandeur."

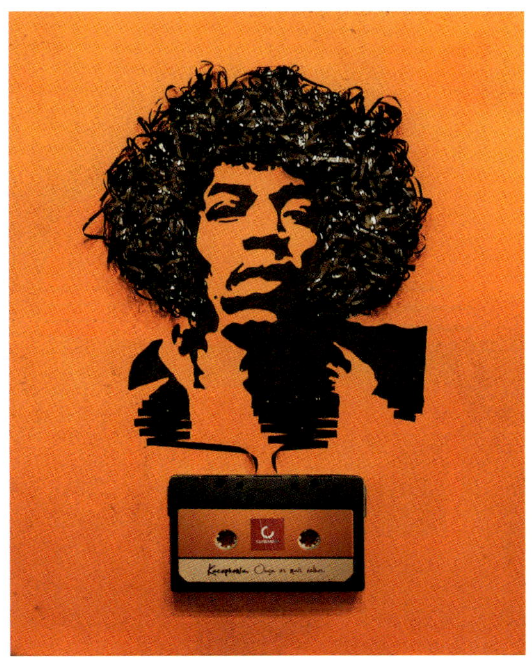

BRÉSIL BRAZIL (2010)
RC Comunicaçao inconnu unknown

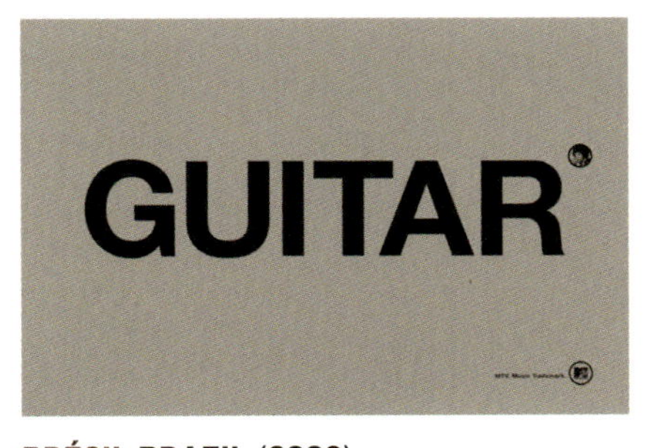

BRÉSIL BRAZIL (2006)
Loducca Publicidade Sao Paulo MTV
Music Trademark
(a little picture of Hendrix replace the ® logo)

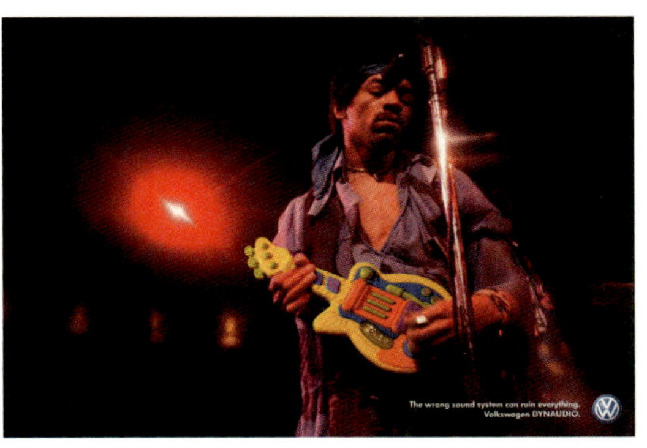

ALLEMAGNE GERMANY (2008)
DDB Dusseldorf Volkswagen Dynaudio System
The wrong sound system can ruin everything

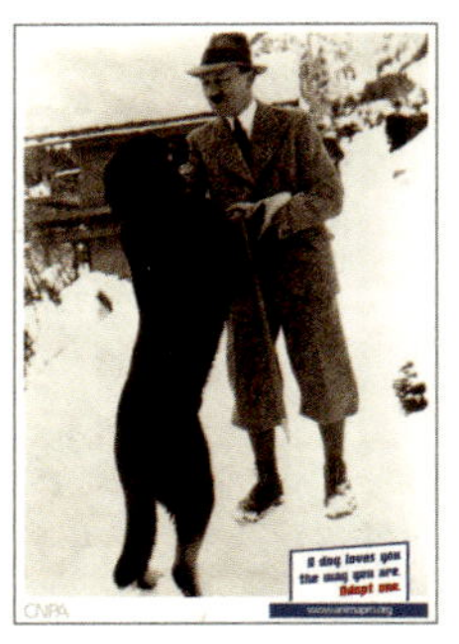

ROUMANIE GERMANY
ROUMANIE **ROMANIA (2006)**
Mc Cann Bucharest
Anima Pro
A dog loves you the way you are. Adopt one

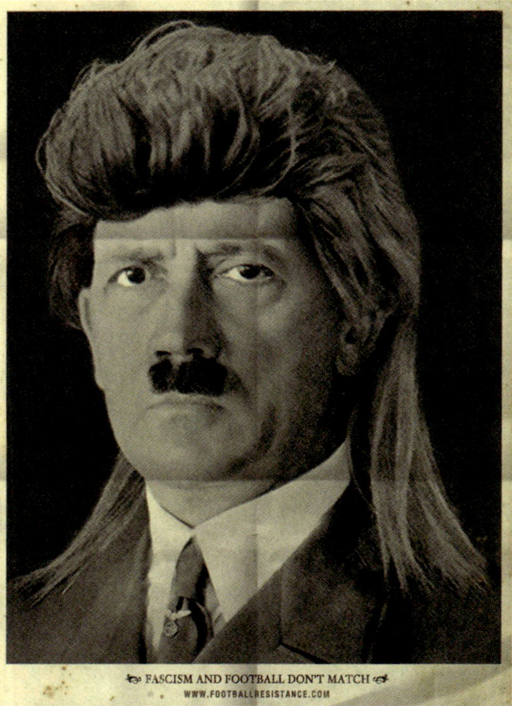

FRANCE **FRANCE (2007)**
CLM/BBDO
Football Resistance
Fascism and football don't match

«Pour moi, s'il y a une référence historique qui devrait être bannie de la pub à tout jamais, c'est bien celle-ci. J'ai été choqué par des annonces que j'ai refusé de sélectionner et qui utilisent l'image du Führer pour vendre des déodorants, de la vodka, du café ou des traiteurs chinois ! Celle-ci est drôle et reste acceptable car c'est pour la bonne cause... »
"For me, if there is a historical reference that should be banned from advertising forever it is this one. I was shocked by the ads – that I refused to select – which use images of the Führer to sell deodorant, vodka, coffee and even Chinese takeaway. This one is funny and only acceptable because it's for a good cause."

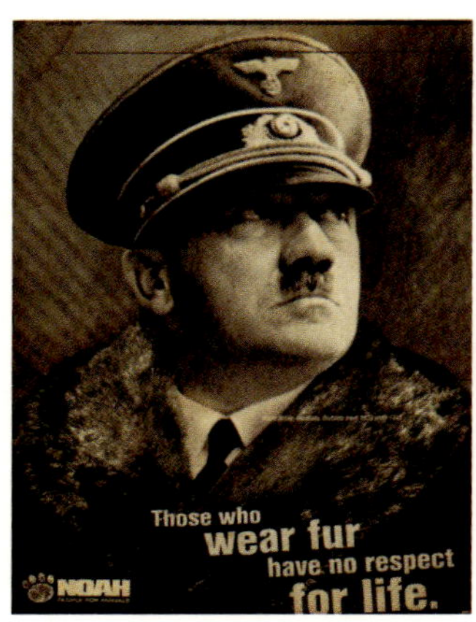

ALLEMAGNE **GERMANY (2004)**
Jung Von Matt/alster
Noah people for animals
Those who wear fur have no respect for life

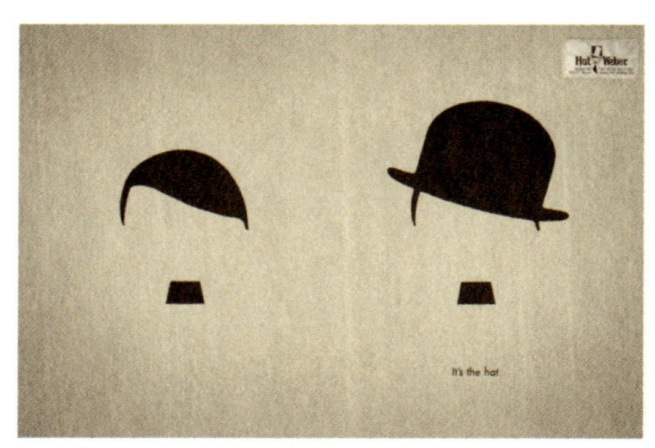

ALLEMAGNE **GERMANY (2008)**
ServicePlan Munich Hut Weber
It's the hat

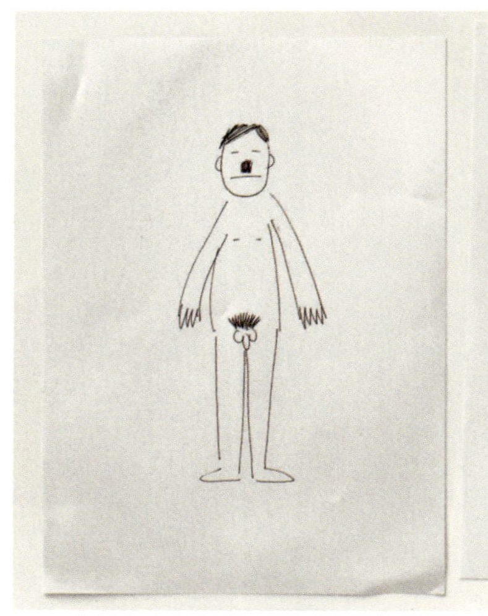
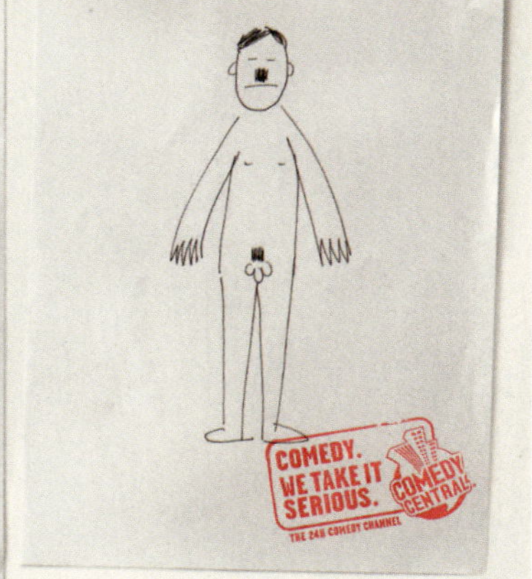

ALLEMAGNE **GERMANY (2007)**
Kempertrautmann, Hamburg Comedy Central

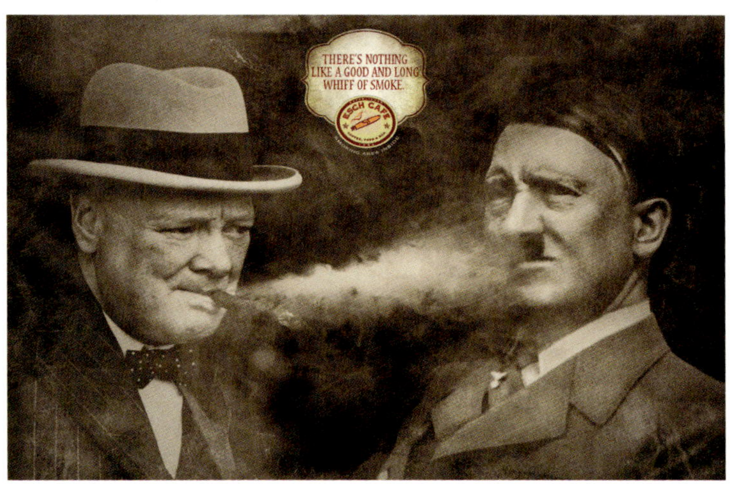

BRÉSIL BRAZIL (2012)
Giovanni DraftFCB Rio · Esch Café
There's nothing like a good and long whiff of smoke

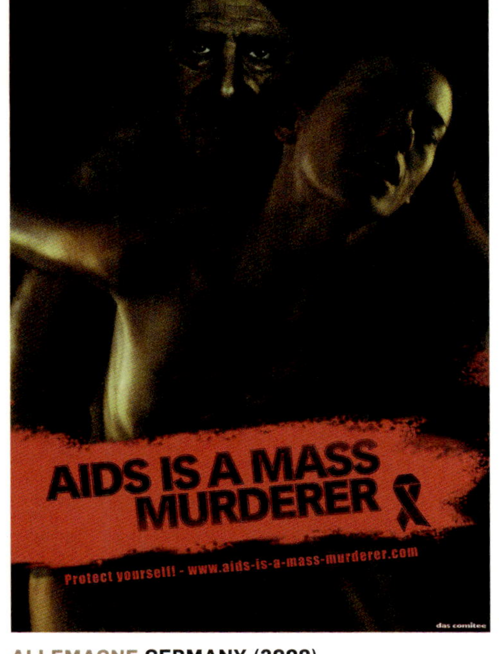

ALLEMAGNE GERMANY (2009)
Regenbogen Berlin · Aids Prevention

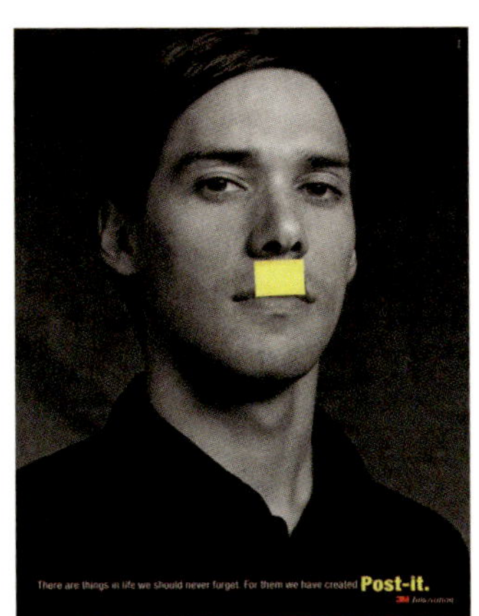

INCONNU UNKNOWN (2006)
Inconnu/unknown · 3M Post-It
There are things in life we should never forget. For them we have created Post-It

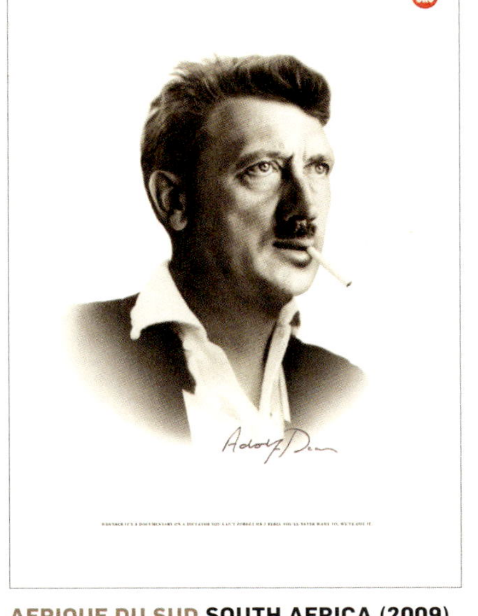

AFRIQUE DU SUD SOUTH AFRICA (2009)
The Jupiter Drawing Room · CNA
(Adolf Dean)
Whether it's a documentary on a dictator you can't forget or a rebel you'll never want to, we've got it.

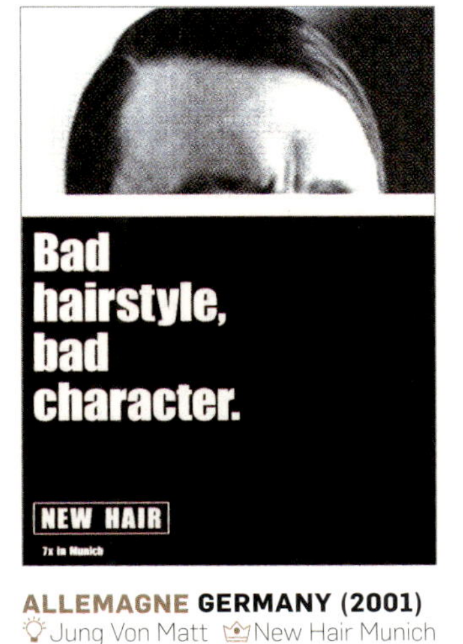

ALLEMAGNE GERMANY (2001)
Jung Von Matt · New Hair Munich

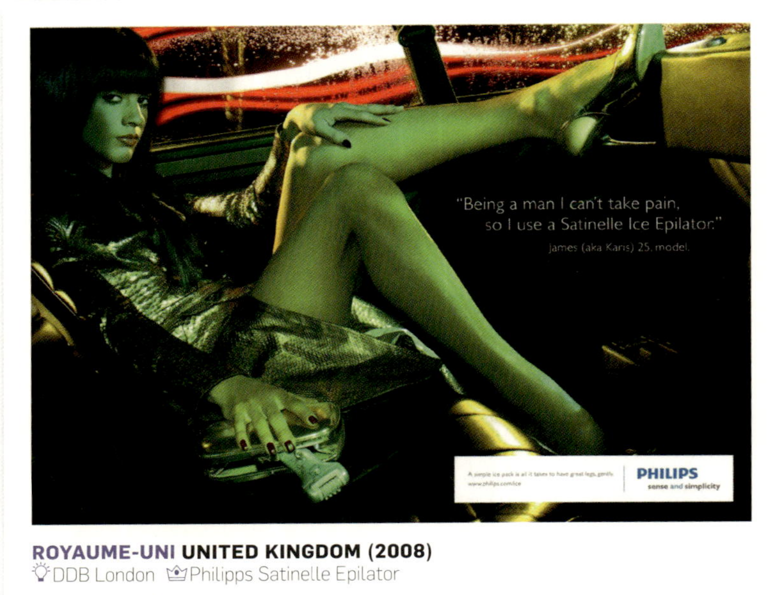

ROYAUME-UNI UNITED KINGDOM (2008)
DDB London Philipps Satinelle Epilator

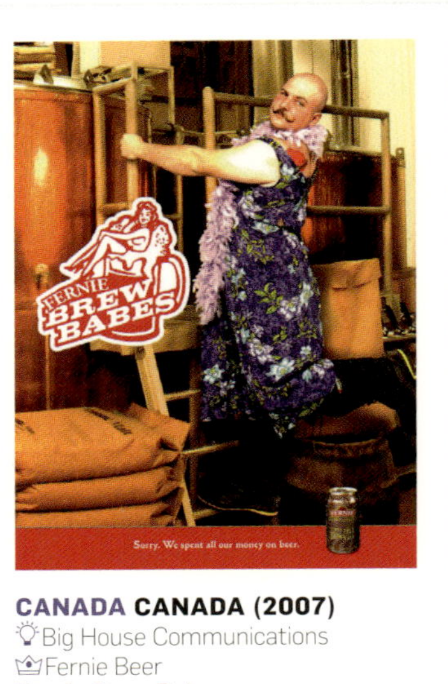

CANADA CANADA (2007)
Big House Communications
Fernie Beer
Fernie Brew Babes
Sorry. We spent all our money
on beer

HOMMES OU FEMMES ?

№ 49

MEN OR WOMEN?

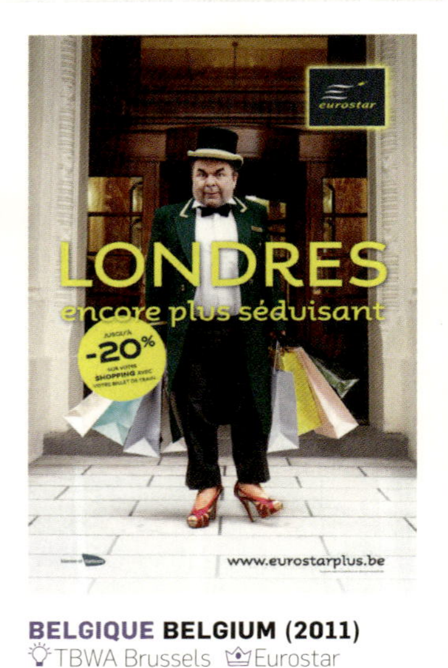

BELGIQUE BELGIUM (2011)
TBWA Brussels Eurostar
London. Even more attractive

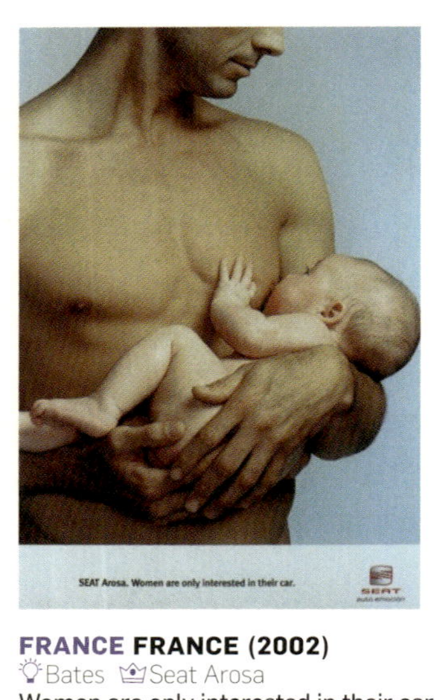
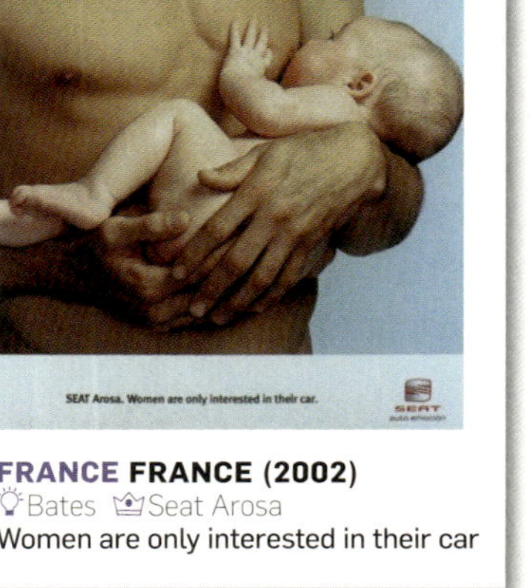

FRANCE FRANCE (2002)
Bates Seat Arosa
Women are only interested in their car

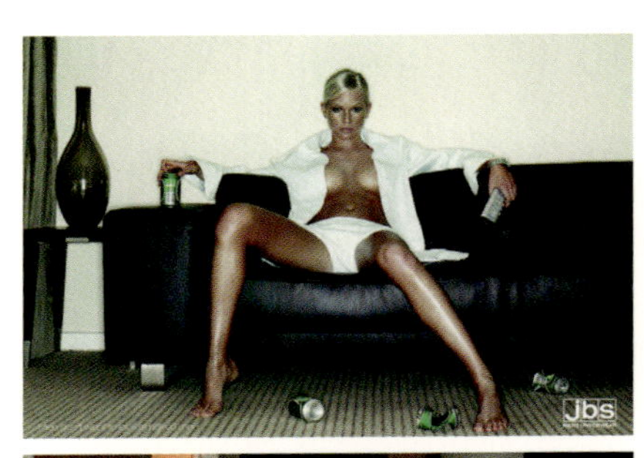
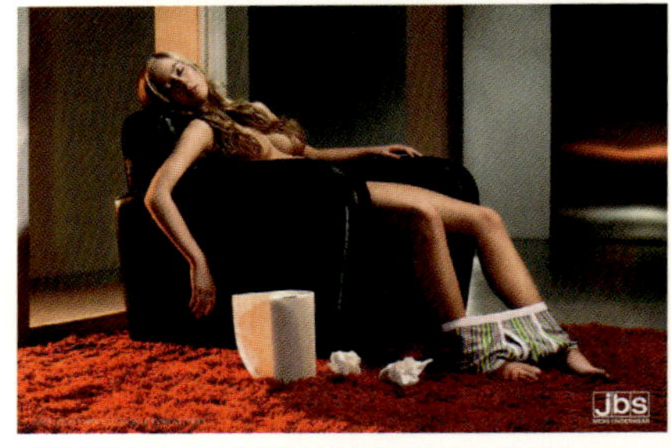
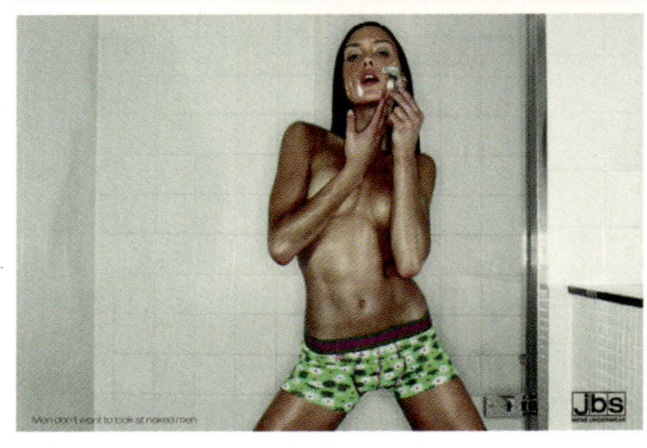

DANEMARK DENMARK (2007)
&Co JBS Men's Underwear
Men don't want to look at naked men

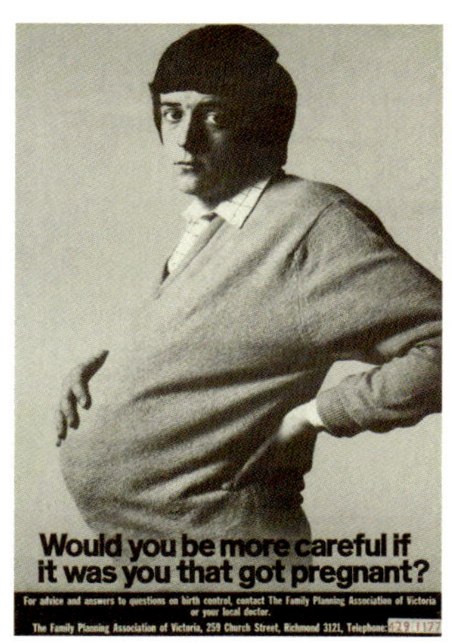

ROYAUME-UNI
UNITED KINGDOM (1980)
Saatchi & Saatchi
Family Planning

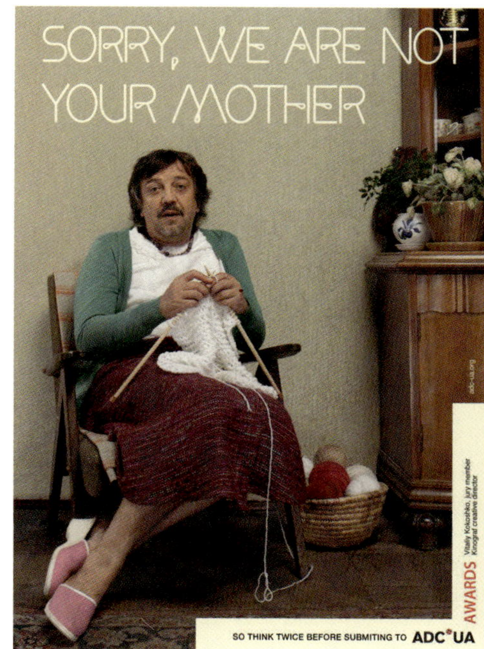

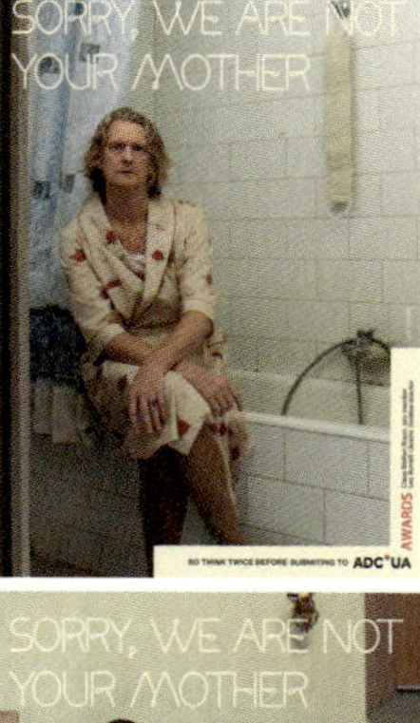

UKRAINE UKRAINE (2010)
Leo Burnett   Art Directors Club Awards
Sorry, we are not your mother. So think twice before submitting to ADC awards

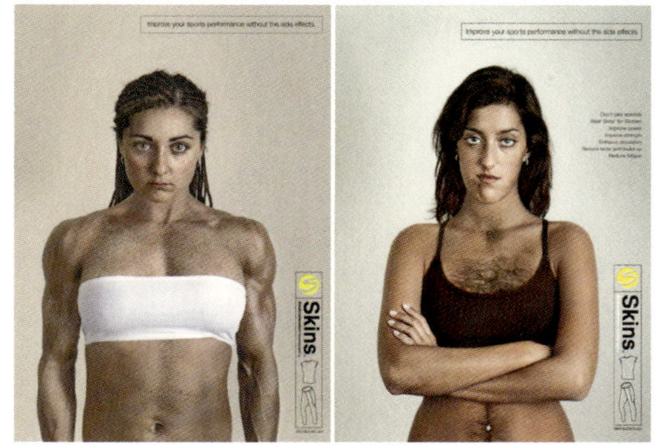

AUSTRALIE AUSTRALIA (2006)
The Furnace   Skins
Improve your sports performance without the side effects

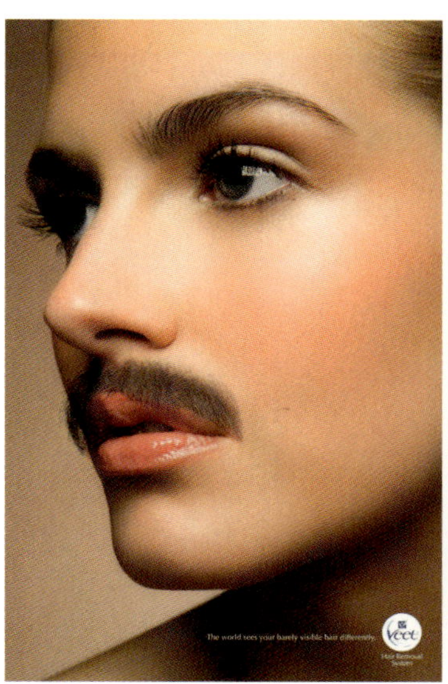
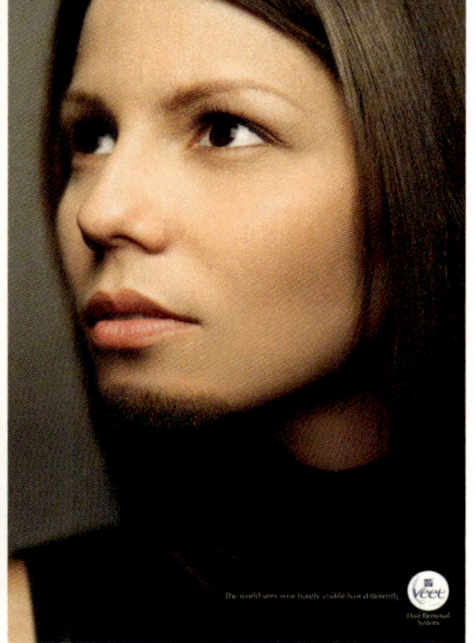

INDE INDIA (2008)
Euro RSCG   Veet Hair Removal System
The world sees your barely visible hair differently

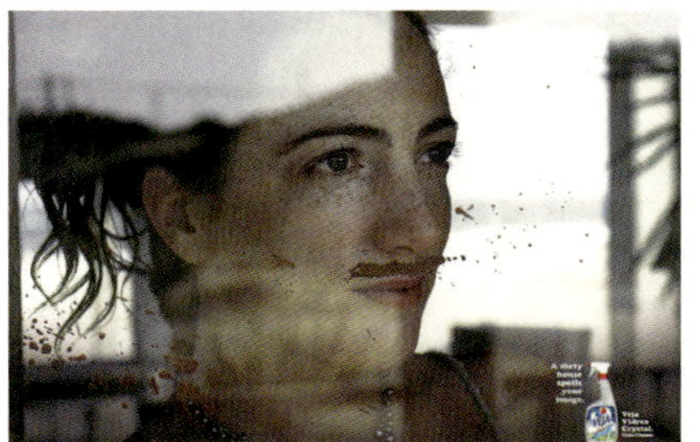

BRÉSIL BRAZIL (2008)
Euro RSCG   Veja Window Cleaner
A dirty house spoils your image

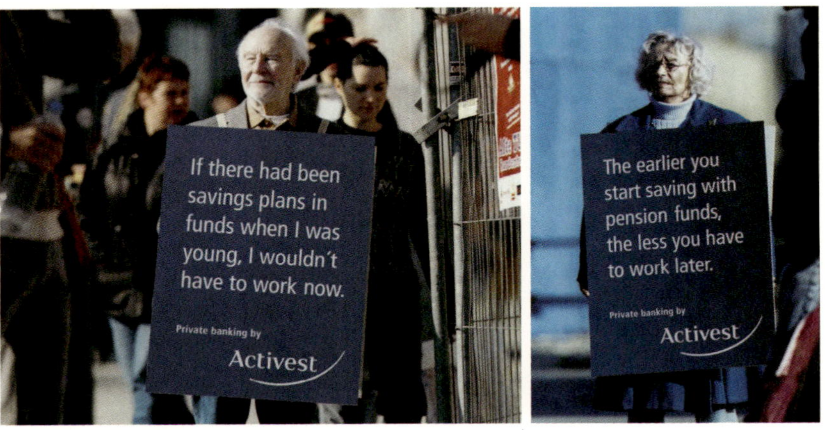

ALLEMAGNE GERMANY (2002)
Scholz & Friends — Activest Private Banking
If there had been savings plans in funds when I was young, I wouldn't have to work now.
The earlier you start saving with pension funds, the less you have to work later

« La plus terrible car elle glace le sang. On est immédiatement révolté de voir des gens âgés forcés de travailler. L'idée, contrairement à d'autres, joue à la fois sur le porteur et sur le message qu'il nous délivre, et pas uniquement sur la drôlerie ou la surprise de la pancarte. »
"The most frightful because it sends chills up the spine. We are immediately revolted when we see older folks forced to work. This idea, unlike others, at the same time plays on the messenger and on the message he gives us, and not only on the comic value and the surprise we see on the sandwich board."

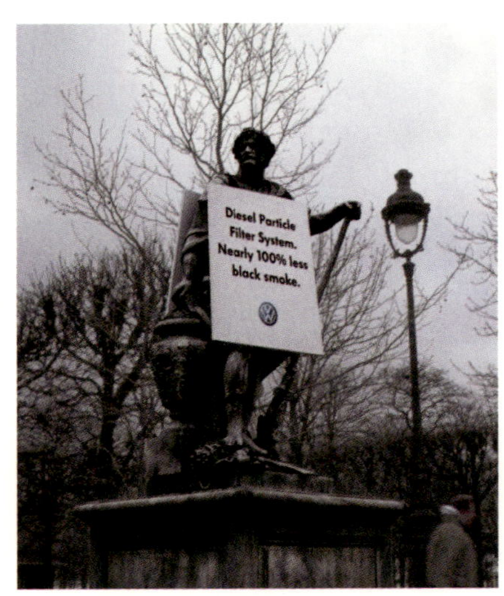

FRANCE FRANCE (2005)
.V. — Volkswagen Diesel Particle Filter
Nearly 100% less black smoke

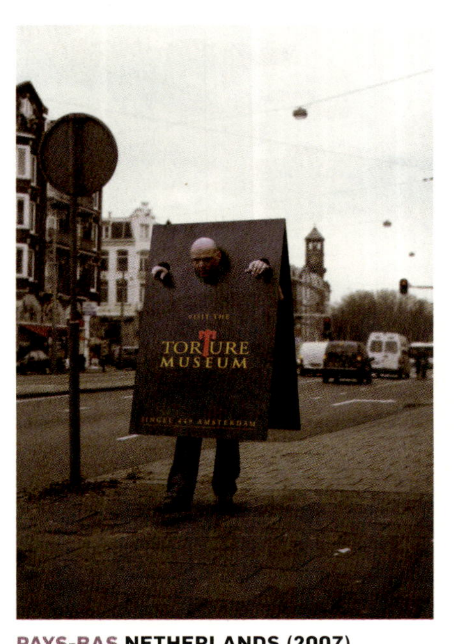

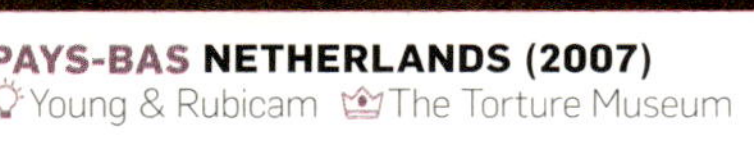

PAYS-BAS NETHERLANDS (2007)
Young & Rubicam — The Torture Museum

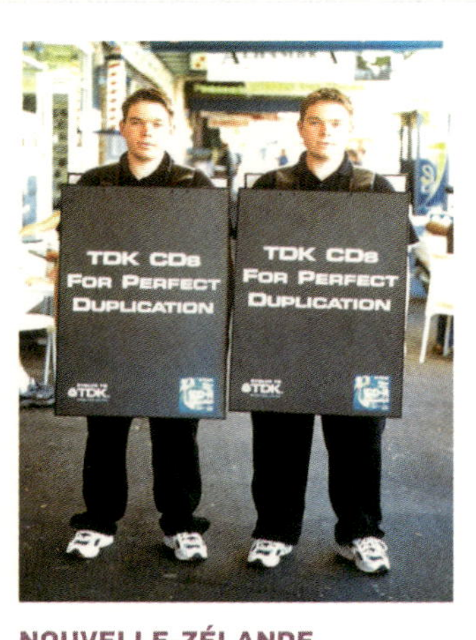

**NOUVELLE-ZÉLANDE
NEW ZEALAND (2002)**
Colenso BBDO — TDK CD's
For perfect duplication

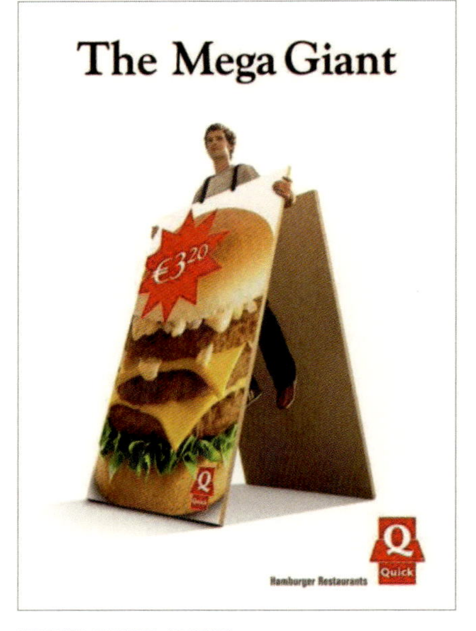

CHINE CHINA (2007)
JWT Beijing — Halls

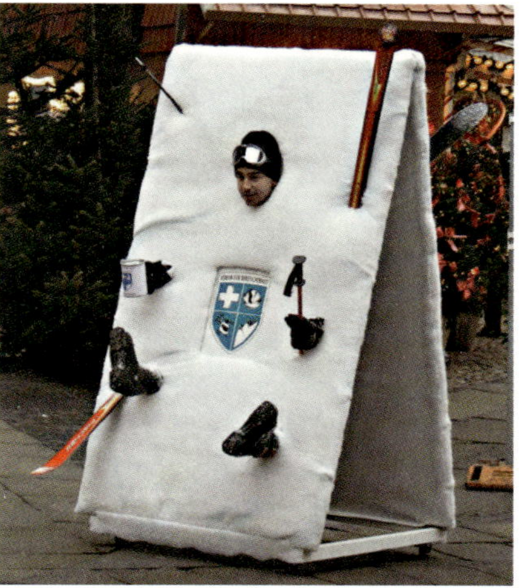

ALLEMAGNE GERMANY (2007)
Scholz & Friends Hamburg
Mountain Rescue Service Fundraising

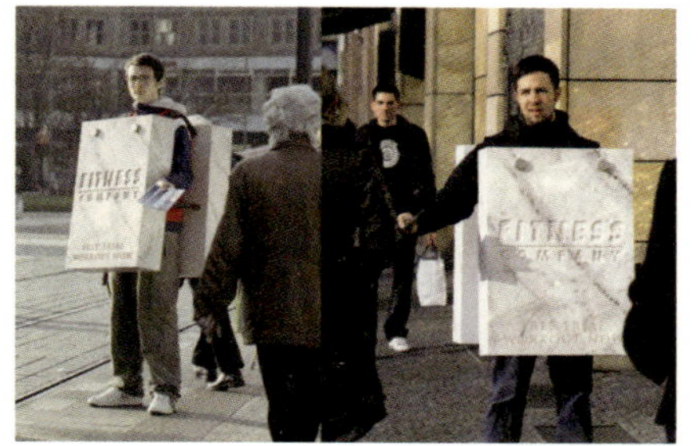

ALLEMAGNE GERMANY (2005)
Scholz & Friends Berlin Fitness Company

HOMMES SANDWICH
Nº50
SANDWICH MEN

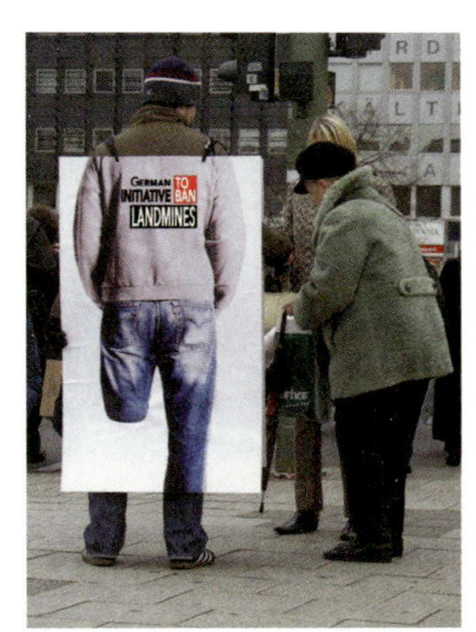

ALLEMAGNE GERMANY (2003)
Scholz & Friends
German Initiative to ban landmines

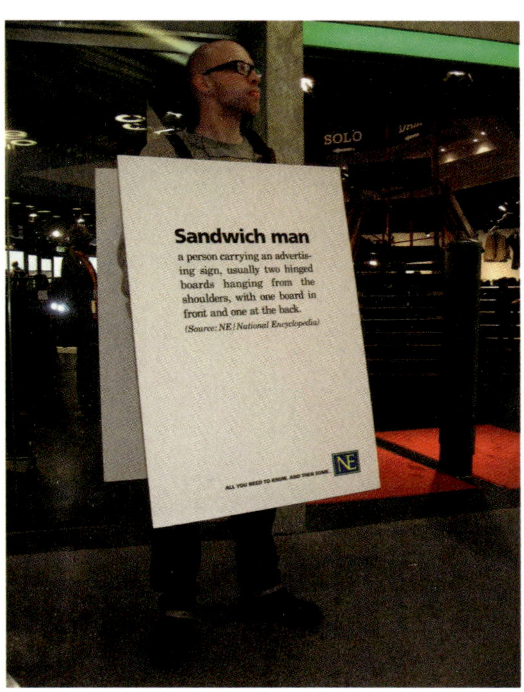

SUÈDE SWEDEN (2007)
Forsman & Bodenfors National Encyklopedin
All you need to know. And then some

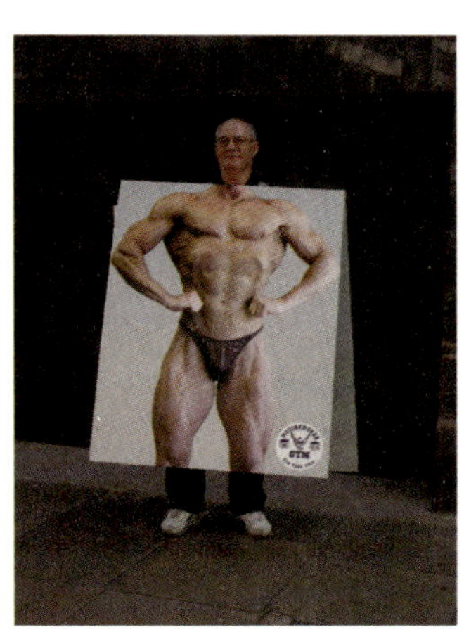

**ROYAUME-UNI
UNITED KINGDOM (2007)**
Lunar BBDO
Muscleworks Gym Club

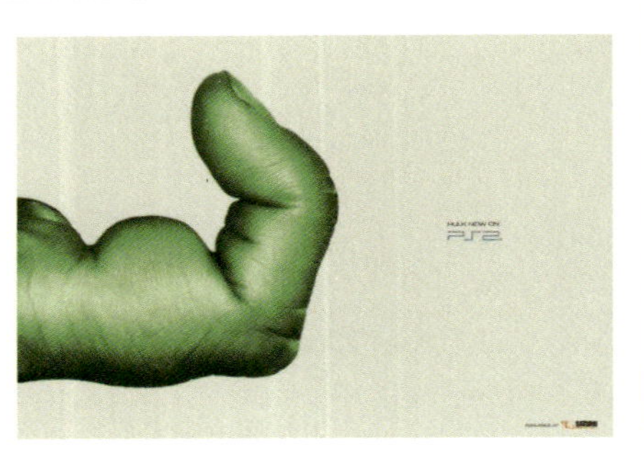

ALLEMAGNE GERMANY (2003)
Jung Von Matt Hamburg Hulk now on sony PS2

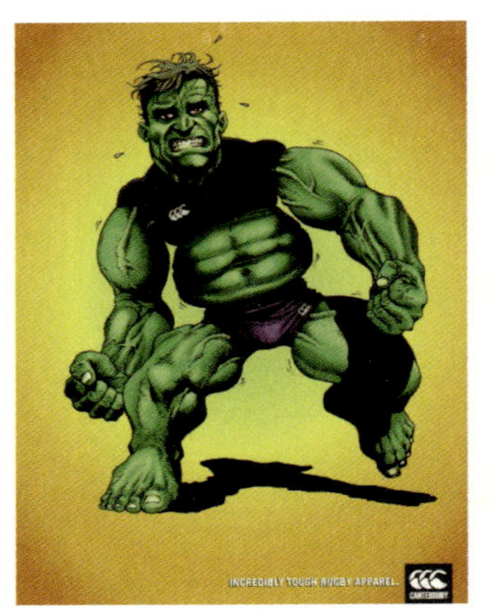

AFRIQUE DU SUD
SOUTH AFRICA (2006)
BBDO Cape Town Canterbury
Incredibly tough rugby apparel

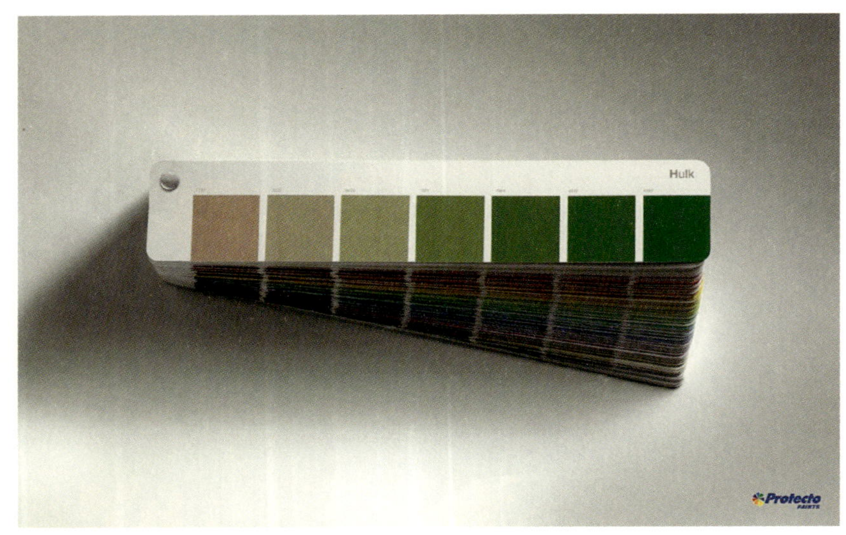

COSTA RICA COSTA RICA (2011)
DDB Proteto Paints
Hulk

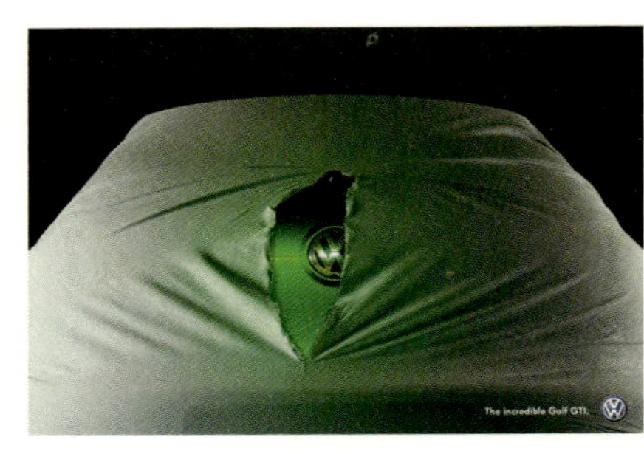

FRANCE FRANCE (2006)
Agence .V. Volkswagen
The incredible Golf GTI

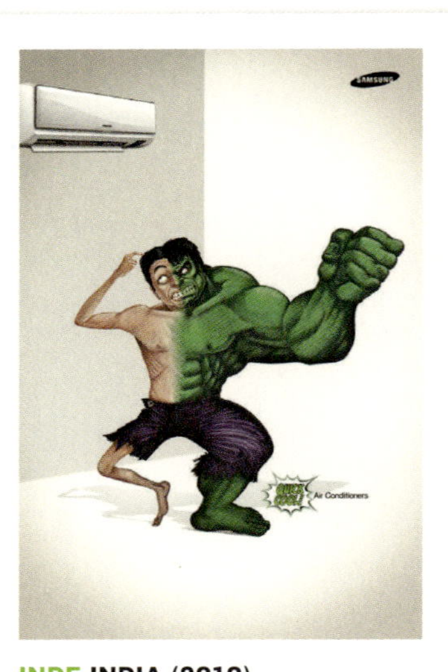

INDE INDIA (2010)
Cheil Samsung
Quick cool air conditioners

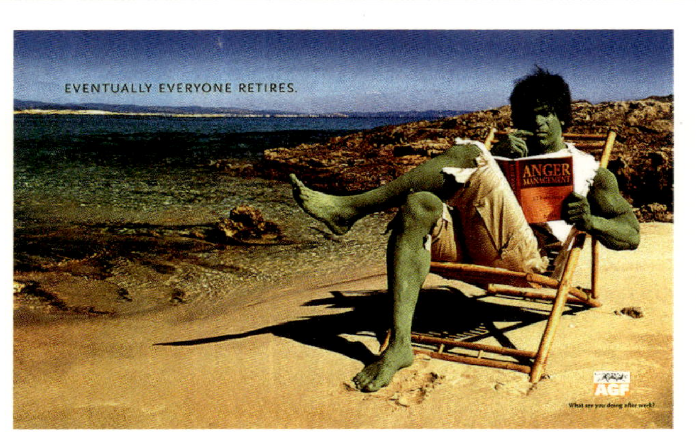

CANADA CANADA (2001)
TBWA Chiat Day Assurances Générales de France. Mutual Funds
Eventually everyone retires

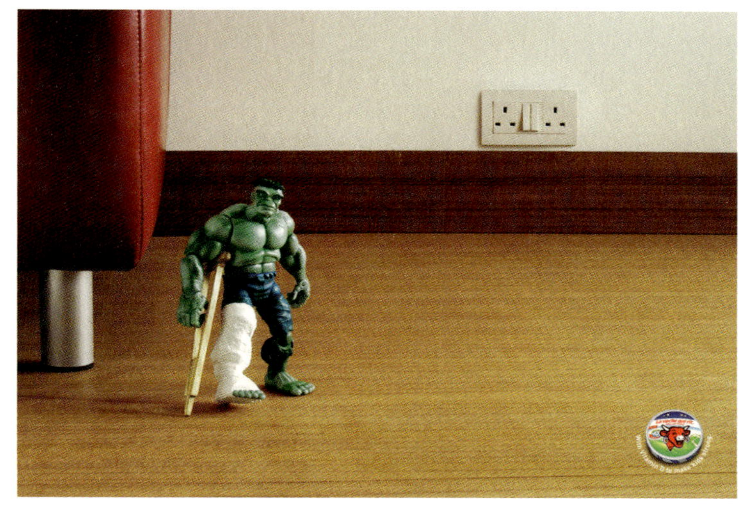

ÉMIRATS ARABES UNIS UNITED ARAB EMIRATES (2006)
💡 Saatchi & Saatchi Dubai 👑 The laughing cow.
With vitamin D. Make kids strong

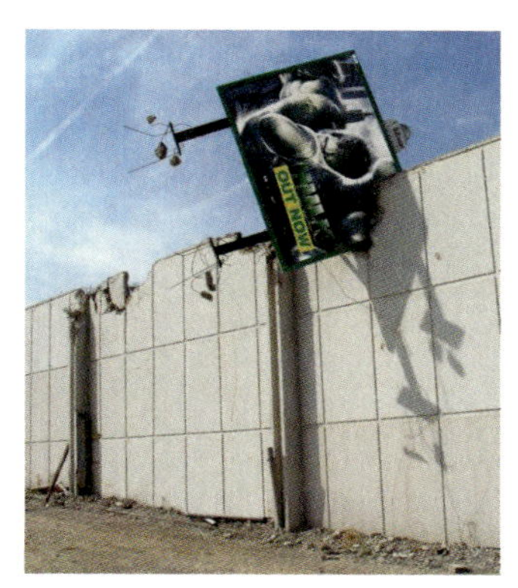

PAYS-BAS
NETHERLANDS (2003)
💡 Amsterdam Advertising
👑 United International Pictures –
Hulk, the movie

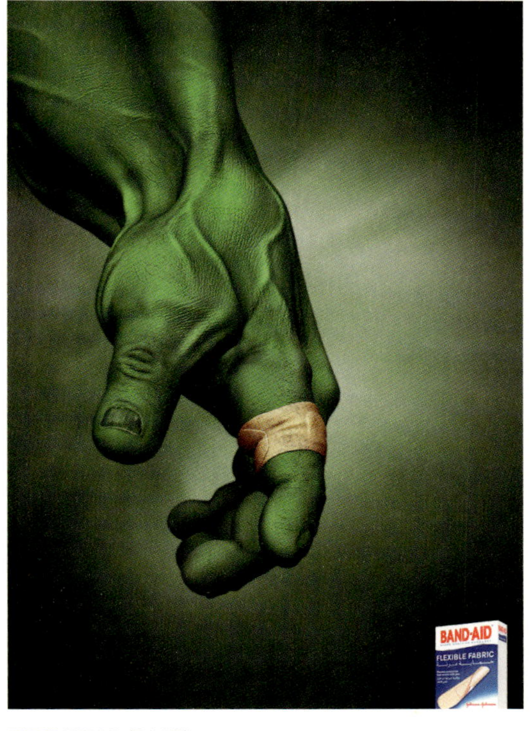

INDE INDIA (2010)
💡 JWT Dubai 👑 Band-Aid
Flexible Fabric

HULK

№51

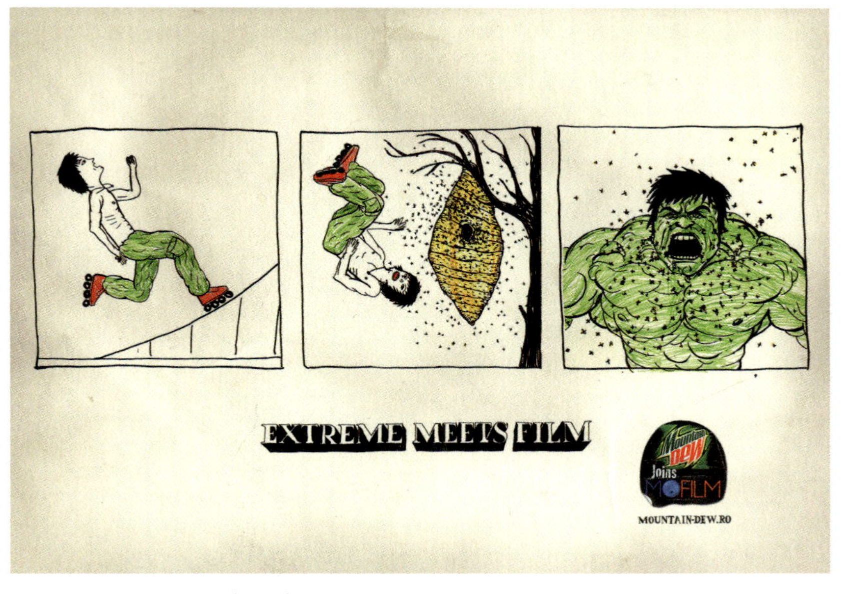

ROUMANIE ROMANIA (2011)
💡 Graffiti BBDO 👑 Mountain Dew MoFilm

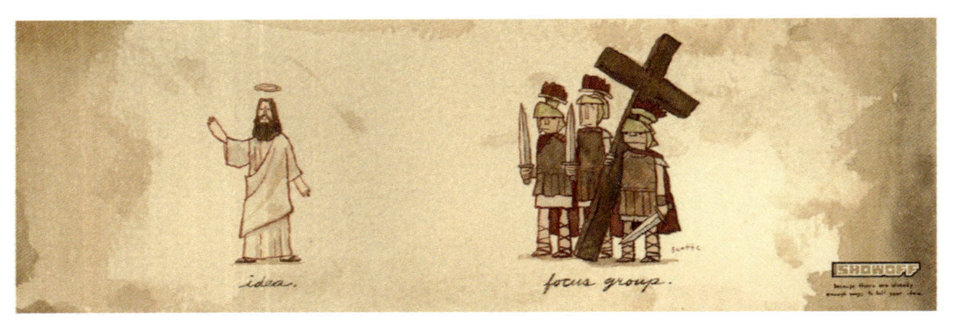

PORTUGAL PORTUGAL (2010)
Fuel Euro RSCG Lisbon   ShowOff Production House
Idea / Focus group. Because there are already enough ways to kill your idea

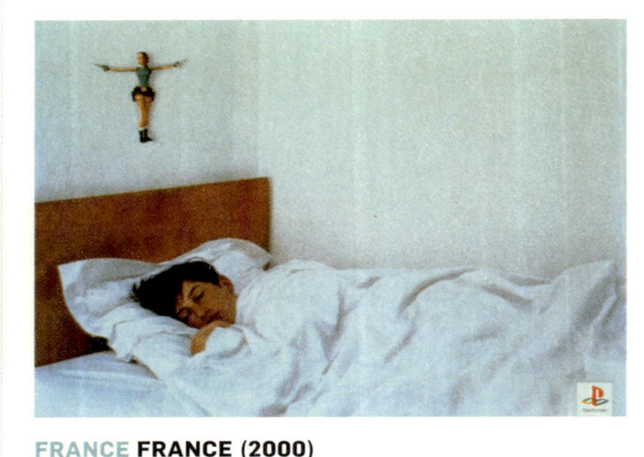

FRANCE FRANCE (2000)
TBWA Paris   Playstation
(Lara Croft replaced Jesus Christ)

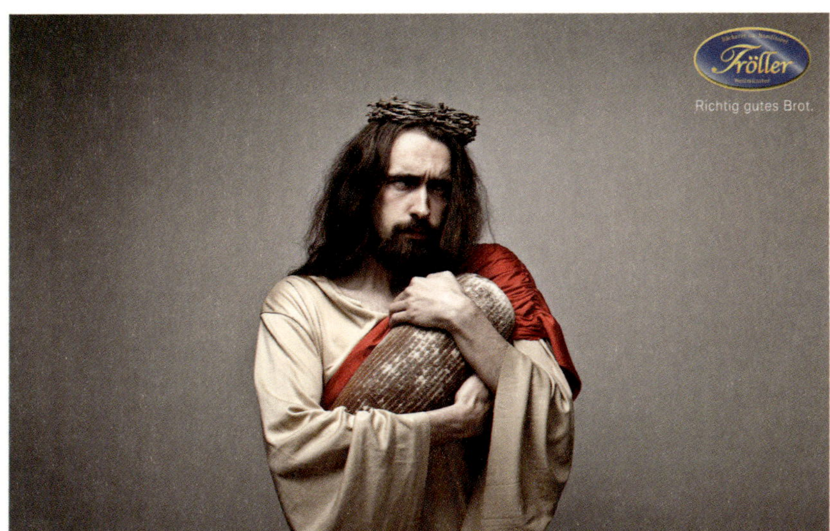

ALLEMAGNE GERMANY (2011)
Lukas Bausch   Tröller
Really good bread

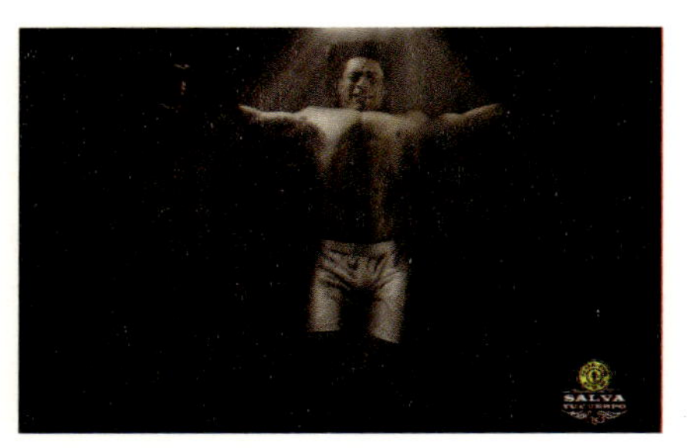

GUATEMALA GUATEMALA (2011)
Red Azul Publicidad   Gold's Gym
Save Your Body

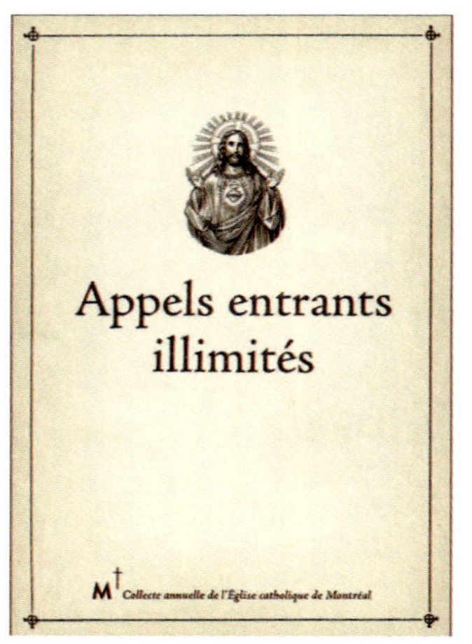

CANADA CANADA (2010)
Bos Montreal   Church of Montreal
Unlimited incoming calls

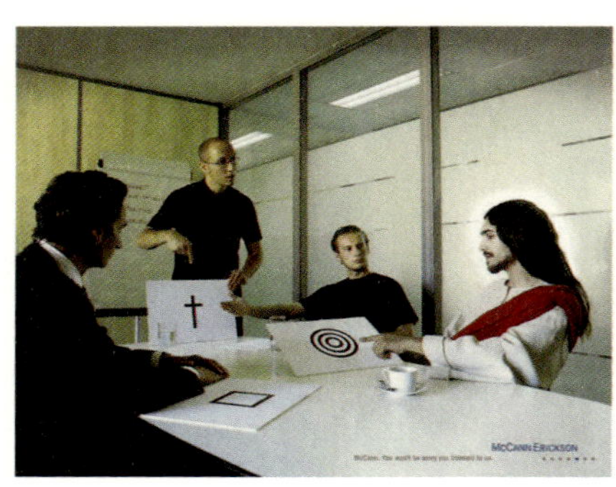

INTERNATIONAL INTERNATIONAL (2007)
McCann Erickson   Agency Self Promotion
You won't be sorry you listened to us

JESUS

№52

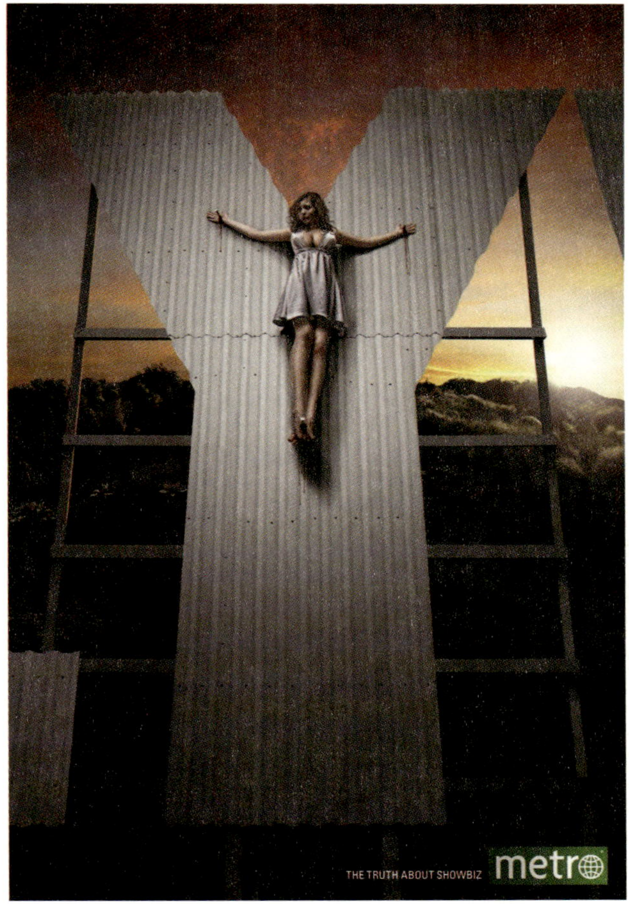

SUÈDE SWEDEN (2008)
Scholz & Friends · *Metro* newspaper
The truth about showbiz

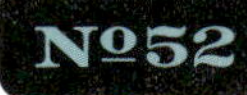

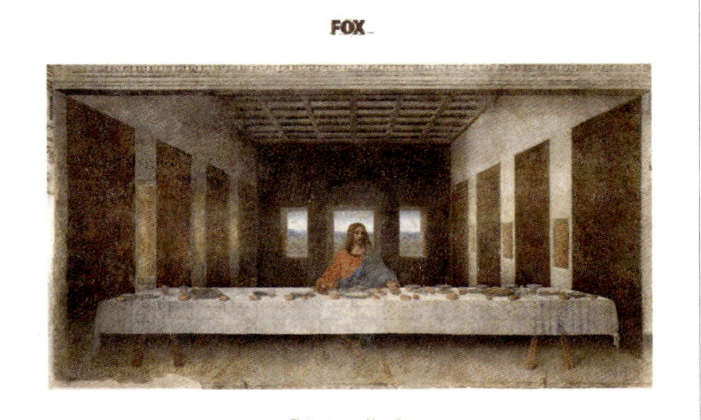

ESPAGNE SPAIN (2008)
Bungalow 25 Madrid · Fox Channel
The best shows at dinner time

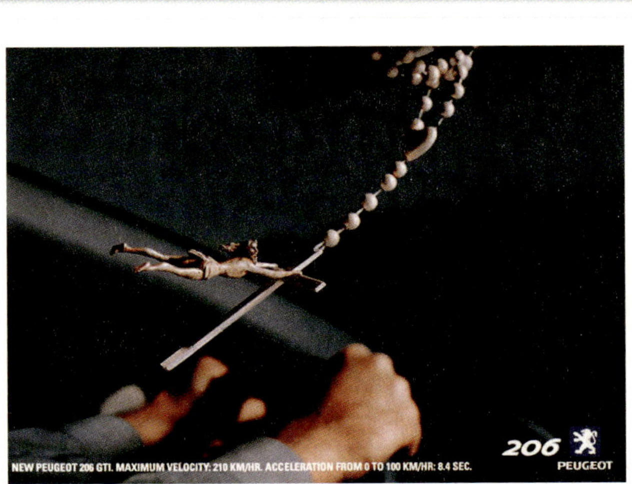

ARGENTINE ARGENTINA (2001)
Craverolanis Euro RSCG · Peugeot 206
Maximum velocity 210KM/H. Acceleration from 0 to 100KM/H: 8.4sec

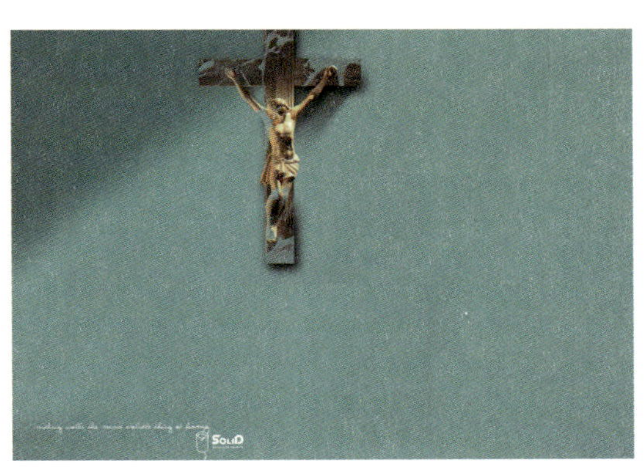

ÉGYPTE EGYPT (2007)
JWT Cairo · Solid Paints
Making walls the most valuable thing at home

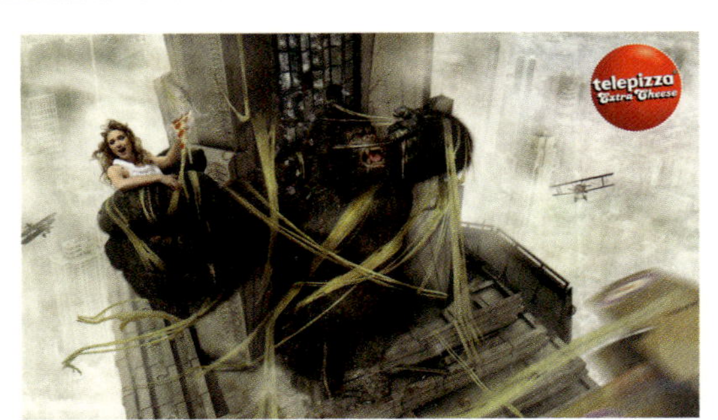

CHILI CHILE (2011)
Nostrum Santiago · Telepizza
Extra Cheese

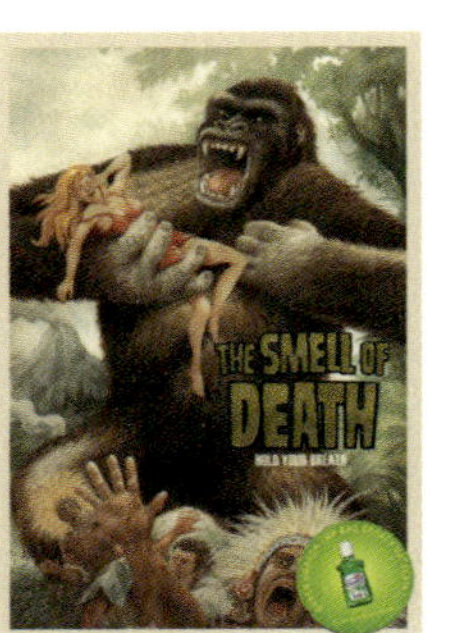

BRÉSIL
BRAZIL (2006)
Publicis
Cepacol Mouth Wash
The smell of death.
Hold your breath.

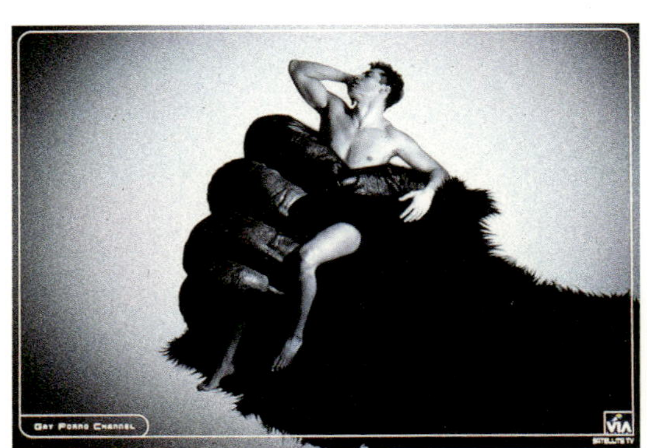

ESPAGNE SPAIN (2000)
Ruiz Nicoli · Via Satellite TV
Gay Porno Channel

KING KONG

Nº53

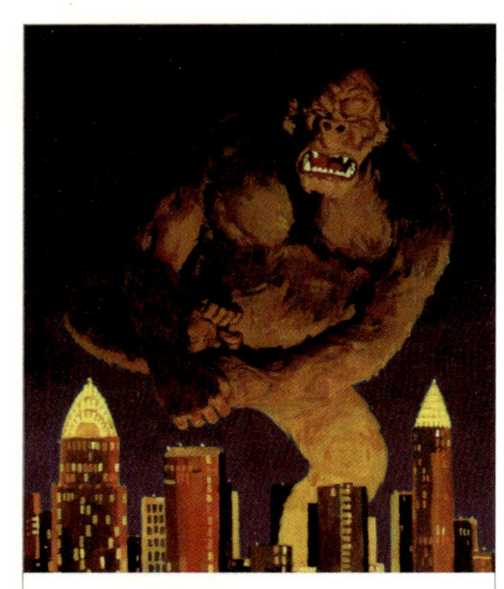

ROYAUME-UNI
UNITED KINGDOM (2005)
DDB London · Volkswagen Polo
Small but tough

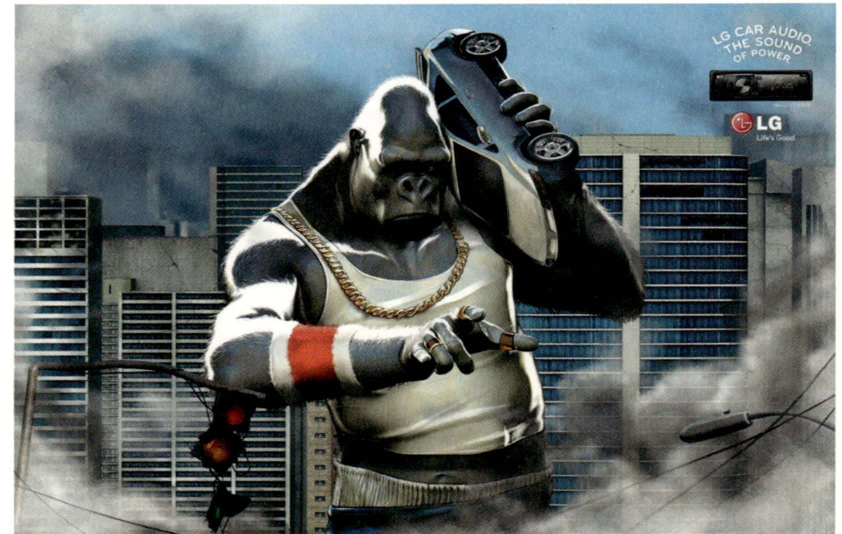

BRÉSIL BRAZIL (2012)
Young & Rubicam Sao Paulo · LG Car Audio System
The sound of power

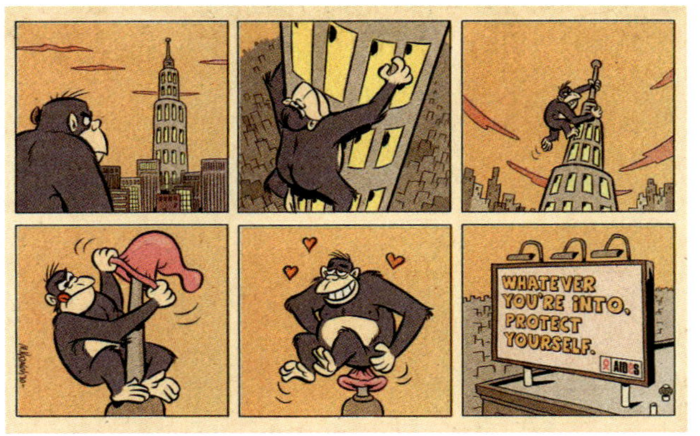

ÉTATS-UNIS UNITED STATES (2011)
Goodby Silverstein & Partners San Francisco — Aides - Aids awareness

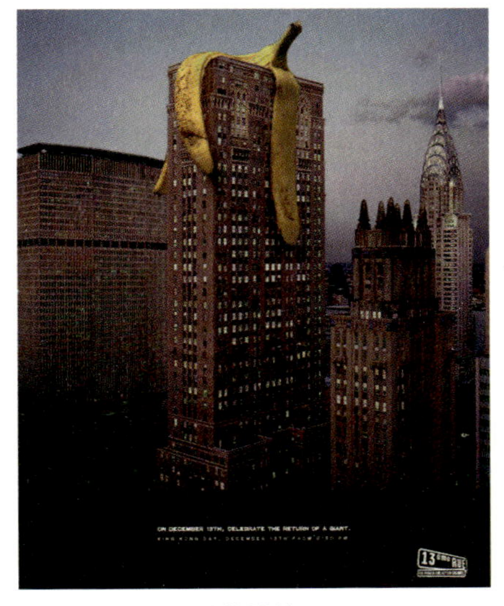

FRANCE FRANCE (1999)
BETC Euro RSCG — 13ᵉ Rue TV Channel
On december 13th, celebrate the return of a giant

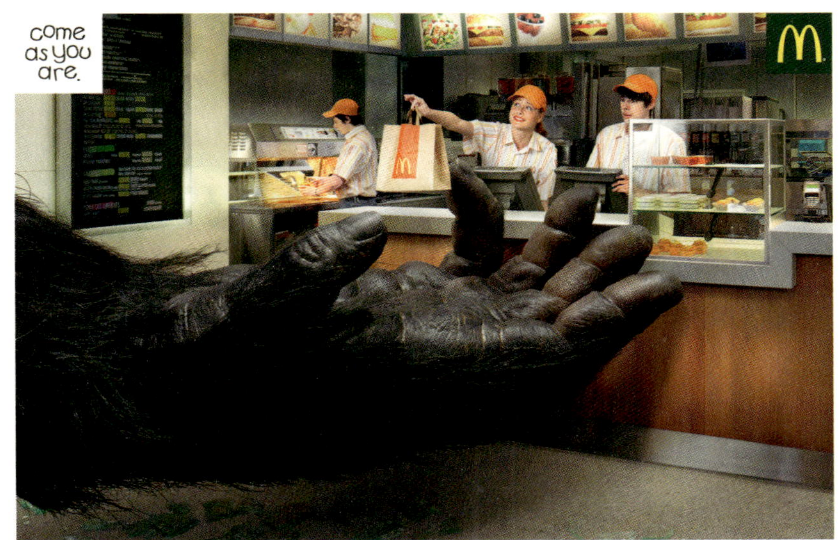

FRANCE FRANCE (2009)
BETC Euro RSCG — Mc Donald's

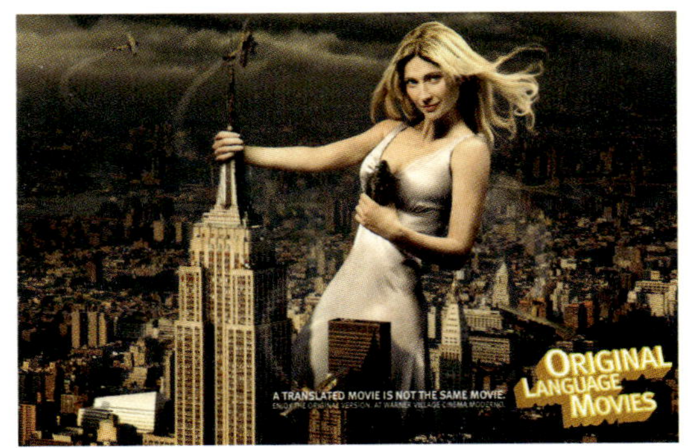

ITALIE ITALY (2008)
BBDO Roma — Warner Village Cinema Moderno
Original language movies.
A translated movie is not the same movie.

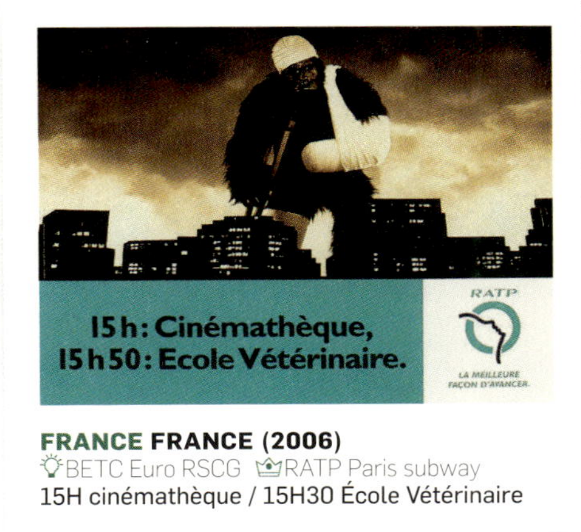

FRANCE FRANCE (2006)
BETC Euro RSCG — RATP Paris subway
15H cinémathèque / 15H30 École Vétérinaire

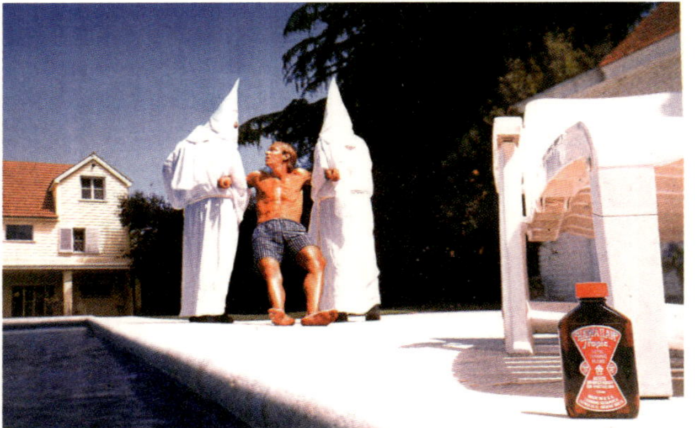

ARGENTINE ARGENTINA (2000)
Grey Hawaiian Tropic

« Je commençais à travailler dans la pub quand cette annonce est sortie et j'avais été frappé par la simplicité et l'immédiateté de cette idée. Mais aussi et surtout par l'humour et le culot que ça avait dû nécessiter de vendre une telle création. »
"I had just begun working in advertising when this came out and I was struck by the simplicity and immediacy of this idea. But above all the humor and the cheek that was needed to sell such a creation."

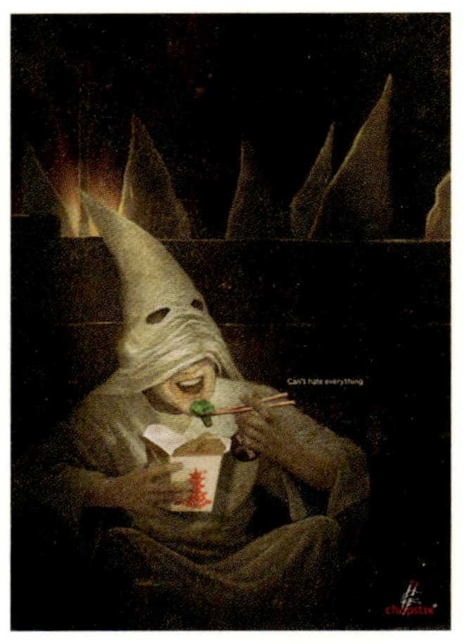

INDONÉSIE INDONESIA (2006)
Dentsu Chopstix
Can't hate everything

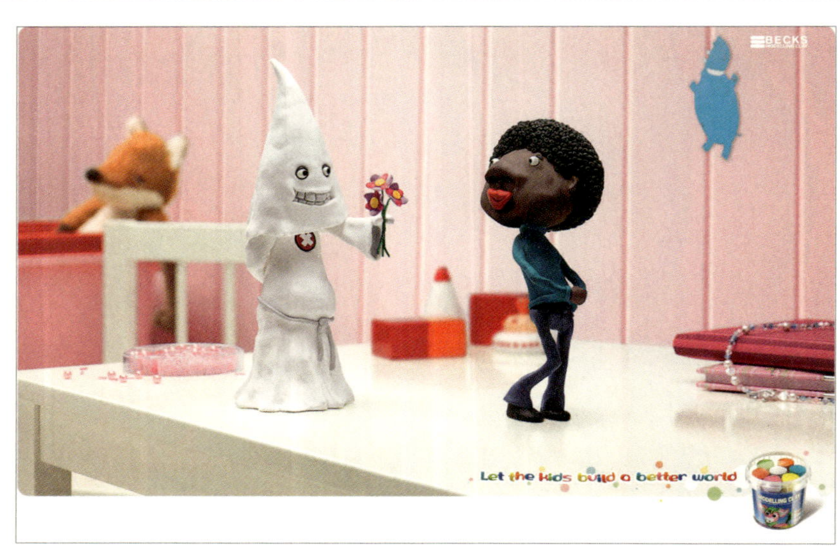

ALLEMAGNE GERMANY (2009)
Scholz & Friends Hamburg Becks Plastilin
Let the kids build a better world

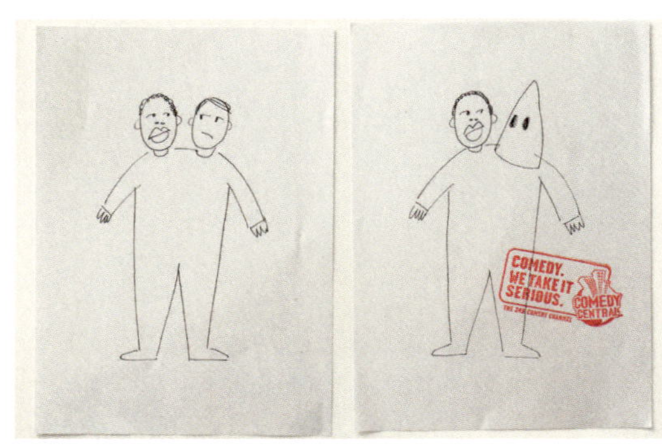

ALLEMAGNE GERMANY (2008)
Kempertrautman Comedy Central Channel

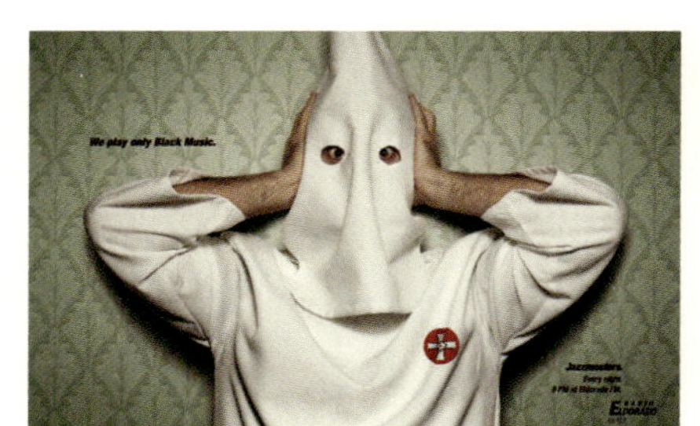

BRÉSIL BRAZIL (2005)
TBWA Radio Eldorado
We only play black music

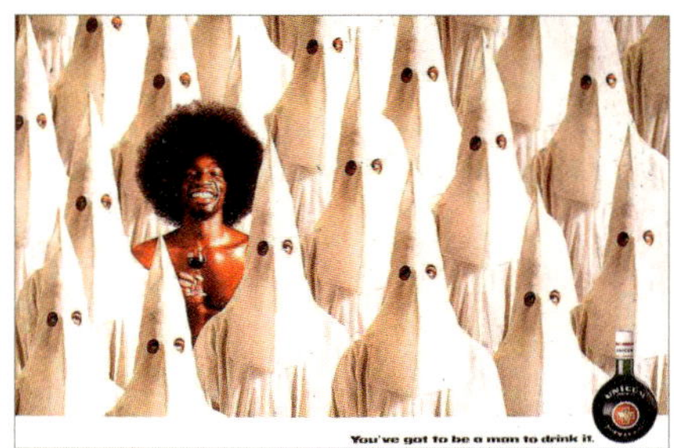

ITALIE ITALY (1998)
Saatchi & Saatchi Unicum (Allied Domecq)
You've got to be a man to drink it

KKK

№54

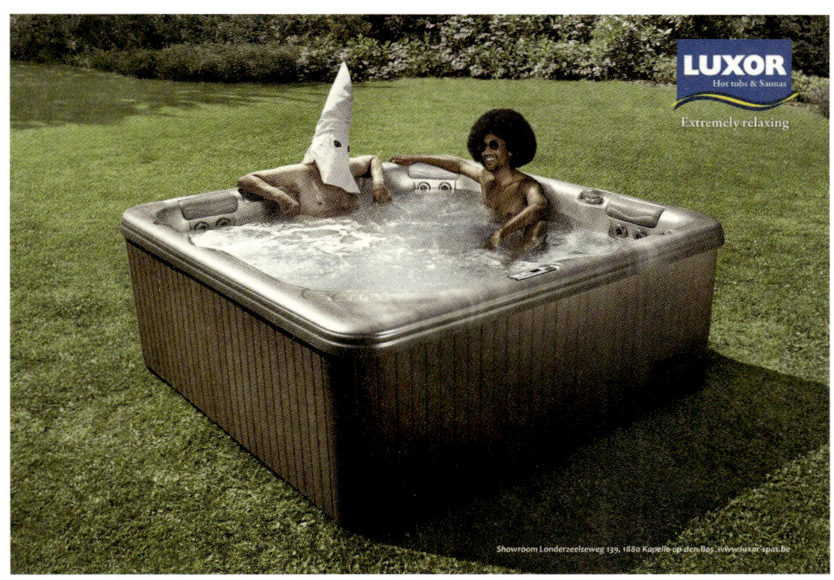

BELGIQUE BELGIUM (2009)
Mc Cann Lowe Luxor Hot Tubs and Saunas
Extremely relaxing

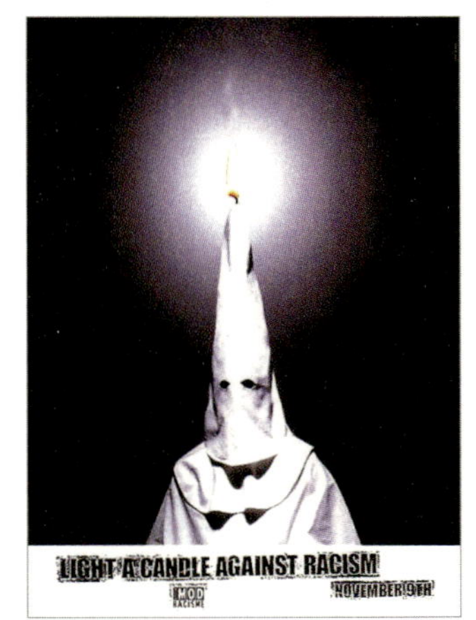

DANEMARK
DENMARK (1999)
Robert Boisen and like minded
Racial awareness
Light a candle against racism

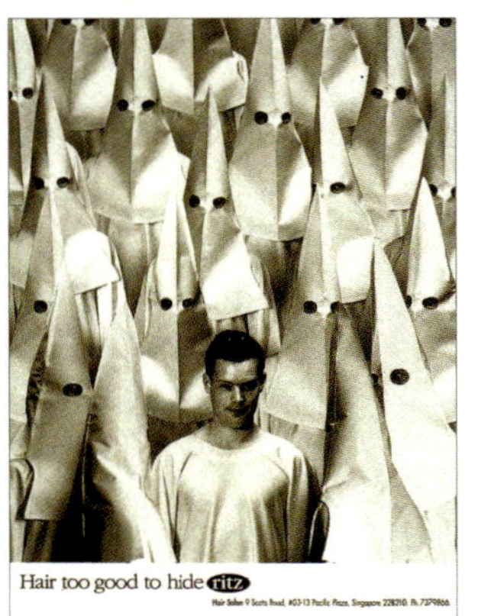

SINGAPOUR SINGAPORE (1999)
DDB Ritz Hair Salon
Hair too good to hide

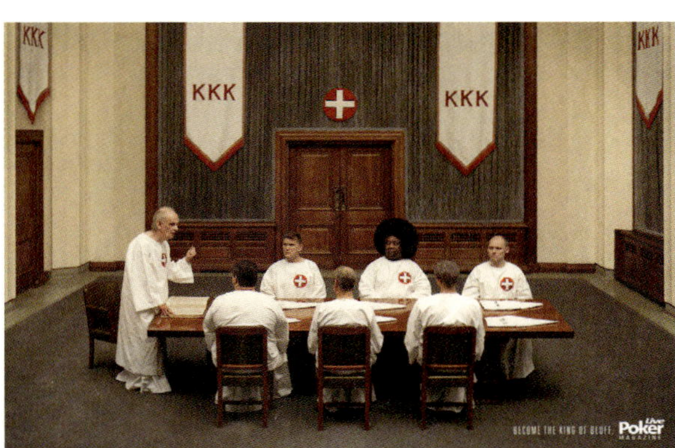

FRANCE FRANCE (2008)
DDB Paris Live Poker Magazine
Become the king of bluff

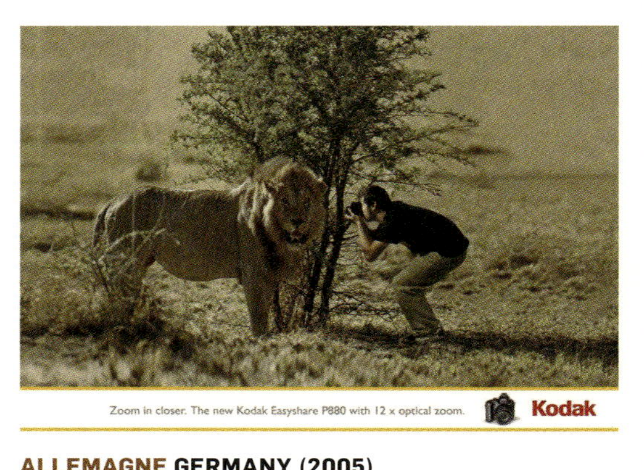

ALLEMAGNE GERMANY (2005)
Ogilvy Frankfurt   Kodak Easyshare P880
Zoom in closer

LIONS

№55

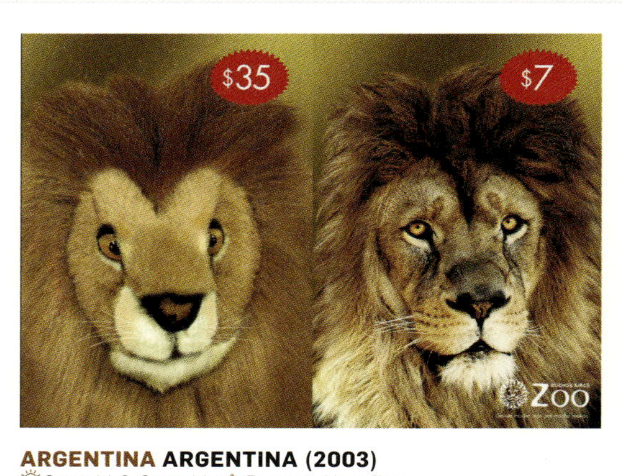

ARGENTINA ARGENTINA (2003)
Saatchi & Saatchi   Buenos Aires Zoo

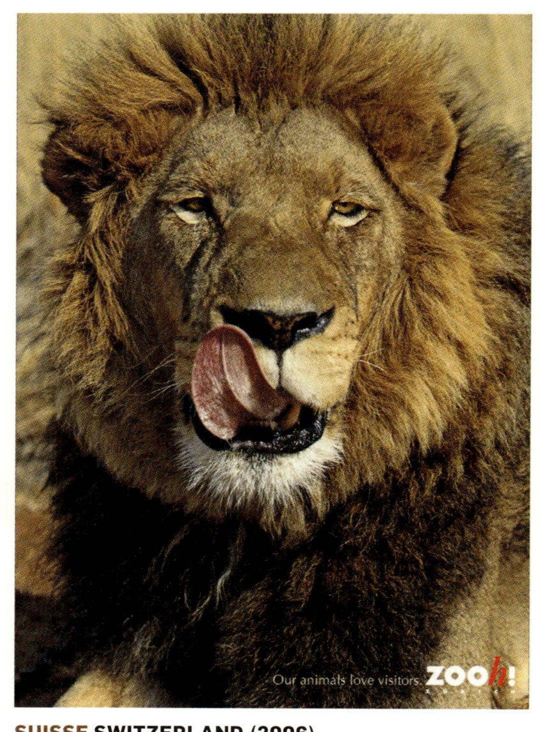

SUISSE SWITZERLAND (2006)
Publicis Zurich   Zoo Zurich
Our animals love visitors

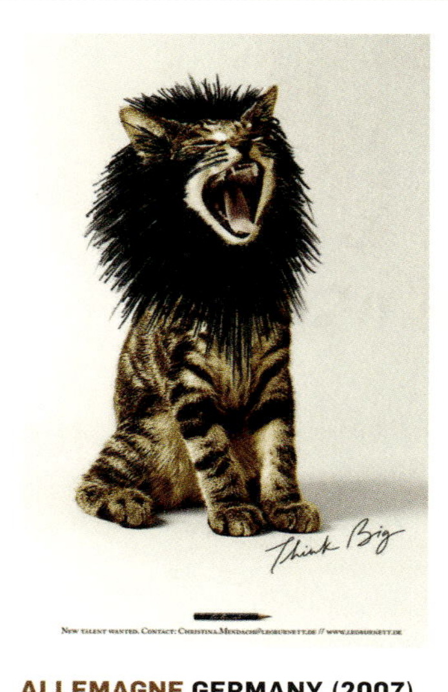

ALLEMAGNE GERMANY (2007)
Leo Burnett Frankfurt
Leo Burnett Recruitment
Think Big. New talent wanted

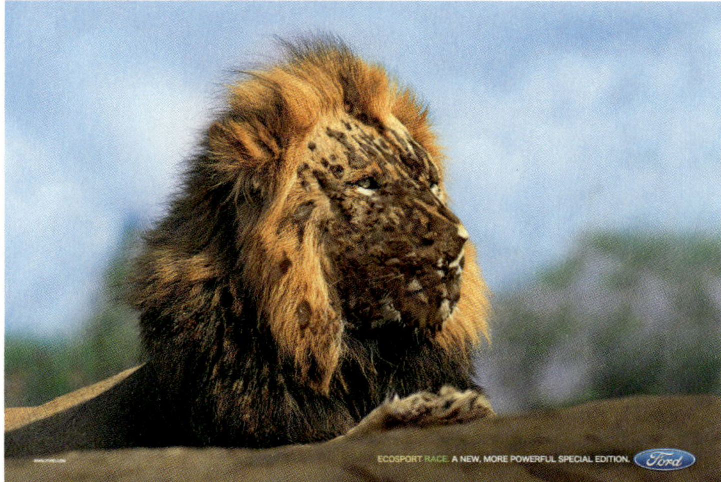

COLOMBIE COLOMBIA (2005)
JWT   Ford Ecosport Race
A new more powerful special edition

« Cette annonce reflète assez bien selon moi l'esprit des possesseurs de 4x4. Des gens sans scrupules qui nous polluent le paysage et salissent la planète. Bien sûr, ce n'est pas ce qu'a voulu dire cette pub, mais j'ai trouvé cette ironie de l'histoire intéressante. »
"This announcement reflects quite well, in my mind, the mindset of SUV owners. Unscrupulous people that pollute the landscape and dirty the planet. Of course it is not really what this ad meant to say, but I found this situational irony interesting."

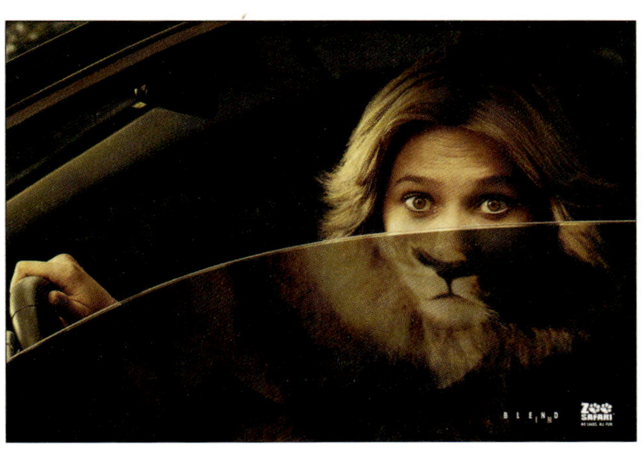

BRÉSIL BRAZIL (2009)
DDB Brazil   Safari Zoo
Blend in

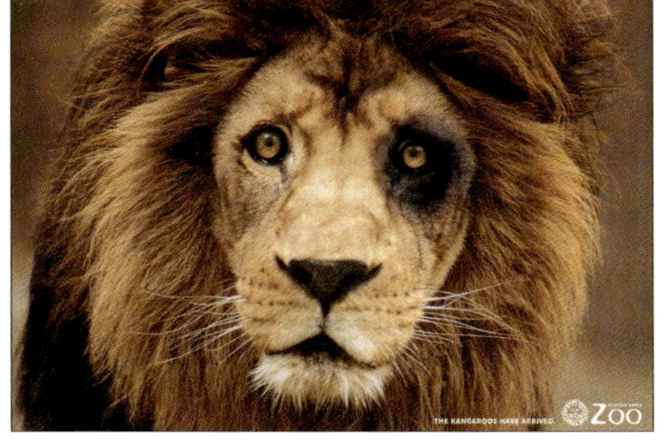

ARGENTINE ARGENTINA (2005)
Saatchi & Saatchi   Buenos Aires Zoo
The kangaroos have arrived

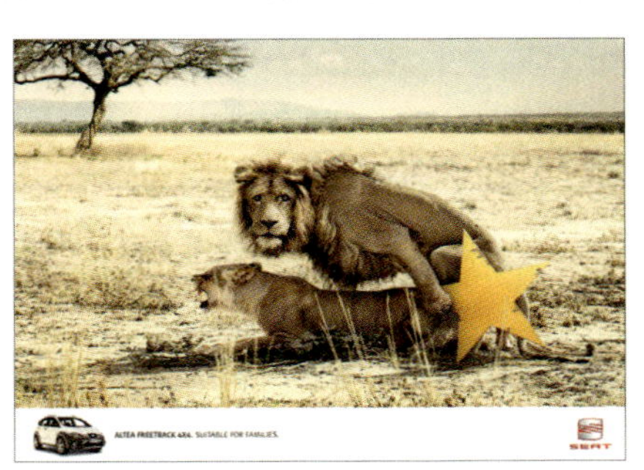

FRANCE FRANCE (2011)
Grey Paris   Seat Altea Freetrack 4x4
Suitable for families

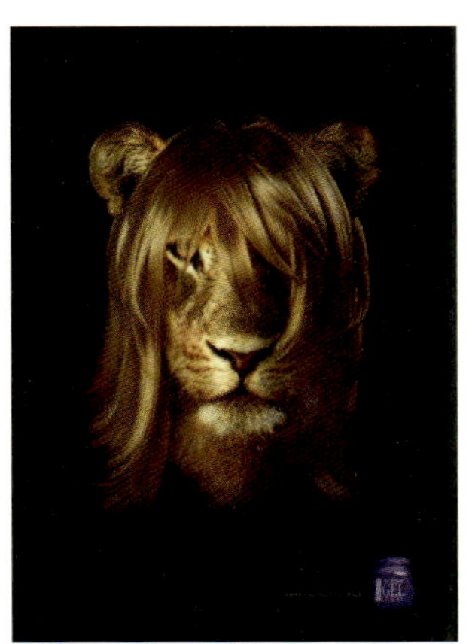

**AFRIQUE DU SUD
SOUTH AFRICA (2005)**
Network BBDO Johannesburg
Sculpting Hair Gel
Tames the wildest hair

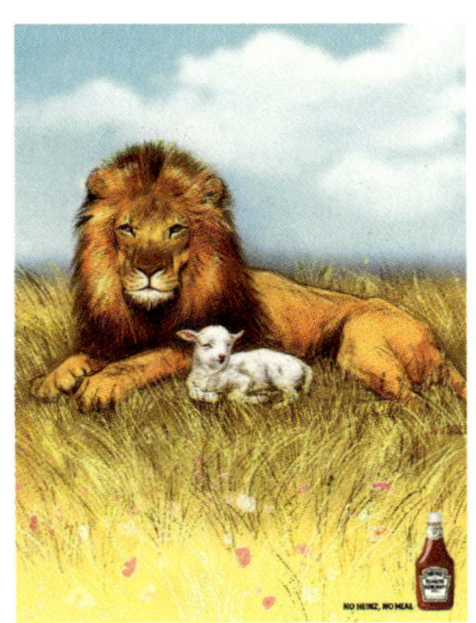

ISRAËL ISRAEL (2008)
Young & Rubicam Tel Aviv
Heinz Tomato Ketchup
No Heinz, no meal

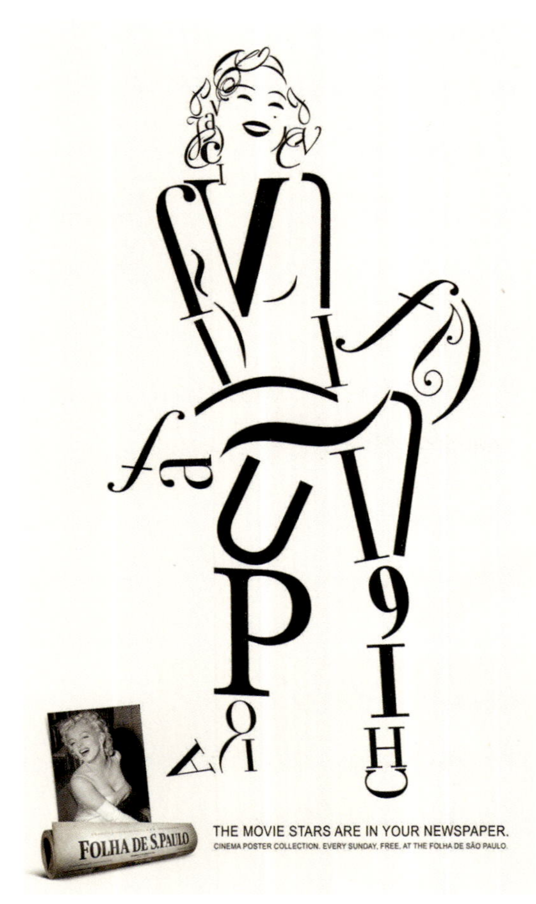

BRÉSIL BRAZIL (2008)
Africa Sao Paulo Folha de Sao Paulo

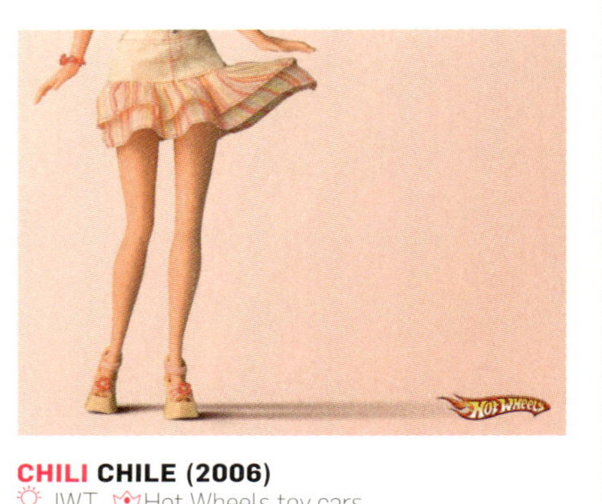

CHILI CHILE (2006)
JWT Hot Wheels toy cars

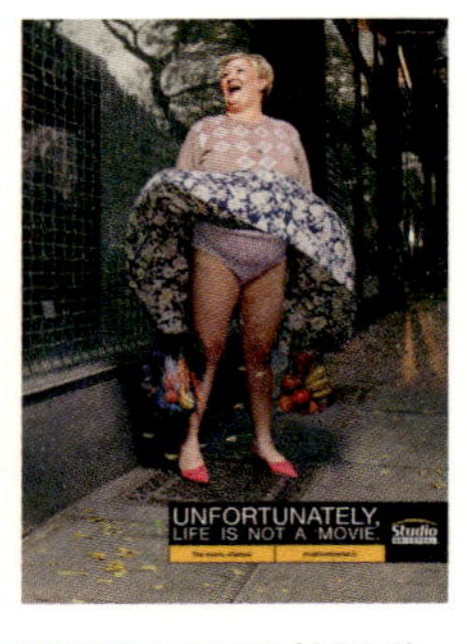

ITALIE ITALY (2005)
D'adda, Lorenzini, Vigorelli, BBDO
Studio Universal
Unfortunately life is not a movie

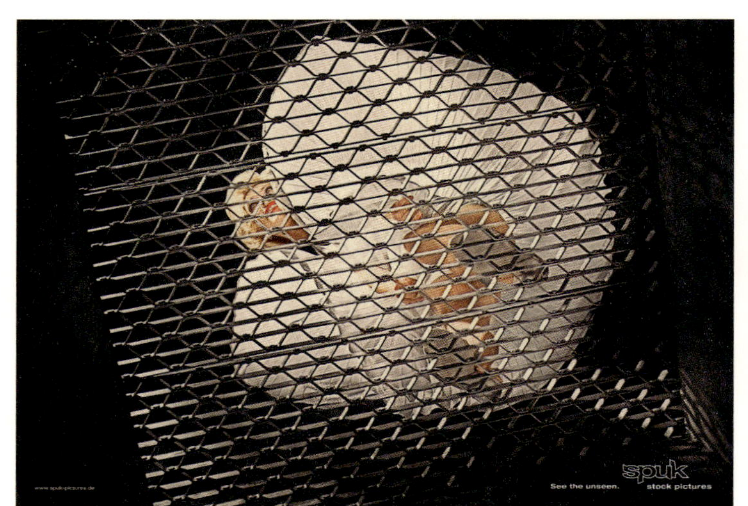

ALLEMAGNE GERMANY (2010)
BBDO Spuk Stock Pictures
See the unseen

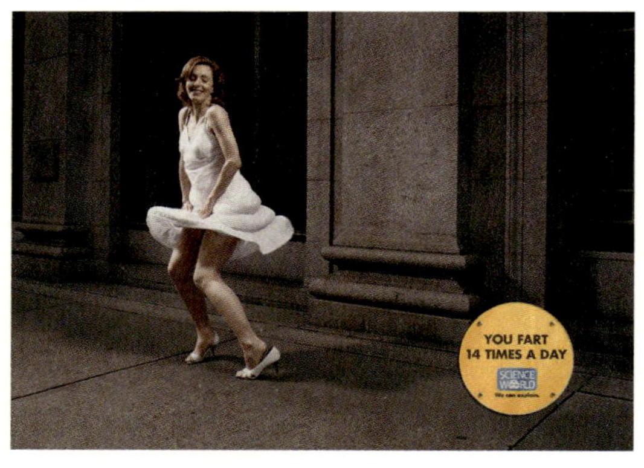

CANADA CANADA (2006)
Rethink Science World
You fart 14 times a day. We can explain

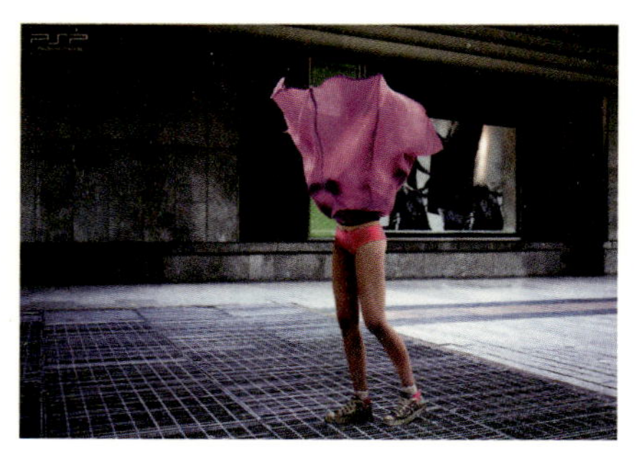

ESPAGNE SPAIN (2008)
TBWA PSP
Playstation Portable

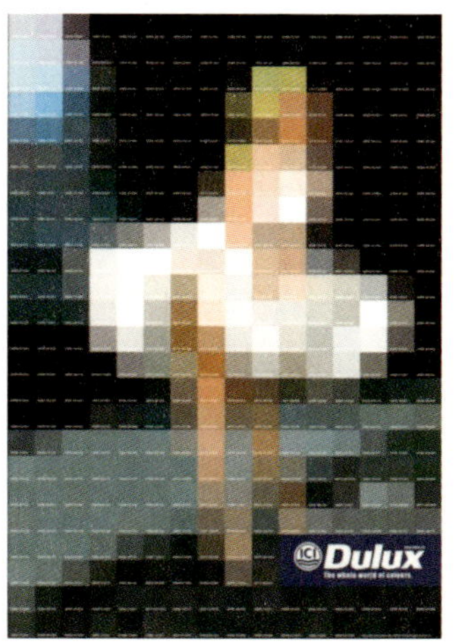

ALLEMAGNE GERMANY (2005)
Jung Von Matt Dulux Paints
The whole world of colours

MARYLIN MONROE

N°56

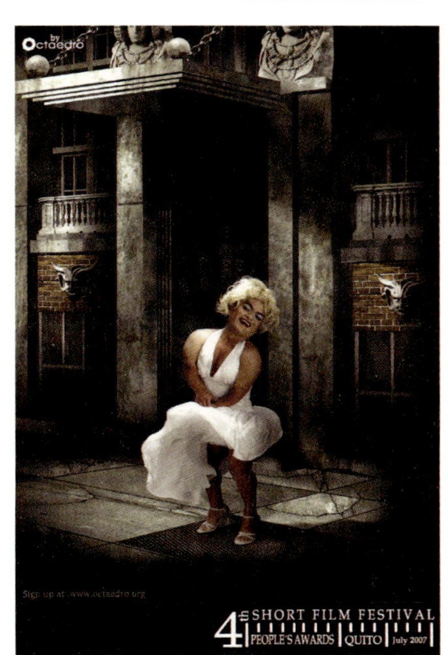

ÉQUATEUR ECUADOR (2007)
JWT 4th Short Film Festival

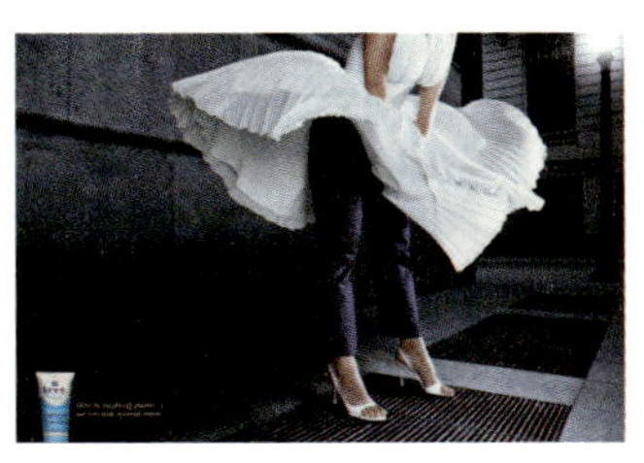

BRÉSIL BRAZIL (2006)
JWT Veet
Veet hair removal cream

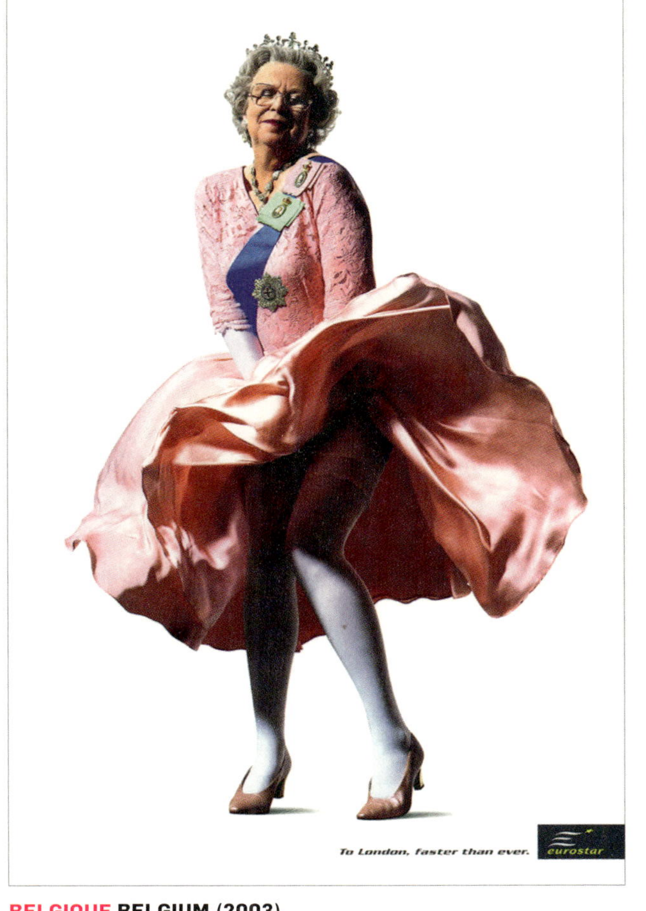

BELGIQUE BELGIUM (2003)
TBWA Brussels Eurostar
To London faster than ever

MC ESCHER

№ 57

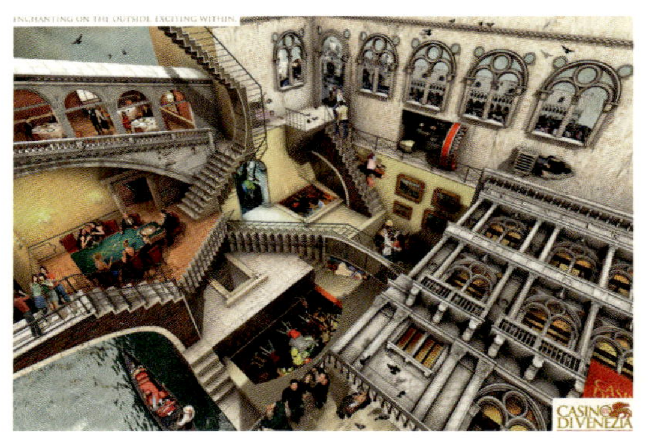

ITALIE ITALY (2009)
ADM Com — Casino Venezia
An infinite emotion

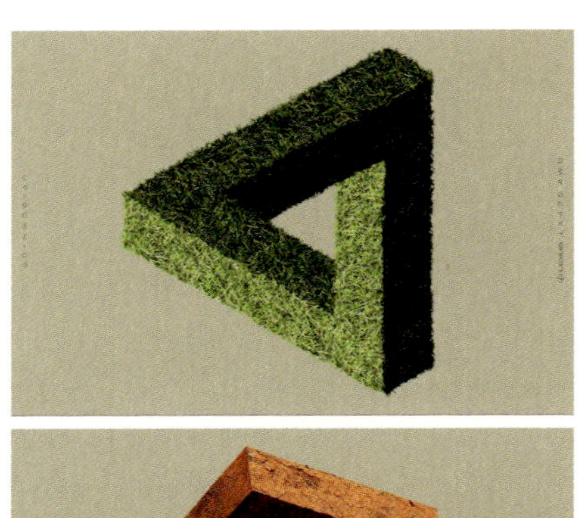

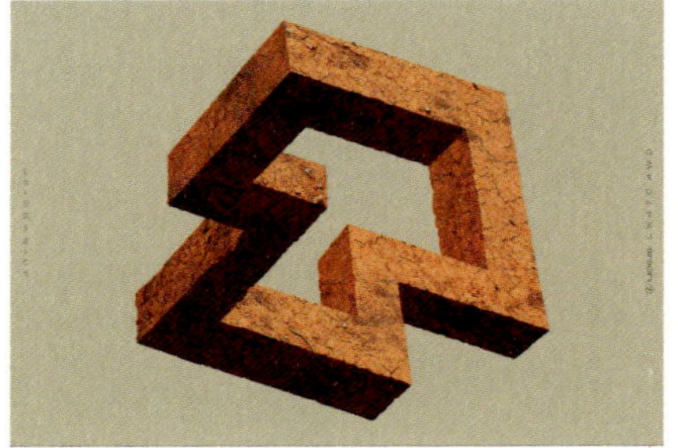

AUSTRALIE AUSTRALIA (2007)
Saatchi & Saatchi Sydney — Lexus LX470 4WD
Up - Down - Up

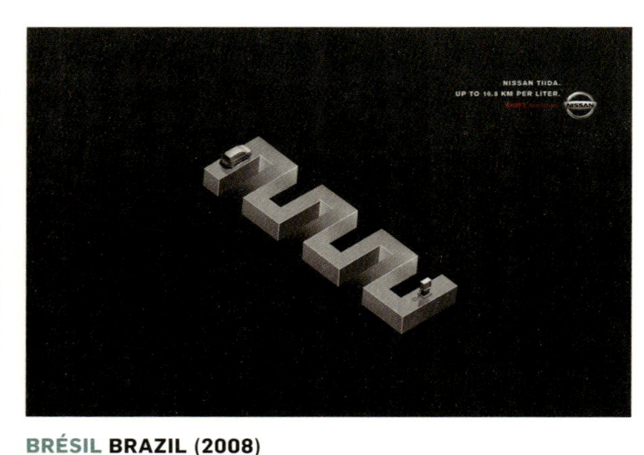

BRÉSIL BRAZIL (2008)
Lew Lara TBWA — Nissan Tiida
Up to 16.8 Km per liter

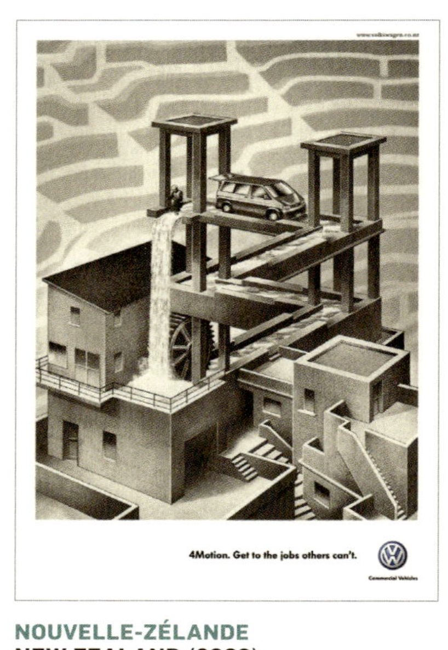
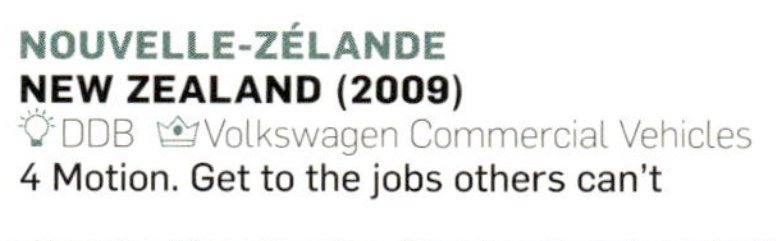

NOUVELLE-ZÉLANDE
NEW ZEALAND (2009)
DDB — Volkswagen Commercial Vehicles
4 Motion. Get to the jobs others can't

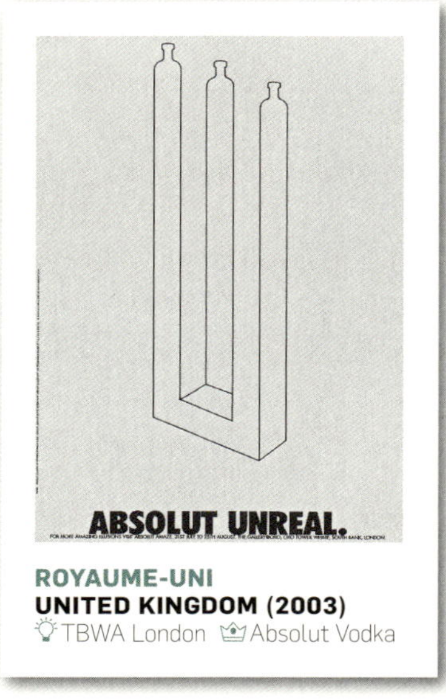

ROYAUME-UNI
UNITED KINGDOM (2003)
TBWA London — Absolut Vodka

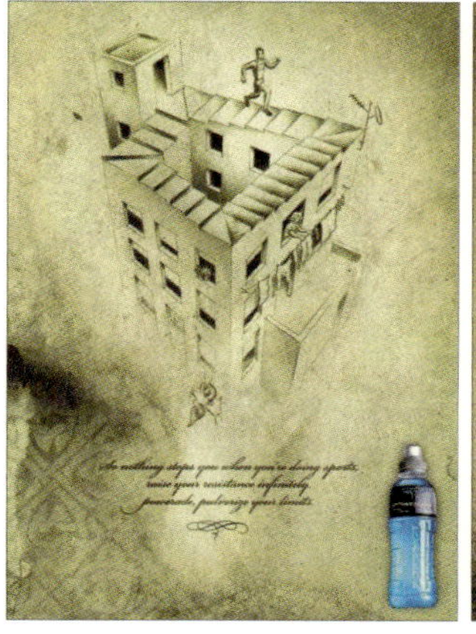

ESPAGNE SPAIN (2003)
Mc Cann Erickson Powerade
So nothing stops you when you're doing sports...

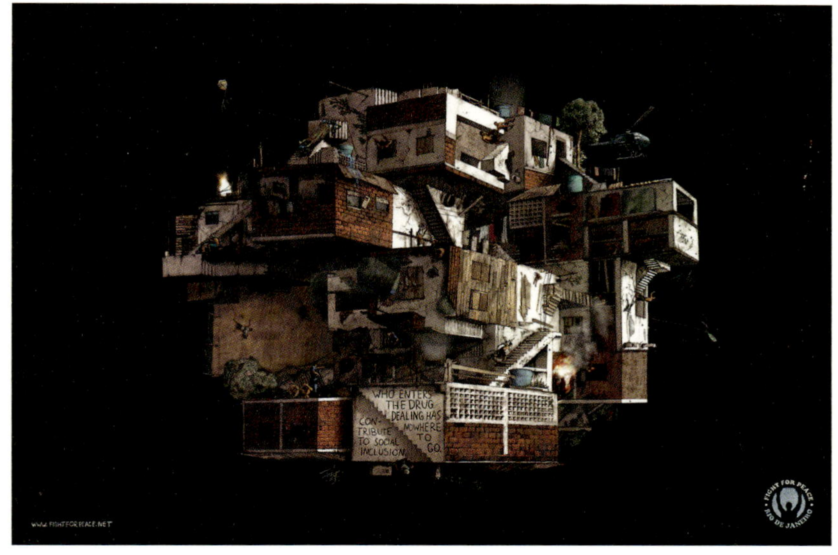

BRÉSIL BRAZIL (2012)
Staff Rio de Janeiro Fightfor peace.net
Who enters the drug dealing has nowhere to go

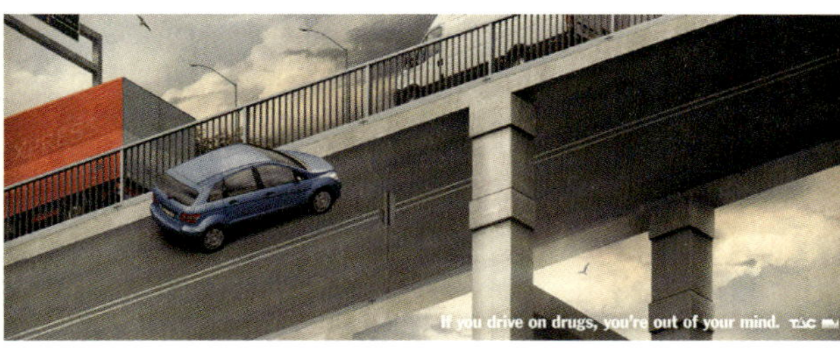

AUSTRALIE AUSTRALIA (2012)
Grey Melbourne TAC. Road Safety
If you drive on drugs, you're out of your mind

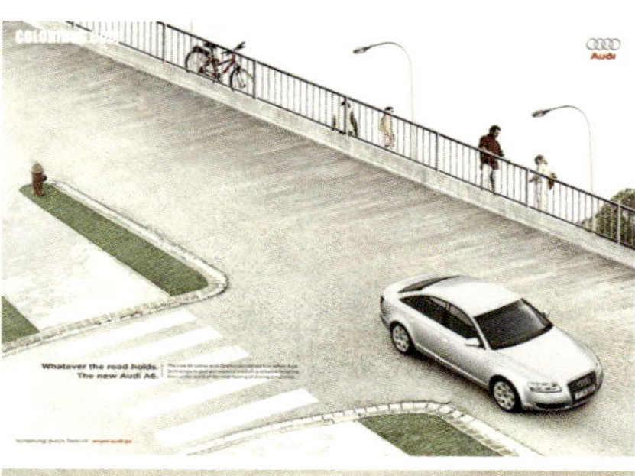

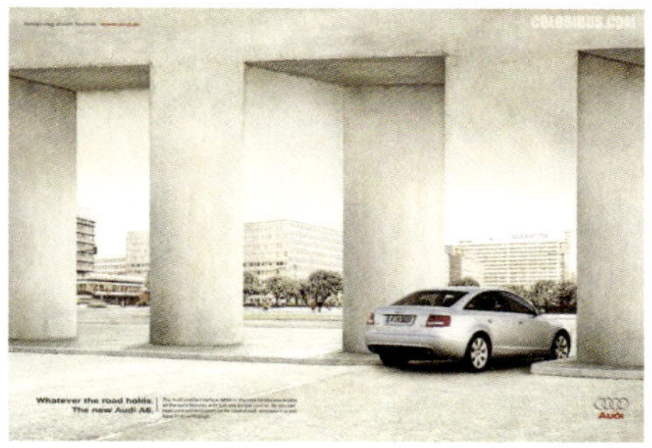

ROYAUME-UNI UNITED KINGDOM (2004)
BBH London Audi A6
Whatever the road holds

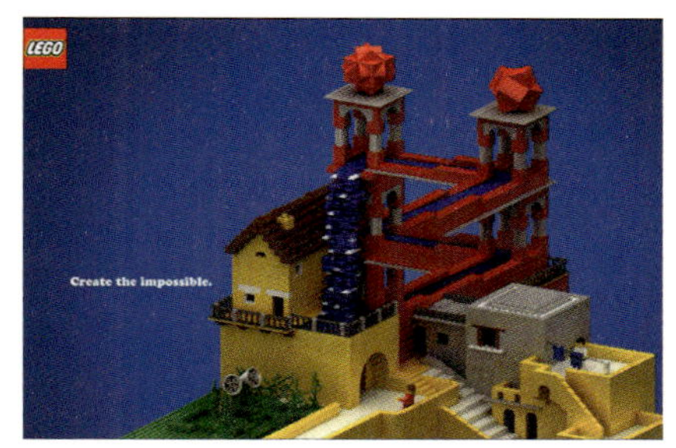

ALLEMAGNE GERMANY (2007)
Jung Von Matt Lego
Create the impossible

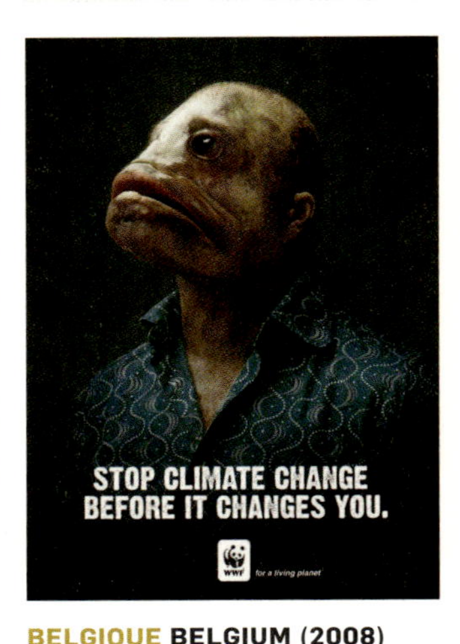

BELGIQUE BELGIUM (2008)
Germaine
WWF For a living planet

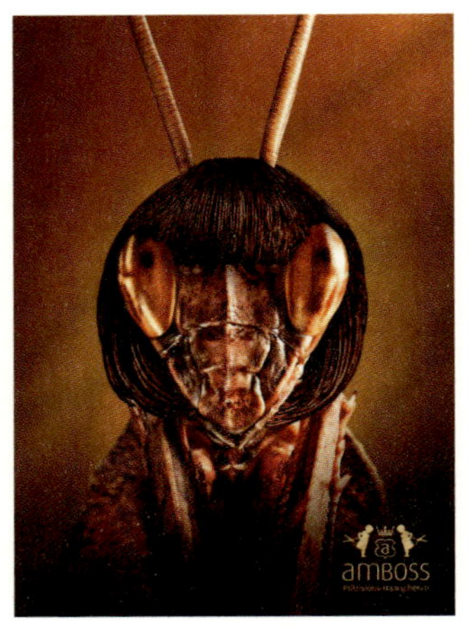

ALLEMAGNE GERMANY (2008)
Saint Elmo'sA gency
For Creative Energy
Amboss Hair Saloon

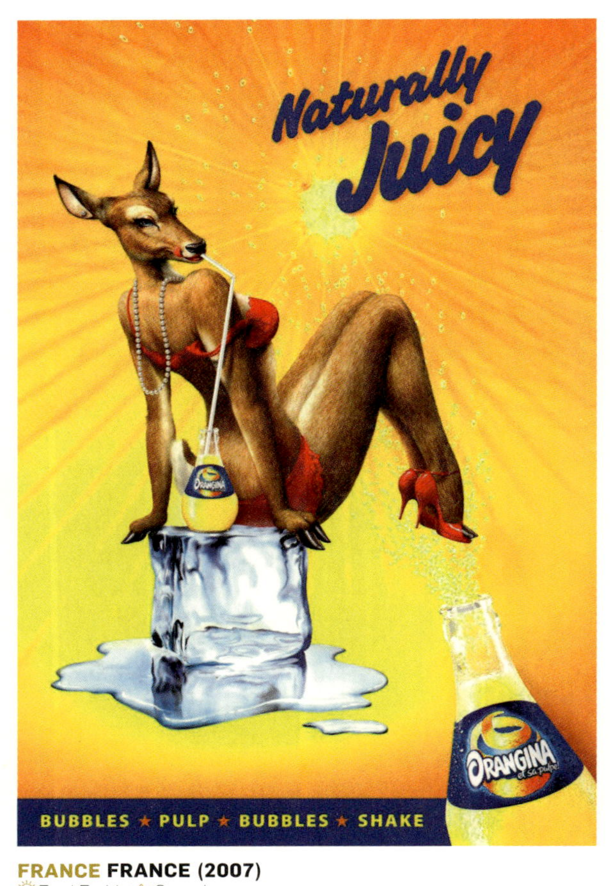

FRANCE FRANCE (2007)
Fred Farid   Orangina

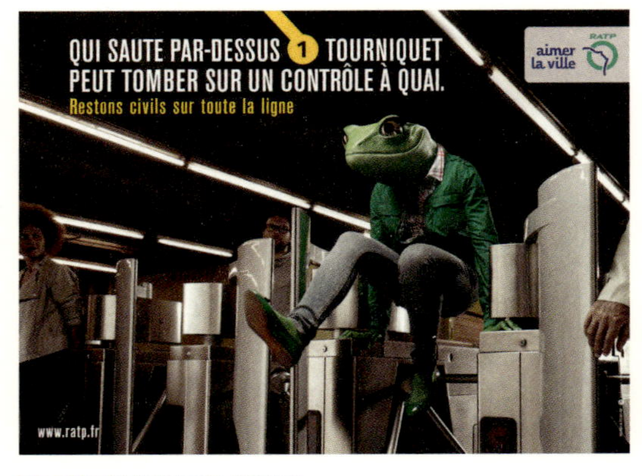

FRANCE FRANCE (2011)
Publicis Conseil   RATP Paris Subway

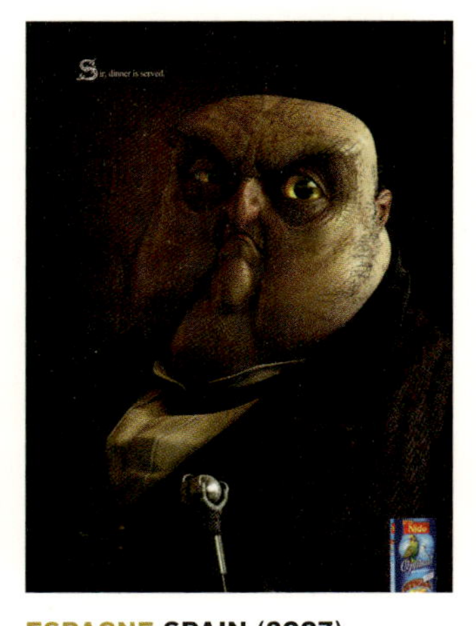

**RÉPUBLIQUE TCHÈQUE
CZECH REPUBLIC (2010)**
Fabrika   Le Cornichon Restaurant
Coq au vin rouge.
Vive la cuisine française

ESPAGNE SPAIN (2007)
DDB   Nido Bird Food
Sir, dinner is served

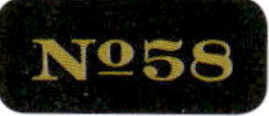

HALF ANIMALS, HALF HUMANS

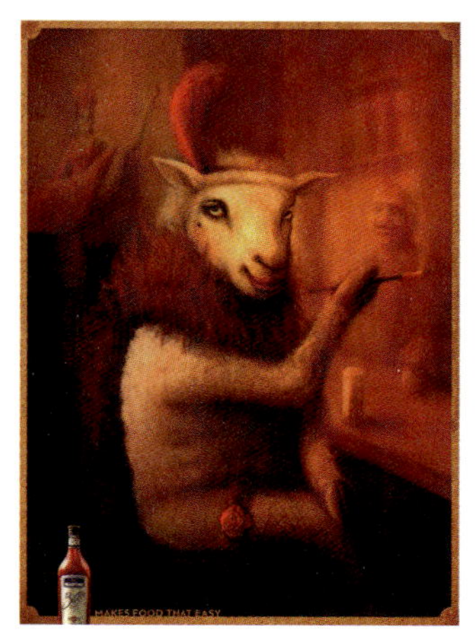

ROUMANIE ROMANIA (2009)
Publicis Martini Bitter
Makes food that easy

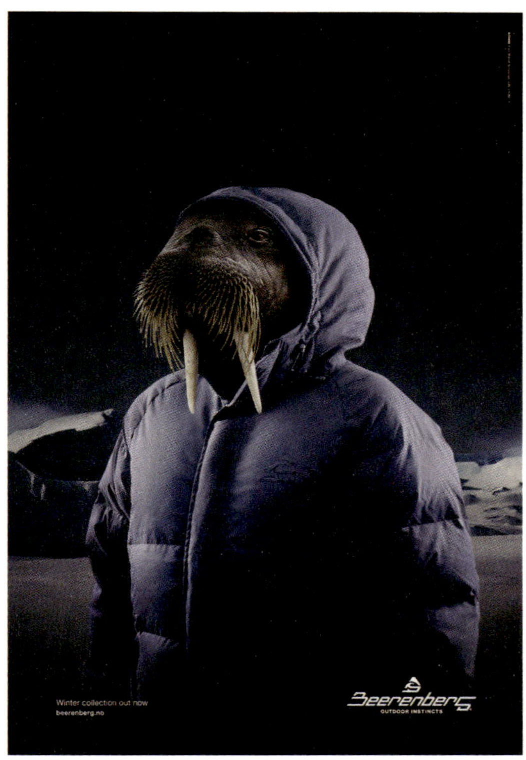

NORVÈGE NORWAY (2009)
Kitchen Leo Burnett Beerenberg
Outdoor Instincts

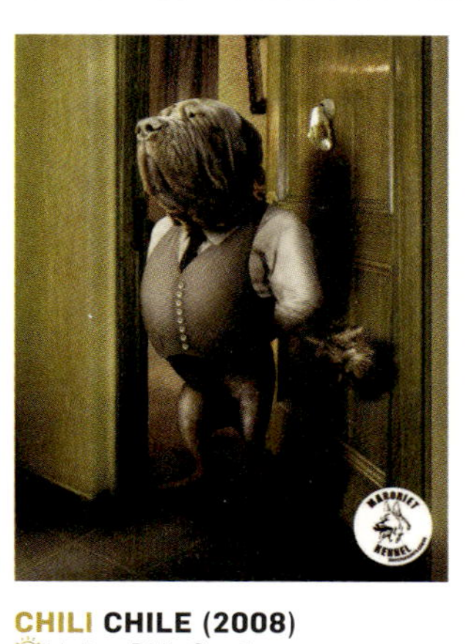

CHILI CHILE (2008)
Unitas RNL Santiago
Kennel Maroriet Dog Training School

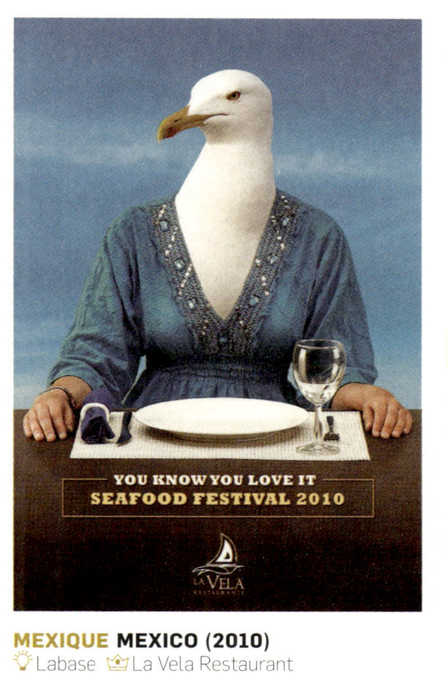

MEXIQUE MEXICO (2010)
Labase La Vela Restaurant

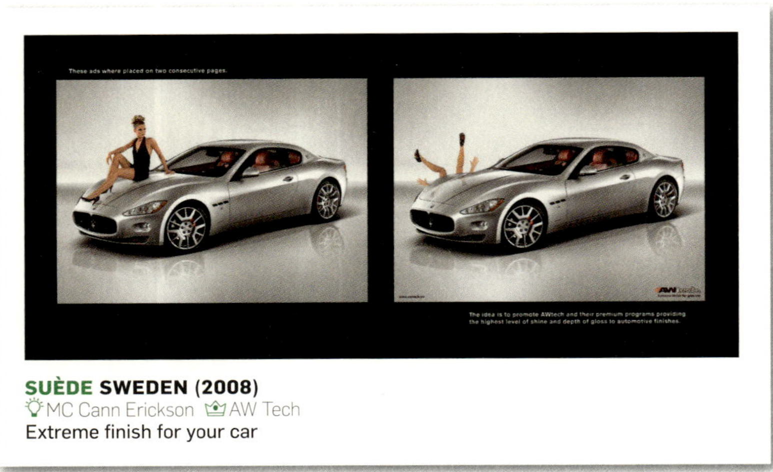

SUÈDE SWEDEN (2008)
MC Cann Erickson AW Tech
Extreme finish for your car

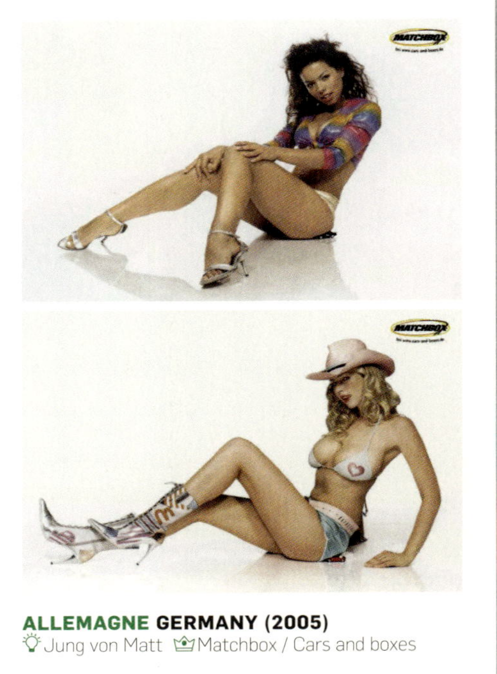

ALLEMAGNE GERMANY (2005)
Jung von Matt Matchbox / Cars and boxes

MODÈLES SUR DES VOITURES

Nº59

WOMEN ON CARS

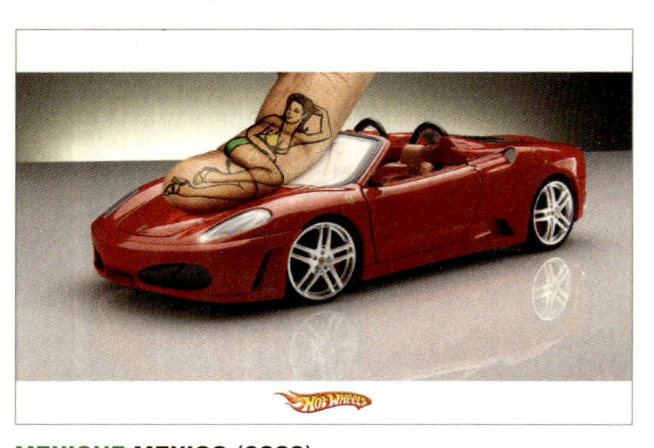

MEXIQUE MEXICO (2008)
Ogilvy & Mather Hot Wheels Toy Cars

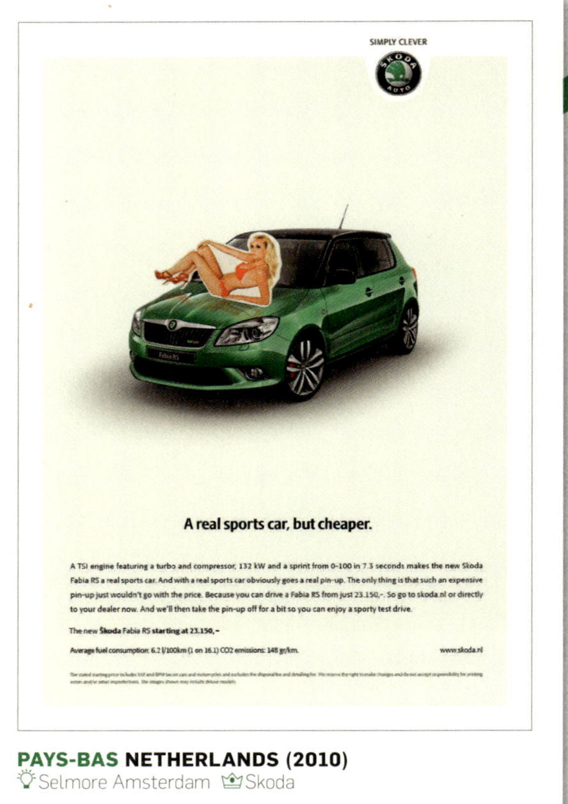

PAYS-BAS NETHERLANDS (2010)
Selmore Amsterdam Skoda

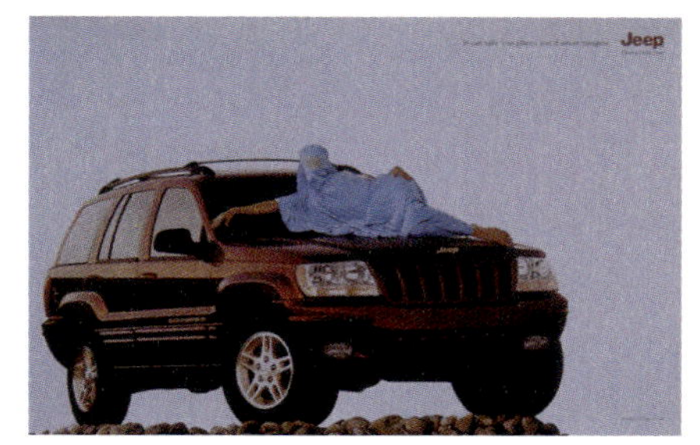

BRÉSIL BRAZIL (2002)
Giovanni FCB Jeep
It can take you places you'd never imagine

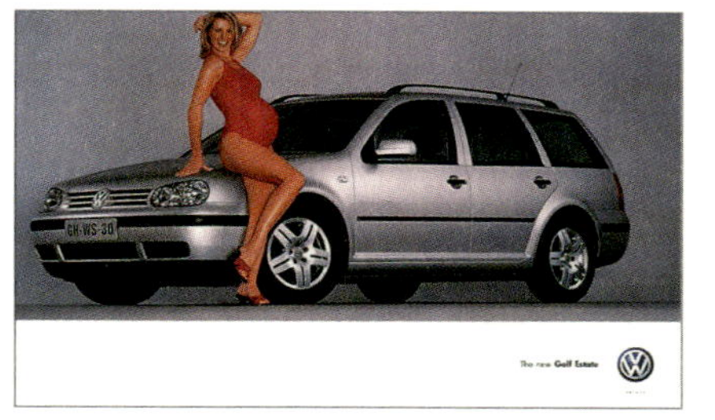

AFRIQUE DU SUD SOUTH AFRICA (2001)
Ogilvy & Mather Volkswagen Estate

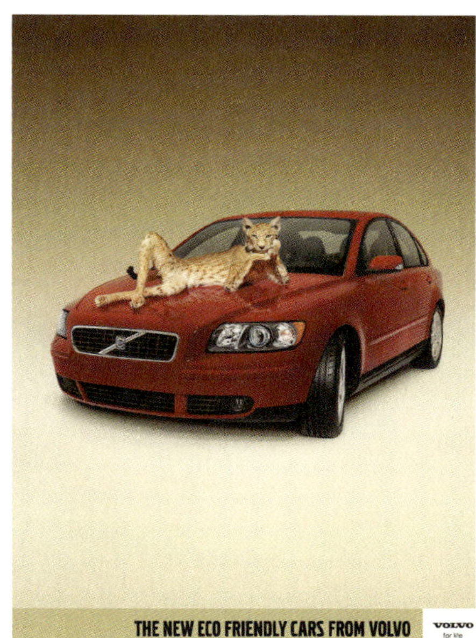

SUÈDE SWEDEN (2005)
Forsman & Bodenfors Volvo

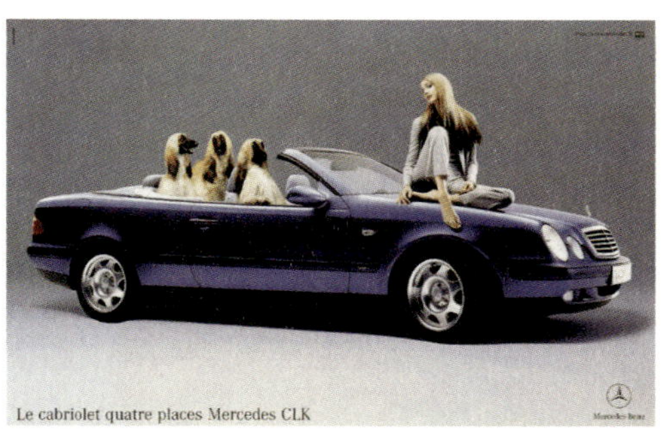

FRANCE FRANCE (1998)
Devarrieuxvillaret Mercedes CLK
Le cabriolet 4 places The cabriolet with four seats

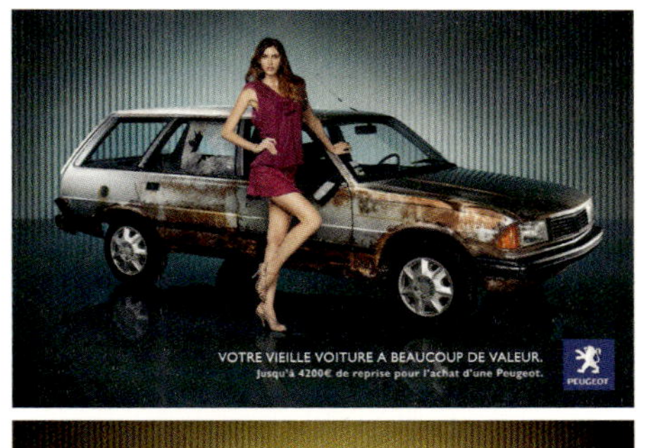

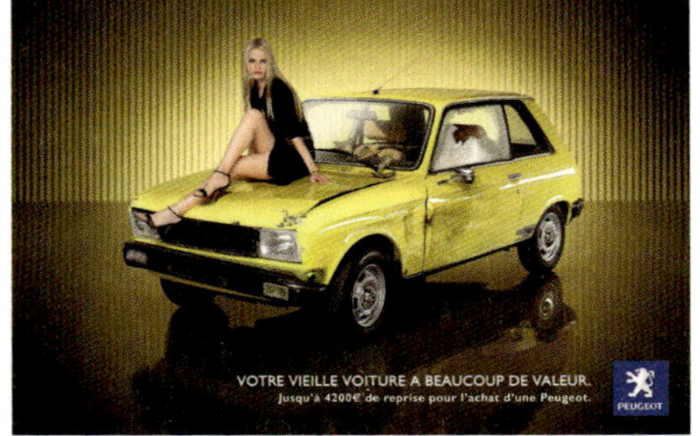

FRANCE FRANCE (2006)
BETC Euro RSCG Peugeot
Your old car is hot property

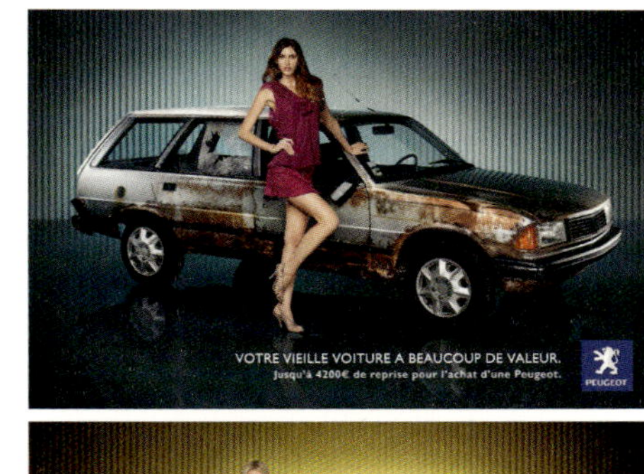

PAYS-BAS NETHERLANDS (?)
BSUR Bob Hahn
Bob Hahn only restores classic Porsches

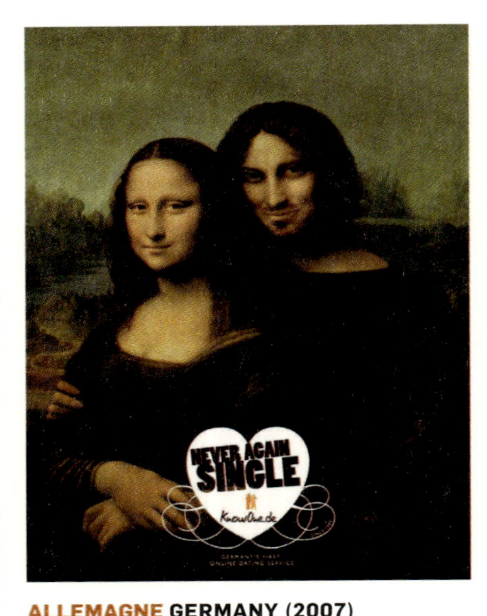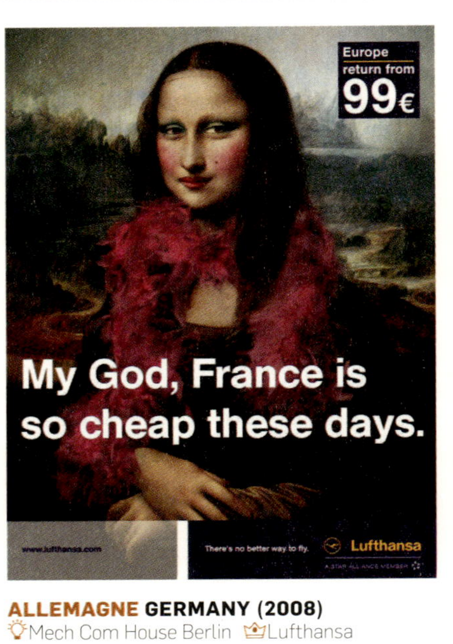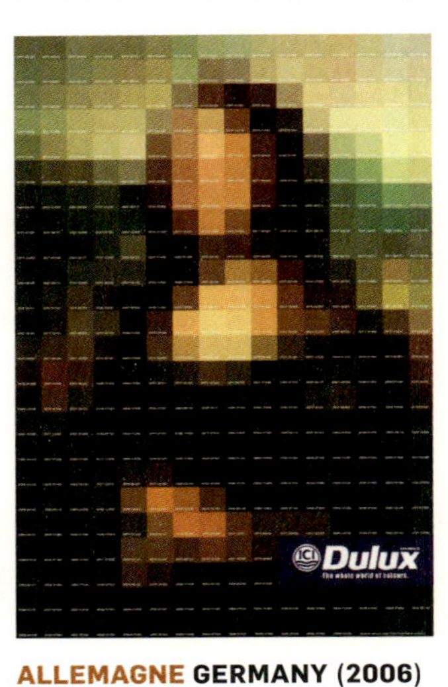

ALLEMAGNE GERMANY (2007)
Schwarzspringer
Knowone.de matchmaking service

ALLEMAGNE GERMANY (2008)
Mech Com House Berlin Lufthansa

ALLEMAGNE GERMANY (2006)
Jung von Matt Dulux
The whole world of colours

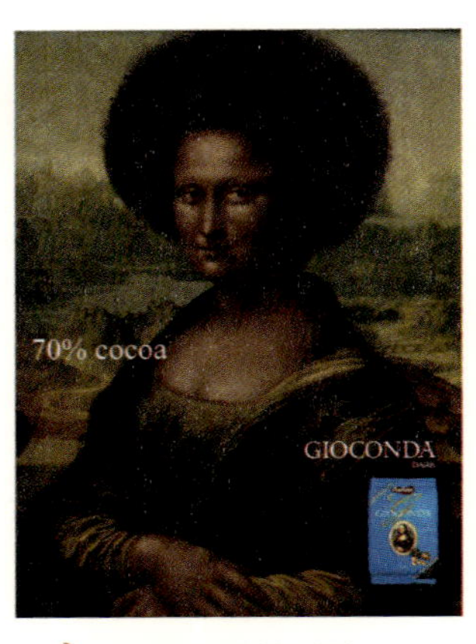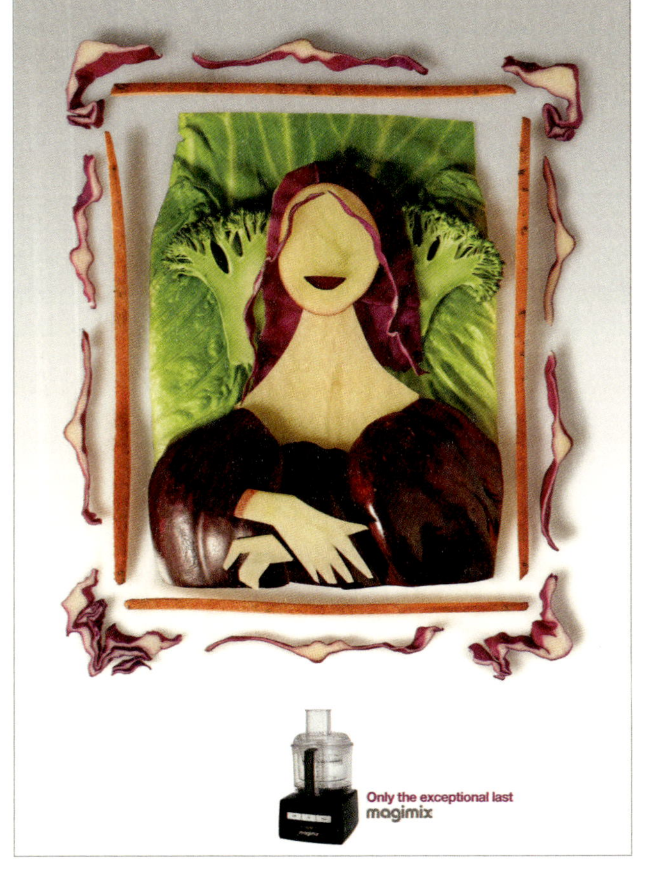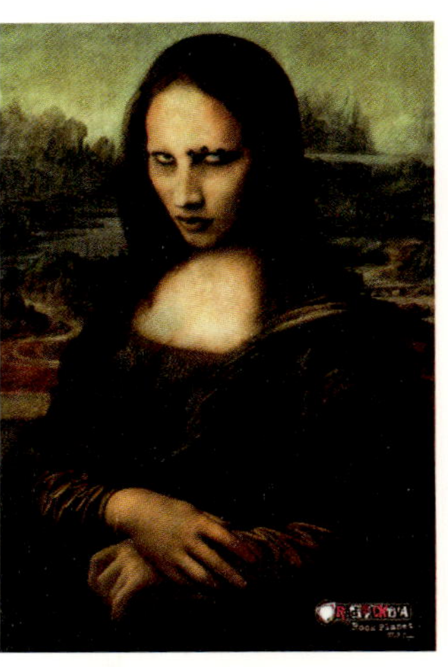

GRÈCE GREECE (2008)
Ogilvy Athens
Gioconda Dark chocolate

ISRAËL ISRAEL (2011)
Young & Rubicam Tel Aviv Magimix
Only the exceptional last

COLOMBIE COLOMBIA (2007)
Ade Bogota Radioactiva
The Rock Planet 97.9 F.M

MONA LISA

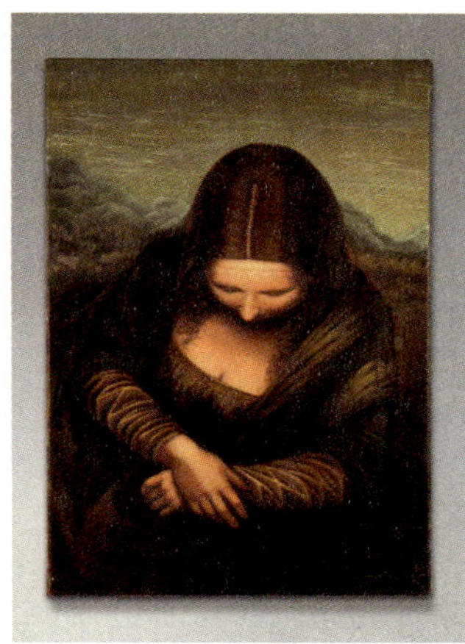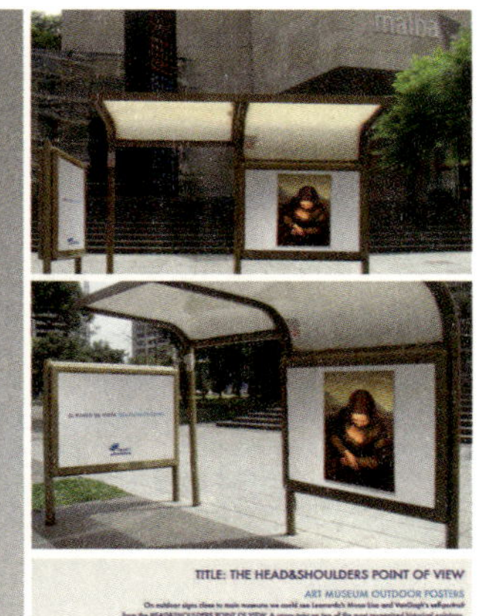

ARGENTINE ARGENTINA (2008)
Saatchi & Saatchi Buenos Aires   Head & Shoulders
The Head & Shoulders point of view

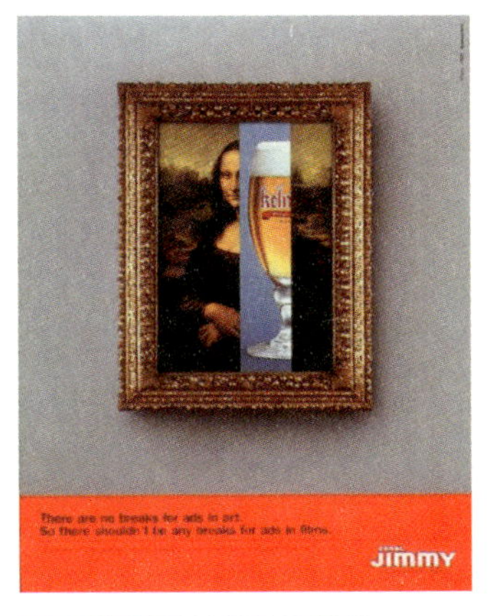

FRANCE FRANCE (2003)
DevarrieuxVillaret
Canal Jimmy Channel
There are no breaks for ads in art.
So there shouldn't be any breaks
for ads in films

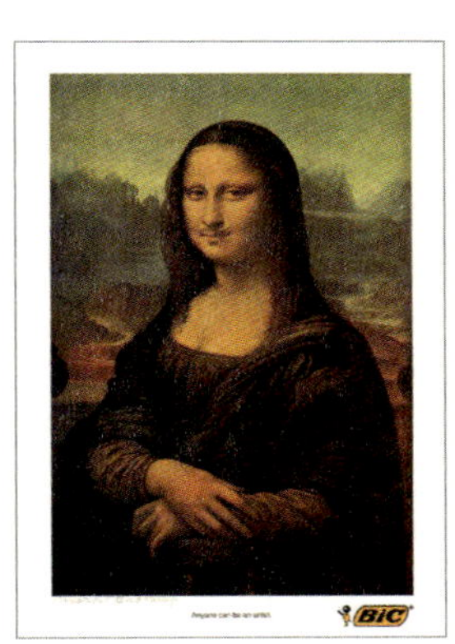

POLOGNE POLAND (2009)
S4   Bic Pens
Anyone can be an artist

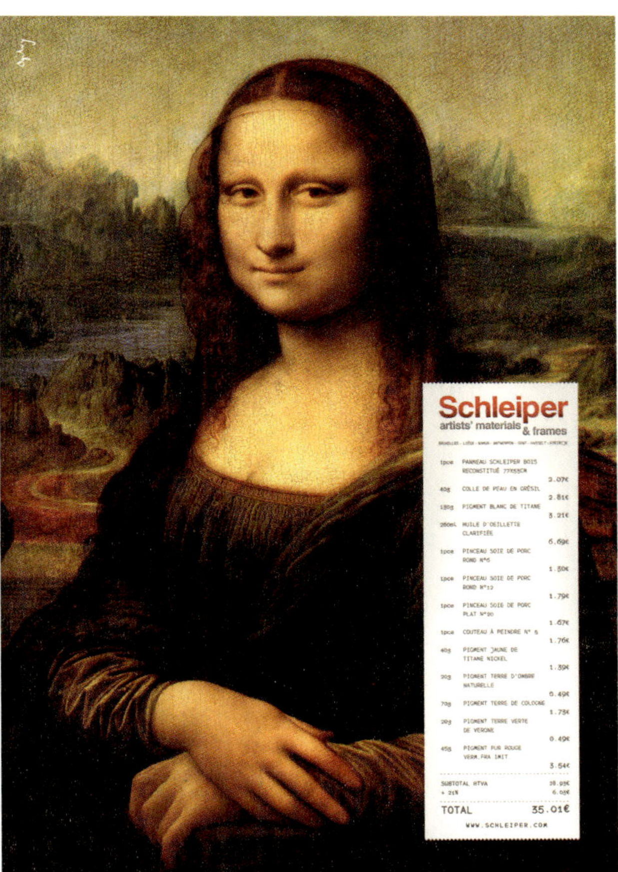

BELGIQUE BELGIUM (2009)
Ogilvy Brussels   Schleiper Artists' Material
Brushes... 1.67€
Paint... 1.76€
Frame... 2.07€
Total: 35€

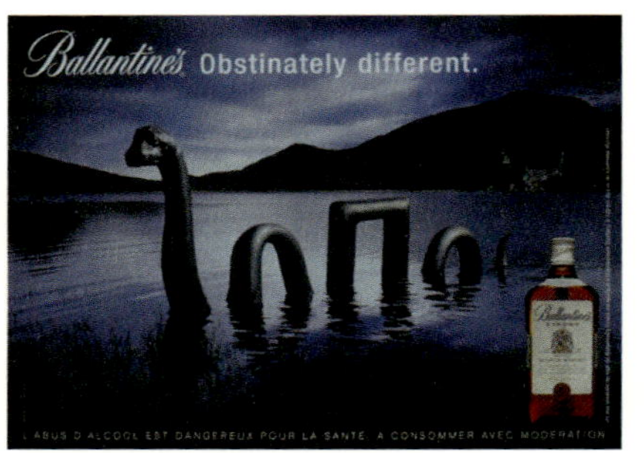

FRANCE FRANCE (2002)
Bates · Ballantine's Scotch Whiskey

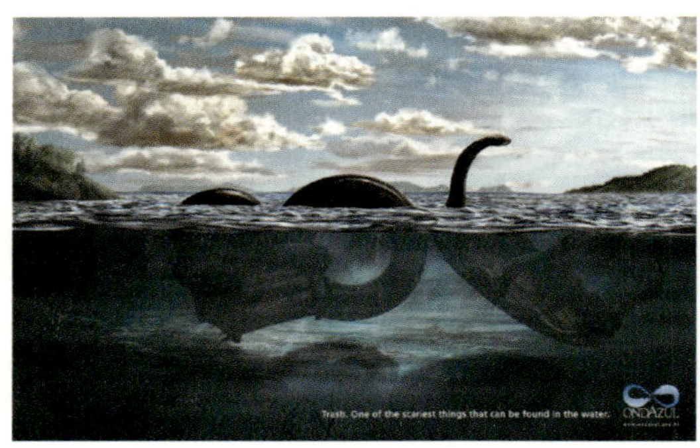

BRÉSIL BRAZIL (2011)
Que Comunicaçao Rio de Janeiro · Ondazul
Trash. One of the scariest things that can be found in the water.

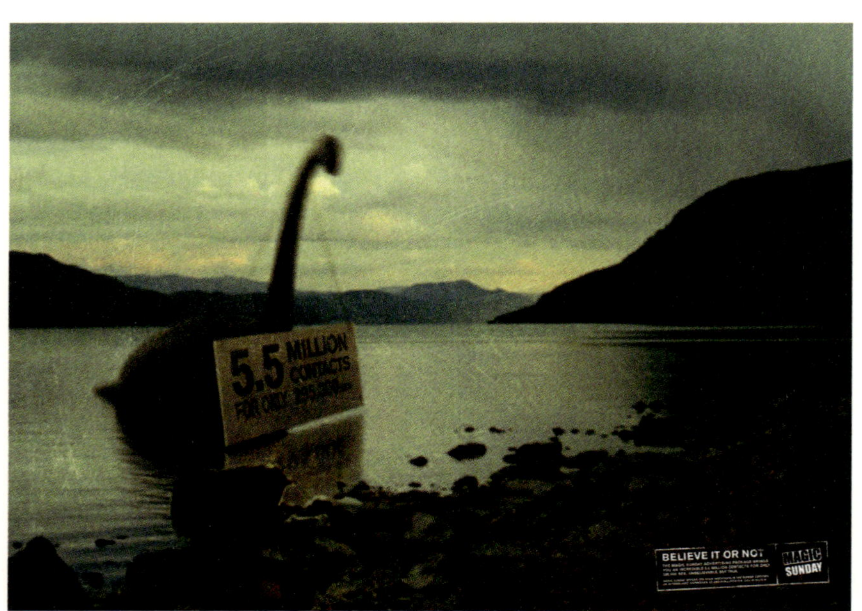

SUÈDE SWEDEN (2008)
Inconnu/unknown · Aftonbladet - Magic Sunday offer

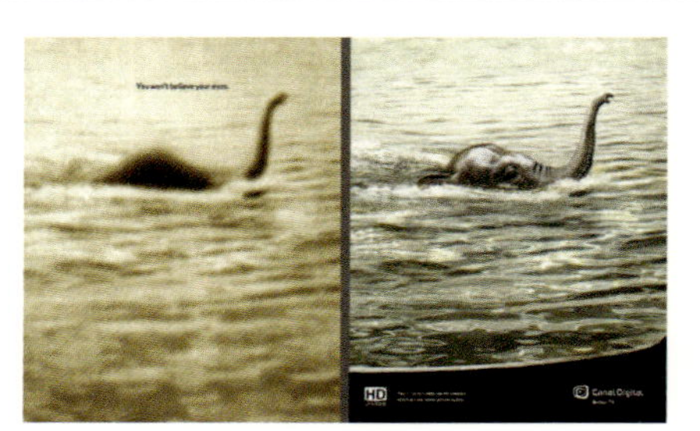

FINLANDE FINLAND (2008)
Family Inc · Canal Digital HD
You won't believe your eyes.
Better picture quality

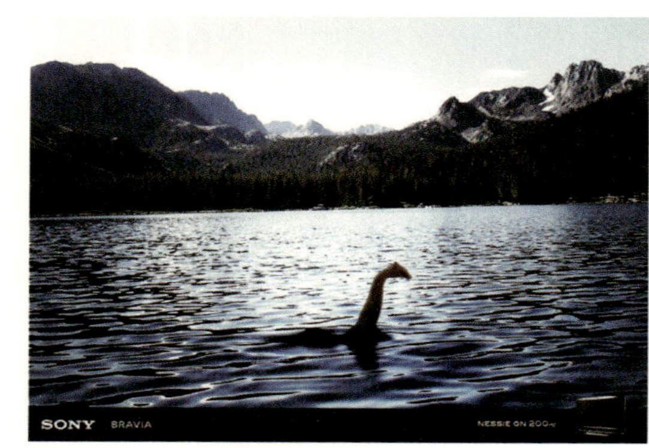

PORTUGAL PORTUGAL (2009)
Lisbon Ad School · Sony Bravia TV
Nessie on 200HZ

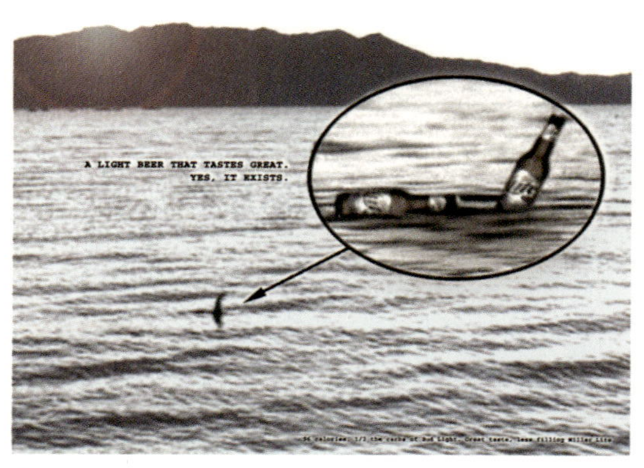

ÉTATS-UNIS UNITED STATES (2004)
Young & Rubicam Chicago · Miller Lite Beer
A light beer that tastes great. Yes, it exists.

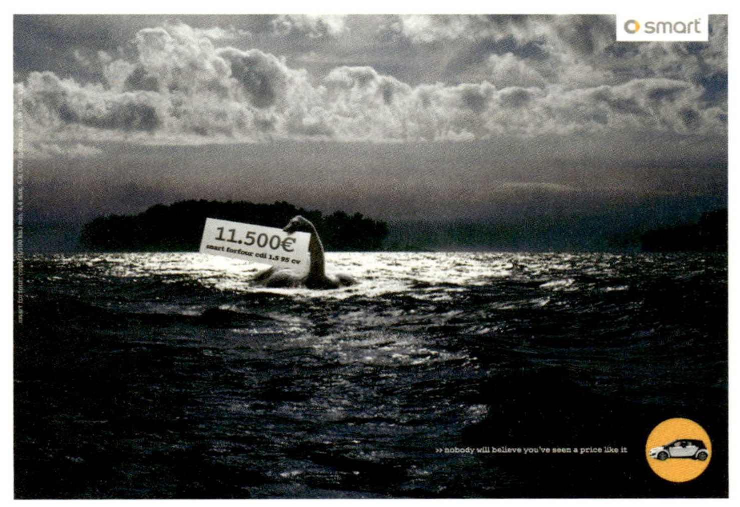

ESPAGNE SPAIN (2007)
Contrapunto Madrid · Smart Forfour
11.500€ Nobody will believe you've seen a price like it

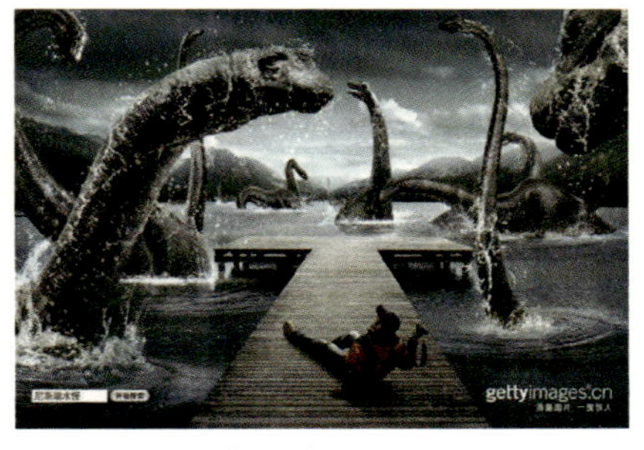

CHINE CHINA (2010)
JWT Shanghai · Getty Images image bank

LE MONSTRE DU LOCH NESS

№61

LOCH NESS MONSTER

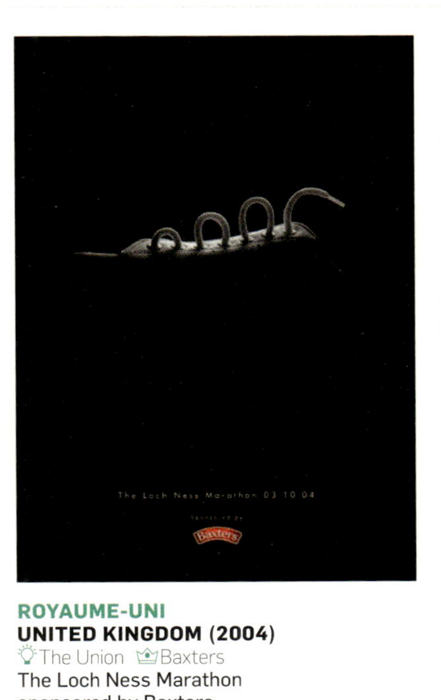

ROYAUME-UNI UNITED KINGDOM (2004)
The Union · Baxters
The Loch Ness Marathon
sponsored by Baxters

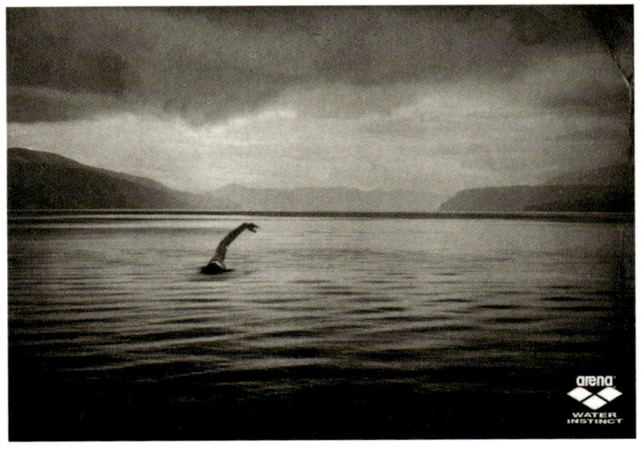

ITALIE ITALY (2007)
Lowe · Arena Swimsuits
Water Instinct

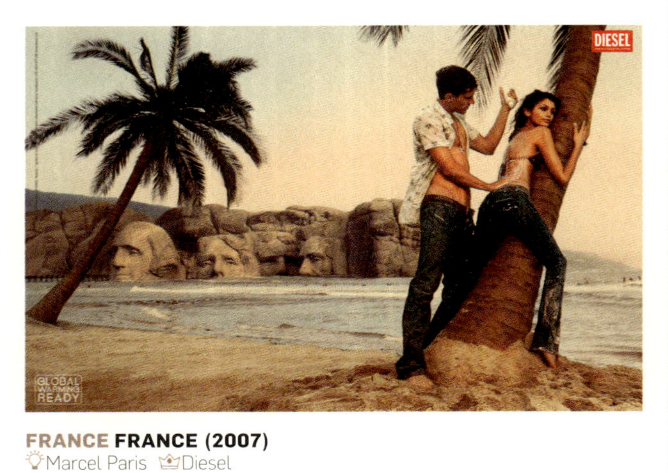

FRANCE FRANCE (2007)
Marcel Paris · Diesel
Global Warming Ready

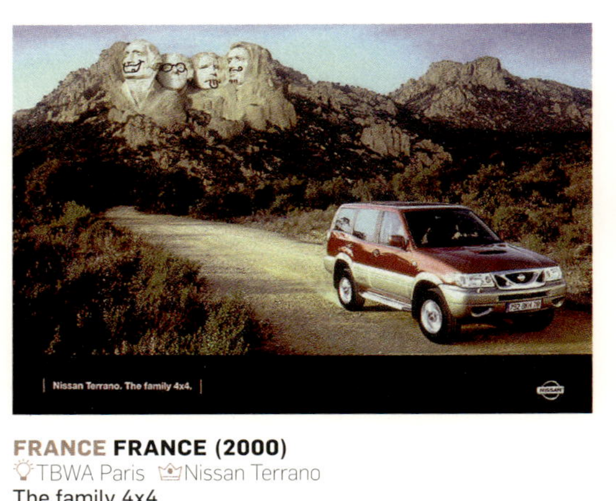

FRANCE FRANCE (2000)
TBWA Paris · Nissan Terrano
The family 4x4

LE MONT RUSHMORE

№62

MOUNT RUSHMORE

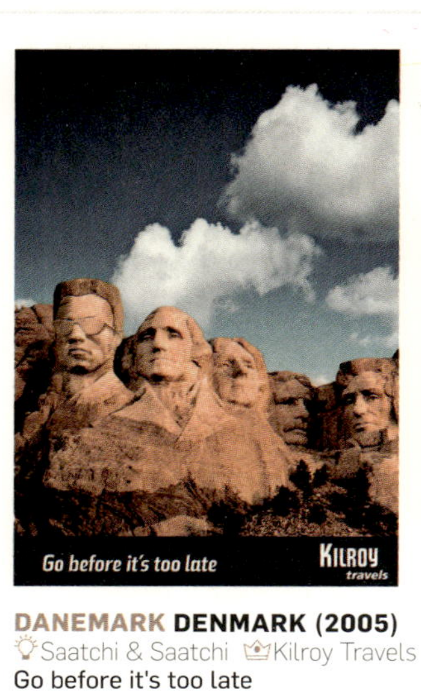

DANEMARK DENMARK (2005)
Saatchi & Saatchi · Kilroy Travels
Go before it's too late

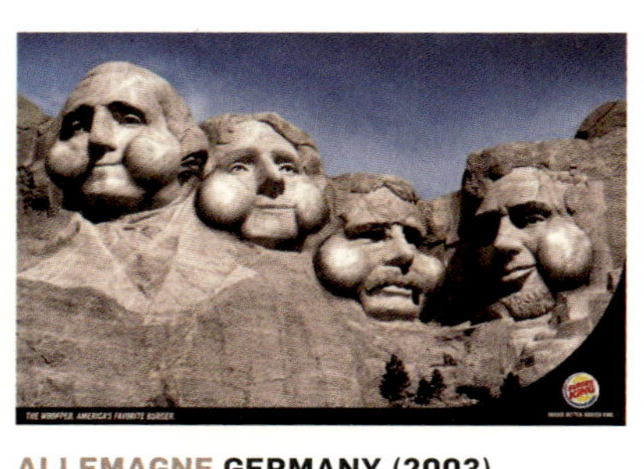

ALLEMAGNE GERMANY (2003)
.Start · Burger King
The whooper. America's favorite burger

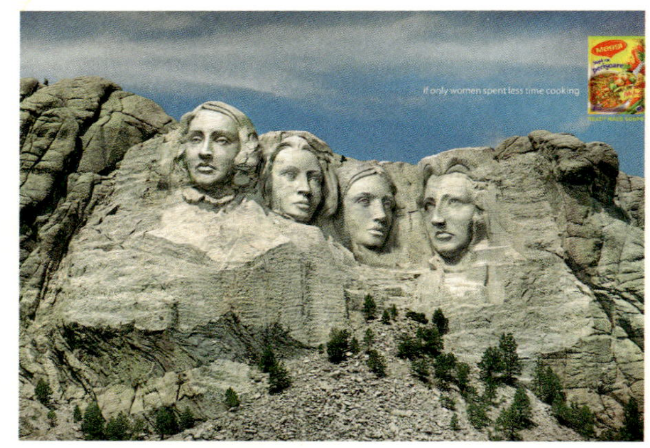

ROUMANIE ROMANIA (2006)
Mc Cann Erickson · Maggi Ready Made Soups
If only women spent less time cooking

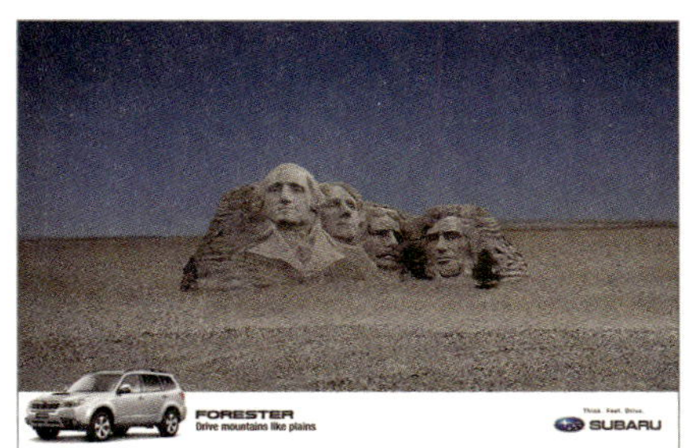

UKRAINE UKRAINE (2009)
Saatchi & Saatchi Subaru Forester
Drive mountains like plains

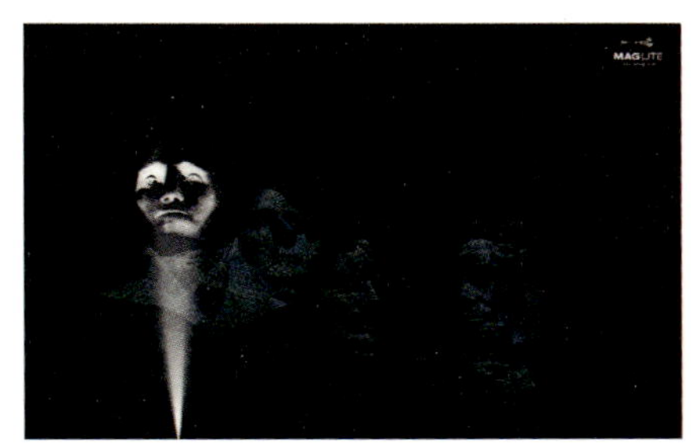

AFRIQUE DU SUD SOUTH AFRICA (2008)
Draft FCB Mag-Lite Torches

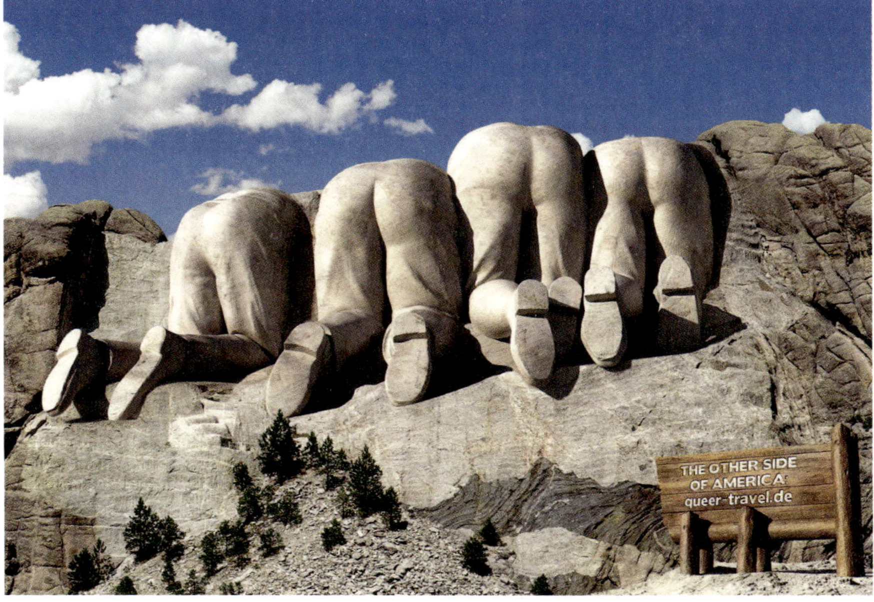

ALLEMAGNE GERMANY (2008)
Scholz & Friends Queer Travel
The other side of america

« Ce qui est fort, c'est que l'on reconnaît immédiatement le monument alors que l'on n'en retrouve presque aucun élément. C'est la plus éloignée de la réalité et la blague la plus osée… donc la plus surprenante.
Je suis sur le cul qu'ils aient pu mener à bien un tel projet. »
"What is strong is that we immediately recognize the monument even though we hardly see any other obvious elements. This is the furthest from reality and the joke is the most daring… so all the more surprising. It knocked me on my ass when I saw that they could actually carry through such a project."

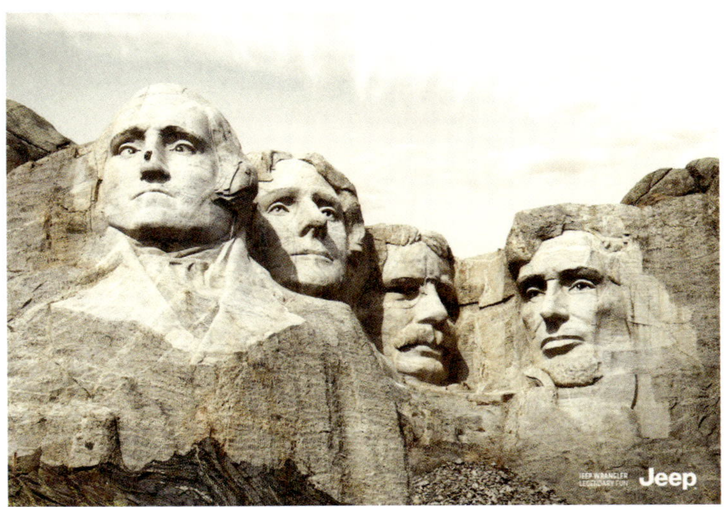

CANADA CANADA (2012)
Publicis Montreal Jeep Wrangler
(There is a small car on the nose of one of the presidents)
Legendary Fun

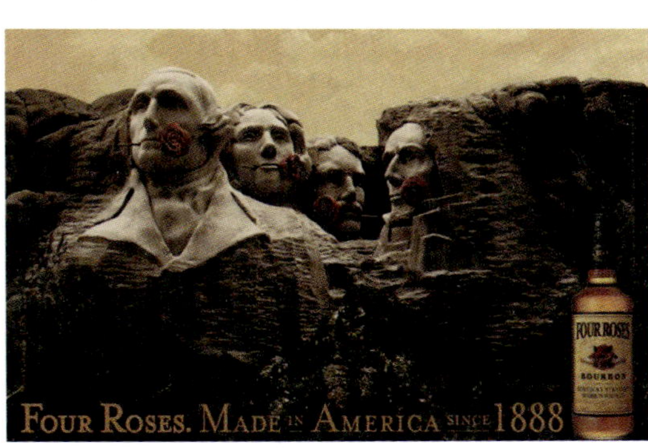

FRANCE FRANCE (?)
BDDP&Fils Four Roses Bourbon
Made in america since 1888

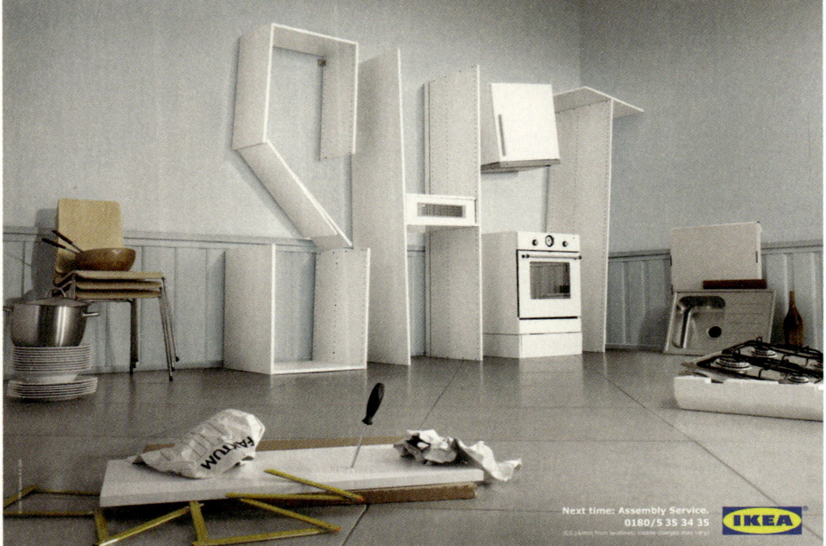

ALLEMAGNE GERMANY (2010)
♡ Grabarz & Partner
☺ IKEA Assembly Service
"shit" - Next time:
Assembly Service 0180 535 34 35

« Les mots me manquent tant l'idée est juste et simple. J'ai envie de dire « merde ! », parce que j'aurais aimé trouver cette idée avant eux. Comme tout le monde, je déteste ces grands moments de solitude que sont le montage des meubles en kit et surtout, cet instant ou l'on se rend compte qu'on a raté une étape et qu'il faut tout défaire ! »
"Words fail me, as the idea is both spot-on and simple. I wanted to say "shit!" because I would have liked to have come up with this idea before them. Like everyone else, I hate those moments of solitude when you are assembling furniture from a kit, and especially that moment when you realize that you missed a step and must undo everything!"

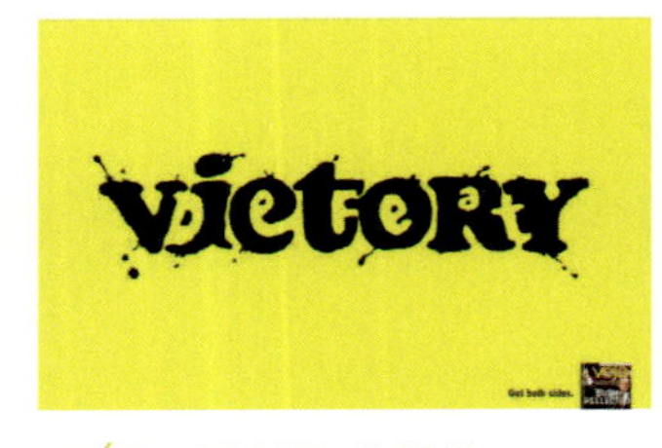

BRÉSIL BRAZIL (2006)
♡ Almap BBDO ♡ Veja Magazine
(Victory / Defeat) Get both sides

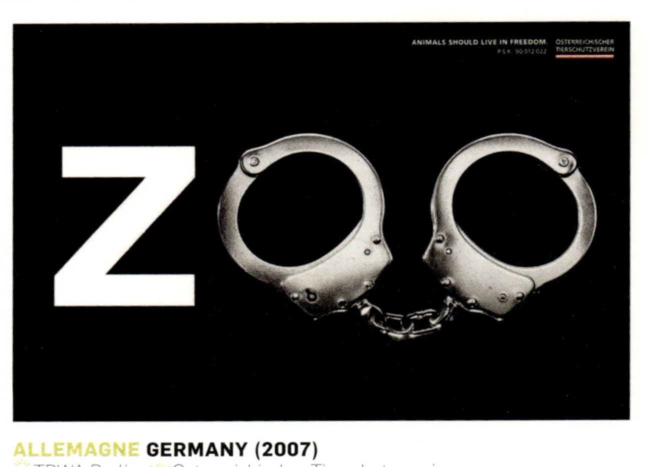

ALLEMAGNE GERMANY (2007)
♡ TBWA Berlin ☺ Österreichischer Tierschutzverein
Animals should live in freedom

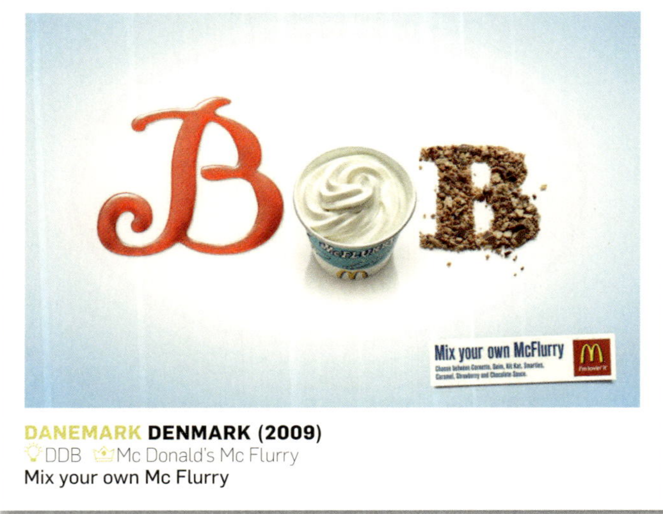

DANEMARK DENMARK (2009)
♡ DDB ☺ Mc Donald's Mc Flurry
Mix your own Mc Flurry

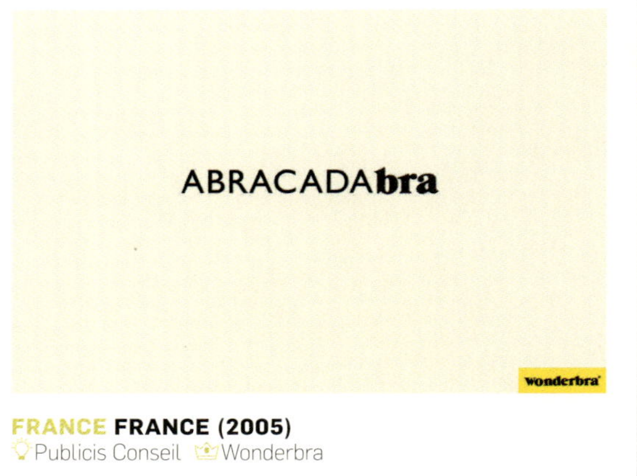

FRANCE FRANCE (2005)
♡ Publicis Conseil ☺ Wonderbra

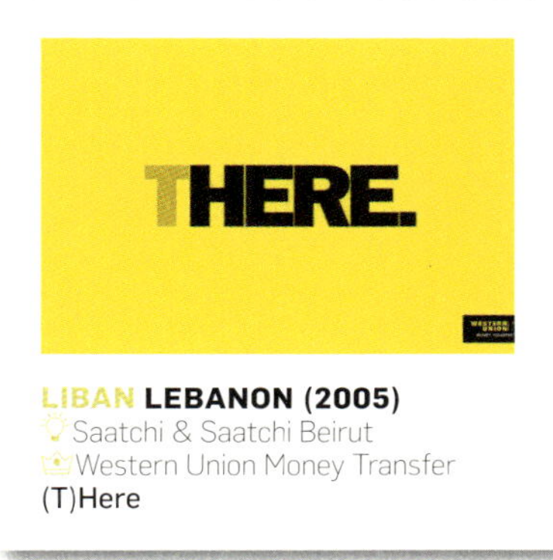

LIBAN LEBANON (2005)
Saatchi & Saatchi Beirut
Western Union Money Transfer
(T)Here

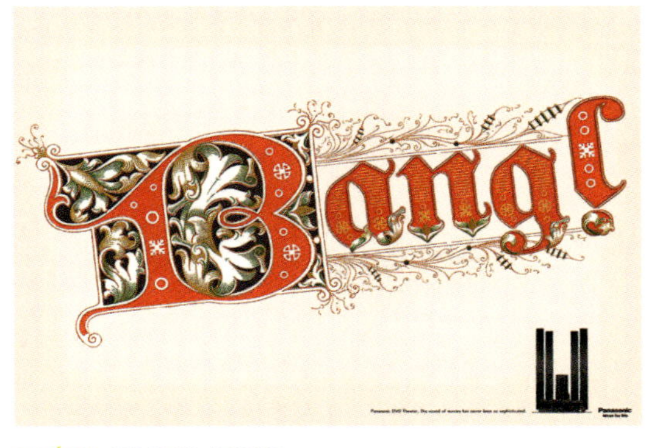

BRÉSIL BRAZIL (2008)
Fischer America Panasonic DVD Theater
The sound of movies has never been so sophisticated

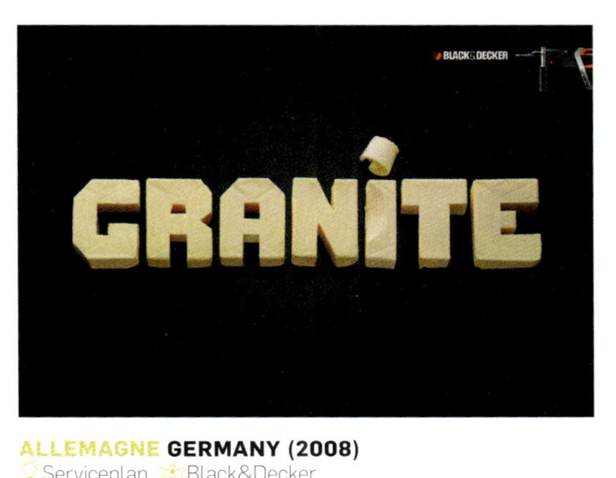

ALLEMAGNE GERMANY (2008)
Serviceplan Black&Decker

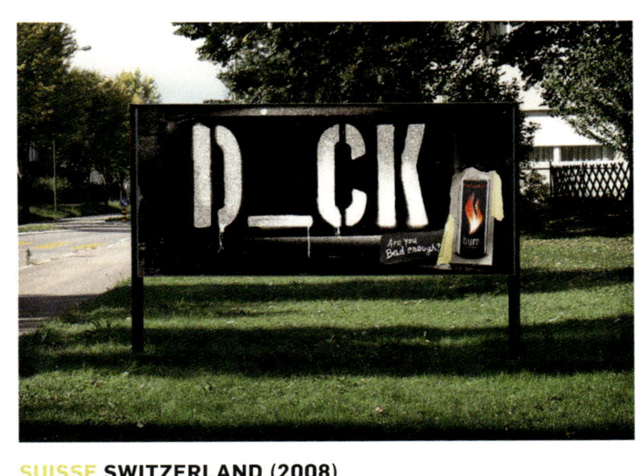

SUISSE SWITZERLAND (2008)
Draft FCB Zurich Burn Energy Drink
(Duck? Dock?... Dick?) Are you bad enough?

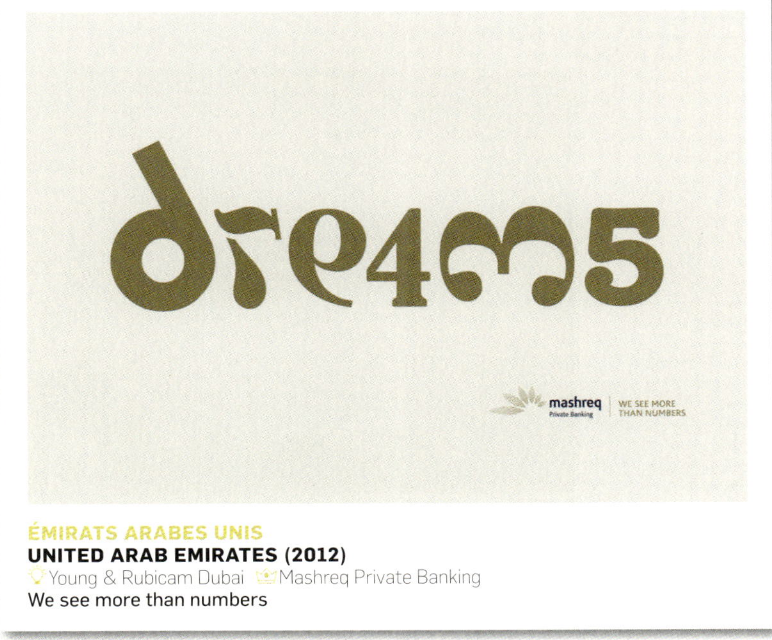

**ÉMIRATS ARABES UNIS
UNITED ARAB EMIRATES (2012)**
Young & Rubicam Dubai Mashreq Private Banking
We see more than numbers

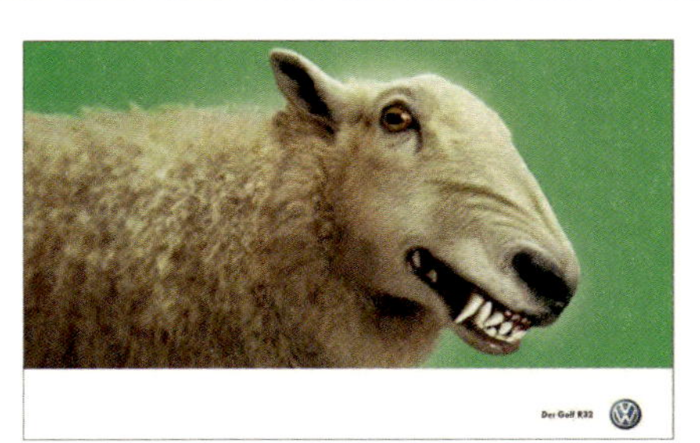
ALLEMAGNE GERMANY (2003)
DDB Berlin Volkswagen Golf R32

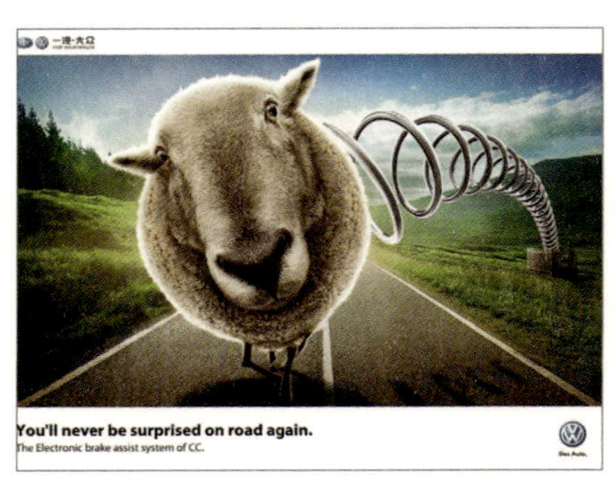

CHINE CHINA (2011)
DMG Beijing
Volkswagen Electronic brake assist system
You'll never be surprised on the road

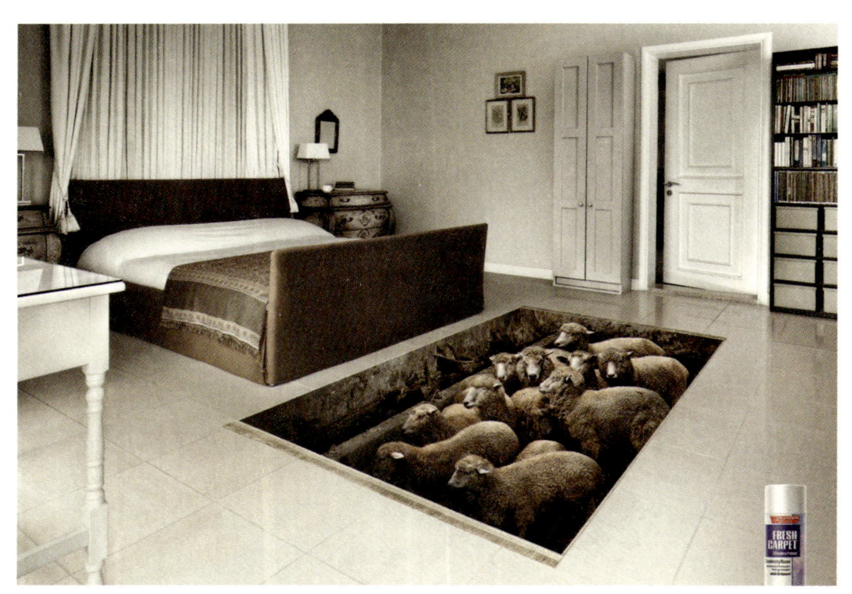

ÉMIRATS ARABES UNIS UNITED ARAB EMIRATES (2012)
Gret Dubai Fresh Carpet Deodorizing mousse

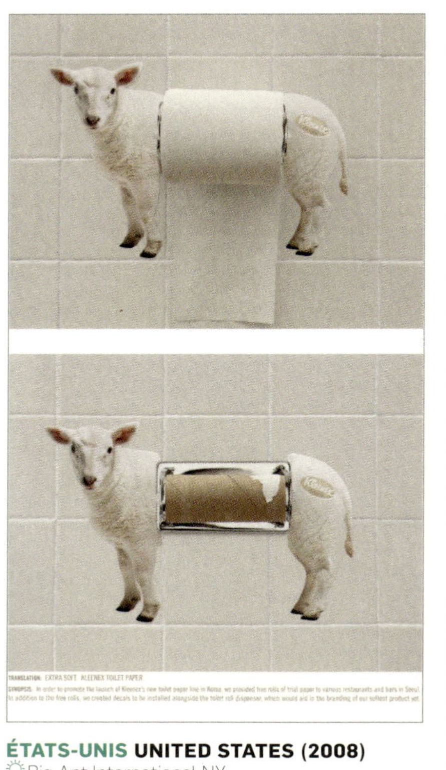

ÉTATS-UNIS UNITED STATES (2008)
Big Ant International NY
Kleenex toilet paper
Extra Soft

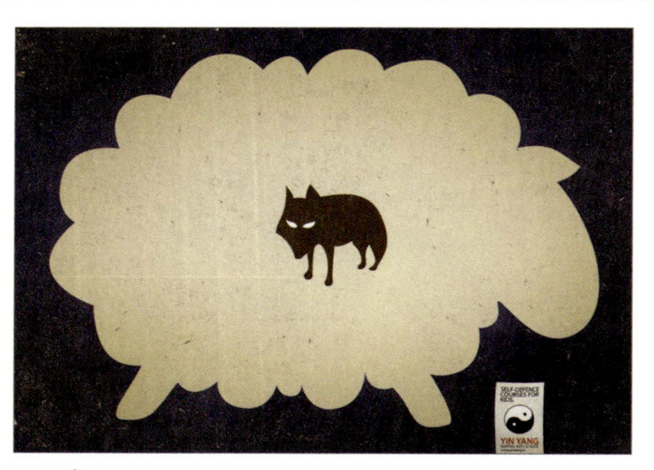

SLOVÉNIE SLOVENIA (2009)
DCC Marketing Yin Yang Martial Arts School
Self-defense courses for kids

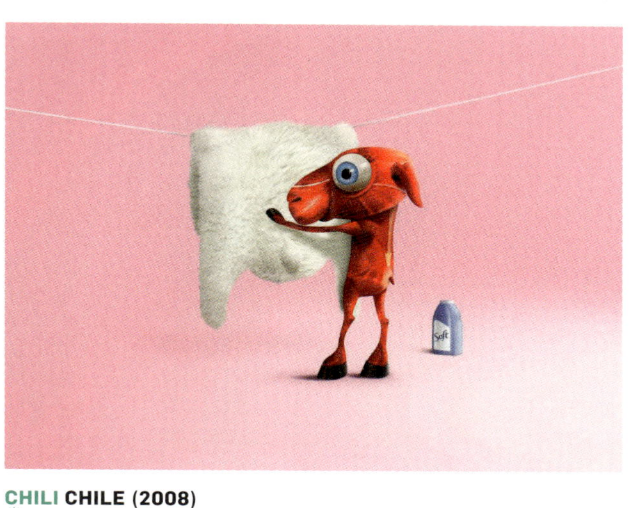

CHILI CHILE (2008)
Ogilvy & Mather · Soft fabric softener

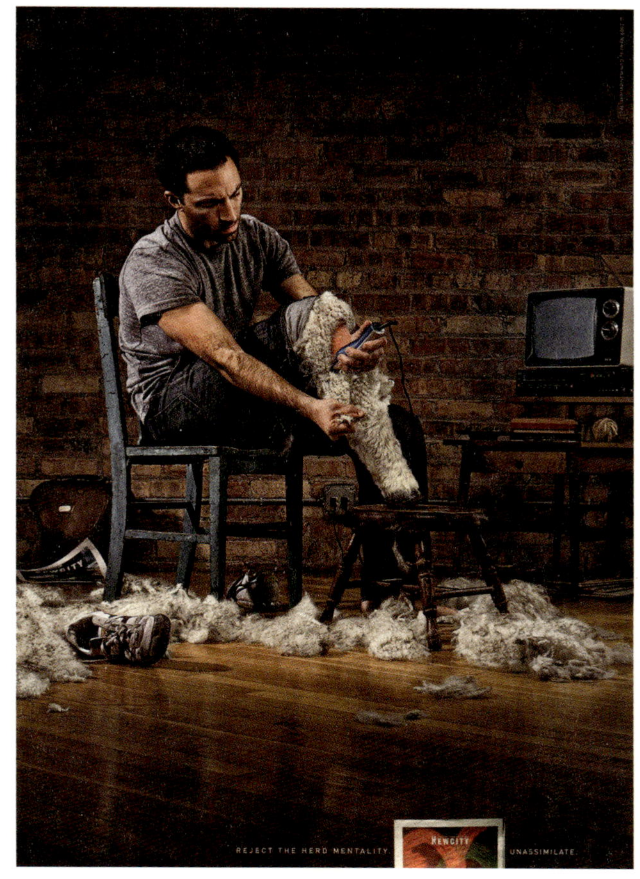

ÉTATS-UNIS UNITED STATES (2009)
Euro RSCG Chicago · Newcity
Reject the herd mentality. Unassimilate

MOUTONS
№ 64
SHEEPS

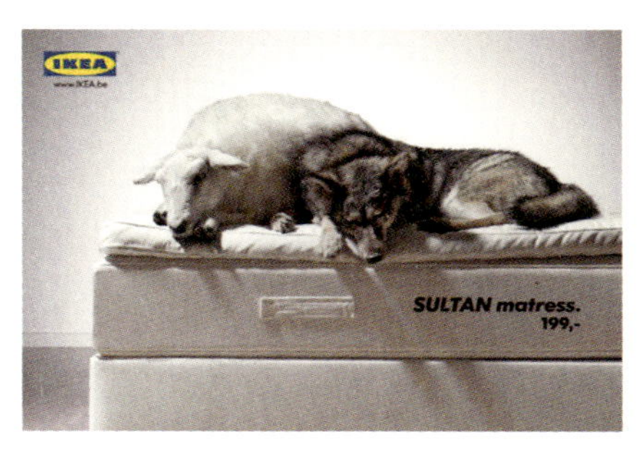

BELGIQUE BELGIUM (2008)
Germaine · IKEA Sultan matress

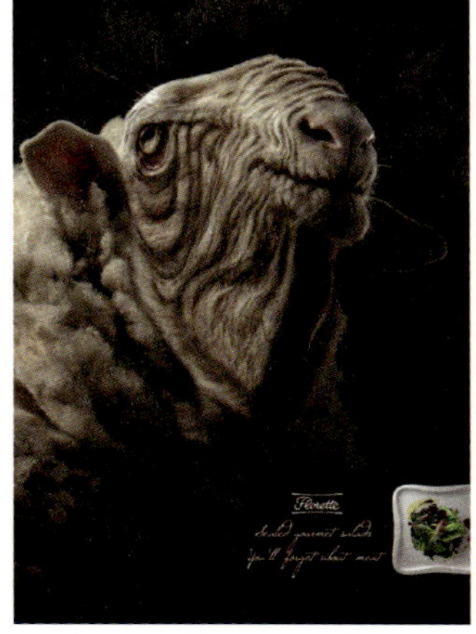
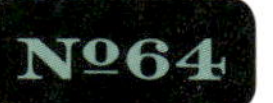

ESPAGNE SPAIN (2008)
Grey Barcelona
Florette Sealed gourmet salads.
You'll forget about meat

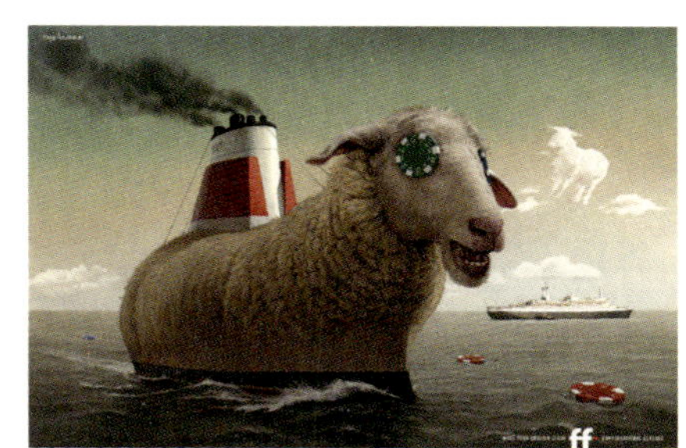

BRÉSIL BRAZIL (2012)
Dim & Canzian Sao Paulo
FF english. Conversational classes
Make your english clear (sheep, chip, ship...)

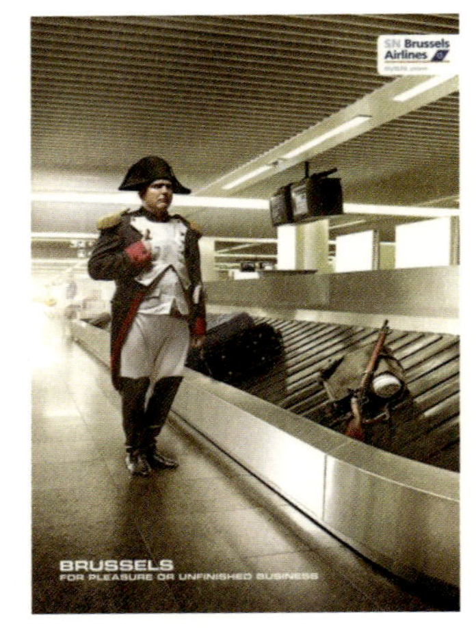

BELGIQUE BELGIUM (2005)
LG&F SN Brussels Airlines

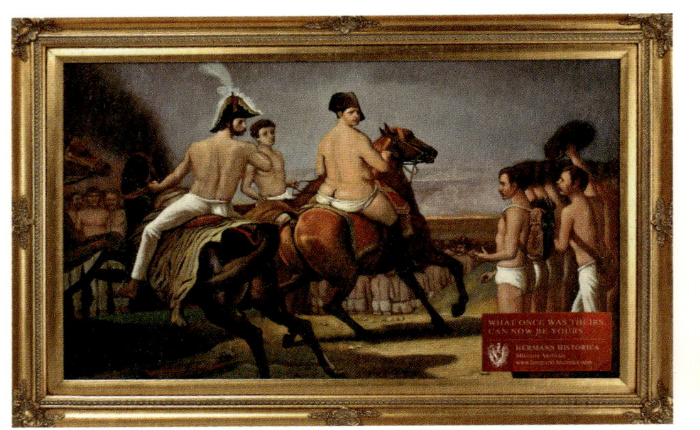

ALLEMAGNE GERMANY (2010)
Heye & Partner Munich Hermann Historica Militaria Auctions
What once was theirs, can now be yours

NAPOLEON

№65

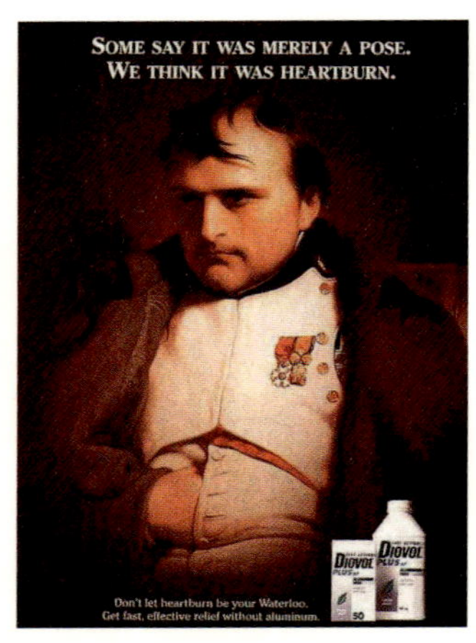

CANADA CANADA (1998)
Bates Diovol Plus
Some says it was merely a pose.
We think it was heartburn.
Don't let heartburn be your
Waterloo. Get fast, effective relief
without aluminum.

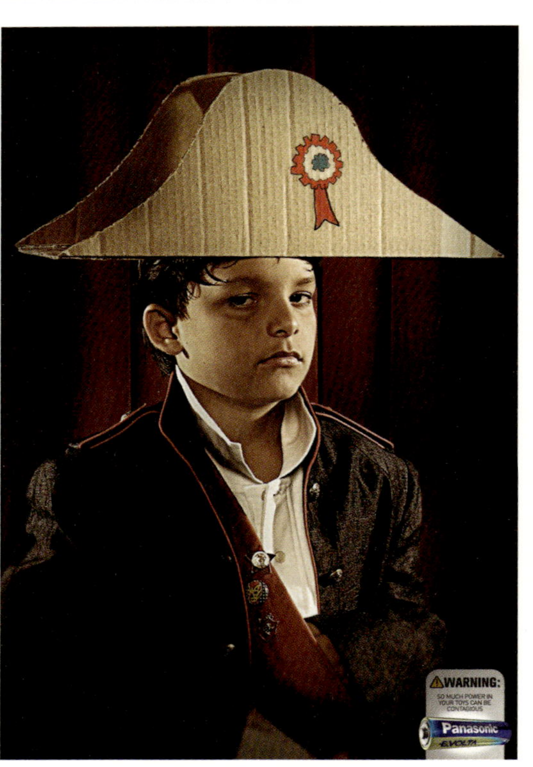

COSTA RICA COASTA RICA (2009)
Publimark Lowe Panasonic Evolta Batteriesv
Warning: So much power in your toys can be contagious

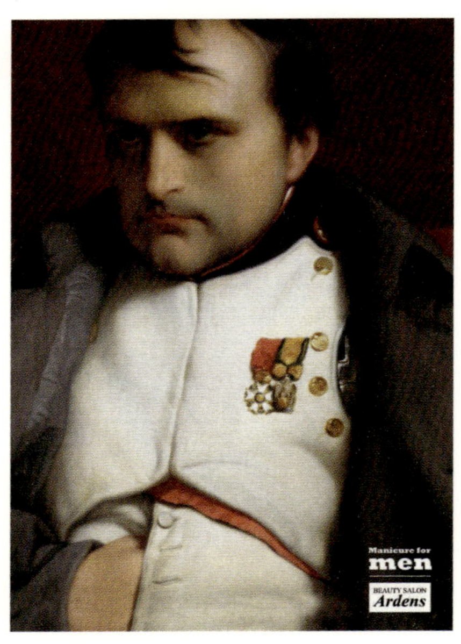

SERBIE SERBIA (2011)
Young & Rubicam Belgrade
Ardens Beauty Salon
Manicure for men

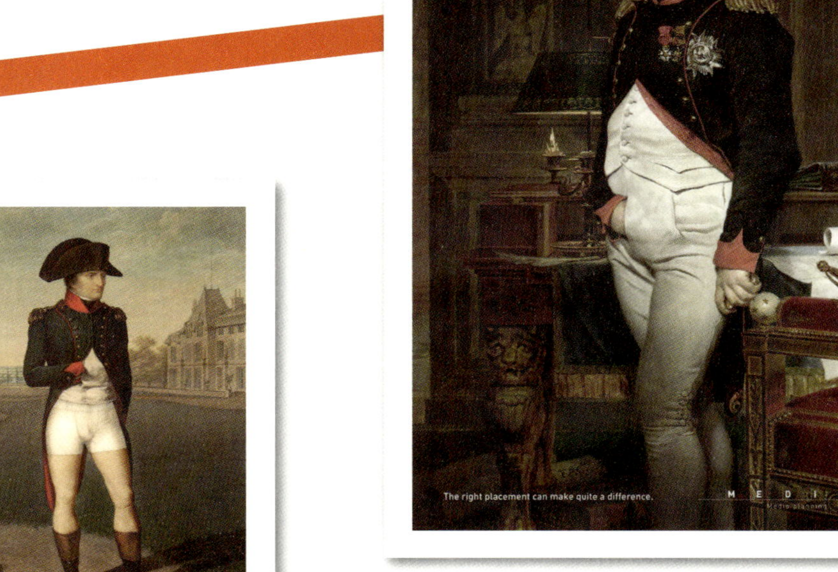

AUTRICHE AUSTRIA (2008)
Demner Merlicek & Bergmann
Media1 Media Planning
The right placement can make quite a difference

« Cette blague est aussi celle qui a été la plus faite en pub avec l'image de Napoléon. L'idée originale était pour le magazine Playboy. Ça n'en reste pas moins celle qui me fait le plus rire. Car elle reste subtile dans la mesure où l'on ne s'en rend pas compte au premier coup d'œil. »
"This joke is also the one that has made the most frequently in advertising with images of Napoleon. The original idea was for Playboy magazine. It none the less makes me laugh the most. Because it stays subtle insofar as you don't appreciate the joke at first glance."

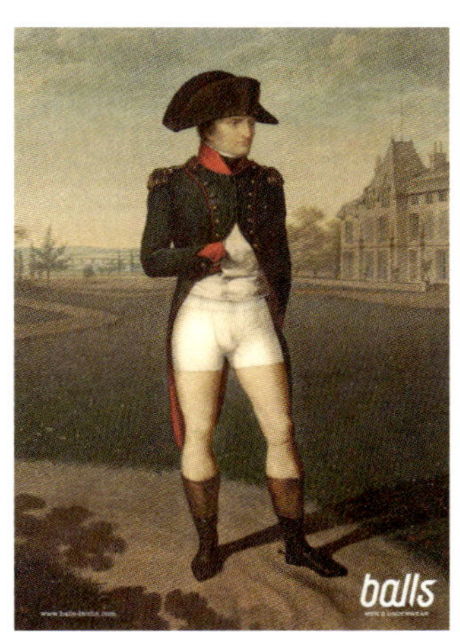

ALLEMAGNE GERMANY (2008)
Glow Berlin
Balls Men's Underwear

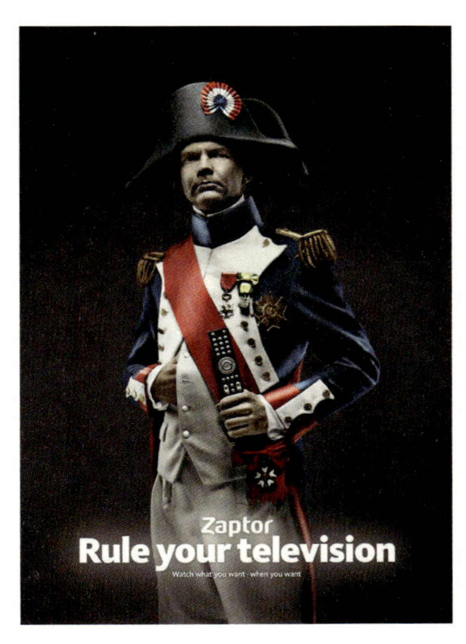

DANEMARK DENMARK (2007)
Hjaltelin Stahl & CO Copenhagene   Zaptor

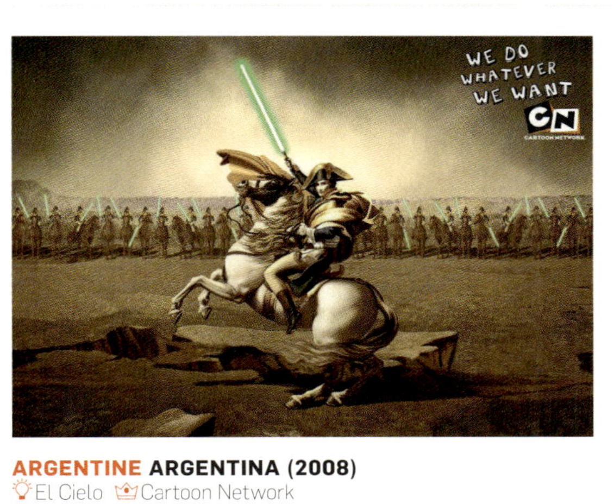

ARGENTINE ARGENTINA (2008)
El Cielo   Cartoon Network

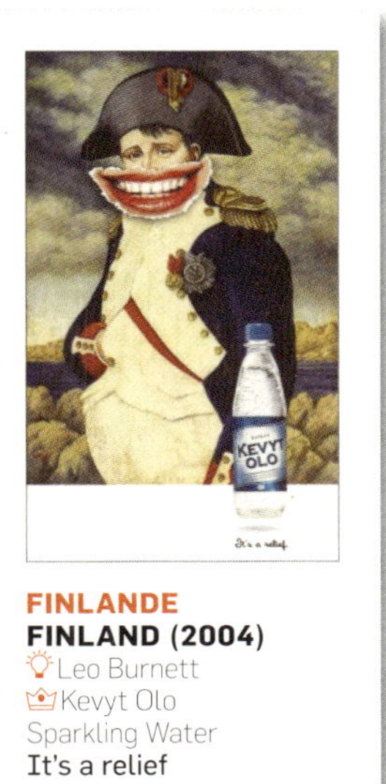

FINLANDE FINLAND (2004)
Leo Burnett
Kevyt Olo
Sparkling Water
It's a relief

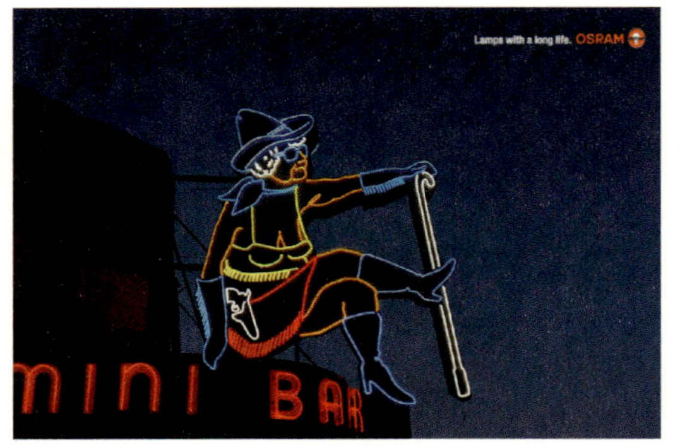

ALLEMAGNE GERMANY (2008)
Springer & Jacoby Osram Bulbs
Lamps with a long life

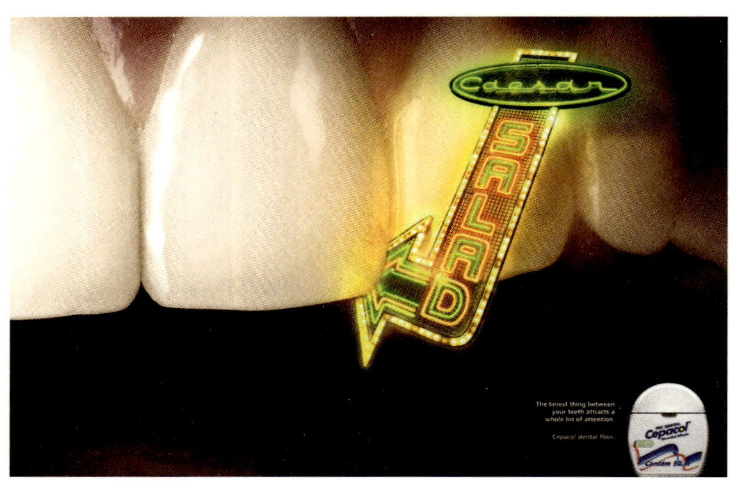

BRÉSIL BRAZIL (2007)
Publicis Cepacol Dental Floss
The tiniest things between your teeth attracts a whole lot of attention

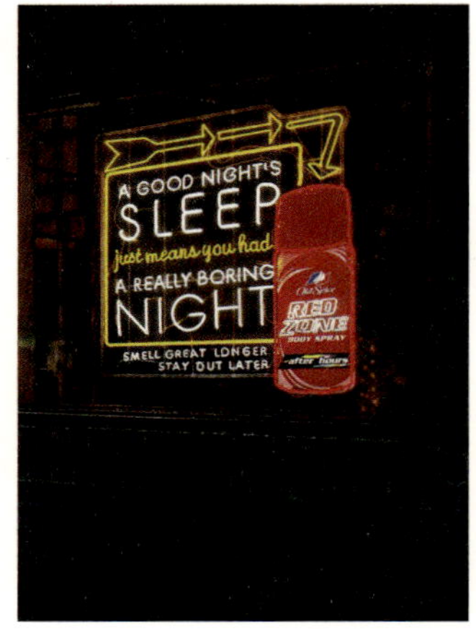

ÉTATS-UNIS
UNITED STATES (2005)
Saatchi & Saatchi New York
Old Spice Red Zone deodorant
A good night's sleep just means you had a really boring night

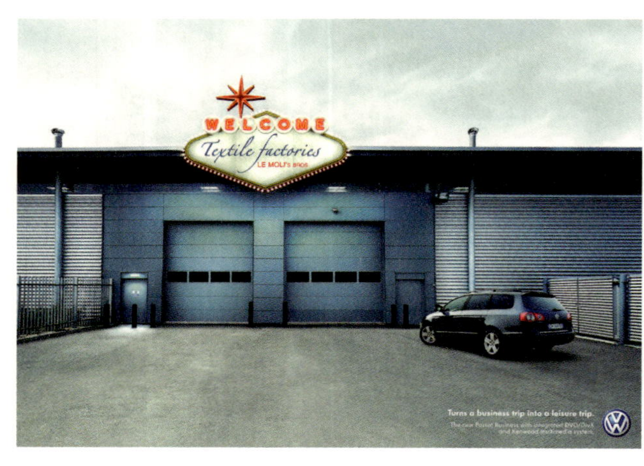

ITALIE ITALY (2008)
DDB Volkswagen New Passat Business
Turns a business trip into a leisure trip

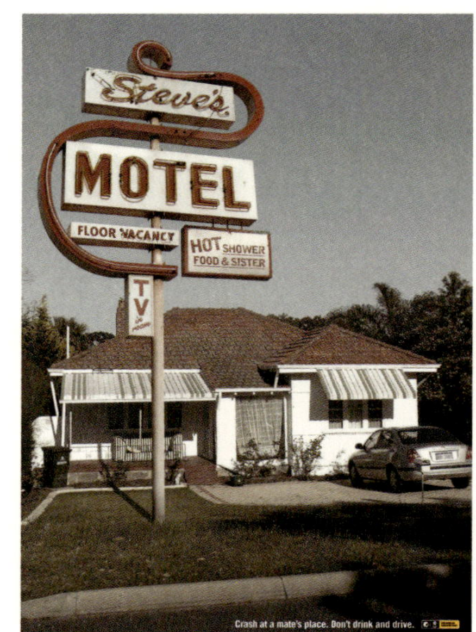

AUSTRALIE AUSTRALIA (2008)
Market Force
Western Australian Office of Road Safety
Crash at a mate's place. Don't drink and drive

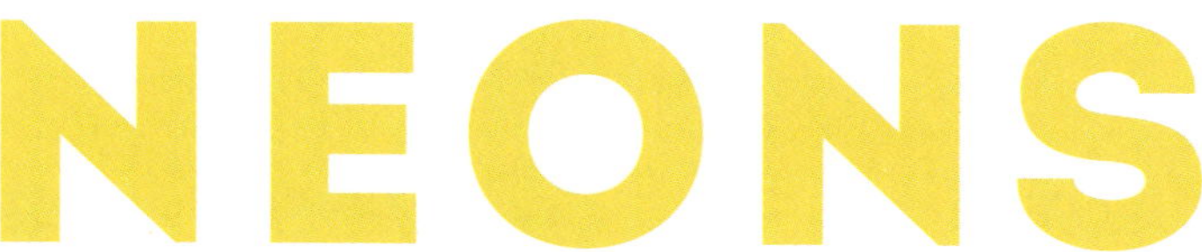

NEONS

№ 66

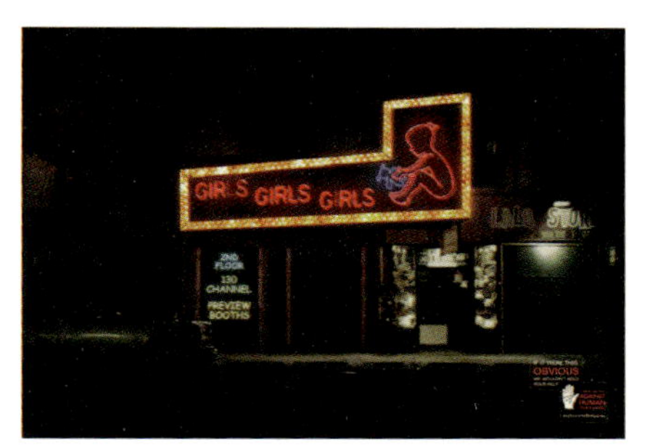

ÉTATS-UNIS UNITED STATES (2007)
Marca Hispanic Miami
Florida Against Human Trafficking
If it were this obvious
we wouldn't need your help

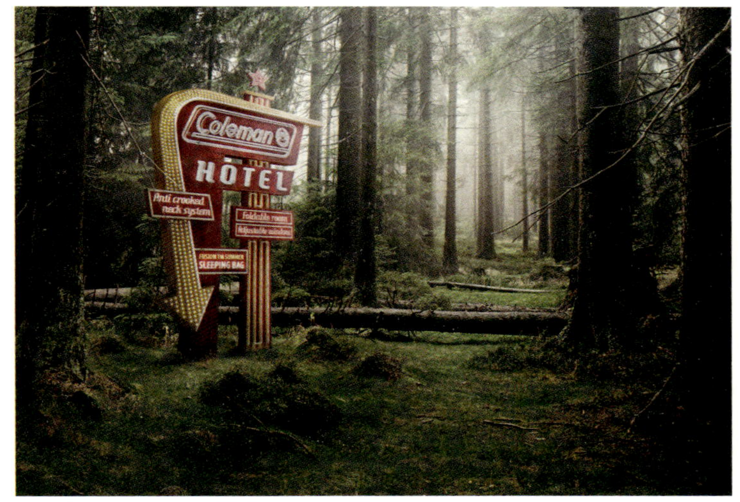

RÉPUBLIQUE TCHÈQUE CZECH REPUBLIC (2012)
Young & Rubicam Coleman Sleeping Bags
"Coleman Hotel: Anti crooked neck system, foldable room, adjustable window…"

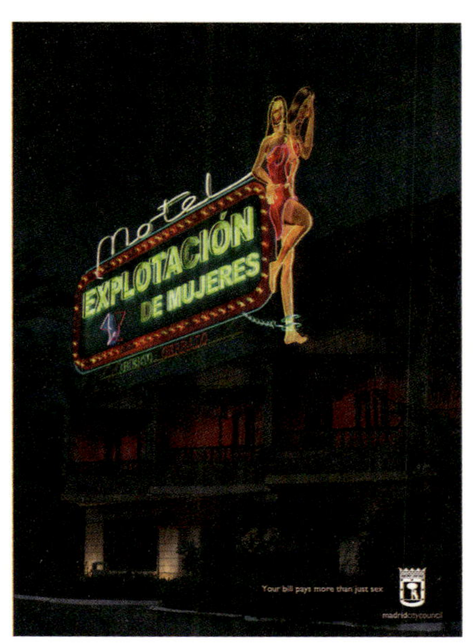

ESPAGNE SPAIN (2007)
Grey Madrid City Council
"Exploitation of women hotel"
Your bills pays more than just sex

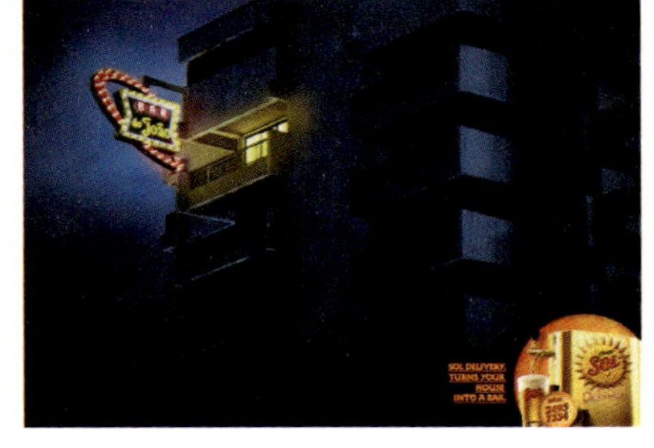

BRÉSIL BRAZIL (2008)
Fischer America Sol Delivery Beer Machine
Turns your house into a bar

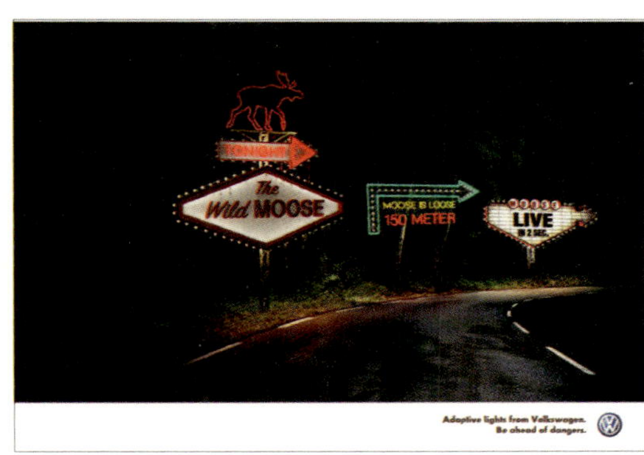

NORVÈGE NORWAY (2010)
Try Oslo Adaptive Lights from Volkswagen
Tonight the wild moose / Moose is loose 150 meter /
Moose Live in 2 sec". Be ahead of dangers

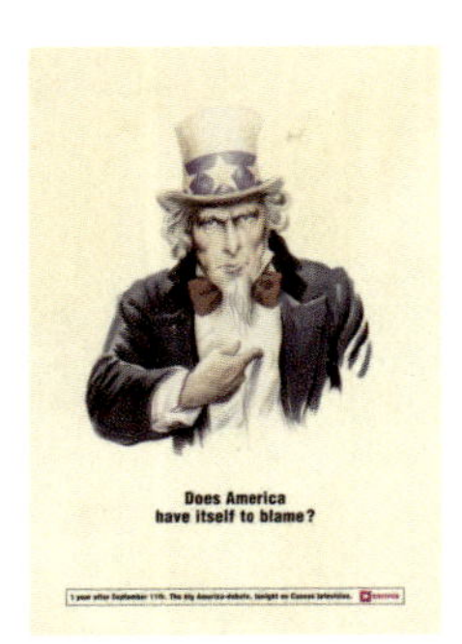

**BELGIQUE
BELGIUM (2003)**
LG&F
Canvas Television
Does America have
itself to blame?
The big debate tonight
on Canvas Television

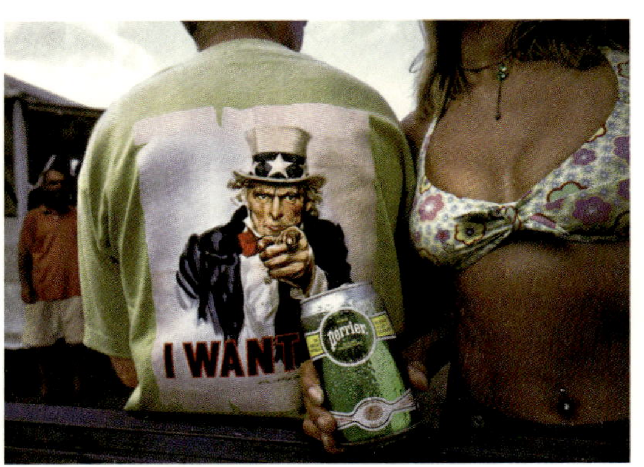

FRANCE FRANCE (2000)
Ogilvy & Mather Paris Perrier

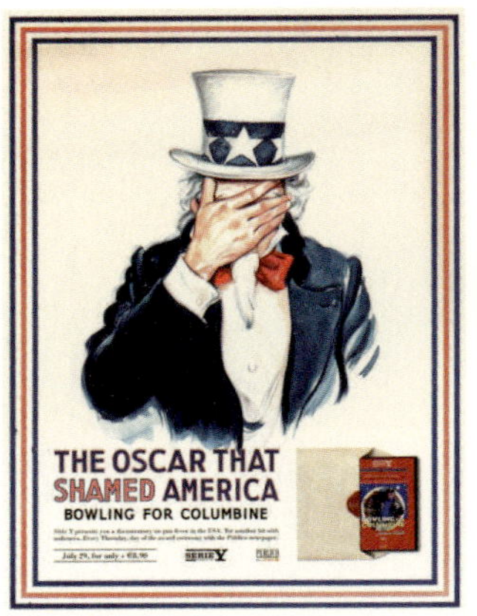

PORTUGAL PORTUGAL (2004)
BBDO
Bowling for Columbine DVD

L'ONCLE SAM
Nº67
UNCLE SAM

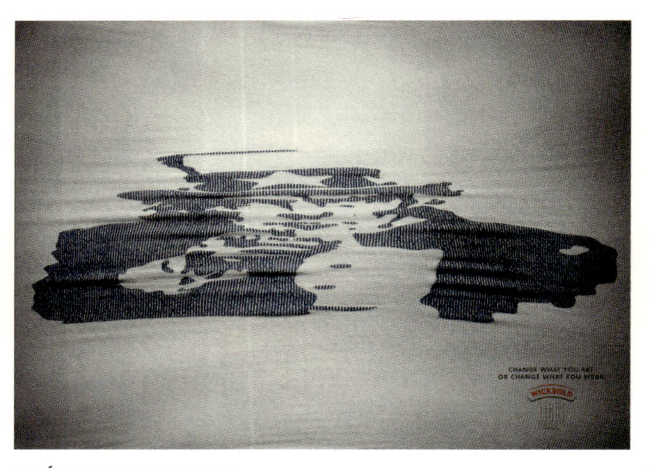

BRÉSIL BRAZIL (2005)
Publicis Sao Paulo Wickbold Light
Change what you eat or change what you wear

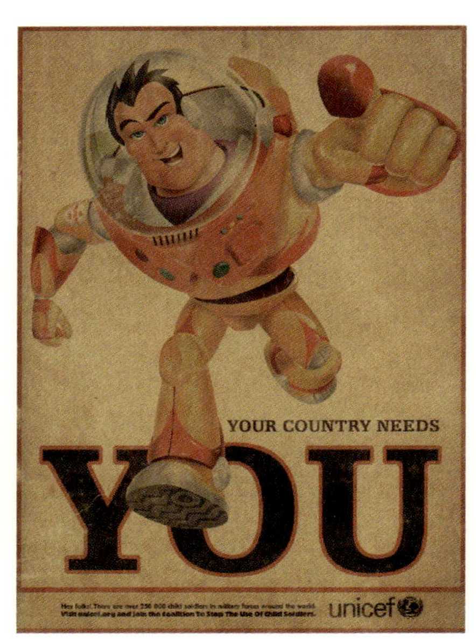

BRÉSIL BRAZIL (2007)
Ogilvy UNICEF
Your country needs you
Hey folks! There is over
250.000 child soldiers...

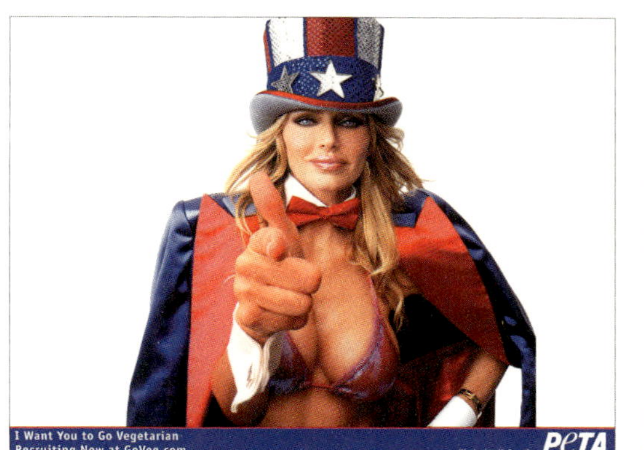

INCONNU UNKNOWN (2011)
Inconnu/unknown Peta
I want you to go Vegetarian (Kimberley Hefner)

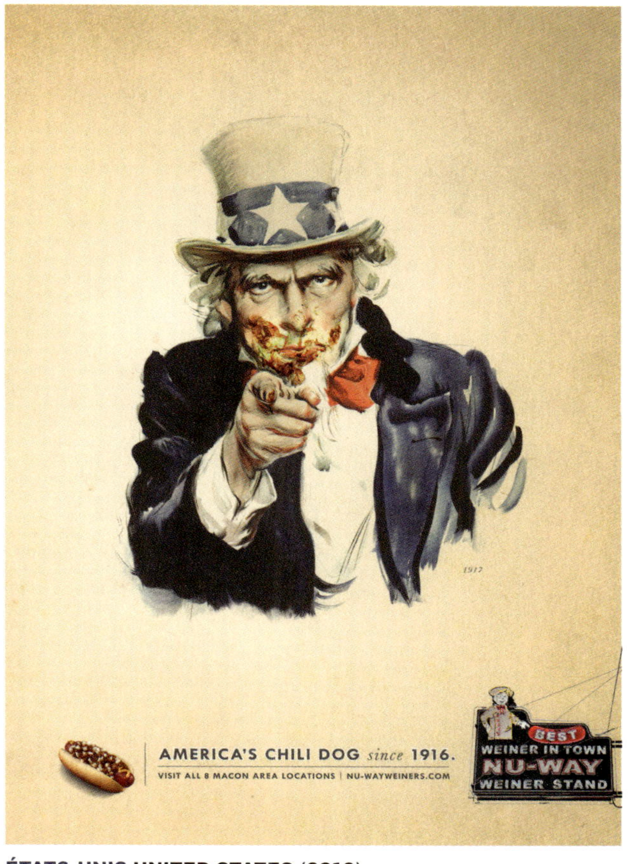

ÉTATS-UNIS UNITED STATES (2012)
Brunner Nu-Way wiener stand

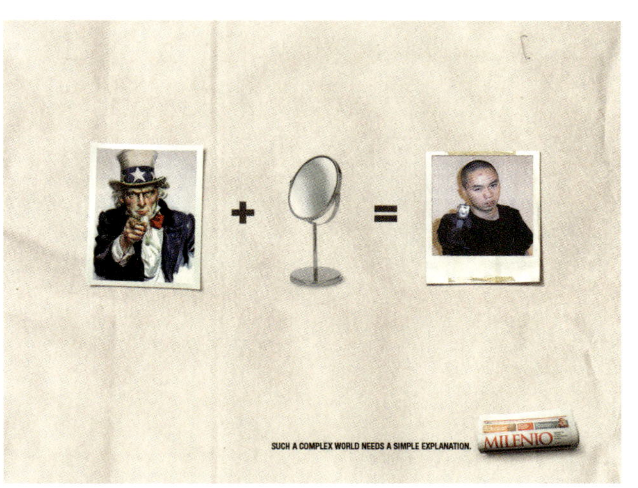

MEXIQUE MEXICO (2007)
Och Milenio Newspaper
Such a complex world needs a simple explanation

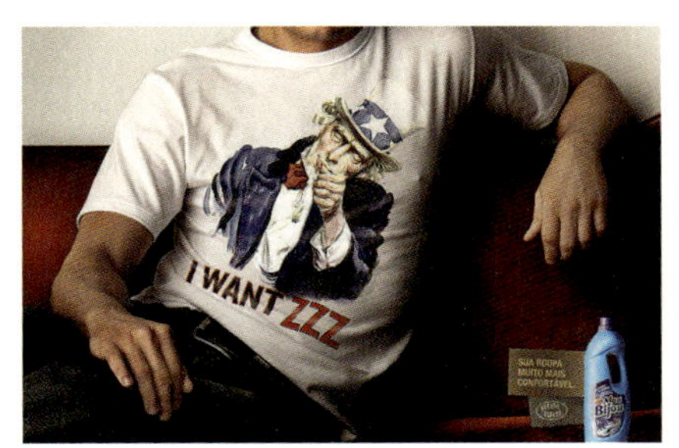

BRÉSIL BRAZIL (2007)
DPZ BomBril Mon Bijou Fabric Softener

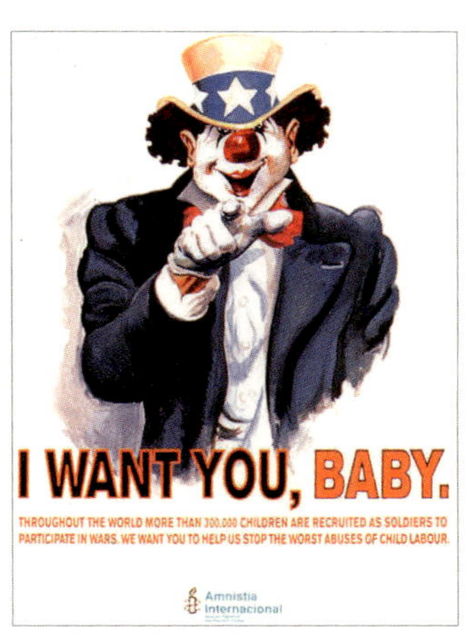

ESPAGNE SPAIN (2000)
Saatchi & Saatchi
Amnesty International
I want you, baby.
Throughout the world more
than 300.000 children are recruited
as soldiers...

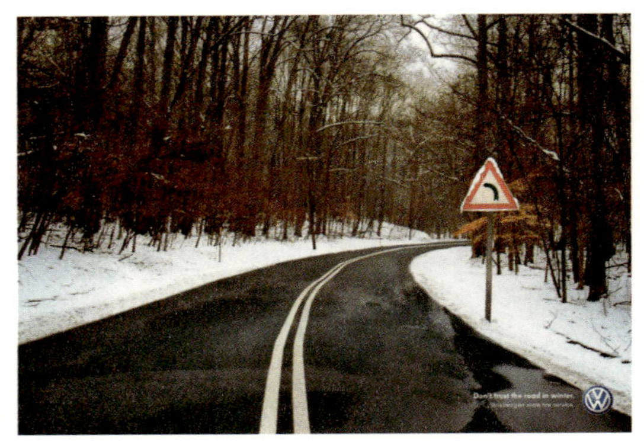

ITALIE ITALY (2008)
DDB · Volkswagen Snow tire service
Don't trust the road this winter

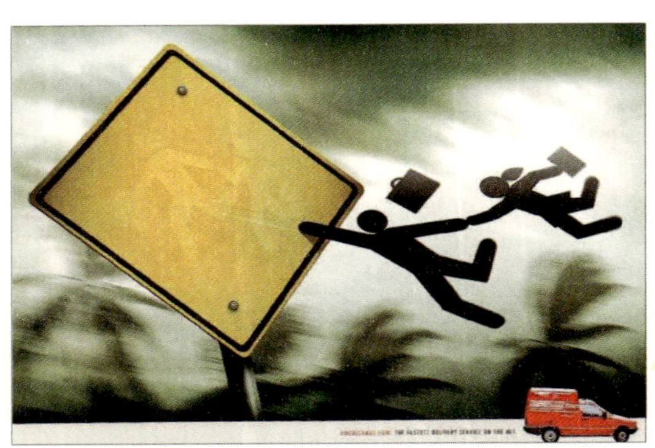

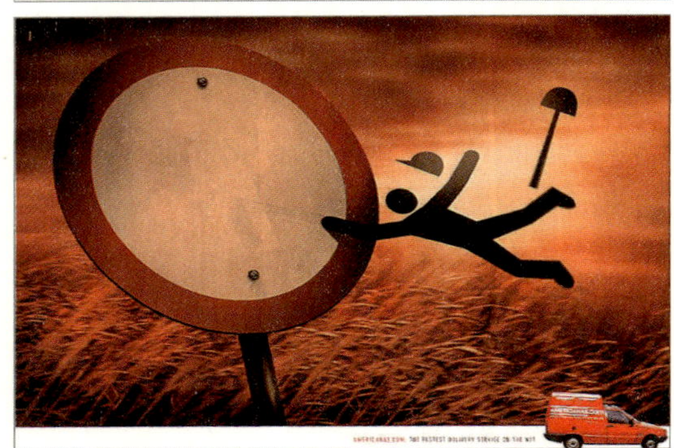

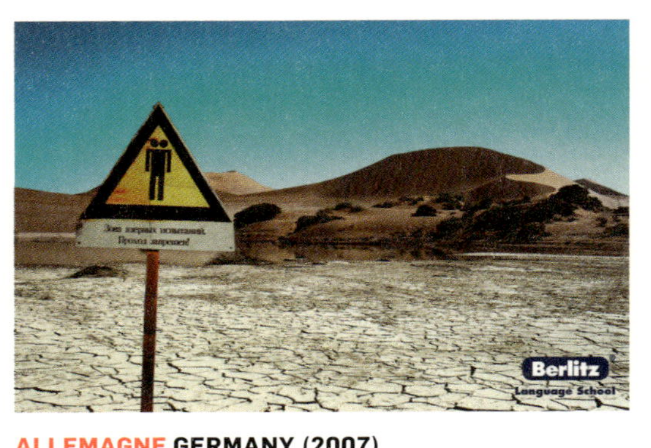

ALLEMAGNE GERMANY (2007)
DDB Dusseldorf · Berlitz Language school

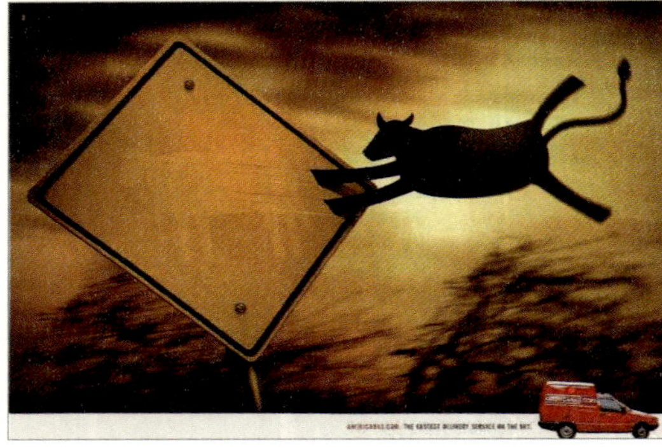

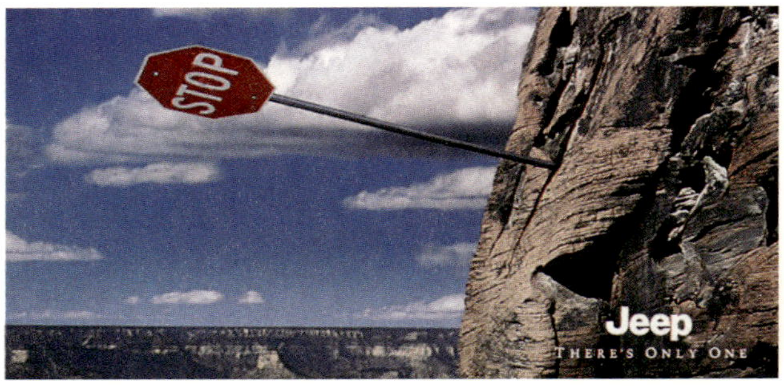

BRÉSIL BRAZIL (2001)
DM9 DDB · Americanas.com
The fastest delivery service on the net

CANADA CANADA (2001)
BBDO · Jeep
There's only one

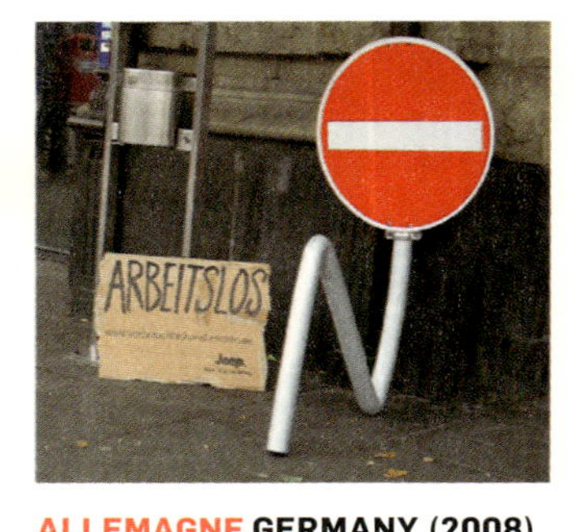

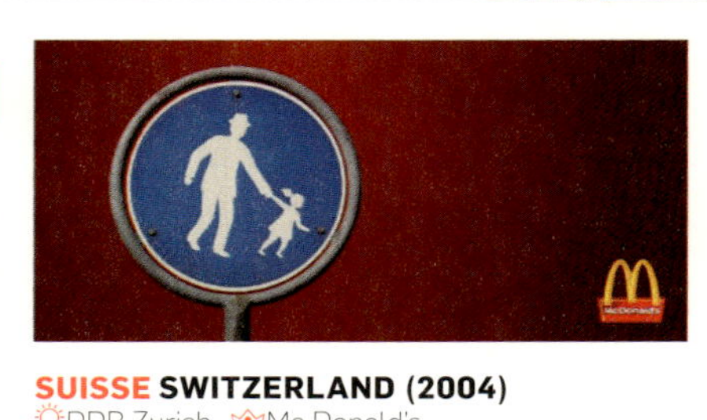

ALLEMAGNE GERMANY (2008)
KNSK · Jeep
Out of work

SUISSE SWITZERLAND (2004)
DDB Zurich · Mc Donald's

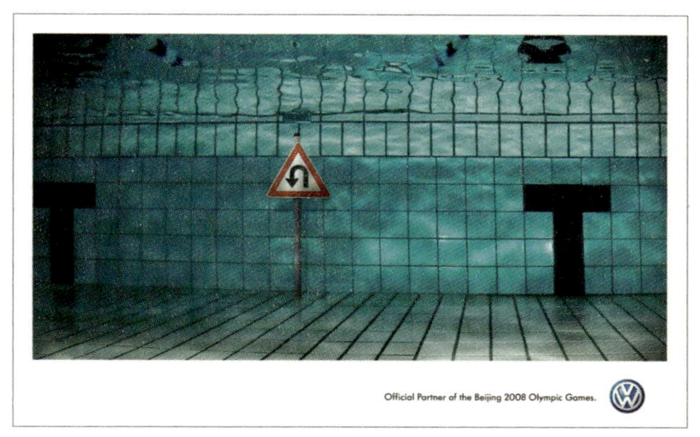

LIBAN LEBANON (2008)
Impact BBDO · Volkswagen
Official partner of the Beijing Olympic games

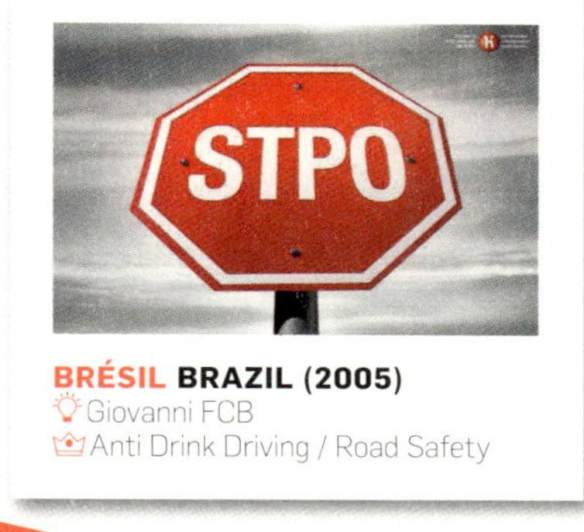

BRÉSIL BRAZIL (2005)
Giovanni FCB
Anti Drink Driving / Road Safety

PANNEAUX DE SIGNALISATION
№68
ROAD SIGNS

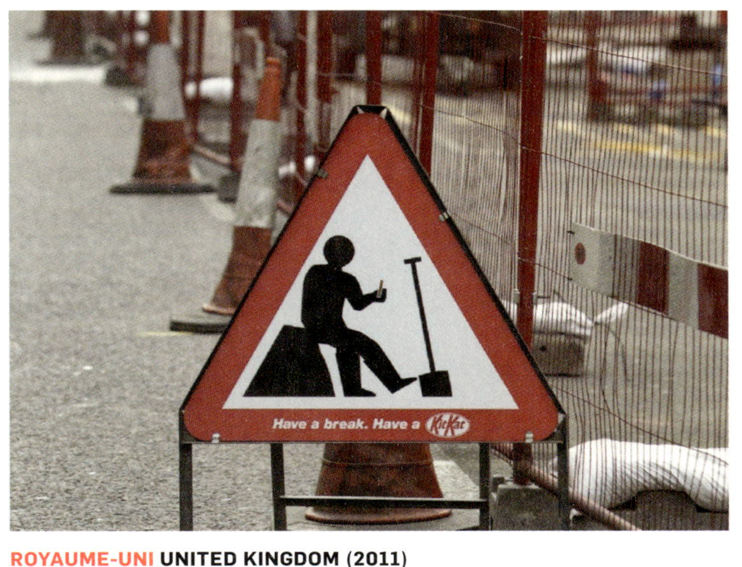

ROYAUME-UNI UNITED KINGDOM (2011)
JWT London · Kit Kat

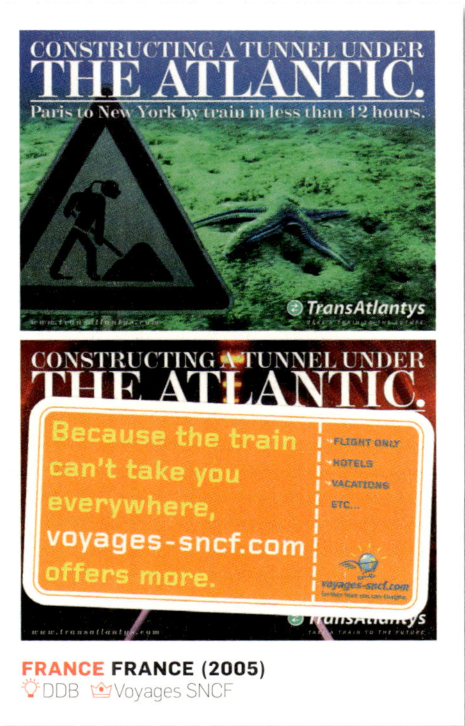

FRANCE FRANCE (2005)
DDB · Voyages SNCF

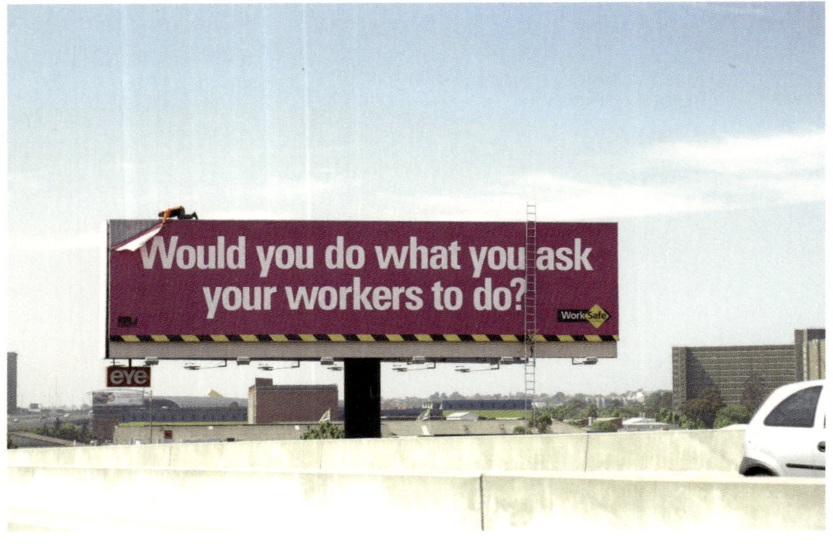

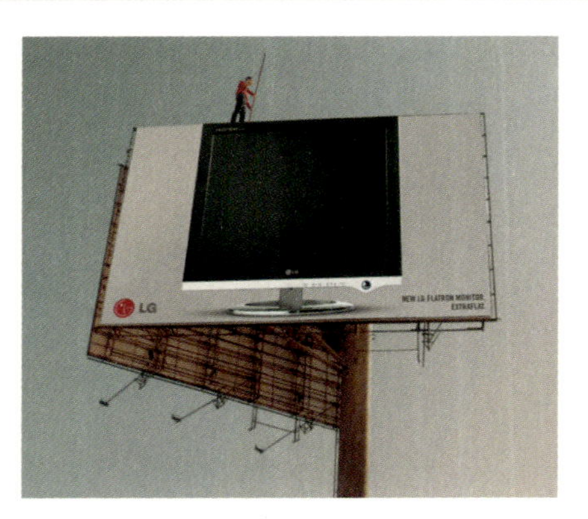

ARGENTINE ARGENTINA (2005)
BBDO Buenos Aires · LG Flatron TV
Extraflat

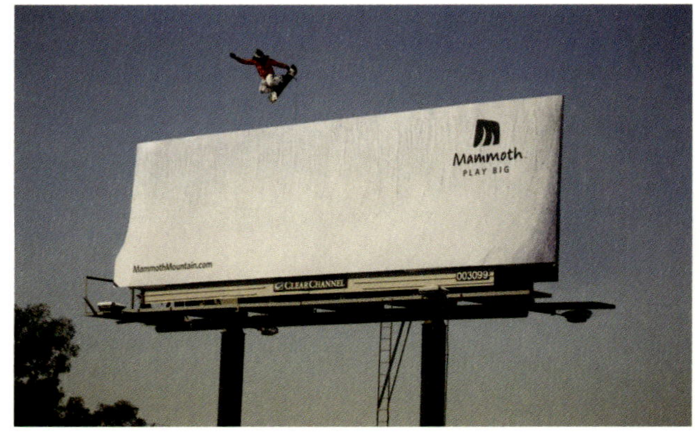

ÉTATS-UNIS UNITED STATES (2009)
David & Goliath · Mammoth Ski Resort
Play Big

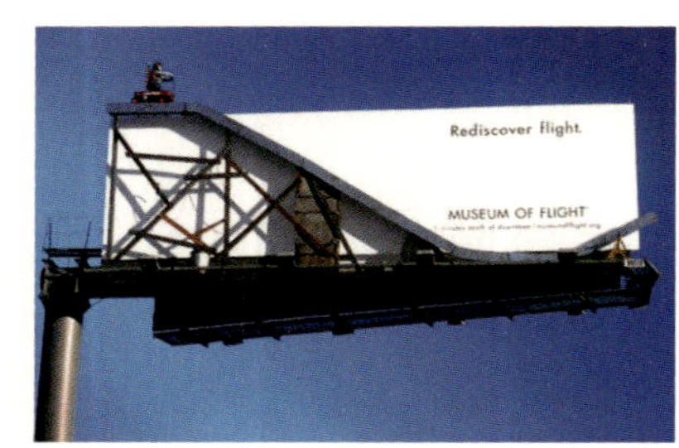

ÉTATS-UNIS UNITED STATES (2002)
Wongdoody · Museum of flight
Rediscover flight

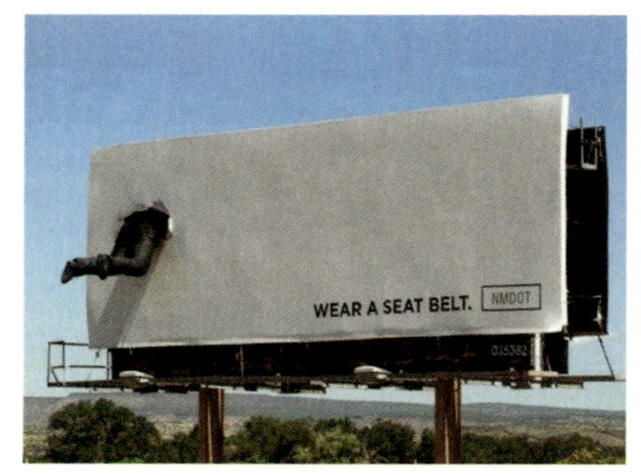

ÉTATS-UNIS UNITED STATES (2011)
Esparza Advertising · Road Safety
Wear seat belt

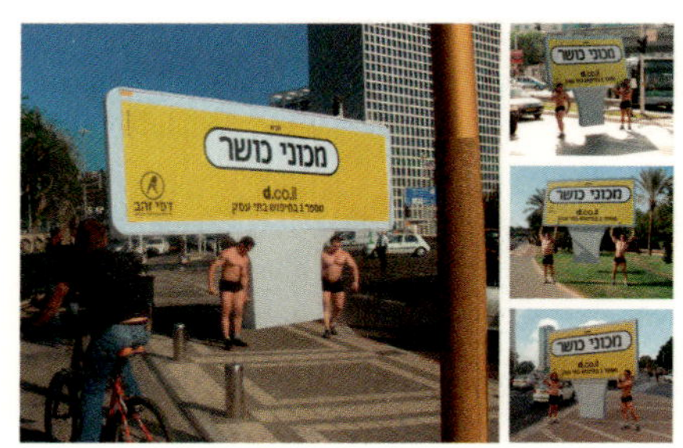

ISRAËL ISRAEL (2009)
Young & Rubicam Tel Aviv · Israel Yellow Pages
(search for) Fitness Club

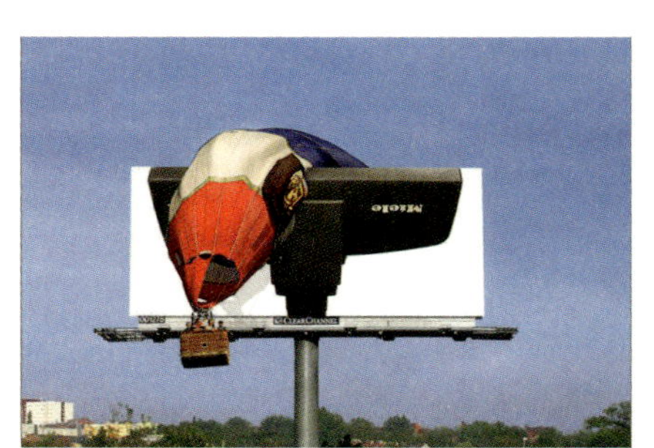

ÉTATS-UNIS UNITED STATES (2006)
Miami Ad School Miele Vaacum
Cleaners

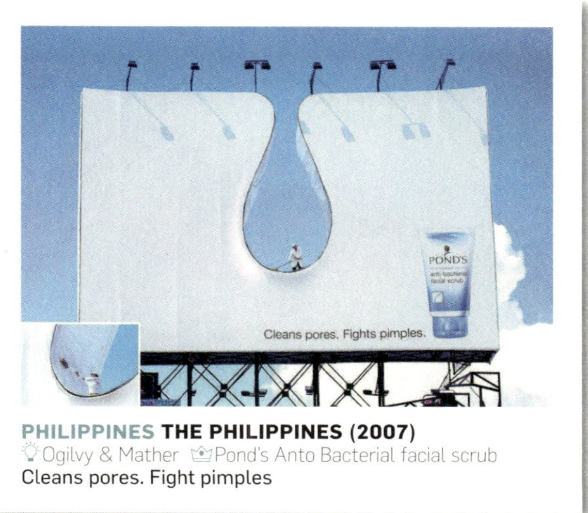

PHILIPPINES THE PHILIPPINES (2007)
Ogilvy & Mather Pond's Anto Bacterial facial scrub
Cleans pores. Fight pimples

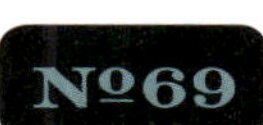

CANADA CANADA (2008)
Zig Toronto IKEA
Decorate for the holidays

PANNEAUX VIVANTS

№69

BILLBOARDS WITH REAL MEN

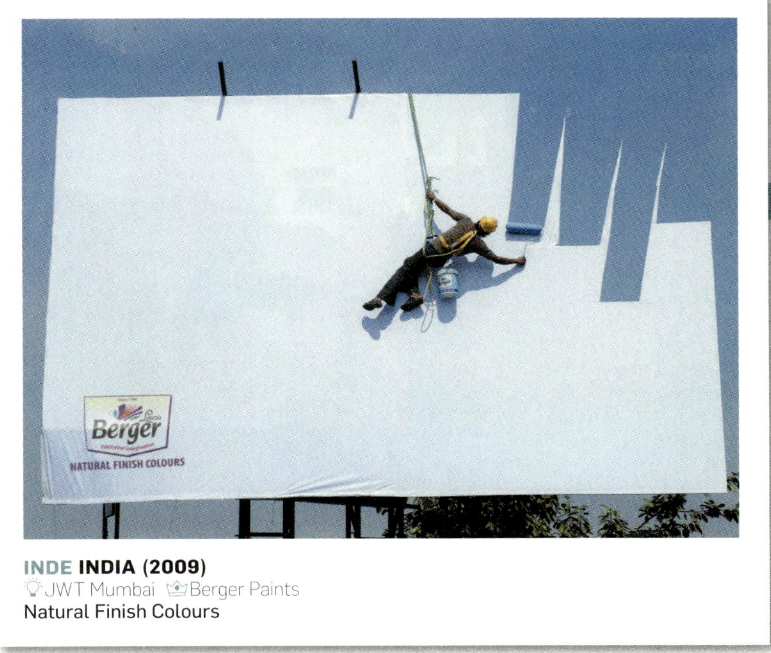

INDE INDIA (2009)
JWT Mumbai Berger Paints
Natural Finish Colours

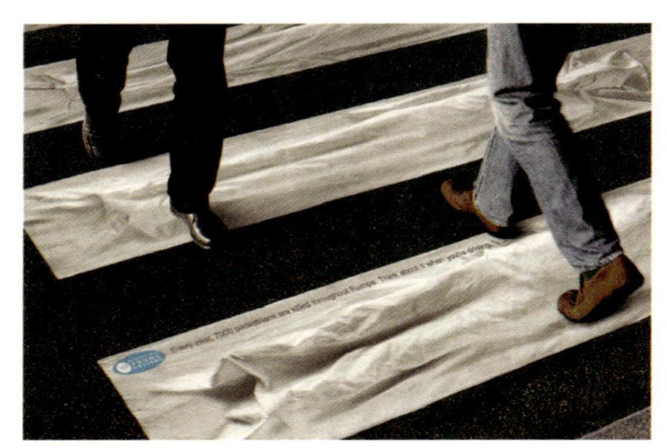

FRANCE FRANCE (2004)
TBWA Paris   Responsible Young Drivers
Every year 7000 pedestrians are killed throughout Europe.
Think about it when you're driving

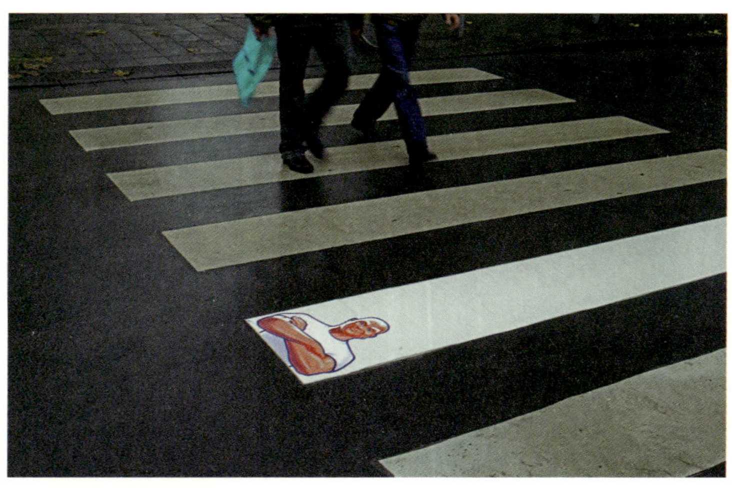

ALLEMAGNE GERMANY (2005)
Grey   Mister Clean

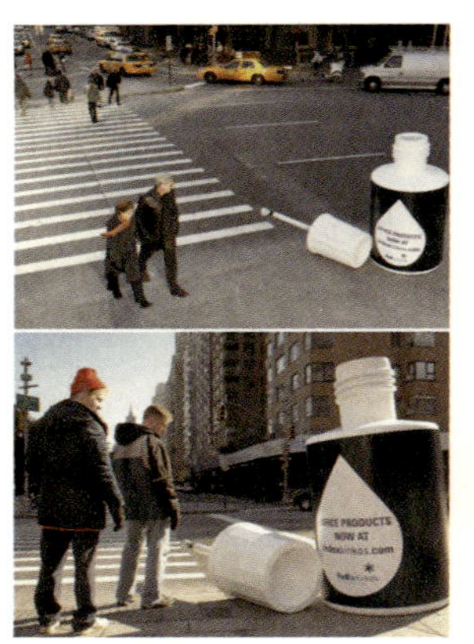

ÉTATS-UNIS
UNITED STATES (2005)
BBDO New York
Fedex Kinkos
Office products
now at FedexKinkos

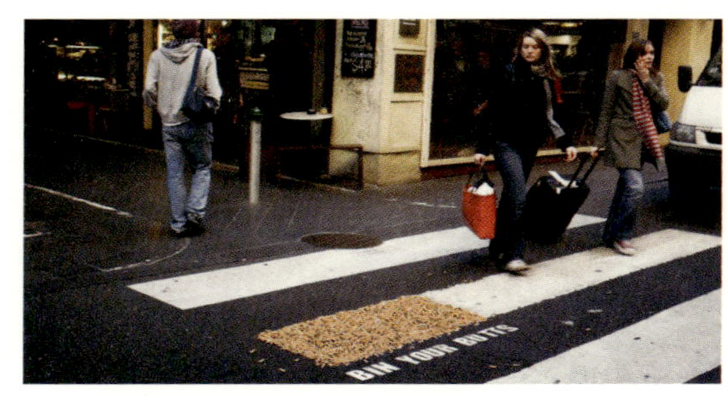

AUSTRALIE AUSTRALIA (2007)
Grey Melbourne   Against cigarette butt litter
Bin your butts

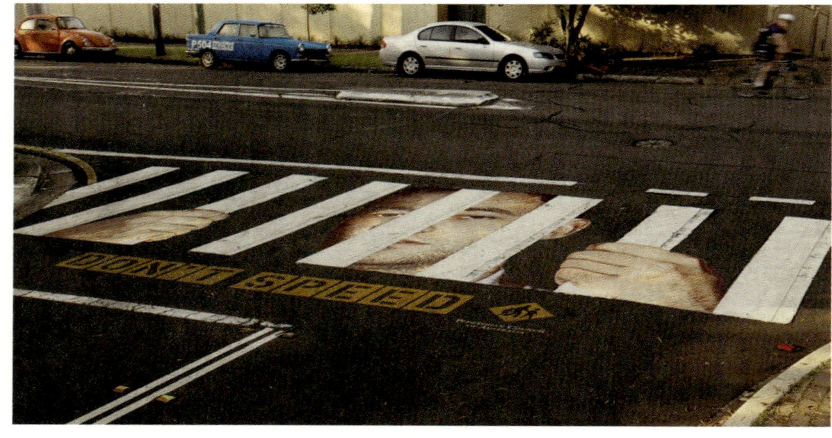

AUSTRALIE AUSTRALIA (2008)
Saatchi & Saatchi Sydney   Pedestrian Council of Australia
Don't speed

PASSAGES PIÉTONS

№ 70

ZEBRAS

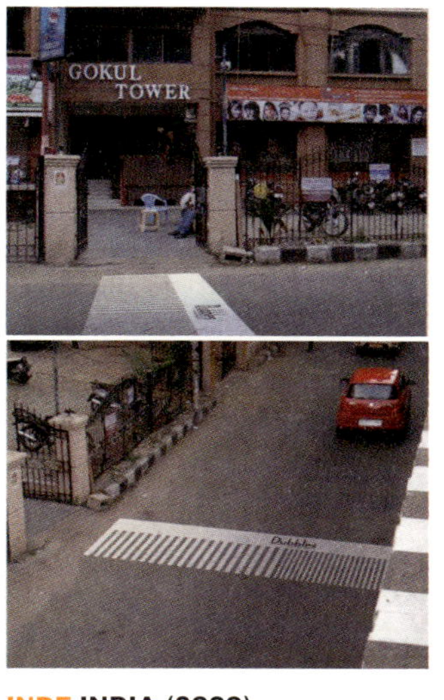

INDE INDIA (2009)
Orchard Advertising Chennai
Bubbles Hair Salon

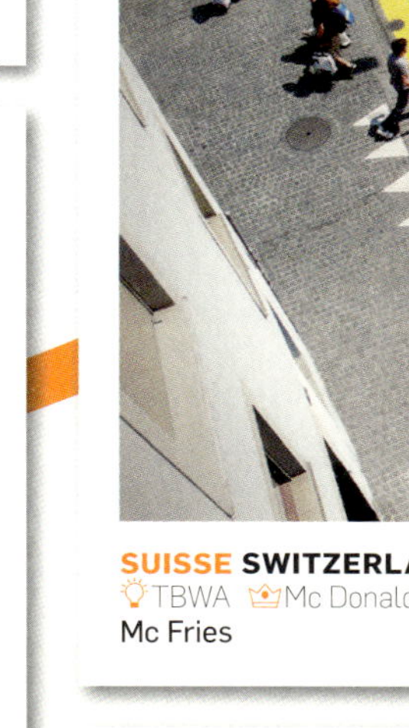

SUISSE SWITZERLAND (2010)
TBWA Mc Donald's
Mc Fries

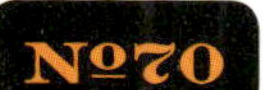

ALLEMAGNE GERMANY (2008)
.start Salzburg Zoo

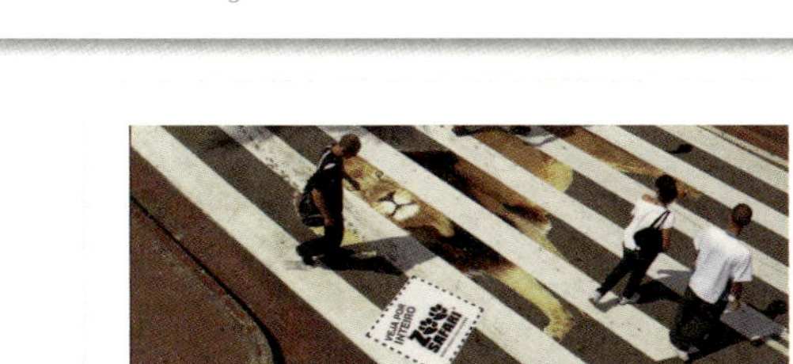

BRÉSIL BRAZIL (2010)
DDB Zoo Safari
No cages, all fun

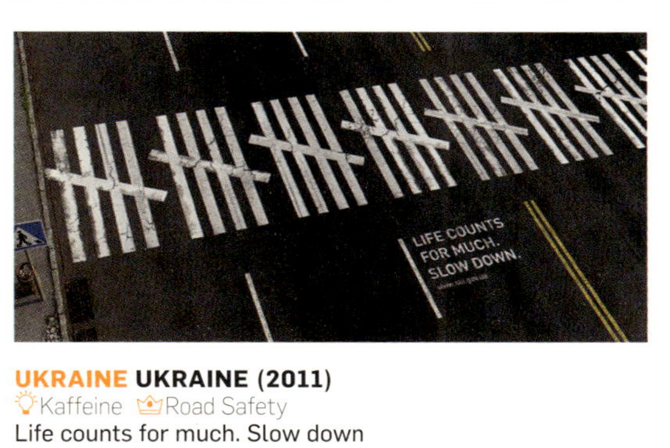

UKRAINE UKRAINE (2011)
Kaffeine Road Safety
Life counts for much. Slow down

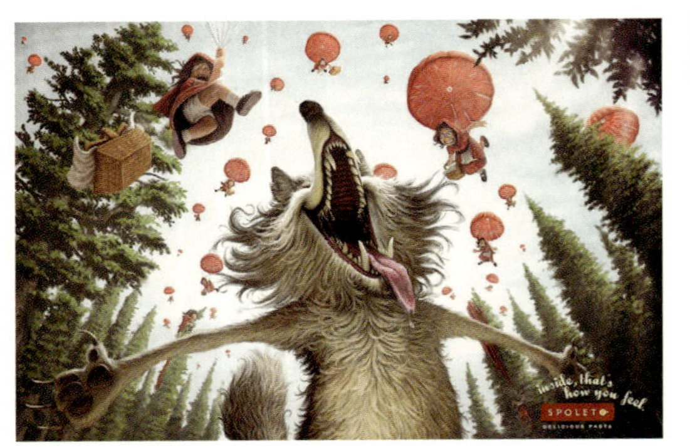

BRÉSIL BRAZIL (2011)
Art Plan Rio de Janeiro Spoleto Delicious Pasta
Inside, that's how you feel

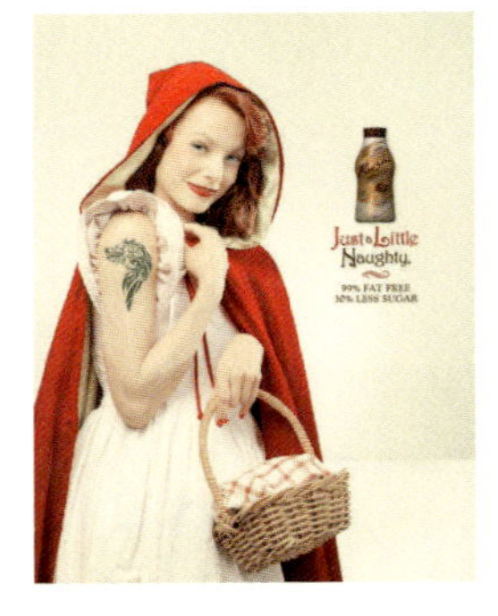

**AUSTRALIE
AUSTRALIA (2005)**
De Pasquale Brisbane
Rush Fat Free drink
Just a little naughty

LE PETIT CHAPERON ROUGE

№71

LITTLE RED RIDING HOOD

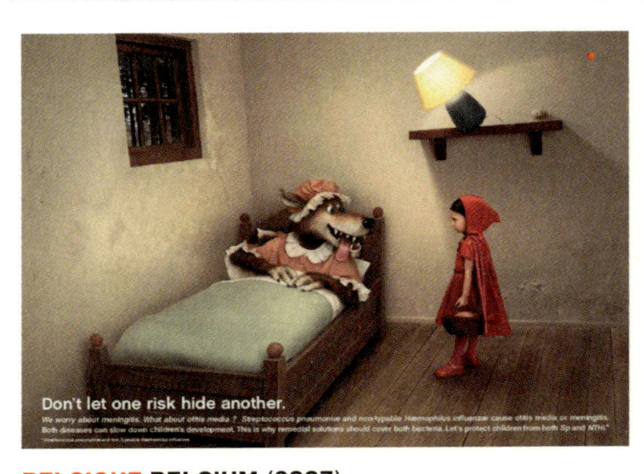

BELGIQUE BELGIUM (2007)
Air Brussels Glaxosmithkline
Don't let one risk hide another

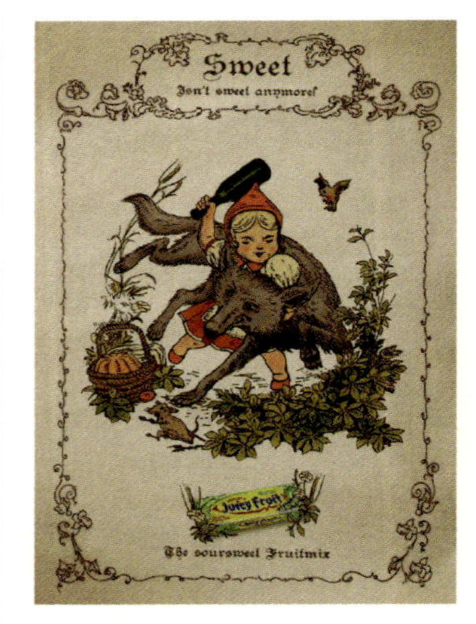

ALLEMAGNE GERMANY (2007)
BBDO Dusseldorf Juicy Fruit
Sweet isn't sweet anymore

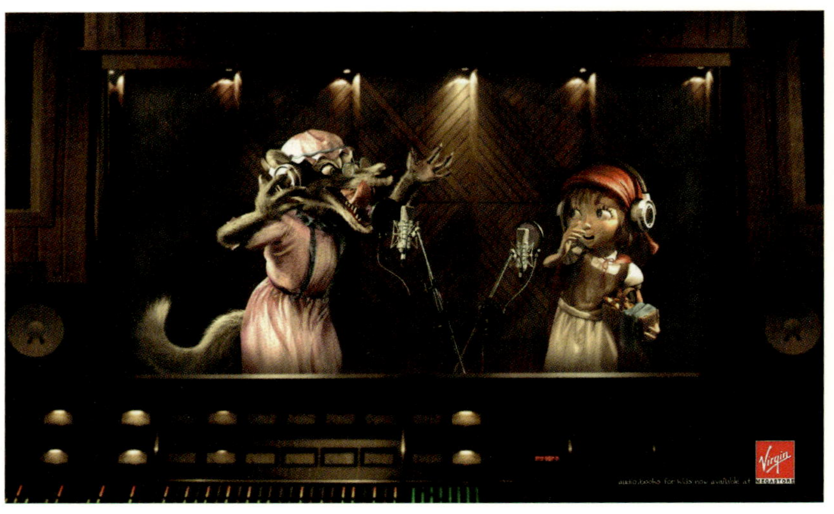

ÉMIRATS ARABES UNIS UNITED ARAB EMIRATES (2009)
JWT Dubai Virgin Megastore
Audio Books for kids now available at Virgin

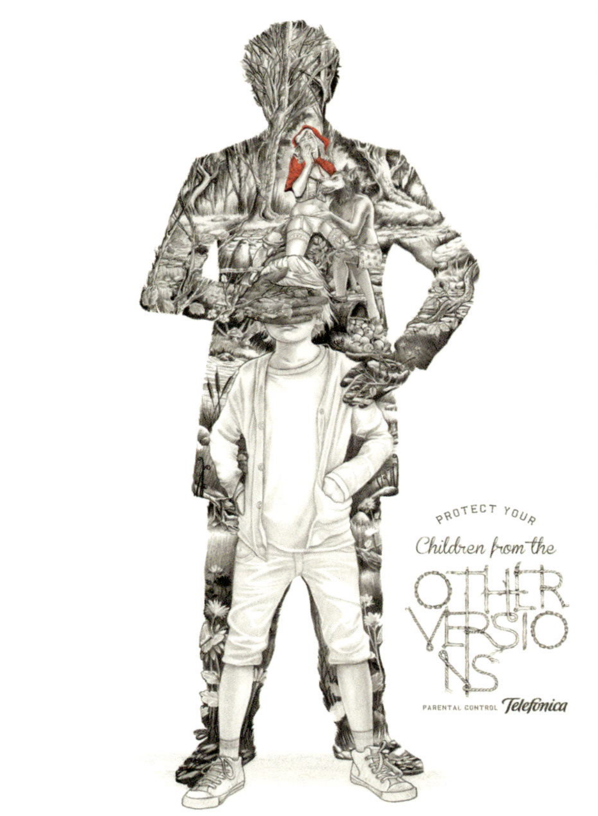

COLOMBIE
COLOMBIA (2012)
Sancho BBDO Bogota
Telefonica Parental Control
**Protect your children
from the other versions**

« Celle-ci est simplement
la plus belle graphiquement
et visuellement. L'illustration
est superbe, et donne envie
d'y regarder de plus près.
Elle fourmille de détails scabreux
et coquins qui en feraient rougir
plus d'un (ou d'une). »
"This is simply the most
graphically and visually beautiful.
The illustration is superb, and
makes you want to take a closer
look. It teems with risqué and
rascally details that could make
you blush more than once
(or at least once)."

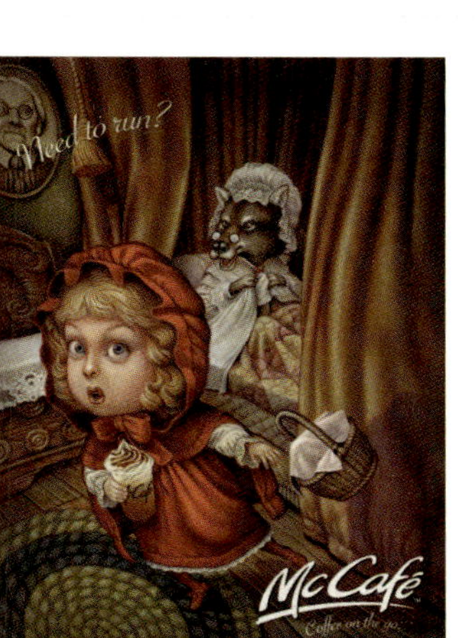

HONGRIE HUNGARY (2006)
DDB Budapest
Mc Café
Need to run? Coffee on the go

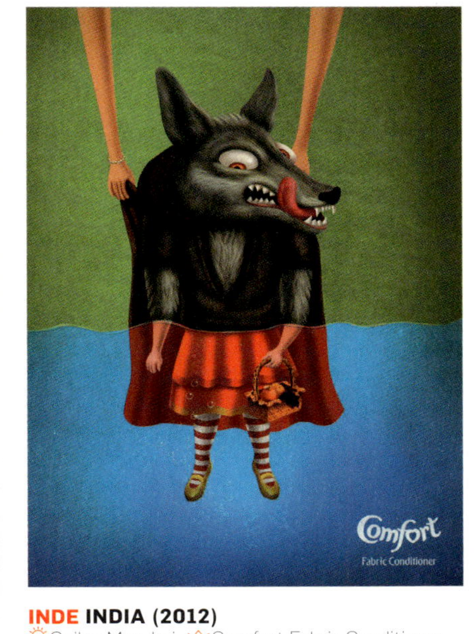

INDE INDIA (2012)
Ogilvy Mumbai · Comfort Fabric Conditioner

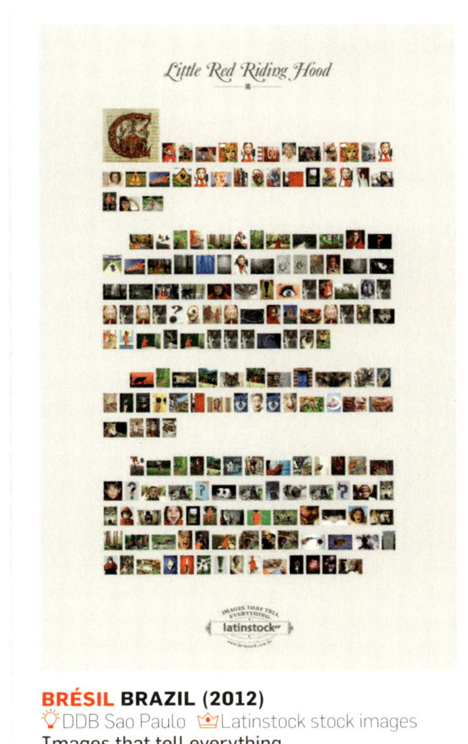

BRÉSIL BRAZIL (2012)
DDB Sao Paulo · Latinstock stock images
Images that tell everything

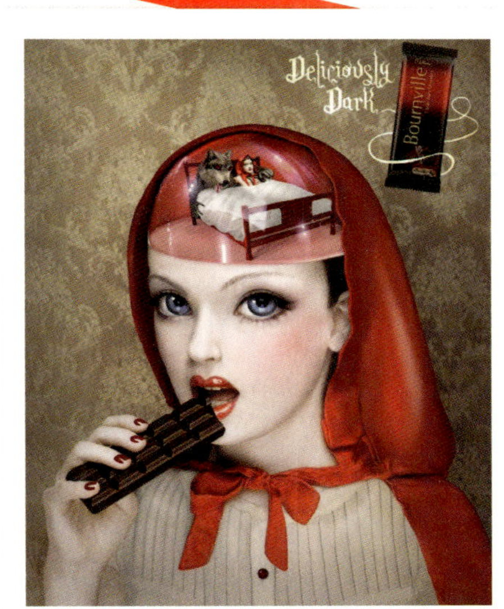

AFRIQUE DU SUD SOUTH AFRICA (2010)
Ogilvy Johannesburg
Bourneville Dark Chocolate
Deliciously Dark

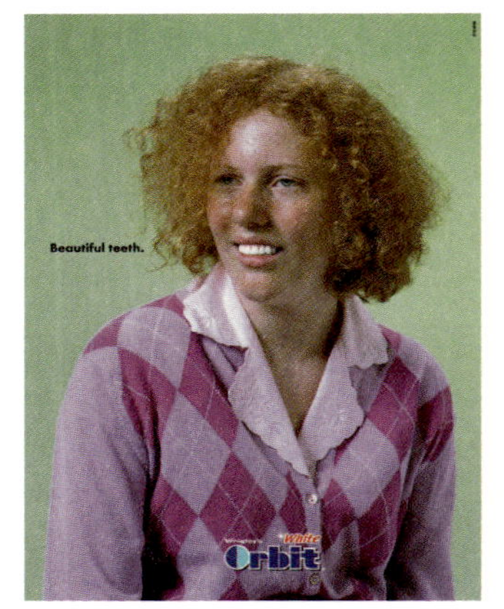

AUTRICHE AUSTRIA (2005)
BBDO · Orbit White
Beautiful teeth

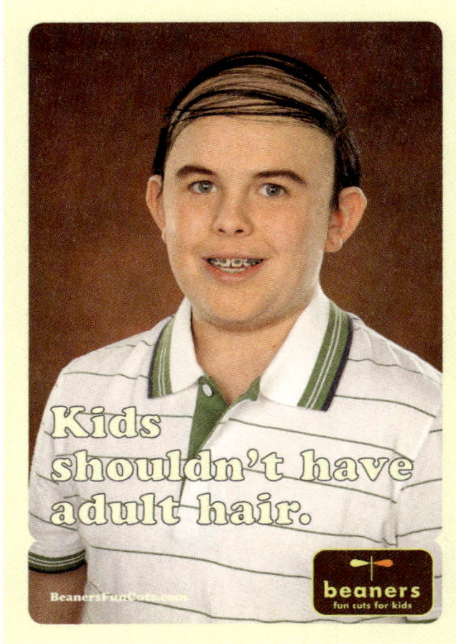

CANADA CANADA (2008)
Trigger · Beaners fun cuts for kids
Kids shouldn't have adult hair

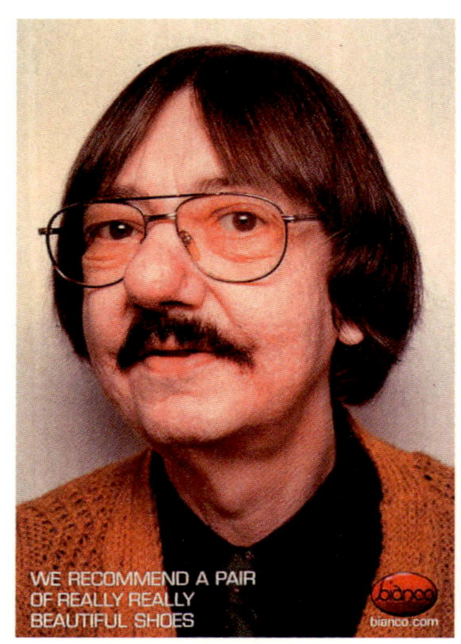
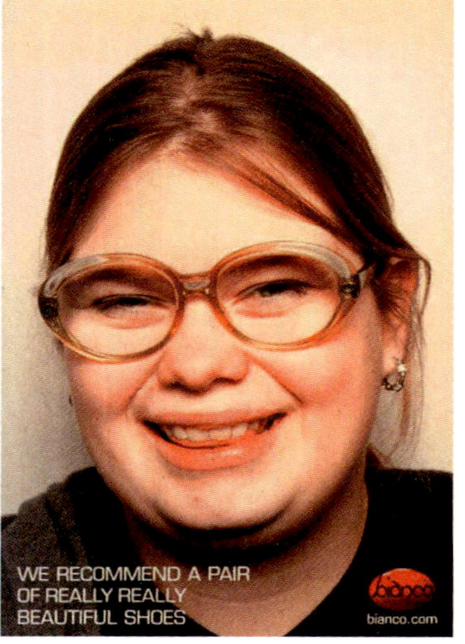

DANEMARK DENMARK (2000)
Grey Copenhagen · Bianco Footwear
We recommend a pair of really really beautiful shoes

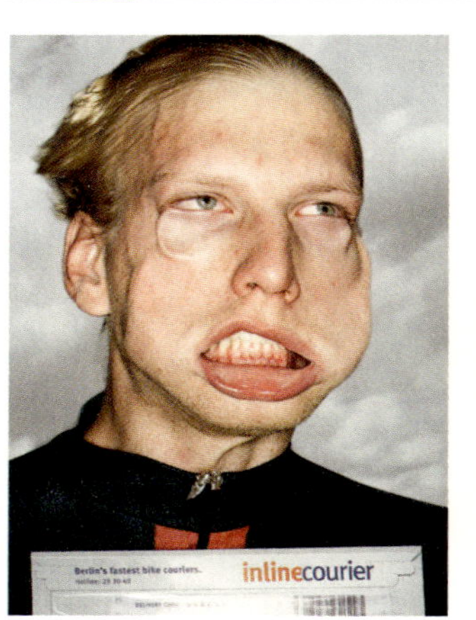

ALLEMAGNE GERMANY (2008)
Scholz & Friends Berlin · Inline Courier
Berlin fastest bike couriers

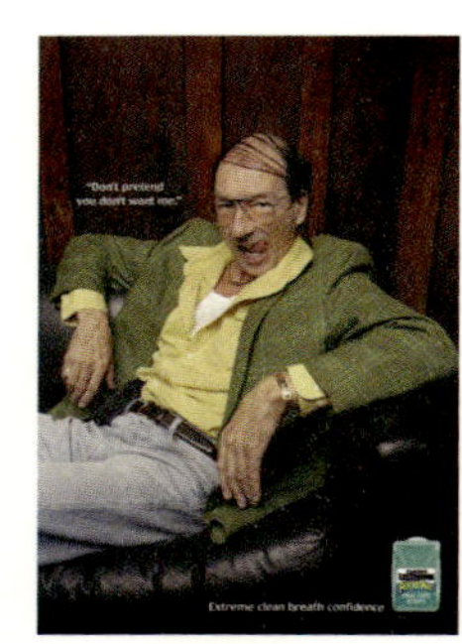

**AUSTRALIE
AUSTRALIA (2006)**
JWT Sydney · Listerine Pocket
"Don't pretend
you don't want me"
Extreme clean breath
confidence

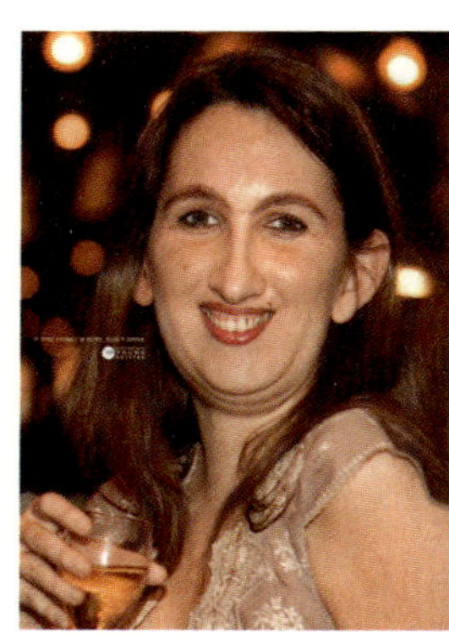
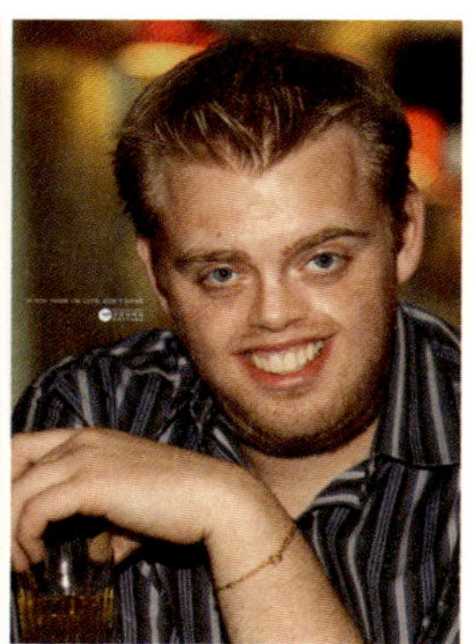

FRANCE FRANCE (2007)
TBWA · Responsible Young Drivers
If you think I'm cute, don't drive

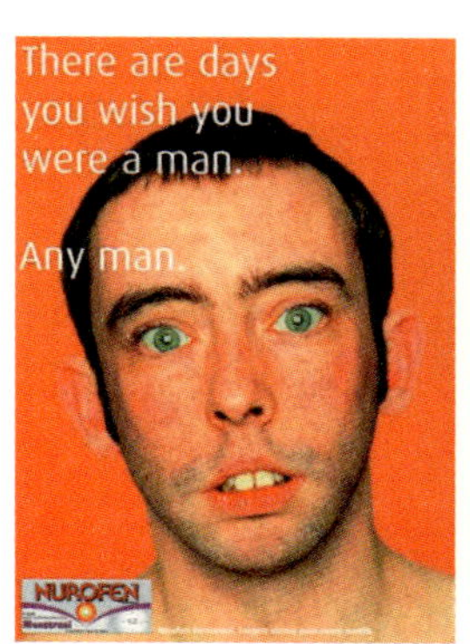
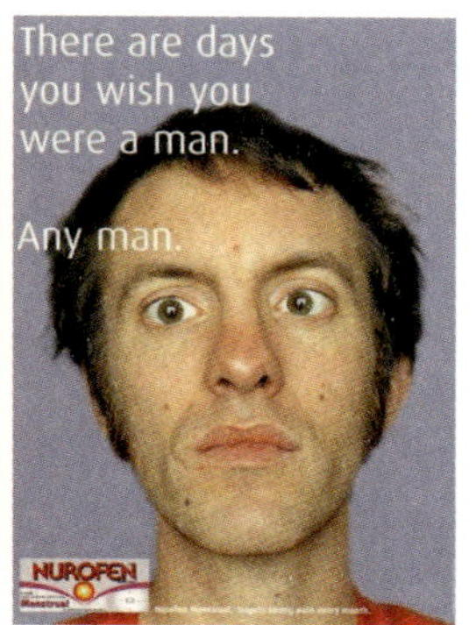

POLOGNE POLAND (2004)
Mc Cann Erickson Warsaw · Nurofen Menstrual
There are days you wish you were a man.
Any man.

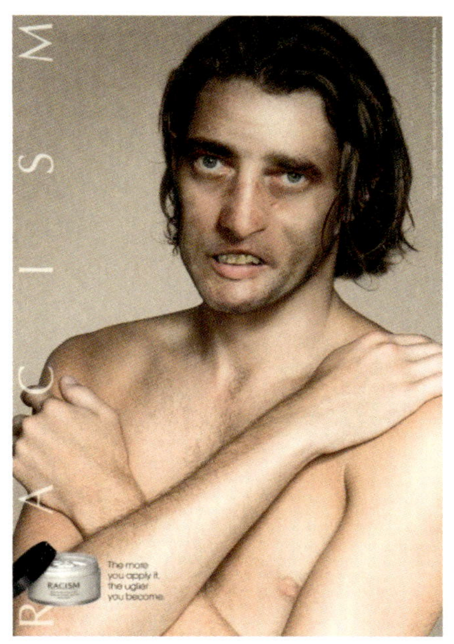

AUSTRALIE AUSTRALIA (2006)
Saatchi & Saatchi · Anti Racism
Racism. The more you apply it,
the uglier you become

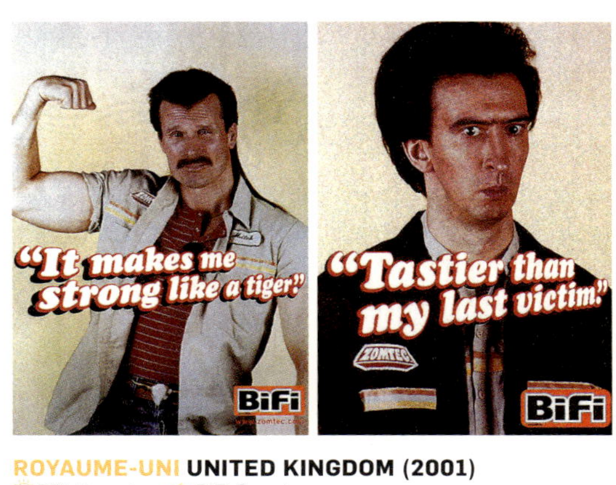

ROYAUME-UNI UNITED KINGDOM (2001)
BBH London · BiFi Snacks

PHYSIQUES INGRATS

№72

UGLY PEOPLE

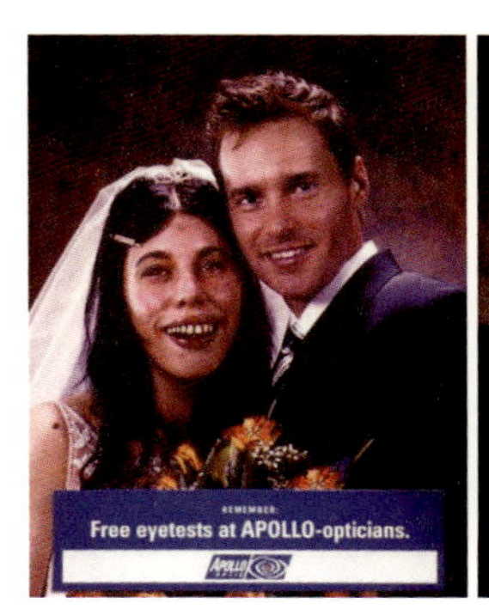
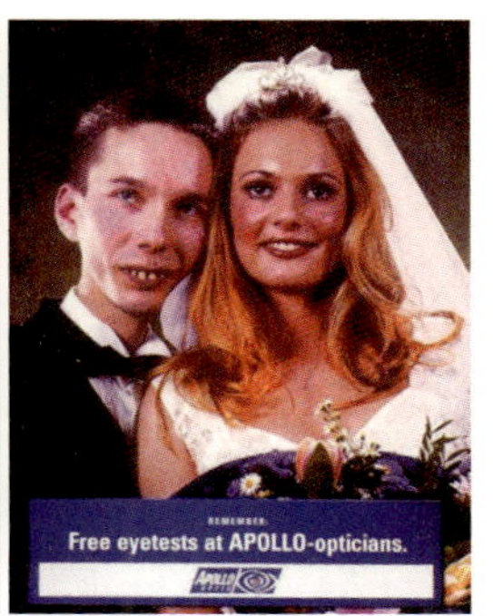

ALLEMAGNE GERMANY (2003)
Jung Von Matt · Apollo Opticians
Remember: Free eyetests

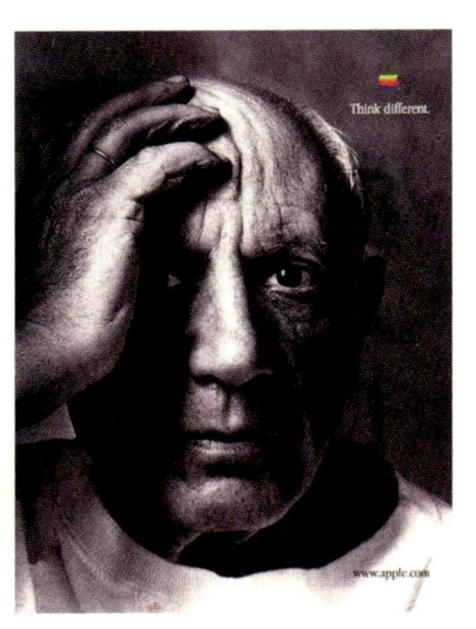

ÉTATS UNIS
UNITED STATES (1998)
TBWA Chiat Day Apple
Think different

PICASSO & CUBISM

№73

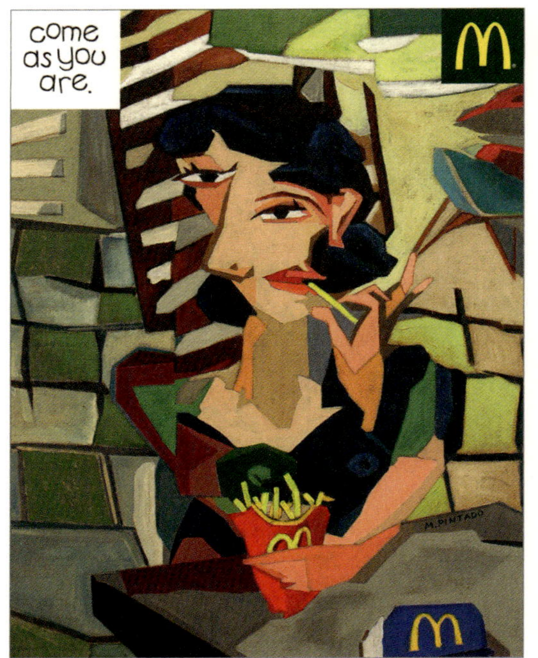

FRANCE FRANCE (2009)
BETC Euro RSCG Mc Donald's

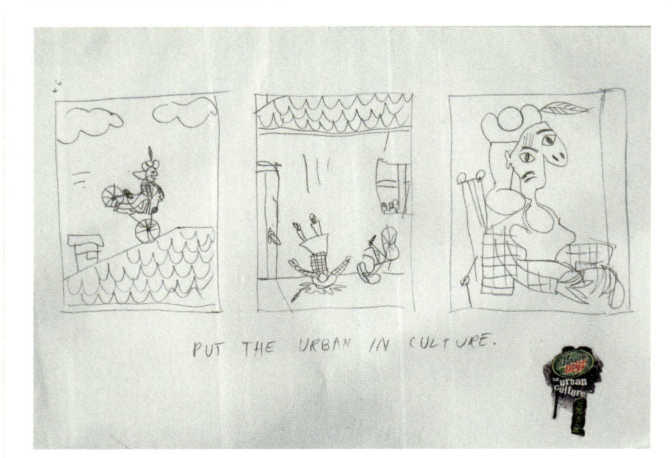

ROUMANIE ROMANIA (2007)
Graffiti BBDO Mountain Dew for Urban Culture
Put the urban in culture

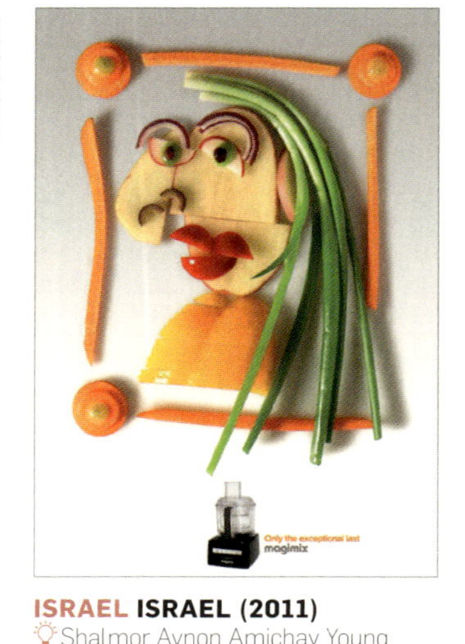
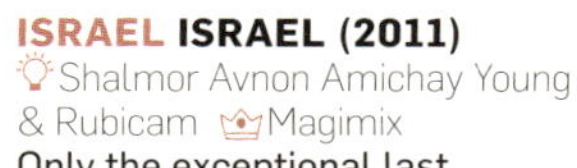

ISRAEL ISRAEL (2011)
Shalmor Avnon Amichay Young
& Rubicam Magimix
Only the exceptional last

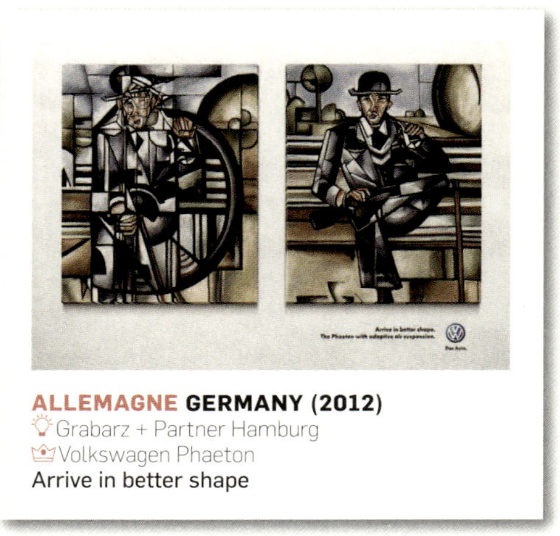

ALLEMAGNE GERMANY (2012)
Grabarz + Partner Hamburg
Volkswagen Phaeton
Arrive in better shape

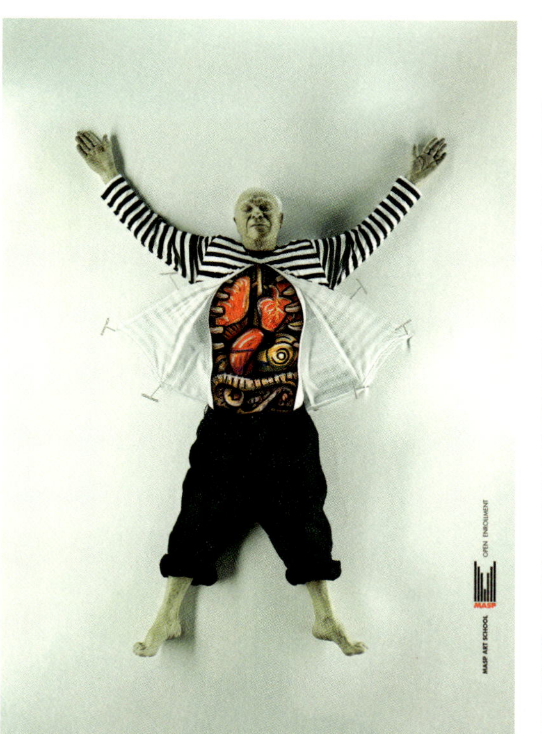

BRÉSIL BRAZIL (2012)
DDB MASP Art School
Open enrolment

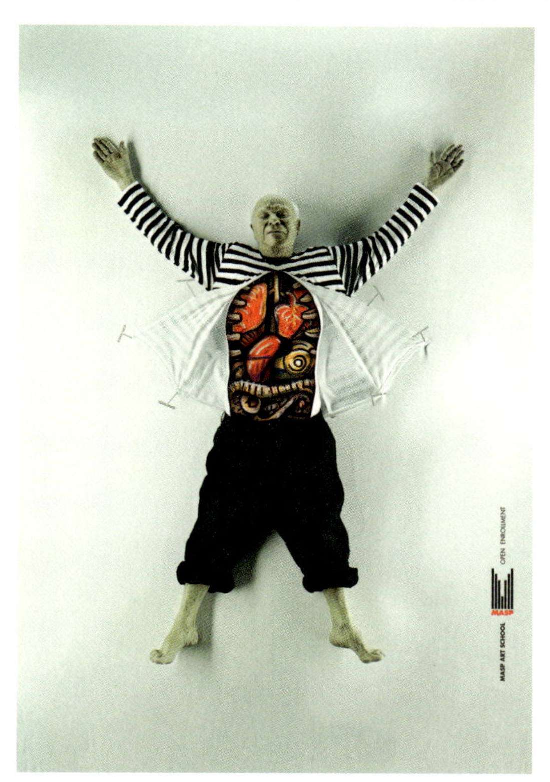

BRÉSIL
BRAZIL (2005)
BBDO Sao Paulo
Bayer Aspirin

INDE INDIA (2007)
Ogilvy & Mather Eraser

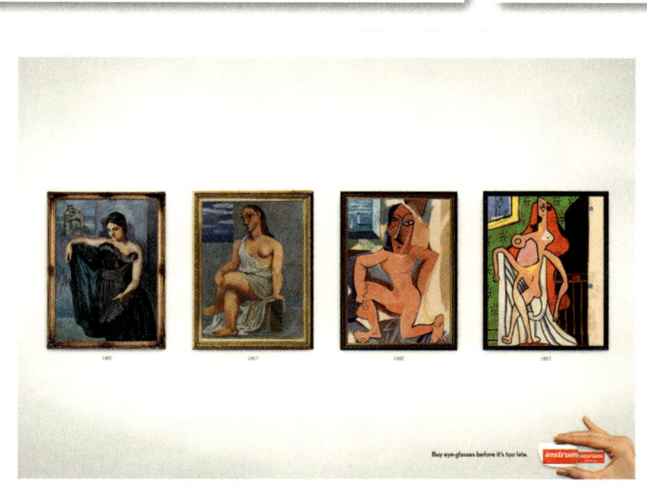

FINLANDE FINLAND (2009)
TBWA PHS Instrumentarium Optician
Buy eye-glasses before it's too late

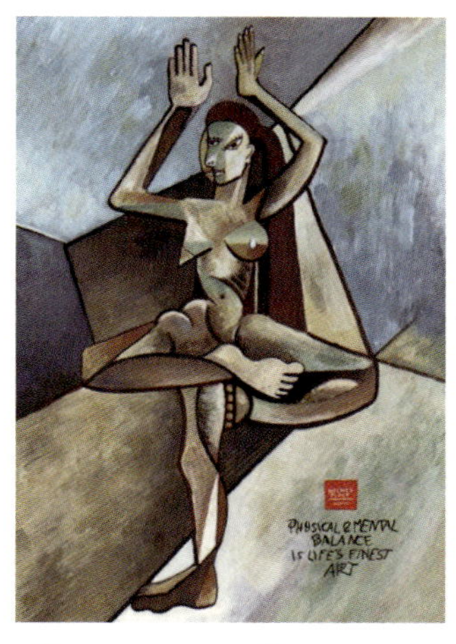

RÉPUBLIQUE TCHÈQUE
CZECH REPUBLIC (2006)
Leo Burnett Helmes Place
Physical & Mental balance
is life's finest art

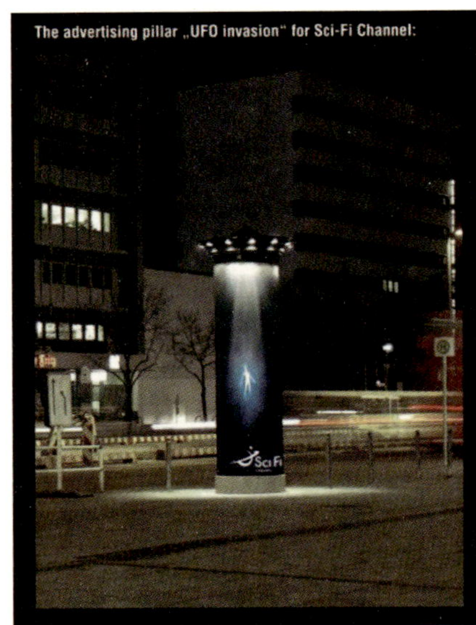

ALLEMAGNE
GERMANY (2006)
Jung Von Matt
Sci-Fi Channel

« C'est vrai que les couronnes qui ornent les colonnes Morris dans certains pays ressemblent étrangement à des soucoupes volantes. Il fallait y penser ! Voilà un Objet Veritablement Non Idiot. »

"It is true that the crowns adorning advertising columns in some countries bear an uncanny resemblance to flying saucers. One has to wonder! Voilà, an Unbelievably Funny Object."

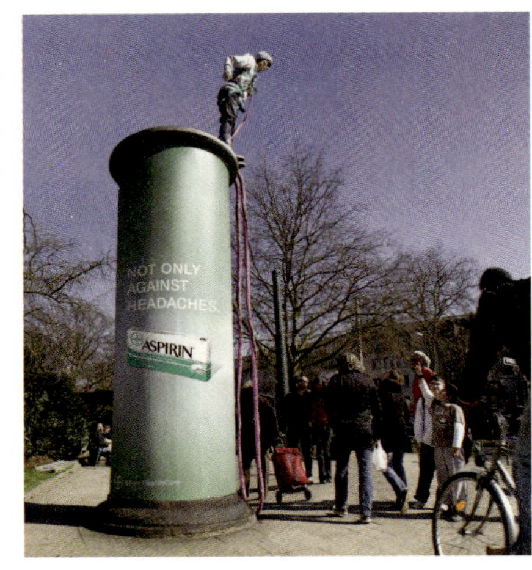

ALLEMAGNE GERMANY (2009)
BBDO Dusseldorf   Bayer Aspirin
Not only against headaches

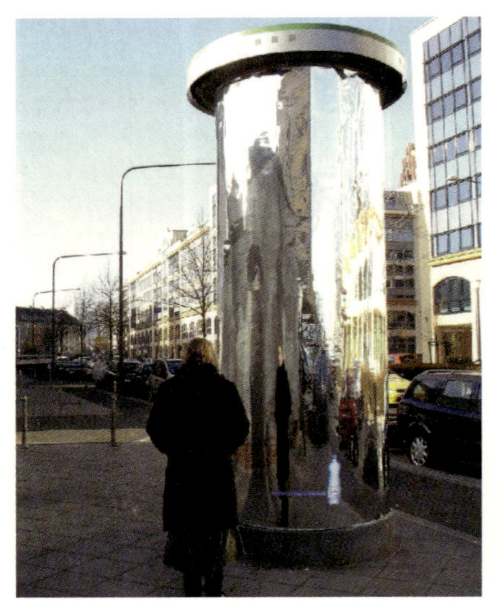

ALLEMAGNE GERMANY (2005)
Publicis Frankfurt   Contrex water

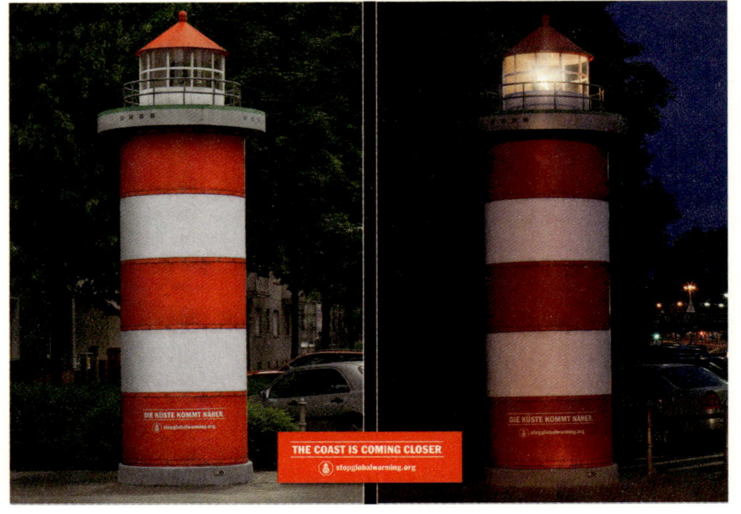

ALLEMAGNE GERMANY (2010)
Ogilvy & Mather Frankfurt   StopGlobalWarming.org
The coast is coming closer

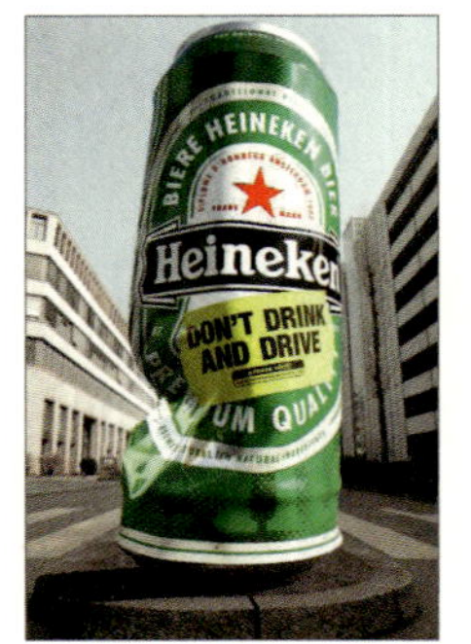

SUISSE
SWITZERLAND (2005)
Publicis Zurich
Road Safety
Don't drink and drive

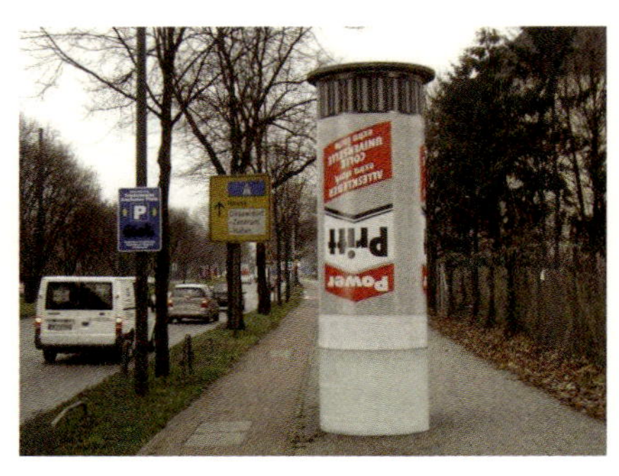

ALLEMAGNE GERMANY (2004)
DDB   Power Pritt Glue

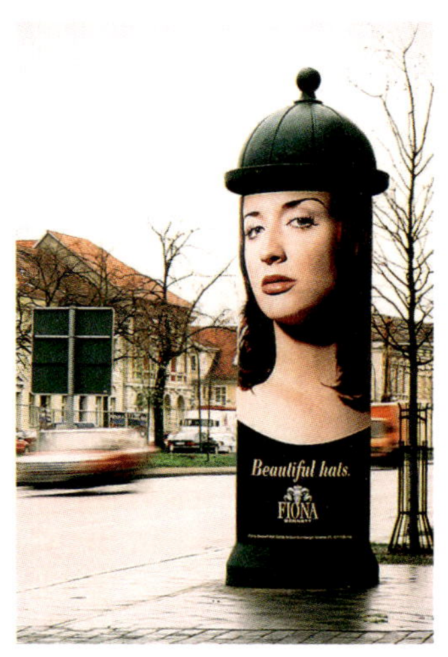

ALLEMAGNE GERMANY (2001)
Scholz & Friends Berlin
Fiona Bennett
Beautiful Hats

PILIERS
№74
PILLARS

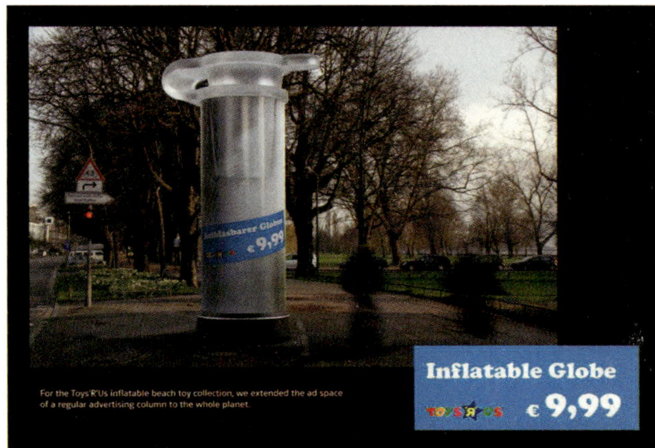

ALLEMAGNE GERMANY (2007)
Grey Dusseldorf   Toys'r us
Inflatable globe 9,99€ at Toys'r us

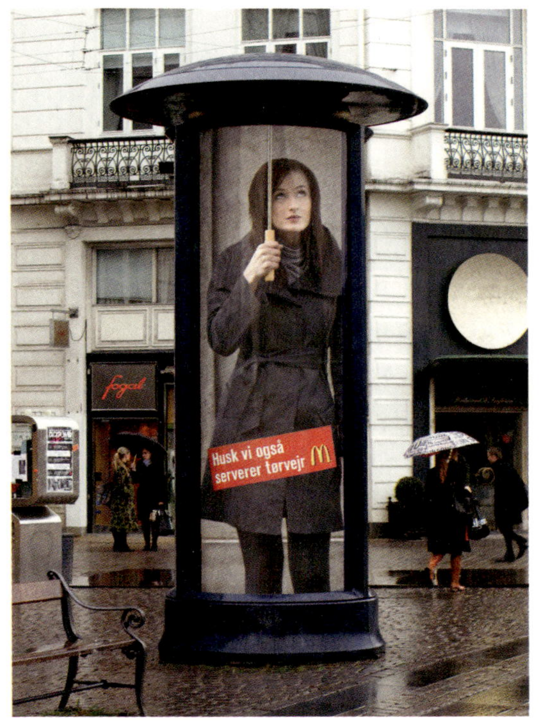

DANEMARK DENMARK (2008)
DDB   Mc Donald's
Remember we've got shelter on the menu as well

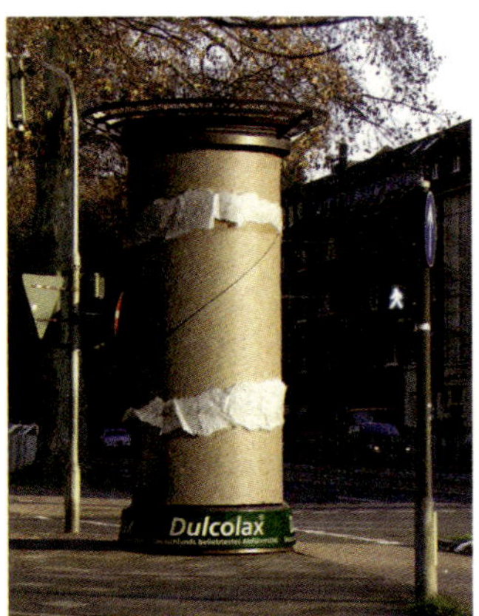

ALLEMAGNE GERMANY (2006)
Euro RSCG Dusseldorf
Dulcolax laxative

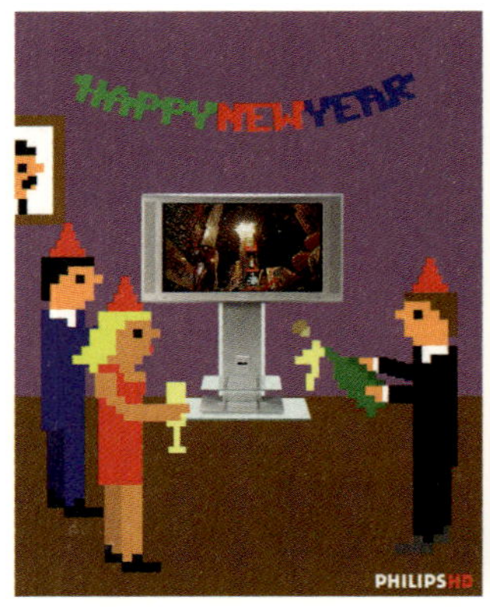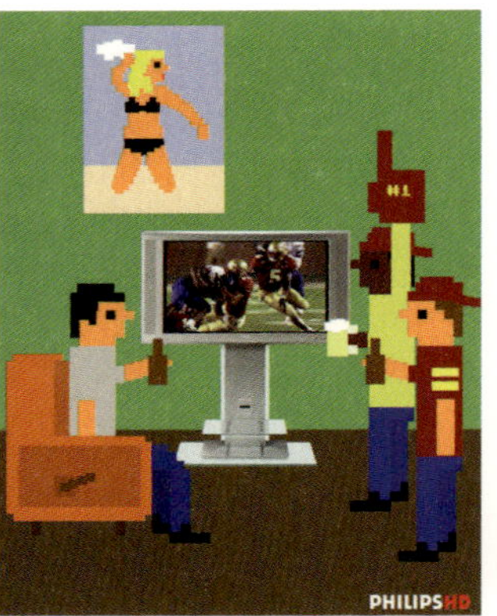

INCONNU UNKNOWN (2005)
Inconnu/unknown Philipps HDTV

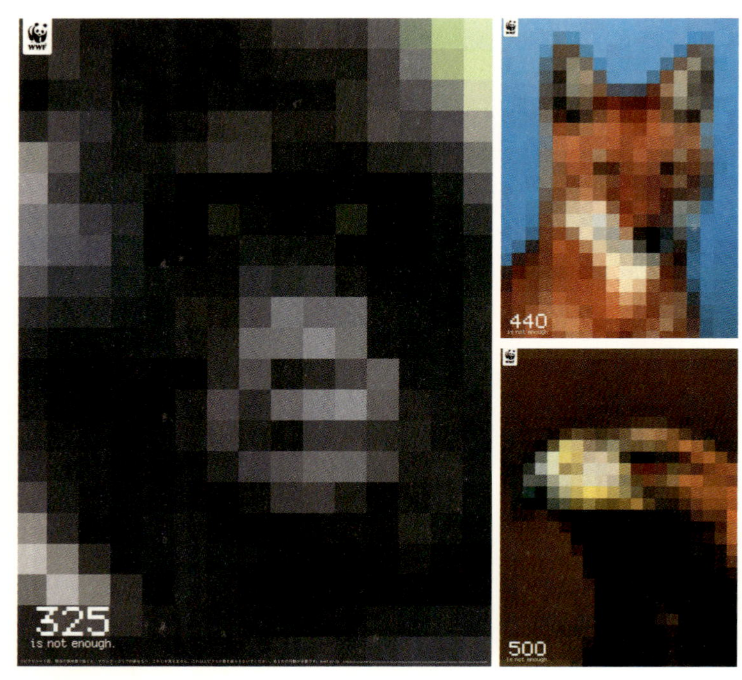

JAPON JAPAN (2008)
Hakuhodo WWF
325 is not enough (gorillas), 440 is not enough (Fox), 500 is not enough (eagles)

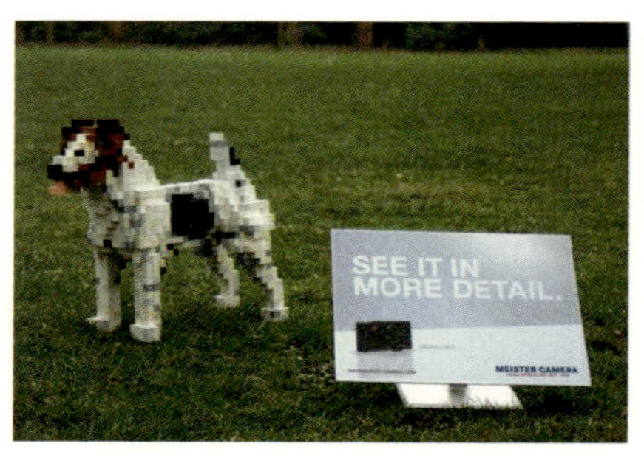

ALLEMAGNE GERMANY (2008)
Philipp Und Keuntje Hamburg
Meister Camera
See it in more detail

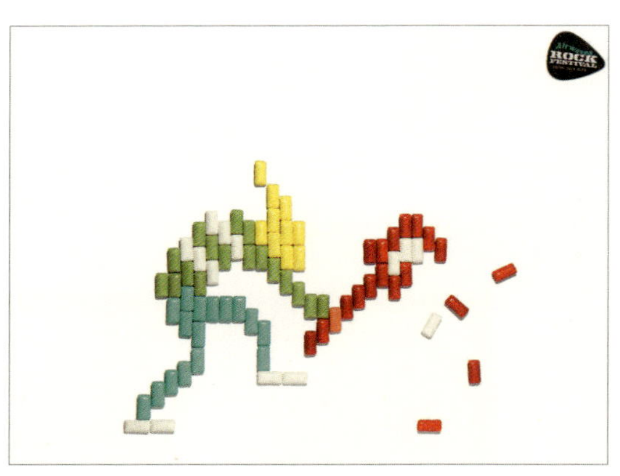

FRANCE FRANCE (2006)
CLM/BBDO Airwaves Chewing Gums - Rock Festival

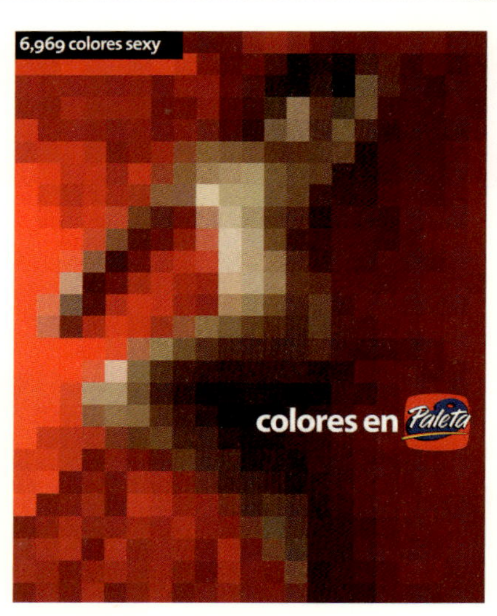

GUATEMALA GUATEMALA (2010)
Garcia Robles Paleta Paints
6969 sexy colors

PIXELS & 8 BIT

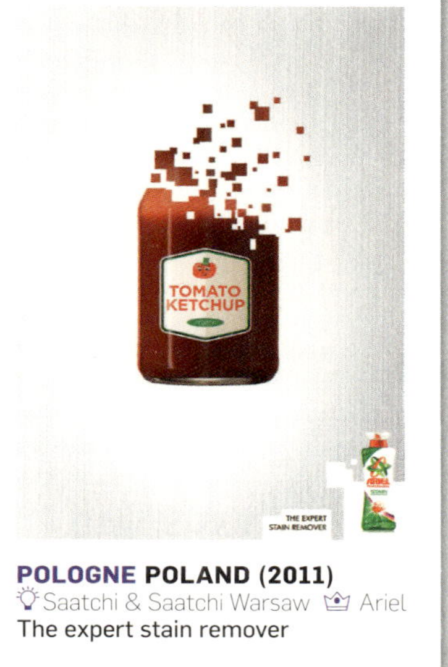

POLOGNE POLAND (2011)
Saatchi & Saatchi Warsaw — Ariel
The expert stain remover

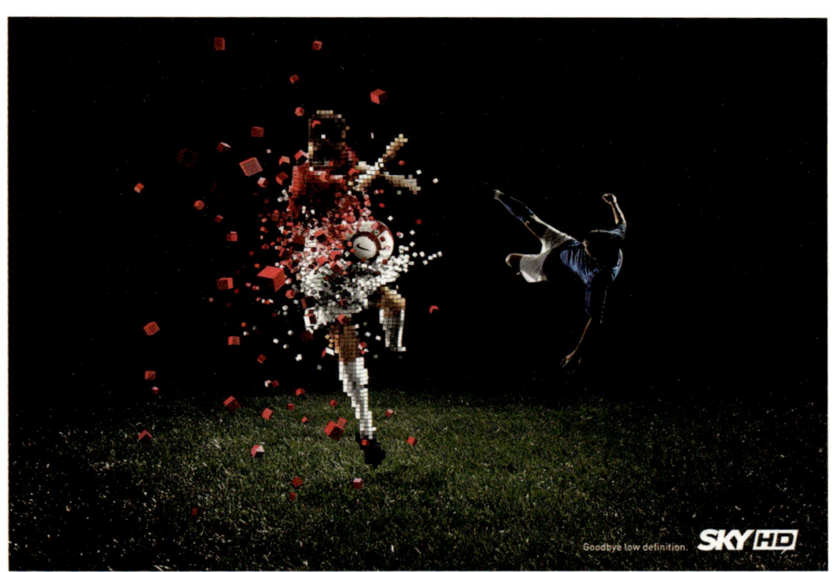

ITALIE ITALY (2009)
1861 Milan — Sky HD
Good bye low definition

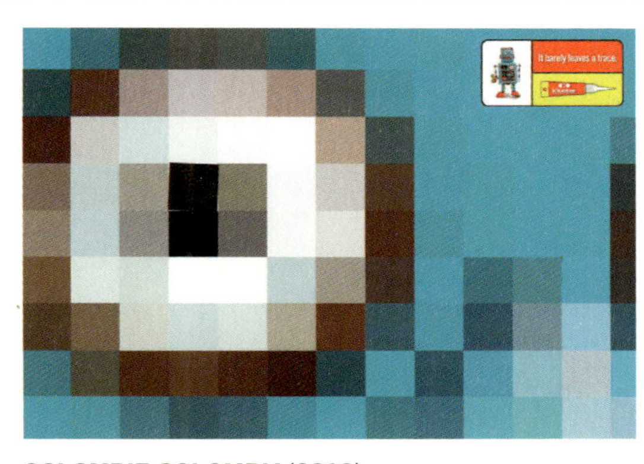

COLOMBIE COLOMBIA (2010)
Young & Rubicam — Klunter Glue
It barely leaves a trace

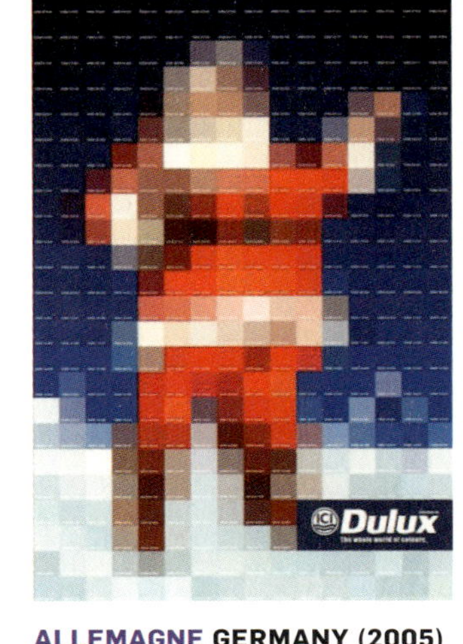

ALLEMAGNE GERMANY (2005)
Jung von Matt — Dulux Paints
The whole world of colours

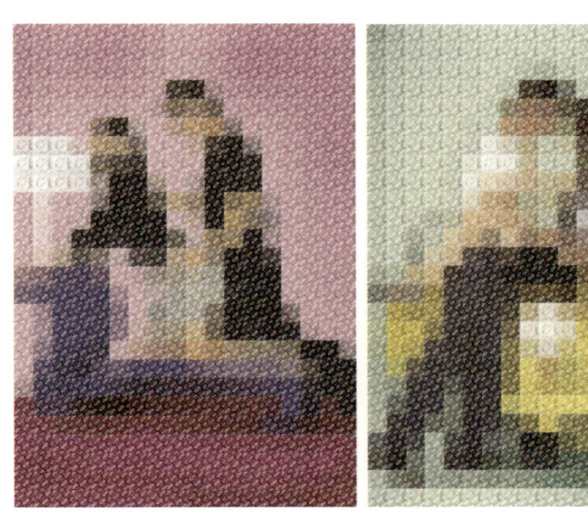

AFRIQUE DU SUD SOUTH AFRICA (2006)
Lowe Bull Cape Town — Durex Condoms

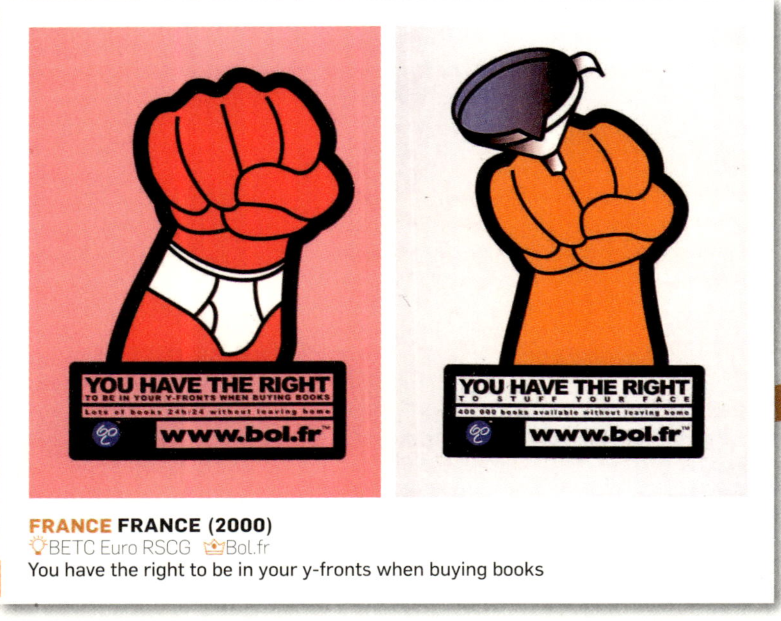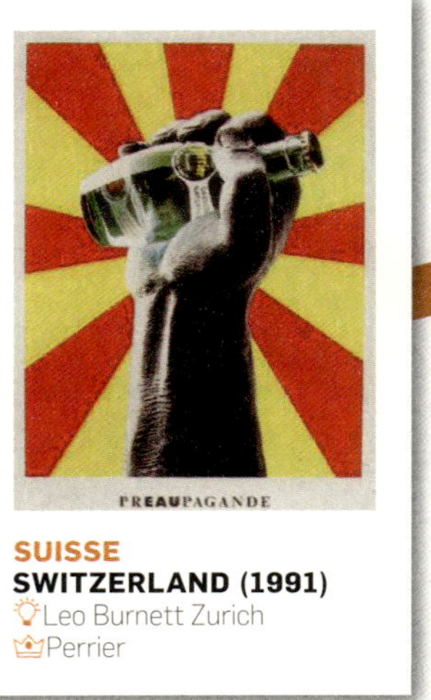

FRANCE FRANCE (2000)
BETC Euro RSCG Bol.fr
You have the right to be in your y-fronts when buying books

SUISSE SWITZERLAND (1991)
Leo Burnett Zurich
Perrier

POINGS LEVÉS
№ 76
HANDS UP

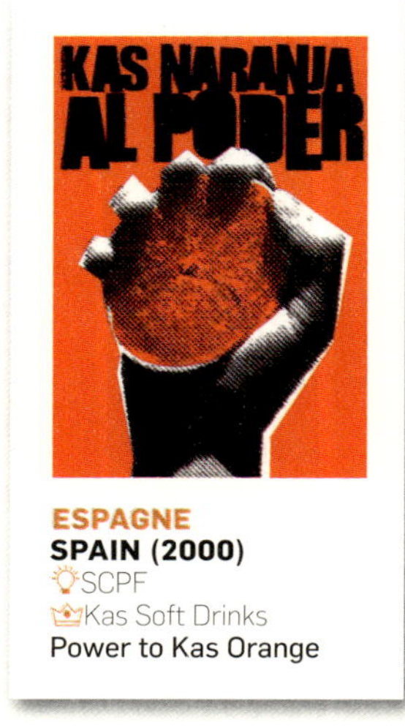

ESPAGNE SPAIN (2000)
SCPF
Kas Soft Drinks
Power to Kas Orange

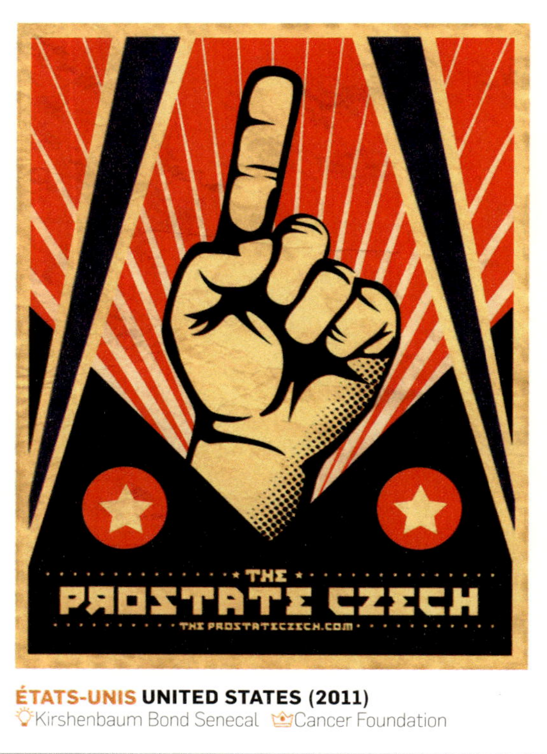

ÉTATS-UNIS UNITED STATES (2011)
Kirshenbaum Bond Senecal Cancer Foundation

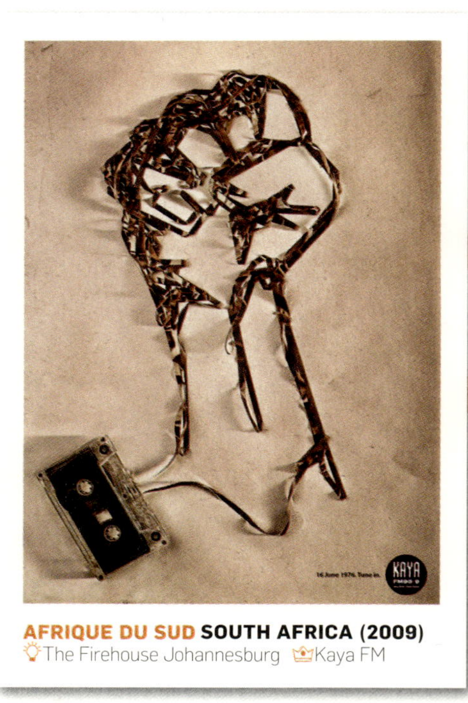

AFRIQUE DU SUD SOUTH AFRICA (2009)
The Firehouse Johannesburg Kaya FM

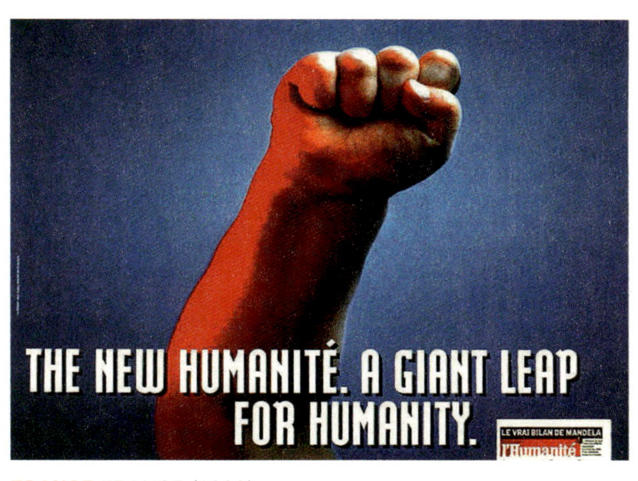

FRANCE FRANCE (1999)
CLM/BBDO *L'Humanité* daily newspaper

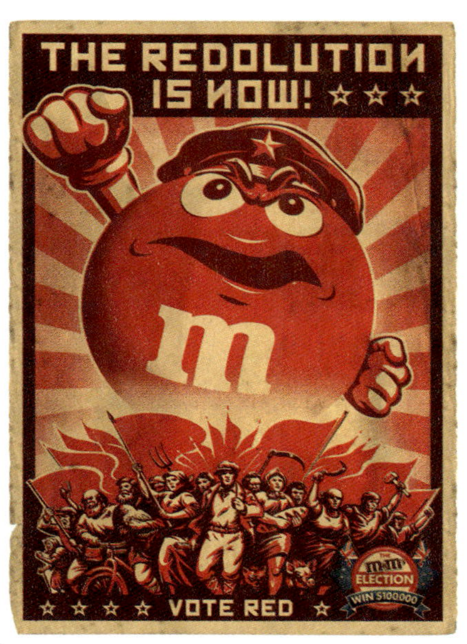

AUSTRALIE AUSTRALIA (2008)
Clemenger BBDO Melbourne M&M's

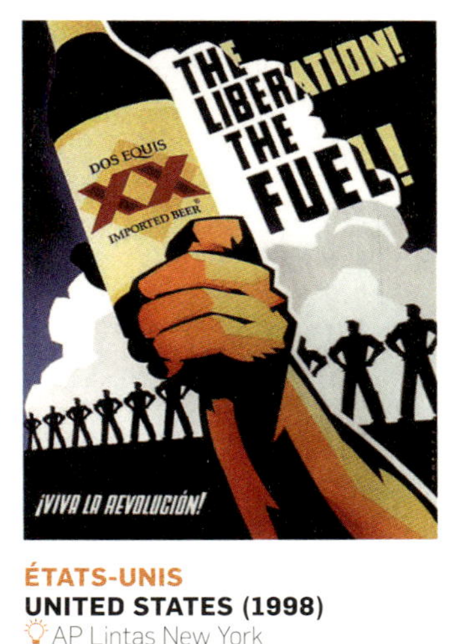

**ÉTATS-UNIS
UNITED STATES (1998)**
AP Lintas New York
Dos Equis Beer

ÉTATS-UNIS UNITED STATES (2010)
Struck Axiom Salt Lake City Shrek Forever After

CANADA CANADA (2008)
Cheil Samsung
Express your strong side

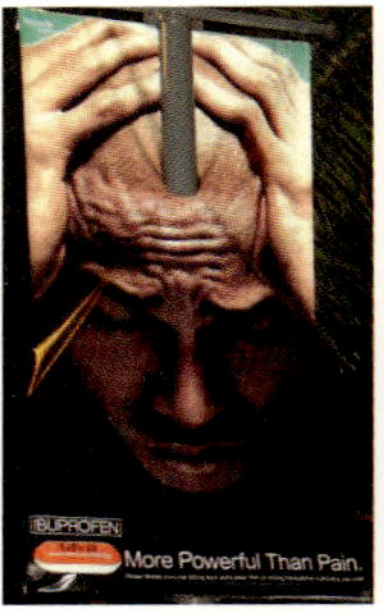
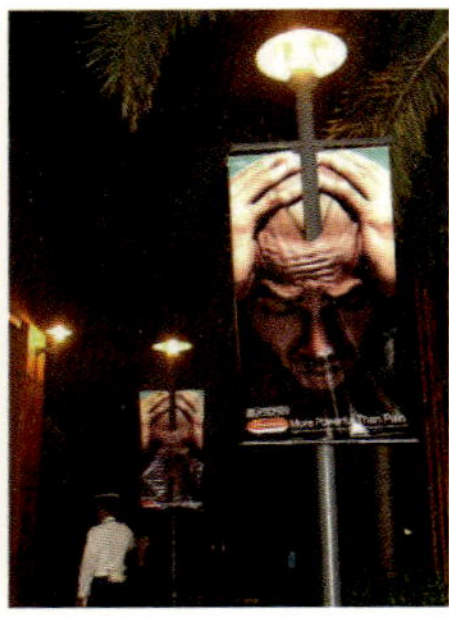

PHILIPPINES **PHILIPPINES (2005)**
TBWA Makati City
Ibuprofen Anti Headaches
More powerful than pain

« L'idée est vraiment lumineuse et je ne dis pas ça parce qu'elle a un lampadaire comme support. Le placement de l'affiche est idéal et extrêmement malin, et c'est ça qui fait mal ! » A really bright idea and I'm not saying this because they use a lamppost as a prop. The placement of the poster is ideal and extremely clever, and that's what burns!

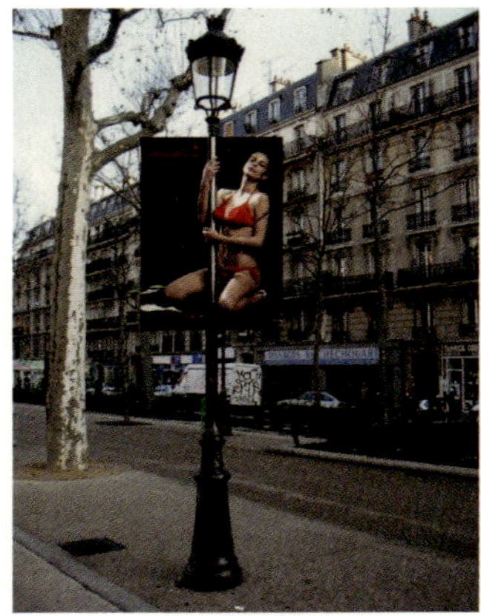

FRANCE FRANCE (2006)
JWT Stringfellow's Night Club

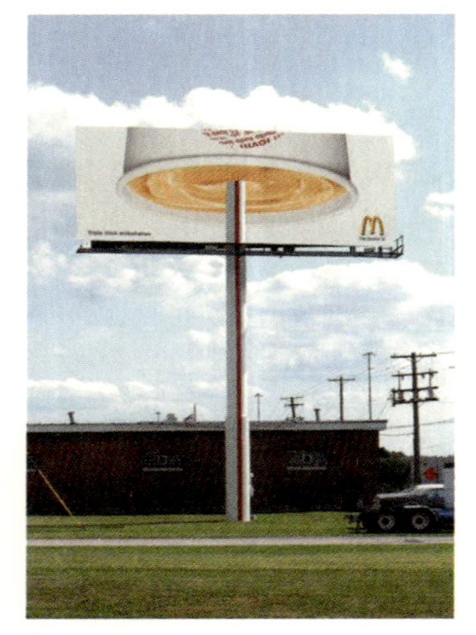

ÉTATS UNIS
UNITED STATES (2005)
Leo Burnett Chicago
Mc Donald's
Triple Thick Milk shake

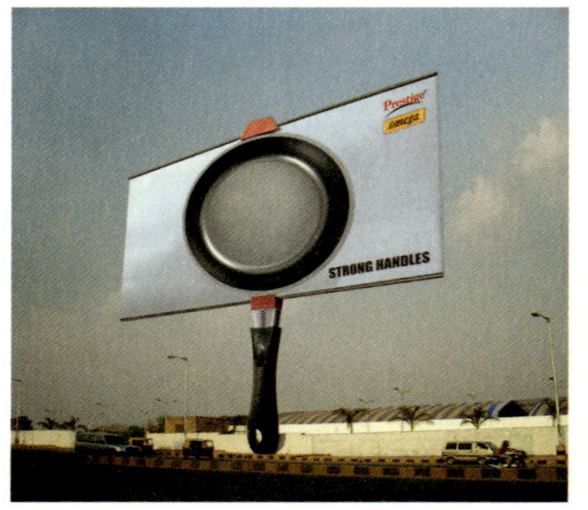

INDE **INDIA (2007)**
Mudra Bangalore
TTK Prestige Omega Fry Pan
Strong Handles

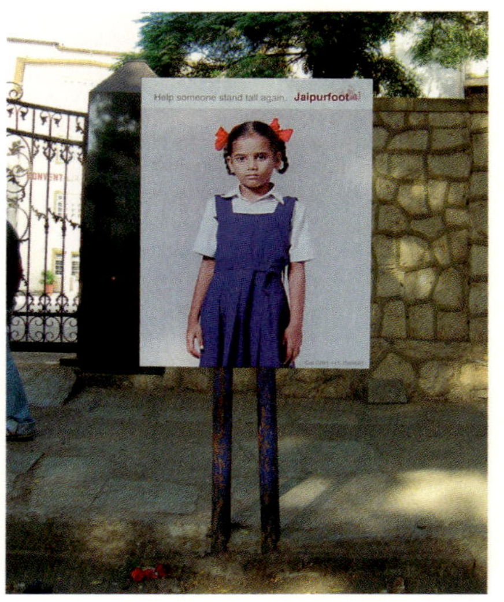

INDE **INDIA (2005)**
Ogilvy & Mather Mumbai Jaipurfoot
Help someone stand tall again

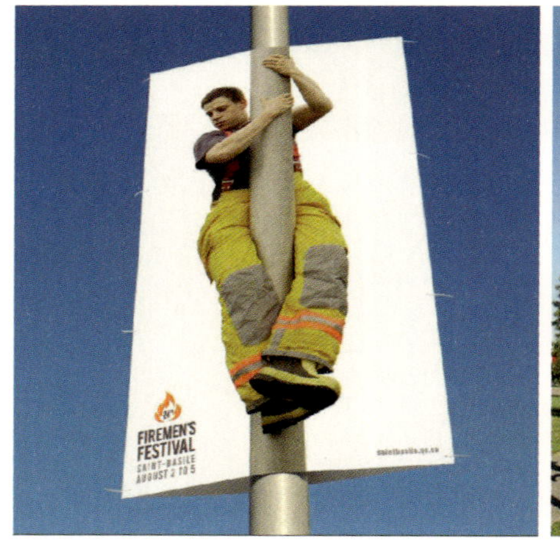
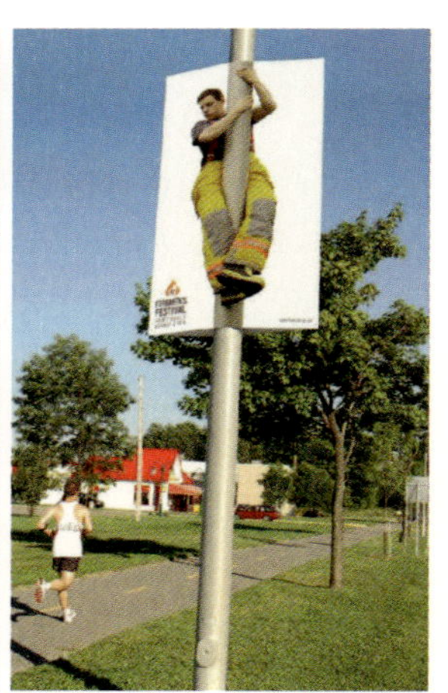

CANADA **CANADA (2007)**
LG2 Quebec Firemen's Festival

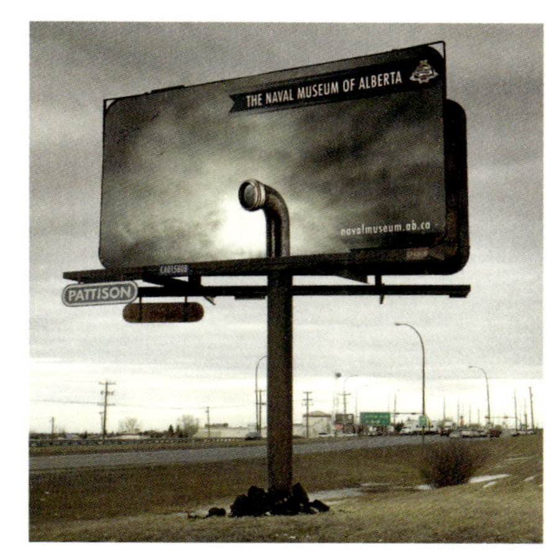
CANADA CANADA (2007)
Trigger Calgary
The naval museum of Alberta

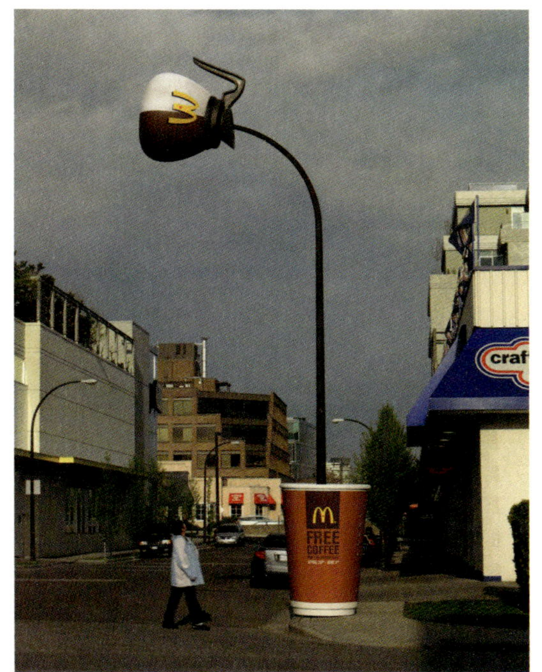
CANADA CANADA (2007)
Cossette Mc Donald's Mc Coffee

POTEAUX
№77
POSTS

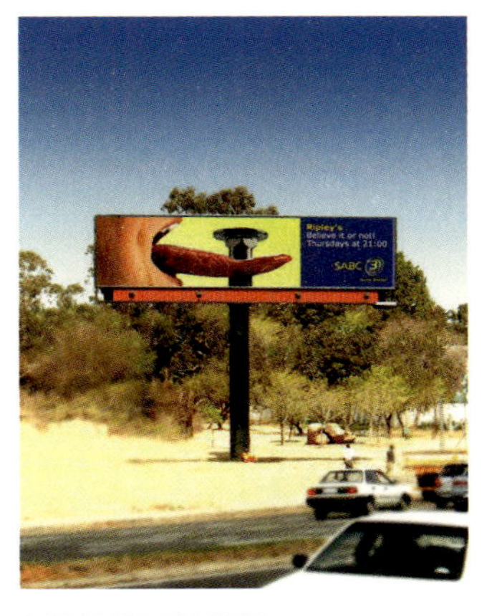
**AFRIQUE DU SUD
SOUTH AFRICA (2004)**
Tequila Johannesburg Ripley's
Believe It Or Not!
Thursdays at 21:00 on SABC3 TV

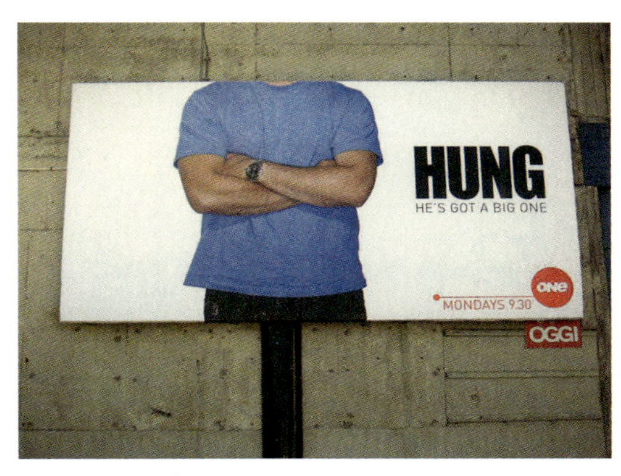
NOUVELLE ZÉLANDE NEW ZEALAND (2010)
Colenso BBDO TVNZ One channel

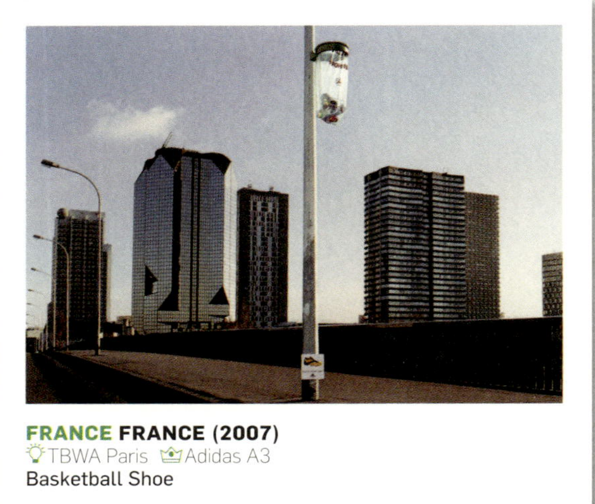

FRANCE FRANCE (2007)
TBWA Paris Adidas A3
Basketball Shoe

POUBELLES PUBLICITAIRES

№78

TRASHVERTISING

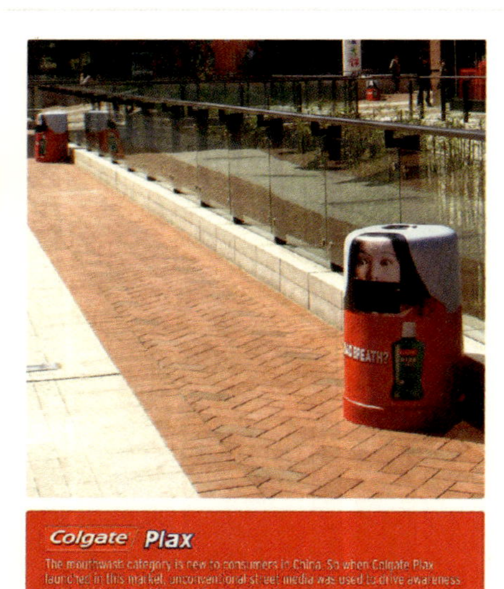

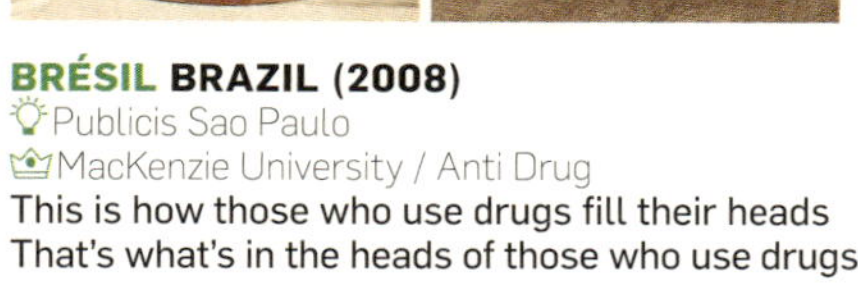

CHINE CHINA (2008)
Young & Rubicam Colgate Plax
Bad Breath?

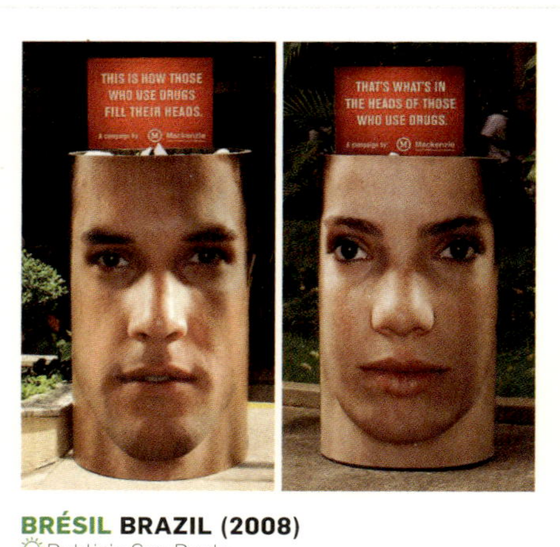

BRÉSIL BRAZIL (2008)
Publicis Sao Paulo
MacKenzie University / Anti Drug
This is how those who use drugs fill their heads
That's what's in the heads of those who use drugs

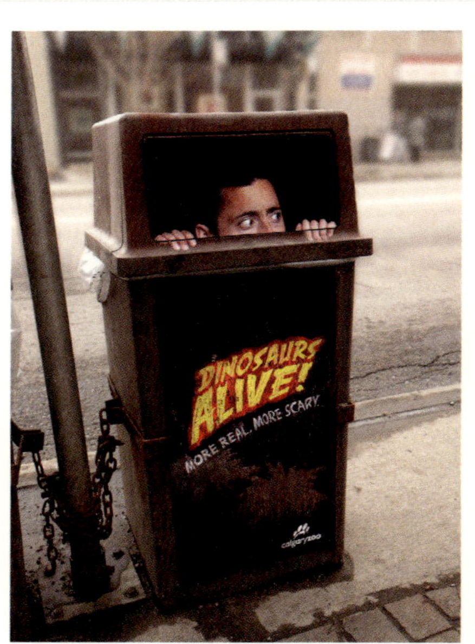

CANADA CANADA (2010)
Trigger Calgary Calgary Zoo
Dinosaurs Alive! More real, more scary

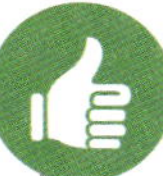

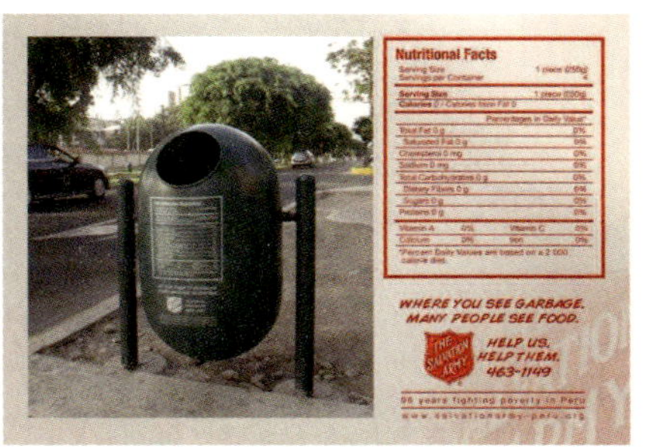

PÉROU PERU (2006)
Draft FCB The Salvation Army
"Nutritional Facts"...
Where you see garbage, many people see food

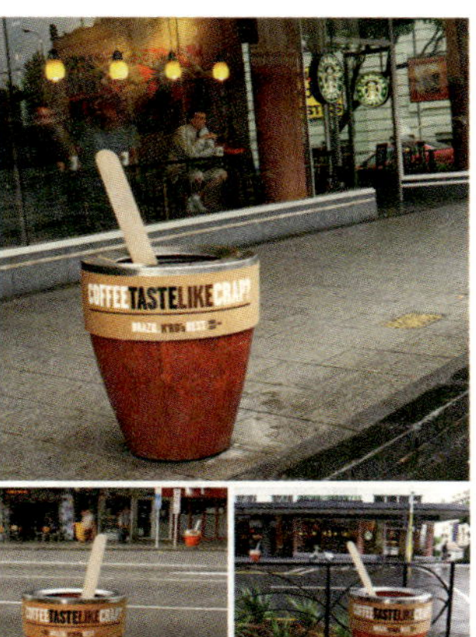

NOUVELLE-ZÉLANDE
NEW ZEALAND (2006)
Draft FCB Café Brazil
(placed outside a branch of Starbucks)
Coffee taste like crap? Brazil Café is best

« Une opération très gonflée qui se moque ouvertement de Starbucks. Et avec tout le respect que je dois à leur incontestable réussite, il faut quand même avouer que certains de leurs cafés allongés sont assez peu savoureux. »
"An overinflated idea that openly mocks Starbucks. And with all due respect to their undeniable success, you still have to admit that some of their coffees are not very tasty."

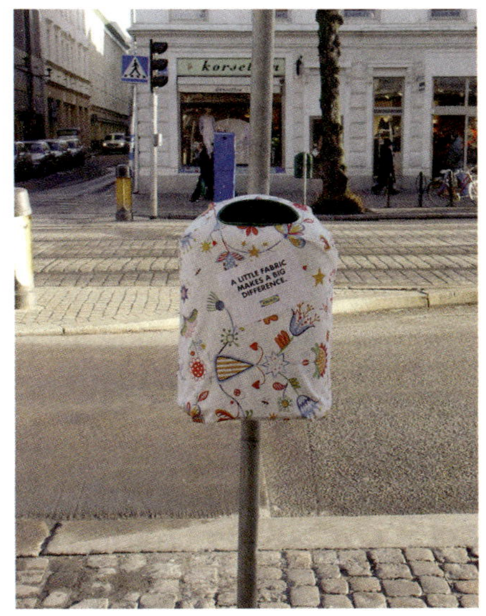

SUÈDE SWEDEN (2004)
Forsman & Bodenfors IKEA
A little fabric makes a big difference

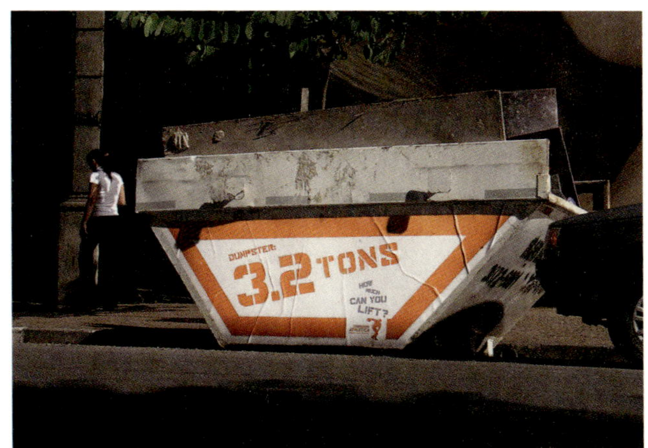

BRÉSIL BRAZIL
DDB Companhia Athletica
Dumpster: 3.2 tons. How much can you lift?

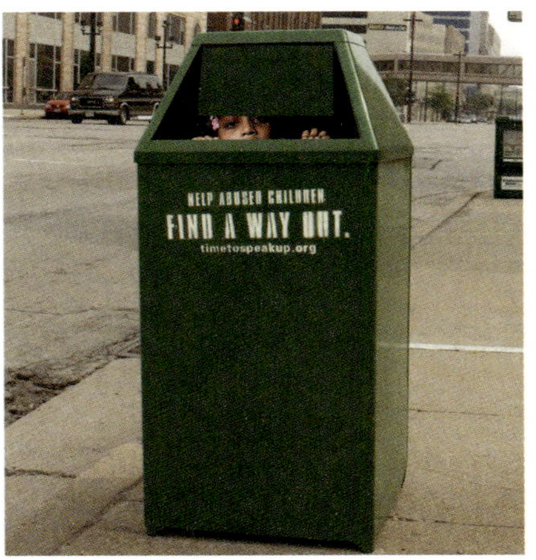

ÉTATS-UNIS UNITED STATES (2007)
Serve Milwaukee timetospeakup.org
Help abused children find a way out

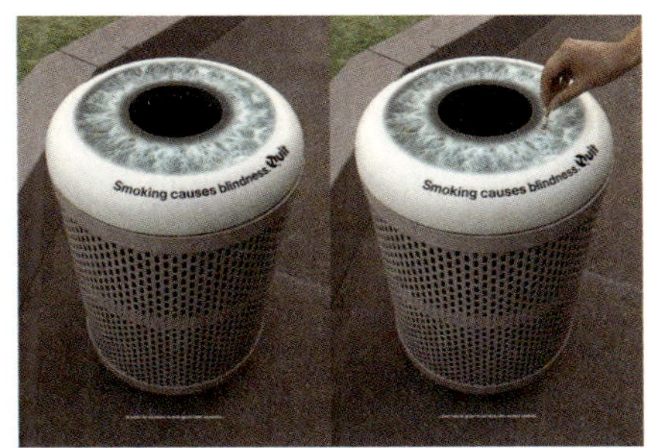

AUSTRALIE AUSTRALIA (2007)
The Campaign Palace Melbourne
Quit Smoking
Smoking causes blindness

POUPÉES RUSSES

RUSSIAN DOLLS

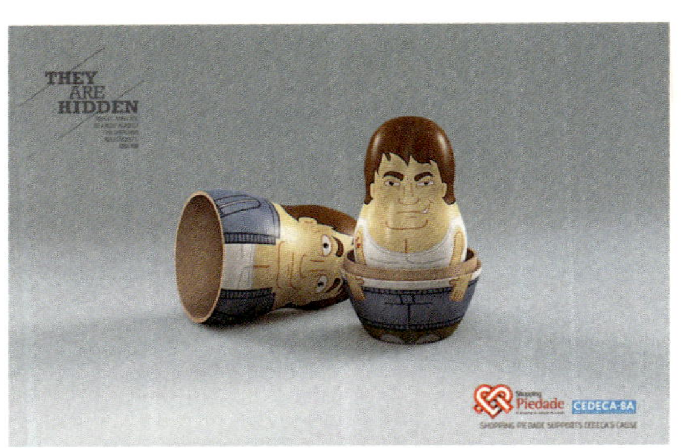
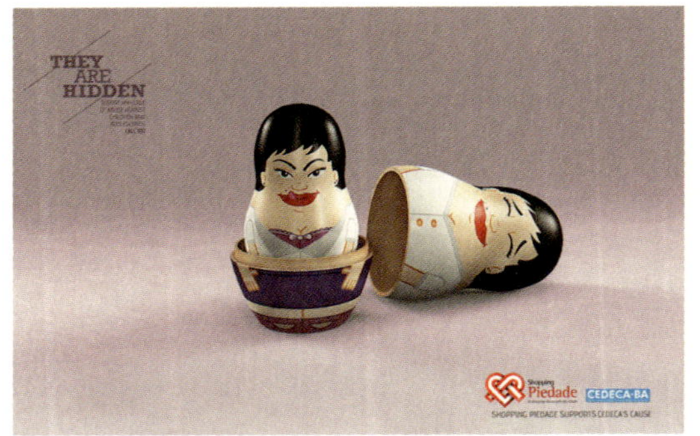
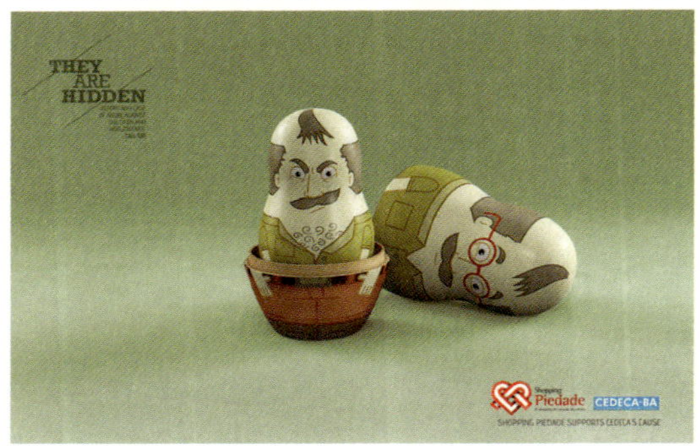

BRÉSIL BRAZIL (2012)
Engenhonovo Propaganda · Cedeca
They are hidden. Report any case of abuse against
children. Call 100

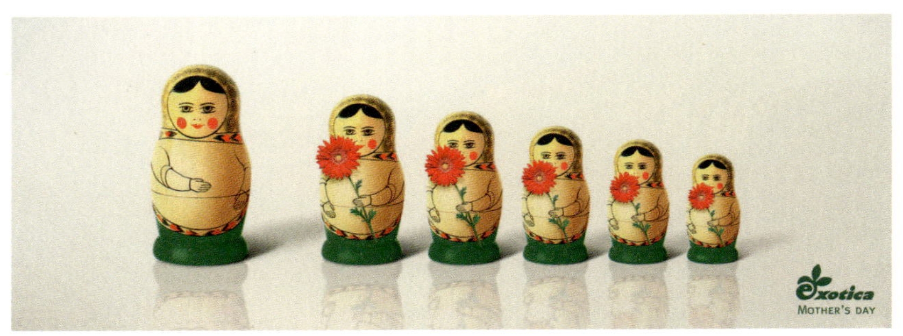

LIBAN LEBANON (2008)
Leo Burnett · Exotica Flowers Shop
Mother's Day

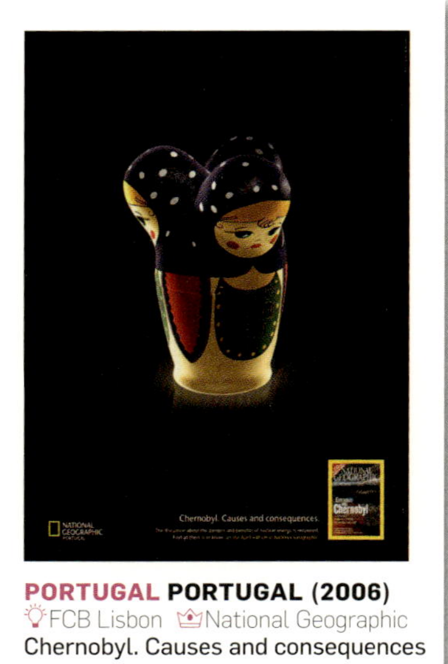

PORTUGAL PORTUGAL (2006)
FCB Lisbon · National Geographic
Chernobyl. Causes and consequences

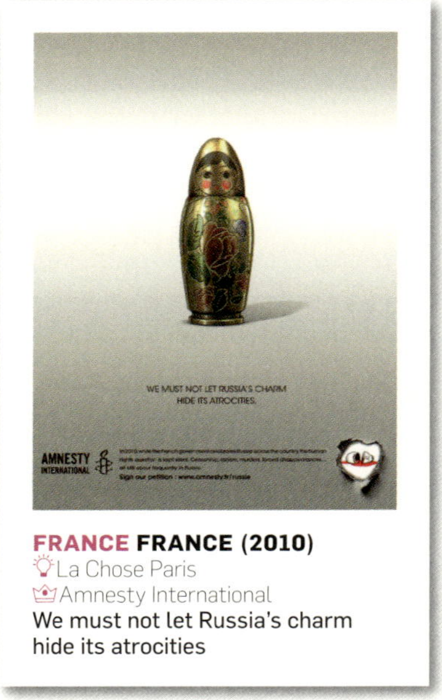

FRANCE FRANCE (2010)
La Chose Paris
Amnesty International
We must not let Russia's charm
hide its atrocities

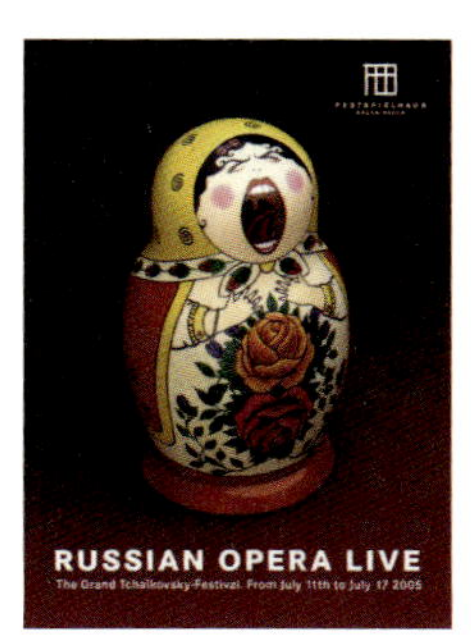

ALLEMAGNE
GERMANY (2005)
Scholz & Friends
Festspielhaus
Baden-Baden
Russian Opera Live

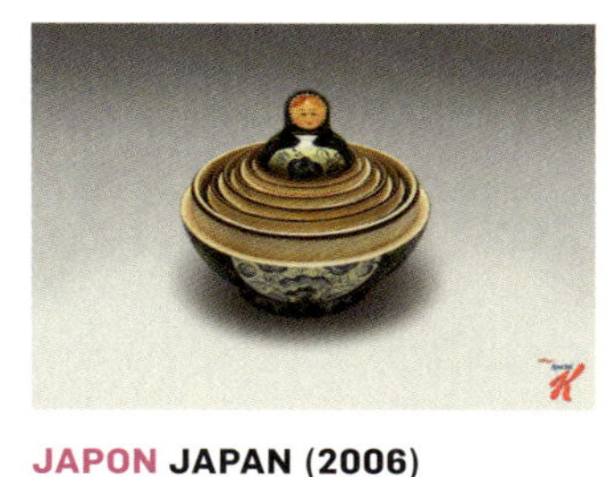

JAPON **JAPAN (2006)**
JWT Kellogg's Special K

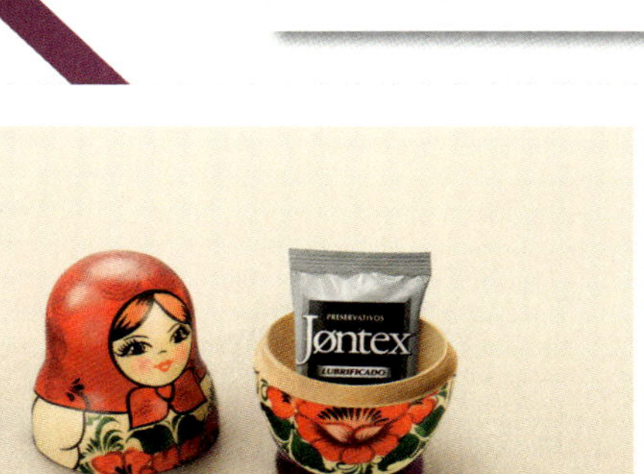

BRÉSIL **BRAZIL (2006)**
McCann Erickson Jontex Condoms

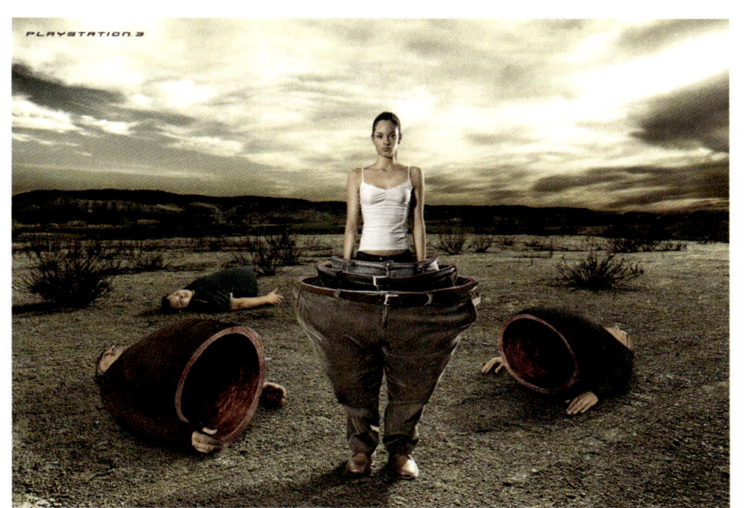

ESPAGNE **SPAIN (2008)**
TBWA Playstation 3

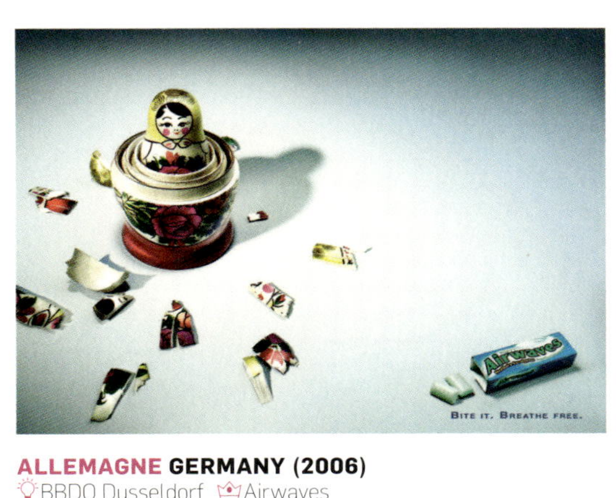

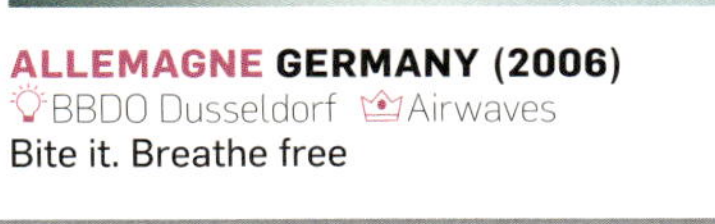

ALLEMAGNE **GERMANY (2006)**
BBDO Dusseldorf Airwaves
Bite it. Breathe free

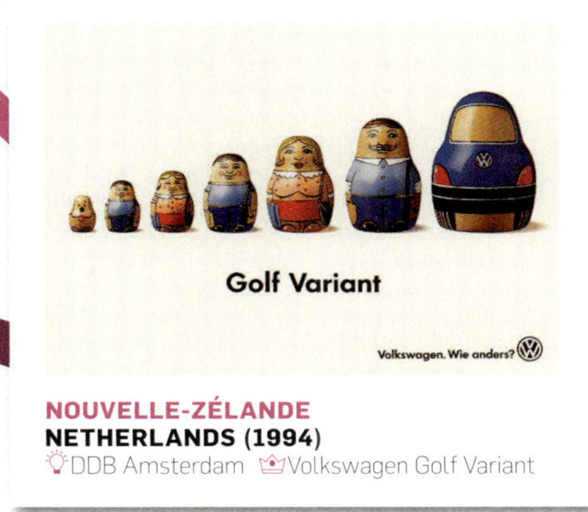

NOUVELLE-ZÉLANDE
NETHERLANDS (1994)
DDB Amsterdam Volkswagen Golf Variant

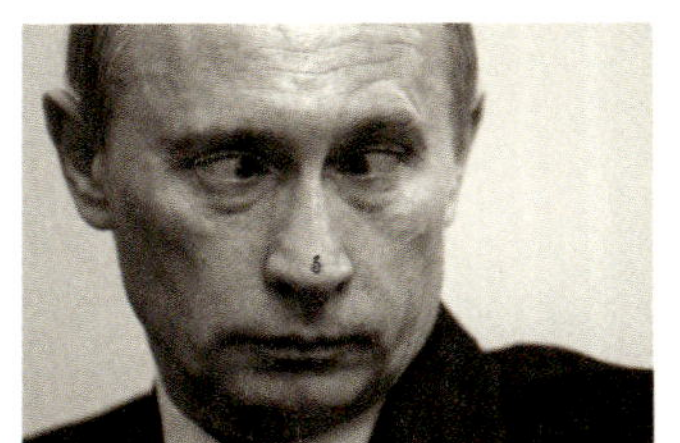
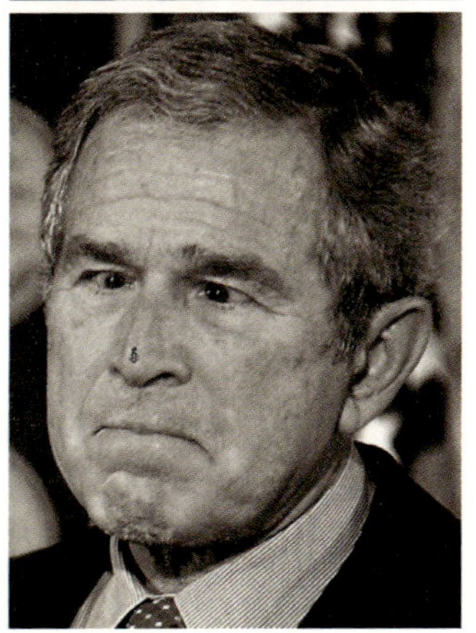

ESPAGNE SPAIN (2008)
Contrapunto
Amnesty International

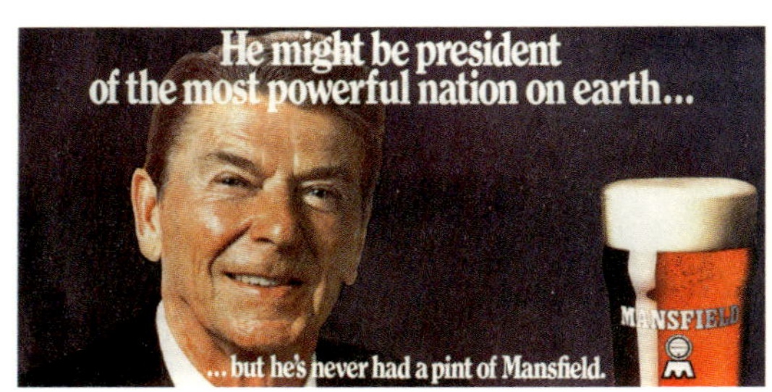

ROYAUME-UNI UNITED KINGDOM (1985)
Cogent Elliot Mansfield Beer
He (Ronald Reagan) might be president of the most powerful nation on earth…but he's never had a pint of Mansfield

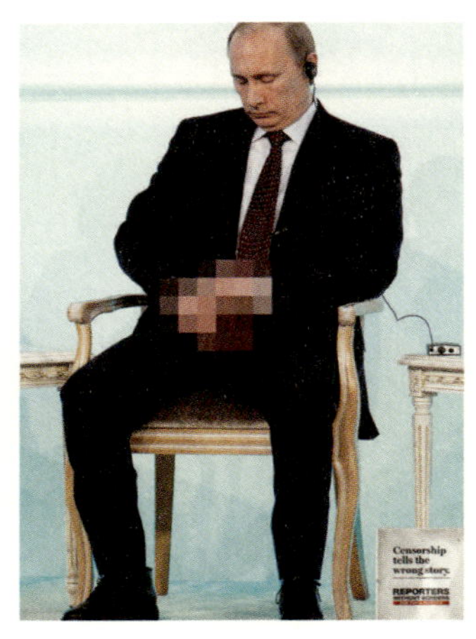

**ÉMIRATS ARABES UNIS
UNITED ARAB EMIRATES (2011)**
Memac Ogilvy & Mather Dubai
Reporters without borders
Censorship tells the wrong story

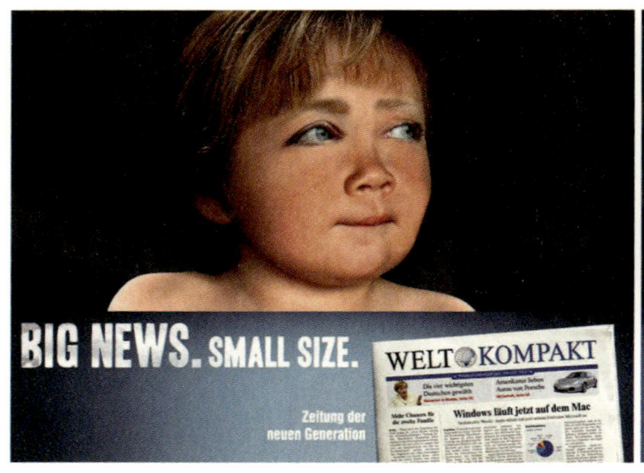

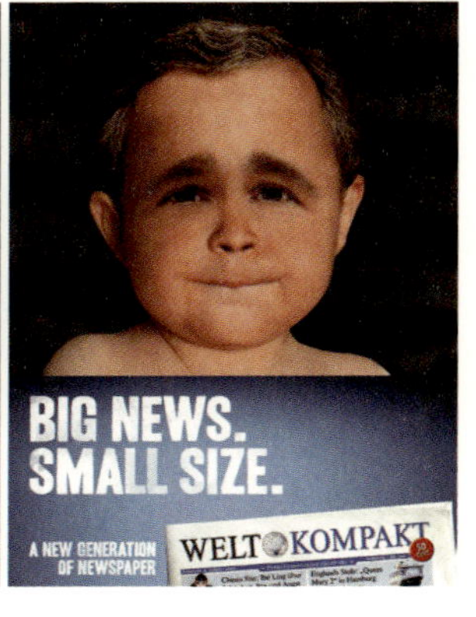

ALLEMAGNE GERMANY (2007)
Jung Von Matt *Welt Kompact* newspaper

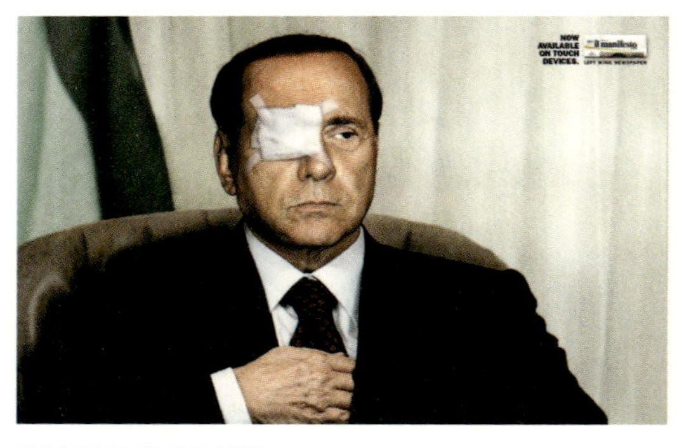

ITALIE ITALY (2011)
SPQR Rome Il Manifesto
Now available on touch devices

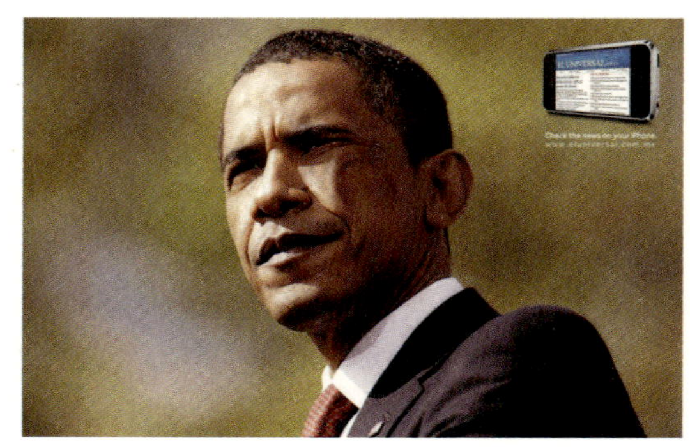

MEXIQUE MEXICO (2008)
BBDO *El Universal* newspaper
Check the news on your iphone

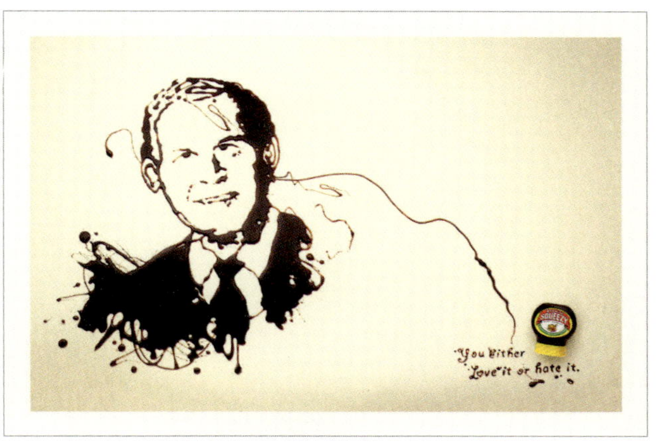

ROYAUME-UNI UNITED KINGDOM (2006)
DDB London Marmite Squeezy
You either love it or hate it

PRESIDENTS

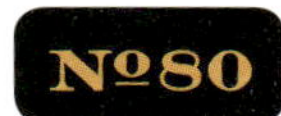
№80

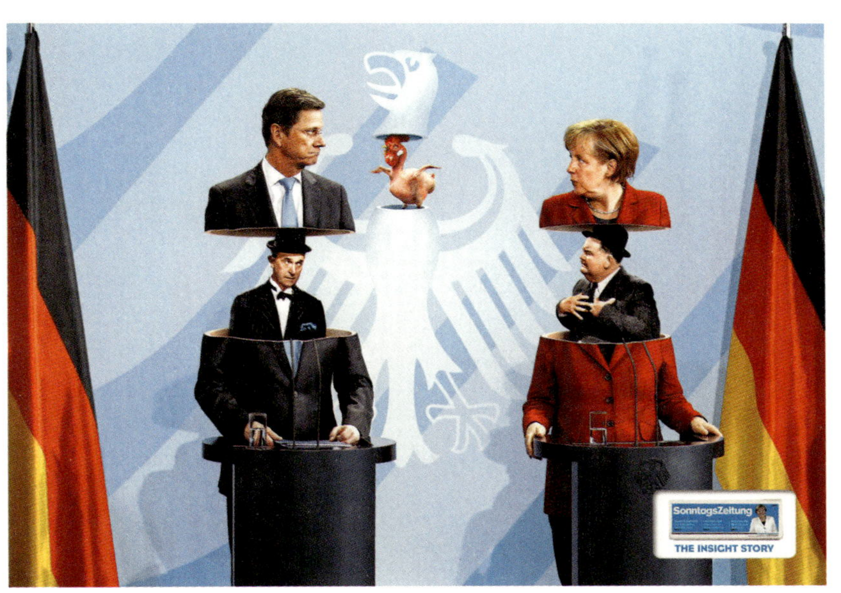

SUISSE SWITZERLAND (2009)
Advico Young & Rubicam Zurich *Sonntags Zeitung* newspaper
The inside story

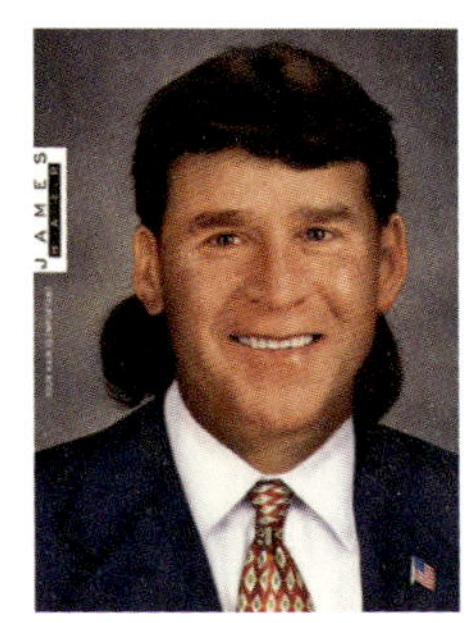

POLOGNE
POLAND (2003)
Leo Burnett Warszawa
James Hair beauty salon
Your hair is important

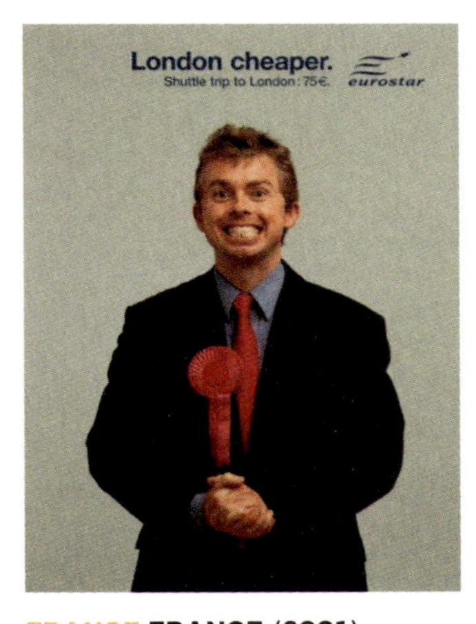

FRANCE FRANCE (2001)
Leg Eurostar

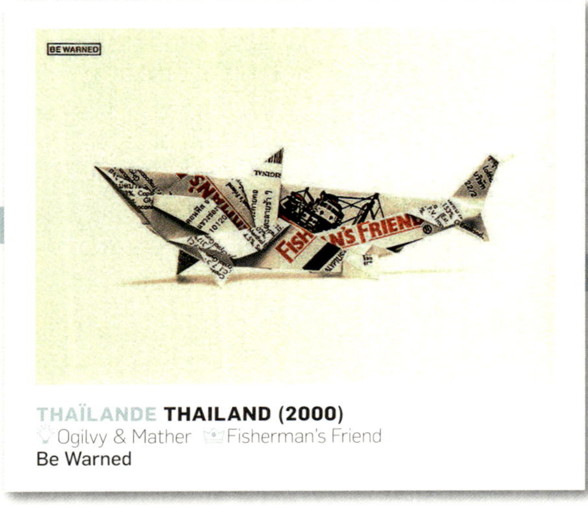

THAÏLANDE THAILAND (2000)
Ogilvy & Mather · Fisherman's Friend
Be Warned

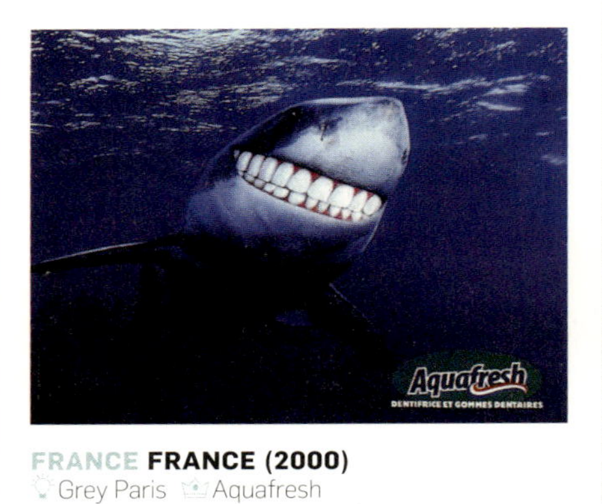

FRANCE FRANCE (2000)
Grey Paris · Aquafresh
Toothpaste and dental gums

REQUINS
№ 81
SHARKS

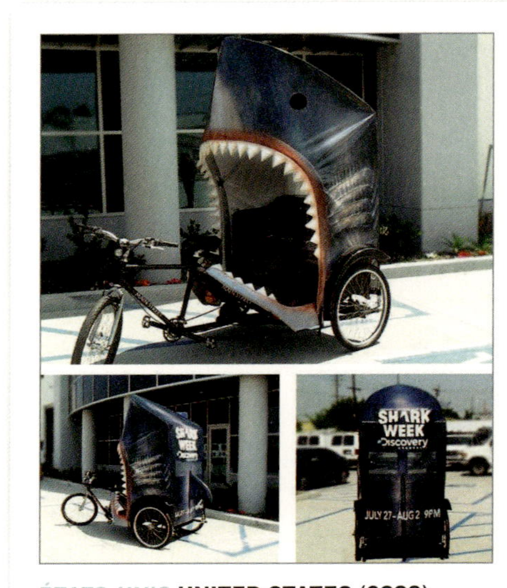

ÉTATS-UNIS UNITED STATES (2008)
InHouse · Discovery Channel
Shark Week on Discovery Channel

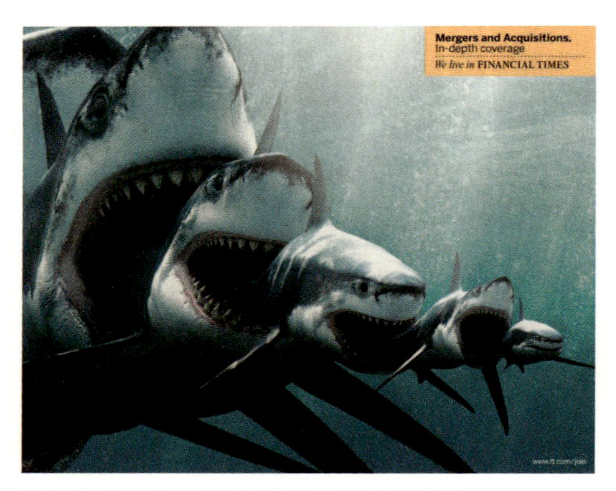

ROYAUME-UNI UNITED KINGSOM (2007)
DDB London · Financial Times Newspaper
Mergers and acquisitions. In depth coverage

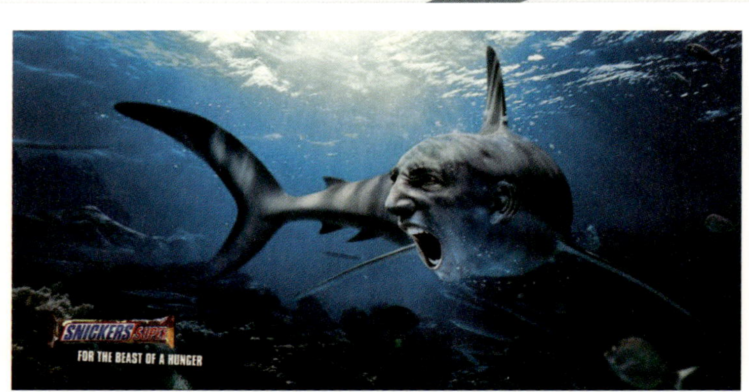

POLOGNE POLAND (2008)
BBDO Warsaw · Snickers Super Size
For the beast of a hunger

DDB & Co Istanbul WWF
"Horrifying / More horrifying" Exploiting
the ecosystem also threatens human lives

« Cette campagne aurait aussi bien pu
figurer dans le chapitre « avant / après ».
Je la trouve très juste et très efficace avec
un minimum d'effets. Comme quoi, on peut
véhiculer un message puissant avec
quelques mots simples et une photo stock
d'une banalité effrayante. »
"This campaign could well have been included
in the "before/after" chapter. I find it very valid
and very effective with minimal effects.
It's proof that we can convey a powerful
message with a few simple words and a stock
photo of frightening banality."

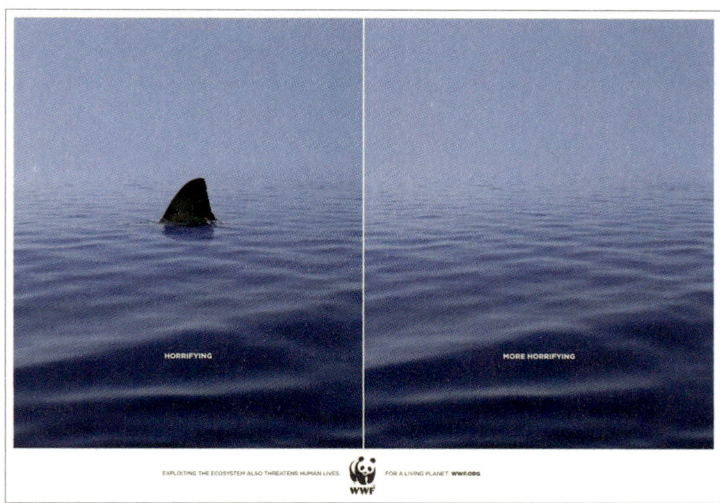

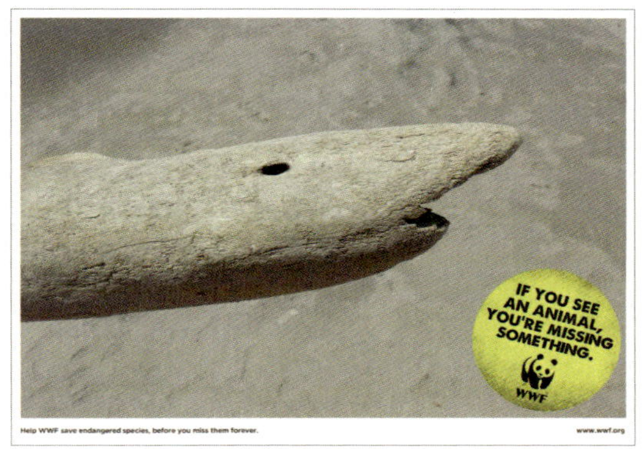

ITALIE ITALY (2010)
Young & Rubicam WWF
If you see an animal, you're missing something
Help WWF save endangered species,
before you miss them forever

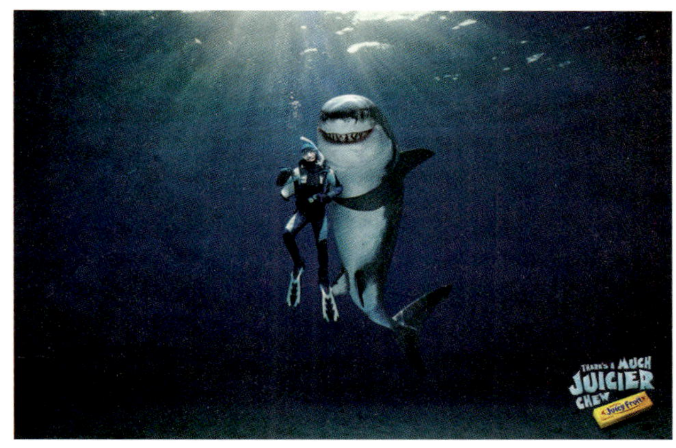

AUSTRALIE AUSTRALIA (2010)
DDB Sydney Juicy Fruit
There's a much juicier chew

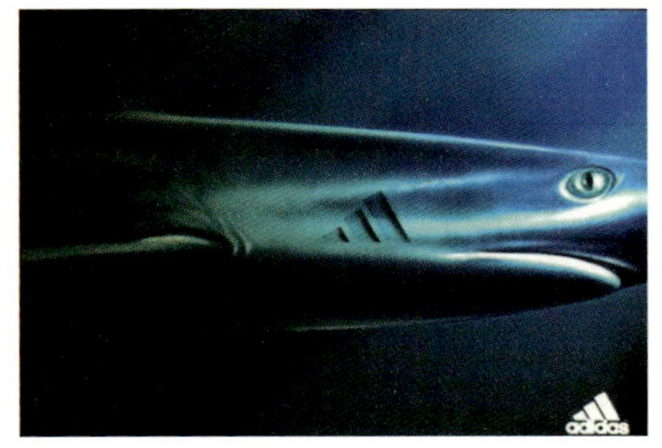

LIBAN LEBANON (2002)
Impact BBDO Adidas

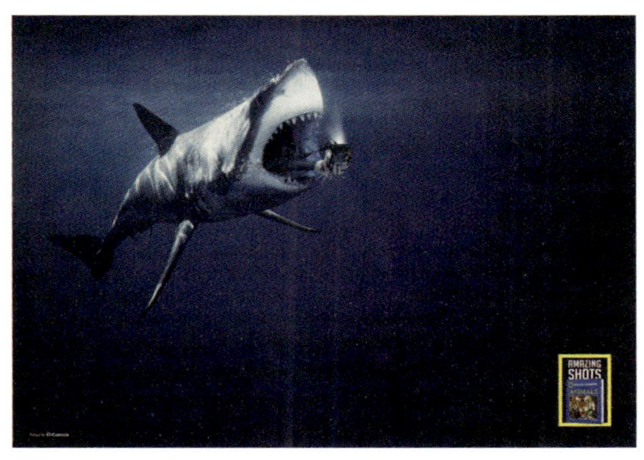

PÉROU PERU (2008)
Circus National Geographic Animals Issue
Amazing shots

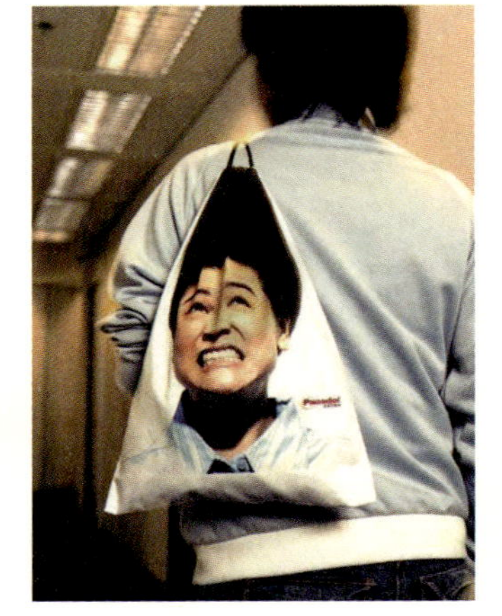
HONG-KONG
HONG KONG (2005)
Ogilvy & Mather
Panadol Extra (Anti headaches)

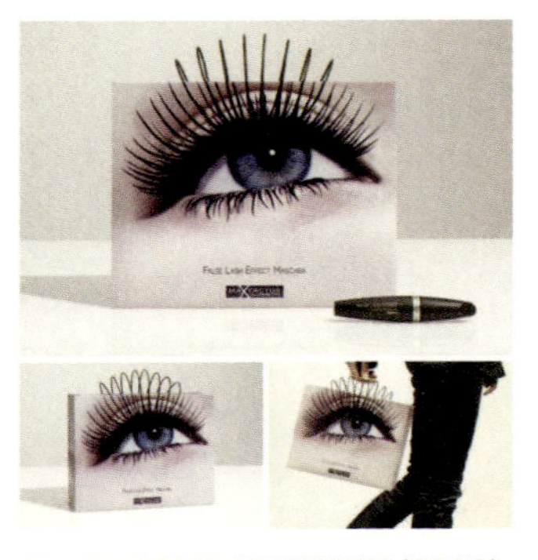
ALLEMAGNE **GERMANY (2009)**
Leo Burnett Frankfurt
Max Factor
False Lash Effect Mascara

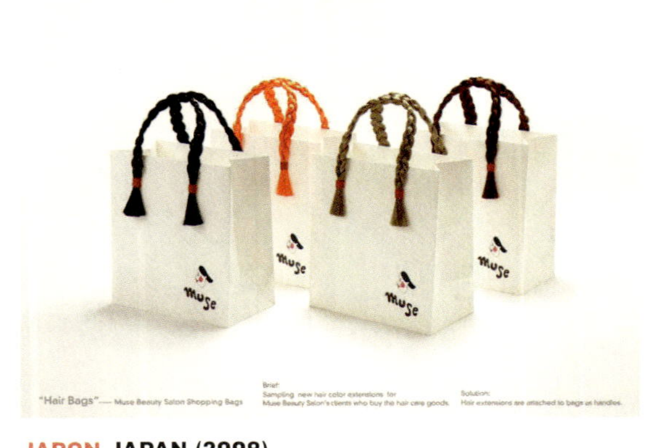

JAPON **JAPAN (2008)**
Tokyu Muse Beauty Salon

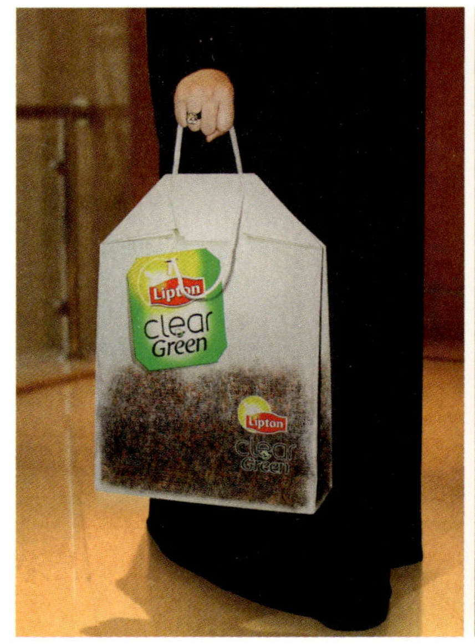

ARABIE SAOUDITE **SAUDI ARABIA (2010)**
DDB Lipton Clear Green Tea

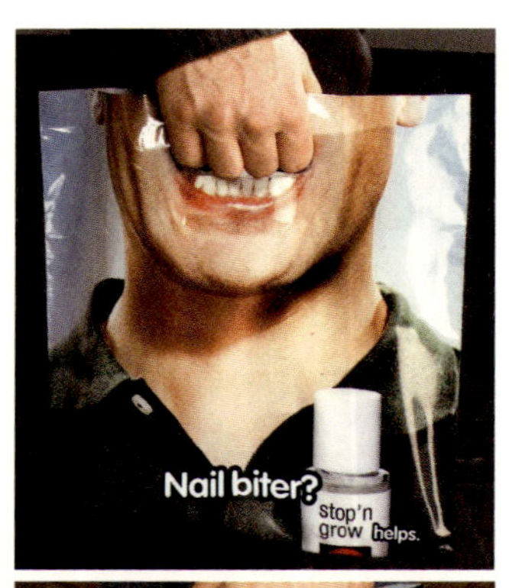

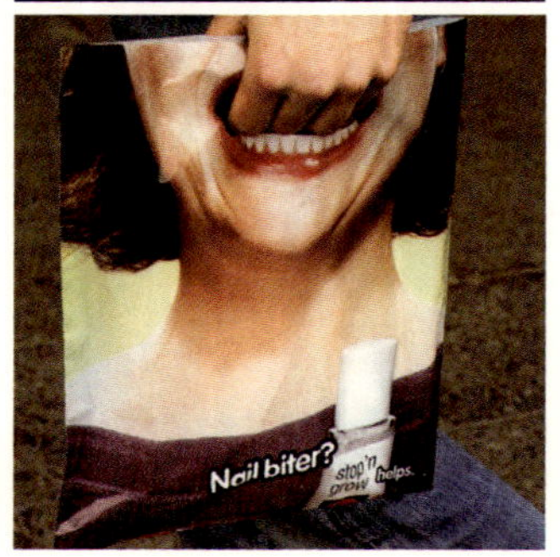

ALLEMAGNE **GERMANY (2008)**
Jung Von Matt Stop'N Grow

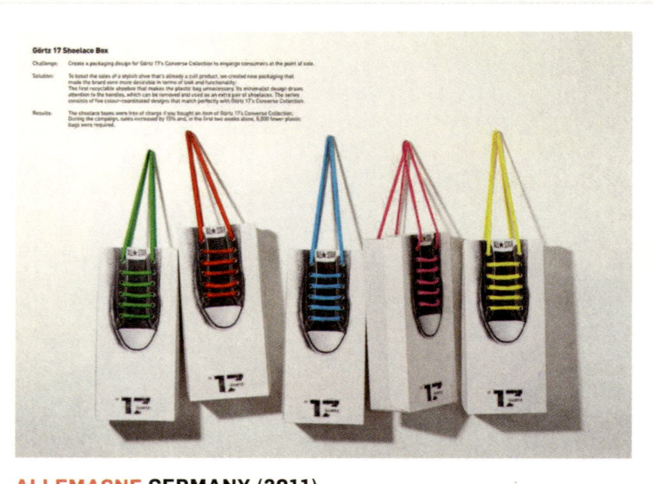
ALLEMAGNE **GERMANY (2011)**
Kempertrautmann Hamburg Görtz Shoes

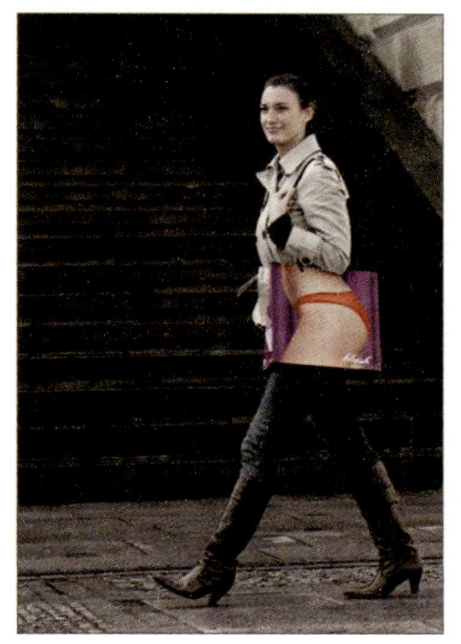

ALLEMAGNE GERMANY (2006)
💡 BBDO Berlin 👑 Blush Lingerie

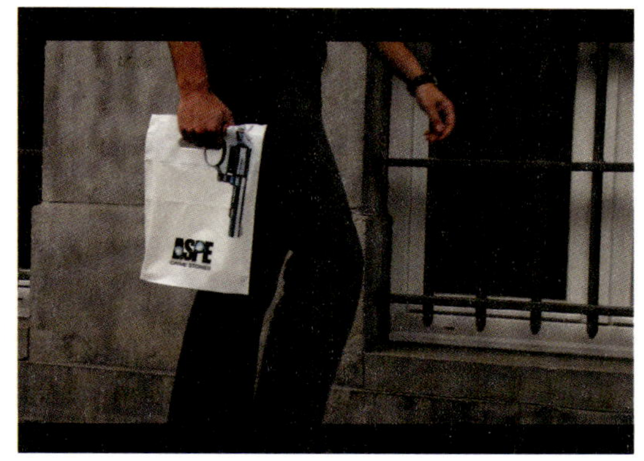

BELGIQUE BELGIUM (2004)
💡 Duval Guillaume 👑 ASPE Crime Stories

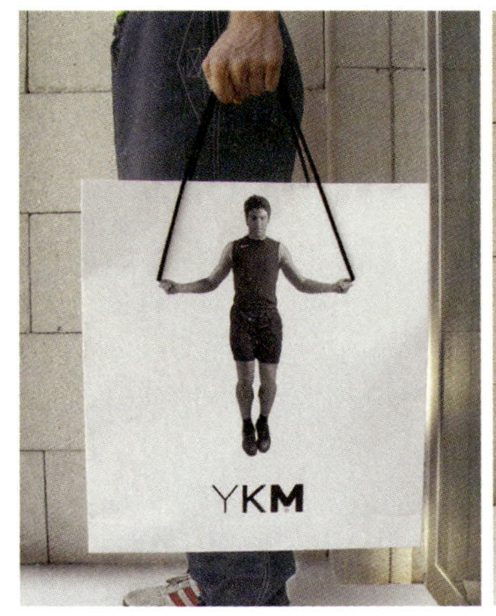

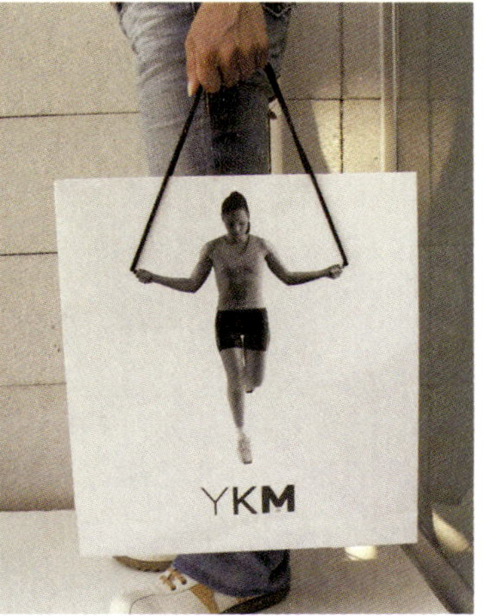

TURQUIE TURKEY (2005)
💡 TBWA Istanbul 👑 YKM department store

SACS
№82
BAGS

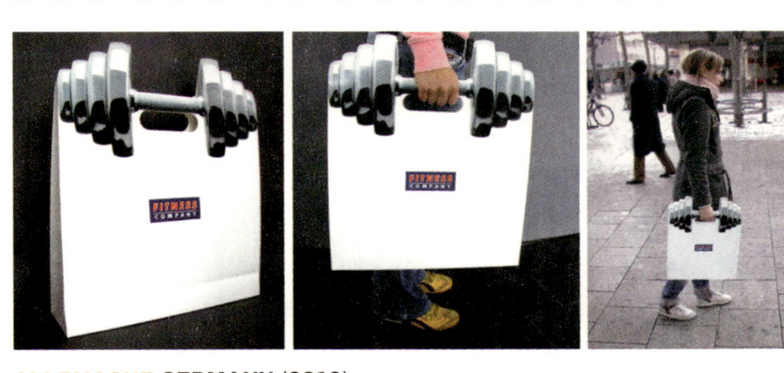

ALLEMAGNE GERMANY (2012)
💡 Publicis Frankfurt 👑 Fitness Company

LE 11 SEPTEMBRE

N°83

NINE ELEVEN

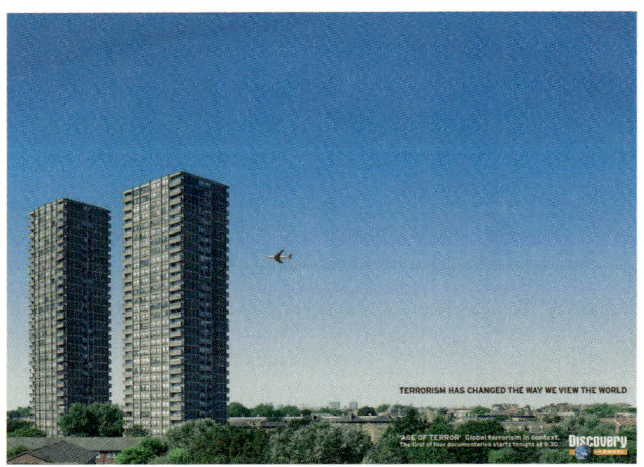

ROYAUME UNI UNITED KINGDOM (2003)
Hooper Galton London · Discovery Channel
Terrorism has changed the way we view the world

« J'aime la justesse de l'observation. Durant les années qui ont suivi le 11 septembre, on n'a plus regardé les tours ni les avions de la même façon. C'est une image d'une terrible banalité et pourtant, elle est très forte. Par ailleurs, je n'aime pas trop les annonces qui comparent le nombre de morts dans des attentats à ceux du tabagisme ou de maladies. »
"I love the accuracy of this observation. In the years since September 11, we don't look at towers and planes in the same way. This is a terribly banal image and yet it is quite strong. At the same time, I really don't like advertising that compares the number of deaths in the attacks with those from smoking or diseases."

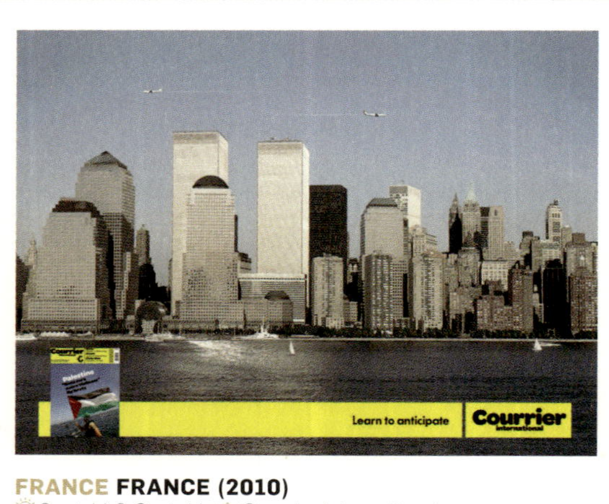

FRANCE FRANCE (2010)
Saatchi & Saatchi · Courrier International
Learn to anticipate

**AFRIQUE DU SUD
SOUTH AFRICA (2003)**
Bates Johannesburg
Exclusive Books
Technology, Terrorism, theatre…

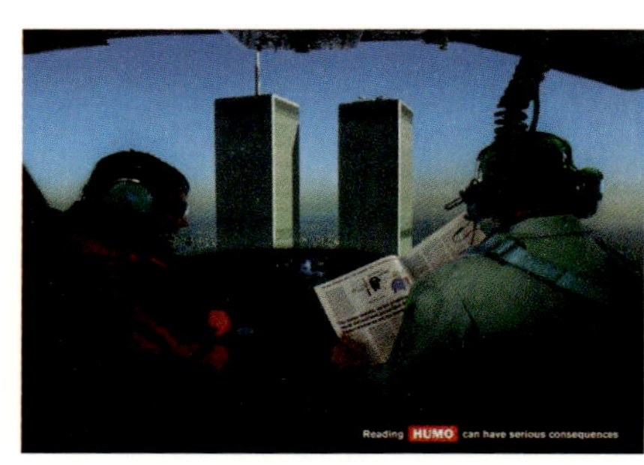

BELGIQUE BELGIUM (2004)
DuvalGuillaume Brussels
Humo Magazine
Reading Humo can have serious consequences

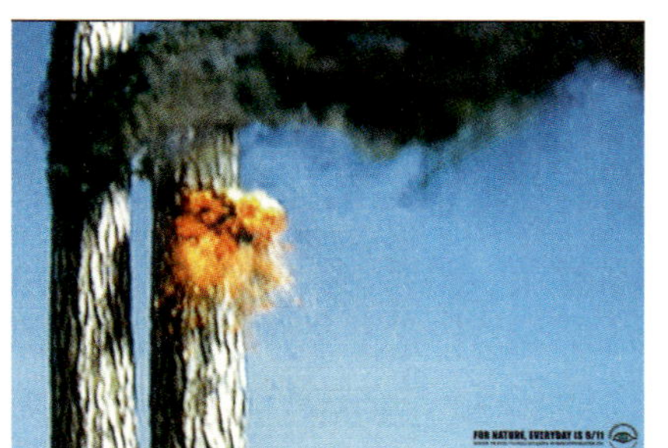

FRANCE FRANCE (2006)
CLM/BBDO Nicolas Hulot Foundation
For nature, everyday is 9/11

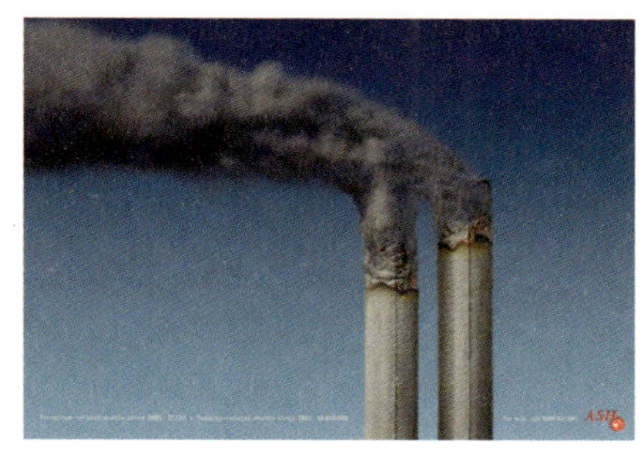

**NOUVELLE-ZÉLANDE
NEW ZEALAND (2008)**
DDB ASH Anti Smoking
Terrorism-related deaths since 2001: 11.337
Tobacco-related deaths since 2001: 30.000.000

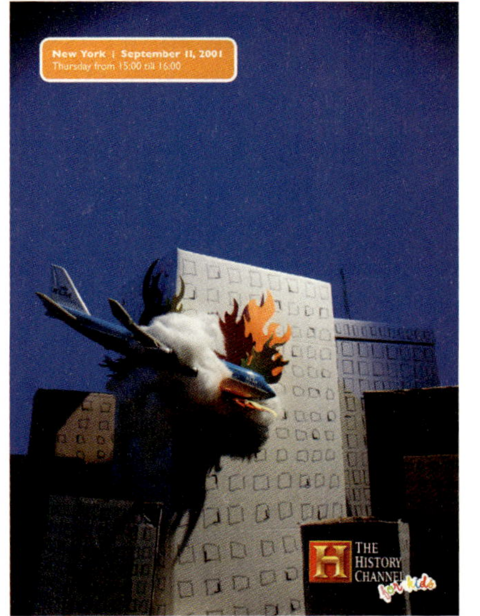

PAYS-BAS NETHERLANDS (2009)
Junior Academy for Art Direction
The History Channel for kids

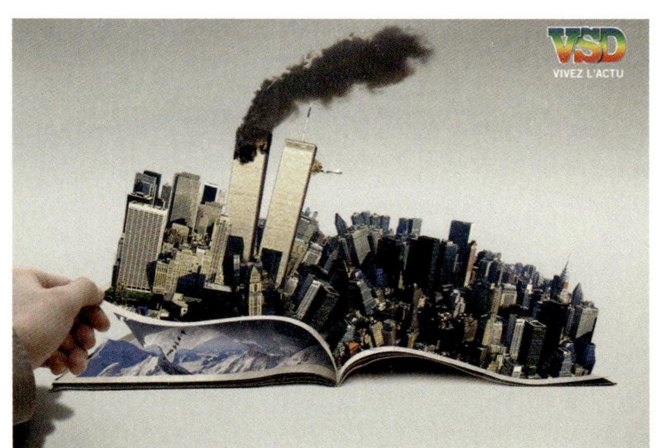

FRANCE FRANCE (2006)
Leo Burnett Paris VSD Magazine
Live the news

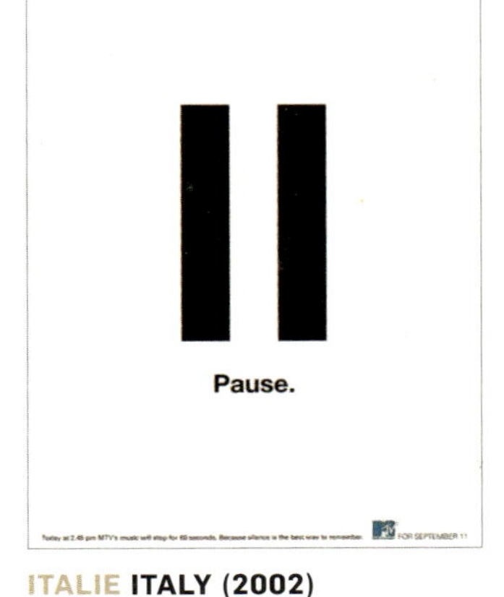

ITALIE ITALY (2002)
Saatchi & Saatchi
MTV For september 11
Today MTV's music will stop for
60 seconds. Because silence is the
best way to remember

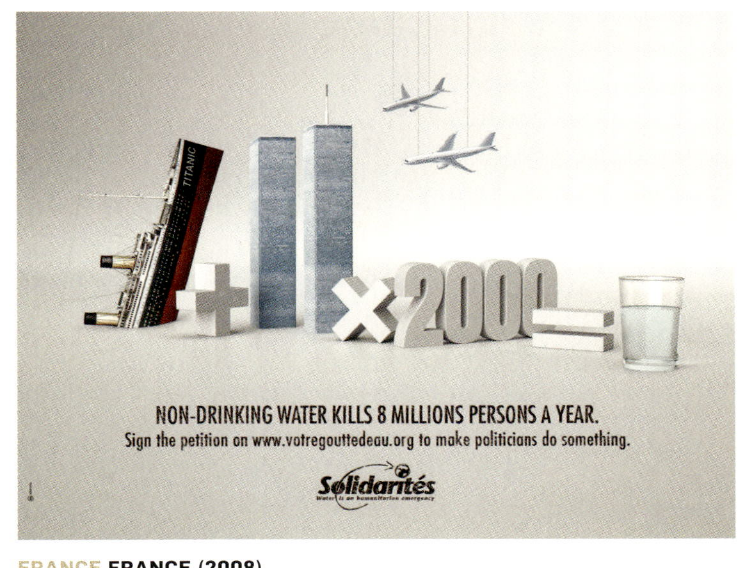

FRANCE FRANCE (2008)
BDDP&Fils Solidarités

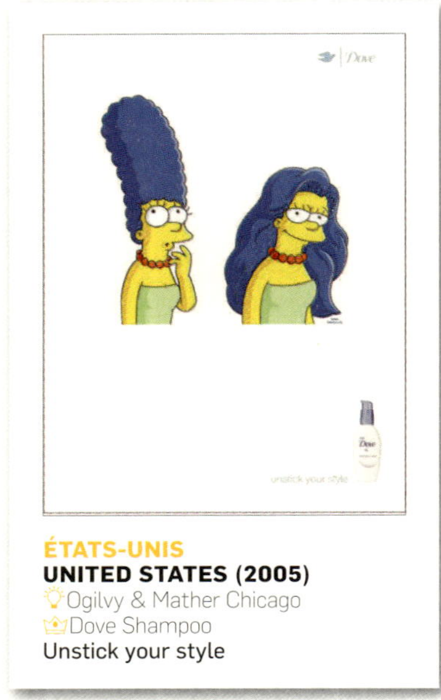

ÉTATS-UNIS
UNITED STATES (2005)
Ogilvy & Mather Chicago
Dove Shampoo
Unstick your style

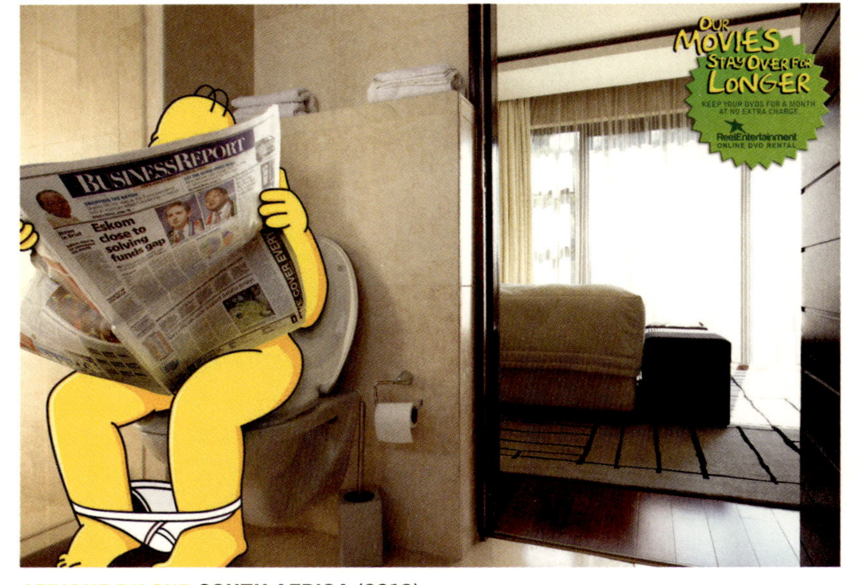

AFRIQUE DU SUD SOUTH AFRICA (2010)
4D Johannesburg   Reel Entertainment online DVD rental

SIMPSONS

№ 84

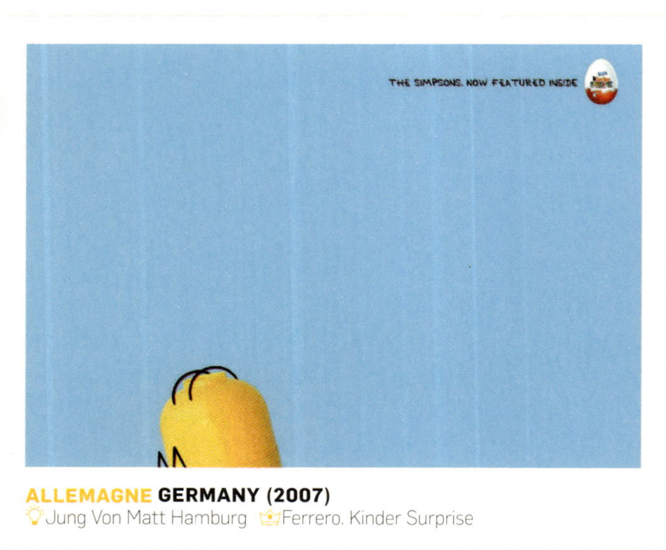

ALLEMAGNE GERMANY (2007)
Jung Von Matt Hamburg   Ferrero. Kinder Surprise

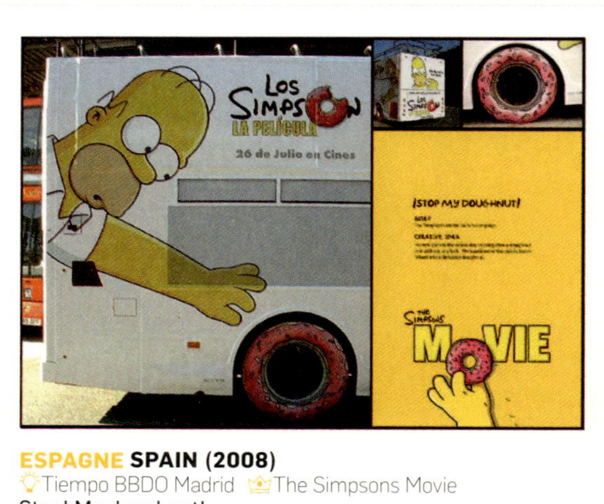

ESPAGNE SPAIN (2008)
Tiempo BBDO Madrid   The Simpsons Movie
Stop! My doughnut!

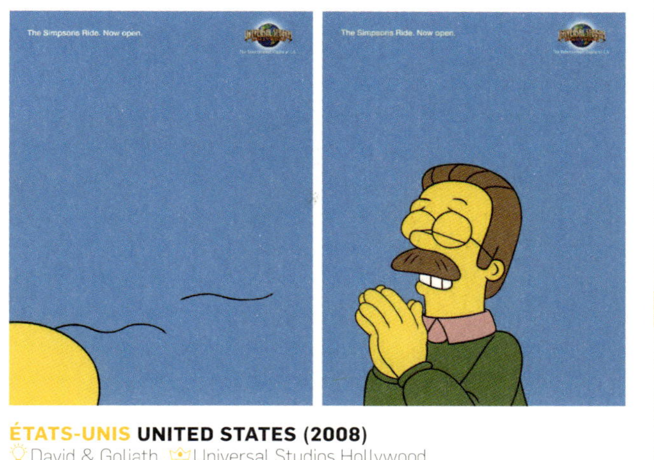

ÉTATS-UNIS UNITED STATES (2008)
David & Goliath · Universal Studios Hollywood
The Simpsons Ride. Now open

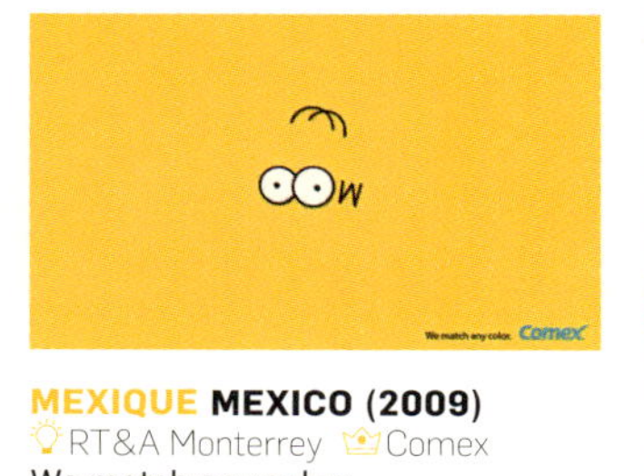

MEXIQUE MEXICO (2009)
RT&A Monterrey · Comex
We match any color

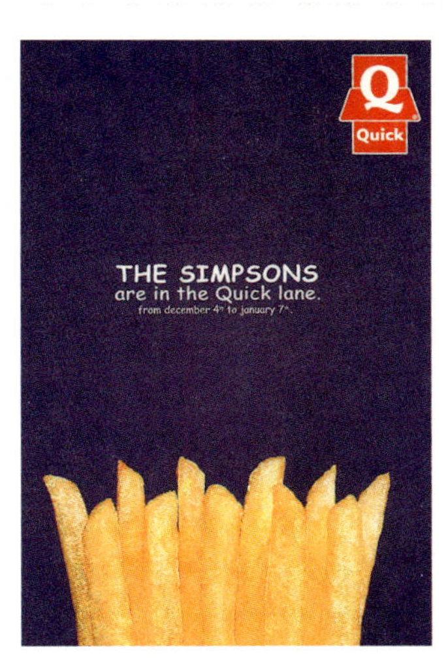

FRANCE FRANCE (2001)
Young & Rubicam
Quick Restaurants

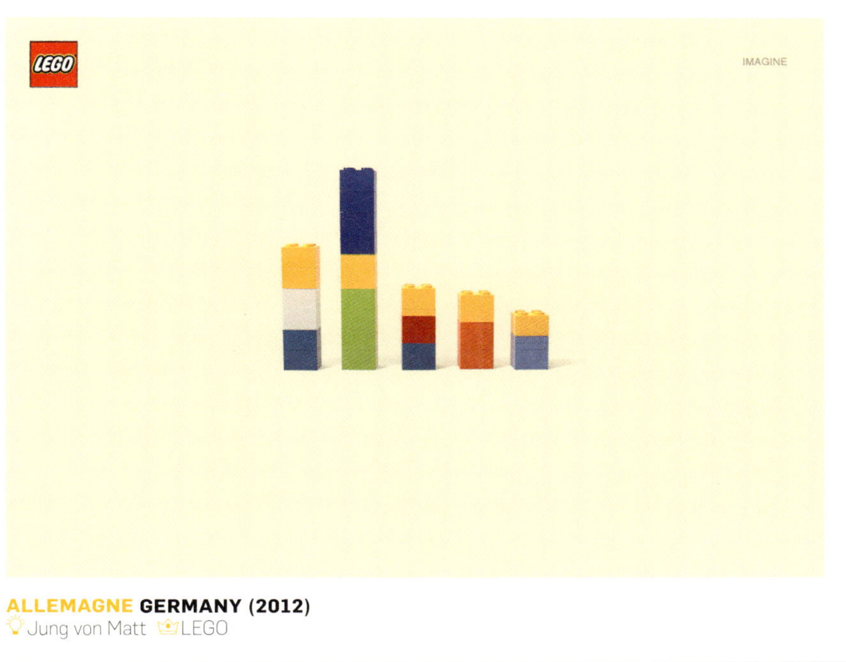

ALLEMAGNE GERMANY (2012)
Jung von Matt · LEGO

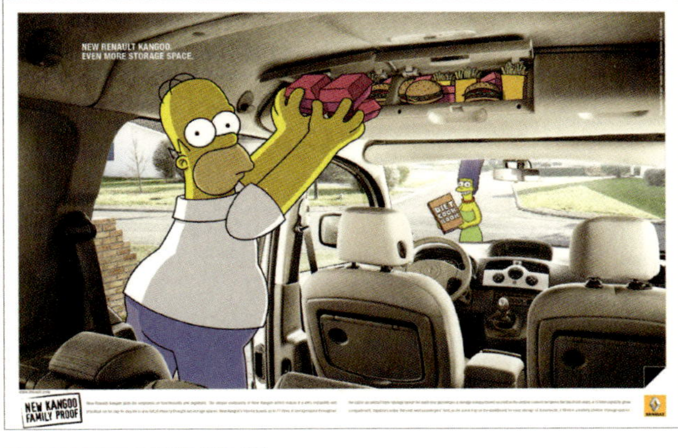

FRANCE FRANCE (2008)
Publicis Conseil · Renault Kangoo
New Renault Kangoo. Even more storage space

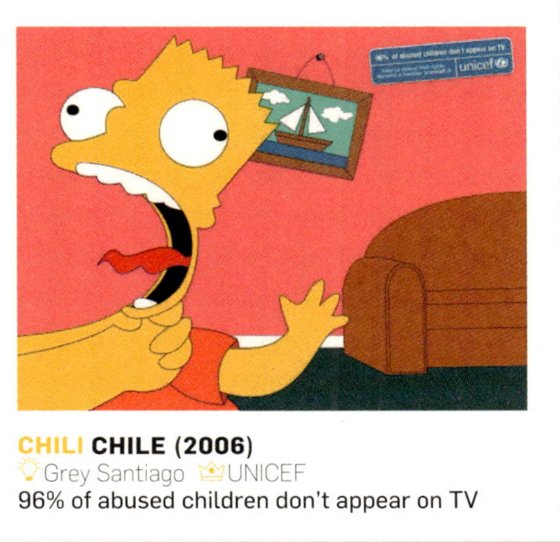

CHILI CHILE (2006)
Grey Santiago · UNICEF
96% of abused children don't appear on TV

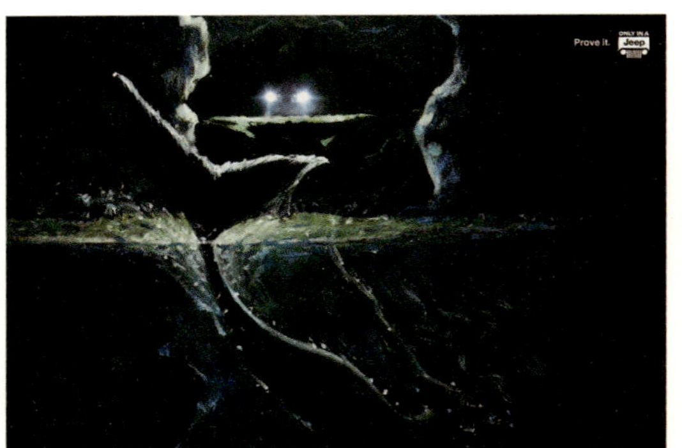

THAÏLANDE THAILAND (2008)
BBDO Jeep
Only in a Jeep. Prove it

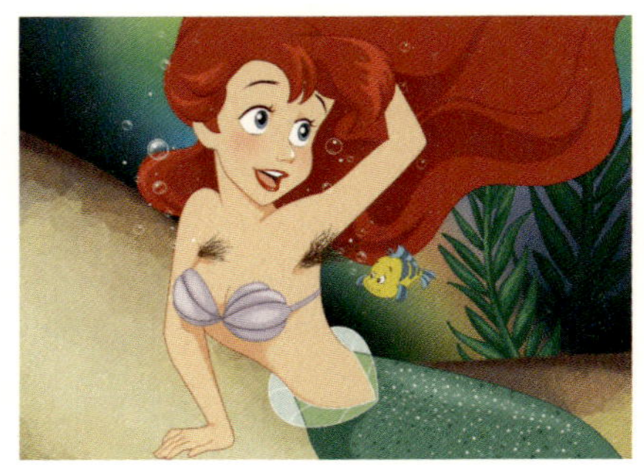

CORÉE DU SUD SOUTH KOREA (2005)
Ogilvy & Mather Seoul Gillette

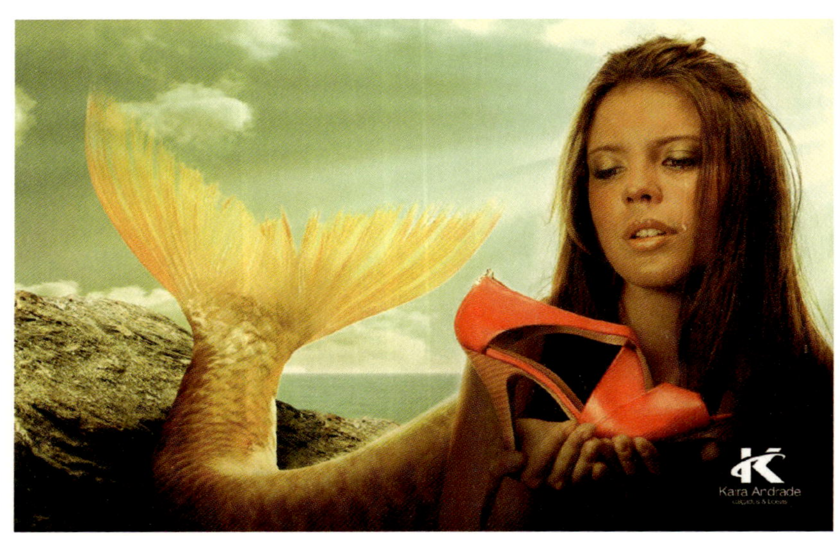

BRÉSIL BRAZIL (2010)
Tata Kaira Andrade Shoes

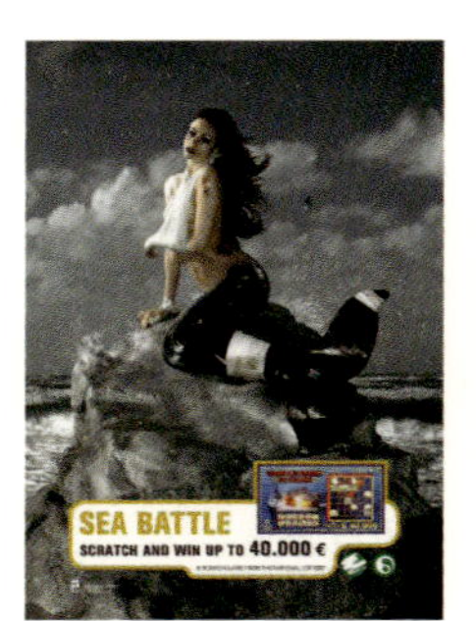

BELGIQUE
BELGIUM (2005)
LG&F Sea Battle
Scratch and win
up to 40.000€

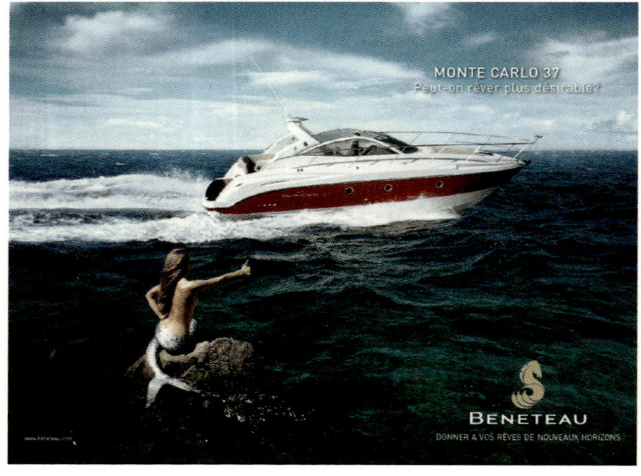

FRANCE FRANCE (2007)
Talents Only Beneteau boats
Peut-on rêver plus désirable?
Can you imagine something more desirable?

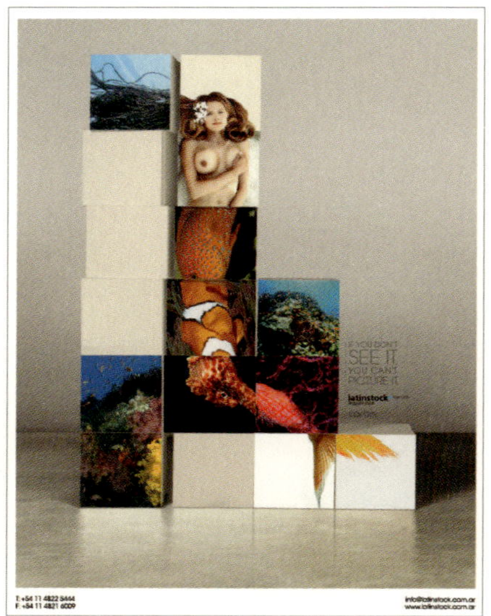

ARGENTINE ARGENTINA (2008)
MC Cann Latinstock stock images
If you don't see it, you can picture it

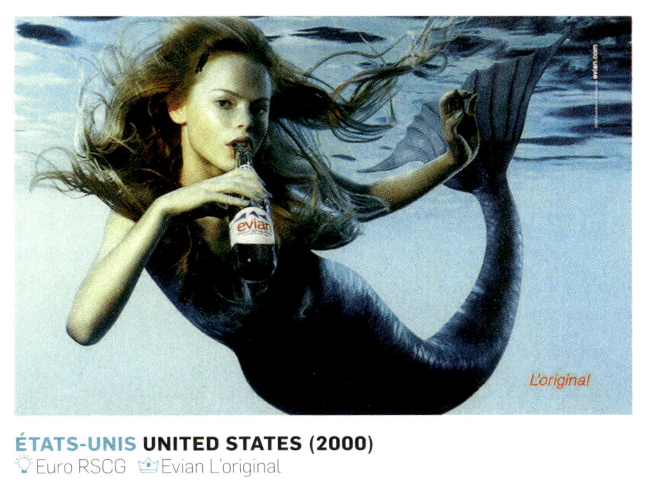

ÉTATS-UNIS UNITED STATES (2000)
Euro RSCG   Evian L'original

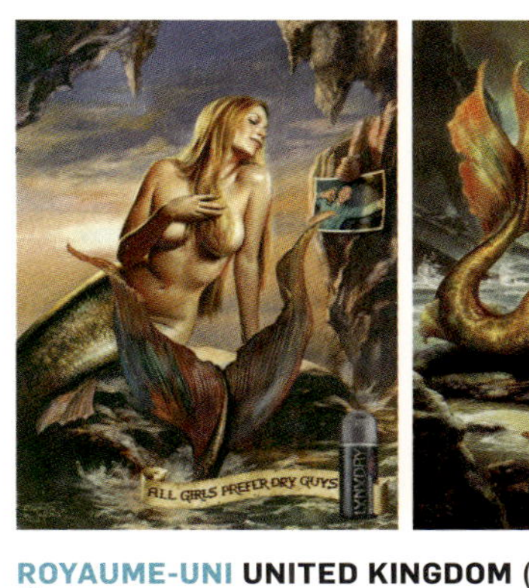
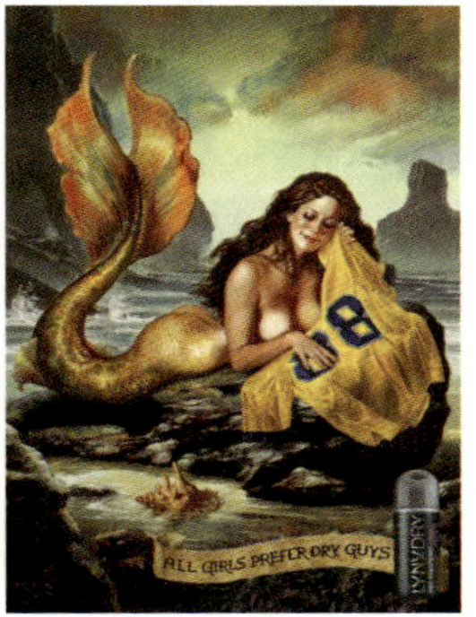

ROYAUME-UNI UNITED KINGDOM (2005)
BBH London   Lynx Dry anti perspiring
All girls prefer dry guys

SIRÈNES

№85

MERMAIDS

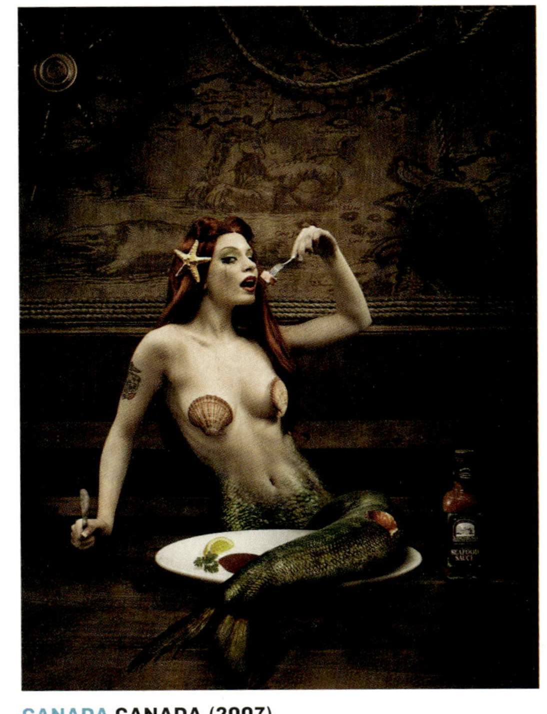

CANADA CANADA (2007)
Wax Calgary   Historic Lynchburg by Wax

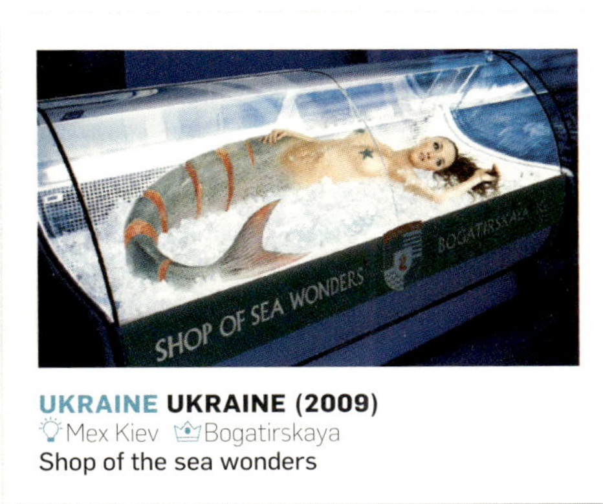

UKRAINE UKRAINE (2009)
Mex Kiev   Bogatirskaya
Shop of the sea wonders

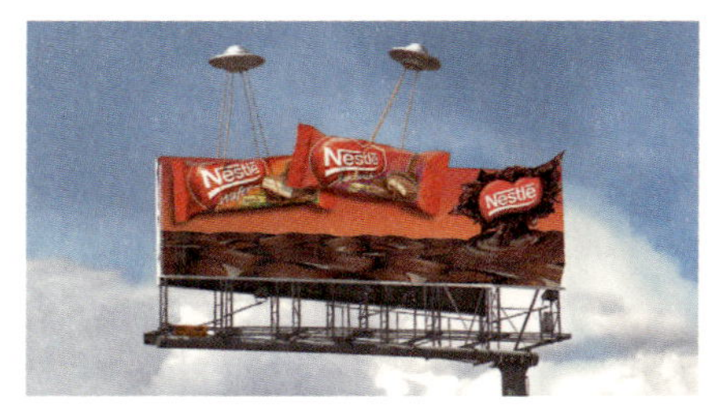

COLOMBIE COLOMBIA (2005)
JWT Nestlé Wafer & Sandwich bars

SOUCOUPES VOLANTES

№86

FLYING SAUCERS

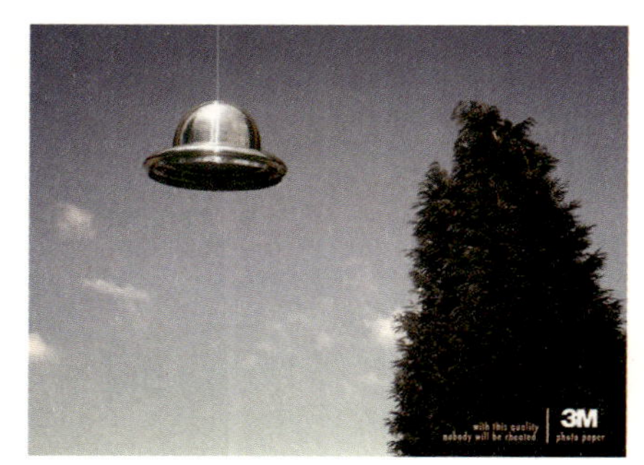

ESPAGNE SPAIN (2009)
Zink Project Madrid 3M Photo paper
With this quality nobody will be cheated

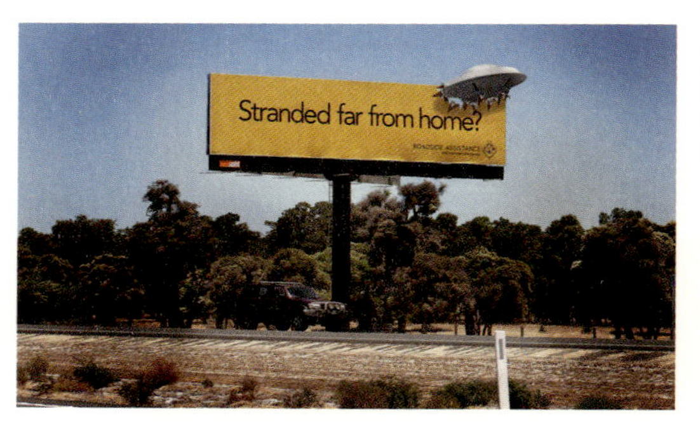

AUSTRALIE AUSTRALIA (2011)
The Brand Agency Roadside Assistance

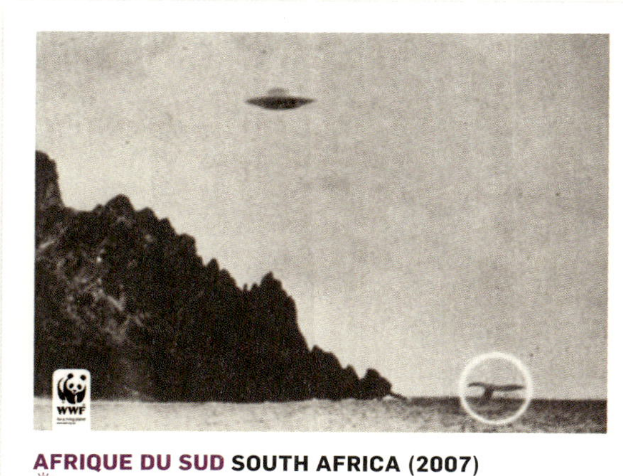

AFRIQUE DU SUD SOUTH AFRICA (2007)
Ogilvy & Mather Cape Town WWF

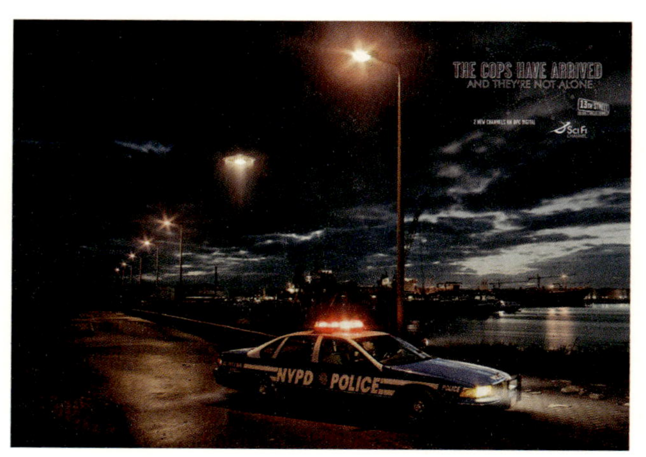

PAYS-BAS NETHERLANDS (2007)
Cake UPC Digital Network 2 New Channels: SciFi & 13th street
The cops have arrived and they're not alone

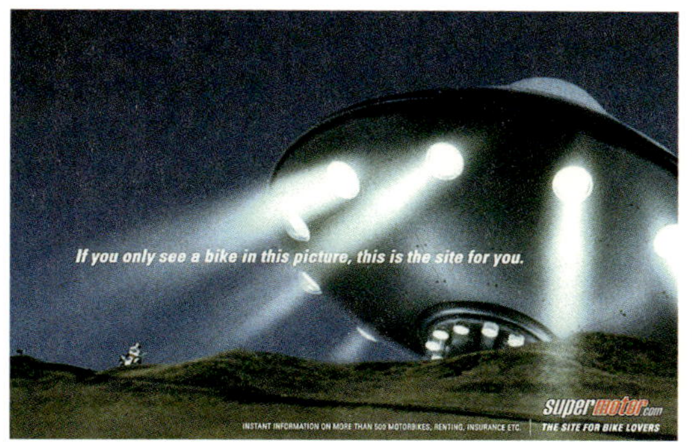

ESPAGNE SPAIN (2001)
Romulo & Remo Supermotor.com the site for bike lovers

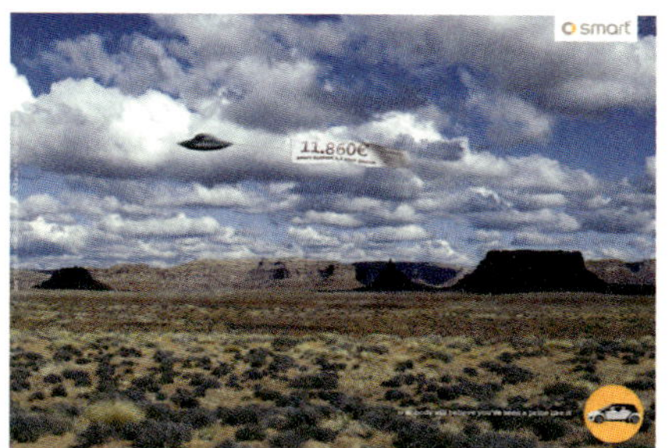

ESPAGNE SPAIN (2007)
Contrapunto Madrid Smart
Nobody will believe you've seen a price like it

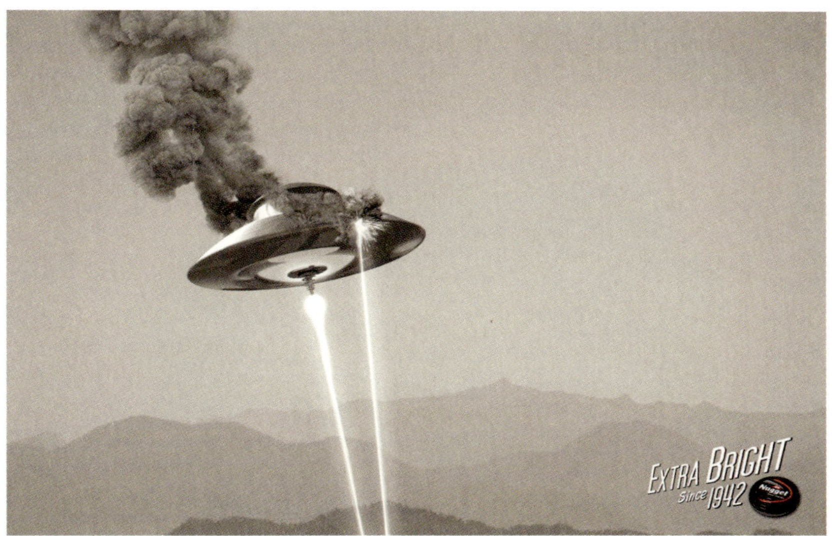

**ARGENTINE
ARGENTINA (2008)**
Euro RSCG Buenos Aires
Nugget shoe shine

« Les ovnis dans la pub, c'est comme les bébés ou les chiens, il faut bien avouer qu'on en a un peu ras la soucoupe. Même quand on est fan de science-fiction, comme moi, on finit par avoir envie de les renvoyer chez eux. Ce que fait assez bien cette annonce. »
"UFOs in ads are like babies and dogs; you must admit that there's really not much more that can be done with them. Even if you're a science fiction fan, like me, you just want to send them back home. That's what makes this ad so good."

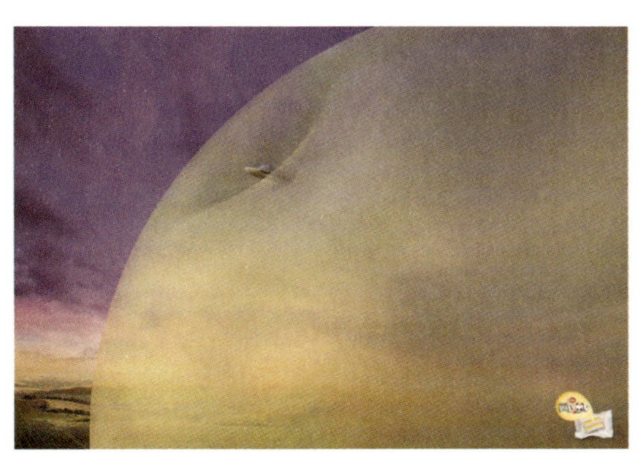

TURQUIE TURKEY (2011)
Leo Burnett Istanbul Crazy Balloon Chewing gum

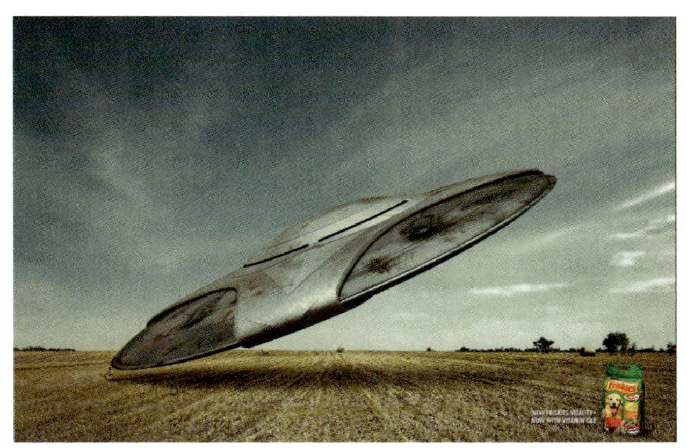

BELGIQUE BELGIUM (2005)
DDB Brussels Friskies Vitality
Now with vitamin C & E

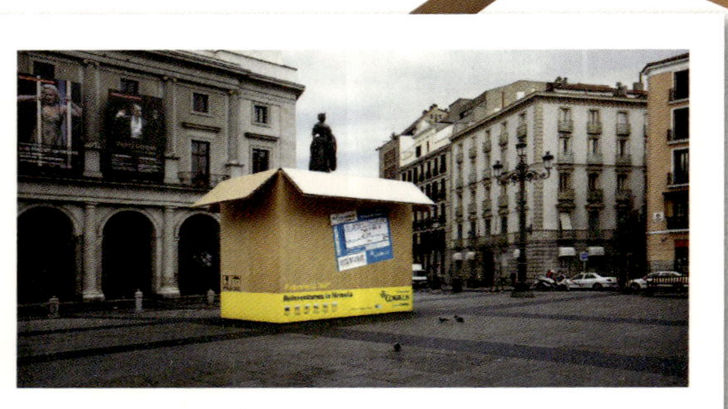

ESPAGNE SPAIN (2011)
Zapping M&C Saatchi Correos

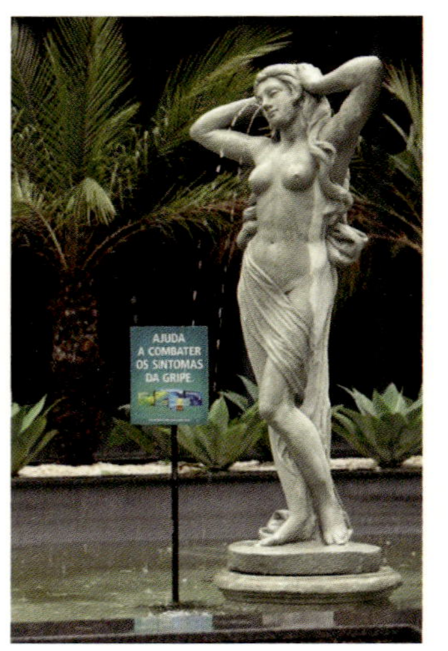

BRÉSIL BRAZIL (2010)
Lew Lara TBWA
Naldecon Cold & Flu Tablets
Help to fight flu symptoms

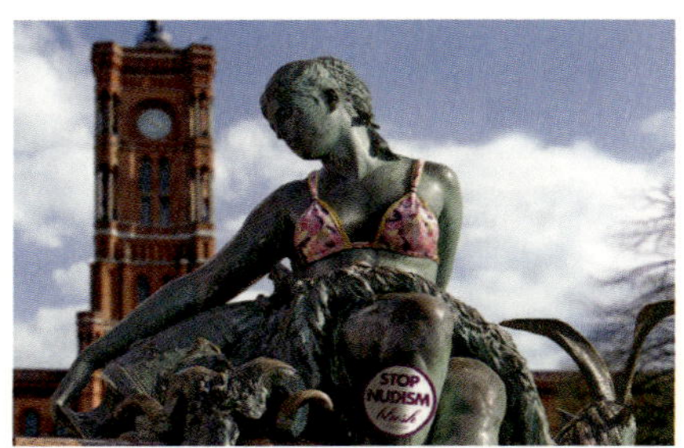

ALLEMAGNE GERMANY (2008)
Glow Blush Swimwear
Stop Nudism

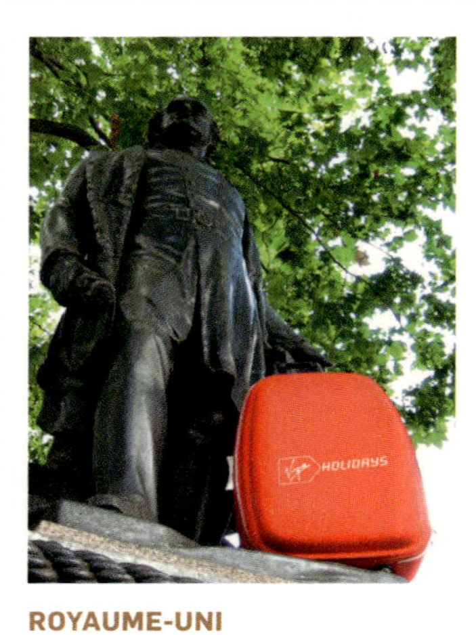

**ROYAUME-UNI
UNITED KINGDOM (2007)**
The Tugboat Virgin Holidays

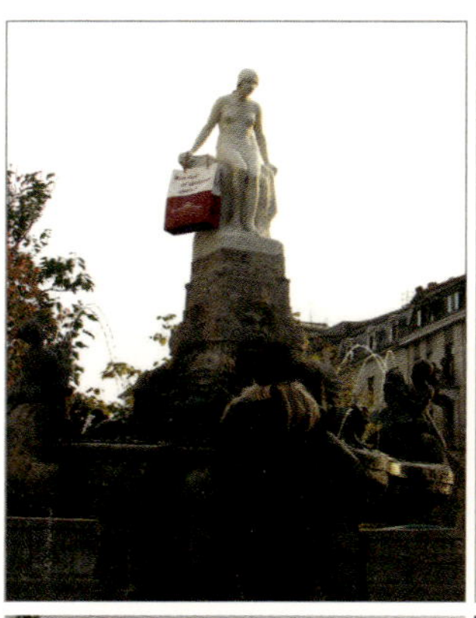

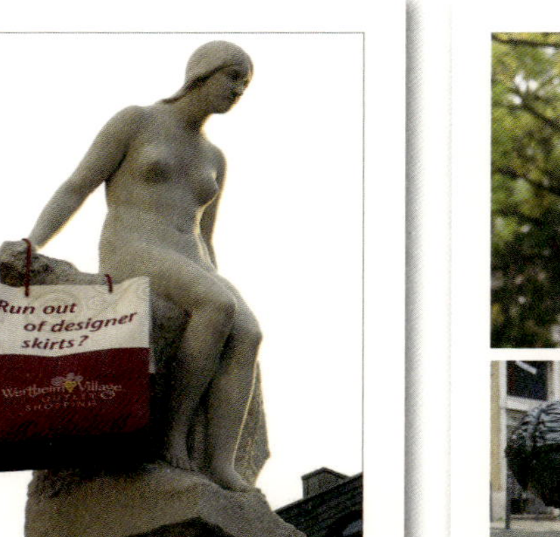

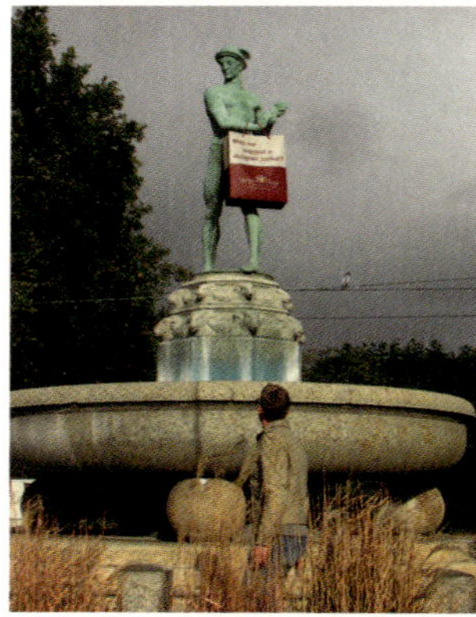

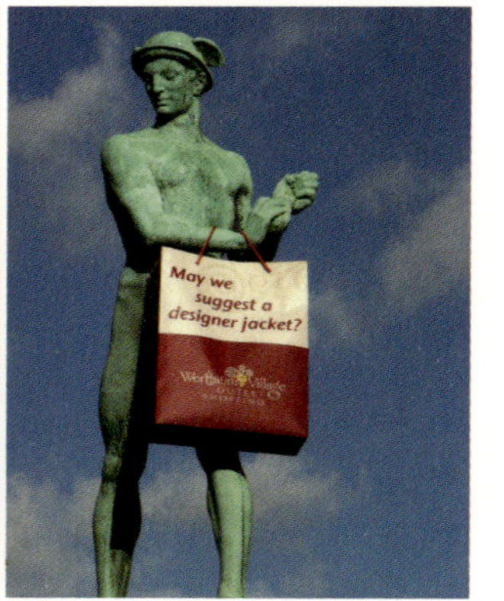

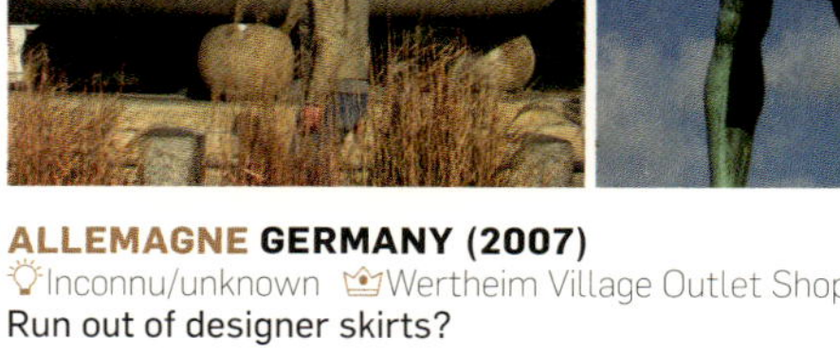

ALLEMAGNE GERMANY (2007)
Inconnu/unknown Wertheim Village Outlet Shopping
Run out of designer skirts?

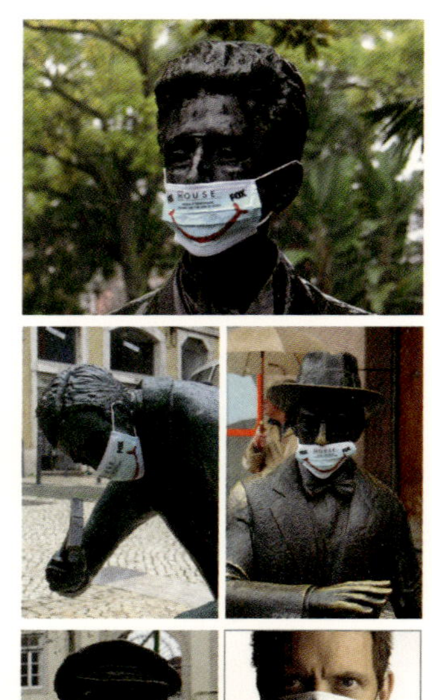

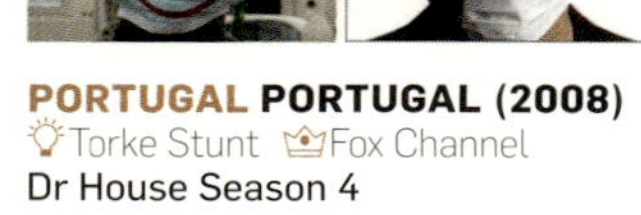

PORTUGAL PORTUGAL (2008)
Torke Stunt Fox Channel
Dr House Season 4

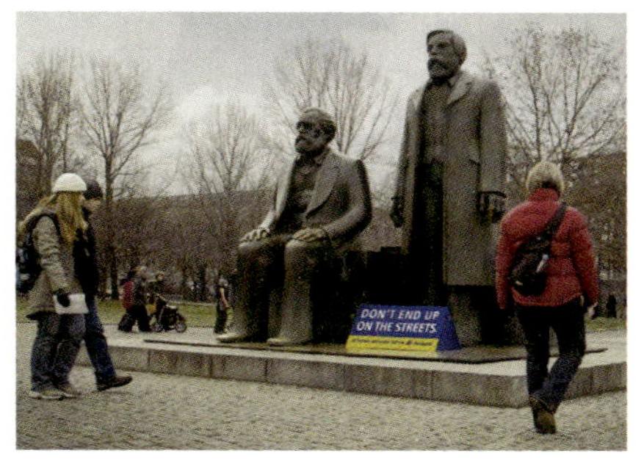
ALLEMAGNE GERMANY (2007)
BBDO Dusseldorf   Postbank
Don't end up on the streets

STATUES

№ 87

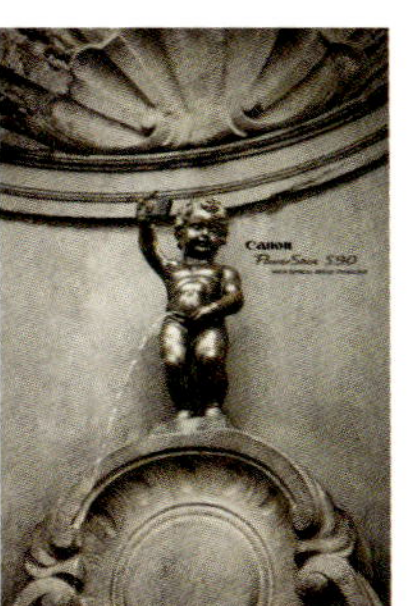
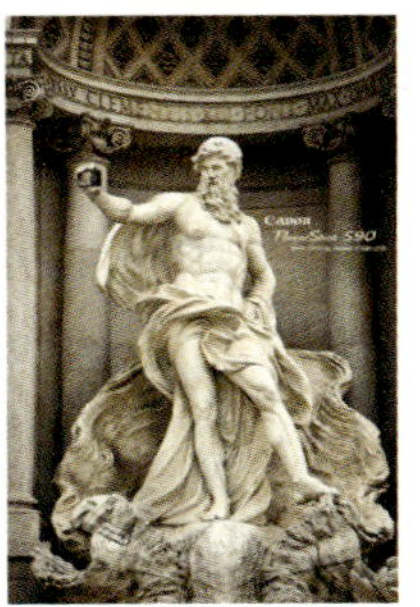

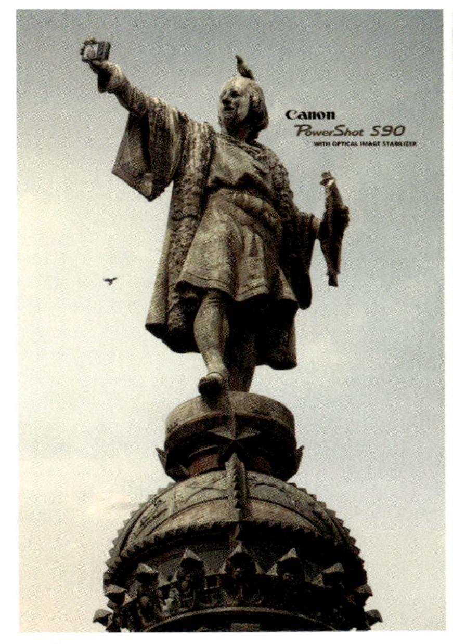
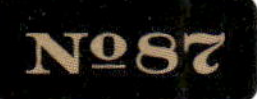
ÉTATS-UNIS UNITED STATES (2008)
Carmichael Lynch
Denver Museum of Nature and Science
Titanic Exhibition

BRÉSIL BRAZIL (2011)
Giovanni Draft FCB   Canon Powershot S90
With optical image stabilizer

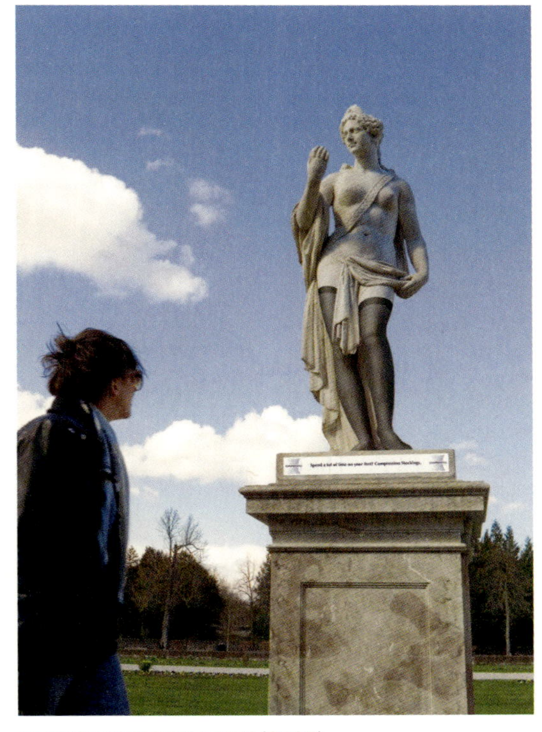
ALLEMAGNE GERMANY (2007)
Heye Group   Compressana compression stockings
Spend a lot of time on your feet?

STATUE DE LA LIBERTÉ

№ 88

MISS LIBERTY

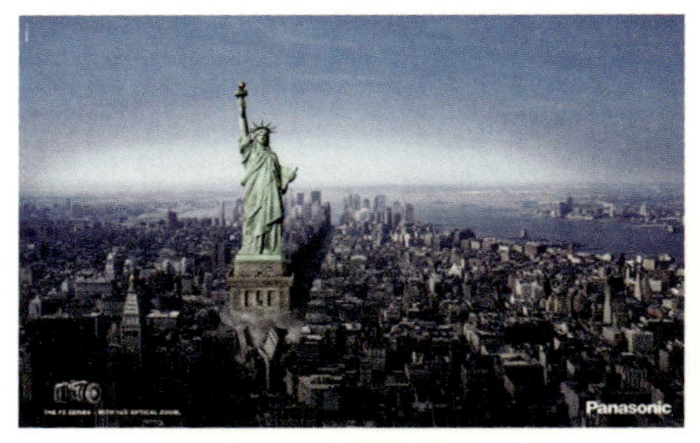

SUISSE SWITZERLAND (2005)
Jung Von Matt Panasonic FZ series
12X Optical zoom

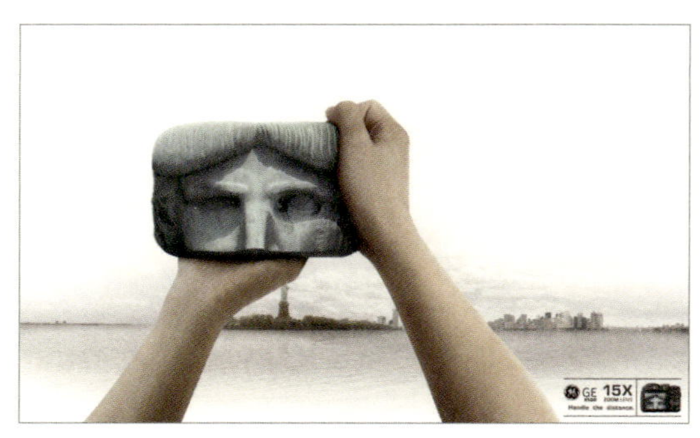

THAÏLANDE THAILAND (2012)
Bangkok Showcase GE X500
15X Zoom lens. Handle the distance

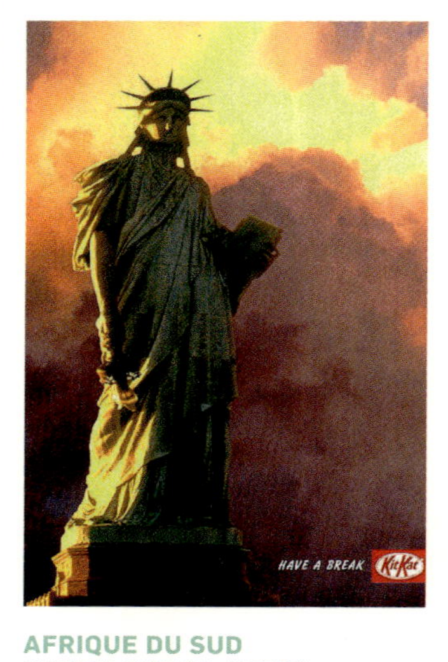

AFRIQUE DU SUD
SOUTH AFRICA (2000)
Ogilvy & Mather Nestlé Kit Kat
Have a break

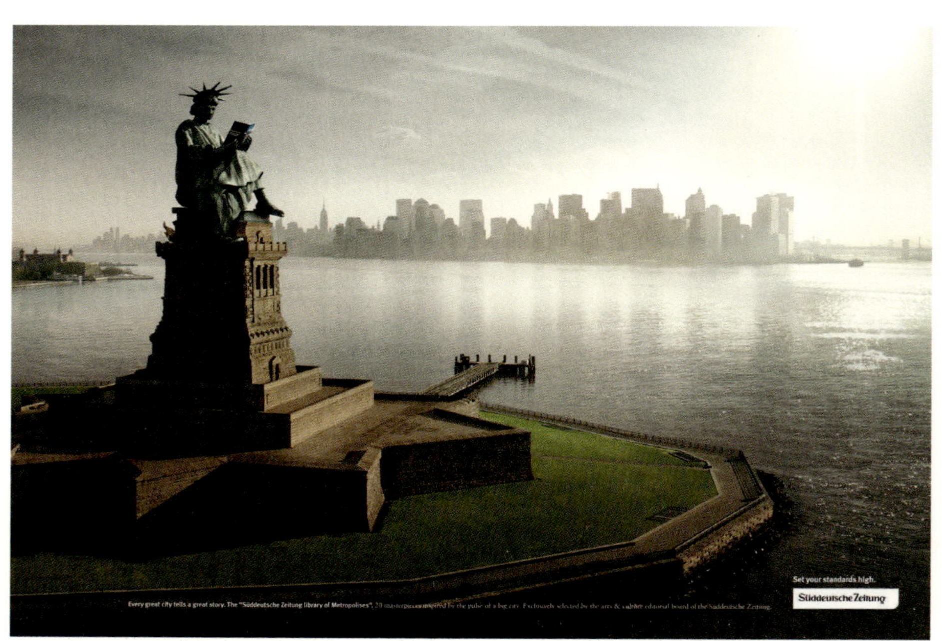

ALLEMAGNE GERMANY (2010)
Heye & Partner Munich *Suddeutsche Zeitung*
Every great city tells a great story

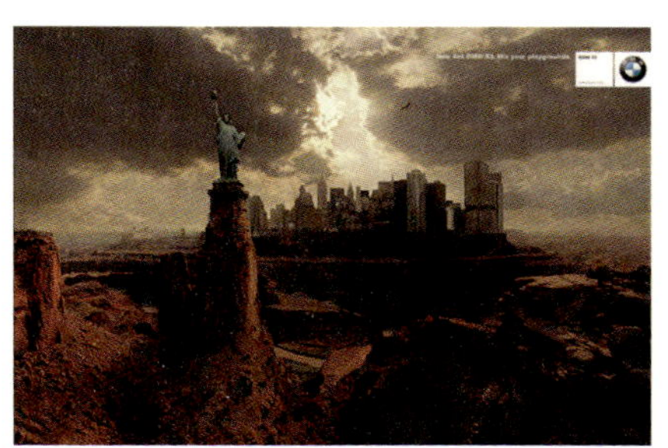

FRANCE FRANCE (2004)
BDDP&Fils · BMW X3
Mix your playgrounds

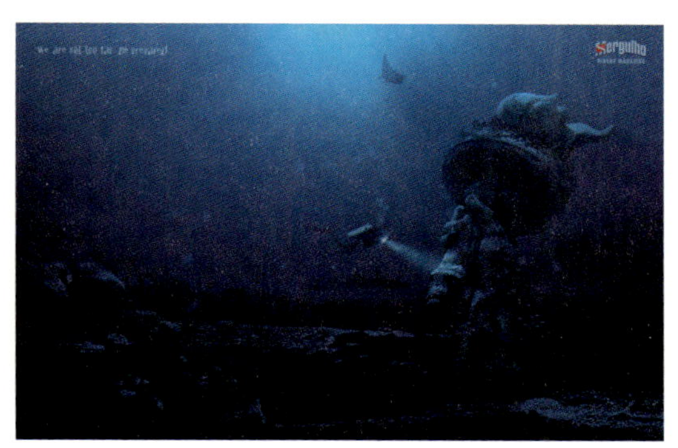

BRÉSIL BRAZIL (2006)
FCB Sao Paulo · Mergulho Divers Magazine
We are not so far. Be prepared

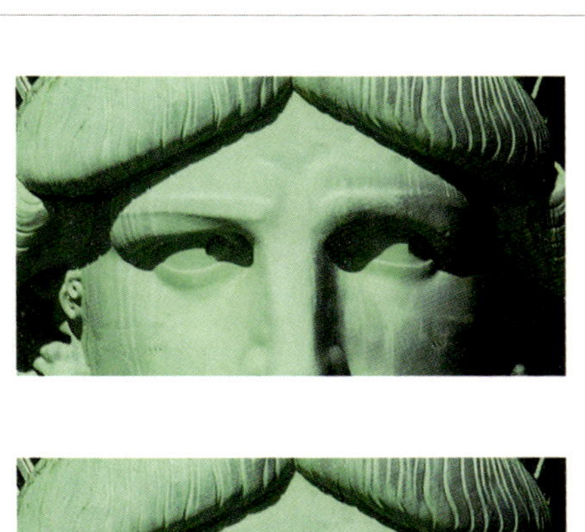

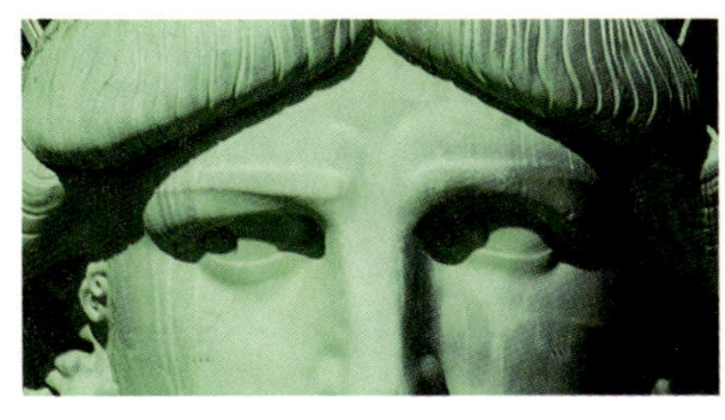

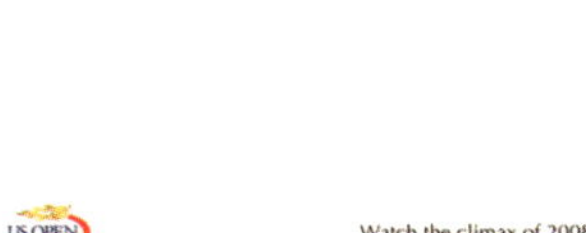

INCONNU UNKNOWN (2008)
Inconnu/unknown · Firstnet
Watch the climax of 2008 US Open live

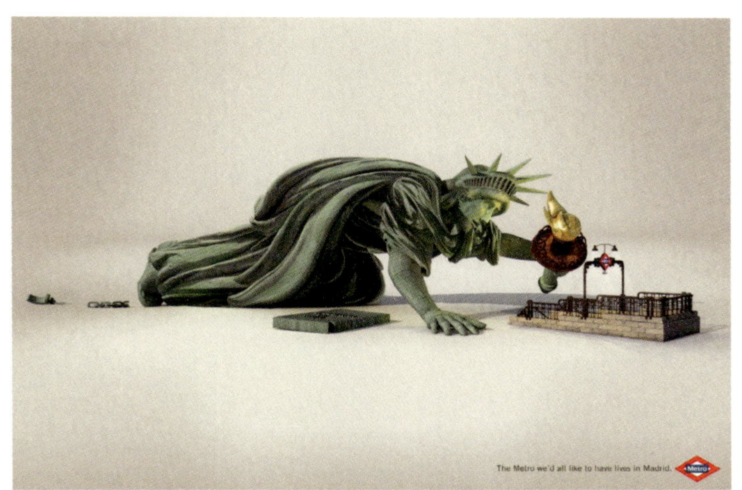

ESPAGNE SPAIN (2009)
Mc Cann Madrid · Metro
The Metro we'd all like to have lives in Madrid

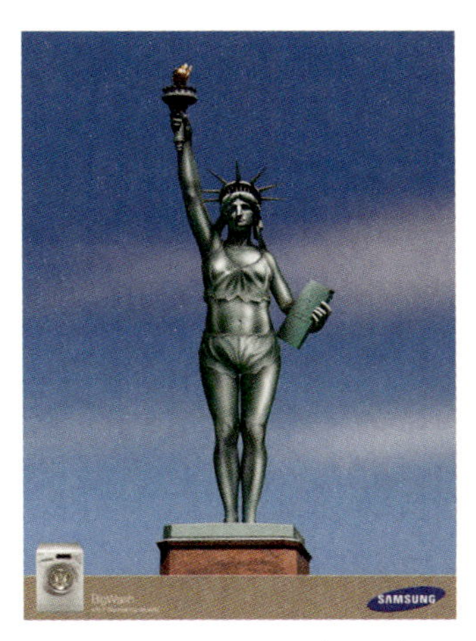

INCONNU UNKNOWN (2006)
Johan H. Ohlson, Zoltan Pinter · Samsung Washing Machines
Big Wash

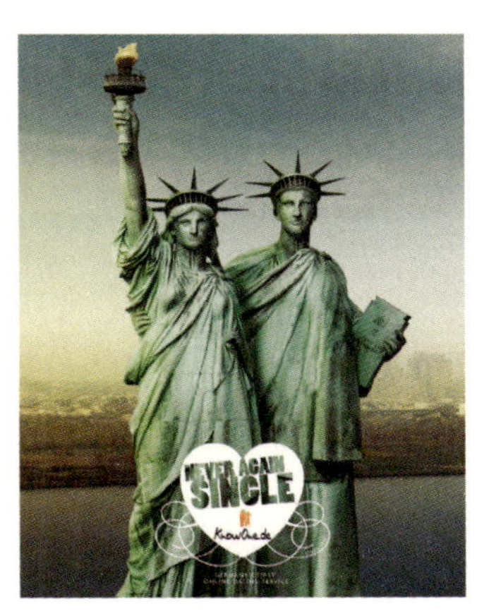

ALLEMAGNE GERMANY (2008)
Schwarzspringer Stuttgart · Knowone.de Matchmaking Service

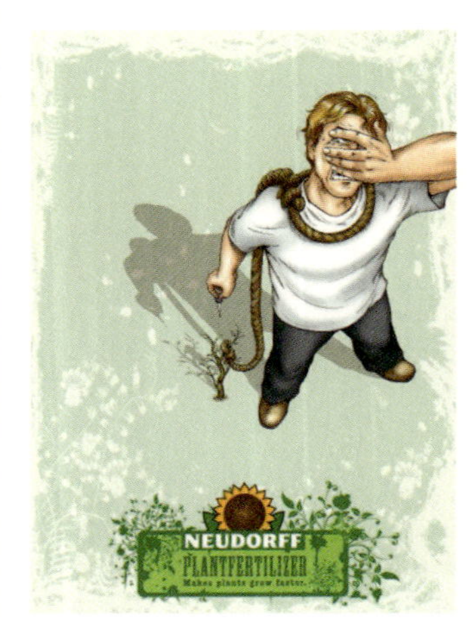

ALLEMAGNE GERMANY (2006)
💡DDB 👑Neudorff Plant Fertilizer
Makes plants grow faster

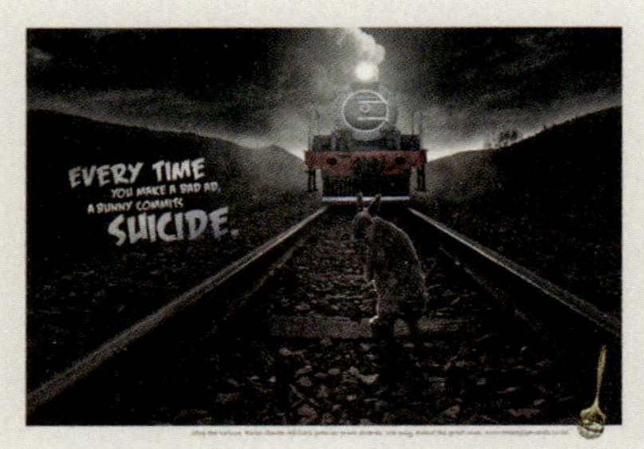

AFRIQUE DU SUD SOUTH AFRICA (2010)
💡King James Cape Town
👑The Eagle Advertising Awards
Every time you make a bad ad, a bunny
commits suicide. Stop the torture,
enter South Africa premier print awards.

**ROUMANIE
ROMANIA (2009)**
💡Mercury 360 Bucharest
👑Anti Tobacco
It's called suicide
because it's your choice

«Difficile de faire mourir de rire
avec quelque chose d'aussi
tragique que le suicide et pourtant
la pub ne s'en prive pas, loin de
là. Je trouve le ton plus juste et
plus fort utilisé de cette manière
et pour servir une cause, que pour
faire une blague trop fumeuse.»
"It is difficult to knock 'em dead
with something as tragic as
suicide and yet this advert does
not hold back, far from it. I find
the tone fairer and stronger this
way, and used to serve the cause
with a smoky joke."

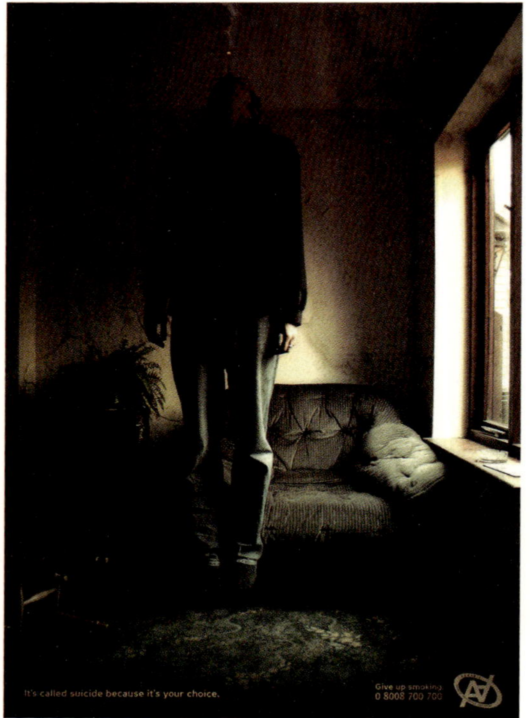

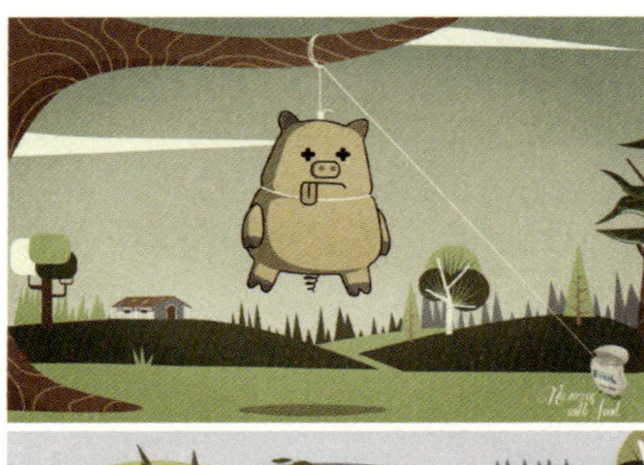
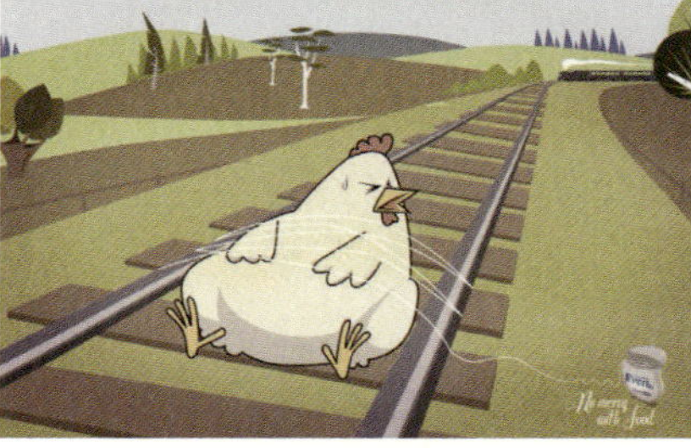

BRÉSIL BRAZIL (2009)
💡RGA Comunicaçao 👑Even Dental Floss
No mercy with food

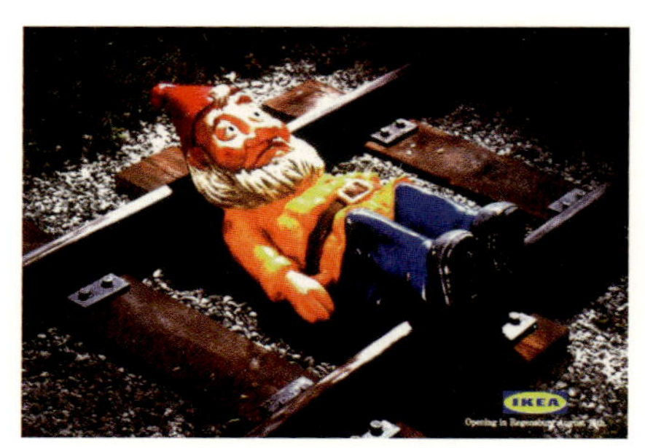

ALLEMAGNE GERMANY (2002)
💡Grabarz + Partner 👑IKEA

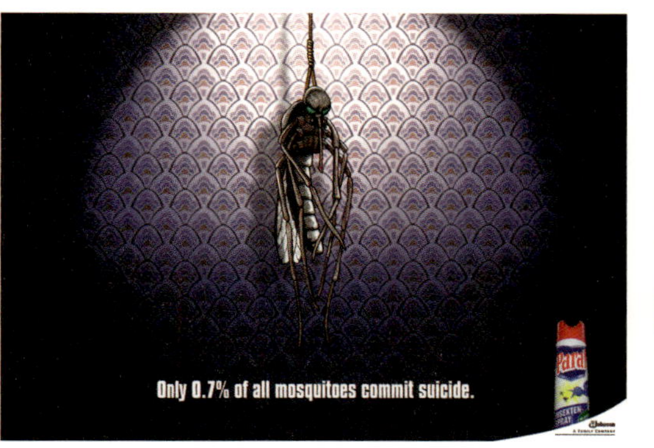

ALLEMAGNE GERMANY (2006)
FCB Hamburg Paral Insecticide
Only 0.7% of all mosquitoes commit suicide

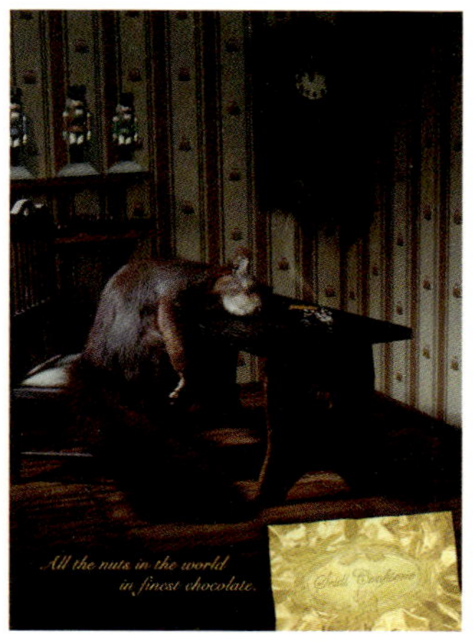

ALLEMAGNE GERMANY (2008)
Serviceplan Seidl Confiserie
All the nuts in the world
in the finest chocolate

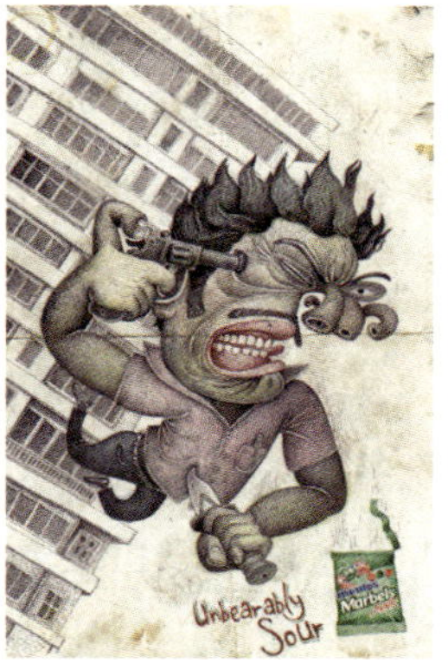

INDE INDIA (2011)
Ogilvy & Mather Mumbai
Mentos Marbels Sour
Unbearably Sour

SUICIDES

№89

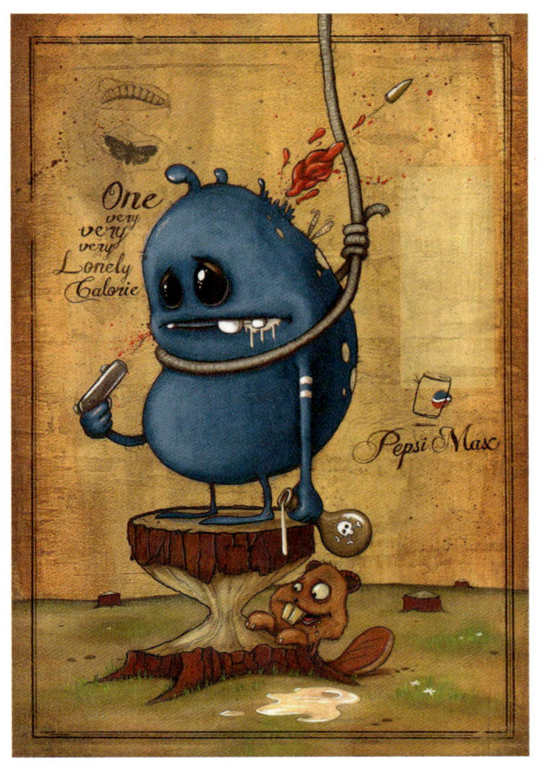

ALLEMAGNE GERMANY (2010)
BBDO Dusseldorf Pepsi Max
One only very very lonely Calorie

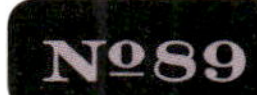

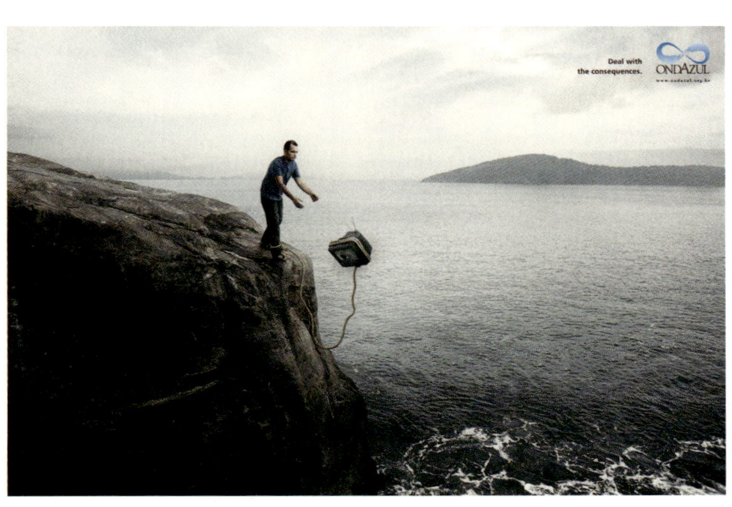

BRÉSIL BRAZIL (2011)
Quê Comunicaçao Rio Ondazul
Deal with the consequences

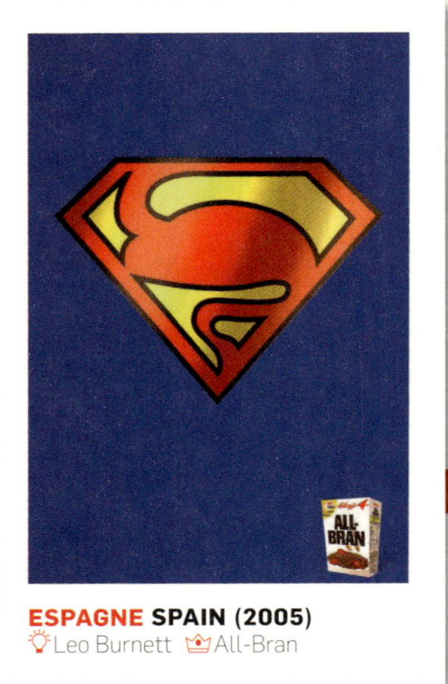

ESPAGNE **SPAIN (2005)**
Leo Burnett · All-Bran

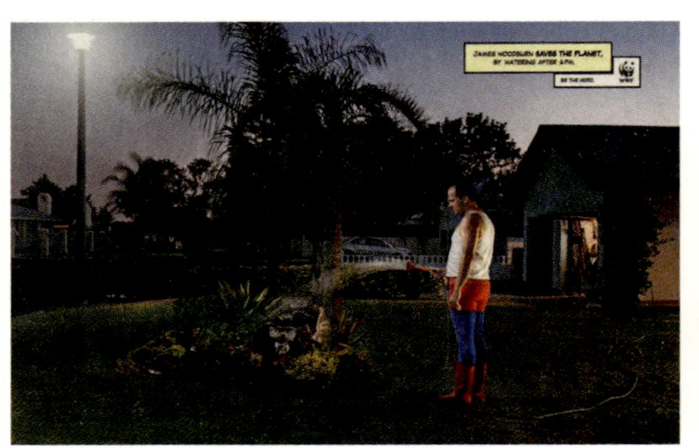

AFRIQUE DU SUD **SOUTH AFRICA (2008)**
Ogilvy & Mather · WWF
James Woodburn saves the planet by watering after 6pm.
Be the hero

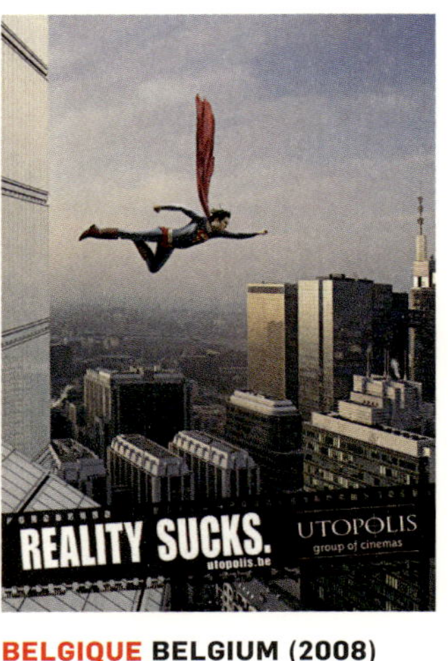

BELGIQUE **BELGIUM (2008)**
Duval Guillaume
Utopolis Group of Cinemas

SUPERMAN

№90

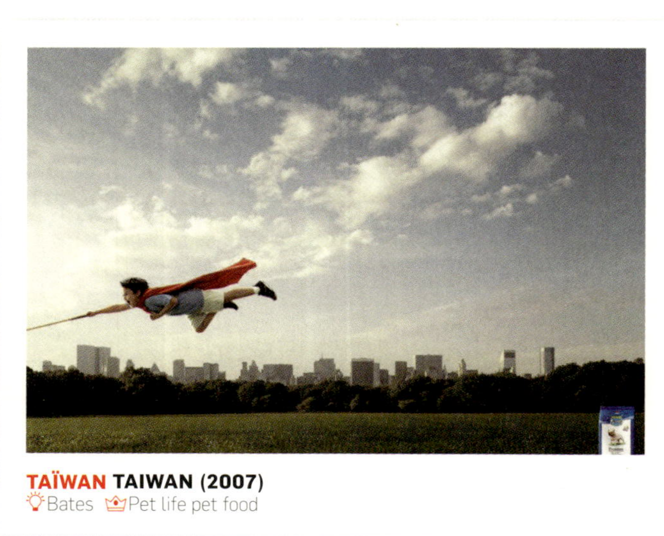

TAÏWAN **TAIWAN (2007)**
Bates · Pet life pet food

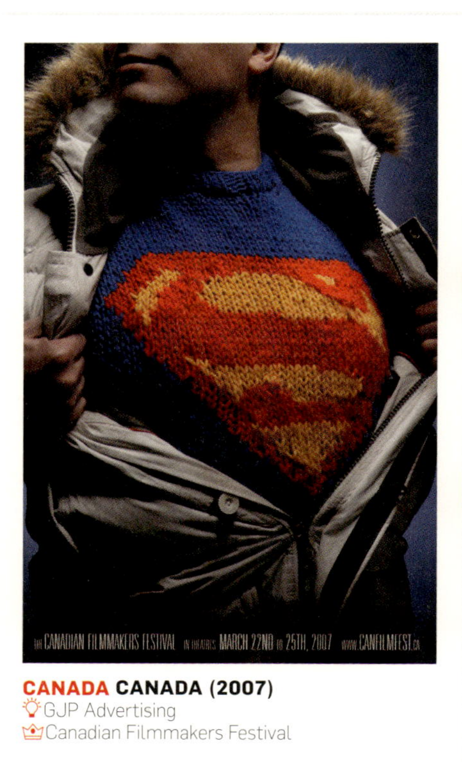

CANADA **CANADA (2007)**
GJP Advertising
Canadian Filmmakers Festival

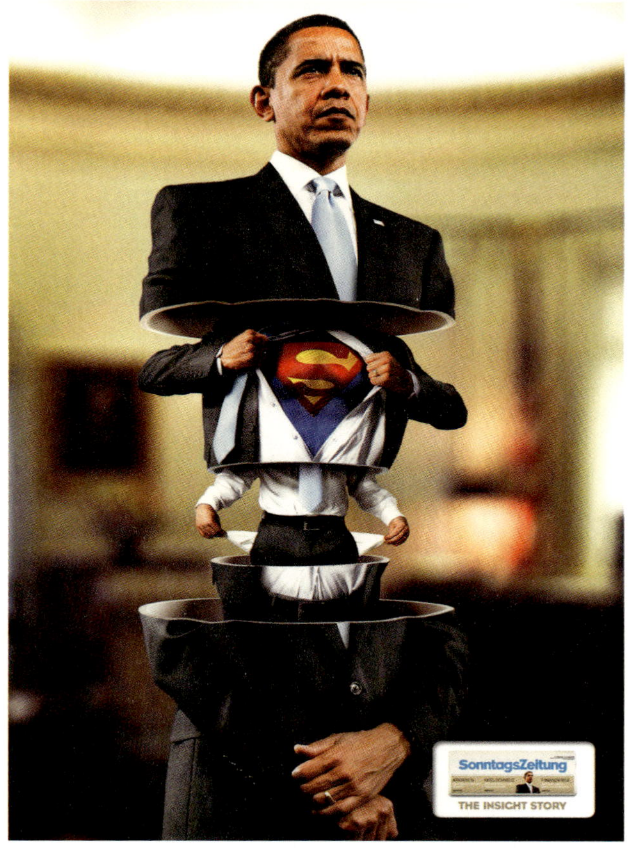

SUISSE
SWITZERLAND (2009)
Young & Rubicam Zurich
Sonntagszeitung newspaper
The insight story

« Celle-ci aurait pu également
figurer dans le chapitre « poupées
russes ». C'est visuellement
la plus étonnante et la plus forte.
Une « super-idée », qui n'est que
l'une des illustrations d'une
« super-campagne » qui aura
au moins eu le pouvoir de
marquer mon esprit. »
This one could also be included
in the "Russian dolls" chapter. It is
visually the most amazing and
the strongest. A "super-idea",
which is just an illustration of
a "super-campaign" that at least
has the power to brand my mind.

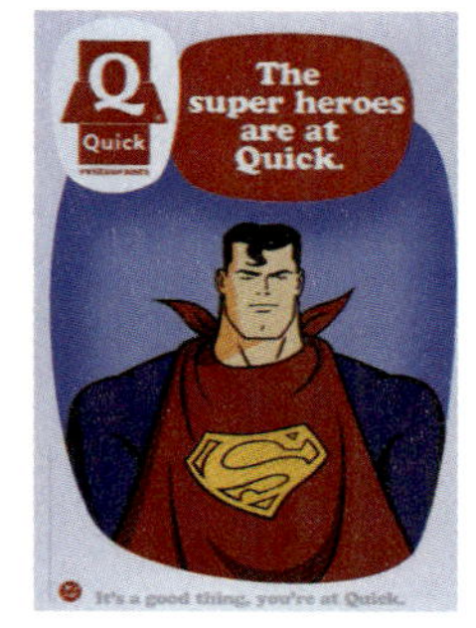

FRANCE
FRANCE (2002)
Young & Rubicam Paris
Quick Restaurants

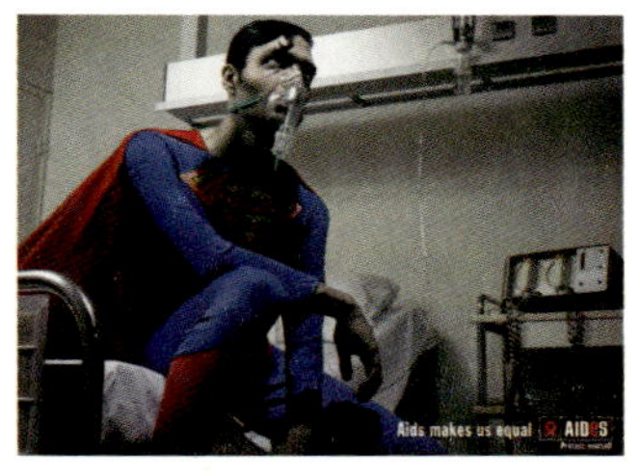

FRANCE FRANCE (2005)
TBWA Paris   Aides
Aids make us equal

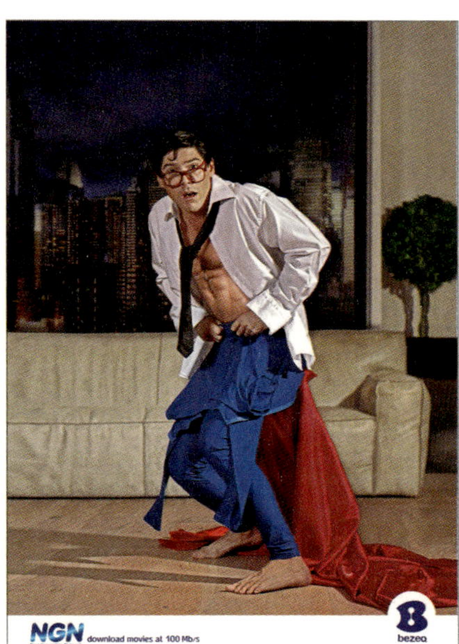

ISRAËL ISRAEL (2011)
Grey Tel Aviv   New Generation Network
Download movies at 100 Mb/s

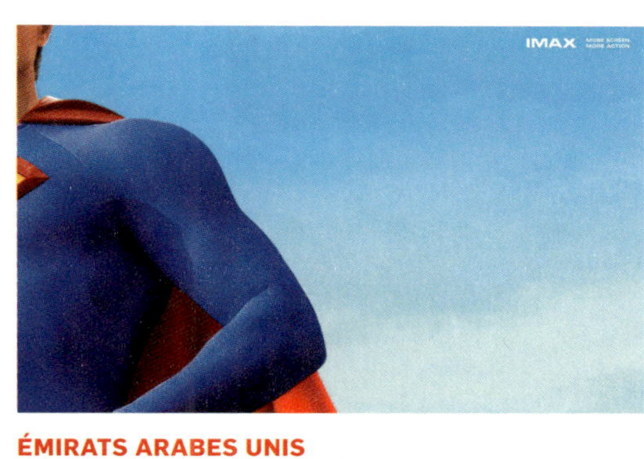

ÉMIRATS ARABES UNIS
UNITED ARAB EMIRATES (2008)
The Tribe   Imax
More screen, more action

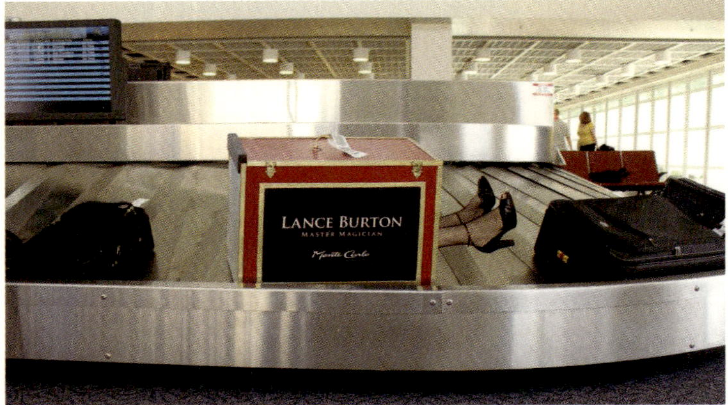

ÉTATS-UNIS
UNITED STATES (2010)
David & Goliath Los Angeles
Lance Burton Master Magician
Monte Carlo

« Celle-ci m'a beaucoup amusée, même si je me demande comment une telle opération a pu avoir lieu vu le niveau de sécurité et de paranoïa qui règne dans les aéroports. Ont-ils fait exploser la valise à la fin ? »
"This one amused me quite a bit, even though I wonder how such an operation could take place given the level of security and paranoia that reigns at airports today. Did they blow up the bag at the end?"

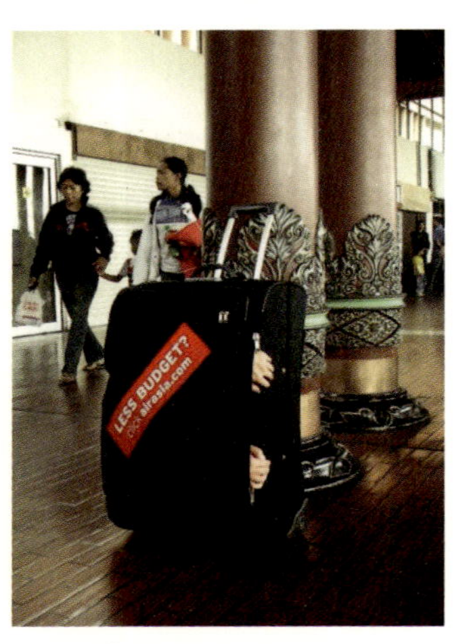

INDONÉSIE INDONESIA (2007)
PlayGroup Air Asia
Low budget? Click Airasia.com

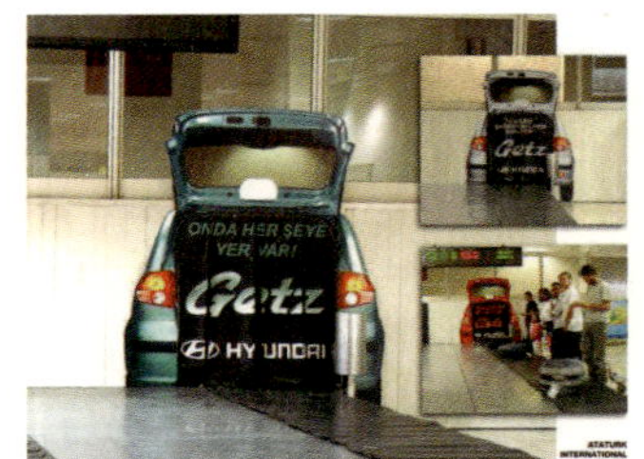

TURQUIE TURKEY (2004)
Ceteris Paribus New Generation Advertising Hyundai Getz

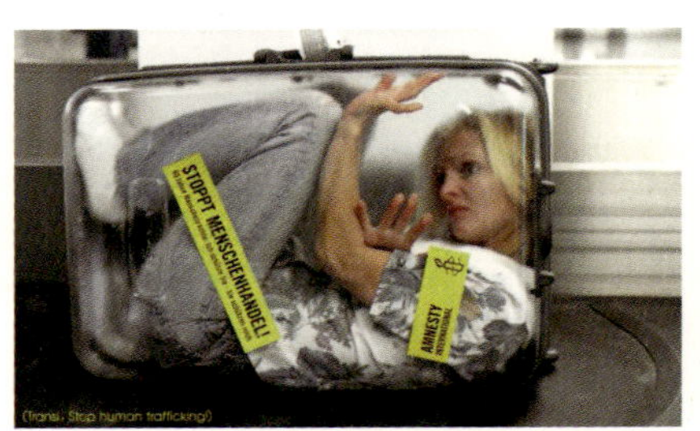

ALLEMAGNE GERMANY (2008)
Serviceplan Amnesty International
Stop human trafficking

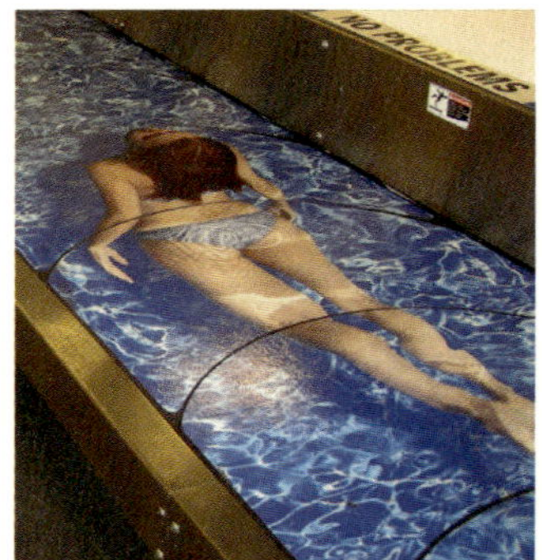

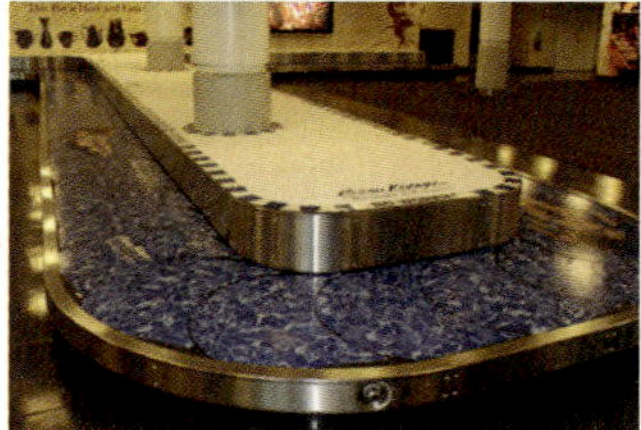

ÉTATS-UNIS
UNITED STATES (2009
Masterminds
Beau Rivage Resort & Casino

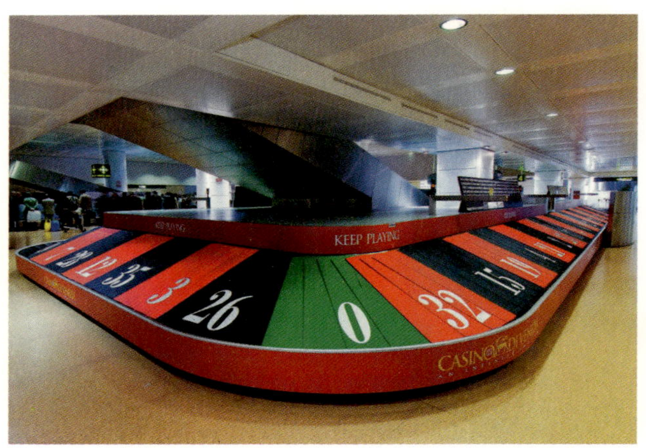

ITALIE ITALY (2007)
ADM Communication Bologna Casino di Venezia
Keep Playing

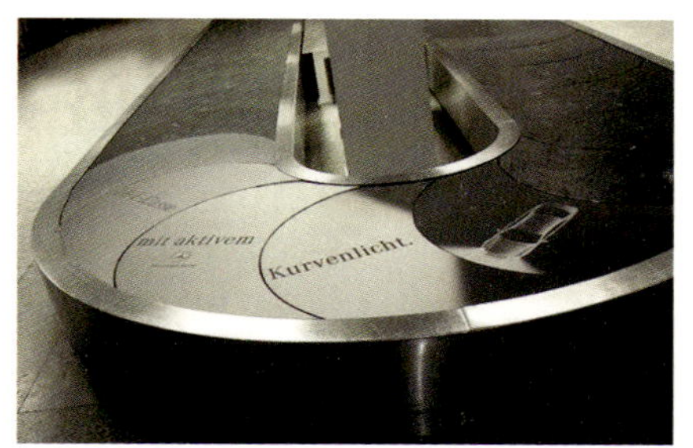

AUTRICHE AUSTRIA (2008)
Springer & Jacoby
Mercedes Adaptative headlights

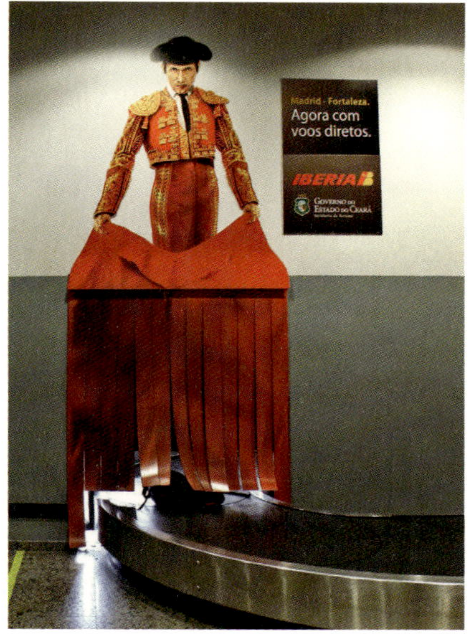

ESPAGNE SPAIN
Inconnu/unknown   Iberia

TAPIS ROULANT À BAGAGES

Nº91

AIRPORT LUGAGE BELT

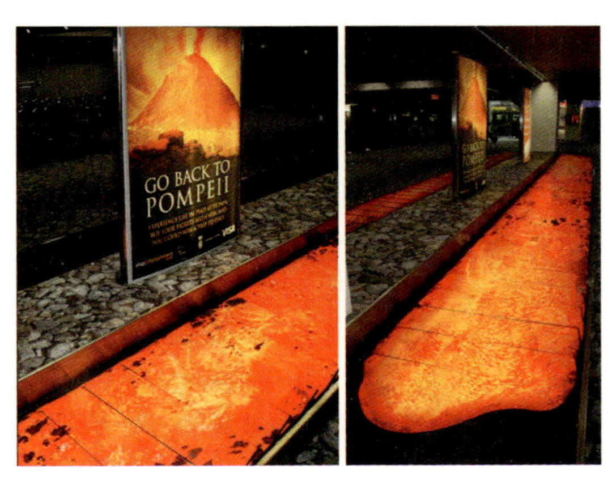

NOUVELLE-ZÉLANDE NEW ZEALAND (2011)
TBWA Tequila Auckland
Visa's sponsorship of the Pompeii exhibit

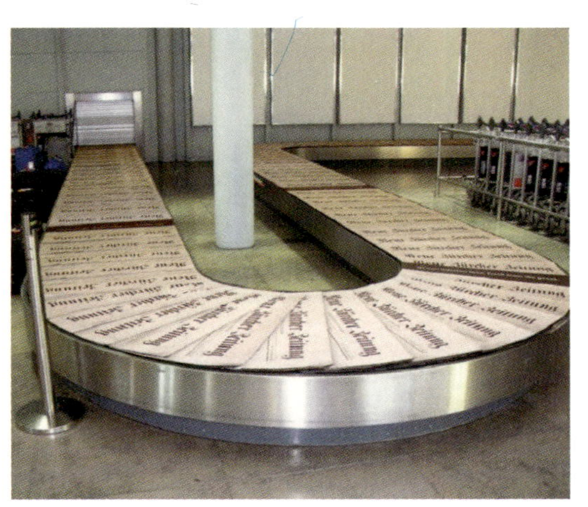

ALLEMAGNE GERMANY (2006)
Jung Von Matt Hamburg   The Zurich Newspaper
Fresh from the press

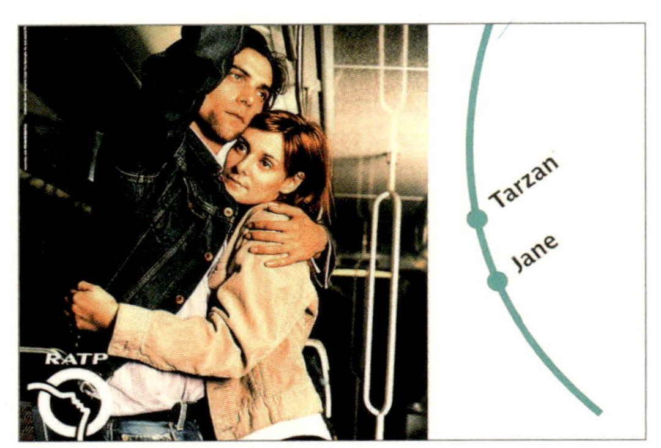

FRANCE FRANCE (2000)
Euro RSCG BETC RATP Paris Subway

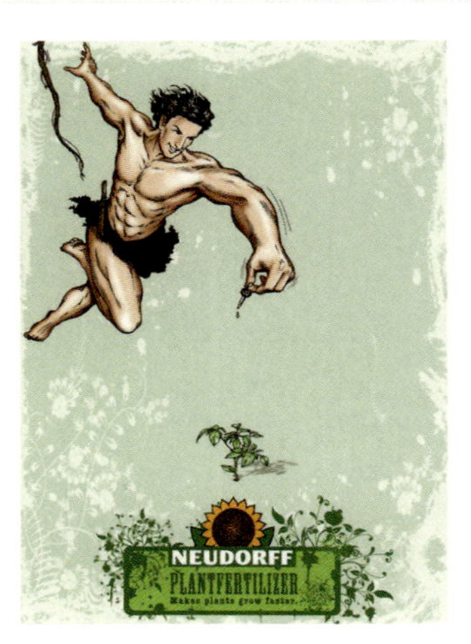

ALLEMAGNE GERMANY (2007)
DDB Dusseldorf
Neudorff Plant Fertilizer
Makes plants grow faster

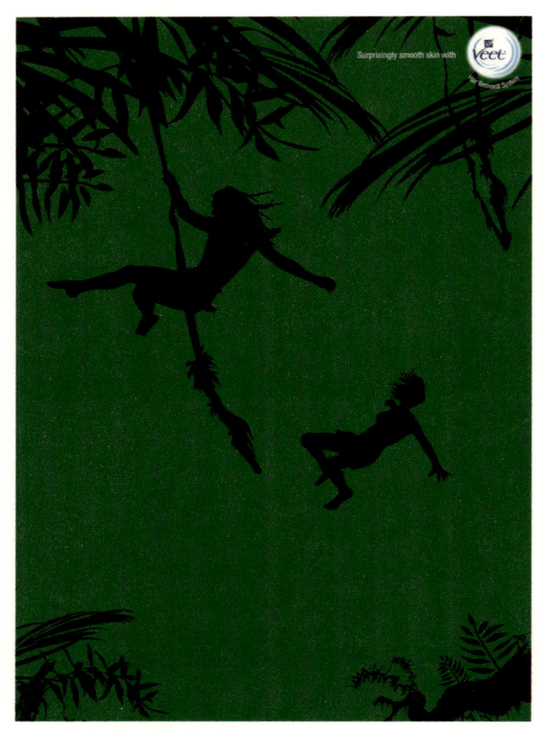

INDE INDIA (2007)
Euro RSCG Delhi Veet Hair removal cream
Surprisingly smooth skin

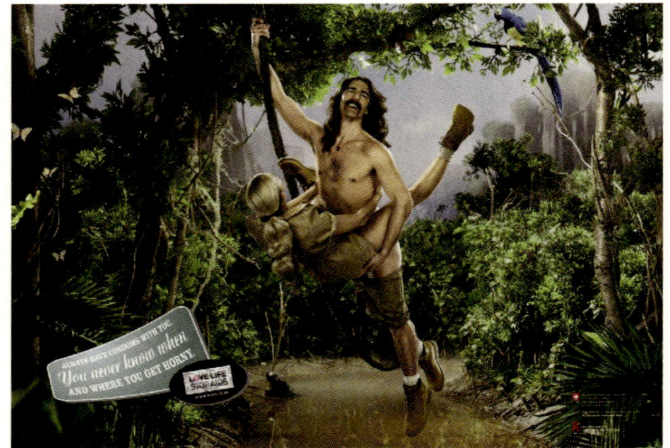

SUISSE SWITZERLAND (2008)
Euro RSCG Zurich Love Life Stop Aids
Always have condoms with you. You never know where you get horny

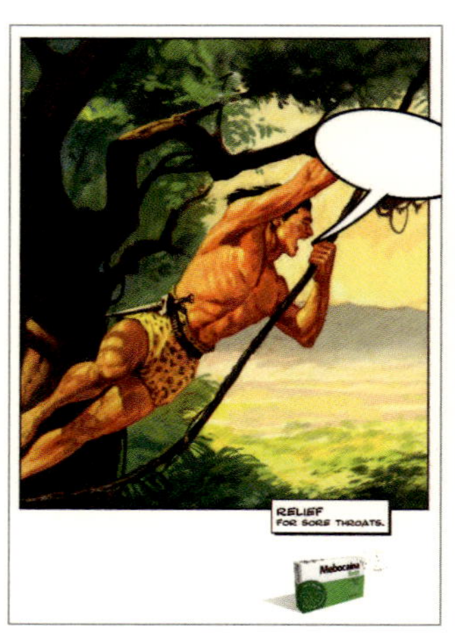

PORTUGAL PORTUGAL (2008)
Euro RSCG Life Mebocaina
Relief for sore throats

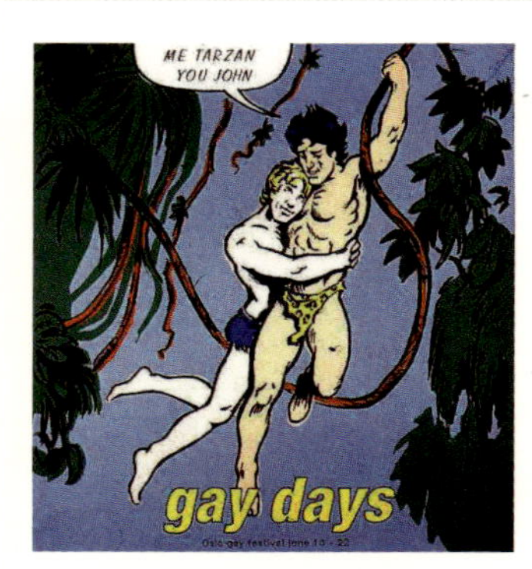

NORVÈGE NORWAY (1998)
Bates Gay Days
Me Tarzan, You John

Nº92

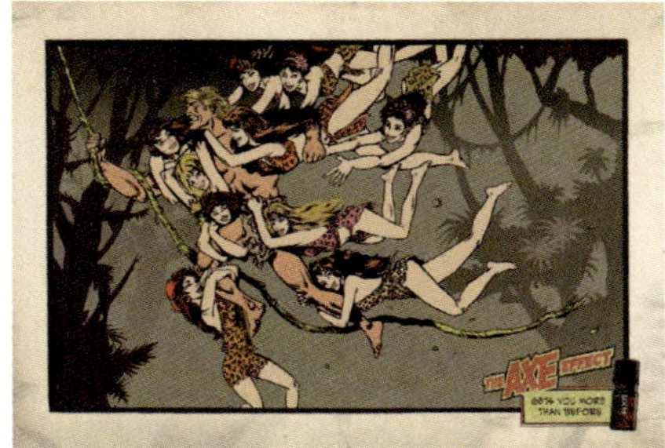

ROUMANIE **ROMANIA (2006)**
Mc Cann — Maggi Ready Made Soups
"Jane, queen of the jungle"
If only women spent less time cooking

SINGAPOUR **SINGAPORE (2008)**
BBH Asia Pacific — AXE Vice
The Axe Effect. Gets you more than before

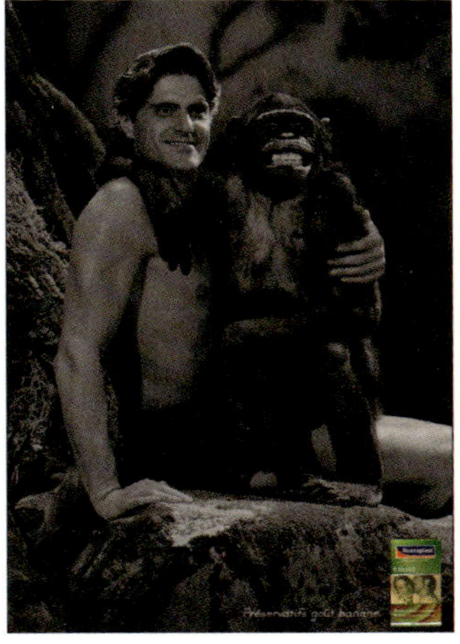

FRANCE **FRANCE (2004)**
TBWA Paris
Hansaplast Condoms
Banana Flavored Condoms

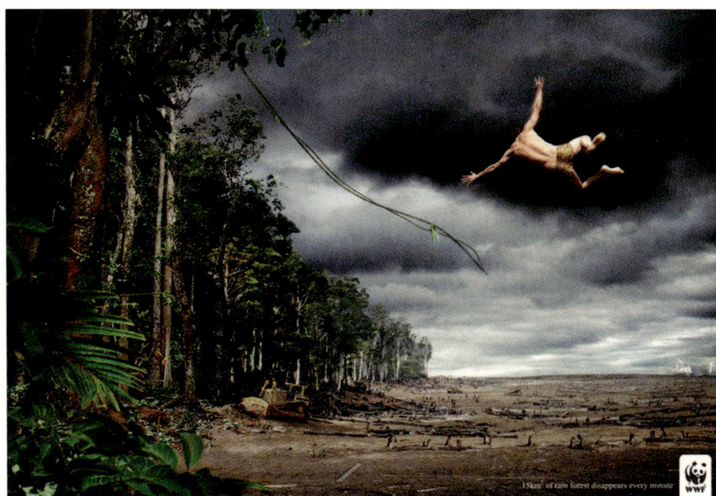

DANEMARK **DENMARK (2007)**
Uncle Grey — WWF
15km of rain forest disappears every minute

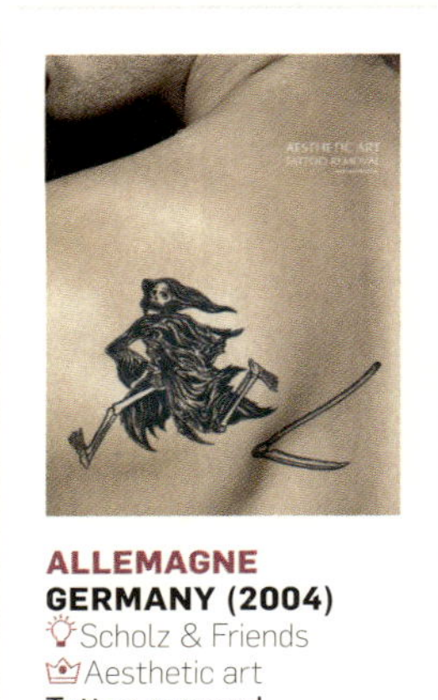

**ALLEMAGNE
GERMANY (2004)**
Scholz & Friends
Aesthetic art
Tattoo removal

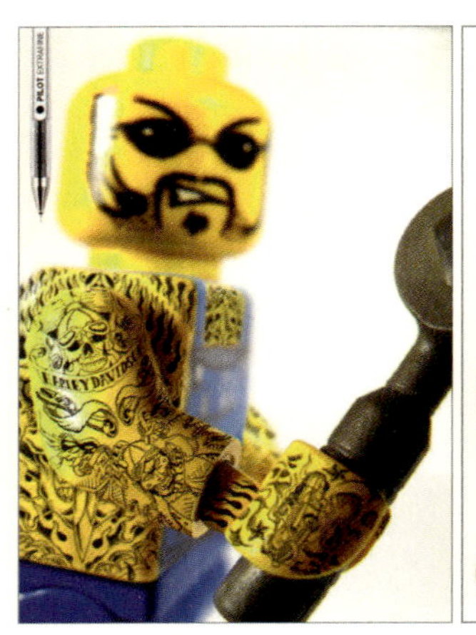

ESPAGNE SPAIN (2010)
Grey Barcelona   Pilot Extrafine

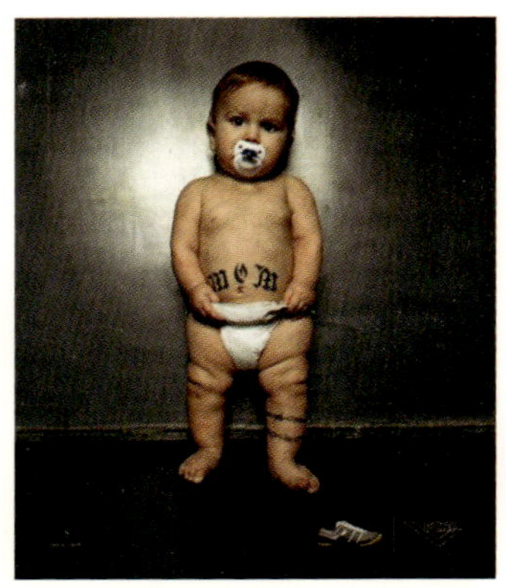

**ÉTATS-UNIS
UNITED STATES (2004)**
Goodby Silverstein & Partners
Pony Shoes

TATOUAGES

№ 93

TATTOOS

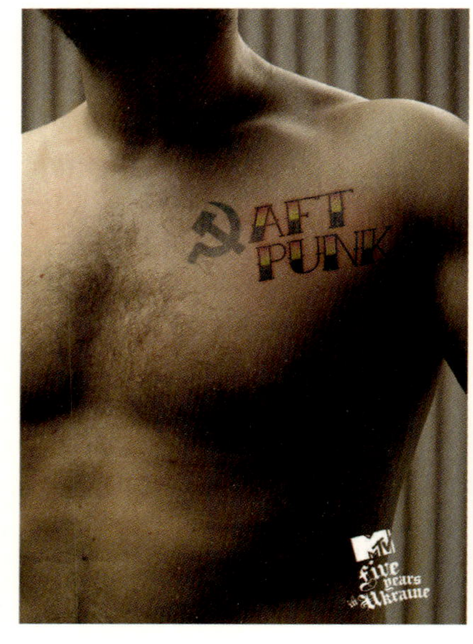
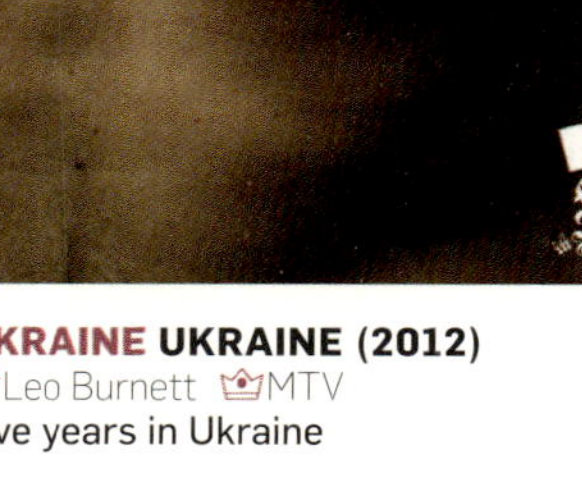

UKRAINE UKRAINE (2012)
Leo Burnett   MTV
Five years in Ukraine

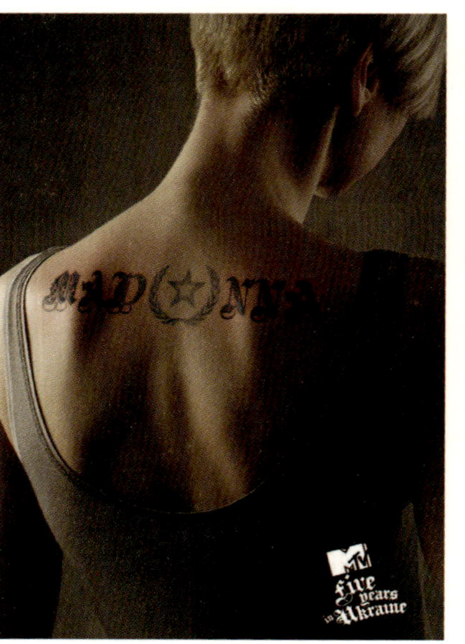

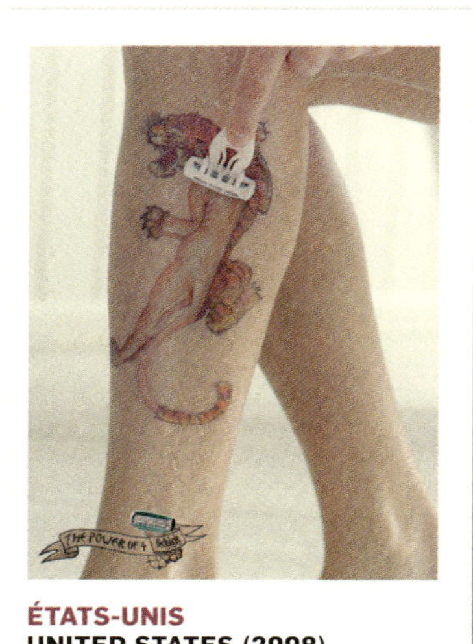

**ÉTATS-UNIS
UNITED STATES (2008)**
JWT   Schick
The power of 4

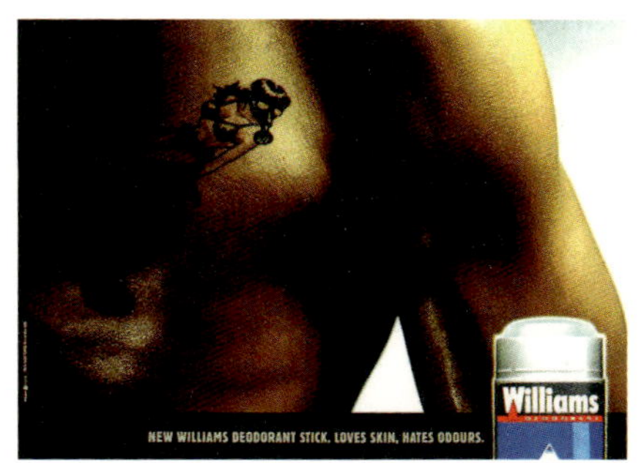

FRANCE FRANCE (1999)
BDDP&Fils Williams deodorant stick
Loves skin, hates odours

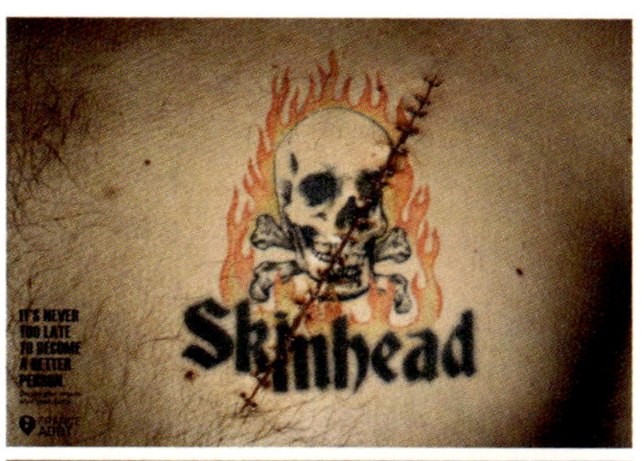

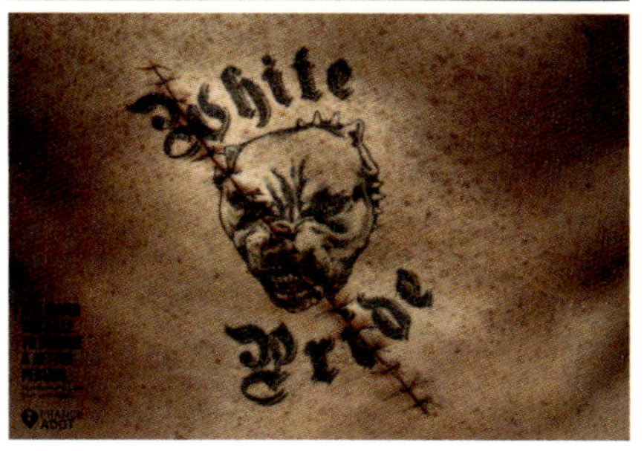

FRANCE FRANCE (2010)
CLM / BBDO France Adot
It's never too late to become a better person

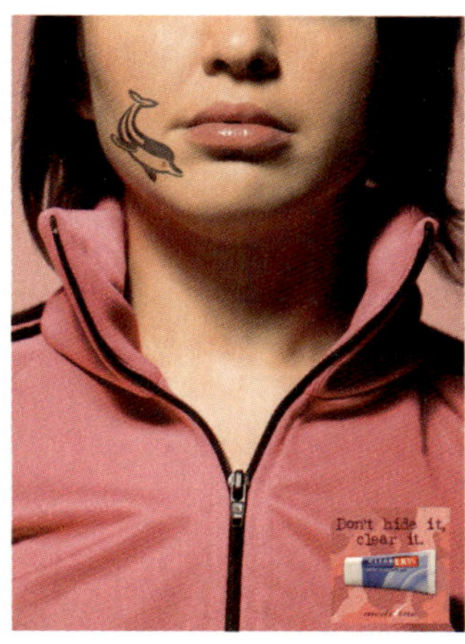

ISRAËL ISRAEL (2009)
Shalmor Avnon Amichay
Young & Rubicam
ClearEx
Don't hide it, clear it

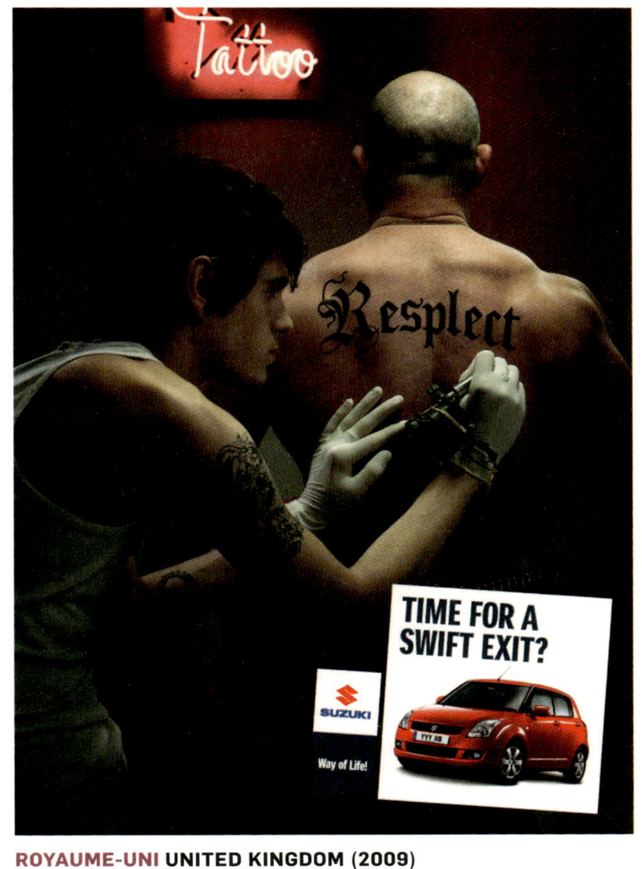

ROYAUME-UNI UNITED KINGDOM (2009)
Nexus H Tunbridge Wells Suzuki Swift

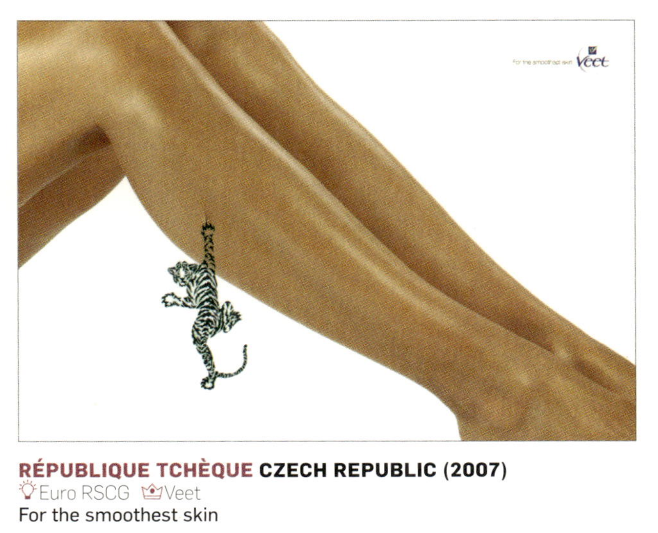

RÉPUBLIQUE TCHÈQUE CZECH REPUBLIC (2007)
Euro RSCG Veet
For the smoothest skin

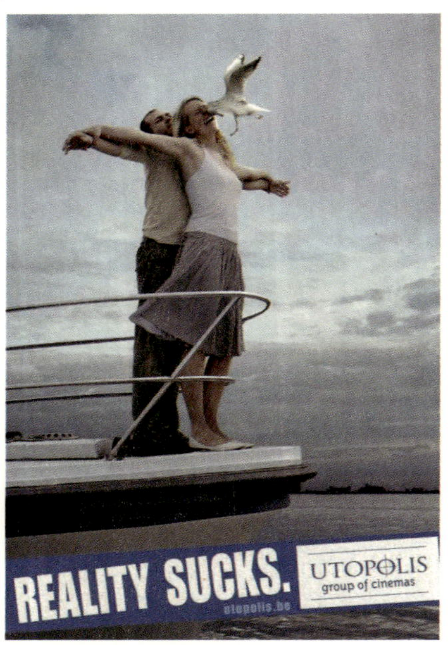

BELGIQUE **BELGIUM** (2007)
Duval Guillaume Antwerp
Utopolis Group of cinemas

« Une idée bien idiote qui va peut-être clouer le bec aux romantiques mais qui permet de casser un peu le mythe et la mièvrerie infinie de cette image. C'est le détournement le plus drôle car le plus tristement réel. »
"A silly idea that could well shut up romantics but also help break a bit of the myth and infinite sentimentality of this image. This hijacking is the funniest because it is the most sadly true."

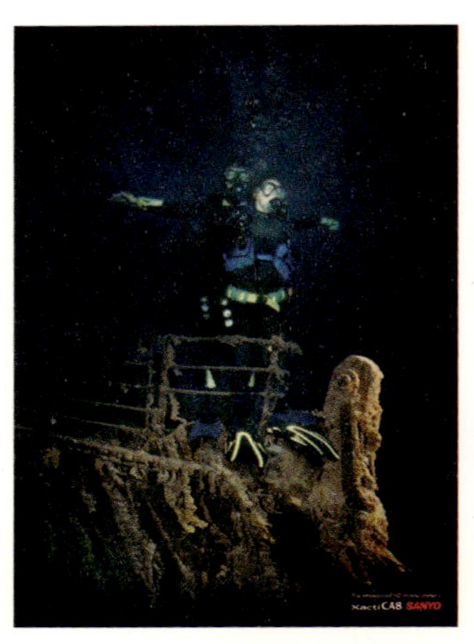

AUSTRALIE **AUSTRALIA** (2008)
Whybin TBWA   SANYO Xaci CA8
The waterproof HD movie camera

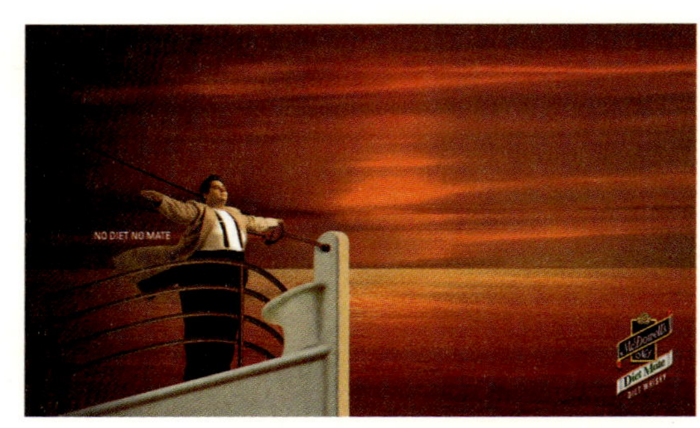

INDE **INDIA** (2007)
Mudra Communications   Mc Dowell's Diet Mate Whisky
No diet no mate

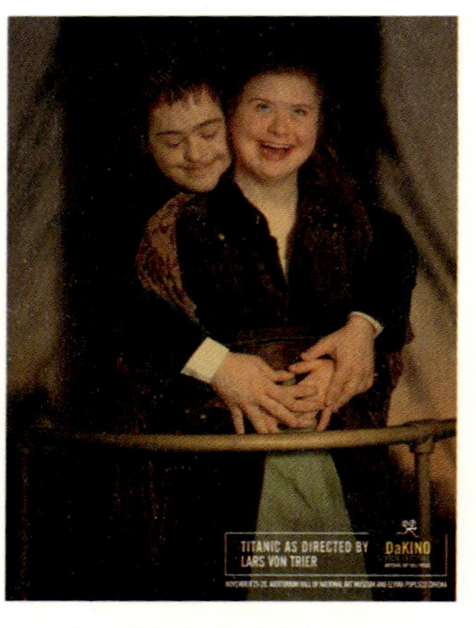

ROUMANIE **ROMANIA** (2005)
Lowe & Partners
DaKino Film Festival
Titanic as directed by Lars Von Trier

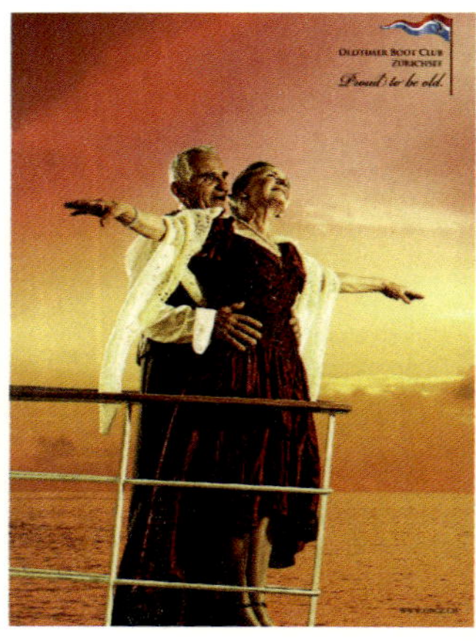

SUISSE **SWITZERLAND** (2010)
KSB Krieg Schlupp Burge
Oldtimer boot club
Proud to be old

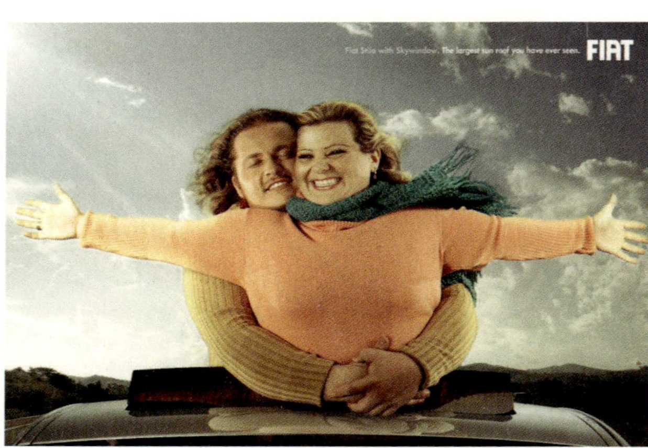

ITALIE **ITALY** (2007)
Leo Burnett   Fiat Stilo with skywindow
The largest sun roof you have ever seen

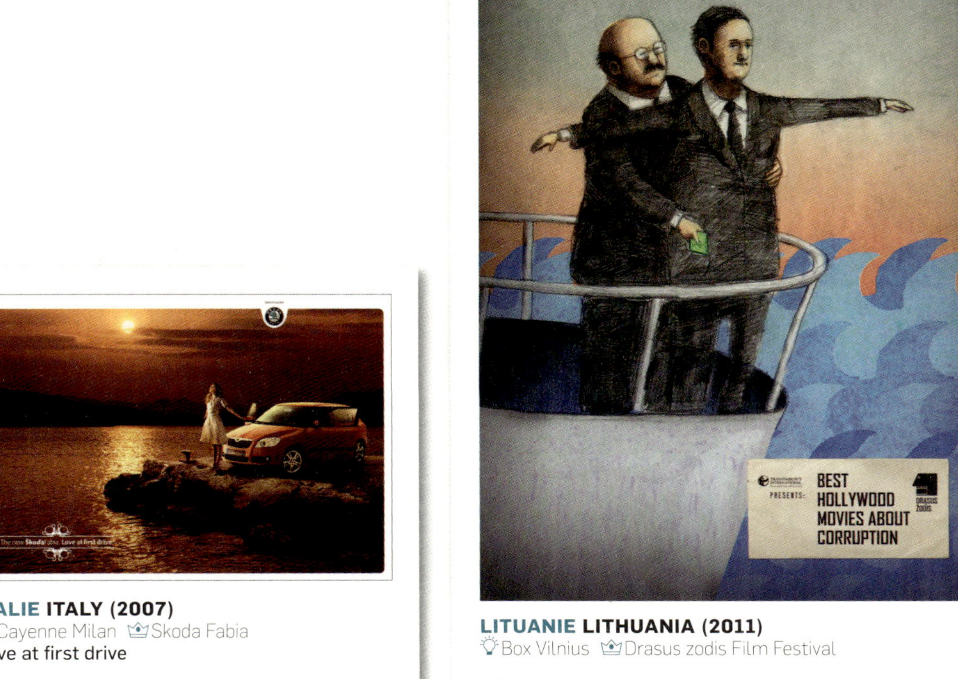

LITUANIE LITHUANIA (2011)
Box Vilnius Drasus zodis Film Festival

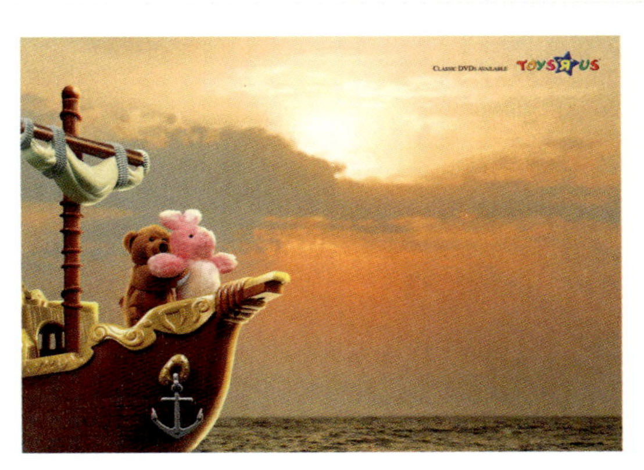

ITALIE ITALY (2007)
Cayenne Milan Skoda Fabia
Love at first drive

TITANIC

№94

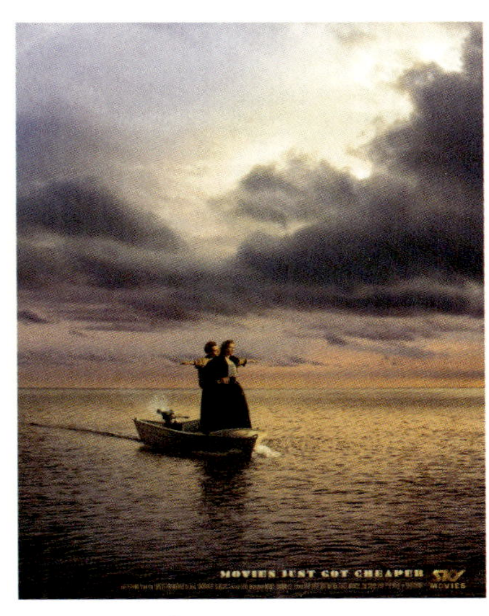

AFRIQUE DU SUD SOUTH AFRICA (2007)
Volcano Advertising Johannesburg Toys'r us
Classic DVDs available

**NOUVELLE-ZÉLANDE
NEW ZEALAND (2009)**
DDB SKY Movies
Movies just got cheaper

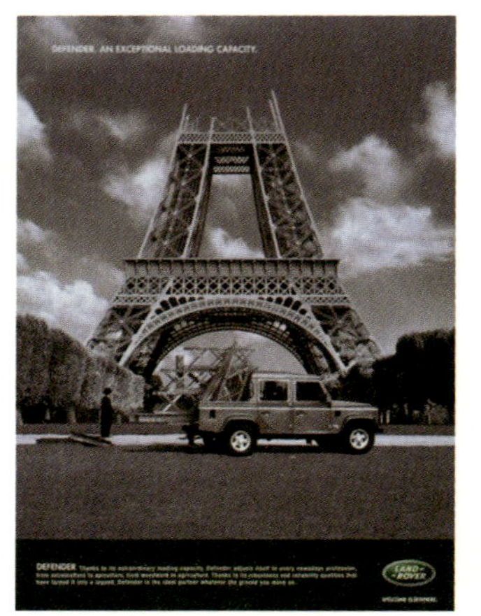

FRANCE FRANCE (2002)
Young & Rubicam
Land Rover Defender
An exceptional loading capacity

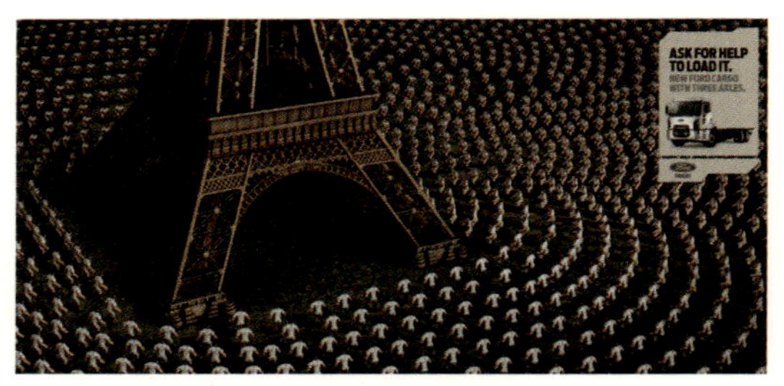

ARGENTINE ARGENTINA (2011)
JWT Buenos Aires   Ford Trucks
Ask for help to load it

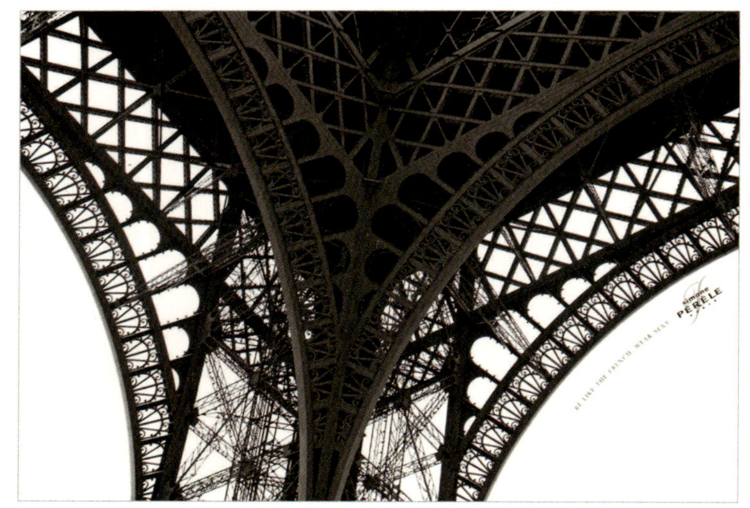

ÉMIRATS ARABE UNIS UNITED ARAB EMIRATES (2008)
Liwa Advertising LLC Dubai   Simone Perele Lingerie
Be like the french. Wear sexy

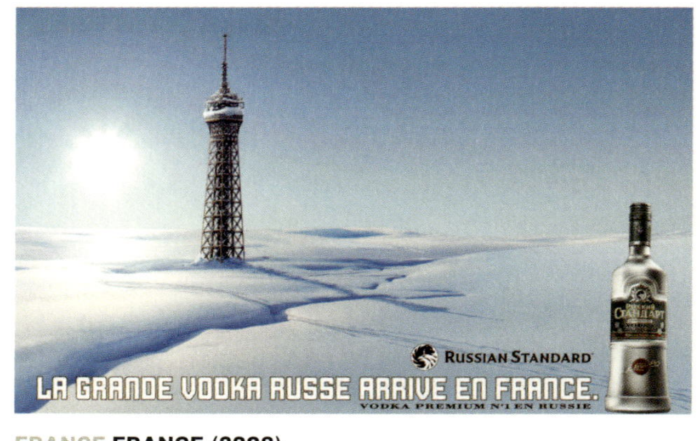

FRANCE FRANCE (2008)
Mc Cann Erickson   Russian Standard Vodka
The great russian vodka arrives in France

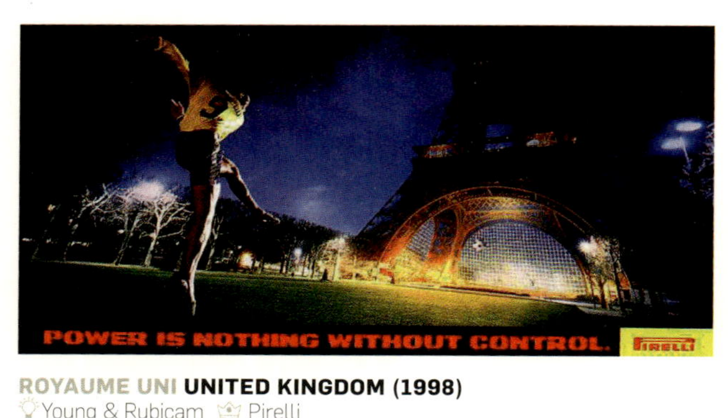

ROYAUME UNI UNITED KINGDOM (1998)
Young & Rubicam   Pirelli

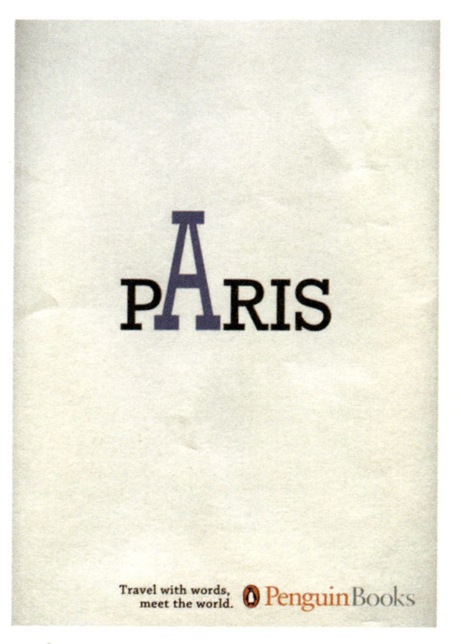

BRÉSIL BRAZIL (2010)
IESP   Penguin Books
Travel the world, meet the world

EIFFEL
TOWER

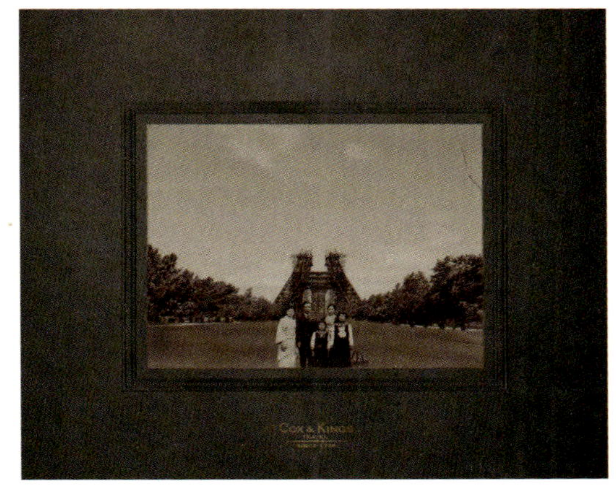

CHILI CHILE (2011)
TBWA Fredrick Santiago Bic Pens
Writes 2 kms

INDE INDIA (2008)
Saatchi & Saatchi Mumbai Cox & Kings Travel
Since 1758

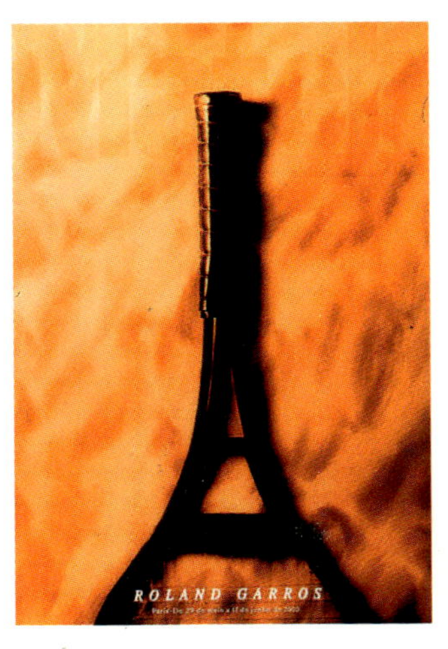

BRÉSIL BRAZIL (2000)
Fischer America
Match Point Magazine
Roland Garros

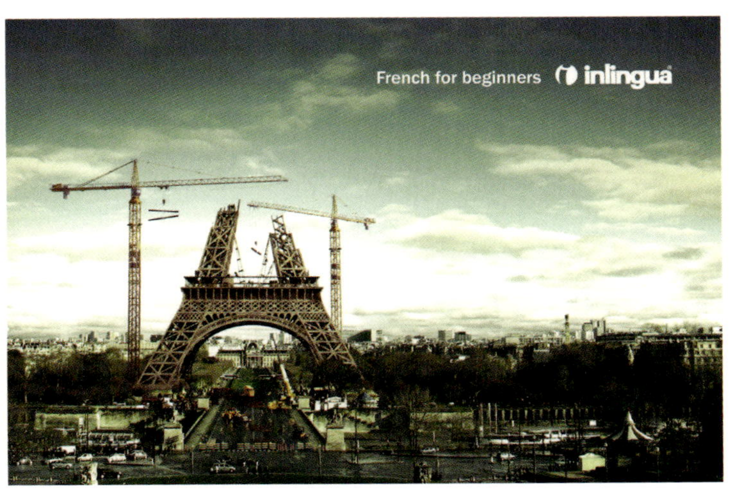

TURQUIE TURQUEY (2010)
TBWA Istanbul Inlingua

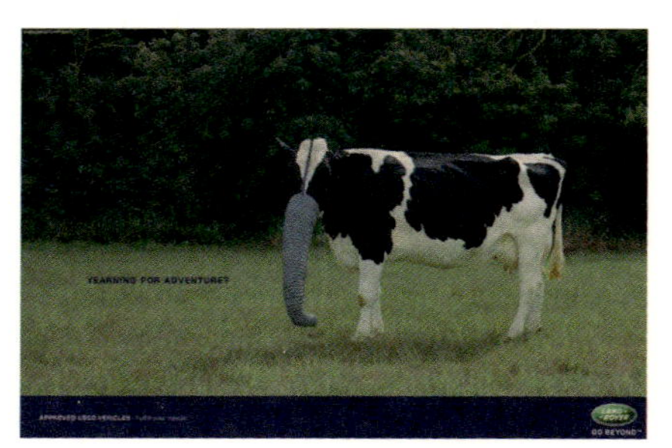

ROYAUME-UNI UNITED KINGDOM (2004)
Rainey Kelly Campbell Roalfe Young & Rubicam
Land Rover approved used vehicules
Yearning for adventure?

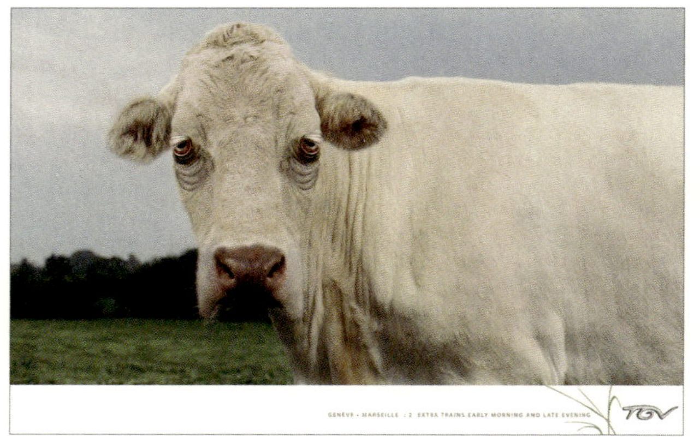

FRANCE FRANCE (2006)
TBWA Paris   SNCF - TGV - Geneve / Marseille
2 extra trains early morning and late evening

VACHES
№ 96
COWS

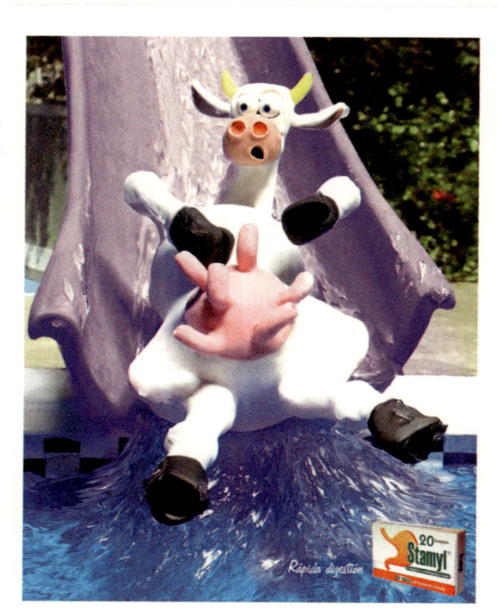

ÉQUATEUR ECUADOR (2009)
Maruri Grey   Fast digestion
Fast digestion

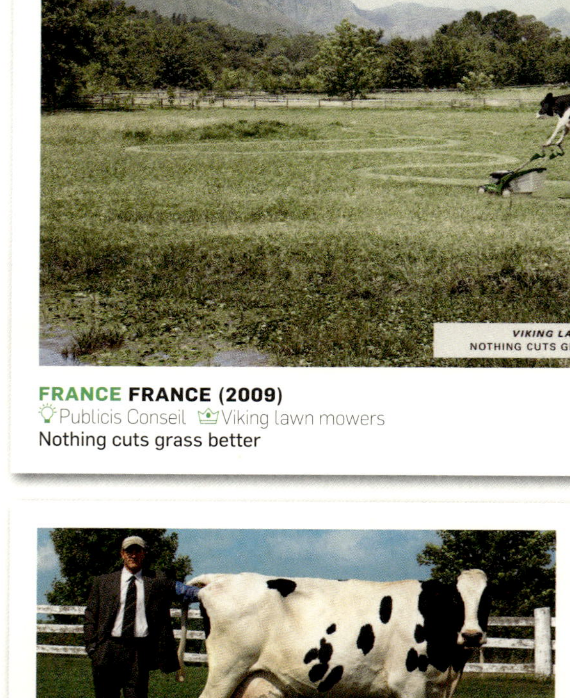

FRANCE FRANCE (2009)
Publicis Conseil   Viking lawn mowers
Nothing cuts grass better

CANADA CANADA (2003)
Saatchi & Saatchi Toronto   Channer's
Look good anytime in a suit

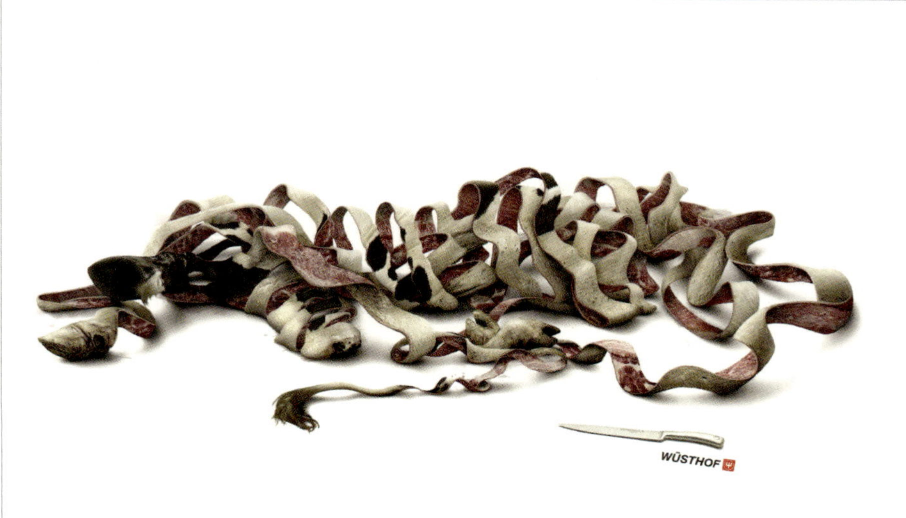

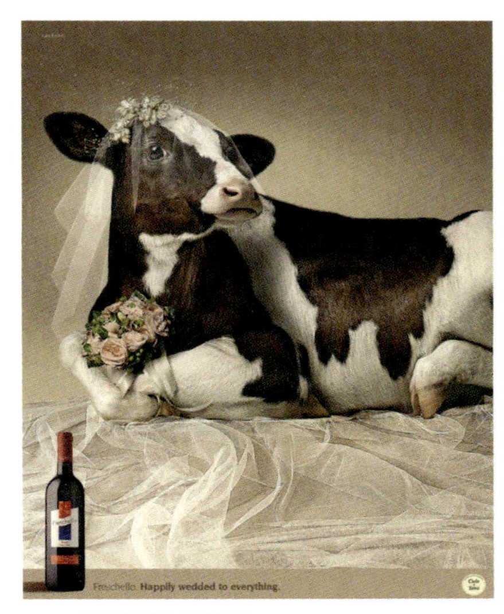

ITALIE ITALY (2006)
Cayenne Milan   Freschello wine
Happily wedded to everything

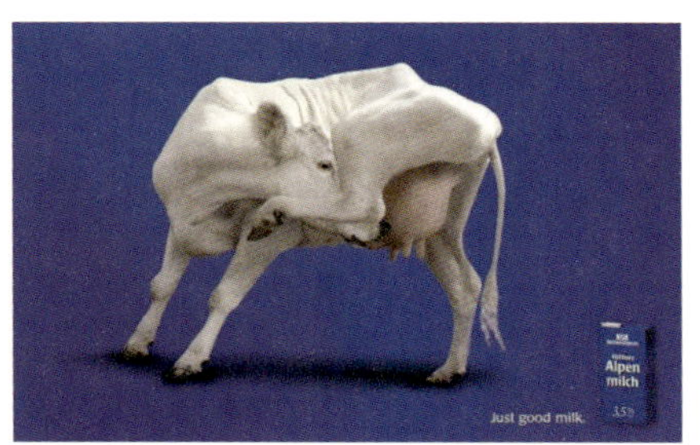

ALLEMAGNE GERMANY (2003)
Kolle Rebbe Hamburg   Alpen Milk
Just good milk

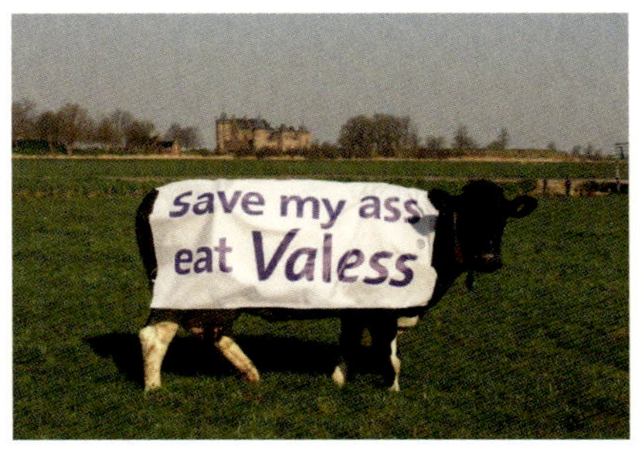

PAYS-BAS NETHERLANDS (2007)
FHV BBDO Amstelveen   Valess
is a dairy based meat substitute product from
The Netherlands. We turned Valess cows into
walking billboards by printing
'Save my ass eat Valess' on cow blankets

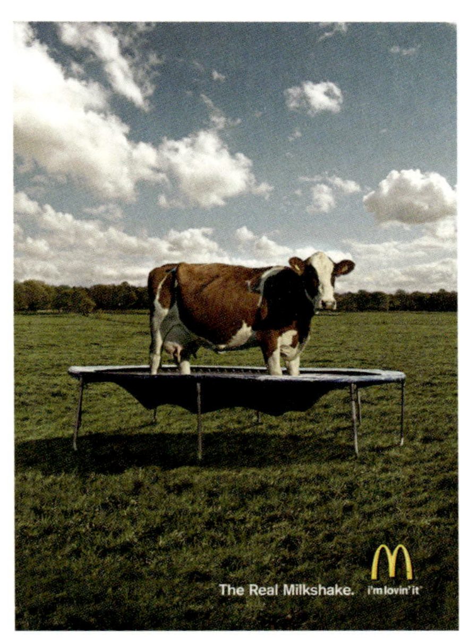

FINLANDE FINLAND (2009)
DDB Helsinki   Mc Donald's
The Real Milkshake

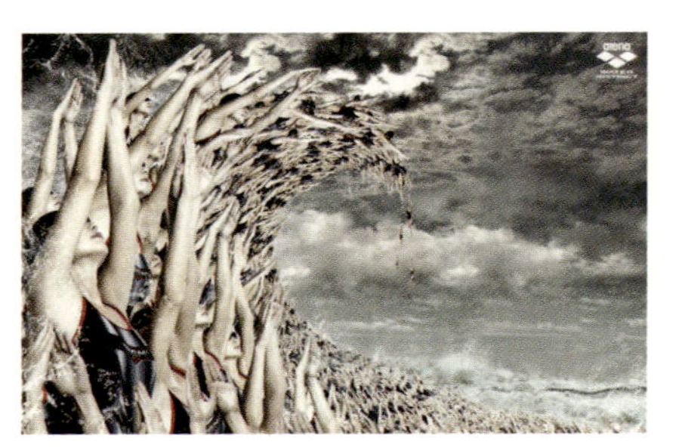

ITALIE ITALY (2009)
Lowe Pirella Milan Arena
Water Instinct

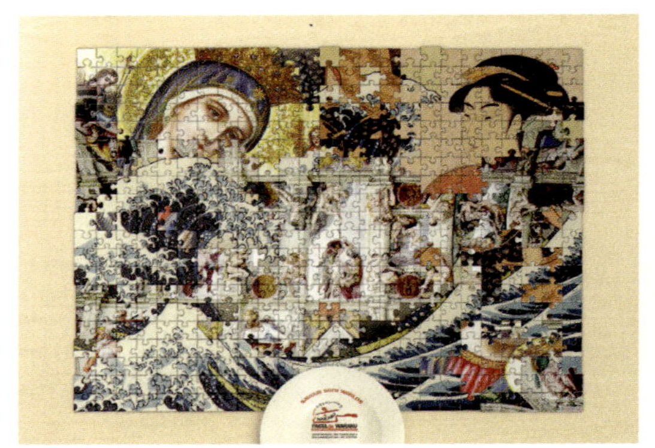

INDONÉSIE INDONESIA (2009)
Bates 141 Jakarta Pasta de Waraku Restaurant
Savour both worlds

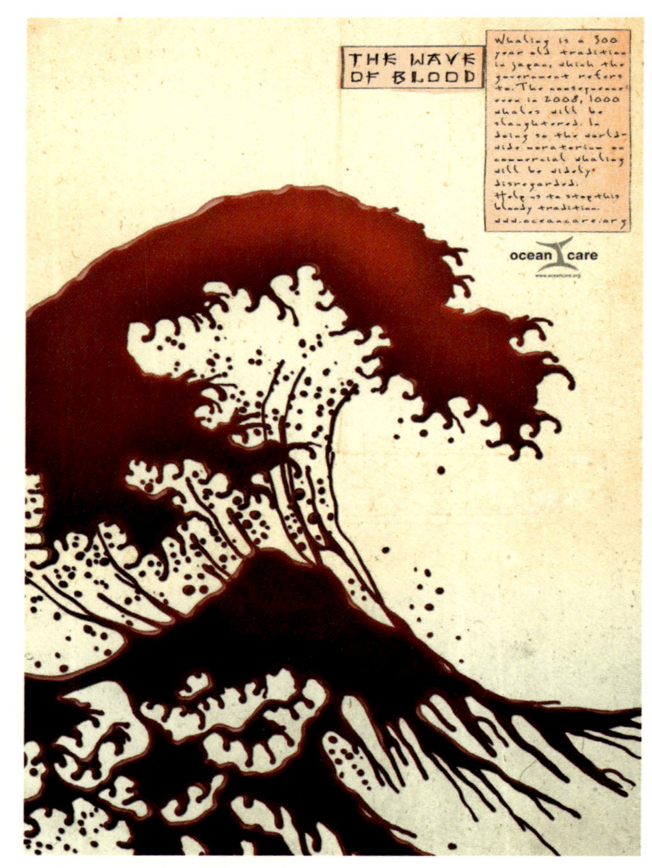

ALLEMAGNE GERMANY (2008)
Ogilvy Frankfurt Ocean Care Whales Protection

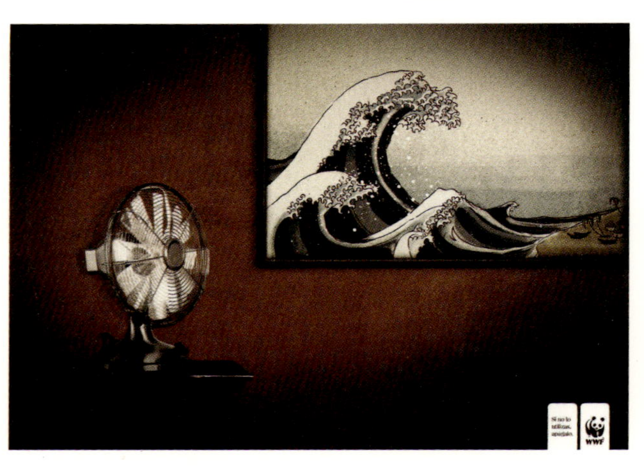

ESPAGNE SPAIN (2010)
BBDO Madrid WWF
Si no lo utilizas apagalo

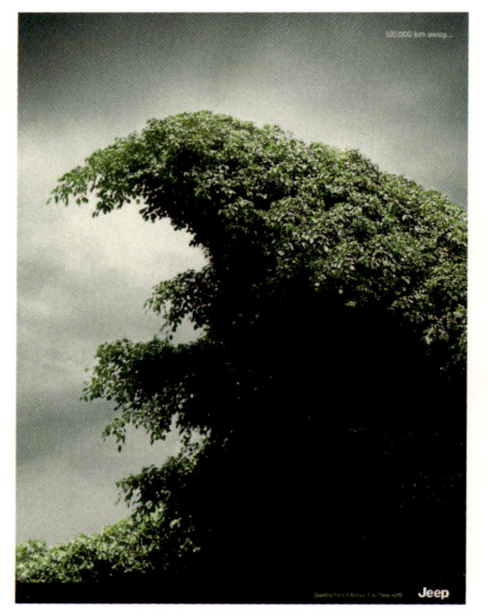

TAÏWAN TAIWAN (2008)
BBDO Jeep
120.000 Km away

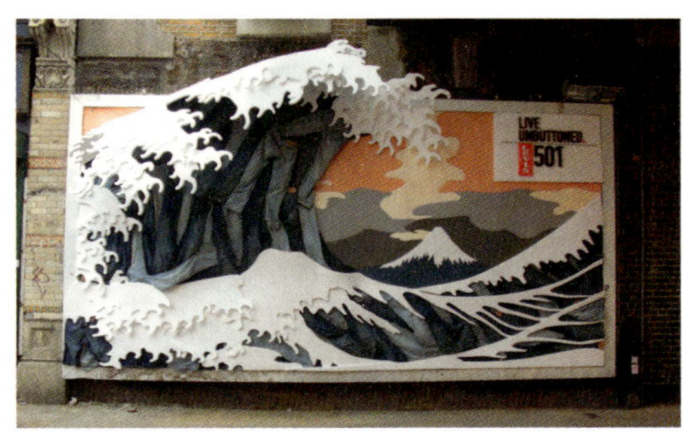

ITALIE ITALY (2009)
Viacom   Levi's 501
Live Unbottoned

LA GRANDE VAGUE D'HOKUSAI

Nº97

HOKUSAI: THE GREAT WAVE

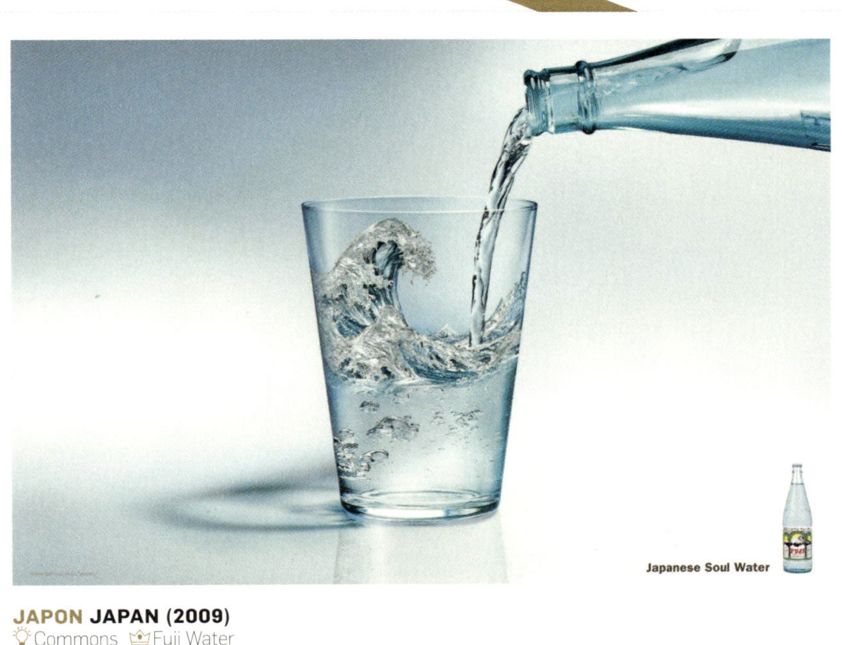

JAPON JAPAN (2009)
Commons   Fuji Water
Japanese Soul Water

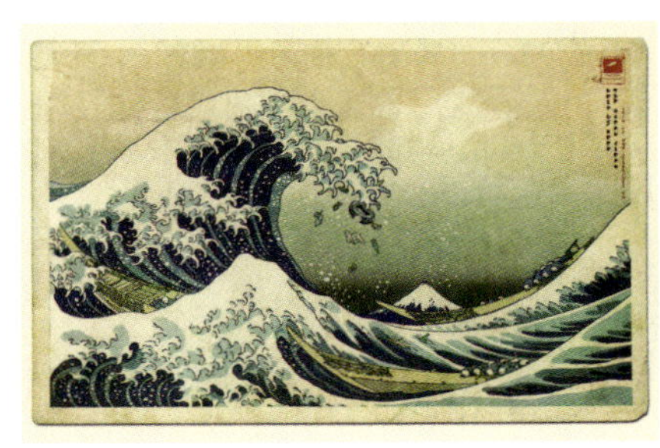

FRANCE FRANCE (2007)
Young & Rubicam Paris   Surfrider Foundation
Let us keep the ocean clean

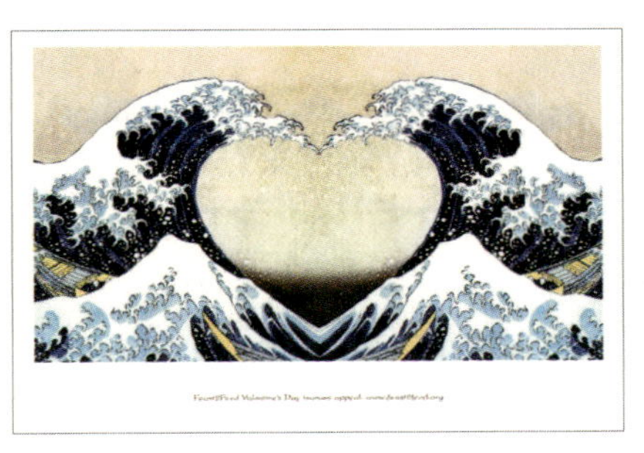

AUSTRALIE AUSTRALIA (2005)
Clemenger BBDO
Valentine Day Tsunami Appeal

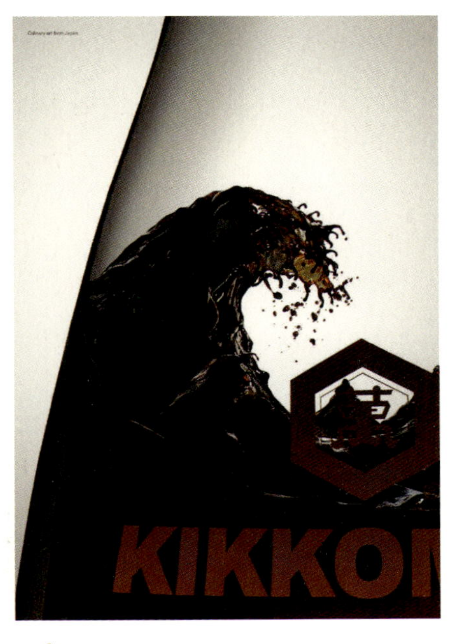

SUÈDE SWEDEN (2008)
Scholz & Friends Stockholm
Kikkoman Soi Sauce
Culinary art from Japan

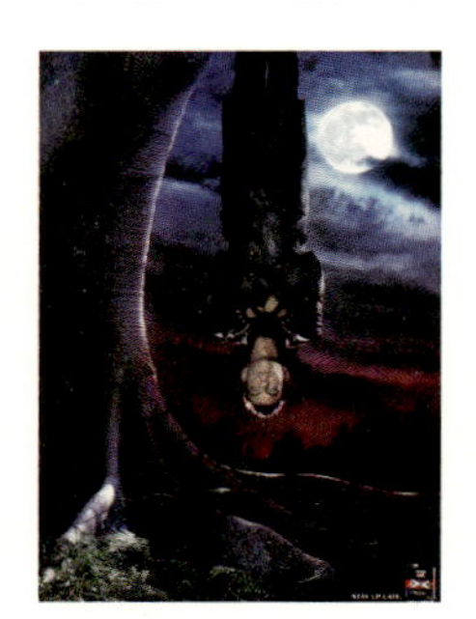

PHILIPPINES
PHILIPPINES (2006)
BBDO Guerrero Ortega Makati City
Pepsi X
Stay up late

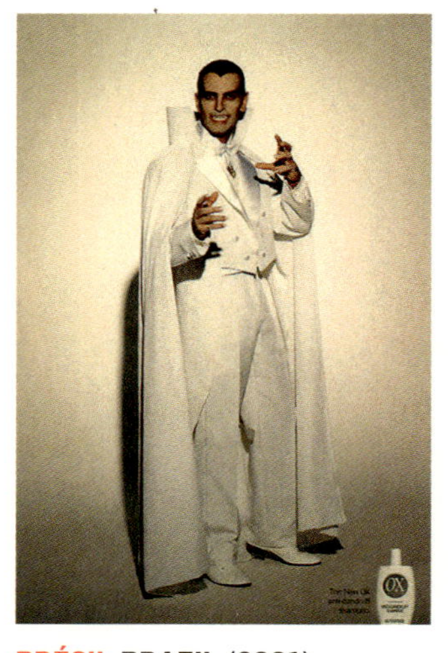

BRÉSIL BRAZIL (2001)
Grottera
OX Anti-Dandruff Shampoo

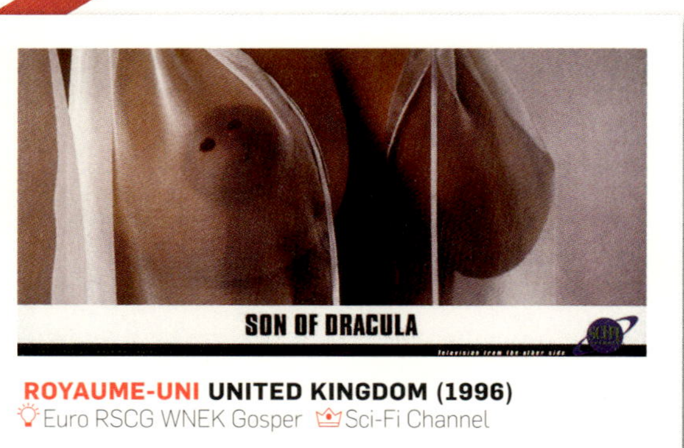

ROYAUME-UNI UNITED KINGDOM (1996)
Euro RSCG WNEK Gosper   Sci-Fi Channel

VAMPIRES

№98

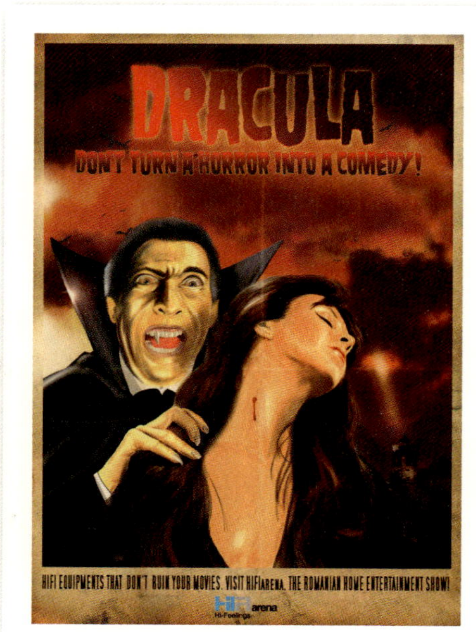

ROUMANIE ROMANIA (2008)
Cohn & Jansen Bucharest   Hi-Fi Arena
Don't turn a horror into a comedy

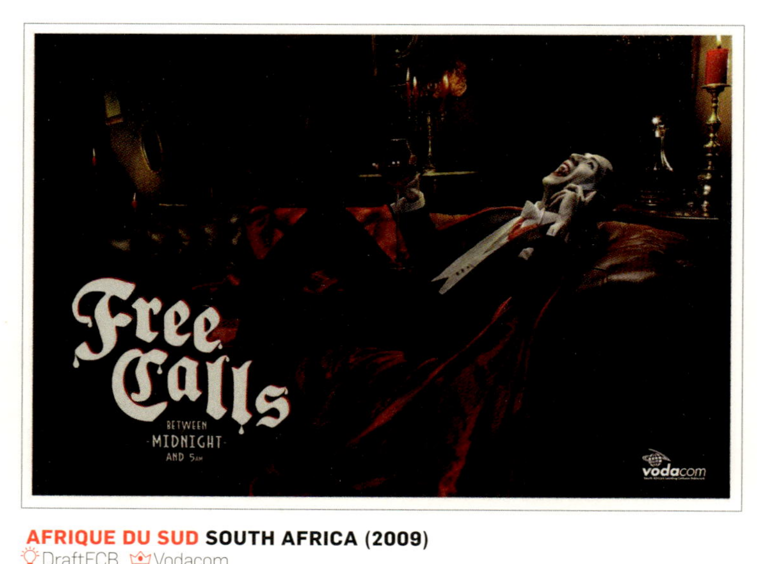

AFRIQUE DU SUD SOUTH AFRICA (2009)
DraftFCB   Vodacom

VAMPIRE BROLLEYS

True Blood is a popular HBO show where vampires walk freely amongst humans. Usually at night. Until now.

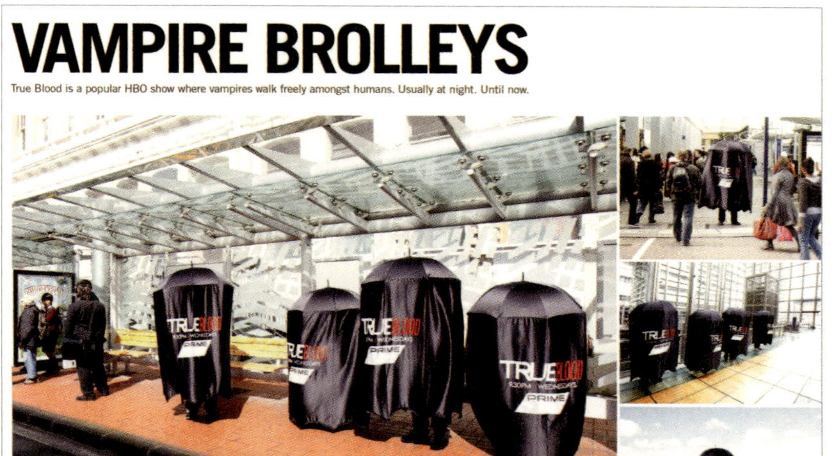

DraftFCB
Prime TV Channel
True Blood 9:30PM wednesdays

« Avec la mode récente des films de vampires, on a vu fleurir toutes sortes de pubs plus ou moins inspirées, à base de dents longues, de sang et de gousses d'ail. Celle-ci est de loin ma préférée et la plus mordante car elle ne ressemble pas du tout aux autres. »
"With the recent fad for vampire movies, we've seen a flurry of all sorts of ads more or less inspired, basically, by long teeth, blood and garlic cloves. This is by far my favourite and the most biting because it does not look like any of the others."

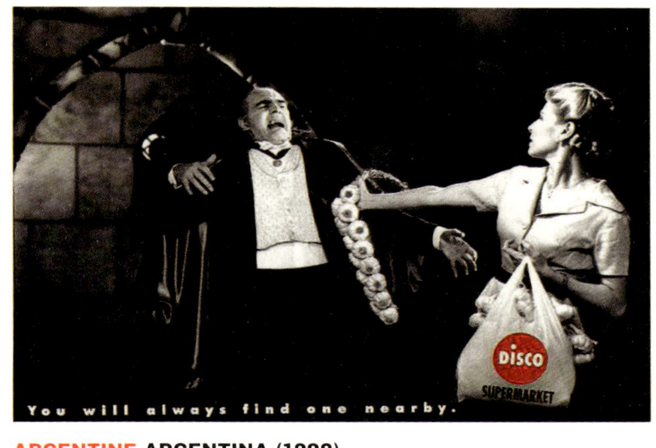

ARGENTINE ARGENTINA (1998)
Young & Rubicam   Disco Supermarket
You will always find one nearby

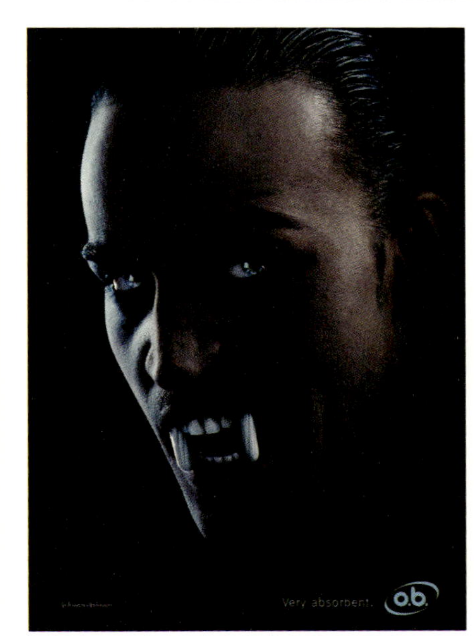

SUISSE SWITZERLAND (2009)
Lowe Group Zurich   OB Tampons
Very Absorbent

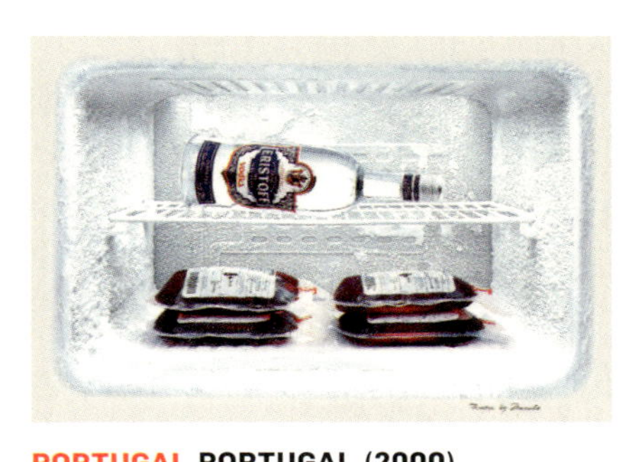

PORTUGAL PORTUGAL (2000)
BBDO   Eristoff Vodka
Freezer by Dracula

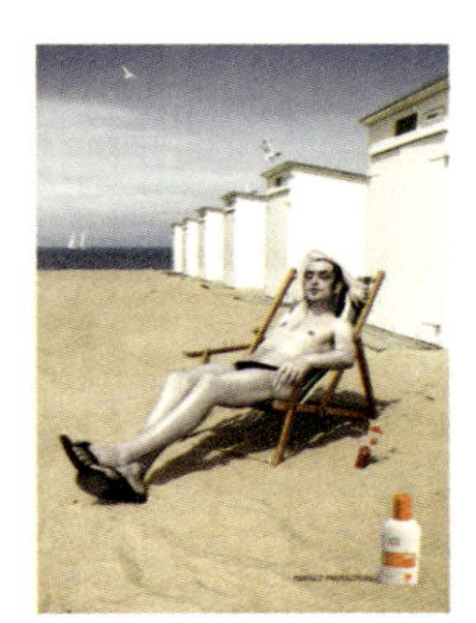

BELGIQUE
BELGIUM (2006)
Duval Guillaume Antwerp
Suncream
Perfect Protection

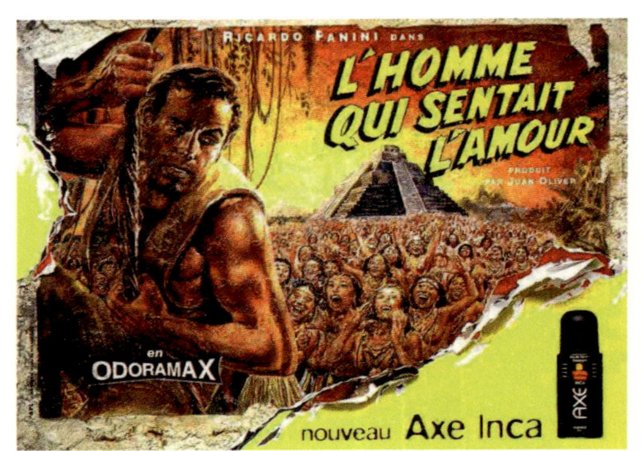

FRANCE FRANCE (1998)
Lowe Lintas Axe Inca
The man who smells love.
In Odoramax

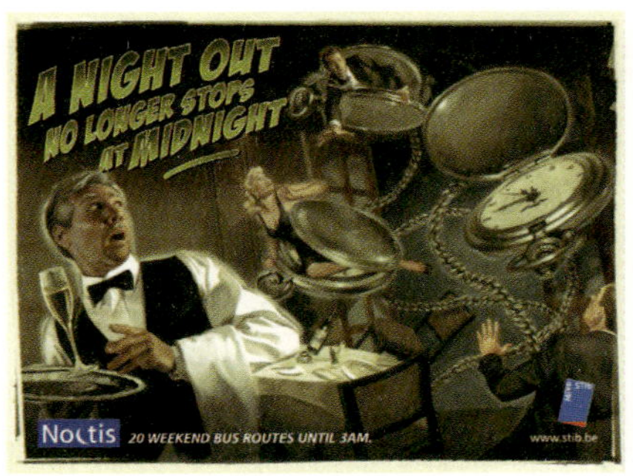

BELGIQUE BELGIUM (2007)
The Retail Company Brussels
Noctis Bus (STIB)
A night out no longer stops at midnight

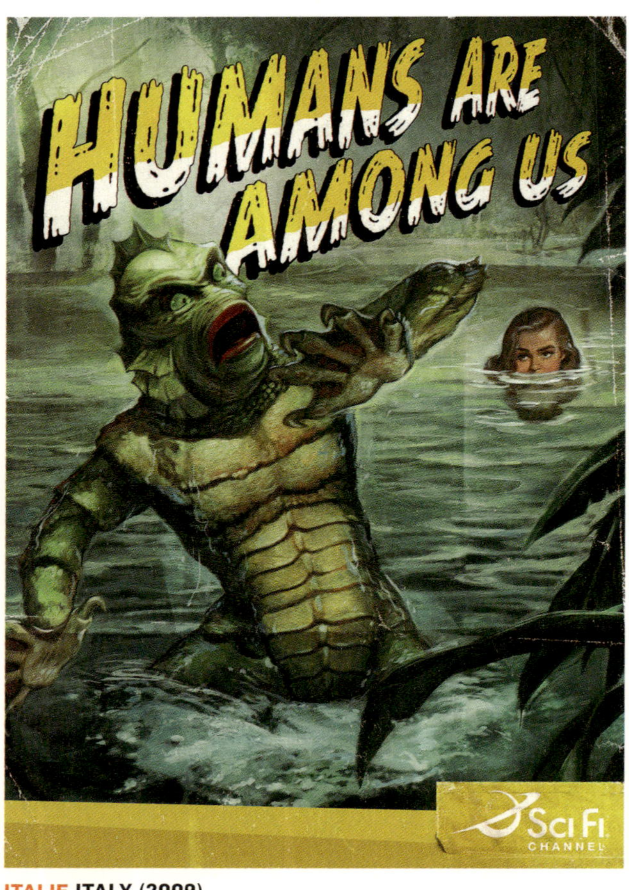

ITALIE ITALY (2009)
Saatchi & Saatchi Milan Sci-Fi Channel

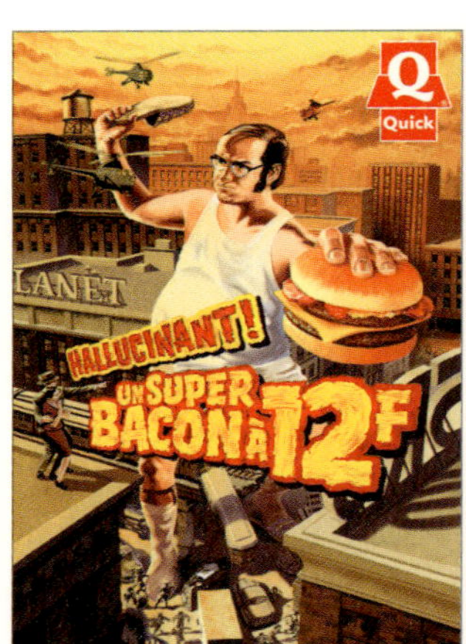

FRANCE FRANCE (2002)
Young & Rubicam Paris Quick Restaurants

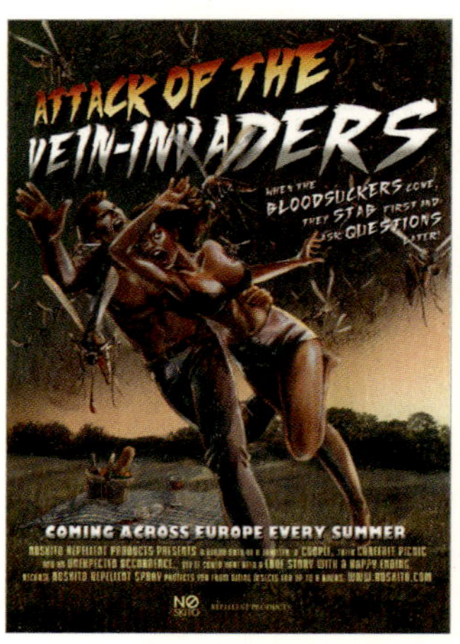

ALLEMAGNE GERMANY (2010)
Grey G2 NoSkito Repellent
Attack of the vein-invaders.
Coming across europe every summer

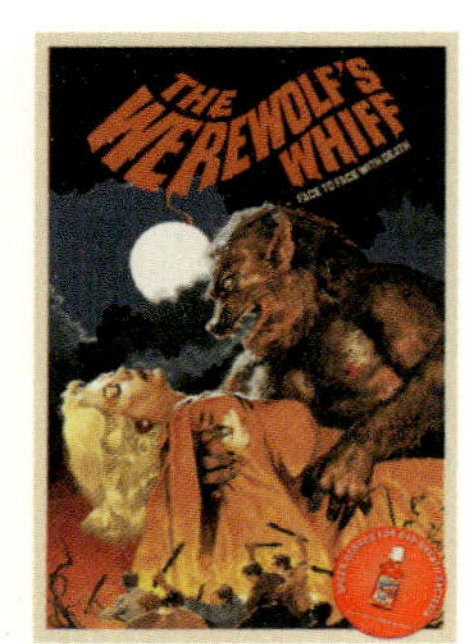

BRÉSIL
BRAZIL (2006)
Publicis
Cepacol Mouth Wash
Sheer horror for bad
breath bacteria

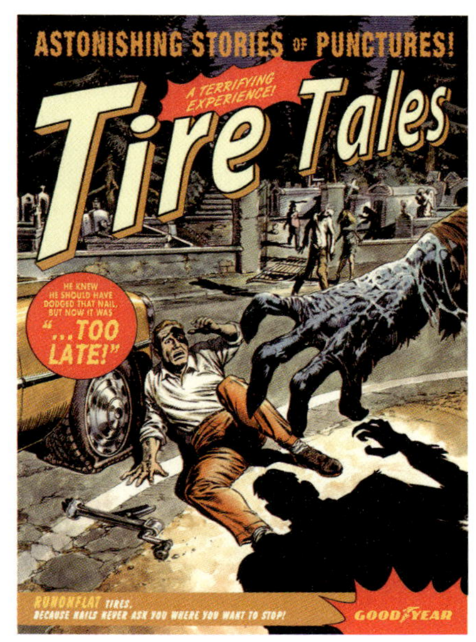

ITALIE ITALY (2007)
Leagas Delaney · GoodYear Tyres

N°99

OLD MOVIES POSTER STYLE

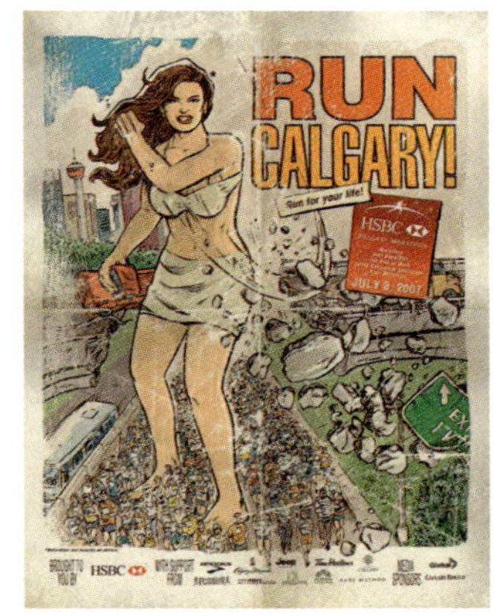

CANADA CANADA (2007)
Rare Method · Calgary Marathon
Run Calgary! Run for your life

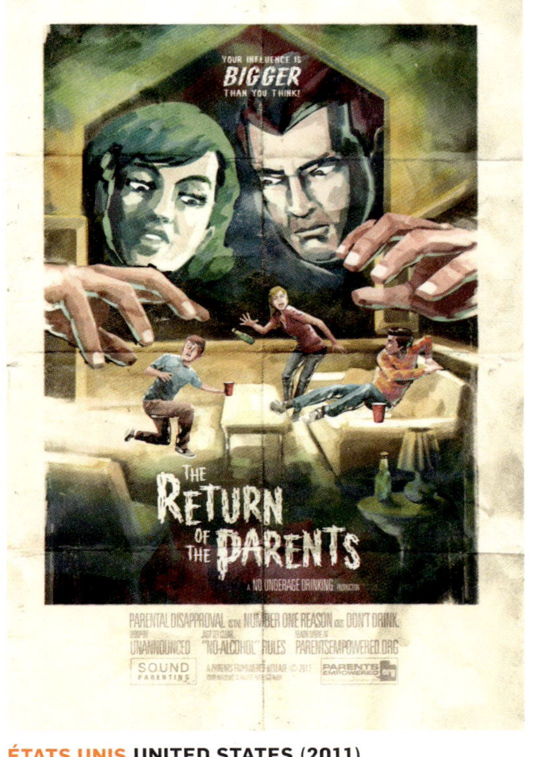

ÉTATS UNIS UNITED STATES (2011)
RR partners Salt Lake City · ParentsEmpowered.org
The return of the parents

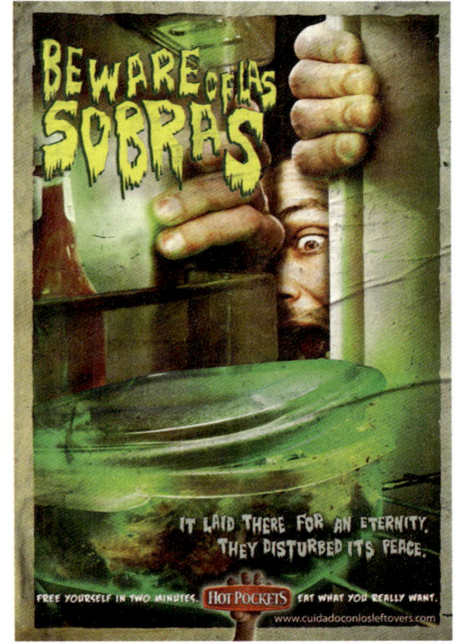

ÉTATS UNIS UNITED STATES (2009)
Casanova Pendrill Costa Mesa · Hot Pockets
Beware of the leftovers.
Eat what you really want

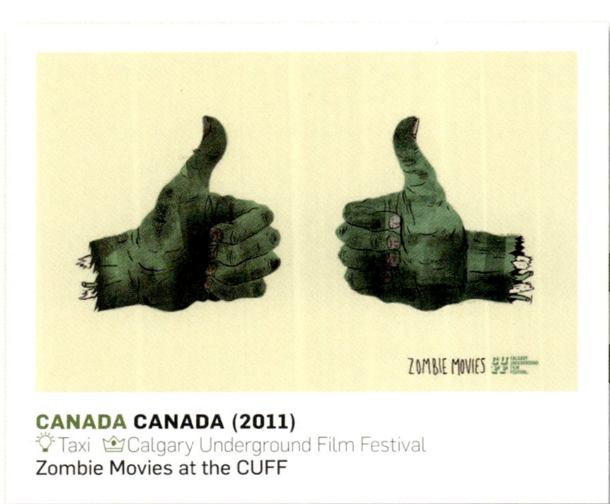

CANADA **CANADA (2011)**
Taxi Calgary Underground Film Festival
Zombie Movies at the CUFF

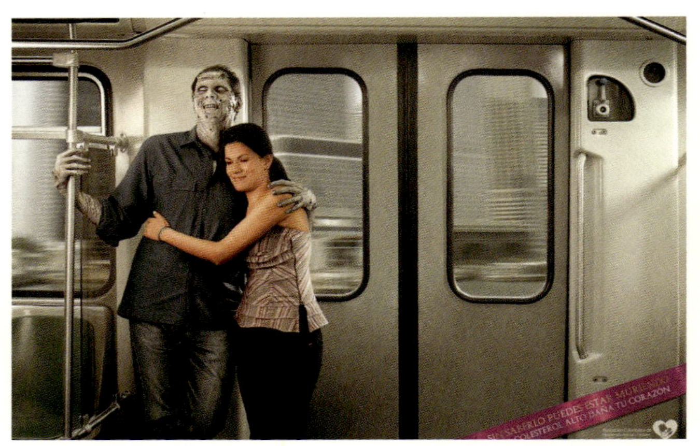

COLOMBIE **COLOMBIA (2007)**
DDB Asociación Colombia de Hipertensión Arterial y Factores de Riesgo cardiovascular
Without knowing you can be dying. High cholesterol injures your heart.

ZOMBIES

№100

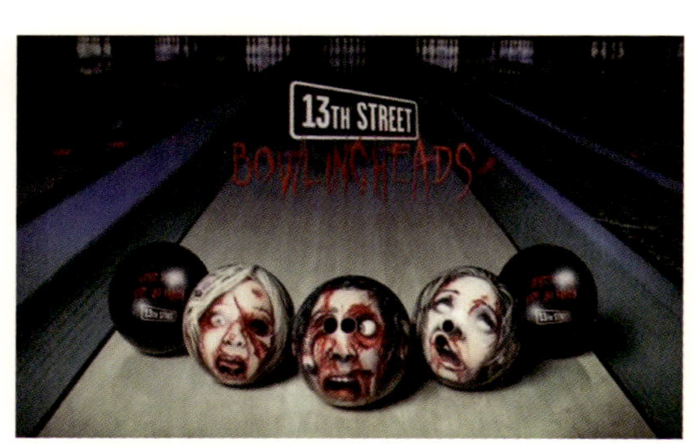

ALLEMAGNE **GERMANY (2008)**
Jung Von Matt 13th street channel
Bowling Heads guerrilla

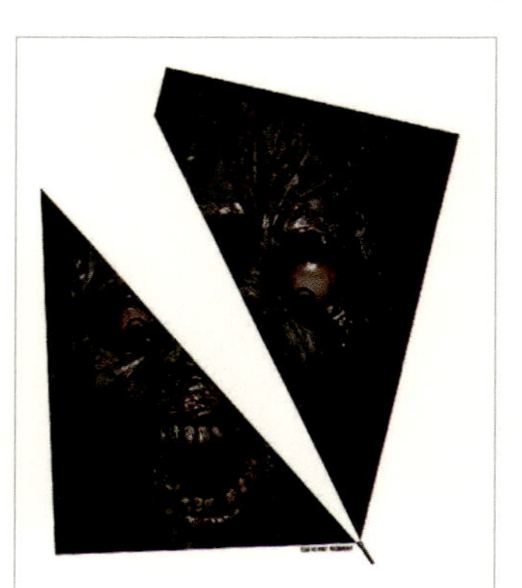

CHINE **CHINA (2008)**
Ogilvy Shanghai
Maxbright torches
Fear no more

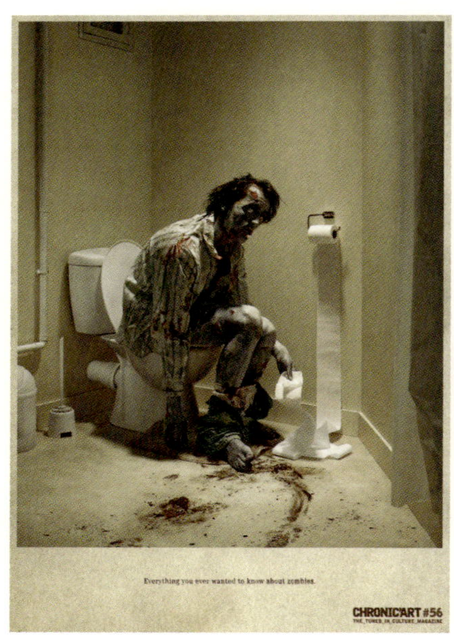

FRANCE **FRANCE (2009)**
DraftFCB Chronic'Art Magazine
Everything you ever wanted to know about zombies

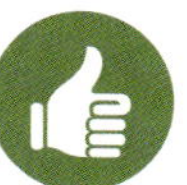

ALLEMAGNE GERMANY (2008)
Jung Von Matt 13th street channel
Zombie stationery (Direct Marketing)

« De loin l'idée la plus drôle et la plus gore.
Ce n'est pas de la pub traditionnelle mais
plutôt du marketing direct.
Et pourtant, ça fait vraiment le trou !
On a immédiatement envie de jouer avec. »
"By far the funniest and goriest idea.
This is not traditional advertising but
rather direct marketing. And it really
hits the nail on the head! We immediately
want to play with it."

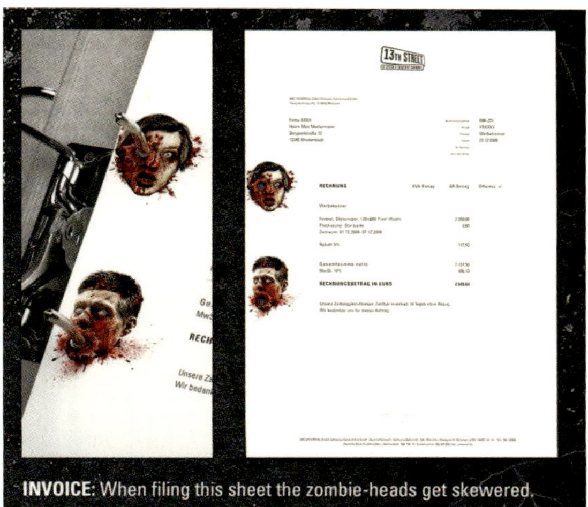

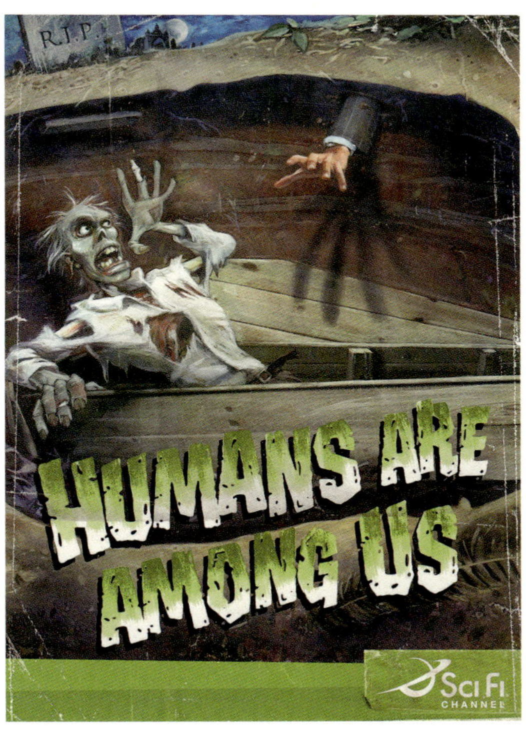

ITALIE ITALY (2009)
Saatchi & Saatchi Milan Sci Fi Channel

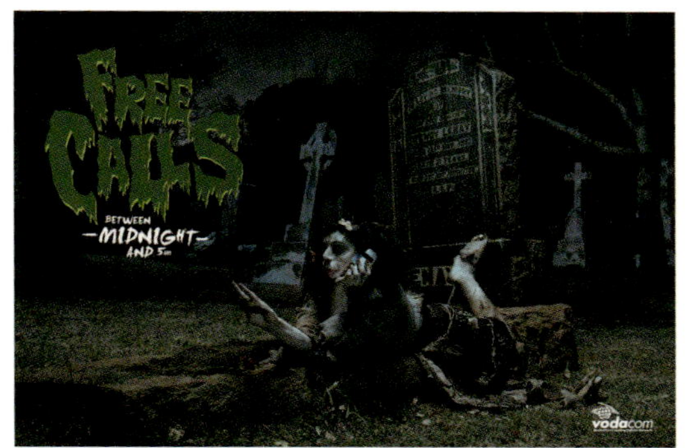

AFRIQUE DU SUD SOUTH AFRICA (2011)
Draft FCB Johannesburg Vodacom
Free Calls between midnight and 5am

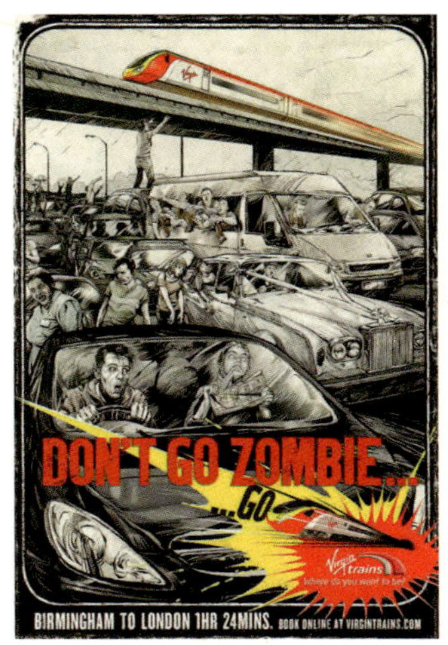

**ROYAUME-UNI
UNITED KINGDOM (2010)**
Elvis Advertising Virgin Trains
Don't go zombie... go Virgin Trains

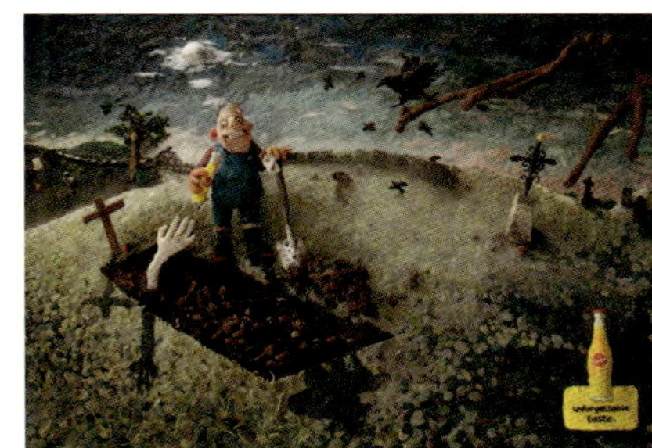

SUISSE SWITZERLAND (2007)
Springer & Jacoby Zurich Sinalco Soft Drink
Unforgatable taste

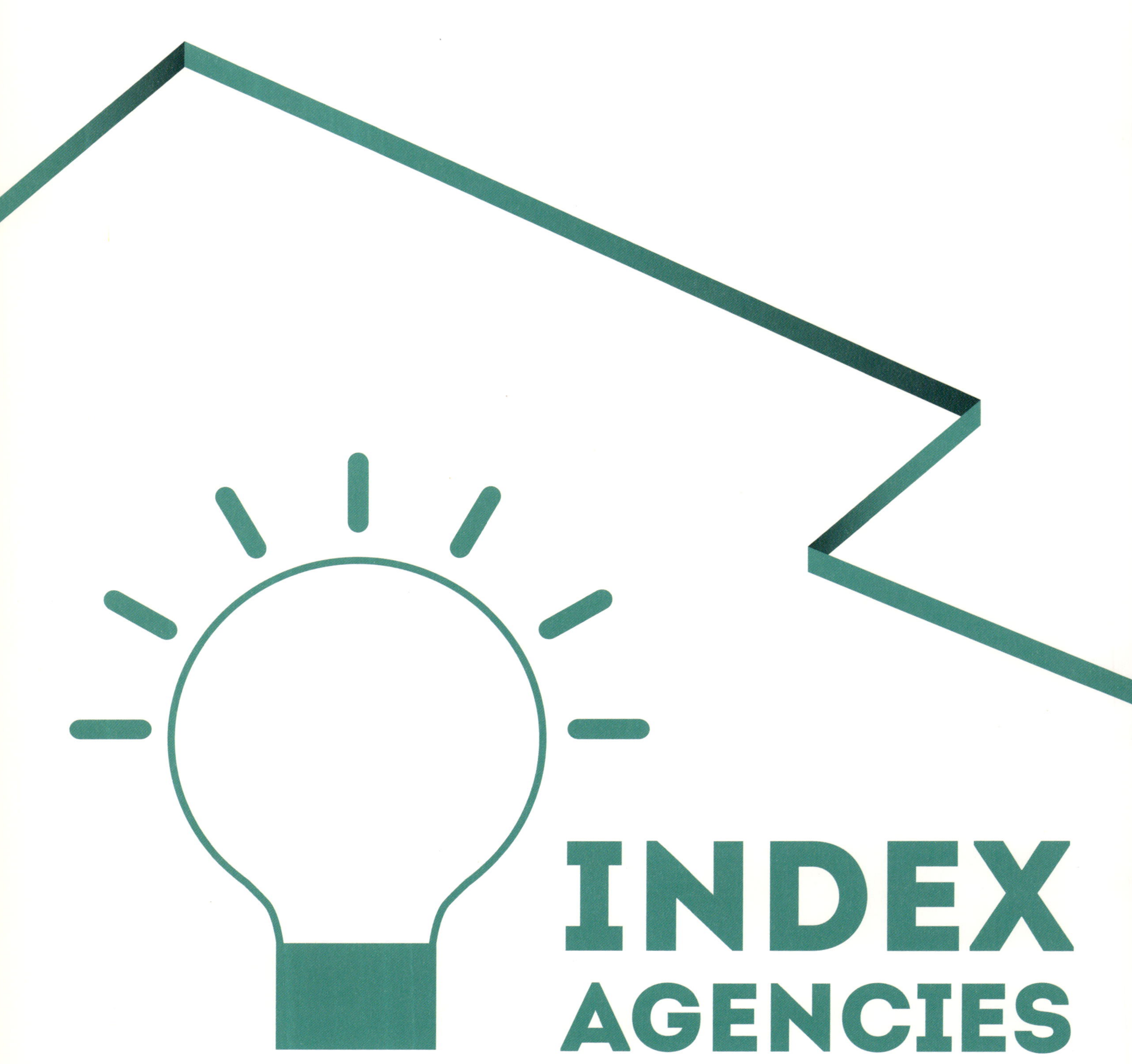

INDEX
AGENCIES

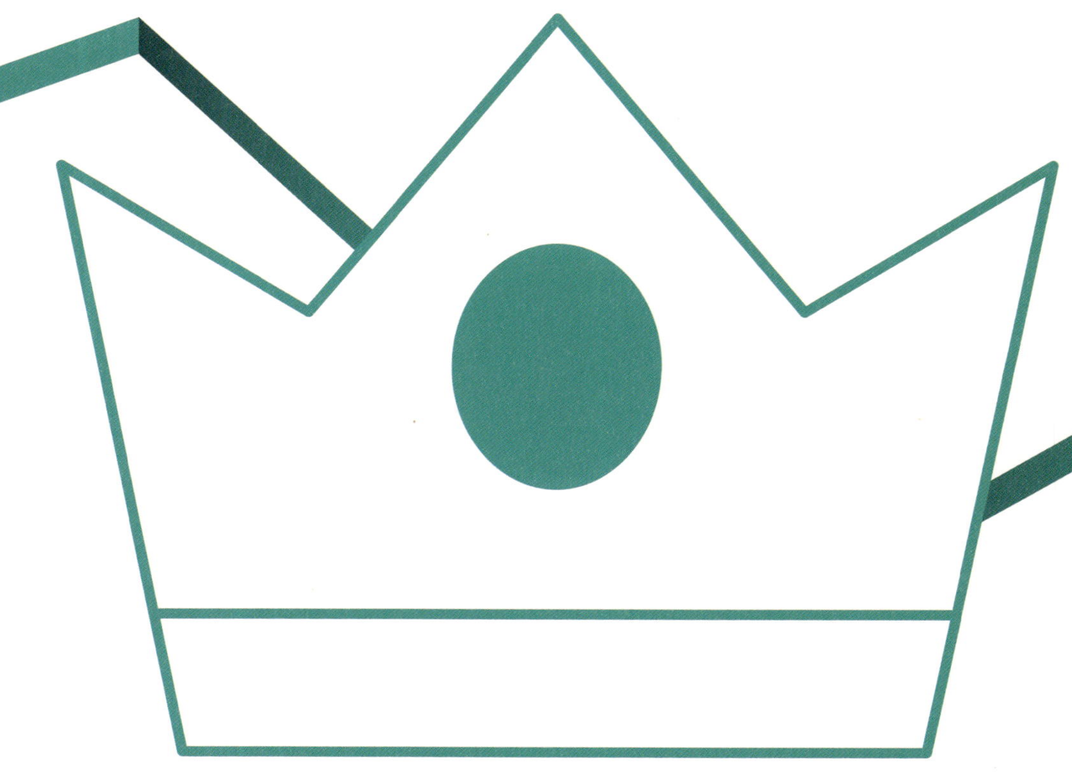

INDEX
CLIENTS

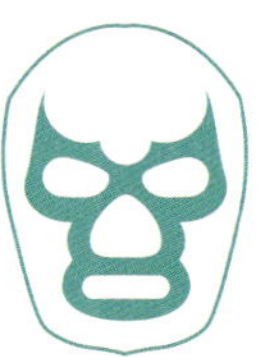

A BOOK BY JOE LA POMPE

A relentless collector of advertisement material, Joe La Pompe has been hosting an influential, eponymously titled blog since 1999. He has worked in advertising (for three of the biggest Parisian agencies), is the author of several books and has written as a columnist for various magazines – currently his musings can be found in *CB News* and *Media Marketing*.

The notoriety of his blog has led Joe to be invited to deliver keynote speeches both in France and abroad. His enigmatic presence recently livened up conferences in Canada and Luxembourg. He has also been on the jury at several festivals and creative competitions.

His blog is listed in the top 25 most influential advertising blogs by BlogRank, and has been recognised by specialist media all over the world. Indeed, as *Business Insider* says: "*Quite simply – this is the blog everyone wants to read and no one wants to be on.*"

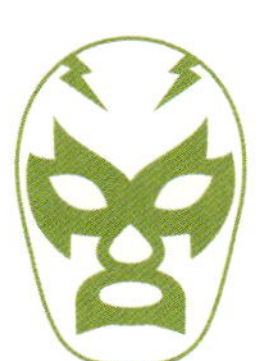

COVER PHOTOGRAPHY Julien Becker
EDITOR Mike Koedinger
ART DIRECTOR Vera Heliodoro
INTRODUCTION France Clarinval

PROOFREADING Aaron Grunwald, Sarah Lambolez
TRANSLATION Aaron Grunwald
COORDINATION Sarah Macri
LAYOUT Olga Krivostsokova
PRINTING Imprimerie Centrale, Luxembourg

PUBLISHER:

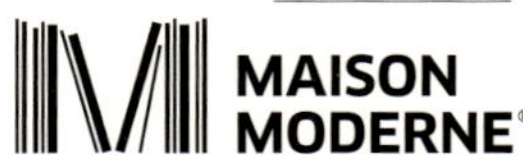

Visit *www.maisonmoderne.lu*

WE INFORM, WE ENTERTAIN, WE INSPIRE.

We are Maison Moderne – Luxembourg's leading and award-winning media group.

We create magazines, books, digital content, events and broadcast TV.

We publish self-initiated projects and we create multi-channel, branded content for clients.

© Maison Moderne ™ used under license by MM Publishing and Media S.A. (Luxembourg) All rights reserved. No part of this book may be reproduced or translated without the express written permission by the publisher.

First edition September 2012
Registration of copyright September 2012
National Library of Luxembourg (www.bnl.lu)

Worldwide distribution:
Gestalten, Berlin
www.gestalten.com
sales@gestalten.com

ISBN 978-3-89955-462-5

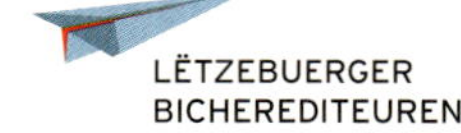
LËTZEBUERGER BICHEREDITEUREN

THE AUTHOR WOULD LIKE TO THANK:

First and foremost Mike Koedinger and his team at Maison Moderne
Pierre Ayroles @p8perplane www.paper-plane.fr
Emptystudio @emptyjonz www.empty-studio.com

And huge thanks for their continued support:

The team at *Media Marketing* and in particular Fred Bouchar, Damien Lemaire and Bart Lombaerts
The team at *CB News* and in particular Margareth Figueiredo, Frédéric Roy, Bertrand Gauthey, Aida de Miguel, Valérie Simon and Anne Valérie Hoh

And equally some support that from time-to-time helped me in different ways (such as encouragement and advice), sometimes even without knowing, or at least not noticing, who was hidden behind the Joe mask:

Babette Auvray (Le jour sans pub, Langue de Pub), Agent-Influence (Dilene Santos and the whole team), CCB Belgium, Philippe Warzee (Pub.be @mediarescue), Jean Philippe Gramond, Pascal Henrard (www.henrard.com), Gabriel Thomas Leclerc (Adicc.com), Patrick Beauduin (Cossette), Hervé Pommier (Sup de création), Bernard Naville, Mehdi El Alj, Pierre Berville, Jean-François Fournon, Pierre Arnaud Gilet, Fred&Farid, Jean-Michel Larsen, Marco Azenha, Michael Bernier, Eric Jannon et Dimitri Guerrassimov, the team at Act Responsible / AdForum: Sophie Guérinet, Isa Kurata, Maud Largaud, Laurence de Lignac and all the others, Andrew Rawlins (EPICA), Stephane Watelet (Télémaque)

The bloggers and twitterers:

@alexisjamet @edouardpetit @LeMonteverdi @fouapa @Vivelapub @TheAmnesic @MathieuFlex @AdTimes @Darkplanneur @CestquilesCreas @AdLand @mikael_colombu @40_cents @culturepub @Petitbrin @myhappywall @inzecity @adsoftheworld @LLLLitl @tristandaltroff @louisaudard @luckthelady @krizofromparis @ecolegraphisme @lareclamefr @pariscomlight @apreslapub @jacinthe_ @sylvainw @paragonanubis @osocio @adada_lu @conceptstorefr (apologies to anyone that I might have forgotten)

My whole family, and all those who've followed my joelapompe.net blog for all these years!

And finally a huge thank you to Christian Blachas to whom I owe so much, and is missed by all the "fils de pub".

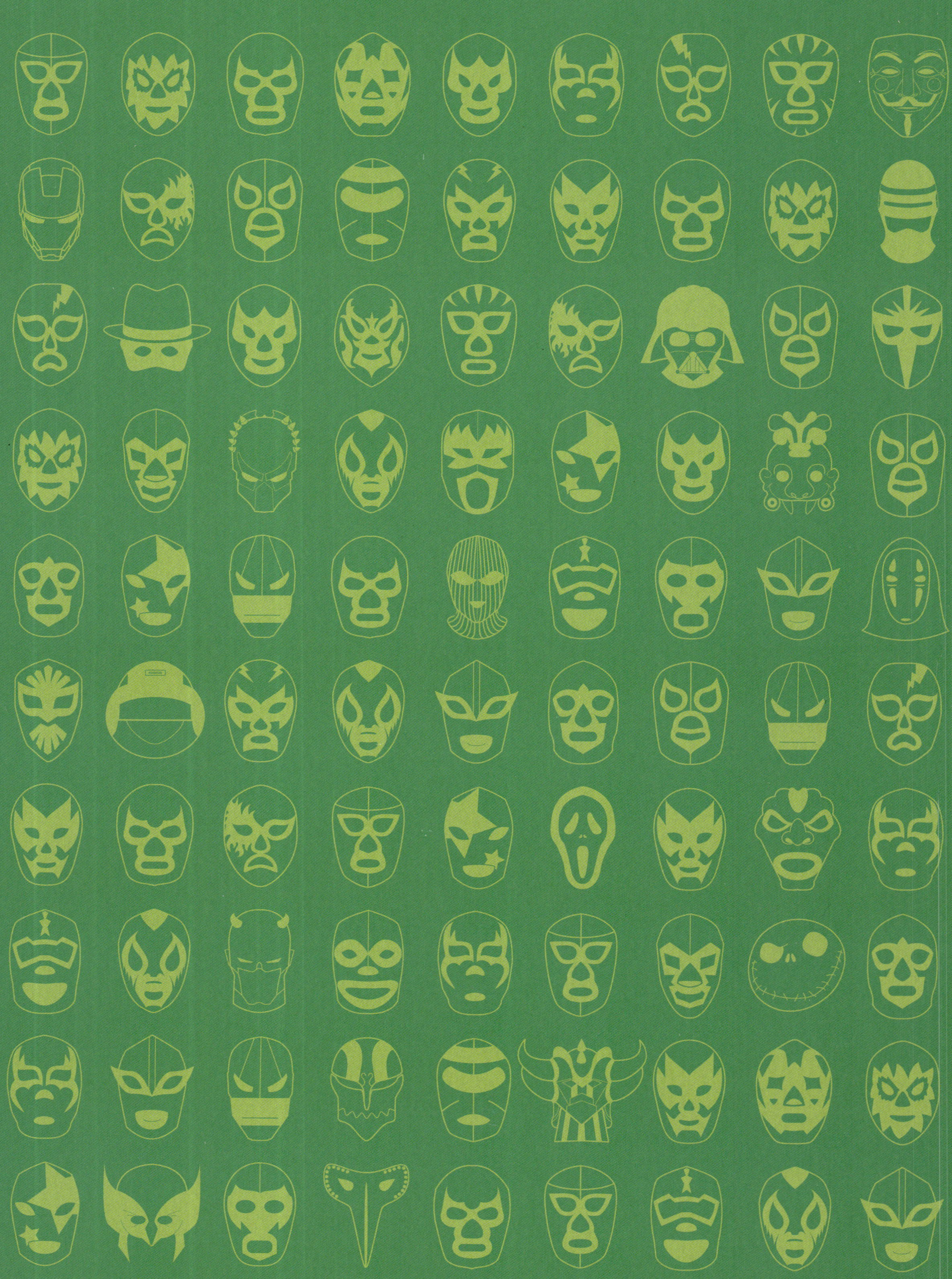